# PATHWAYS IN THE NINETEENTH-CENTURY BRITISH TEXTILE INDUSTRY

# PATHWAYS IN THE NINETEENTH-CENTURY BRITISH TEXTILE INDUSTRY

*Edited by*
*Philip A. Sykas*

**Volume I**
**The Waste Textile Industries**

Routledge
Taylor & Francis Group
LONDON AND NEW YORK

First published 2023
by Routledge
4 Park Square, Milton Park, Abingdon, Oxon OX14 4RN

and by Routledge
605 Third Avenue, New York, NY 10158

*Routledge is an imprint of the Taylor & Francis Group, an informa business*



*British Library Cataloguing-in-Publication Data*
A catalogue record for this book is available from the British Library

*Library of Congress Cataloging-in-Publication Data*
Names: Sykas, Philip Anthony, editor.
Title: Pathways in the nineteenth-century British textile industry / edited by Philip A. Sykas.
Description: New York, NY : Routledge, 2022- | Includes bibliographical references and index. | Contents: v. 1. — v. 2. — v. 3. |
Identifiers: LCCN 2021055700 (print) | ISBN 9780367221546 (set) | ISBN 9780367222765 (v. 1 ; hardback) | ISBN 9780367222772 (v. 2 ; hardback) | ISBN 9780367222789 (v. 3 ; hardback) | ISBN 9780429273551 (ebook) | ISBN 9780429274190 (v. 1 ; ebook) | ISBN 9780429274206 (v. 2 ; ebook) | ISBN 9780429274213 (v. 3 ; ebook)
Subjects: LCSH: Textile industry—Great Britain—History—19th century.
Classification: LCC HD9861.5 .P38 2022 (print) | LCC HD9861.5 (ebook) | DDC 338.4/76770941—dc23/eng/20211112
LC record available at https://lccn.loc.gov/2021055700
LC ebook record available at https://lccn.loc.gov/2021055701

ISBN: 978-0-367-22154-6 (set)
eISBN: 978-0-429-27355-1 (set)
ISBN: 978-0-367-22276-5 (volume I)
eISBN: 978-0-429-27419-0 (volume I)

DOI: 10.4324/9780429274190

Typeset in Times New Roman
by Apex CoVantage, LLC

# CONTENTS

# VOLUME I: LIST OF IMAGES

## Part 1



## Part 2



## Part 3

## Part 4



## Part 5

## Part 6



## Part 7

# VOLUME I: TIMELINE

| | |
|---|---|
| 1792 | William Thompson set up a mill to spin waste silk yarns at Galgate near Lancaster |
| 1801–1802 | Patents of Thomas Parker, William Telfer and Alexander Affleck of Glasgow, for machinery to recover fibrous raw materials from manufactured textiles |
| 1806 | Conjectured date that Israel Davis adulterated Spanish wool with wool pulled from old blankets, and realised full prices in Yorkshire |
| 1807 | James Holdforth began spinning silk waste at Leeds |
| 1809/1813 | Conjectured date of first shoddy cloth by Benjamin Law and Benjamin Parr of Batley |
| 1815 | First rag pulling machine of sawtooth construction by Joseph Archer for Benjamin Law and Benjamin Parr |
| 1818 | Joseph Jubb and others construct woollen rag pulling machines |
| 1820 | George Hall began dealing in woollen rags for shoddy grinding at Clerk Green, Batley |
| c1820–1825 | Rag pulling machine for woollen rags modified to use conical teeth and dubbed the 'devil' |
| 1821 | Marshall and Co. of Leeds begin carding and preparing of tow by machinery |
| 1822 | Hick Lane Mill established in Batley to weave shoddy cloth |
| 1822 | J. S. Alioth of Basle began spun silk production, moving to Arlesheim in 1824 |
| 1827 | Marshall and Co. of Leeds began tow processing for fine work |
| 1828 | Output of rag trade estimated at 9,000 packs shoddy (*Wool Year Book*) |
| 1830 | Shoddy from Denmark exported to Britain by Marcus Gottlieb Galthen Bech |
| 1834 | Experiments with mungo production begun |
| 1842 | Busfeild Ferrand's denunciation of the shoddy trade as 'devil's dust' |

| | |
|---|---|
| 1844 | Abolition of import duties on foreign wool entering Britain, including rag wool |
| 1844 | London Sack Protection Society formed to recover empty sacks |
| 1849 | William Garnett Taylor of Manchester patented a hand-operated linting machine |
| 1850 | First hard waste opening machinery for worsted (Leather 1917) |
| 1851 | P. and C. Garnett, machine makers, founded |
| 1851–1855 | Experimental phase in the development of extract wool (wool extracted from blends with cotton) |
| 1852 | Lyon Playfair's lecture before the Society of Arts touching on recycling |
| 1853 | Crone, Fenton and Aldred patent for extracting wool from cotton and wool mixtures (no, 1891) |
| 1855 | First power-driven linting machine devised by William Robinson of Chesterfield, from experiments begun around July 1854 |
| 1856 | Frédéric Quinson patented a waste silk combing machine in France that was put into practical use around 1870 |
| 1858 | A process of recovering stearine from wash water was put in place at Kingholme Woollen Mills, Dumfries |
| 1859 | Lister and Warburton's first silk comb |
| 1861–1865 | Lancashire cotton famine stimulated interest in waste processing and mixture fabrics |
| 1862 | Joseph Rhodes of Morley gained knowledge of Mathias Stirn and Sons' improvement of the rag machine for mungo grinding, and patented it in Britain, hence known as Rhodes's cover |
| 1865 | Low woollen goods market opened at the Piece Hall, Halifax, Saturday, 7 January. Previously there was only a market at Rochdale |
| 1865 | The silkworm disease pebrine caused the French and Italian silk industries to collapse, making supplies scarce |
| 1866 | James Tomlinson patented his first machinery for hackling and opening hemp |
| 1867 | Celestin Martin of Verviers, Belgium, was commended at the Paris *Exposition Universelle* for the superior clearness of yarns made from burry wool by carbonisation |
| 1868 | Cottolene, a lard substitute from cottonseed oil, marketed in the United States |
| 1868–1869 | Samuel Cunliffe Lister patents velvet looms for weaving spun silk yarns |
| 1869 | Manchester Cotton Waste Dealers Exchange set up |

| | |
|---|---|
| 1870 | Jean Sebastien Bolette, Belgian engineer, introduces the steel tape for dividing carded fleece into strips for condensing |
| c1870 | Carbonisation of wool/cotton blends came into general use after twenty years of secretive practice (Leather 1917) |
| 1871 | Lister and Reixach joint patent for face-to-face weaving velvet loom |
| 1871 | William Charles Jones established a cotton waste business in Manchester |
| 1873 | Archduke Rainer Ferdinand von Hapsburg invited displays concerning waste consumption for the Vienna exhibition |
| 1875 | *Textile Manufacturer* began publication, first monthly trade journal devoted to the interests of the textile industries |
| 1877 | Oakum picking removed from allowed types of hard labour punishment |
| 1877 | John Henry Leather patents a toothed wire for Garnett waste opening cylinders that allowed setting in double rows |
| 1881–1884 | Concerns over potential transmission of disease by rags led to investigations by Henry Franklin Parsons M.D. for the Local Government Board |
| 1889 | *Textile Mercury* began publication, the first textile trade weekly |
| 1889 | Cordite (using nitrocellulose in the form of guncotton) introduced as replacement for gunpowder |
| 1911 | Rag Flock Act banning sale of uncleansed rag flock |
| 1912 | Bradford Corporation extracted from their sewage over £30,000 worth of grease, the effluent of worsted manufacturers in the city |
| 1912 | *Waste Trade World* began publication, a weekly journal dedicated to waste and old material trades |

# VOLUME I: REFERENCES


Anderson, Christopher Gangadin. *London Vagabond: the Life of Henry Mayhew* (London: published by the author, 2018)

Beaumont, Roberts. *Woollen and Worsted: The Theory and Technology of the Manufacture of Woollen, Worsted, and Union Yarns and Fabrics*, 2 vols. (London: The Library Press Ltd., 1916).

Bevan, G. Phillips (ed.). *British Manufacturing Industries*, vol. 5 (London: Edward Stanford, 1876).

Brewer's *Dictionary of Phrase and Fable* (London: Cassell, Petter and Galpin, 1870).

Burnley, James. *The History of Wool and Woolcombing* (London: Sampson Low, Marston, Searle and Rivington Ltd., 1889.

Caldwell, S.A.G. *The Preparation and Spinning or Flax Fibre* (London & Manchester: Emmott & Co., 1931).

Carter, H. R. 'Shoddy and Mungo and their Manufacture' *Waste Trade World*, 1:4 (25 May 1912), pp. 13–14; 1:10 (6 Jul 1912), p. 6; 1:13 (27 Jul 1912), pp. 13–14; 1:19 (7 Sep 1912), p. 6.

*Cassell's Household Guide to Every Department of Practical Life being a Complete Encyclopaedia of Domestic and Social Economy*, 4 vols., new and rev. ed. (London: Cassell and Co., 1869–1871).

Charley, William. 'Flax and its Products in Ireland: Letter XIV', *Journal of the Society of Arts*, 8:373 (13 Jan 1860), pp. 124–128.

Cookson, Gillian. 'The West Yorkshire Textile Engineering Industry, 1780–1850' (PhD thesis, University of York, July 1994).

Cookson, Gillian. *The Age of Machinery: Engineering the Industrial Revolution, 1770–1850* (Woodbridge, Suffolk: The Boydell Press, 2018).

Cooper, Timothy. 'Peter Lund Simmonds and the Political Ecology of "Waste Utilisation" in Victorian Britain', *Technology and Culture*, 52:1 (Jan 2011), pp. 21–44.

'"Cures" for alcoholism. The Leyfield (Hayden) Cure', *The British Medical Journal*, 1 (2145), 8 Feb 1902, p. 355.

'Death of Mr. Joseph Boden', *Alderley & Wilmslow Advertiser*, 14 Oct 1910, p. 5.

Desrochers, Pierre. 'Victorian Pioneers of Corporate Sustainability', *Business History Review*, 83:4 (Winter 2009), pp. 703–729.

Du Cane, Capt. E. F. 'On the Utilisation of Prison Labour', *Journal of the Society of Arts*, 19:965 (19 May 1871), pp. 529–539.

Elliott, Isabelle M. Z. (based on material collected by Elliott, James Rawlings). *A Short History of Surgical Dressings* (London: The Pharmaceutical Press, 1964).

Eyre-Todd, George. 'Peter Fyfe' in *Who's Who in Glasgow in 1909. A Biographical Dictionary* . . . (Glasgow: Gowans and Gray Ltd., 1909), p. 74.

Gee, N. C. *Shoddy and Mungo Manufacture: Its Development, Ancillary Processes, Methods and Machinery* (Manchester: Emmott & Co. Ltd., 1950).

Hart, Ernest (ed.). 'Flock Beds', *The Sanitary Record: A Journal of Public Health*, 4:29 (Jan 1876), p. 73.

Hewitt, F. O. *Bibliography of the Technical Literature on Silk* (London: Hutchinson's Scientific and Technical Publications, 1946).

Hill, Samuel. *A Plan for Reducing the Poor's-Rate, by Giving Permanent Employment to the Labouring Classes: with Some Observations on the Cultivation of Flax and Hemp* . . ., 2nd ed. (London: J. Harding, 1817).

Hoffman, Frederick L. 'Mortality from Consumption in Dusty Trades', *Bulletin of the Bureau of Labor*, 17:79 (Nov 1908) (Washington: Government Printing Office, 1909), pp. 633–875, notably sections on 'Hemp and cordage manufacture', pp. 757–762; 'Shoddy manufacture', pp. 813–817; 'Rag industry', pp. 817–821, and 'Upholsterers', pp. 821–825.

Humpherys, Anne. *Travels into the Poor Man's Country: The Work of Henry Mayhew* (Athens, GA: University of Georgia Press, 1977).

Jubb, Samuel. *The History of the Shoddy Trade: Its Rise, Progress and Present Position* (London: Houlston and Wright, 1860).

Koller, Theodore. *The Utilization of Waste Products: A Treatise on the Rational Utilization, Recovery, and Treatment of Waste Products of All Kinds*, 3rd ed. (London: Scott, Greenwood and Son, 1918).

Lister, Samuel Cunliffe. 'Spun Silk', *Journal of the Society of Arts*, 21:1088 (26 Sep 1873), pp. 851–852.

Local Government Board. *Reports to the Local Government Board on Public Health and Medical Subjects: Reports on Rag Flock.* N.S. no. 27 (London: HMSO, 1910).

Lock, Charles G. Warnford (ed.). Spon's Encyclopaedia of the Industrial Arts, Manufacturers, and Commercial Products, 5 vols. (London: E. & F. N. Spon, 1882).

Ludlam, Albert James. *The Craft of Mattress and Bedding Production* (London: The Furniture Record Ltd., 1947).

Malin, John Christopher. The West Riding Recovered Wool Industry, ca. 1813–1930. PhD thesis, University of York, 1979.

Marsden, Richard. *Cotton Spinning: Its Development, Principles, and Practice* (London: George Bell and Sons).

Marwick, William H. 'Some Quaker Firms of the Nineteenth Century. II.', *Journal of the Friends Historical Society*, 50:437 (1962), pp. 17–36.

Melville, Herman. *Redburn: his first voyage. Being the Sailor-boy Confessions and Reminiscences of the Son-of-a-Gentleman, in the Merchant Service* (New York: Harper & Brothers, 1850).

Murphy, William S. 'Ch. VI Carding' and 'Ch. VII Gilling', in *The Textile Industries: A Practical Guide to Fibres, Yarns & Fabrics in Every Branch of Textile Manufacture* (London: Gresham Publishing Co., 1910), vol. 2, pp. 43–101.

Ormerod, Frank. *Wool* (Constable and Co. Ltd., 1918).

'Obituary: Eli Sowerbutts', *Geographical Journal*, 23:6 (Jun 1904), pp. 792–793.

'Obituary: Mr. Howard Priestman', *Manchester Guardian*, 8 Dec 1931, p. 10.

Reuss, F.W. "Old French Rag Merchants and Exporters", *Waste Trade World*, 3:9 (28 Jun 1913), pp. 8–9.

Reuss, F. W. 'Milestones in my Life', *Waste Trade World*, 4:14 (31 Jan 1914), pp. 10–11.
Rimmer, W. G. *Marshalls of Leeds: Flax-Spinners 1788–1886* (Cambridge: University Press, 1960).
Sala, George Augustus. 'Old Clothes', *Household Words*, 5:108 (17 Apr 1852), 93–98.
Sala, George Augustus. *Looking at Life; or, Thoughts and Things* (London: Routledge, Warne, and Routledge, 1860).
Simmonds, Peter Lund. *Waste Products and Undeveloped Substances: or, Hints for Enterprise in Neglected Fields* (London: Robert Hardwicke, 1862).
Simmonds, Peter Lund. 'The Employment of Waste Silk', *Journal of the Society of Arts*, 21:1090 (10 Oct 1873), pp. 871–882.
'Strength of Army Cloths Compared', *The New York Times*, 18 Aug 1918, p. 18.
Tardieu, Ambroise. *Dictionnaire d'hygiène publique et de salubrité, ou Répertoire de toutes les questions relatives à la santé publique*, 2nd ed. (Paris: J.-B. Ballière et Fils, 1862).
Thornley, Thomas. *Cotton Spinning (Honours, or Third Year)*, 2nd ed. (London: Scott, Greenwood & Son, 1907).
Warner, Sir Frank. *The Silk Industry of the United Kingdom: Its Origin and Development* (London: Drane's, 1921).
White, Noel D. 'Spun Silk: Its Manufacture and Uses', *American Dyestuff Reporter*, 25:2 (27 Jan 1936), pp. 27–30 & 53–54.
Zipser, Julius. *Textile Raw Materials and Their Conversion into Yarns*. Translated from the German by Charles Salter (London: Scott, Greenwood and Co., 1901).

# ACKNOWLEDGEMENTS

A project like this is intimately bound up with a love of libraries and archives, books and booksellers, old prints and documents, catalogues and bibliographies. I am grateful to all who keep this material world alive, often in spite of diminishing budgets and reduced hours. Those institutions that have contributed to this project include Manchester Central Library, the John Rylands Library, Chetham's Library, and the several university libraries in my home city of Manchester. The British Library, the National Art Library and the National Archives have long been favourite haunts; and more recently I have added the Brotherton Library (Leeds), the Mitchell Library (Glasgow), the National Library of Scotland and the Bodleian Library to my literary purlieus. To the (usually anonymous) librarians and archivists in these places who have answered my queries or those who have fetched and returned materials, I am indebted.

One who deserves particular mention is Kirsty McHugh, Curator of the John Murray Archive and Publishers' Collections at the National Library of Scotland. To her dedication, I owe the identification of contributors to *Chambers's Journal*. Liane MacIver of *The Times* archive (News UK) confirmed authorship of an article in that newspaper. Sue Hurley, Archivist of the Saddlers' Company kindly searched records for me, as did Andrew Filarowski, Technical Director of the Society of Dyers and Colourists, Helen Farrar, Curator of the Bradford College Textile Archive, and Corin Williams, Editor of *Materials Recyling World*. Curator Matthew Watson of Bolton Museums, Archivist David Tilsley of the Lancashire Record Office, Rebecca Unsworth of the Textile Institute, and Maria C. Thiry of the American Association of Textile Chemists and Colorists, were particularly helpful with rights and permissions.

Research of this nature is hugely facilitated by the availability of digitised books and journals. The free websites of the Internet Archive, the Hathi Trust, Google Books, Grace's Guide and The Gazette were instrumental to efficient working. The Gallica site of the Bibliothèque Nationale de France and the Portail Persée of the Persée partnership were equally useful for French historical literature. My personal subscription to the British Newspaper Archive was immeasurably important in searches for publication dates, life stories of lesser-known people and company histories. Institutional subscriptions to Proquest and Gale databases were also heavily tapped. Yet all these sources cannot satisfy the foraging requirements for an addict of textile trade literature. In 2020, I made a madcap purchase of an eighty-year run of the *Textile Manufacturer*, a quantity so large that customs officials were reluctant to believe this could be for my personal use. But during the pandemic lockdown, access to this journal proved its worth on multiple occasions.

The period during which this series came to fruition saw the death of three friends and colleagues who would have so much appreciated these works: the art librarian Harlan Sifford, the textile curator Linda Eaton, and the weaving and German language expert Ute Bargmann. I hope these volumes may be worthy of their memory.

# NOTES ABOUT TRANSCRIPTION

The transcriptions in this series aim to be as accurate as possible a rendition of the author's words, and to preserve as much of the original format as may be meaningful. Original capitalisation and italicisation has been retained where possible. Historical and idiosyncratic spellings have also been retained. However, evident unintentional typographical errors have been silently corrected in the text in order to allow quotation without the need for the Latin adverb *sic*. Otherwise, corrections are made in the annotations, where, for example historical variations in spelling are adjusted, or proper names amended.

Original punctuation has been respected but, with reticence, a comma has occasionally been added or removed to aid reading or meaning. And single sentence paragraphs have occasionally been combined with previous or subsequent paragraphs when this has aided sense. Ditto marks in tables have sometimes been expanded for clarity. Where abbreviations have been expanded to aid the modern reader, this is signalled within the headnotes.

### A warning about offensive text

In much British writing of the nineteenth century, casual racism, anti-Jewish and anti-Irish remarks surface. African ethnicities are often found characterised as less than civilised. Prejudice against Jewish people arises in remarks about uncleanliness, and negative attitudes to Irish people are conveyed by association with poverty. Names carrying a pejorative sense are used as a literary device with the intent of othering: *Mumbo Jumbo* for the African, *Ikey* for the Jewish man, and *Pat* for the Irishman. It has not been considered necessary to annotate each instance, but attention has been given where such prejudice is important to the context or meaning of the individual text. Some may question why I have reproduced such objectionable texts. The intention has been principally to retain historical integrity, but also to make available to scholars of race and racism examples that may be of use.

# INTRODUCTION TO *PATHWAYS IN THE NINETEENTH-CENTURY BRITISH TEXTILE INDUSTRY*

> I do not think altogether the worse of a book for having survived the author a generation or two.
>
> Hazlitt, 'On Reading Old Books'

The works compiled in this series of volumes have little of the 'pure silent air of immortality' treasured by Hazlitt in his essay on old books, and indeed part of their value is that they preserve much of 'the dust and smoke and noise' of the time when they were current literature.[1] Written for a particular time and audience, many of these texts served their purpose and then passed quickly out of memory. This series looks at historical sources focused on three thematic areas: the waste textile trades, the commercial warehouse and the calico printing industry. These texts are revived here, not as period pieces, and not just because of their historical value in encapsulating social, business and technical knowledge, but also because of what they offer us today on strategies of innovation, global trade and sustainable manufacturing.

Often viable ideas and inventions do not take root because societal values mitigate against their growth. Nineteenth-century British society was enclosed in a frame of mind that was not only rigidly defined by class, but also one with an urge to classify. Hierarchies of value were applied widely, not only to textile fibres and fabrics but to discarded garments and rags. Ranks were ascribed to the location of urban buildings, and to the floor levels within these buildings, as well of course, to occupations and matters of aesthetic taste. Such concepts of higher and lower goods and purposes limited the freedom to apply all manner of useful ideas. Instead, they led to the promotion of less edifying systems, such as phrenology, or positively harmful beliefs in racial superiority. Revisiting historical texts offers not only a window on the past, but an opportunity to revive and reassess the innovations of the time in order to draw new connections with current projects.

## The waste textile trades

Class and textiles were inextricably combined in the nineteenth-century mindset. This was at the heart of the great anxiety surrounding the rag and shoddy trade, that 'the offcast of every class of the population, from the wealthy of the West-end to the tramp and vagrant of the East' were intermixed in the recycled product.[2] Even rags were expected to respect class, and the wounds of the gentry were bandaged with lint made from fine linen although ordinary linen would have served as well.[3] In the nineteenth century, recycling of textile waste ran up against cultural prejudices more strongly than technological barriers. Fear of contagion in an era of cholera, the associations of reconstituted substances with adulteration, and class-based bias against materials tainted by poverty – all these imparted a negative character to rags and regenerated textiles. Reinforcing these disincentives, the best-known example of textile reprocessing – converting old rope into oakum for caulking wooden ships – was used as a punishment, connecting it in the public consciousness to criminality and prisons.

The satisfactory quality of the end products of the textile waste industries – if the composition of products using recycled waste could have been revealed – might eventually have mitigated negative feelings, but these predominating cultural attitudes were powerful motivation for concealment rather than announcement. Less sullied by their origin were virgin fibres that were either by-products of manufacture, or gatherable through increasingly efficient processing of raw materials. But even these suffered the undignified names of droppings, fly, strippings and sweepings, hardly suited to public advertisement.

These cultural shortcomings were somewhat counterbalanced by the perceived good of eliminating waste. Domestic practices of *waste-not, want-not* prudence inculcated from childhood the values of a waste-free manner of living. It was to such homely virtues that the chemist Lyon Playfair first appealed in a public lecture of 1852, 'Chemistry, like a prudent housewife, economises every scrap',[4] going on to join feminine thrift to another cultural pillar, the model provided by nature, wherein every substance degrades and is re-utilised. Nevertheless, when it came to the insertion of waste-derived textile fibres into cloth, concealment became a stigma in itself. In 1862, the writer of the essay 'Social Wastes and Waste Lands' asserted:

> that quality and make of goods are now so delusive and disguised since machinery has been applied to the manufacture of cloths of every description, that none but [the manufacturers] themselves know of what it is made; and the public only learn by wear and tear that they are not what they bought them for.[5]

Despite the poor reputation of textiles incorporating waste fibres, quality was not necessarily compromised, and the main aim of textile production using waste fibre was lowering of cost, thereby enabling luxury-style fabrics to reach a wider market. Notwithstanding honest commercial intentions, the use of waste, no matter how economically or morally laudatory, was never able to become an open selling point in the nineteenth century. The lingering sense of abasement attached to the waste textile trades in the past appears to have led to their neglect as a foundation for contemporary recycling studies. Even the term *waste* can be implicated in this problem. As soon as a practical use is found for refuse material, it is no longer waste – an anomaly that many writers on the topic have confronted. The heading of *waste* has been adopted here because it was widely promulgated and recognised in nineteenth-century literature.

What can we learn from the waste textiles of the past? Firstly, a lifetime of use could contribute valued properties to textile material; the medical use of lint was based upon softening through multiple alkaline washings, a character not possessed by fresh linen. Even quite radical treatments to recuperate fibres from intermediary or end products by tearing and shredding still left intact their unique *worn* character. For example, mungo – torn from felted broadcloth – was able to add qualities of smoothness and sheen to high-calibre woollen cloths that were not achievable with raw wool. So we find textile materials can gain desirable properties through use and reprocessing.

The British textile industries were segregated by fibre type, allocated to different geographical regions, with the waste textile industries following much the same pattern. With hindsight, this segregation can be seen to have slowed the spread of waste textile technology across the major types. We can now see that the development of waste textile machinery was to divide along processing lines rather than fibre type, aligning with either the carded or combed categories of spinning. Breakers, carders and condensers characterised short-staple processing, with gills and combs the tools of long-staple working. Bridging across fibre divisions gave new insights; Samuel Lister's experience with the wool comb provided him with a lead in the treatment of waste silk. Such cross-fertilisation was probably encouraged by the larger machine-making firms located in warehousing centres like Manchester or Leeds. Machine-makers were able to apply understandings gained in the sphere of wool to that of cotton or silk uninhibited by fibre-based regional separation. However, local crossover of technologies was also possible, demonstrated by divergent techniques for rag flock production, with Yorkshire following the shoddy devil model, Gloucestershire the paper beater model and Surrey the fulling stocks model. Innovation was nourished where textile technologies and mechanical technologies intersected.

A century earlier, William Lewis (c1708–1781) had drawn attention, in his *Commercium Philosophico-technicum*, to the interrelations between the arts that remained separated by the lack of mutual knowledge:

> The discoveries and improvements made in one art, and even its common processes, are generally little known to those who are employed in another, so that the workman can seldom avail himself of the advantages which he might receive from the correlative arts. . . . To enquire therefore by experiment into the different means of producing one effect, and trace it through all the arts . . . appeared to be the most rational and

> direct means . . . of procuring an useful intercourse and communication of knowledge . . . of enriching one art with the practices, materials, and sometimes even with the refuse-matters of another.[6]

While wool waste textiles were assorted to both combed and carded branches (the worsted and woollen divisions of the industry), long-fibred silk and linen paralleled the combed branch, and mixture fabrics the carded branch. Cotton waste, on the other hand, developed upon independent lines that gave rise to new textile structures and products. Possibilities for cotton re-use followed more closely upon staple length, with shorter fibres employed for filling and stuffing yarns wherein fibres are not subject to tensile stresses. Non-woven structures like batting, medical cotton wool, and engine-cleaning waste ensured that there was little fibre which could not be repurposed.

Victorian innovation in mixture fabrics, especially combining cotton with wool (vegetable with animal fibre), led to particularly intractable problems when reprocessing the waste of such mixtures. The solutions adopted involved destruction of the least valuable fibre, for example, carbonisation of cotton to extract wool. With contemporary mixtures of synthetic and natural fibres, the difficulties have increased, but technologies have also expanded in areas of materials separation such as ultrasonication. The long-standing challenge of fibre separation may ultimately act as a stimulus to design solutions that find replacements for blended-fibre fabrics.

The incessant Victorian impulse to classify was turned into a strength that contributed to the success of nineteenth-century rag recycling. The re-use of rags ultimately depended on the efficiency of systems of grading. Sorting of rags into a myriad of fibre, colour and quality categories by experienced and knowledgeable women made it possible to re-use materials with reduced processing, notably without dye-stripping, and with the least amount of re-dyeing.

Textile recycling often involves other forms of trade-off. Henry Franklin Parsons made the insightful statement that the hygienic advantage of washing wool rags, 'is gained at the cost of a certain amount of river pollution; the streams carrying off the organic matter, which would otherwise find its way to the land as manure'. Already, the complex balance between competing forms of pollution was being highlighted. Parsons also noted that although washing 'would in all probability remove any infectious matter adhering to the rags [it did not give], however, any protection to the work-people. On the contrary, the additional handling required in the early stages would tend in the opposite direction'.[7] More than a century has passed but the issues of textile recycling remain embedded in their materials, structures and processing, linking the present day with the past.

## The commercial warehouse

Business historian Roland Smith saw the emergence of the warehousing system in Manchester as one of the most startling changes in its cotton industry: 'In 1820,

126 officially termed warehouses were listed in the Township Rate Books and only nine years later the number had increased to nearly one thousand'.[8] These early warehouses were often converted dwellings or cellars but soon warehouses developed into a special class of architecture. Warehouse architecture had to resolve issues of constricted urban access, lighting, fire safety and ventilation. But even before this, the commercial warehouse came to represent a new practice of doing business.

Samuel Bamford suggests it was the Scottish brothers William Grant (1770–1842) and Daniel Grant (1784–1855) who introduced a stronger sociability to attracting warehouse custom. Their firm, William Grant and Brothers, had a warehouse at 1 Lower Cannon-street, Manchester, from 1804 when they entered the calico printing trade. Bamford recalled:

> They soon showed their English neighbours the way to do business; they were indefatigably on the alert for customers, and whilst other tradesmen stood at their doors bowing to country buyers – for it was never the custom then to stop them and ask them in – the Grants with quick eyes were on the look out, and seldom permitted a stranger to pass without offering him the inspection of their "stock of unequalled prints at the very lowest prices." Whilst others coldly looked on, they were often successful in making a sale; and thus, by means of an innovation on the old form of trading, they . . . soon established a good connection, and laid the foundation for their subsequent extraordinary and deserved prosperity.[9]

Some niceties of business were slow in arrival. In 1825, the Manchester Commissioners of Police recorded an expense for painting numbers upon doors: 'A Commissioner observed that the numbers on the doors in Back George-street were extremely irregular; the dwelling-houses were numbered in one way, and the warehouses in another; and this caused much trouble and inconvenience, and sometimes mistakes, in the delivery of parcels.'[10] Warehousing signboards appear as a later innovation, arising from the increasing array of specialist textiles available by 1840 that created a need for greater ease of identity. By good fortune, Benjamin Love's *Hand-Book of Manchester* preserves the babel of textile signage of the time.[11]

To cope with burgeoning variety and scale of business, the design of new warehouse buildings was modified to enable efficient receipt and stockpiling of goods, and to facilitate their display and sale to wholesale customers, while not neglecting discreet credit-checking and packing. A raised ground floor enabled a functional basement storey, and the lighting of five floors was supplemented by roof lights above a central well. Light was of the essence for sale of decorative cloth, with prints accorded the top floor, while grey goods could be consigned to the basement. With the invention of prismatic pavement lights, even the lower storey enjoyed reasonable natural illumination. Contemporary descriptions of the warehouse experience accord great pride to the systems of message communication between floors. These enabled checking of credit while the customer was moving from floor to floor placing orders. Later innovations were conveniences such as customer lifts that made examining goods on upper floors a less strenuous undertaking.

At the start of the nineteenth century, goods made in the North were sent to London for warehousing and shipping. The growth of regional banking and insurance enabled provincial cities to become warehousing centres, with Manchester, Glasgow and Dublin in leading roles. Alongside their regional staples, the new commercial warehouses began to introduce luxury goods – ribbons, artificial flowers and lace – as well as haberdashery and hosiery, becoming rivals to the London houses. It was the expansion into these *fancy* trades that marked the full emergence of the commercial warehouse, able to satisfy all needs on one site. The transition was marked on the outside by the more decorative palazzo style making warehouses resemble Venetian palaces, and on the inside by grand staircases and extensive displays of goods.

At the heart of the warehouse system was the division into departments each headed by a buyer responsible for acquisition of stock and accountable to the business partners for its timely sale. Under each buyer was a team of senior and junior salesmen and apprentices. They were supported by entering clerks and counting house clerks who handled the paperwork and accounts. Specialising in a particular category of goods enabled salesmen to thoroughly know their stock and efficiently serve the wants of their wholesale customers. Everything sold was available to see and handle, and great orderliness was required to show, then repack and return goods to stock. Long hours were characteristic of warehouse work but the introduction of the Saturday half-holiday in 1843 was a hard-won concession. Leo Grindon described the prior situation:

> In winter it was quite a common thing to see every window in the principal warehouses illuminated up till nine, ten, even eleven pm., and the longest and sweetest of midsummer Saturday evenings often sank to sleep in the crimson west before ever a door was locked or a lad set free.[12]

To enable long hours, salesmen and apprentices often lived in tied premises adjoining, making warehousing a way of life. For a working-class lad, obtaining warehouse work was seen as satisfying most ambitions. Archibald Prentice derided the pretensions observed in the early Glasgow scene where 'The assistant in a warehouse, who receives a salary of £50 a-year, dares not be seen in conversation with a weaver, for fear it might be supposed he kept *low* company'.[13] By mid-century, with the steady increase in sale of ready-made clothing items, workrooms were set up and women hired for making up such items on-site. John Roberton's report of 1860 suggests at that time these workrooms were little better than sweatshops, but improvements were slowly introduced. We can see in the commercial warehouse the various innovative features that were adopted by retailers in the introduction of the department store.

From the 1830s, warehousing began to divide along the lines of the home trade serving the domestic market, and the shipping trade serving various export markets. In Manchester, the shipping trade grew largely in the hands of foreign merchants, many of whom became naturalised and added greatly not only to the wealth, but to the culture of the city. Manchester welcomed the foreigner in this context, but assimilation was not easy for the first generation. In the velveteen trademark dispute of 1880, for example, the naturalised Louis Behrens with his imperfect English was still seen as a foreigner. Export houses brought new marketing methods, with great attention paid to packing and labelling goods so that brands could be readily recognised abroad by sight. With the language barrier, and natural wariness of deception, purchasers abroad depended on visual cues to confirm quality, and insisted on consistency. Understanding the complexities of packing for different markets became a competitive advantage for British-based merchants over their new rivals at the start of the twentieth century. The commercial warehouse, in the form of the shipping house corresponding with agents stationed abroad, became the dominant model in the global textile trade of the nineteenth century. Methods of advertising, display, branding, grading of goods all had origins in the commercial warehouse and its international trading practices – revealed equally in the development of corresponding practices to deceive buyer and seller.

## The calico printing industry

In calico printing, the nineteenth century experienced a nexus of the leading branches of innovative activity. George Dodd emphasised the tripartite contributions in design, mechanics and chemistry. All three manifested across the century, although with varied concentrations of intensity. The century opened with a burst of activity in transfer engraving and cylinder printing that saw the mastery of mechanised printing by the 1840s. This intersected with steady and regular advancements in colouration that showcased colour innovations as fashion trends up to the 1870s. The last part of the century witnessed a focus on export styles of printing that elicited developments in design alongside colouration, effects less well-known because they were seldom seen in European contexts.

Chemical technology became the prime symbol of advancement, and calico printing the representative industry taking advantage of new chemical knowledge. 'Hence in every large print-work there is either a partner or a manager thoroughly versed in practical chemistry; and the drug or chemical department in such establishments shows the importance attached to this matter'.[14] Charles O'Neill, more than any other author, related the fits and starts of the developments in mordants, dyes and processes for calico printing. His accounts reveal how much the history of synthetic dyes has been written with hindsight, whereas at the time of their development, there was not a clear advantage to synthetic dyes as a general category. Economic factors were the crucial determinant of how innovation was received.

The fervour of attention to developments in colouration, and anxiety surrounding retaining competitive advantage from them, is brought out by John Mercer junior's account of his father's discoveries. His description contains numerous examples of the rapid diffusion of new chemical processes. After Mercer's introduction of the chlorination of wool in the early 1840s, his firm was 'able to print the most splendid Royal Blues and had a run of about a year before it became generally known'. Mercer gave the process to connected printworks in Sabden, but 'Sabden people let it slip in about a year after they got it; a man from a neighboring printworks pirated the secret from one of the workmen and set off through England, Scotland and France selling the process'.[15]

Mechanical innovation in calico printing developed more incrementally. Thomas Bell's oft-cited patent of 1783 for cylinder printing was not workable, but by the 1790s, a practicable single-colour printing machine was introduced. It was not until the 1820s that printing two colours in register became common, and three-colour printing was still in the experimental stage until 1830. Improvements in machine printing required advancement in adjunct areas, such as cylinder making, mandrels to hold and drive the cylinders, doctor blade materials, and construction of backing cloths. William Turnbull's article on the cylinder printing machine shows the level of sophistication reached after a century of incremental improvements.[16] Countering the Arts and Crafts movement's call for a return to craft-based production, Turnbull demonstrated how machinery extended the range of human skill.

It is a mistaken notion that innovation proceeded unidirectionally toward mechanised production. Hand-block printing competed with cylinder printing into the 1840s when, with the regulation of child labour, production became more costly. However, for printing expensive silk and wool materials or complex furnishing patterns, block printing retained its advantage into the next century.[17] It was a distinctive blend of artisan and machine production that characterised calico printing. Charles F. Sabel and Jonathan Zeitlin noted that calico printworks operated more as 'groupings of artisans' shops under one roof than factories organised on the assembly-line model'.[18] Flexibility, not speed, was a factor of crucial importance for the industry; old equipment was retained knowing that outmoded techniques could return to fashion.[19] Creation of new products and expanded assortments of goods were the means used by the British calico printer to outdo competition. From the boasts of *miles* of production in the first half of the century, outputs moved toward smaller-scale runs and sales based on pre-sampling in the second half. The combination of an artisanal with an industrial mindset appears to have motivated and sustained innovation.

In the early part of the century, designers were trained from young working-class men in the printworks who showed artistic promise. In the absence of academy-based presumptions about design, they produced work that prefigured later modern movements in the arts. The mid-century saw the dominance of "French" design, but we learn from William Mercer that the typical Paris studio was a multinational mixture of Alsatians, 'a few Frenchmen from different provinces, a sprinkling of Germans, Dutch, Flemings, seldom more than one or two Parisians, and perhaps a solitary Englishman'.[20] In the last part of the century, British calico printing design was dominated by work for export markets. Designs were developed from advice given by agents stationed at destination ports, or adapted from models collected in the export regions – what would now be called cultural appropriation. The impetus of closely imitating hand work through mechanical means stimulated new printing techniques. From the 1880s, an appreciation of Japanese patterns, accessed through imports of worn-out *katagami* stencils, helped revitalise British design for both home and export markets. We can see that throughout the century, innovation in design largely emanated from cross-cultural fertilisation, but it was equally stimulated by new developments in colouration and mechanical technologies.

## Reflections

Ultimately, it takes a free attitude of mind to take a different perspective. Farrar Fenton's Captain Corbett realised that if papermakers could separate cotton from wool by chemically destroying the wool, then the opposite must be possible – retaining the wool and eliminating the cotton.[21] Samuel Cunliffe Lister wrote,

> My very ignorance was the cause of my doing what I otherwise should not have done. A practical silk spinner would at once have said, "There is plenty of good waste; why bother with this rubbish?" . . . But not being a practical silk spinner and knowing little or nothing about silk or silk waste, I thought I would try and see what could be done with it.[22]

Closely occupied with the day-to-day running of their businesses, nineteenth-century manufacturers and merchants were largely exposed to alternative ideas through engagement in written communication channels: through journals of patents, trade journals, newspapers and reviews of national and international industrial exhibitions. These texts were increasingly accompanied by images and plans, visual stimuli likely to spawn ideas that could cross industrial divisions based on fibre types and localisation. The trade journals that arose in the last quarter of the century offered a chance to publish for the first time to many of the technical writers selected for this series. Often they were writing toward the end of a career in industry or education, summing up a lifetime's experience. Others adopted a more literary standpoint in the form of reminiscences, bringing to vivid detail working lives whose incident might otherwise have been lost in the even tenor of the everyday. The most varied group of authors contributed to literary magazines, showing an aspiration to reach outside a class-bound life. Occasionally young, like William Drennan, who wrote upon completion of his warehousing apprenticeship, they were more often seasoned men who had stumbled in the treacherous path to business success; Daniel Puseley altered his name and mythologised his past to obscure his bankruptcy history and pursue a literary career. But the important point is that they wrote from experience. In this selection, a significant number of authors have been identified for the first time, and their biographies sketched out. The modern reader will note that there are few women's voices, but the noteworthy roles women played in the industrial world are nevertheless brought to attention. Likewise, the part of immigrants to Britain in the textile field is brought into view, if not in their own voices. Nevertheless, diverse and divergent voices have been sought, providing an elliptical view rather than an artificially sharpened focus.

Tasked with describing the year's advances in textile manufactures for 1883, Alan Summerly Cole, authority on the textile arts, raised the question, 'Would it be an advance if design and method of manufacture were improved, but the quality of material had deteriorated?' Cole outlined the positions of two camps, the *perfectibilian* that insisted on progress, and the *deteriorationist* that saw only corruption. Taking the side of advancement in manufactures which he saw characterised by vivacity in design, he nevertheless regretted 'a sort of hard effect in form. . ., a result of accustoming designers to the sight of mechanical designs. A similar character is even present in the appearance of hand-made works'.[23] More than a century later, Cole's reflection remains relevant, and to it we must add whether an innovation can be considered an advancement if it does not further environmental sustainability and social equity. The class system and imperial mentality impaired visions of social equality in the nineteenth century. However, in the narrow confines of textile commerce, there grew in Britain an appreciation of the foreigner at home and the tastes of the consumer abroad. More widely, the rational interests of nineteenth-century business began to align with environmental interests.[24] In 1873, Archduke Rainer Ferdinand went so far as to propose that the extent to which the waste materials of industry were utilised be considered 'a measure of the degree of industrial development and capability'.[25] A fresh look at nineteenth-century achievements in the textile industries can be both surprising and humbling.

## Notes

1 W. Hazlitt, 'On Reading Old Books', *Table-Talk: or, Original Essays* (Paris: A. and W. Galignani, 1825), vol. 2, p. 135.

2 P. Fyfe, 'What the People Sleep Upon', *Various Lectures – 1892–1904* (Glasgow: Corporation of Glasgow, 1908), Lecture 9, pp. 1–11 (on p. 3).

3 C. M. Smith, 'Lint', *Chambers's Journal*, 23:59 (17 Feb 1855), pp. 104–106 (on p. 105).

4 Lyon Playfair (1818–1898), British chemist, delivered this passage in a lecture before the Society of Arts, 7 January 1852: 'On the chemical principles involved in the manufactures of the Exhibition as indicating the necessity of industrial instruction', published in *Lectures on the Results of the Exhibition delivered before the Society of Arts, Manufactures, and Commerce, at the suggestion of H.R.H. Prince Albert, President of the Society* (London: David Bogue, 1852), p. 124.

5 Ajax (pseud.). *Social Wastes and Waste Lands; Flax v. Slave-Grown Cotton: Being a Glance at the Commercial and Social State of the Nation. . .* (London: Simpkin, Marshall & Co. Manchester: Dinham & Co., 1862), pp. 20–21.

6 W. Lewis, *Commercium Philosophico-technicum; or, the philosophical commerce of arts: designed as an attempt to improve arts, trades, and manufactures* (London: printed by H. Baldwin for the author, 1763), pp. xii–xiii.
7 H. F. Parsons, 'On the Manufacture of Rag Flock in Reference to the Possible Dissemination of Infectious Disease by this and other Products of Woollen Rags', *Fifteenth Annual Report of the Local Government Board, 1885–86: Supplement containing the Report of the Medical Officer for 1885* (London: HMSO, 1886), Appendix A, no. 7, note 4.
8 R. Smith, 'Manchester as a Centre for the Manufacture and Merchanting of Cotton Goods, 1820–30', *University of Birmingham History Journal*, 4:1 (1953–54), pp. 47–65 (on p. 63).
9 S. Bamford, *Early Days* (London: Simpkin, Marshall and Co., 1849), p. 189.
10 'Commissioners of Police', *Manchester Courier*, 8 Jan 1825, p. 3.
11 B. Love, *The Hand-Book of Manchester . . . being a second and enlarged edition of "Manchester as it is"* (Manchester: Love and Barton, 1842), p. 230.
12 L. H. Grindon, *Manchester Banks and Bankers: Historical, Biographical, and Anecdotal*, 2nd ed. (Manchester: Palmer & Howe, 1878), pp. 174–175.
13 A. Prentice, *Letters from Scotland by an English Commercial Traveller Written During a Journey to Scotland in the Summer of 1815* (London: Longman, Hurst, Rees, Orme and Brown, 1817), pp. 199–200.
14 G. Dodd, 'A Day at a Lancashire Print-Work', *Penny Magazine*, 12:727 (29 Jul 1843), pp. 289–296 (on p. 292).
15 J. Graham, 'Some of the Practical Discoveries of John Mercer Esquire of Oakenshaw, as Furnished to Me by his Son John for the Information of the Royal Society, 15th November 1847', 'History of the Printworks of the Manchester District from 1760 to 1846'. Manchester Archives, Ms. ff 667.3 G1, pp. 463–469 (on p. 468).
16 'The Calico Printing Machine. By a Calico Printer', *The Dyer and Calico Printer*, 2 (Mar–Oct 1891), pp. 35–36, 53, 73, 89, 105, 121, 139, 157.
17 See E. Honey, 'Fabric Printing. Block Work and Machine Printing Compared', *The Dyer and Calico Printer*, 14 (Aug–Oct 1894), pp. 115, 132, 148.
18 C. F. Sabel and J. Zeitlin, 'Historical Alternatives to Mass Production: Politics, Markets and Technology in Nineteenth-Century Industrialization', *Past and Present*, 108 (Aug 1985), pp. 133–176 (on p. 150).
19 See O'Neill on the unexpected revival of block printing from 1857 to 1859. C. O'Neill, 'The Printing and Dyeing of Calico, Silk, and Woollen Fabrics', *Record of the International 1862 Exhibition* (Glasgow, Edinburgh and London: William Mackenzie, 1862), pp. 356–364 (on p. 360).
20 W. Mercer, 'Designers' Ateliers in Paris', *Chambers's Journal of Popular Literature, Science and Arts*, 7:176 (16 May 1857), pp. 305–308 (on p. 306).
21 F. Fenton, 'Woollen Shoddy. Its Invention, History, and Manufacture', *Textile Manufacturer*, 7:76–82 (15 Apr–15 Oct 1881), pp. 131–132, 172–173, 208–209, 251–252, 287–289, 328–329, 365–367.
22 S. C. Lister, *Lord Masham's Inventions. Written by Himself* (Bradford: The 'Argus' Printing Works, 1905), pp. 52–62.
23 A. S. Cole, 'The Year's Advance in Art Manufactures. No. V. – Textiles: Lace, Tapestry, Stuffs', *The Art Journal*, (1883), pp. 149–152 (on p. 149).
24 See the work of Pierre Desrochers: 'Learning from History or from Nature, or Both? Recycling Networks and their Metaphors in Early Industrialization', *Progress in Industrial Ecology*, 2 (2005), pp. 19–34. 'Victorian Pioneers of Corporate Sustainability', *Business History Review*, 83:4 (Winter 2009), pp. 703–729.
25 Cited in English translation by Peter Lund Simmonds in *Waste Products and Undeveloped* Substances, 2nd ed. (London: Robert Hardwicke, 1873), p. 1.

# INTRODUCTION TO VOLUME I

## The Waste Textile Industries

> Instead of a disgrace to our manufacturing industry, the employment of mungo and shoddy is a credit to the age, for waste is a sin against the present and future generations.
>
> Bevan, G. Phillips (ed.). *British Manufacturing Industries*, vol. 5 (London: Edward Stanford, 1876), p. 50

In introducing the art of fish-scale embroidery, *Cassell's Household Guide* advises, 'A knowledge of how to utilise trifles which would otherwise be valueless, will often enable the housewife to render her home attractive without expending that money which might be required for other purposes'.[1] Reclaiming waste was so thoroughly ingrained in female education and domestic economy that it usually passed without regard. However, in moving to the masculine sphere and the scale of industrial economy, the utilisation of waste materials came to take on an important visibility in the nineteenth century. Many nineteenth-century writers drew attention to the contradiction of applying the term *waste* to substances that had been found of valuable use. However, *waste* was conveniently applicable to both by-products and re-used goods – new and old materials. The term *waste* in this context also served to associate with industry moral values of prudence and thrift. The utilisation and re-utilisation of fibre residues was not new to the nineteenth century, but the mechanisation of processes leading to large-scale production and an increased range of products was the wonder of the age. Waste from each of the major textile fibres followed its own path toward mechanisation, had its own geographical centres, and its own markets. Looking first at writers on the general subject of waste, the subsequent chapters will treat individual fibre-based industries: bast fibre, wool, cotton, silk; then the development of the rag processing, ending with a chapter on repurposed textiles.

### Part 1 'A credit to the age': the utilisation of waste

The utilisation of waste was a symbol of modernity. This was often made evident by citing the transformative power of chemistry. Peter Lund Simmonds indicated

DOI: 10.4324/9780429274190-1

that 'modern chemistry has taught us how, out of the most vile and apparently the most worthless rubbish, the most useful and frequently the most beautiful things may be elaborated'. The Victorian mind delighted in the paradox of the low made high with its Biblical echoes. Simmonds continued:

> Rags are the common emblem of poverty, and to say that a man is in a ragged condition is the worst thing that can be said of him; but rags are, in fact, a great source of wealth, and one of the staples of our commerce.[2]

It is appropriate that Simmonds's papers head this volume as his writings on waste were amongst the first to treat the subject across the industrial and imperial landscape, and they held considerable influence, both reflecting and shaping the popular understanding of waste.

The philosophy first espoused by Simmonds was the imitation of nature: 'we perceive in nature how nothing is wasted, but that every substance is reconverted, and again made to do duty in a changed and beautified form'. Yet the insightful industrialist was one who 'rescued from the manure-heap' products that could serve wealth creation before re-entering nature's cycle. This value-adding economic argument was eventually extended, supported by the providential belief in nature as an infinite resource for humankind. Simmonds shifted in his thinking about waste, leaving behind the moral imperative to reduce pollution, and moving toward the exploitation of 'undeveloped' colonial raw materials. An underlying driver was the rag shortage of the 1850s – rags needed for papermaking upon which the expanding publishing industry depended. The search for papermaking substitutes in colonial fibre plants was seen as a means of maintaining Britain's competitiveness amongst its European neighbours. But the association of waste with unutilised natural resources became a means of legitimising interference in colonial ecologies for the purpose of capitalist profit.[3]

Speaking in 1917, Charles Walter Leather, proprietor of the iconic Garnett company and authority on machinery for processing reclaimed wool, reflected upon progress in the textile waste trade over the course of a century. He returned to a definition of waste as the residues or by-products of industry, and was an early proponent of zero waste, claiming that 'The acme of industrial economy is the profitable employment of every atom of material'. Britain maintained an impressive range of reprocessed fibre and products made from it, from the lowest saddle-stuffings to fine costume cloths, selling both fibre and end products, so that few opportunities for re-use were missed. However, while praising the organisation of the rag trade centred in the West Riding of Yorkshire, Leather chided the English manufacturer for putting short-term profit above improvement of the trade. Citing the Belgian expertise at purifying fine wool mixed with cotton, the French proficiency in removing burrs from wool, and German improvements in rag processing machinery, Leather saw Continental firms making greater advancement than their British counterparts. He returned to Lyon Playfair's 1852 metaphor of the prudent housewife's economising in order to describe the direction of future progress,

progress that would allow every scrap to be recycled as in the chemistry of nature. Cottonseed was the shining example: it was 'garbage in 1860, a fertiliser in 1870, a cattle food in 1880, and a table food and many other things in 1890'.

## Part 2 Hard labour: oakum and tow

> From six in a bed in those mansions of woe,
> Where nothing but beard, nails, and vermin do grow,
> And from picking of Oakum in cellars below,
> Good Lord, deliver us!
>
> *The Poor Man's Litany* (c1811)

The unravelling of tarry old rope into its component fibre, making oakum, was associated with the prison and poorhouse long before the nineteenth century. Perhaps considered as a preventive measure to unfit a criminal's hands for the delicate work of pickpocketing, the original intent of oakum picking as punishment more likely lay in an enforced meditation on 'the rope' as means of execution, and the work necessary to undo a twisted lifetime. It was to become more simply a form of repellent labour designed to prevent inmates finding any comfort in their environment. Already, in 1817, Samuel Hill pointed out the unsound economic basis of such work:

> One hundred and fifty persons capable of labour, in St. Giles's Poor-house (as appears from the books), earned by picking oakum, in the years ending at Lady-day 1817, *72l. 4s. 6d.* which, after deducting the percentage of the Master of the Poor-house, and the wages of the Over-looker, would not amount to one halfpenny per day for each person.[4]

But Henry Mayhew's account of the *Criminal Prisons of London* (1862) shows that the practice of textile working as punishment continued; his writing brings to life through skilful simile the dusty atmosphere and peculiar smell that characterised the work. Oakum was used, along with pitch, mainly for caulking ships, although the finer grades also found medical use for wound dressing – the tar acting as an antiseptic.[5]

In 1871, the Surveyor-General of Prisons showed that other forms of prison work (matmaking, shoemaking, tailoring) were valued ten to twenty times more than oakum picking, but still maintained the necessity of penal labour, such as cranking or pumping.[6] Prison reforms of 1877 finally dropped oakum picking as hard labour, and in the post-punishment era, oakum largely fell out of public consciousness. A 1926 article in the trade journal the *Textile Manufacturer* reminded readers that oakum was 'still picked' – now efficiently by machine, and it presented business opportunities. This article serves to reintegrate the story of oakum with the Victorian shipyard and the maintenance of vessels. However, it is unlikely that late Victorian sailors any longer relished oakum as an alternative to tobacco as did Melville's seamen, finding an epicurean 'nutty delight' in the aromatic heart of the rope.[7]

The production of fine textile yarns always necessitates the rejection of a quantity of fibre shorter in length, tangled or irregular in texture that would otherwise prevent a smooth, even yarn. Tow is the flax fibre rejected in the process of combing (hackling) during the production of linen. Utilisation of such refuse material necessitated economical means of processing in keeping with its lesser value, so mechanical methods were sought. A notebook kept by John Marshall of Leeds records experiments made in the 1820s to card and prepare tow by machinery. These notes provide evidence of the difficulties of engineering complex processes involving multiple factors, and the extended periods of time that such experimental endeavours entailed. Marshall and Co. was a bold innovator in adjunct fields as well, being a pioneer of the green roof. The newest of the firm's mills was described in 1843 as being arranged on a single storey with a roof area of nearly two acres covered with grass, 'To "take a walk in the fields" on the top of a factory . . . is the impression likely to be made at first glance'.[8]

Moving to Peter Sharp's account of tow carding and preparing written in 1882, it is interesting to note how much of Marshall's experimental work had become codified in the intervening decades. Although machinery and settings had grown in sophistication, the same basic mechanisms and parameters of adjustment remained. Refinement had come in understanding precisely which settings to use for a given quality of tow to achieve a particular end quality of yarn.

## Part 3 The 'low wools': shoddy and mungo

Sir George Head provides our first picture of the shoddy industry when it was still a novel business. Head had to dismiss the less reputable origins of shoddy – 'from the scarecrow or the gibbet' – reflecting the prejudices faced by the trade in 1835. Nonetheless, it had been taken up by the fashionable London tailor, George Stultz, for constructing the swelling collars of the dandy. By contrast, children working the rag machine suffocated under a cloud of foul-smelling dust that rendered them 'in appearance like so many brown moths'. Walter White takes up the story when shoddy had risen to a 'national institution' in the 1850s with the addition of mungo. Mungo was a radical phenomenon because the cheaper fibre brought broadcloth in reach of the masses, overturning a long-held sartorial distinction. But while these low wools were democratising, they were not revolutionary; they perpetuated the existing hierarchy, wherein the paletot of the gentleman was easily distinguished from the pilot coat of the practical man. White was fascinated by the low origins of shoddy, and in his account there remains genuine surprise that rags can give rise to prosperity. He ends by bolstering extant social norms through an image of uncultured shoddy operatives in awe of *true* West Country broadcloth.

Once the reclaimed wool industry had gained commercial success and a measure of respectability, the origins of shoddy became a topic of interest, and also of heated dispute from rival claimants to the honour of 'discovery'. Samuel Jubb wrote the first extensive history in 1860, which has become widely known.[9] Less familiar is Farrar Fenton's rival history published in parts in the *Textile Manufacturer* in 1881, but never released in book format. Fenton, unlike the Yorkshire trade historians, looked beyond the county and raised some novel material from oral sources that deserves consideration. Making Fenton's account available here enables the debate over the origins of shoddy to be revisited, and adds his unique viewpoint to the uncontested later history of the trade.

Professor Roberts Beaumont wrote for students and practitioners in the wool industry. Extracted here are his texts of 1888 and 1922, his first and last word on what he termed 'substitute' wools, in order to avoid deprecating associations. His definitions and descriptions of the varieties of waste and their characteristics form a secure groundwork, and make the point that reclaimed wool is not deficient in the normal properties of the fibre. Rags made from excellent fulling wool will produce mungo of good felting properties, enabling the use of reclaimed wool to produce textiles of high quality. Essential to this goal is the initial task of rag sorting, usually performed by women skilled in the physical judgements of handle required to allocate the different sorts. Subsequent machine processing was aimed at forming an evenly blended and uniform product.

The history of the *waste* wool industry can be read in the scale of the partnerships and companies that processed material, alongside the network of adjunct firms that serviced those companies, not least the machine-makers. Company histories provide an insight into the human level of entrepreneurial activity: entry into business followed by expansion, success or failure. Most businesses began as family firms and small partnerships, some being incorporated as limited companies, especially late in the century. With the great expansion of industry, commercial directories became lucrative ventures, and provide a means to view firms within their geographical concentrations. The 1893 directory of the London Printing and Engraving Company was one such venture that innovated with its attempt at short business biographies. At this time, we can see that telephone numbers joined telegraphic addresses as an item of prestige as well as contact.

Shoddy's tainted reputation entered the English language as a synonym for shabbiness and pretence. The staying-power of this image problem probably owes much to shoddy's rich affordances as a metaphor for debasement and deceit, in keeping with class-based anxieties over the advancement of the 'lower orders'. Real evidence for widespread sale of cloth lacking in quality or durability is absent, and it is likely the purchaser of shoddy received value for money. Where deceit occurred, it was mainly at the retail level, not in manufacturing. Curiously, the prejudice against shoddy offered opportunities for further deceits as entertainingly recounted by Alexander Cook in *Old Time Traders*.

Howard Priestman's 1913 article on 'pulled wool' provides a perspective on the shoddy industry at the height of specialisation. He emphasised the sorting process, which if performed well avoided the necessity of re-dyeing, as well as the need for skilful blending requiring astute judgement. Of immense value to the historian, Priestman provides contemporary and localised meanings of wool terminology.

## Part 4 The waste of one is the raw material of the next: cotton waste

Cotton waste within textile production, as opposed to its use in papermaking, was concerned with fully exploiting the raw material rather than reprocessing rags into cotton fibre. In preparing cotton for spinning fine yarns, much of the fibre was rejected but could be taken up and spun for other purposes. Cotton fabrics evolved to make full use of residue material, with fine cottons having a symbiotic relationship with fabrics that utilised the refuse created in their making. Also, during the nineteenth century, greater efficiency was achieved in extracting more of the fibre from the cotton boll and seed, driven especially by the precarity of cotton supply. Our first article, from the premier issue of the trade journal *Waste Trade World* in 1912, introduces the subject by drawing attention to the numerous everyday products in which cotton waste was a component. A companion article, from the same journal, focuses on reclaiming the ultimate residues of cotton processing – the dirt. When working on an industrial scale, all residues can quickly become practical problems. If the only end use was agricultural, the seasonal nature of consumption meant that the processor either had to create adequate storage, or pay for removal during the off-season. This article also clarifies a terminological point – that cotton waste was referred to as *shoddy* by those in this branch of the trade.

Only a limited amount of cotton waste was re-used on-site by spinners; most was sold on to dealers. A pair of articles from 1868–1869 on the Cotton Waste Dealers' Exchange of Manchester mark the transition of such dealing from marginal to respectable. A new generation coming of age in the middle of the century sought to disassociate itself from the intemperate and sharp business practices of the past, while viewing with pride their ability to transform waste material into a valued commodity. The growth of the trade during the subsequent decade is witnessed by Eli Sowerbutt's 1882 *Cotton Waste Dealers' Directory* containing over 700 entries covering a spread of twenty waste trade specialities. Geographically, Manchester and Oldham had the largest concentrations of waste cotton dealers, with significant numbers at Bolton, Bury, Heywood, Rochdale and Stockport. Notable are five female dealers suggesting that entry to the field was more open than other mercantile trades. Included is Ann Stanyer née Wooleston (c1823–1891) who came from a family of rag merchants, and whose daughter Sarah Townend Stanyer (1851–1913) followed her mother into the business. Edwards and Bercry's 1888 trade directory of Manchester provides brief sketches of six firms involved in the waste cotton trade, highlighting the development from engine-cleaning waste to sponge cloths and packing cloths – as well as the growth of cotton wadding and cotton wool as items of consumption.

The processing of waste cotton entailed modifications of the ordinary mechanical spinning process to deal with three additional difficulties: (1) the need to tear apart 'hard' (previously spun) waste or deal with dirty 'soft' waste, (2) the resulting wide variation in fibre length that necessitated additional blending for uniformity, and (3) the fragility of the carded roving that required consolidating by *condensing* (crosswise rubbing) to make it strong enough to be handled by machinery. The still-tender roving required insertion of twist to maintain strength while stretching during the spinning process. Joseph Nasmith, writing in 1892, does an admirable job of making such complexities intelligible, and if we find the text somewhat technical, it is instructive that it introduces the subject at the level of the student aiming to become a mill manager. There follows a description of a complete cotton waste plant from 1889 highlighting the adaptations of machinery introduced to make possible the spinning of cotton waste.

Thomas Thornley, in 1901, directing his attention to students for the cotton spinning examinations, located the sources of waste cotton in spinning mill processes, defining their particular characters and quantities. He adds to the general material introduced by Nasmith, refining the specialist vocabulary. In Thornley's definitive 1912 text on cotton waste, he describes in detail the composition of the main fabrics using cotton waste.

The remaining articles on cotton waste, from the end of our period, bring out particular features of British industrial practice, in sales or production. In 1913, Henry Brougham Heylin described business practice in the cotton waste line whereby mills contracted sale of their waste on an annual basis. It appears that the cotton waste dealer suffered from low esteem on the part of the mills who took little care with bagging or maintaining bagged waste in good condition. Frank Nasmith's lecture of 1916 indicates the divergent directions of British and Continental practice. While British manufacturers used short-fibred soft cotton waste mainly in a secondary role for stuffing and backing yarns, Continental manufacturers, especially in Germany, developed soft cotton waste as a material in its own right to make woven and knitted fabrics that imitated wool. The interruption of trade by the war necessitated a change in direction in Britain, but it is significant that war had not diminished admiration for the achievements of German industry, nor the close following of German developments through exhibition of samples by the Board of Trade. Sam Wakefield's 1917 treatment of waste is concerned with its monetary value. Accurate accounting methods reveal the losses waste could incur; a small fraction of a penny per pound generated a large figure over the course of a week. He admonishes that the average workperson – even the foreman – is oblivious to waste and requires educating in waste reduction.

The American Bureau of Foreign and Domestic Commerce kept a close eye on British textile practice. A report of 1918 identified a double profit in the form of cleaning cloths made from waste cotton: the cloths were easily washed and the oil with which they were saturated was recovered. One firm sold them with a contract to wash and mend for a specified period, thereby recovering many tons of oil. Finally, in 1920, W. C. Jones Ltd. dealt with the perpetual image problem of the waste industry by a sophisticated promotional campaign. Waste was to be seen as a precious material in its own right 'for there are some effects which can only be got from waste – effects which cotton, no matter how expensive, cannot give'.

## Part 5 An 'uninviting aggregation of rubbish': spun silk

We begin this section with a piece of juvenile literature by William Claxton from 1913 that captures facts, myths, social values and anxieties bound up in the subject of waste silk. Silk, the highest class of textile fibre, also generated the greatest waste. Extolling industry and invention, Claxton followed the well-trodden story that such waste was sold as rubbish until Samuel Cunliffe Lister's innovations in silk combing that enabled waste silk to resemble *true* silk. But successful conversion to a substitute silk brought fears of adulteration and false selling. Claxton resolves this unease with the assertion that waste yarns could imitate silk for a time, but their origins would soon be revealed by wear. As in social life, birth determined class, and mobility was not appreciated, even in textile fabrics.

James Burnley's contribution on Lister to the popular 'Fortunes Made in Business' series in 1881 presented the accepted view of Lister's contribution to waste silk spinning, but emphasised the end products enabled by the new industrial scale production and the extended range of waste convertible to attractive yarns. The development of face-to-face velvet weaving and plush silks is highlighted alongside a range of non-elite products: 'silk cleaning-cloths for machinery, bath-towels, floor-cloths, dish-cloths, and so forth'. Samuel Cunliffe Lister was not content with Burnley's account with regard to the credit given to Isaac Holden for the wool comb. In 1905, he penned his version of events which it seems fair to juxtapose with Burnley's. As regards invention of the comb for waste silk, James Warburton, Lister's joint patentee, enjoys sympathetic treatment here, even though the two men separated soon after this collaboration.

In 1905, Joseph Boden provided a welcome corrective to the Lister mythology. Silk manufacturers evidently knew that the outer layers of silk cocoons had long been converted to floss silk yarns, and the inner layers into wadding, but Boden cites specific examples predating Lister, and names the early firms. Boden provides a commercial view of the waste silk manufacture, an industry beset by rapidly fluctuating prices of raw material, and keen European competition.

Finally, Hollins Rayner's article of 1901 provides a dealer's perspective, introducing the range of silk wastes on offer in Eastern and European markets, and the merchanting practices followed in examining and buying. The prowess of the Chinese dealer in taking advantage of the lax inspection processes of the British buyer is recounted disparagingly – with an imperialist view. However, the source of the proliferation of quality terms, such as 'extra extra extra selected' is explained with a touch of humour and admiration for his Chinese counterparts, with the knowledge that such grade inflation arose at home as well as abroad.

## Part 6 'Complete metamorphosis of the rag': rag flock

Dr Henry Franklin Parsons's report on rag flock, written for the Local Government Board in 1884, reviews with great clarity how rag flock was produced, variations in different geographical centres, and the different classes of rag used. He then enters on an assessment from the perspective of human health, and in doing so, reveals a great amount of detail about working conditions and practices. Parsons's account is slanted in favour of the manufacturer, but maintains a convincing argument that there was little actual evidence for disease transmission through wool textiles in the context of rag processing.

Peter Fyfe's 1904 lecture 'What the People Sleep Upon' was the rallying cry that eventually led to the Rag Flock Act of 1911. Deciding from the start that wool flock was an evil, instead of the balanced approach of Parsons, Fyfe struck upon the idea of comparing the rinse water from rag flock to raw sewage. Finding less quantity of bacteria in the sewage, Fyfe made the appalling suggestion that 'it would be safer to sleep on a bed filled with sewage'. In case this did not convince his audience, Fyfe also employed the class argument, that the lady purchasing an economical bed for her servant 'takes into her otherwise well-appointed home a centre of disease potentiality', disease that could transfer from servant to family.

Paul Hasluck, describing materials for upholstery in 1904, gives an insight into how flocks fit within the range of available stuffing materials at this time. The upholsterer, required to produce for a full gamut of furnishings, budgets and climates, was at the forefront of testing new materials, both raw and recycled.

The escalating agitation over the issue of unwashed wool flock took to the pages of the medical journal *The Lancet* from 1906 to 1907 in a sequence of correspondence and notes assembled around the scornful title 'Loathsome Bed Stuffing'. It was implied that the horse in its fresh straw enjoyed a cleaner bed than the average city dweller. Blame is laid at the door of competition for cheapness, thereby signalling a shift from long-accepted free trade economic doctrine to a desire for a more regulatory regime.

This section ends with the section on rag flock from an extensive series of articles on the 'Inside of a Mattress' published in *The Cabinet Maker* between 1924 and 1928. This marks the rehabilitation of rag flock to a praiseworthy commodity, seen to emerge from the rag processing machinery 'cleansed, purified and carded – standard rag flock – an entirely new product' – a 'complete metamorphosis'. Images aid our understanding of the range of types available. Rag flock had expanded to include mixtures of wool with cotton, and even jute, using 'only such rags . . . as are quite useless for any re-manufacturing process or blending with wool for the making of cheap cloths'. In this way, rag flock played a major role in eliminating textile waste.

## Part 7 Dolly shops and 'things done with'

This section moves on to textiles that are repurposed, rather than converted back into fibre for re-use. Cleansing and reshaping could erase the material's ancestry and enable its *translation* into a new article. One site of exchange of materials for such re-use was the dolly shop: 'the name popularly given in London to a shop where rags and other kinds of old articles are bought, and over the door of which a black doll is usually suspended'.[10] Adalbert Hoppe detailed this as a black wooden doll in white clothing.[11] The white garments are explained when it is known that the black doll was formerly a shop sign denoting the sale of India muslins.[12] However, the route of its descent from elite fabrics to rags is not clear. Nor was its original meaning widely remembered, as evidenced by Thomas Hood's cartoon of an indignant African in London, appalled by the seeming execution of a black child.[13]

The first article in this section, written by Charles Manby Smith in 1855 during the Crimean War period, concerns sheet lint for medical use in dressing wounds. Linen softened and purified by years of use and washing was the preferred source material for such dressings. Jewish entrepreneurs contracted with institutional users of linen (hospitals, prisons, schools, etc.) for larger and more consistent provision of such rags than could be provided by the dolly shops. Jewish populations were often closely linked to the rag and second-hand clothing trade, and nineteenth-century accounts are seldom clear of antisemitic innuendos of unfair dealing, even while admitting the tight margins and the difficulties of making a profit in such trades. The appeal of Smith's article, however, is its focus on the female lint-maker, pursuing her skilled but monotonous and wearisome trade in the dingy attics of London's back streets.

In another essay treating the lowly hemp or jute sack, Smith tackles, in 1854, a problem astonishingly modern in nature – the practicalities of returnable containers, and how to encourage their return. Because flour and grain sacks were provided for free, consumers did not respect the rights of the owner over this property. Private enforcement and legal remedies being costly, and failing to resolve the problem, owners dreamed of a throwaway single-use item that would counteract the sheer tempting utility of sacks, a utility that invited re-use as containers or conversion to floor, wall or roof coverings, amongst other possibilities. Again, Smith highlights an overlooked cadre of female workers making a meagre living, here facing a new threat of competition from the sewing machine.

In 1864, Andrew Wynter responded to the question of what becomes of old clothes with surprising revelations about their transformations and travels. Black cloth garments were cut up to make caps in France. The red tunics of the British infantry were destined for waistcoats of working-class Dutchmen, while scarlet officers' coats became facings for civil uniforms of Russian officials. Black velvet waistcoats from country towns were the source of material for Jewish skullcaps in Germany or Poland.

We conclude with Clara Matéaux's 1881 account of the rag and bone trade, appropriately titled 'Things That Are Done With'. As with many works for juvenile readers, this article strongly conveys core cultural narratives. First there is the awesome capacity of modern industry to transform materials – here conducting things that are 'done with' to a pristine new start. Admiration is bestowed on those with the insight to envisage creating value from such discarded things. But there is also a more disturbing class narrative. While sorters in the factory are represented as skilled in performance of a difficult task, even if *crouching* at low stools or barefoot, outdoor workers are portrayed as a different race: the 'hill people'. Likened first to ants and then to crows, the women hidden by sacking aprons and straw hats, hold on to their humanity only by virtue of their ability to sing and be useful. While mechanical equipment is able to purify waste, the human operative is enmired by close contact with disagreeable materials rather than dignified by the work.

The nineteenth-century waste textile industries inhabited a territory redolent with anxieties about class. Movement of textiles from low to high triggered emotional discomfort, provoked by associations with foreigners, beggars, criminals and contagion. Only if the manufacturer was able to completely cleanse and renew the fibre, to effect not transmigration but metamorphosis, could the suspect fibre gain full acceptance. Paper, with its near-elemental transformation that imitated nature and left the rag in a state of visual purity, was first to win public esteem. Then the virgin waste fibres like tow, spun silk and cotton, with their evocation of good housewifery, and clever business practice producing value from refuse, gained favour. Shoddy and flock, of more dubious origins, lingered much longer on the edge of approbation, flock requiring legislation to enter respectability, and shoddy remaining the textile that dared not speak its name.

## Notes

1 *Cassell's Household Guide*, new and rev. ed. (London: Cassell and Co., 1869–71), vol. 3, p. 280.

2 Simmonds, Peter Lund. *Waste Products and Undeveloped Substances: or, Hints for Enterprise in Neglected Fields* (London: Robert Hardwicke, 1862), p. 8.

3 Timothy Cooper has expounded upon waste as a driver for capitalist modernity in 'Peter Lund Simmonds and the Political Ecology of "Waste Utilisation" in Victorian Britain', *Technology and Culture*, 52:1 (Jan 2011), pp. 21–44.

4 Hill, Samuel. *A Plan for Reducing the Poor's-Rate, by giving permanent employment to the labouring classes: with some observations on the cultivation of flax and hemp . . .*, 2nd ed. (London: J. Harding, 1817), p. 16.

5 Elliott, Isabelle M. Z. (based on material collected by James Rawlings Elliott). *A Short History of Surgical Dressings* (London: The Pharmaceutical Press, 1964), pp. 51–52.

6 Du Cane, Capt. E. F. 'On the Utilisation of Prison Labour', *Journal of the Society of Arts*, 19:965 (19 May 1871), pp 529–539.

7 Melville, Herman. *Redburn: his first voyage. Being the Sailor-boy Confessions and Reminiscences of the Son-of-a-Gentleman, in the Merchant Service* (New York: Harper & Brothers, 1850), pp. 340–342.

8 Dodd, George. 'A Day at a Leeds Flax-mill', *Penny Magazine of the Society for the Diffusion of Useful Knowledge*, 12:754 (Dec 1843), supplement, pp. 501–508, (on p. 504). Reprinted in *The Textile Manufactures of Great Britain by George Dodd* (London: Charles Knight and Co., 1844), p. 157. See also Combe, James. 'Description of a Flax Mill recently erected by Messrs. Marshall and Co. at Leeds', *Institution of Civil Engineers. Minutes of Proceedings, Session 1842*, 2 (1844), pp. 142–145.
9 Jubb, Samuel. *The History of the Shoddy Trade: Its Rise, Progress and Present* Position (London: Houlston and Wright, 1860).
10 *Chambers's Encyclopaedia: a Dictionary of Universal Knowledge for the People* (London: W. & R. Chambers, 1880), vol. 3.
11 Hoppe, Adalbert. *Englisch-Deutsches Supplement-Lexikon* (Berlin: G. Langenscheidt's Verlagsbuchhandlung, 1871), p. 124.
12 Brewer, Ebenezer Cobham. *Dictionary of Phrase and Fable* (London: Cassell, Petter and Galpin, 1870), p. 237.
13 Hood, Thomas (ed.). *The Comic Annual*, 1839. A story was elaborated from the *Comic Annual* cartoon by the *Exeter and Plymouth Gazette*, 23 Feb 1839, p. 4.

# Part 1

# 'A CREDIT TO THE AGE'

## The utilisation of waste

*Fig. 1* View of a blending or mixing room at Redmayne and Isherwood Ltd., Kirkham, manufacturers of cotton and engine waste.

*Source*: *Concerning Cotton: a brief account of the aims and achievements of the Amalgamated Cotton Mills Trust Limited and its component companies* (Manchester: ACMT Ltd, 1920), n.p. Manchester Metropolitan University Library.

## Editorial Headnote

### Simmonds, Peter Lund. 'On the Utilization of Waste Substances', *Journal of the Society of Arts*, 7:325 (11 Feb 1859), pp. 175–188. Courtesy of RSA, London.

### Simmonds, Peter Lund. 'On the Useful Application of Waste Products and Undeveloped Substances', *Journal of the Society of Arts*, 17:846 (5 Feb 1869), pp. 171–178. Courtesy of RSA, London.

Peter Lund Simmonds (1814–1897) was born in Aarhus, Denmark, but adopted around 1818 by George Simmonds (c1789–1841), Lieutenant in the Royal Navy, with his Danish wife Serine Sophie Amalia née Mørup, and raised in Hampshire. In 1831, he was sent to Jamaica to work as a bookkeeper on a sugar plantation. His biographer, David Greysmith, observed, 'The West Indies, in this tumultuous period of slave emancipation, made a deep impression on him; the experience formed the basis for all his later interests' (Oxford DNB). Not long after his return to England in 1834, Simmonds began his career in journalism, and in 1844 he launched *Simmonds' Colonial Magazine* which he edited for five years. As a voice for the interests of colonists, Simmonds carried on correspondence across the British Empire, and ingested colonial views. Projecting the potential benefits of the natural resources of the Empire was seen as a means of gaining political support for colonial efforts.

Simmonds's association with the Society of Arts began when he was engaged to catalogue the animal specimens from the Great Exhibition selected for a collection of trade products displayed at the South Kensington Museum and later at Bethnal Green. He became a member in 1855, and was given a life membership in 1862 in recognition of his 'services in application of sciences to the arts' ('Obituary', *J. Society of Arts*, 45:2343, 15 Oct 1897, p. 1150). The two papers extracted here are among sixteen he delivered before the Society. The first was read 9 February 1859 and, after appearing in the Society's journal, was reprinted in a supplement to the *North British Agriculturist* (23 Feb 1859, pp. 182–183), and extracted in other newspapers. The other paper, read 3 February 1869, did not receive the same wide news coverage, perhaps because the ideas were familiar through Simmonds's book *Waste Products and Undeveloped Substances: or, Hints for Enterprise in Neglected Fields* (London: Robert Hardwicke, 1862).

We can trace in Simmonds's lectures of 1859 and 1869 the consolidation of a shift in his orientation to the subject. In the 1850s, he still saw waste as the residue of raw materials used in manufacturing processes 'which it is the province of others . . . to collect and utilize'. By the end of the 1860s, with the utilisation of residuary matters perceived as largely in place within the major industries, particularly textiles, the term waste was associated with natural products lying 'undeveloped'. This expanded definition of waste moved away from the reduction of industrial pollution toward the exploitation of colonial ecologies for economic profit.

# 1

# SIMMONDS, PETER LUND. 'ON THE UTILIZATION OF WASTE SUBSTANCES' AND 'ON THE USEFUL APPLICATION OF WASTE PRODUCTS AND UNDEVELOPED SUBSTANCES'

*Journal of the Society of Arts* (11 Feb 1859), pp. 175–180; (5 Feb 1869), pp. 171, 177–178.

## On the utilization of waste substances

The announced title of the paper I am about to read scarcely expresses accurately the subject I propose to discuss, but it would be difficult to find one which should embrace and define all the matters to be treated of. There are many substances already utilized, which are to all intents and purposes waste or refuse substances; and there are very many others not used, which are also waste substances, and well worthy of the attention of practical men. The subject is highly important in its commercial bearings, whether the substances utilized are limited or extensive, because they all lead to a watchfulness and thriftiness which converts waste matter to some profitable use.

Viewed in its collective form, it has not occupied that prominent degree of attention which it demands; and although I cannot hope to bring forward much that is new, yet the hints and details respecting some of these reconversions and applications of waste materials may lead to thought, and prove profitable in other quarters, while they will probably elicit in the subsequent discussion much interesting information on these and other substances.

When we perceive in nature how nothing is wasted, but that every substance is reconverted, and again made to do duty in a changed and beautified form, we have at least an example to stimulate us in economically applying the waste materials we make, or that lie around us, ready to be utilized.

Some subjects of this kind have already occupied the special attention of the Society, and among others I may allude to those of fish-guano by Mr. Horace Green and Mr. Lawes (*Journal*, Vol. ii., p. 87);[1] the Utilization of the Sewage of Towns, by Mr. Fothergill Cooke (Vol. v., p. 49);[2] "The utilization of the slags or

 DOI: 10.4324/9780429274190-3

molten mineral products of smelting furnaces," by Dr. William H. Smith (Vol. iii., p. 335)[3] &c.

In every manufacturing process there is more or less waste of the raw material, which it is the province of others following after the original manufacturer to collect and utilize. This is done now to some extent, more or less, in almost every manufacture, but especially in the principal ones of the country – cotton, wool, silk, leather, and iron. But new industries spring up from time to time, and out of the waste of these, much commercial wealth has yet to be drawn.

In the desultory observations I am about to offer, I shall group the waste substances, for convenience, under the ordinary divisions of Animal, Vegetable, and Mineral.

First then, as to the ANIMAL PRODUCTS: –

In the woollen manufacture a considerable portion of the raw material is scattered as waste; but there are a number of "waste merchants" in different parts of the country who buy up everything like wool, and send it to Leeds, Dewsbury, and Batley, to be made into shoddy or mungo. Being mixed with some new wool, it is spun into yarn, and made into broadcloth, doeskins, pilot cloths, druggets, and coarse carpeting. The reproduction of a woven fabric from material formerly regarded as entirely waste and useless for such purposes, is a striking illustration of the adaptive ingenuity of the present day.

Besides the woollen rags collected at home, others are imported. These are torn up by machinery, and their fibrous material entirely separated; this is then spun into "low numbers," and made into a coarse description of woollen cloth, used for baize, table-covers, &c.

The rag-grinder takes the cloth, when thrown aside by the wearer, cuts it into particles, which he forcibly tears asunder, and thus re-models them into raw material, to be again used by the first consumer. And of such consequence is this last process to the trade, that the 16 rag machines in the town of Leeds alone are capable, in full work, of producing 3,605,760 lbs. of raw material in a year, or (upon the average of 9 lbs. to the fleece,) of adding to the annual stock of wool the fleeces of 400,000 sheep.

A recent visitor to the woollen districts of Yorkshire has discovered that pilot cloth is shoddy; that glossy beavers and silky-looking mohairs are shoddy; that the Petershams so largely exported to the United States are shoddy; that the soft, delicate cloths in which ladies feel so comfortable, and look so graceful, are shoddy; that the "fabric" of Talmas, Raglans, and paletots, and of other garments in which fine gentlemen go to the Derby, or to the Royal Academy Exhibition, or to the evening services in St. Paul's and Westminster Abbey, are shoddy. And if Germany sends us abundance of rags, we send to Germany enormous quantities of shoddy in return. The best quality manufactured at Batley is worth ten shillings a yard; the commonest not more than one shilling.

Even the greasy cotton wads with which engineers wipe their machinery enter into the material of some qualities of shoddy. But there are woollen rags that are not good enough for shoddy, and these are used as manure for the hops in Kent, so we get shoddy in our beer as well as in our broadcloth. Two-and-a-half lbs. of dry woollen rags, we are told, are equal to 100 lbs. of farmyard manure, or 15 lbs. of liquid blood, when applied to land.

In addition to the rags and tailors' clippings, worsted stockings, carpeting, skirtings, and such like, are pulled to pieces and reworked.

The flocks made at the "raising gig"[4] from pilot cloth in the wet state, are cleaned and dyed, and used in the manufacture of certain yarns. These flocks are also used for stuffing mattresses, seamen's bedding, and common articles of furniture. There is still, however, some "mill waste" which cannot be worked up again for shoddy, namely, that portion of the wool waste which is so saturated with oil and grease, that the fatty matter is heavier than the wool. This is called "creash,"[5] and forms a very valuable manure.

A process is now in operation at the Kingholm woollen mills, near Dumfries, by which the hitherto refuse water of the washing houses is converted into valuable commercial material.[6] By means of mechanical appliances and chemical action, the refuse formerly turned into the river Nith to the injury of the salmon, is made to produce stearine, which forms the basis of composite candles, as well as a cake manure that sells at 40s. per ton.

Teall's patent for recovering the fat from waste soap liquors is chiefly applicable to wool-scourers' soap-waste,[7] and is conducted in the following manner: –

The fluid, as obtained from the wool-scourers, is run into large tanks, where it is treated with sulphuric acid, which causes the fat to separate from the soap and rise to the surface, carrying with it all the impurities removed from the wool. The semi-solid product, after separation from the water, is, according to Professor Anderson,[8] subjected to pressure in powerful Bramah presses, when the oil or grease is expressed; and a dark brown cake, still containing some oil, along with small quantities of woollen fibre and other impurities, is left.

This refuse substance, which contains about 71 per cent. of organic matter and 8 per cent. of alkaline salts, is sold for manure. Glue-makers' refuse has long been employed as a fertilizer in the vicinity of tan and glue works, and with good success when applied to any kind of crop, as from its putridity it acts rapidly. It is worth about 36s. per ton.

Poake,[9] a name among fellmongers for the collected waste arising in the preparation of skins, which consists of lime, oil, and hair, in various proportions, is also bought for manure.

Wool, ground very fine and dyed, is now extensively used in the manufacture of flock-paper hangings. The wool that comes off the sheep-skins, after soaking in the lime-water of the tan-pits, is sold, when washed, at 3d. to 5d. the pound. We import 2,340 tons of woollen rags annually, valued at £21,658; and flock for paper-stainers to the extent of 1,350 cwts., of the further value of £5,400.

In the carpet manufactories, the waste from the carpet looms is used for stuffing mattresses, &c.; another portion of the waste from the looms and winder-wheels is used for making prussiate of potash,[10] and the general mill-waste for manure.

There are many light articles of ladies' dress, such as balzarines, orleans, coburgs, alpacas, &c., which are formed by an admixture of a warp of cotton with a weft of worsted, or of mohair, alpaca, &c. Now, after these are worn out or thrown aside, they are comparatively valueless, from the mixture of the two substances, but, by a chemical process, the cotton is now destroyed, and the wool, the most valuable substance of the two, is recovered for future use in making woollen cloth. I have here specimens of dresses first, as collected from the dust-hole; secondly, after boiling in acid; thirdly, the recovered wool, teazed into Bromley wool,[11] the refuse dust being used as manure; and, finally, cloth made of one-fifth long wool and four-fifths of this Bromley wool.

Cow-hair, from the tanneries, is used for mortar and for making felt; but, in some parts of the continent, they make ropes and carpets of it, and stuff sofas and chair-cushions with it instead of with horsehair.

The waste shavings in whalebone cutting are employed as a stuffing material by upholsterers, and for filling firegrates in summer; and all the refuse goes to the farmer for manure, or to the prussiate maker, to be used with other animal substances, woollen waste, rags, hoofs and horns, button-makers' refuse, bone drillings and filings, to form those beautiful salts.

We import yearly about 21,000 cwts. of raw knubs and husks of silk; the husk which covers the chrysalis, after the best silk is reeled, is used for bed covers, or spun for common silk stuffs. This offal amounts to 10 per cent. of the weight of raw silk. The gum has to be discharged from the husks and knubs; these are bleached and the dressed waste cut to a uniform length for carding. It has then to be twisted into skeins, rovings, and cops. The Chinese, not content with using the silk thread of the cocoon, with their usual thriftiness, determining that nothing shall be wasted, eat up the chrysalis itself.

. . .

The street pickers and sewer rakers, and the persons who frequent the river banks, &c., gather up rags, bones, metal, old boots and shoes, – in fact, anything that can be sold or reconverted to a useful purpose.

The boots and shoes go to the translators, vampers, and clobberers, as they are technically termed in Monmouth-street and the purlieus of Petticoat-lane and Rag Fair, where, by the use of the heel-ball and clobber, a mixture of ground cinders and paste, the crevices and breaks of our old "understandings" are filled up; and, when the cement is dry and a few nails and stitches are added, they are polished and disposed of to those who patronize or can only afford cheap shoe-leather.

## Vegetable substances

There are some again who buy only the clippings of tailors, shirt and cap makers, and others engaged in the manufacture of dress. These gatherings are either sold to the piece brokers, or to the shoddy maker.

The itinerant clothesmen of the metropolis are pretty numerous, although I have no precise account of their numbers. In conjunction with the china and glass pedlars, and the vendors of growing plants and flowers, they collect worn-out garments, hats, boots and shoes, &c., which are renovated and made "better than new," for home sale, either in Holywell-street, the Minories, and the neighbourhood of the Tower, or in Monmouth-street, and such localities. Then there are the wardrobe purchasers, whose advertisements are seen continually in the *Times*, requiring garments for export. These classes furnish a considerable portion of the "apparel and slops," to the value of £2,000,000 sterling, annually exported, half of which goes to Australia.

The extent of this waste material trade, if I may so term it, may be estimated by the number of persons engaged in it in London, as gleaned from the pages of the Post-office Directory. This number, however, is necessarily far below the mark, as it only includes housekeepers, and many in the suburbs are omitted. There are, I find, 354 clothes salesmen; (these, perhaps, are not all vendors of *old* clothes, but include some of the outfitters,) an undefined number of wardrobe dealers, 160 rag merchants, 564 marine store dealers, 19 bone dealers (10 of whom are bone boilers), and 3 bone crushers.

Rags are the common emblem of poverty, and to say that a man is in a ragged condition is the worst thing that can be said of him; but rags are in fact a great source of wealth, and one of the staples of our commerce, for, besides our large home collection, we import cotton and linen rags, on the average of years, of the value of more than a quarter of a million sterling; and the whole quantity used in the kingdom is estimated to exceed one million sterling. During the late war there was an enormous demand for linen rags by the apothecaries to scrape into lint. Unless persons then have carefully examined the vast amount of the cost of rags, they can form no idea of their great importance. To make one pound of paper it takes one and a quarter pounds of rags.

Our imports of rags and other materials for making paper, in the last few years, have been as follows: –

| *Years* | *Quantity Tons.* | *Value £.* |
|---|---|---|
| 1854 | 11,415 | 255,910 |
| 1855 | 9,414 | 219,323 |
| 1856 | 10,284 | 230,116 |
| 1857 | 12,196 | 272,848 |

The largest quantities come from Prussia, the Hanse Towns, Russia, and Italy.

In New York there are more than 1,000 professional rag pickers, 100 wholesale rag dealers, besides 700 licensed and unlicensed junk shops, which buy rags from housekeepers and rag pickers, and sell them to the rag-dealers.

. . .

Not only would the finding of a plentiful and good substitute for rags be of great importance in a pecuniary point of view, but it might be the means of preventing the spread of malignant diseases. Many a case of small-pox, yellow fever, plague, and cholera, are to be traced to the filthy rags carried from place to place.

The lowest price of common rags is £15 per ton, to which is to be added the loss of one-third before such rags are reduced into "half-stuff."[12] Good linen rags are worth £28 to £30 per ton. One of our largest and best paper-makers has declared that "it is nonsense to talk of paper made solely from linen rags; linen rags," he says, "cannot be found, nor, indeed, any other rags in sufficient quantity to supply an increased demand; and that unless a new material be found, paper making will be at a stand-still."

Mr. F. B. Houghton[13] has recently patented a process for making paper from any description of woody fibre, which is especially applicable to the manufacture of paper from flax-straw, or flax refuse. Flax-straw (shoves) can be procured at 50s. a ton, about 2½ tons making one ton of paper. Waste flax (the refuse of the scutching mills, from which no profitable results are obtained) can be procured at a mere nominal price, as it is burnt or thrown away. Now, as our imports of rough or undressed flax amount to 81,000 tons a-year, and our home growth of flax is extensive, there being 100,000 acres under culture in Ireland, there is plenty of raw material available.

. . .

Cotton waste is the refuse cotton of the mill, being the "strippings" from the card, after the cotton has passed through the machine, the "flyings" or the portions which fly off from the card whilst the machine is in motion, the "droppings" and "blowings" which collect under the blowing machine in which cotton is cleaned, and the "sweepings" or gatherings from the floor of the card room.

The value of cotton waste varies with the price of cotton; strippings and blowings are worth about one-half to two-thirds that of cotton; and droppings, blowings, and sweepings, one-tenth to one-eighth.

The waste of cotton made during the process of manufacture, is, according to Mr. Ashworth, wrought into coarse sheets and bed-covers, which are sold at prices varying from 6d. to 9d. per lb.[14] The residue of the waste is used for the manufacture of paper, the cleaner portion being for writing-paper; and the sweepings from the floors of factories supply a large proportion of the paper mills of Lancashire with the raw material of the paper which is used for the printing of books and newspapers. The actual quantity of waste made must be very considerable upon a consumption of 800 or 900 million pounds of cotton annually.

Estimating it at 15 per cent., the usual allowance, there is at least 50,000 tons of cotton waste available, which, added to 20,000 tons of linen waste, and the same amount from rope and canvass, gives a large quantity to be worked up again. Previous to 1841 cotton waste was only used for making very common papers, but straw pulp being more generally used now for this purpose, cotton waste is chiefly worked up for printing-paper.

There are in Oldham 127 cotton waste dealers; in Manchester 82; and in other towns in Lancashire 244; so that there are probably 500 cotton waste dealers in the district. In America waste cotton is employed for the manufacture of articles of furniture, after the manner of papier mache; it is compressed into wood that takes a very beautiful polish.

The quantity of oakum sold in Liverpool, we are told amounts to 1400 tons a year, valued at £28,000, and the quantity used in London no doubt exceeds this, looking at the extent of shipping and the other uses to which it is applied.

Of codilla, or tow,[15] the refuse or waste fibres knocked out of hemp and flax in cleansing and carding it, we imported in 1857 nearly 13,000 tons, valued at £378,000. It is made into bags, sheeting and yarn, and used for other purposes.

By machinery in the United States and on the Continent, the cotton surrounding the seed is taken off, and can be sold to carpet manufacturers and paper-makers. At Antwerp, it realises about 12s. 6d. to £1 the cwt. Recently, in speaking after Mr. Wray's paper on American cotton cultivation (see *Journal*, vol. vii., p. 86),[16] I pointed out in detail the enlarged and very important uses of the cotton seed, formerly a waste substance, and the valuable commercial products now obtained from it, and I need not, therefore, enter again into the details, but I may exhibit a specimen of refined cotton seed oil, now coming extensively into use to mix with rape oil for burning, and to adulterate olive oil.

. . .

Thus we perceive that the sweepings of our cotton and flax-mills, the outside wrappers of the cotton bales, however discoloured or dirty, the weeds of our fields, thistles and couch grass, the stalks of reeds and canes, sawdust and pine-shavings, the refuse of the Irish flax scutching mills, moss and furze,[17] our cast-off garments, the beggar's rags, old sacks, and worn-out ropes, all of which we should be troubled to dispose of, are converted by the paper-maker into an article indispensable to civilized man.

## On the useful application of waste products and undeveloped substances

About fifteen years ago, in a paper read before the Society, I threw out various suggestions as to the useful applications of "Some Unappreciated and Unused Articles of Raw Produce from different parts of the World,"[18] for which the Council did me the honour to vote me their silver medal. Just ten years ago, I again called the attention of the members to the "Utilisation of Waste Substances."[19] These notes I afterwards amplified into a popular volume, published under the title of "Waste Products and Undeveloped Substances," which passed through a large edition, and is now out of print.[20] From the very many interesting papers that have since been read before the Society on the utilisation of other waste substances, and knowing from personal experience, and a close investigation at the different International Exhibitions with which I have been officially connected, that many of these hints and suggestions have developed themselves into important industries, I have thought that a short notice of the application and progress made with some of these formerly waste products might not be without interest.

I am aware that there is a kind of contradiction of terms in the expression of the utilisation of waste, since by the utilisation of all residuary matters there will be no waste in any manufacturing operations. There are many natural products, however, yet lying waste or undeveloped, to which attention will one day be prominently turned, as new demands arise to be supplied. My desire is to press upon the attention of all persons engaged in the useful arts the importance of the prevention of waste, and I shall advert briefly to the utilisation of the refuse products of certain manufactures and processes of domestic economy, with the hope of suggesting to those engaged in other trades the profits which might accrue to themselves, and the benefits which would result to mankind, from the useful application of these hitherto worthless residues.

In our great textile industries all the residue and nominal waste is pretty generally utilised; the waste from the cotton, woollen, and silk manufactures is all fully appreciated. Thus we import some 25,000 to 30,000 cwts. of silk waste to be used up. There are at least 60,000 tons of cotton waste in the cotton manufacture, which, added to 20,000 tons of linen waste, and the same quantity from rope and canvas, gives a large total to be worked up again for various purposes.

The enormous increased production of wool in the last ten or fifteen years has somewhat lowered prices, but has not done away yet with the using up of shoddy or re-converted woollen rags. Besides the large quantity of shoddy and mungo produced at home, we import 22,000,000 pounds of woollen rags, torn up to be used as wool. The use of shoddy in the last fifteen years has assumed gigantic proportions.

It has been well observed that the combination of shoddy with wool, together with the use of cotton warps, is the most valuable adaptation of materials in the history of the woollen trade which the ingenuity of man has discovered. By it multitudes of the humbler classes are enabled to obtain useful and comfortable articles of clothing, which formerly were beyond their means. Nor does it stop here. An immense mass of material, once thought all but valueless, has been rescued from the manure-heap, and made subservient to the wealth, industry, and comfort of millions. A feeling of prejudice or a smile of ridicule may rise at the thought, but manufacturers and consumers owe more to it than they are ready to admit. The manufacturers of pure wool goods are deeply indebted to it, for it has allowed them a full supply, which they could not have had, except at ruinous prices.

It often happens that the value of a thing is only discovered after its loss. Stop the supply of shoddy, and you may reasonably expect to double the present price of wool, and deprive millions of their warm and cheap winter garments, and their light and useful summer ones. Stop the supply of shoddy, and you will close one-third of the woollen mills in the kingdom, and bring distress upon the West Riding of Yorkshire.

. . .

Few persons have any idea of the enormous quantity of steel hoop and wire manufactured for the millions of crinolines used, and as fashion gradually changes, the utilisation of these cast-off hoops becomes of consequence. Thousands of these are said to be thrown into the streets of New York and other large American cities, where they are a nuisance and a plague to passengers. The *chiffoniers* utterly reject them, as not worth picking up, and the dustmen do not like them, as they are not very portable. Some witty journalist suggests they might be used with a pole in the centre for a rosary or trellis work in gardens. At any rate some plan should be adopted to utilise this great waste of steel in cities, so that old crinolines may be gathered with as much avidity as old rags and papers are now.

. . .

In conclusion, I may state that I have only skimmed over the surface of this great subject; for, to have enumerated only the various useful applications of residues or waste which have been made in the last ten years would have occupied all the time at my disposal this evening. It may, however, be confidently asserted, that as man advances in scientific knowledge, he will discover means of utilising everything now considered as waste, and we shall realise the fact that the Great Creator has made nothing in vain. Certainly the thanks of the community at large are due to the long labours of the Society of Arts in collecting, publishing, and discussing every subject and suggested improvement calculated to benefit the wide domains of Art, Manufactures, and Commerce, on which not only so materially depends the progress of our commerce and our high status among European nations, but also the well-being, the intellectual advancement, and the artistic taste of our people.

## Notes

1 H. Green, 'On Pettitt's Fisheries Guano', and J. B. Lawes, 'On Fish Manure as a Substitute for Guano', *Journal of the Society of Arts*, 2:57 (23 Dec 1853), pp. 88–95.
2 W. F. Cooke, 'On the Utilisation of the Sewage of Towns by the Deodorising Process Established at Leicester, and the Economical Application of it to the Metropolis', *Journal of the Society of Arts*, 5:212 (12 Dec 1856), pp. 49–61.
3 W. H. Smith, 'The Utilization of the Molten Mineral Products of Smelting Furnaces', *Journal of the Society of Arts*, 3:123 (30 Mar 1855), pp. 335–41.
4 Pilot cloth is given a thick nap on its face using the gig which raises the nap with teasles mounted in a cylinder that brush against the cloth. Wet raising leaves the pile lying flat on the surface covering the weave.
5 The Oxford English Dictionary gives 'creesh' as a Scottish word for grease or fat.
6 Robert Scott and Sons began wool manufacture at Kingholm in 1844. From 1856, Kingholm Mills were continued by John Lindsay Scott (1815–1888), and in 1865 the firm was incorporated as a limited company, J. Lindsay Scott and Co. The process of recovering stearine and fertiliser from wash water was put in place by September 1858 when it was reported in the *Dumfries Courier*, and reprinted widely in other papers.
7 William Teall (c1809–1882) of Wakefield, engineer, was granted patent No. 1431 for 'an improved method of treating and working soapy or greasy waters in order to obtain the greasy substances therefrom', 22 June 1855. He became head of Teall, Simpson and Co. Ltd., of the Patent Stearine Works, Wakefield.
8 This was Thomas Anderson (1819–1874), appointed Regius Professor of Chemistry at the University of Glasgow in 1852. In 1857, Anderson was called upon to report whether a proposed grease works using Teall's patent was likely to cause a nuisance; he judged it would be beneficial (see 'Mr. Teall's Patent Grease Works in Eglinton Street', *Glasgow Herald*, 9 Nov 1857, p. 5).

9 The Oxford English Dictionary shows 'poak' as the preferred spelling, and this is the form Simmonds used in his *Dictionary of Trade Products* (London: G. Routledge and Co., 1858), p. 293.
10 Potassium ferrocyanide.
11 The term 'Bromley wool', sometimes used to describe shoddy, here refers to 'carbonised' wool. Carbonising is the chemical process of extracting wool from cotton mixtures. The name Bromley wool was used in at least one case to avoid paying a higher customs duty on shoddy for an export to New York (see *Liverpool Albion*, 5 Jun 1865, p. 15).
12 Paper pulp.
13 Frederick Burnett Houghton (1824–1888), papermaker.
14 Ashworth, Henry. 'Cotton: Its Cultivation, Manufacture, and Uses', *Journal of the Society of Arts*, 6:277 (12 Mar 1858), pp. 256–270 (on p. 261).
15 Codilla is the refuse of the scutching process, and tow the refuse of the hackling process, the initial processes of separating bast fibre from stem material in preparation for spinning.
16 L. Wray, 'The Culture and Preparation of Cotton in the United States of America, &c.', *Journal of the Society of Arts*, 7:318 (24 Dec 1858), pp. 77–89.
17 Gorse (*Ulex Europaeus*).
18 *Journal of the Society of Arts*, 3:106 (1 Dec 1854), pp. 33–42.
19 *Journal of the Society of Arts*, 7:325 (11 Feb 1859), pp. 175–88.
20 *Waste Products and Undeveloped Substances; or, Hints for Enterprise in Neglected Fields* (London: Robert Hardwicke, 1862). The book had a second edition in 1873, and a third in 1876.

## Editorial Headnote

## Leather, C. W. 'Utilisation of Waste Products', *Journal of the Textile Institute*, 8:1 (1917), pp. 9–19.

Charles Walter Ikin Leather (1873–1939) was born in Ilkley, the eldest son of mechanical engineer John Henry Leather (1842–1912). In 1865, the senior Leather was appointed resident manager for the machine-making firm P. and C. Garnett, also becoming a partner. Founded in 1851, the Garnett firm had become specialised in machinery for processing textile waste. John Henry Leather was to purchase the firm from its surviving founder Peter Garnett (1825–1900) in the 1890s. Leather's patented 'improvements in the method of securing toothed wire in the periphery of carding or waste opening cylinders formed of metal' (No. 3057, 9 August 1877) were key to the firm's success. These wires were used to densely clothe the cylinders of the firm's machines for opening wool waste; the importance of the brand was such that its name was given to the process, called *garnetting* wool.

Charles W. I. Leather, after completing a mechanic's apprenticeship in Oldham, joined his father at Garnett's Wharf Works in Cleckheaton, eventually taking over as managing director by 1910. He was a pioneer of profit-sharing, and in 1903 launched a scheme for employees at P. and C. Garnett Ltd. In 1906, he married Maude Scarth (1883–1975), daughter of textile magnate Sir Charles Scarth (1846–1921). The couple's sons Charles Ikin Leather (1907–1984) and Richard Walter Leather (1913–1966) were to follow in their father's footsteps as joint managers of the firm. On his death, Leather left a considerable estate valued at £67,654. Leather's obituary in the *Yorkshire Post and Leeds Intelligencer* noted,

> He was recognised as an authority on machinery dealing with all descriptions of waste materials. He was a member of Bradford Wool Exchange for more than 40 years, being well known to a large circle in the textile trade. He was also actively associated with the work of the Wool Research Association at Torringdon, and at Bradford Technical School, and he wrote frequently on textile and economic questions.
>
> (8 Sep 1939, p. 10)

This lecture was read at a meeting of the Yorkshire Section of the Textile Institute held at the George Hotel, Huddersfield, on 12 December 1916. Leather concluded the discussion following the lecture by an observation that the use of wastes had been explored more extensively abroad, and summoning the British manufacturer to devote more time and resources to experimentation. The printed version came out in the Institute's March number. It received notice in the *Textile Manufacturer* where it was described as a 'comprehensive paper' (43:508, 15 April 1917, p. 110). Leather supplemented his own experience by copying and adapting material on wool fat, cottonseed oil and dyestuffs from a work by Henry Grattan Kittredge (1841–1909), 'The utilization of wastes and by-products in manufactures with special reference to the decade of 1890–1900' (*Twelfth Census of the United States: Census Bulletin*, no. 190, 16 Jun 1902, pp. 3–26).

# 2

# LEATHER, C. W. 'UTILISATION OF WASTE PRODUCTS'

*Journal of the Textile Institute* (1917), pp. 9–19.

The further the subject of waste and by-products is inquired into, the more complex and large is it found to be. In this paper, many branches are touched upon without entering closely into the technicalities of any particular branch. As a matter of fact, many papers could be prepared by technical experts on many branches of the subject. Most of the matter for the present paper was collected prior to the war. The statistics presented are pre-war statistics, retained in order to obviate erroneous impressions as to what the country does by comparison with other countries.

Disparaging remarks are often heard about the use of shoddy and waste in clothing, &c., and there has been a tendency to regard this use as associated with doubtful or dishonest practises. Such remarks have only indicated the prevalence of a considerable amount of ignorance on the subject. Few people seem to realise to what extent shoddies and wastes are used and to what extent their use has enabled us to have clothing at a really moderate price. It is impossible to say, exactly, but I am strongly of opinion that wool clothing, stockings, underwear, &c., would have been almost double in price were it not for the employment of shoddies and wastes. Generally speaking, in regard to all waste products, it is impossible to measure statistically the addition to the wealth of the country by the turning to useful purposes of residues and by-products formerly thrown away or left to rot. The volume preserved and turned to useful account must be enormous, and in every instance cited in this paper the utilisation has resulted in definite cheapening of products to the consumer. The subject is one that is vitally associated with the progress of every industry and inseparably connected with the development and prosperity of every form of manufacturing. The acme of industrial economy is the profitable employment of every atom of material in whatever form presented or however obtained.

The signification of the word "waste," as given by different authorities, may be considered. The definitions in some of the older dictionaries are interesting.

Webster's Dictionary says: "That which is of no value, worthless remnant, refuse, especially the refuse of cotton, silk or the like."[1]

Worcester's Dictionary says: "Something of little or no account or value, as the refuse of cotton or silk."[2]

DOI: 10.4324/9780429274190-4

The Century Dictionary says: "Rubbish, trash, rejected as unfit for use, refuse, hence of little or no value, useless, stuff that is left over or that is unfitted or cannot readily be utilised for the purpose for which it was intended, overplus or rejected material, refuse, as paper scraps in a printing office or bindery, or shreds of yarn in a cotton or woollen mill."[3]

Thus, it will be seen from that which follows later in this paper that things formerly described as waste or rubbish are now to be regarded as valuable raw materials for industries.

Archduke Regnier, President of the Imperial Commission, Vienna exhibition, 1873, said: – "The consumption of paper, the quantity of letters exchanged, the extension of public libraries and the use made of them &c., are often taken as a measure of the actual degree of civilization of a nation. An extensive and refined use made of the waste materials of industry and housekeeping might be considered with equal right as a measure of the degree of industrial development and capability. It would also scarcely be possible to find in the processes of manufacture and in agriculture an instance which shows to the same extent the really creative force of science and the characteristic tendency of a nation to economise, as its endeavour to keep, like nature, entirely within the circle of reproduction."[4]

I will endeavour to deal with some of the waste product trades separately, and will first take the rag trade, as it is one of the oldest and most important, and is especially interesting to people living in Yorkshire. Some idea of its importance may be gathered from the following pre-war figures.

As far as I have been able to gather, the approximate weight of clean wool which goes into consumption in this country annually is, in round figures, about 350,000,000 lbs. The worsted trade deals with about 230,000,000 lbs. of this, leaving about 120,000,000 lbs. for the woollen trade. But besides this, in the woollen trade nearly 200,000,000 lbs. of pulled rags are employed as well as nearly 30,000,000 lbs. of noils[5] and wastes, by-products from the worsted trades. So that in the woollen trade about two-thirds of the total weight of the wool material used consists of pulled rags and wastes. It will be readily realised, therefore, what an enormously important part is played by pulled rags in the manufacturing of the cheap wool goods, and how very badly off we should be without them for warm clothing, &c.

In addition to the above weights, we export about 14,000,000 lbs. of pulled rags.

It may be somewhat confusing to those not actually connected with the trades when I refer to the worsted and woollen trades. A few words of explanation may be advisable at this point. Roughly speaking, the French description of the two trades is the simplest. They describe the worsted trade as "Combed Wool," and the woollen as "Carded Wool." There are some few exceptions to which these descriptions do not correctly apply, but, generally speaking, for the purposes of a non-technical discussion, these definitions answer very well.

In the worsted or combed wool trade, the object is to get rid of the shortest fibres, fluff, or any other objectionable material which is noil, and to retain the longest and best fibres.

In the woollen system, everything and anything goes through the carding machine and condenser. It is for this reason that so much shoddy or mungo can be employed.

It may be interesting to give a short history of the rag-pulling industry and the wonderful little machine which turns rags, old and new, into spinning fibre. So far I as I have been able to learn, it is doubtful whether the actual machine was ever patented. There was, however, a patent for a somewhat similar machine taken out by three Glasgow gentlemen in the year 1801. Their names were Thomas Parker, William Telfer, and Alexander Affleck, instrument makers, and the patent was No. 2,469.[6] True, the patent was entitled "Preparation and manufacture of flax, hemp, &c." But the specification contained the following statement: – "Our said invention is also to prepare or reduce articles made from flax, hemp, silk, wool, cotton or other materials, after the same have been in use or otherwise, into the best state of which they are capable in order that they may be recovered and again made use of as materials of manufacture."

The same patentees obtained a further patent in the following year for improved machines for the same purpose, in connection with which it was stated explicitly "To recover materials of manufacture from articles that have been made of flax, hemp, silk, wool, cotton, &c., by reducing or teasing down the materials into states capable of being again manufactured."[7]

So far as I have been able to ascertain, this is the earliest reference to rag-pulling, although, I believe, in the West Riding of Yorkshire it has been generally believed that a man named Law, of Batley,[8] in the year 1811, was the first individual to produce artificial wool, or pulled rags. It appears that besides the three Glasgow gentlemen who patented the aforementioned rag-teasing machine, there was also a man in the South of England who pulled rags. This was Mr. John Coxeter,[9] of Greenham Mills, near Newbury, Berkshire.

On June 25th, 1811, the said Mr. Coxeter laid a wager that he would take the wool from the sheep's back, sort it, card it, and spin it, spool, warp, and weave the yarn, mill, dye, dry shear and press the cloth, and have a complete suit made from it between morning and night. This was duly performed in 13 hours and 20 minutes, and Mr. Coxeter won his wager.[10] A feast was given in celebration of the feat; a whole sheep was roasted on the village green and 120 gallons of strong beer distributed amongst the spectators. Mr. Coxeter gave a dinner to forty friends and at that dinner made a speech in which was this important statement: – "So great are the improvements in machinery which I have lately introduced into my mill, that I believe in twenty-four hours I could take a coat off your back, reduce it to wool, and turn it into a coat again."

I cannot trace whether there was any connection between the machine patented in Glasgow and those Mr. Coxeter was actually using. Yet it is clear, from the foregoing statements, that other people had actually pulled up rags for re-manufacturing purposes.

Mr. Law, of Batley, is usually looked upon as the pioneer of the rag pulling industry, and he is also famous for having introduced the word "mungo." The story is that Mr. Law showed some of the pulled material from old cloth to a prospective purchaser, and the latter suggested that material was too short in the fibre and would be of no use. Mr. Law's reply in broad Yorkshire was, "It mun go," meaning "It must go." And "mungo" became the name for wool pulled from hard rags. In every country in the world where wool is produced from such rags, the material is known by the Yorkshire name "mungo."

To those not in the trade, it may be well to describe, roughly, the difference between shoddy and mungo. Shoddy is the material pulled from unmilled rags, such as stockings, jerseys, vests, flannels, blankets, and other soft rags. Mungo is made from rags of suitings, new tailors' clippings, felts, etc. Then there is also another rag wool known by the name of "extract." This is obtained from rags containing cotton. All rags are sorted and graded, and the seams and selvedges containing sewing cotton are usually separated. There are many cloths, such as gaberdines, rainproof coats, various forms of Bradford dress goods, and many other goods which frequently contain a large proportion of cotton. All such goods are now carbonised in order to destroy the cotton. As mechanical means are unavailing, a chemical process is employed – carbonisation. Cellulose, the basis of all vegetable fibres, is composed of carbon, hydrogen, and oxygen. When acted upon by certain acids, such as sulphuric acid and hydrochloric acid, the hydrogen and oxygen are withdrawn in the form of water, and there remains the carbon; hence the term carbonization. The wool, a more complex compound, containing also sulphur and nitrogen, remains unaltered. There are two methods of carbonisation – wet and dry. The first is employed for some new wools to free them from straw, wood splinters, burrs, etc.; the latter – the dry system – involves treatment of the wool rags by hydrochloric acid fumes in order to destroy the cotton warp or weft. Carbonisation came into general use in the 'seventies, after twenty years of secrecy in certain mills.

The rag trade is now very highly organised. The old rags are collected by "rag and bone" men in various towns, and then go to dealers, who roughly sort them, the cotton being eliminated from the woollen goods. Then they are sent to large merchants, who further classify them. A large proportion from all parts of the world come to Dewsbury and Batley, where they are carefully sorted and graded in qualities and shades, the rags made from fine wools being graded together and frequently dyed to one shade, opened and carded, and sold as carded shoddy; or, after sorting and grading, the rags are re-exported. It is computed that there are some 400 or 500 firms in the rag trade in the West Riding of Yorkshire. They have naturally drawn together greater facilities for doing business than exist elsewhere. One of the most interesting developments is the system of selling rags at auctions. The leading auctioneers belong to old-established firms with excellent reputations. Some sell country collections only, while others receive consignments from every part of the world. It is worth while for anyone to pay a visit to one of these sales in Dewsbury, and I recommend all who have not seen one to pay a visit.

I may say that many of the waste and shoddy merchants in England have often expressed surprise that English manufacturers allow so much of the best quality shoddies, wastes, and noils to leave this country instead of using them here. The merchants say that English manufacturers appear to prefer to buy the cheaper and inferior qualities.

I must add that the flocks which come from the finishing machinery of cloth mills are curled and used largely for stuffing bolsters and pillows. Cheap, low-class rags, unfit for re-opening purposes, are used for pulling up for the filling of cheap furniture and cheap mattresses. This trade has been somewhat improved by John Burns's Rag and Flock Act,[11] but still I consider our cheaper mattresses among the dirtiest and most insanitary of any used in a civilised country. Those used by the Americans, French, and many Continental countries are infinitely more wholesome. It is a curious thing that although we in England pride ourselves so much on our cleanliness, yet much of our bedding is among the most insanitary in the world.

The shortest refuse of all, after the wool rags have been used as far as possible, goes as manure for the hop fields of Kent and Hereford.

Before entirely leaving the subject of rag pulling, I wish to remark that some of the Continental firms have got somewhat ahead of us in the construction of rag machines. If we had paid more attention to detail in construction and finish, and had applied certain improvements which make the machine more efficient and more convenient to work, the position would have been better. They have given more attention to detail than English machine makers.

From observations during my numerous visits to Continental countries, I have come to the conclusion that one German firm has supplied the greater proportion of the rag machines bought on the Continent during the last ten years. This firm has supplied well-designed and well-constructed machines, and has obtained a higher price for them than that which English makers usually secure. This raises an interesting point as to whether the English machine maker or the English manufacturer is the more to blame for this state of things. Is it that an English maker would not alter his design and his models, or is it that the English manufacturer would not pay a sufficiently high price to enable him to get a better article? I am afraid that there has been a tendency on the part of most users of machinery in this country to consider too much the question of the price of the machine, and not enough the results obtainable.

I may now turn for a few minutes to the thread waste branch, that is, the spinning and weaving wastes from the woollen, but chiefly from the worsted mills. I have already stated that about 30,000,000 lbs. of waste from the worsted trade are used as raw materials in the woollen trade in Great Britain. Now, although this weight is only comparatively small when compared with the weight of rags employed, still the value per pound of waste is usually very much greater than pulled rags, for when opened, they are usually a more valuable raw material and for many purposes are almost equal to new wool.

With regard to worsted spinning wastes, previous to the year 1850 hard spinning wastes were used for cleaning waste or thrown on the fields as manure. In the year named, the first waste opening machine was built, and I believe the first machine used was by a firm of carpet manufacturers. I understand that when the first machine was built, the original maker went to see this firm of carpet manufacturers. They took him out into their yard and showed him a heap of hard spinning waste and asked him if he could do anything with it. He took a sample away with him, returned home, put it through the machine, and returned it by messenger the same day. Before breakfast next morning, one of the carpet firm was at the office of the machine maker with a cheque in his hand and a request that the machine should be sent on immediately.

I believe that after the machine maker had sold a few machines he realised that he had made a mistake, as he saw that he would have made a much larger fortune had he put up a number of machines at his place, collected the waste which he could get for practically nothing, and opened it and sold it at 4d., 6d., 8d., or even more per pound.

At the present time, I estimate that nearly 100,000,000 lbs. of worsted thread wastes must be treated annually in the world, and to give an idea of the value of some of this material, I may say that the market price in 1913 for some of the pulled wastes from fine botany wools was as high as 22d. per pound.

Most of the pulled wastes are used in the woollen trade, but certain classes of wastes can be so successfully treated to-day that they can be combed and used for certain classes of worsted yarns, especially in the hosiery yarn trade. This is also done with mohair wastes to a certain extent.

Pulled wastes are employed in a number of trades, and can be found to a certain extent in best Scotch tweeds, in West of England suitings, in flannels, blankets, hosiery yarns, woollen carpet yarns, in medium class suitings and cap cloths, such as are made in Yorkshire districts, and in quite good class ladies' dress goods made on the Continent; they are also used in felt making. Some of the cheaper wastes are pulled up for stuffing saddles and horse collars and also for mattresses and cushions. I could go on for a long time enumerating the different purposes for which different wastes are used. I must mention one very interesting class of material, which shows how the waste from one trade can be converted into a valuable raw material for another, and that is the press cloth, which is used in the cottonseed crushing industry. This is very strong material, made from very strong and good worsted yarn. After it has become saturated with grease and seed from the seed pressing it is thrown away, and this material is shaken and pulled up again, and it is a valuable raw material in the woollen trade, especially for woollen carpet yarns.

Noils are another important waste product from the worsted industry. They are the short material combed out in the combing process. Noils are mixed with wools and shoddies for making cheap and medium ladies' dress goods, shawls, blankets, flannels, felts, and innumerable other goods, some of which have been already mentioned. Many of the noils and other wastes from the worsted cards, etc., are carbonised to get rid of the bits of vegetable matter. Many of the fine wool noils go to the felt industry for hats, etc. As most of you are aware, a large proportion of these noils and other wastes containing vegetable matter, coming from the worsted industry, were sent to Verviers, in Belgium, to be carbonised, as the firms in that district had made a special study of this kind of work. They are, I believe, able to obtain superior results on most classes of material.[12] Since the war there has been a great extension of carbonising plants in this country, and it is to be hoped that the experience gained will enable us after the war to retain most of the trade in our own country.

I may say that at one time English worsted spinners looked upon burry wool as almost a waste product. As they were the wealthiest buyers of wool 30 to 40 years ago, they endeavoured to buy wool as free from burr as possible, so that the French, Belgians, and Germans had to buy the burry wools and make the best of them.

The French have always, therefore, been ahead of us in the mechanical treatment of burry wools, and have been able to practically get rid of the burr by carding and combing only. In fact, they have been able to treat burry wools by mechanical means only, with results that would have been thought impossible in England, at any rate up to a short time ago, except by carbonising. It may be added that the conditioning-house test for burry wools in France requires that there shall not be more than one bit of burr in 12 yards of combed top.

In the silk trade a large amount of waste, at one time considered of little value, is made. Now, the re-working of waste silk has become an important and profitable industry. Lord Masham, then Samuel Lister,[13] of Manningham Mills, was the first to successfully treat this waste silk. It is not quite waste, as the term is usually understood in the textile trade. It is a part of the cocoon left over after the long-fibred silk has been obtained, and is really a good fibre. Many beautiful goods are made from it at Manningham, in Switzerland, Germany, and France. There is also spinning waste from this waste silk, which is now opened successfully and used for yarns for the making of bags. In France and Switzerland it is so well treated that it is mixed again with the raw material and used for yarns for the plush trade and other valuable purposes. Japanese silk rags, old, and formerly thrown out as manure, are now being opened, carded, and spun into yarn and used in the manufacture of rugs, mats, etc.

The wool industry furnishes a number of materials formerly regarded as waste but now utilised in the industry itself and for pharmaceutical and other purposes.[14] One important by-product is wool grease, and another is "suint." The sheep obtains from the soil of the pastures upon which it feeds a considerable portion of potash, which, after circulating through the system of the animal, is excreted with other matter from the skin and attaches to the wool. This excretion is known by the French as "suint." Formerly, when the wool was cleaned, the suint was allowed to go to waste, and even now a large portion is permitted to go to waste with the wash waters. The encrusting matters attached to the wool, besides the dirt, consist of wool fat (soluble in ether or benzine), and wool perspiration (soluble in water). The wool fat is a mixture of a solid alcoholic body, cholesterine, together with iso-cholesterine, and the compounds of these bodies with several of the fatty acids.[15] Wool perspiration consists essentially of the potassium salts, oleic acid and stearic acids, and possibly other fatty acids; also potassium salts of volatile acids like acetic and valerianic,[16] and small quantities of chlorides, phosphates, and sulphates. Thus, the yolk of wool contains many elements of recognised value in the arts and manufactures.

When the potash salts are evaporated and ignited, they yield a product of the potassium carbonate, and it is estimated that 2,200,000 lbs. of this product is annually saved from the wool wash waters of the mills and scouring establishments of France and Belgium. When the suint is submitted to dry distillation, it yields a residue containing carbonate of potash, nitrogenous carbon of great value, for the manufacture of yellow prussiate of potash.[17]

In 1895, a plant for treating wool by the "solvent" process was put in operation by the Arlington Mills, of Lawrence, Mass., and was the first plant of its kind in the world to prove commercially and technically successful.[18] This plant has a capacity to degrease 50,000 pounds of wool every ten hours, and has been run to its full limit ever since it was started. After an experience of 10 years with the solvent process, the Arlington Mills have built a new plant with capacity of from 200,000 to 250,000 lbs. of wool every ten hours.[19]

The fat products obtained are applicable to the following uses: –

(1) As a base for ointments and other pharmaceutical and toilet preparations, on account of penetrating, lubricating, and softening qualities.
(2) As a leather and belt dressing, and, when freed from resinous matter, as a lubricant in conjunction with certain lubricating oils.
(3) As a lubricant for wool and other animal fibres. This can be used to advantage to increase the specific gravity and viscosity of certain lubricating oils.[20]

I may say that the Bradford Corporation extracted from their sewage over £30,000's worth of grease in 1912 which had run away from the various combing establishments in the city.

The cotton waste trade is also of considerable importance, but, of course, the value of the treated material does not approach that of the wool wastes and shoddies.

First of all we have the linters waste, which is the short fibre taken from the cotton-seed, by a second ginning process after the ginning proper. These linters are largely used for the medical wadding trade, and most medical wadding is made from such waste, which is first of all bleached. Linters waste is also very extensively used in the United States and Canada for making mattresses, and a very clean, wholesome bed it makes.

Cotton spinning wastes and card wastes are opened, cleaned, carded, and spun into yarns for sheetings, towels, flannelettes, cretonnes, cheap hosiery, bed covers, cotton blankets, sponge cloths, candle-wicks, etc. The hardest cotton threads, which cannot be successfully opened for re-spinning purposes, are used for wiping waste and sold in huge quantities to railway companies, dockyards, engineers' shops, etc. Old curtains are now successfully pulled up for mixing with this cleaning waste.

Cotton rags were formerly practically only considered fit for the paper-making trade, but now more valuable uses have been found for hundreds of tons. Some of the best black cotton linings are pulled up for very cheap hosiery yarns and for mixing in the woollen trade. Other rags are pulled up for spinning into coarse yarn for Belgian blankets, and large quantities are now shredded into thread again to mix with wiping wastes. Some cotton rags are now used in the manufacture of artificial silk on the Chardonnet system.[21] They are opened, cleaned, and bleached, and then dissolved in ether and alcohol. The resulting solution is then forced out of the mixer and into the hydraulic press, which then passes it through a filter under great pressure, whereby all undissolved cotton and impurities are eliminated.

From the reservoirs, the solution is forced through small capillary tubes, forming fine filaments, a dozen or more of which are combined constitute a thread, which is finally wound on a bobbin.

Closely allied to cotton manufacturing is the cotton-seed oil industry, in which there has been a great revolution within late years in the utilisation of the cotton-seed, obtaining most valuable commercial by-products – which at one time were allowed to go to waste with the seed in the form of manure. Cotton-seed was garbage in 1860, a fertiliser in 1870, a cattle food in 1880, and a table food and many other things in 1890.[22]

The manufacture of cotton-seed oil and all of its resultant by-products furnishes one of the best examples of the developments of a business based upon the utilisation of a waste product. One of the principle uses of cotton-seed oil is the manufacture of a compound – a mixture of lard, oleo stearine, and refined cotton-seed oil, making a most palatable and economical food. Another product of cotton-seed oil, white cottolene, is a mixture of oleo stearine and cotton-seed oil.[23] This product marks, perhaps, the highest development of cotton oil as a food product.

Cotton oil is also used in the making of salad oils, packing sardines in the oleomargarine industry, for miners' and cathedral lamps, tempering oils, oils for heavy tool-cutting machines, and for mixing with putty.

The cheapness of cotton-oil compared with other fats, as well as its excellent soap-making properties, has caused it to be largely used by soap makers in America. Cotton-seed oil is used today to a great extent by bakers. It is also used as a substitute for olive oil. Chemists and physicians now recognise cotton oil as a high-class food product.[24]

There are many by-products used in the dye-house, and in the dyeing industry which have contributed largely to the great progress made in manufacture within the last one or two decades. Of these by-products, the most conspicuous and valuable are those obtained from coal tar or gas tar, which not many years ago formed waste material difficult to get rid of. It could not be thrown into the streams because of pollution, nor could it be disposed of by burial because of its destructive effect upon vegetation. It had to be disposed of by burning. These by-products have now become of the highest value, not only for the production of saccharine, dyes, and high explosives, but for medicines and disinfectants, and for the production of a saccharine substance several hundred times sweeter than sugar. The list of uses to which these materials can now be converted is a long one. Naphthalene, one of the products of gas tar, formerly a troublesome waste, by its tendency to choke gas pipes and otherwise make itself obnoxious, is now one of the most valuable substances for the preparation of dyestuffs. The manufacture of alizarin, an artificial preparation of the by-products of tar, has destroyed the madder industry of Europe, or practically so. The aniline by-product of gas tar is a most productive source of colouring matter, its derivatives being almost without number, and producing every shade of colour imaginable. By means of a synthetic process, certain constituents of coal tar can be combined for the production of artificial indigo, equal in all respects to natural indigo, at a cost that makes it an article of much commercial value. Naphtha is a well-known product of coal tar used in dissolving gums, resinous substances, etc., indiarubber and gutta-percha, and for many other purposes. Perhaps the most important products of this tar are benzol, from which aniline colours are obtained, and naphthalene and anthracene, from which alizarin and purpurin are obtained. Benzol is, of course, now largely used for motor cars.[25]

The limits of one paper does not permit of my dealing with the slaughter-house by-products, such as hides, bristles, parchment, gelatine, glue, or with by-products from the metal and mining industries, such as furnace gas for motive power, slag and slag wool, etc.

I will now conclude with a quotation from a speech by Lord Playfair,[26] made a good many years ago, in which he said: – "Chemistry, like a prudent housewife, economises every scrap. The clippings of the travelling tinker are mixed with the parings of horses' hoofs from the smithy, or the cast-off woollen garments of the poorest inhabitants, and soon afterwards, in the form of dyes of the brightest hue, grace the dresses of courtly dames. The bones of dead animals yield the chief constituent of lucifer matches. The dregs of port wine, carefully rejected by the wine drinker in decanting his favourite beverage, are taken by him in the morning as seidlitz powders.[27] The offal of the streets and the washings of coal gas re-appear carefully preserved in the lady's smelling bottle, or are used by her to flavour blanc-manges for her friends. This economy of the chemistry of art is only an imitation of what we observe in the chemistry of nature."

## Notes

1 *An American Dictionary of the English Language by Noah Webster, LL. D. thoroughly revised and greatly enlarged by Chauncey A. Goodrich . . . and Noah Porter. . .* (Springfield MA: G. & C. Merriam and Co., 1889), p. 1194.

2 *A Dictionary of the English Language by Joseph E. Worcester, LL. D.* (London: Frederick Warne and Co., 1884), p. 1649. This definition is attributed to Simmonds; 'the refuse of cotton or silk' is one definition of waste given in P. L. Simmonds's *A Dictionary of Trade Products* (London: G. Routledge and Co., 1858), p. 406.

3 *The Century Dictionary: an Encyclopedic Lexicon of the English Language. Prepared under the Superintendence of William Dwight Whitney. . .* (New York, The Century Co., 1895), vol. 8, p. 6388. The quoted version recombines several entries from the dictionary.

4 Archduke Rainer Ferdinand von Hapsburg (1827–1913) wrote this in a circular inviting displays concerning waste consumption for the 1873 exhibition. It was quoted in English translation by Peter Lund Simmonds in *Waste Products and Undeveloped* Substances, 2nd ed. (London: Robert Hardwicke, 1873), p. 1.

5 Wool noils are the short fibres that fall out when combing wool.

6 The patent was granted 3 February 1801 to Thomas Parker of Broomward near Glasgow, and William Telfer and Alexander Affleck of Glasgow, mathematical instrument makers.

7 Patent no. 2607 of 1802.

8 Benjamin Law (c1773–1837).

9 John Coxeter (1772–1816).

10 The wager of 1000 guineas was made by Sir John Throckmorton (1754–1819), who wore the suit. John Coxeter coordinated the production. The story was reported in the *Manchester Mercury*, 9 July 1811, p. 4. This account clarifies that two sheep were shorn for the wool, and the same roasted for the celebratory feast.
In 1816, the leases of the Greenham factory were advertised for sale by assignees due to bankruptcy; the machinery was sold the following year, but did not include rag-teasing equipment.

11 The Rag Flock Act 1911 was introduced during the tenure of John Elliot Burns M.P. (1858–1943) as President of the Local Government Board.

12 Verviers was a major European wool centre in nineteenth-century Europe, remaining an important hub into the twentieth century. Already in 1867, the exhibits of Celestin Martin of Verviers at the Paris Exposition Universelle were commended for the superior clearness of the carded result when starting with burry wool. See G. Leach, 'Report on Carded Wool, Woollen Yarns, and Woollen Fabrics' in *Reports on the Paris Universal Exhibition, 1867* (London: Eyre and Spottiswoode, 1868), vol. 3, pp. 67–77.

13 Samuel Cunliffe Lister, 1st Baron Masham (1815–1906).

14 These paragraphs on wool fat are largely abridged from Kittredge (pp. 13–14), where the chemical composition of the yolk of wool is attributed to Sadtler's *Industrial Organic Chemistry*, 3rd ed., p. 306.

15 The composition of lanolin (wool fat) is described as it was then understood. Cholesterine, now known as cholesterol, is one of the alcoholic components.

16 Valeric or pentanoic acid: $CH_3(CH_2)_3COOH$.

17 Potassium ferrocyanide.

18 Arlington Mills was established in 1865. It grew to an extensive scale, and processed both wool and cotton.

19 This paragraph is closely adapted from Kittredge (p. 16). In the Kittredge version, it is stated that the new plant was then building, after an experience of six years. This implies that Leather may have first adapted the material for a lecture around 1906.

20 This compilation is taken from Kittredge (p. 15).

21 Hilaire de Chardonnet (1839–1924) extruded and spun nitrocellulose to form silky fibres. The process was commercialised in 1891.

22 This paragraph is closely taken from Kittredge (p. 18) who attributes it to Frederic G. Mather, *Popular Science Monthly*, 45 (May 1894), pp. 104–108 (on p. 104).

23 Cottolene was a lard substitute produced and marketed in the United States from 1868.

24 These paragraphs on cottonseed oil are largely taken from Kittredge (p. 20), probably derived from Mather (see note 22).

25 This paragraph on dyeing is closely taken from Kittredge (p. 21).

26 Lyon Playfair (1818–1898), British chemist, delivered this passage in a lecture before the Society of Arts, 7 January 1852: 'On the chemical principles involved in the manufactures of the Exhibition as indicating the necessity of industrial instruction', published in *Lectures on the Results of the Exhibition delivered before the Society of Arts, Manufactures, and Commerce, at the suggestion of H.R.H. Prince Albert, President of the Society* (London: David Bogue, 1852), p. 124. Leather has somewhat abridged the original passage.

27 A laxative containing tartaric acid and sodium potassium tartrate.

# Part 2

# HARD LABOUR

## Tow and oakum

*Fig. 2* The large oakum room (under the silent system) at the Middlesex House of Correction, Coldbath Fields. See Ch. 3 this volume.

*Source*: Mayhew, Henry. *The Criminal Prisons of London* (London: Charles Griffin, 1862), opp. p. 300. Author's collection.

*Fig. 3* Oakum carding machine by Tomlinsons (Rochdale) Ltd. See Ch. 4 this volume.

*Source*: *Textile Manufacturer*, 52:618 (15 Jan 1926), p. 201. Author's collection.

*Fig. 4* Tow carding at Marshall and Co., Leeds. A factory hand feeds prepared tow onto the divided apron, and the carded tow emerges above, where portions are consolidated by small rollers into slivers collected in nearby cans. See Ch. 5 this volume.

*Source*: Dodd, George. *The Textile Manufactures of Great Britain* (London: Charles Knight and Co., 1844), p. 165. Author's collection.

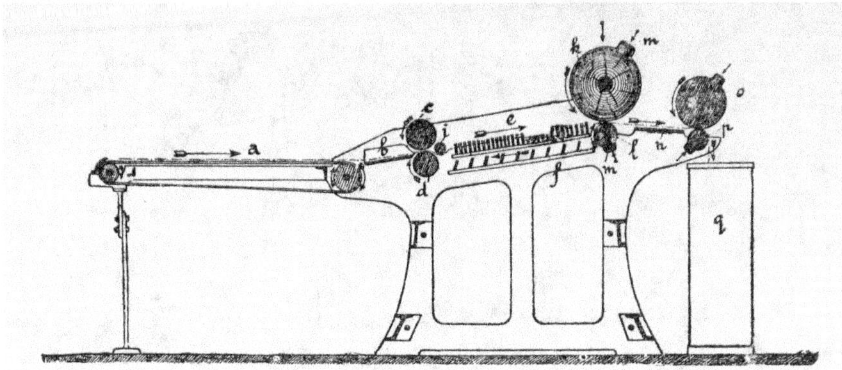

FIG. 139.—Gilling Machine for Flax (vertical longitudinal section).

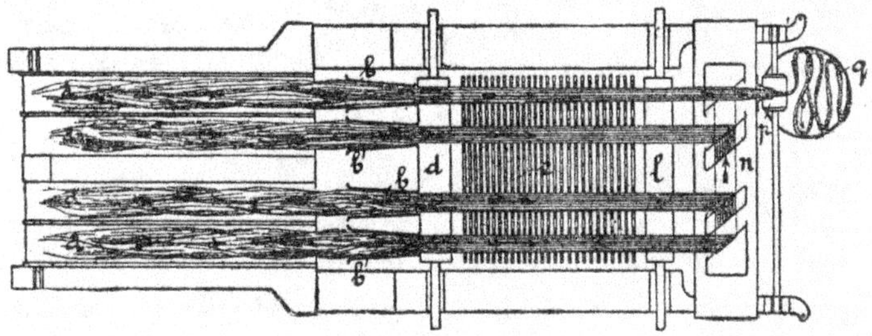

FIG. 140.—Flax Gilling Machine (plan view).

*Fig. 5* The gilling machine in cross-section and plan. The gills (e) comb through the fibre in the direction of the arrow and then drop to return to their starting position. See Ch. 5 this volume.

*Source*: Zipser, Julius. *Textile Raw Materials and Their Conversion into Yarns*. Translated from the German by Charles Salter (London: Scott, Greenwood and Co., 1901), p. 247. Author's collection.

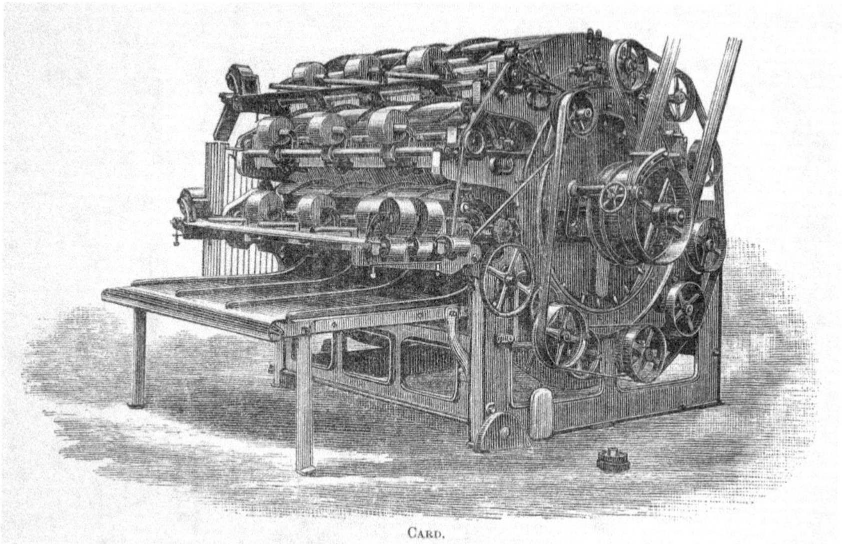


*Fig. 6* The tow carding machine. The feed apron and the condenser rollers that deliver the carded sliver are on the same side of the machine; the canisters where the sliver is coiled at the side of the machine are not shown. See Ch. 6 this volume.

*Source*: Sharp, Peter. *Flax, Tow, and Jute Spinning*, 2nd ed. (Dundee: James P. Mathew & Co., 1886), p. 96. Author's collection.

## Editorial Headnote

**Mayhew, Henry. 'House of Correction, Coldbath Fields: Oakum Picking', 'Of the Interior of Tothill Fields Prison', and 'The Female Work and Work-rooms at Tothill Fields Prison', in Mayhew, Henry and Binney, John. *The Criminal Prisons of London and Scenes of Prison Life* (London: Charles Griffin, Bohn and Co., 1862), pp. 310–313, 400–402, 476–477.**

Henry Mayhew (1812–1887) is best known for his work as a journalist and as editor of the seminal study of urban street life, *London Labour and the London Poor*. This began as articles in the *Morning Chronicle* from 19 October 1849 to 12 December 1850, then developed as a serial from December 1850 to February 1852 after he left the newspaper, before taking its final form in a four-volume set of books published in 1861–1862. Mayhew and his fellow researchers were adept at recording the colourful spoken idioms of the London streets. John Binny, born around 1834 in Scotland, was author of the section on 'Thieves and Swindlers' in *London Labour*, and it was Binny who was employed by the publishers Griffin and Co. to complete the prisons work serialised by Mayhew as 'The Great World of London', so that it could be published as a single volume. The sections extracted here were completed by Mayhew in July and August 1856. Compared to *London Labour*, Mayhew's attitude toward his male prison subjects showed more sympathy, founded on a conviction that the roots of crime lay in poverty, although women still received less empathic treatment.

Mayhew's original categorisation of people was based upon their inducement, ability or willingness to work. But in oakum picking, he uncovered work used as a form of punishment, a concept almost calculated to breed a dislike of work, and sneer at any idea of prisoner reform. There is a hint that the hardening of hands consequent on oakum picking might reduce the adeptness of prisoners for crimes requiring manual dexterity. However, Mayhew's aim is to show the pointlessness of the labour. The statistics that account for hours, quantities and monetary values, not only authenticate the account, but demonstrate the poor economic value of hand-production of oakum.

The completed book appeared 19 April 1862 in a large cloth-bound volume sold at 10s. 6d. It received some praise for its readability, but did not achieve the impact of *London Labour*, for which it was seen as a concluding piece. *Criminal Prisons* did not receive another edition until Augustus M. Kelley brought out a facsimile in 1968, followed by Frank Cass in 1971, with an edition for its 'Victorian Times' series.

# 3

# MAYHEW, HENRY. 'HOUSE OF CORRECTION, COLDBATH FIELDS: OAKUM PICKING', 'OF THE INTERIOR OF TOTHILL FIELDS PRISON', AND 'THE FEMALE WORK AND WORK-ROOMS AT TOTHILL FIELDS PRISON'

*The Criminal Prisons of London* (London: Charles Griffin, Bohn and Co., 1862), pp. 310–313, 400–402, 476–747.

## Oakum picking

There are three distinct rooms where the prisoners pick oakum, one in the misdemeanour prison, and the two others in the felons' prison. We shall choose for our illustration and description the larger one in the felons' prison. It has lately been built on so vast a plan that it has seats for nearly 500 men. This immense room is situated to the west of the main or old prison, close to the school-room. It is almost as long as one of the sheds seen at a railway terminus where spare carriages are kept, and seems to have been built after the same style of architecture, for it has a corrugated iron roof, stayed with thin rods, spanning the entire erection. We were told that the extreme length is 90 feet, but that does not convey so good a notion of distance to the mind as the fact of the wall being pierced with eight large chapel windows, and the roof with six skylights. Again, an attendant informed us that there were eleven rows of forms, but all that we could see was a closely-packed mass of heads and pink faces, moving to and fro in every variety of motion, as though the wind was blowing them about, and they were set on stalks instead of necks.

On the side fitted with windows the dark forms of the warders are seen, each perched up on a raised stool. The bright light shines on the faces of the criminals, and the officer keeps his eye rapidly moving in all directions, almost as if it went by clock-work, so as to see that no talking takes place. If a man rest over his work


DOI: 10.4324/9780429274190-6

for a moment and raise his head, he sees, hung up on the white walls before him, placards on which texts are printed. One is to the effect that "IT IS GOOD FOR A MAN THAT HE BEAR THE YOKE IN HIS YOUTH;" another tells the prisoners that "GODLINESS WITH CONTENTMENT IS A GREAT GAIN;" whilst a third counsels each of them to "GO TO THE ANT, THOU SLUGGARD, CONSIDER HER WAYS, AND BE WISE."*

We went to the wall where the warders were, and looked up the sloping floor at the dirty gray mass of life; the faces of the men seemed like the flesh showing through a tattered garment.

* One of the peculiarities of Coldbath Fields is the frequent display of Scripture texts, printed in a large bold type, and hung up on every conspicuous part of the prison walls. We believe that this idea originated with the present kind-hearted governor himself – a gentleman whose endeavours to improve the religious feelings of the prisoners under his charge are, from the evidences so plentifully distributed about the prison, unceasing and most enthusiastic. But we doubt very much whether a criminal is to be affected by a printed display of Bible quotations. On the contrary, we rather believe that the constant sight of such placards tends so to accustom him to the religious warnings, that at last be ceases to notice them altogether, and pays no more attention to them than we do to the pattern of the paper on our walls. The obtruded texts become, as it were, part of the furniture, and the felon at last passes them by, giving no more heed to the principles inculcated by them than we do to a notice-board, which, having once read, we do not stop each time we go by to re-peruse. Over the report-office, in the entrance hall of the prison, is placarded, "SWEAR NOT AT ALL," which we before noticed, remarking that in a prison conducted on the silent system such a command appeared to us somewhat superfluous. In explanation, the governor tells us that the men, when reported and brought before him, often accompanied their expostulations of innocence with oaths such as "Strike me dead!" "Upon my soul!" &c., and that it was on that account he had the text placed over the entrance door. It would appear, however, that the language of the prisoners has not been much improved by the placard, for the same form of vehement asseverations is said to be still indulged in, nor is it *likely* that a line or two of print should change men, who pay no regard to the laws of society, into persons of gentle speech. Besides, the experiment of these silent warnings has been often tried and failed. The Mohammedan has the very cornice of his ceiling, and the arabesques on his walls, decorated with quotations from the Koran, and yet he cannot order a cup of coffee, or converse on the most ordinary topic, without swearing, "By Allah!" or "By the Prophet!" at every dozen words. The Pharisees, again, are known to have had their phylacteries covered with short passages from the Bible hung about their necks. The old Puritans, too, were accustomed to interlard their conversation with oaths, such as "By God's wounds!" "By God's blood!" "By the agony of Christ!" and yet, although these phrases were intended to carry with them a scriptural sound, everybody of the present day would certainly denounce them as improper and revolting. Again, the same fanatics loved to put up religious signs even at their drinking booths, as "GOD ENCOMPASSES" (now corrupted into the "GOAT AND COMPASSES"), or, in Saxon English, "GOD IMBUTES" (literally, God surrounds – God is *about*, but now transmogrified into the "GOAT AND BOOTS"). The Bible texts on the walls of Coldbath Fields seem to us of the same *blasphemous* character. To our minds – we confess it boldly – they appear very much like using the most solemn phrases "*in vain*," *i.e.*, idly, or when the mind is not fitted to appreciate them; and surely the plastering the walls of a prison with those religious posting-bills only teaches thieves to adopt the *cant*, rather than feel the *spirit*, of true piety. Suppose every hoarding in the public thoroughfares was to be covered with texts, would the public be a bit better for it, think you? or, rather, would not men be rendered worse, and taught to use Scripture as a slang – to chatter it, as Catholic beggars do their Latin prayers without thinking of what they themselves are saying, and merely as a means of imposition upon others.

The building was full of men, and as silent as if it merely contained so many automata, for the only sound heard was like that of the rustling of a thicket, or, better, the ticking of clock-work – something resembling that heard in a Dutch clockmaker's shop, where hundreds of time-pieces are going together.

The utter absence of noise struck us as being absolutely terrible. The silence seemed, after a time, almost intense enough to hear a flake of snow fall. Perfect stillness is at all times more or less awful, and hence arises a great part of the solemnity of night as well as of death. To behold those whom we have seen full of life and emotion – some wondrous piece of breathing and speaking organism, reduced to the inanimateness of the statue, is assuredly the most appalling and depressing sight we can look upon. The stillness of the silent system, however, has, to our minds, even a more tragic cast about it; for not only is the silence as intense and impressive as that of death itself, but the movements of the workers seem as noiseless, and therefore unearthly, as spectres. Nor does the sense of our being surrounded by some five hundred criminals – men of the wildest passions, and almost brute instincts, all toiling in dumb show and without a single syllable escaping from their lips – in any way detract from the *goblin* character of the sight.

The work-room at the dumb asylum is not half so grim or affecting a scene as the five centuries of silent oakum-pickers at Coldbath Fields; for, at the latter place, we are conscious that the wretched mutes before us *would* speak if they dare, so that we cannot help thinking of the struggling emotions pent up in the several hundred crushed spirits before us. Either the men must have been cowed by discipline into the insensibility of mere automata, or else what gall and bitterness, and suppressed fury, must be rankling in every bosom there, at the sense of having their tongues thus *virtually cut out*. Nor can we help thinking that the excision of the organ of speech itself (after the manner that barbarous nations deal with offending slaves) would be less inhuman as a punishment; for to leave the tongue in a man's mouth, and yet to deny him the liberty of using it (when every little event in life, every act we witness, every feeling we experience, as well as every thought that passes through the brain, suggests some form of speech from the mere force of association; and when, therefore, the restraint imposed upon a man's lips for the whole of his imprisonment must be one long round of irritation upon irritation – a continual series of checkings and curbings of natural impulses, sufficient to infuriate even the best regulated and least irritable natures) – this is surely a piece of refined tyranny, worthy of the enlightenment, if not the humanity, of the nineteenth century. We are well aware of the evil consequences that ensue when unrestricted intercourse is permitted among criminals; but because thieves and vagabonds become more corrupt by speaking together on bad subjects, surely that affords no sound reason why we should deny such people the right of speech altogether, and so cut off from them the only means that all persons have of improvement, viz., by moral and intellectual communion with other minds.

The quantity of oakum each man has to pick varies according to whether he be condemned to hard labour or not. In the former case the weight is never less than three, and sometimes as much as six, pounds; for the quantity given out depends upon the quality of the old rope or junk, *i.e.*, according as it is more or less tightly twisted. The men *not at hard labour* have only two pounds' weight of junk served out to them.

Each picker has by his side his weighed quantity of old rope, cut into lengths about equal to that of a hoop-stick. Some of the pieces are white and sodden-looking as a washer-woman's hands, whilst others are hard and black with the tar upon them. The prisoner takes up a length of junk and untwists it, and when he has separated it into so many corkscrew strands, he further unrolls them by sliding them backwards and forwards on his knee with the palm of his hand, until the meshes are loosened.

Then the strand is further unravelled by placing it in the bend of a hook fastened to the knees, and sawing it smartly to and fro, which soon removes the tar and grates the fibres apart. In this condition, all that remains to be done is to loosen the hemp by pulling it out like cotton wool, when the process is completed.

By the rays of sun-light shining through the window, you can see that the place is full of dust; for the bright rays are sharply defined as those streaming through a cathedral window. The shoulders of the men, too, are covered with the brown dust almost as thickly as the shirt-front of a snuff-taker. A prisoner with a bright tin water-can is going the round, handing up drink to the workers, who gulp it down as if choked.

"You're getting too close together on that back seat," presently a warder shouts to some men on a form against the wall, and who instantly separate, till they are spaced out like tumblers on a shelf.

We left the building for a time, and when we returned, we found a man lying on the stone floor with a bundle of picked oakum supporting his head, and a warder unbuttoning his shirt and loosening his waistcoat; he was in an epileptic fit. His face had turned a bright crimson with the blood flown to the head, so that the clenched teeth between his parted lips seemed as white as a sweep's. The other prisoners went on working as though it were no business of their's. After a few minutes a thrill ran down the limbs of the prostrate man, he began to draw in his extended arms, his tightly closed hands opened, and the eyelids quivered. "How do you feel now, my man?" asked the warder; but the only answer was a deep-drawn breath, like that of a person going into cold water.

"We often have such cases," said the officer to us. "After letting them lie down for half an hour they are all right again, and go back to their oakum as well as ever."

As the day advanced, the pieces of old rope by the prisoners' sides disappeared bit by bit, and in their place the mound of treacle-brown oakum at their feet grew from the size of a scratch wig to that of a large pumpkin. At length the men had all completed their tasks, and sat each holding on his knees his immense tar-coloured ball, waiting to take his turn to go to the scales and have his pickings weighed. Then the silence of the room, which has all along been like that of a sick chamber, is suddenly broken by the warder calling out, "The first three men!" The voice seems so loud, that it startles one like a scream in the night-time. Three gray forms rise up obediently as shepherds' dogs, and, carrying their bundles before them, advance to the weighing-machine. Now the stillness is broken by the shuffling of feet, and the pushing of forms, as prisoner after prisoner obeys the command to give in his oakum.

Two officers stand beside the weighing-machine, and a third, with a big basket before him, receives the roll as soon as it has been passed as correct. If a prisoner's oakum be found to be light, he is reported and punished; many, we were told, are wont to get rid of their junk, and so ease their labour by perhaps a pound.

"This won't do," says the warder, pointing to the puffy hemp in the scales; "it's half a pound short."

"It's all I had, sir," answers the man. "Ask them as was next me if I haven't picked every bit."

"Report him!" is the warder's answer; and his brother officer writes down the number of the culprit in a book.

When the men had fallen into line, and been marched off to their different yards, we inquired of one of the warders if oakum-picking was a laborious task. "*Not to the old hands*," was the answer. "We've men here that will have done their three or four pounds a couple of hours before some of the fresh prisoners will have done a pound. They learn the knack of it, and make haste to finish, so as to be able to read; but to the new arrivals it's hard work enough; for *most thieves' hands are soft*, and the hard rope cuts and blisters their fingers, so that until the skin hardens, it's very painful."

The quantity of rope picked into oakum at Coldbath Fields prison would average, says the governor, *three and a half tons per week*, which, at the present price of £5 the ton, would produce the sum of £17 10s.

## House of correction, Tothill Fields

"You can pass them in now," said the warder; and the order was no sooner given than the keys rattled in the locks of the nearest exercising-yard, and the gates groaned as they turned heavily on their hinges. "Pass on," said one of the warders; and then the boys from "6 and 7" came filing along, one after another, in a continuous stream, each with his small canvas satchel of books dangling from his hand; these were immediately followed by the urchins from "3 and 4," and when this yard was emptied, those from "1 and 2" kept up the apparently endless line.

We now entered the oakum-room at the end, as we said, of yard 7 and 8, and found the interior of the shed somewhat like a large barn, with the whitewashed tie-beams and rafters showing overhead. The shed was filled with seats, that ranged from one end of the long room to the other, and stood on a slightly-inclined plane, so as to have the appearance of a large booth at a fair or stand at a race-ground – with the exception that the side which is usually open at such places was, in the prison, fitted with the peculiar lengthy windows that, in the district of Spitalfields, are termed "long-lights." Here was the same tarry smell of oakum as is peculiar to all such places.

At the time of our entry, the serving out of the oakum for the day's labour was going on. At one end of the room was a warder, sitting beside a small box of hooks and a pair of large, buttermonger-like scales. Near these stood three boy-prisoners, with baskets of brown, tarry, old junk, and bits of rope close beside them. One of the boys placed a bundle of the junk into the scale-pan, whilst another stood by with the weights in his hand – two pounds in one and one and a half in the other – and placed either the heavier or the lighter one in the scale, according as the lad to whom the bundle of strands was served out was older or younger.

"Boys of sixteen," said the chief warder to us, "have two pounds of junk given out to them; those under sixteen, one and a half pound; and those under nine years of age, only one pound. Some of the young ones, however, who have been in the prison many times before, have one and a half pound to do; and they manage it better even than the older lads."

The oakum is ready weighed into parcels of the various quantities before it comes to the work-room, and being sorted into different baskets, it has, in the morning, only to be served out. The weights, however, are placed in the scale at the same time, so that the prisoner may see that he gets no more than his fair allowance.

As we stood beside the warder at the end, the boys came filing past the scales, the balance clicking the while, as the several bundles were thrown from the baskets into the pan, and the hooks rattling in the box as each of the prisoners dipped into it.

In a few minutes the lads were all busy at their day's work, with the hooks tied just above the knee; some "fiddling away," as the prison phrase goes, at the unravelled yarn passed across the hook, and others rolling the loosened strands backwards along the other thigh, which seemed to be coated with glue, from the tar with which it had got to be covered, while the atmosphere of the place grew gradually hazed with the dust of the abraded tow flying in the air.

A death-like silence prevailed throughout the place, and round the room the warders sat on high, lawyer's-clerk-like stools, with their eyes intently fixed on the young urchins, and ready to put a stop to the least attempt at communication among them.

"They are kept at the oakum-work for nearly five hours altogether in the day," the chief warder informed us; "and they are expected," he added, "each to do the quantity served out to them in that time. They begin at a quarter past seven, and continue working till half-past four, with the intervals of an hour and three-quarters for their meals during the day, as well as an hour for exercising, and another hour and three-quarters for schooling and Divine service."

We afterwards learnt, on visiting the oakum-store, that there is, altogether, about from 24 to 26 cwt.[1] of oakum picked, on an average, every week, in Tothill Fields prison. Of this quantity, the boys do nearly one-half, or between 11 and 12 cwt.[†]

In the oakum-room, at the period of our visit, there were altogether about some 150 of mere children congregated together. Some of the boys, seated on the lower forms, were dressed in a suit of prison-blue, marking that they were imprisoned for misdemeanours, and *not* sentenced to hard labour. Others were habited in suits of iron-gray, to note that they have been sentenced to be kept at hard labour, being known technically as "summary boys," *i.e.*, they had been committed by the magistrates, rather than after trial. Others, again, had yellow collars to the waistcoats of their gray suits, and this was to mark them as "sessions'" prisoners, or, in other words, as those who had been tried and found guilty of larceny or felony. All the boys wore striped tricolour woollen night-caps, which were arranged, by tucking down the peak, into the form of an ordinary day-cap. Besides these vestiary distinctions, there were others, which consisted of letters and marks attached to the left arm – such as either a large figure 1 or 2, in yellow cloth, to denote the class of prisoners to which they belonged – the third-class prisoners being unmarked, and consisting of such as had been sentenced to be imprisoned for fourteen days or under. The second-class prisoners, however, on the other hand, were under imprisonment for three months; whilst the first were those who had more than three months' incarceration to undergo. Moreover, some of the boys had red marks, besides the yellow ones, to indicate the number of times they had been previously committed; others, again, had badges, showing that they were imprisoned for two years, whilst others had a yellow ring on the left arm, to denote that their sentence was penal servitude.

Once conversant with these distinctions, it was indeed a melancholy sight to look at that century and a-half of mere children in their prison clothes. Some were so young, that they seemed to need a nurse, rather than a jailer, to watch over them; others, again, had such frank and innocent-looking faces, that we could not help fancying they had no business there; whilst others had such shamelessness and cunning painted in their features, that the mind was led insensibly towards fatalism, and to believe in criminal races as thoroughly as in cretin ones.

† We were furnished with the following official account of the quantity of oakum picked at this prison. . . . Total picked by the boys in the week 11cwt. 3qrs. 3 lbs. . . . Gross quantity of oakum picked by boys, per annum, about 31 tons. This, at £4 10s. per ton, which is the price paid for the picking, gives, as the yearly earnings of gross number of the boys employed in oakum-picking, £132. Therefore, each boy-prisoner employed at oakum-picking may be said to earn about 17s. per annum by their labour. Now, by the official returns, we find that the average cost per head of the prisoners at Tothill Fields is within a fraction of £8, so that it follows that there is a loss of very nearly £7 a-year upon each of the boys so employed.

## The female work and work-rooms at Tothill Fields prison

The several forms of labour pursued at this prison are oakum-picking, straw-plaiting, knitting, and laundry-work; whilst the majority of the work done goes to the county lunatic asylum at Hanwell.

In these work-rooms one sees almost the same large assemblages of criminals as at Coldbath Fields, and the sight of the dense mass of female infamy, clad in the one monotonous prison dress, and all as silent as death, produces an intensely powerful effect upon the mind; whilst the contemplation of such an immense variety of feature, impresses the beholder with a sense that every form of physical as well as moral ugliness is here presented to his view; for there is scarcely one well-formed, and certainly not one innocent-looking, face to be detected among the wretched crowd, and in the countenances of many the marks of premature disease, or of long-continued ill-treatment, or confirmed dissipation may be noted – the lingering bronzy traces of the blackened eye – the blotched and crimson cheeks, and the cancerous nose – together with the callous and brazen smile on every lip, and startling shamelessness in every glance – of the young as well as old – all serve to make up a picture and a scene that has not its parallel for hideousness in the civilized world.

The oakum-room is a large shed similar to that in the boys' prison, and situate at the end of C 8 yard. Here we found some 200 and odd women ranged upon several long benches, and with the warders stationed round the room – the work differing in no way from that already described in connection with the boys; while the most ghost-like silence reigned throughout the place – there being no attempt made either to instruct or occupy the minds of the prisoners during the operation.

The females under the age of 16, as well as those staying in the nursery, have 1 lb. of oakum to pick per diem, whereas the boys under the same age have to do 1½ lbs.; and the females of 16 years and upwards, 1½ lbs., whilst the elder boys have 2 lbs.

In the course of the week preceding our visit, there had been, on an average, 187 women and girls employed at oakum-work daily, and these had picked altogether a few pounds more than 13 cwt. during that time, which is at the rate of 2 cwt. and 20 lbs. for the whole of the females, and not quite 1 lb. 5 oz. for each daily – the average for the boys being a fraction more than 1 lb. 6 oz. each per diem. Accordingly, it will be found that there is rather more than 33 cwt. of oakum picked by the female prisoners collectively in the course of the year, and this, at the price of £4 10*s*. the cwt. paid by the contractor for the picking, would make the aggregate earnings of the women and girls employed at this work amount to very nearly £150, or a fraction more than 15*s*. each per annum, whilst the boys, severally, earn about 17*s*. per annum.

The women are all clad in close white caps with deep frills, and a loose blue and white spotted dress, so that, from the colours being more marked than those in the boys' prison, the sight of the assembly has a far more peculiar effect. Some of the prisoners have a number stitched upon their arm, to indicate that they are there for three months and over, and entitled to the first-class diet; whilst the arms of other are marked with a cloth figure of 2, as a sign that their term of imprisonment is less than three months and more than twenty-one days. A large proportion of the women, on the other hand, have no such marks upon their sleeves, and these are what are technically termed "days' women," being there merely for a week or two, and mostly in default of payment of some small fine.

## Note

1 In imperial measures, one quarter (qtr) is 28 pounds (lbs); four quarters or 112 lbs is one hundredweight (cwt), and twenty hundredweight is one ton.

## Editorial Headnote

### Pickworth, Charles Newton (ed.). 'The Manufacture of Oakum. A Little-known Branch of the Textile Industry', *Textile Manufacturer*, 52:618 (15 Jun 1926), pp. 201–202.

This article appeared in the 'Textile Machinist' section of the journal. Articles for this section might be assisted by the machine making firm, when the title would be fittingly underscored by the company name. However, this piece seems to have originated from a genuine editorial interest that is also manifest in the non-technical character of the writing, and its focus on the end product and its use, rather than on the illustrated machine.

Charles Newton Pickworth (1861–1955) was appointed editor of the *Textile Manufacturer* in 1895. With a mechanical engineering background, he also edited the *Mechanical World* for Emmott and Co. which was the proprietor of both journals. Upon the fiftieth anniversary of the former publication in 1925, he explained,

> It has been our practice to make announcement of all new machinery and appliances as soon as the makers were willing to release such information for publication. . . . [I]n this service the journal has consistently encouraged the adoption of the latest and best types of machines.
>
> (Jubilee Number, Dec 1925, p. 13)

In so doing, the journal aimed to promote the textile industry as a whole. While the article on oakum drew attention to a regular advertiser, Tomlinsons of Rochdale, the aim seems genuinely to highlight an opportunity for production of a product in short supply.

Rochdale machine makers Robert Tempest (1816–1866) and James Tomlinson (c1824–1881) had formed a partnership by 1854 when they began patenting improvements in machinery for fibre processing. The partners split in September 1862, with each carrying on separately. By February 1866 when he patented his first machinery for hackling and opening hemp, Tomlinson had moved to the Soho Iron Works, and his name became associated with the successful company. At the time of Tomlinson's death, his personal estate was valued at £16,575.

In 1877, the Prison Commissioners instituted reforms such as separating young offenders from old, and abolishing 'the treadwheel, shot-drill, and oakum-picking, etc., for more useful methods of work, facilities for education, improved workshops and sanitation', throwing into shadow the time-worn associations of oakum with punishment by hard labour. Oakum faded into the normality of mechanised production and became little heard of. The West Hartlepool *Northern Daily Mail* ran a short item announcing 'Oakum Still Picked' (24 Jun 1926, p. 5) evidently sourced from this article, and summarising the major points of interest for their shipbuilding community.

# 4

# PICKWORTH, CHARLES NEWTON (ED.). 'THE MANUFACTURE OF OAKUM. A LITTLE-KNOWN BRANCH OF THE TEXTILE INDUSTRY'

## *Textile Manufacturer* (15 Jun 1926), pp. 201–202.

It is a far cry from the prisoner laboriously hand-picking oakum in a gaol a hundred years ago, to the scientifically constructed machinery which produces the stuff to-day. But in the early days of the nineteenth century – when all our ships were timber built throughout – practically the whole of the oakum required by the Government dockyards and for private enterprise was hand-picked in prisons. To-day there is an enormous increase in the use of oakum. Notwithstanding the changes that have come over shipbuilding in the last hundred years, the vastly increased number of vessels afloat demands oakum in far greater quantities than before.

Practically the whole of the world's requirements are nowadays produced under ordinary modern industrial conditions, and yet comparatively few firms are engaged in the industry to-day. In the United Kingdom, the names of the oakum-manufacturing firms can be numbered almost on the fingers of one hand. As a matter of fact, the business of oakum manufacturing is practically confined to the United Kingdom, Holland and Scandinavia. A certain amount is produced in the U.S.A. This is to be wondered at, because there is usually far more oakum wanted than is available, and the best qualities often sell at prices from £70 to £90 per ton.

The best oakum is manufactured from old-tarred hemp rope. This material has the advantage of having been tarred and "seasoned" by use, so that the wherewithal for waterproofing the oakum is present at the commencement of manufacture. It is usually cut into three-feet lengths on a circular cutting machine, such as is used in the waste trade for cutting thrums, etc., and subsequently treated on a hackling machine. The latter consists of a feed table and a pair of fluted rollers, which lead the lengths of rope against the coarsely toothed cylinder preforming the actual operation of "hackling." A cursory inspection of a hackling machine at work makes one realise what a punishing job the hand-picking of rope junk was, and still is. Nevertheless, very heavy ships' ropes are usually untwisted by hand, even to-day.


DOI: 10.4324/9780429274190-7

After hackling the material undergoes the principal operation of the process – *i.e.*, carding, or "spinning," as it is quite wrongly called in the trade. It is done on a special oakum carding engine, constructed on lines similar to those of a cotton card, and comprising a main cylinder, a doffer, a complement of workers and clearers, and the necessary feeding and delivery arrangements. In addition to the doffing comb, the machine is fitted with traversing "balling heads," which have the purpose of making the oakum into regular cheeses weighing some 2¾ lb. to 3 lb. each. These "balling heads" virtually take the place of the condenser on an ordinary condenser card.[1] The sliver of which they are made is fairly strong, owing to the long staple of the product. Normally it has a breaking strain of about 1 lb., but this, of course, varies according to the quality of the material. It is usually doffed and "balled" in three to five strands, each about 1 in. wide.

It is sent to the shipbuilder in this cheese form. The caulker, seated upon the ship's deck, has a cheese of oakum pierced through the centre by an iron spike, which is stuck upon the deck in front of him. As he uses his caulking tools, he unrolls the sliver and drives it between the deck boards. It is extremely probable that the craft of caulking underwent no change until shortly before the war, when caulking machines were put on the market, and in the biggest European and transatlantic shipyards they are now fairly commonly used.

The partial exclusion of the human element in the process of caulking, however, operated in an unforeseen way. The sliver of oakum was found to be too weak to withstand the pulling or dragging action of the caulking machine. A workman can gently unroll the sliver from the cheese. If it breaks he can easily manipulate it by twisting the two broken ends together, and continue his job. But this is not so easily accomplished with the mechanical device. The speed of the latter gives it a great advantage, however. Hence the simple expedient of putting sufficient twist into the oakum sliver to enable it to withstand rougher usage without breaking was resorted to.

To prepare oakum for use in the mechanical caulker the cheese is removed from the carding engine and mounted upon a small horizontal twisting frame which, although adjustable within certain limits, is designed expressly to give the very small amount of twist required for the necessary strength. It will be obvious that this must be reduced as far as possible, because a tight rope of oakum could not be effectually driven between the deck boards of a ship. There is still an enormous quantity of oakum produced for hand-caulking, and, as stated above, the operation for the finishing of this ends with the production of the traversed cheese from the oakum carding engine.

The lower qualities of oakum, which are characterised by a shorter staple, and by the fact that additional tarring is resorted to, consist of small quantities of old ships' ropes mixed with larger quantities of new hemp or old bagging which has been specially opened. The manufacture may sometimes be cheapened by the inclusion of various other inferior waste fibres.

When the oakum is manufactured from old-tarred rope, little, if any, additional impregnation is necessary, but when a high percentage of hemp, bagging waste, etc., is used, the hackling machine's operation, which is to "open" the baled material, as well as to disintegrate old rope, is followed by that of the impregnation plant. This consists of a copper-lined tank filled with Archangel tar, or a similar product – the lower the quality of oakum the cheaper the liquor. It is kept fluid and at a high temperature by submerged steam coils.

The uncarded oakum is then dropped in this tank, and the surplus liquor is afterwards removed by mangling, or the material is passed between calenders running in contact with the fluid. In any case, only a small amount of tar is permissible in the material when it reaches the carding engine. If it carries an excessive amount it is obvious that satisfactory carding is rendered impossible. Excepting the smell, a slightly darkened colour, and a certain stickiness of "handle," there is little evidence of the existence of tar in the finished product.

We are indebted to Tomlinsons (Rochdale) Limited for the accompanying illustration of an oakum carding engine, and it is rather interesting to note that this firm of engineers are the only makers of complete oakum-manufacturing plant in the world.

## Note

1 These instruments consolidate the strands created by dividing the carded fleece, not by the condenser to follow subsequent spinning processes, but by the baller for their end use.

## Editorial Headnote

## Marshall and Co., Leeds. Notebook on Processes. 'Carding' and 'Tow Preparing', pp. 10–14 & 18. Brotherton Library, University of Leeds, MS200/36.

This modest notebook, bound in red morocco with stormont-marbled paper sidings, is entitled 'Processes'. Written from 1826 to 1829 by John Marshall (1765–1845), it documents trials in carding and preparing tow by machinery that had started in 1821 at Marshall and Co. The notes are all the more valuable for citing the experiments that disappointed as well as those which worked. Success and failure were evaluated in terms of particular givens, such as the staple length of the tow, or factory output needs; but complaints of customers were also remarked. As well as changing the running speed of different parts of the machinery, the size, spacing, number and density of wire clothing of the various types of rollers could all be varied, making for great complexity.

Starting with an opened sheet of fibres, the object of carding is to clean and straighten the textile fibres and lay them in a given direction resulting in a sliver – a thick, soft strand that can be drawn and spun into yarn. Carding rollers are covered with a sort of wire brush with the wire teeth slanted in one direction; when brushes with teeth sloped in opposing directions and turning in opposite directions are brought close to each other, they comb through the fibre straightening it, whereas if the teeth slope in the same direction, the fibrous fleece is removed (doffed) from one cylinder.

The carding machine has a large central rotating cylinder, the *swift*. The prepared sheet can be fed to the swift by fluted rollers and a *licker-in* roller with teeth slanted in the direction of revolution of the swift so that the swift can completely take up the fibre. Along the circumference of the swift, *worker* rollers alternate with *strippers*. A worker rotates in the same direction as the swift with teeth sloping opposite to the direction of rotation; this allows it to pick out tangled groups of fibres. The strippers rotate in the same direction with teeth also sloping in this direction so they draw out the tangled fibres from the workers and feed them back to the swift. A *fancy* roller has fine long teeth bent only at a slight angle that are positioned to come into touch with the teeth of the swift. By this means it lifts the fibres toward the surface of the cylinder ready for the doffer roller which matches the workers in orientation so that it picks the carded fibre off the swift. From there it is fed into the sliver-forming apparatus.

Gilling is a different method of straightening fibres using *fallers* which are horizontal bars studded with spikes (the spikes are here called *heckles*). These comb out the fibres gripped by the front (or retaining) rollers, and carry the fibres forward to a delivery roller. The sequence of bars is called fallers because before they reach the delivery roller, an eccentric cam knocks the bars down where they are received by another shaft that moves them back to the starting place. The difference in speed between the retaining and delivery rollers determines the amount the fibre bundles are stretched, or the *draw* – at Marshall's a factor of six times.

Gilling, or *preparing* as it was alternatively called, was more effective than carding in straightening long-staple fibres.

The experiments with carding and gilling of tow at Marshall and Co. were prompted by economic considerations. Not only was tow a cheaper raw material that offered wider profit margins, but tow was available in quantity as a by-product of the company's preparation of linen yarns. Over half the flax fibre processed for linen was rejected as tow.

# 5

# MARSHALL AND CO., LEEDS. 'CARDING' AND 'TOW PREPARING'

## Notebook on Processes, pp. 10–14 & 18. Brotherton Library, University of Leeds: MS200/36.

**Carding.** June 1829. The principal changes in our cards previous to 1823 were the substitution of plain doffing rollers for fluted ones; & of single broad sheets of 22 & 33 inches wide instead of several narrow ones. Both these were material improvements particularly the broad sheets. We also tried much finer card than we had before used for covering our engines but in this we failed from the card being much too close set & the load far too great so that the tow was rolled rather than carded & all these finest cards were afterwards taken off. In 1823 we found that we had overloaded our tow preparing machine by extending the spinning without a corresponding extension of preparing. We were obliged to card very heavy; the yarn uneven & quality complained of. It therefore became evident that a great extension of tow preparing was necessary. We proposed to make the cards more effective by giving them 2 workers & cheaper & simpler by using a doffing cylinder & crank instead of a flexible sheet & rollers. The 2 workers were found advantageous though not to any great degree. The cylinder after a variety of trials we finally concluded not to be so effective or perfect for the length of staple our tow has, as the flexible sheets. We made them double cards 2 slivers of 22 inch to save expense & space. The crank we could not manage at the speed we then doffed at.

Hitherto we had run our carding engines about 100 rev pr minute of the Swift & boxed up nothing but the Fancy & its stripper.[1] We now increased the speed of the Swift first to 150 & then to 200 rev pr minute & boxed the card completely up. At first trying various means as by gratings & openings to let the dirt out at the bottom, but lastly having only the opening below the doffing shut & boxing all the rest as close as possible. This increased speed was a very great assistance in rendering our carding at once nearly twice as effective as before. The speed of the feeding & doffing we kept nearly as before; & afterwards as we increased our cards & diminished our weights we made our feeding sheets & rollers go twice as slow as at first & one hand[2] which at first spread only for one sliver eventually spread for 2. We found that slow feeding & then doffing produced the best result both in the first & second cards; & reduced the speed of the feeding of the 2nd cards putting up twice as many slivers.[3] The feeding rollers were also reduced in

DOI: 10.4324/9780429274190-8

size; & carrying rollers place[d] close to the doffing rollers which enabled us to bring away a much thinner sliver than we could have done without. The next step was a spreading frame detached from the card: the tow being spread & lapped up in a sheet & put up behind the first card thus avoiding the expence which would otherwise have attended our light carding, one hand now spreading for 4 or 5 ends. Also a doubling frame by which the first card slivers are wrapped onto a bobbin & then put up behind the second card rendering a great number of doubles practicable & feeding the card very much more perfectly than before.

Having improved the tools for the heckling machines by increasing the space between the rows of pins & putting fewer rows into a stock; we applied the same principle to card fillet; diminishing the number of rows per inch & putting in more pins in each row, & of finer wire. We found this [to] make a much better card, more efficient in penetrating & splitting the tow & more easily doffed & kept clean: & we were enabled to use finer cards than before. The fancy card was found to be much better with the wire perpendicular to the leather; it raised the tow better when running considerably slower & diminished the chance of spoiling the Swift by the Fancy being allowed to touch it.

Mr Smith of ~~Glasgow~~[4] Deanston[5] when here mentioned that for some of his cotton cards he used a flexible revolving sheet instead of flats; which was stripped by a revolving brush & that brush by a hutch. This induced us to try a flexible sheet instead of workers: at the same time we made the card a single one of 22 inch & much lower than the other cards: & applied a doffing crank to the doffing sheet instead of rollers. The sheet worker appears to work on a better principle than the rollers, keeps the tow straighter does not break it so much, nor make so much flyings & waste: we have not yet been able to make a sheet nearly so true as a roller else there can be no doubt of its greater efficiency in carding out the knots. We are now trying to make the sheet true by giving it another boss to support it in the centre: making the ribs of cast metal, brass, or run steel, & covering it with 3 inch fillet instead of a broad sheet: which it is very difficult to get of leather of equable thickness & strength.

The doffing crank answers perfectly well; makes fewer errors than the rollers; & does not afford a receptacle for masses of waste & dirt like the rubbers of the rollers. The feeding rollers are again reduced in diam$^{r}$. They are now 1½ cast iron, 2½ covered. The Swift cast iron turned: Fancy & strippers sheet iron covered with composition.

We now run our first cards 200 rev & second 150 for fine work, for coarse both 200. A speed of 150 makes fewer flyings & does not break the tow so much. We tried 100 rev. for the second card but at that speed had great difficulty to doff the Swift perfectly & keep it clean.

We have also tried carding three times over for the coarse tow Mill A:[6] but did not find any advantage in it. The same number of A hand being the person operating the carding machine cards carding three times over instead of twice must card heavier, or quicker, which is a bad thing & counterbalances the advantage of another action between the Swift & the feeding rollers. With fine tow it would be still less applicable. A blowing machine is still a desideratum: we tried a shaking machine imitating the action of a hand in shaking tow up with a stick, but it run the tow into strings & was not effective in cleansing it. The machine however is ill constructed & s[c]arcely a fair trial of the principle. Also tried batting by hand on a frame covered with strings similar to the cotton process for the fine tow: but was not efficient & far too expensive.

**Tow Preparing.** June 1829. In 1821 or 1822 we began to apply gill preparing to tow; we first used it in Mill A to replace the worst roller roving frames as they wore out. We had a small circular you[7] plate containing 12 fallers with broad heckles of 5 rows of pins ¾ long: with wire strippers between the fallers: front roller 2½ diam$^{r}$ 1½ face: draw 6. Bobbin 6 in traverse 4 inch bottom.

In these frames the great distance between the heckles: the small number in action at once & the width of the tools were great imperfections. Lawson & Walker[8] even at the time making twisting frames for Salop:[9] & Bolton our model maker[10] had left us & gone to them: & they were making a considerable quantity of Tow gill preparing. We got a draw$^{g}$ frame from them: circular plate larger than before 5⅝ in diam$^{r}$ containing 25 fallers much closer together than before & the slides made so as diminish the distance of the nip & to make the fallers fall suddenly: the frame had 4 carriages 8 slivers of 3 inch broad each, pirn ¾ in draw 6. We had a number of draw$^{g}$ frames & some roving from the Foundry on this plan except that we had only 2 carriages 4 slivers in each frame & 2 necks to each roller.

In 1827 we made a new addition of tow preparing for fine work: barrel the same size as before but with 30 fallers: front roller 2 inch diam$^{r}$ breadth of face first 2 & afterwards 1½ draw 6. Distance of nip 1¾ inch in the other frames 2¾ in. Roving 4 spindles to a carriage bobbin 4 inch traverse 2⅝th bottom: breadth of boss ⅝th pirns ½ inch N24 wire.[11] These frames were made by Cawood & Mirfin.[12]

We had great trouble with the strippers or guards in these frames the heckles being so close to them as continually to get damaged by striking against them. We took the strippers off & found we could do perfectly well without them.

## Notes

1 Boxed up means enclosed; higher running speeds would have produced more dust and fly.
2 Hand indicates the person distributing the prepared fibre on the feeding sheet.
3 This suggests two swifts (cards) are worked in tandem here for a coarse followed by light carding. That is probably the meaning of *double cards* in the previous paragraph.
4 Crossed out in original manuscript.
5 James Smith (1789–1850), mechanical engineer and agriculturalist. Smith's early aptitude was recognised by James Finlay and Co., where he was appointed manager of the firm's Deanston Cotton Mills from the age of eighteen. He remained for thirty years, introducing many improvements and mechanical inventions. He is also known through his work *Remarks on Thorough Draining and Deep Ploughing* (1831), describing the agricultural practice developed on his model farm at Wester Deanston.
6 Marshall's three Leeds mills were called A, B and C.

7 Possibly the word *screw* is meant here. The faller combs of the gill were often driven forward by screw shafts.

8 Lawson and Walker was established in 1812 by the partners (and brothers-in-law) Samuel Lawson (1782–1866) and Mark Walker (1787–1874) at Hope Foundry in Leeds. Walker's grandson Frederick William Dixon Walker (c1854–1930) later wrote:

> Before starting in business with his brother-in-law, Mr Samuel Lawson, he was apprenticed to Mr. Farmery, a Leeds engineer, and afterwards worked in three of the most famous engineering shops of the early years of the nineteenth century – Mr. Matthew Murray, Leeds, Messrs. Fawcett and Littlewood, Liverpool, and Mr. Henry Maudslay, London.
>
> (*Yorkshire Post and Leeds Intelligencer*, 2 March 1915, p. 3)

Samuel Lawson served his apprenticeship at Murray and Wood (fl. 1794–1826). For more information on Lawson, see G. Cookson, 'The West Yorkshire Textile Engineering Industry, 1780–1850'. PhD thesis, University of York, July 1994.

9 Marshall and Co. had a mill at Castle Foregate, Shrewsbury, Shropshire, in addition to its three mills in Leeds.

10 This may be John Bolton, a Leeds machine maker who went bankrupt in 1837 (*London Gazette*, 17 Nov 1837, p. 3005).

11 The delivery roller is known as a boss.

12 Cawood and Mirfin was a Leeds firm of machine makers. The engineer William Mirfin (c1781–1840s) was partner with John Cawood (c1777–1846), son of the ironfounder Martin Cawood (1756–1824), who established the Leeds Foundry. John joined his father in partnership until setting up in a separate firm in 1821, probably Cawood and Mirfin. After Martin Cawood's death in 1824, the Leeds Foundry became the principal site for his son's subsequent firm: John Cawood and Son. Cawood and Mirfin's premises were offered for lease by John Cawood in 1842 (*Leeds Times*, 3 Dec 1842, p. 1). At John Cawood's death, he left debts that eventually caused the firm to go into bankruptcy in 1848.

## Editorial Headnote

### Sharp, Peter. 'Tow Carding' and 'Tow Preparing', *Flax, Tow, and Jute Spinning: A Handbook Containing Information on the Various Branches of these Trades,* 2nd ed. (Dundee: James P. Mathew & Co.; Edinburgh and Glasgow: John Menzies & Co.; London: Simpkin, Marshall & Co., 1886), pp. 97–100, 107–108.

Peter Sharp (c1858–1930), was born in Armagh, Ireland, the eldest son of Scottish parents James Sharp (1830–1895) and his wife Christina née Cadenhead (1830–1899). The family returned to its native Aberdeen in the 1870s, where Peter served his apprenticeship with the old-established manufacturing firm of Messrs. Richards and Co., at Broadford Works, a leading house in the heavy flax trade. By 1881, he was manager of a flax mill, possibly where he had trained. On becoming examiner in linen manufacture for the City and Guilds of London Institute in 1885, the *Aberdeen Free Press* wrote, 'This appointment, which is for a period of four years, is quite an honour to Mr. Sharp, and is an evidence that among linen manufacturers his technical knowledge is considered of no mean order' (2 Sep 1885, p. 4). By the time of his marriage to Isabel Fulton Shanks (1859–1943) on 14 January 1886, he and his father had created a merchant firm, James Sharp and Son, specialising in flax, linen and tow. The company was based in Dundee with a branch in Aberdeen. In the early 1890s, Peter took over sole management, and his father died a few years later.

The company got into financial straits in 1896 and matters became worse in 1898 when Richards and Co. suspended payment. Sharp's firm was placed into trusteeship to try to recover the debts. Probably as a consequence, Sharp emigrated to New York where he carried on in the same line. In 1902, his business card was noticed in the American *Cordage Trade Journal* by a former associate: 'Peter Sharp & Co., 45 Leonard St., New York. Agents for W.F. Malcolm & Co., London. C. Wemaere, Lille. Hemp, Jute, Flax, and Tow. Waste and Oakum Merchants' (*Dundee Evening Post*, 20 May 1902, p. 5). Sharp returned to Scotland (probably after the war), and began a flax preparation works at The Shore in Perth around 1920. After a serious fire in March 1923, it appears the works was not rebuilt, and that Sharp retired from active business.

The first edition of the spinning handbook was available at the start of February 1882, priced at 5s. *The Dundee Courier* praised the book for its fluent style, neatly arranged tables and good index (8 Feb 1882, p. 4). The *Dundee Advertiser* included a lengthy and critical review with compliments for the section on tow carding, but pointing to the lack of a chapter on flax hackling (11 Feb 1882, p. 7). This gap was remedied in the second edition which came out at the end of May 1886. A third edition appeared in time for Christmas 1896, and publisher's advertisements suggested it as a suitable gift. Reviewers emphasised sixteen new illustrations of machinery as a key attraction. Having become a student textbook, it ran to a fourth edition in 1907. A fifth edition was said by the author to have been in preparation at the end of 1923, but does not appear to have reached fruition.

# 6

# SHARP, PETER. 'TOW CARDING' AND 'TOW PREPARING'

*Flax, Tow, and Jute Spinning* (Dundee: James P. Mathew & Co.; Edinburgh and Glasgow: John Menzies & Co.; London: Simpkin, Marshall & Co., 1886), pp. 97–100, 107–108.

### Tow carding

Carding is one of the most important branches in a spinning mill, and especially in the primary processes through which tow passes before reaching the spinning room. Difficult as it is to give any practical guidance in the manipulation of the flax fibre over the various machines, it is still more difficult to do so in carding. The objects in carding are various, depending on the material, and the purpose for which it is intended, *e.g.*, separating the fibre from shive, nap, and dirt; cutting the fibre; also, sorting the tow by various doffers, and delivering in a sliver for the drawing frames. In order to judge how any given tow should be carded we must have the material before us, and, knowing the yarn into which it is to be made, see the defects which it is essential to remove for that yarn, and, by an acquaintance with the qualities of our material, such as strength, &c., strive to arrange our carding so as to perform the work with the least possible damage to the fibre, and with the least possible waste.

In tows, as in flax, we have a wide range of material, from the fine, and sometimes combed, for wet-spun yarns, to the coarse, for sacking, canvas, &c. The quality of the material to be operated on differs so much that, in order to give an account of carding, we would require to give an example of the many different varieties of tows, for which we require different carding. Generally speaking, one carding is sufficient for Baltic tow, the shive, dirt, &c., being easily thrown out, owing to the dry and open nature of the material. In Scotland a great quantity of the tow worked is Baltic, hence carding is accomplished in a different manner from that adopted in the case of the finer tows in Ireland. In the majority of Scotch mills only one card is used, acting as a breaker and finisher, and it is only in cases of very dirty tow that two separate cards are used. I shall give, farther on, the particulars of a card adapted for from 3 to 4 lbs. per spindle. The speed of the cylinder varies according to the nature of the material and the purpose for which it is intended, as does also the speed of the workers and strippers, &c. Cylinders

 DOI: 10.4324/9780429274190-9

6 ft. by 5 ft., generally run 150 to 200 revolutions per minute. By varying the speed of one or the whole of the strippers and workers we can throw out much or little dirt. Fast driving of the strippers under the card is liable to throw out fibre as well; but where it is essential to drive these fast for cleaning, a tin cylinder may be placed under, between the worker and stripper, allowing the shive and dirt to fall, and keeping the fibre in. Where two cards are used, the workers and strippers may be driven slower than in a single card with similar material and work to perform. Hand-made tow, such as Archangel, Kama, Jaroslav, and machine tow off the same, as well as Rjeff,[1] are so clean that the straightening and opening up of the fibre are the principal requirements; but some of these tows, and especially those off the hackling machines, are very full of naps, and require more carding, especially if for light yarns. Some hand-made tows of this class require opening and teasing before going to the card, and this is accomplished best by manual labour or by an open teaser. The evil effects of over-carding will, however, be very readily seen in these, owing to the weak nature of the fibre. Doffing by means of a roller is applied to cards of this description, and this process differs from the mode applied to cards for fine tows, as in these doffing knives are used. In a breaker and finisher card two doffing rollers are generally used, while with two separate cards and for light sizes, such as 3 lbs., the finisher has sometimes only one doffing roller. Generally, however, the slivers from cards having two doffing rollers are delivered into one, as by taking away the best or top sliver the remaining one would be left poor, and the fibre very short. The principal objections to twice carding are, the greater amount of waste, the breaking up of the fibre, and the risk of ends getting away. To this has to be added the extra cost, as lapping machines or cans have to be used.

If only one card is employed, it is essential to run first through a teaser flax used as tow, codillas, rope tow, &c., for the purpose of putting it into working form for the finisher.

## Setting cards, clothing, &c.

In setting cards the clothing required varies according to the material being worked. This is also the case with the clothing on workers and strippers. The distance of the workers and strippers from the cylinder also varies, they being set further off at the beginning than at the end, the distance depending on the length of fibre and nature of material under process. The diameter of the workers and strippers is also varied according to the length of fibre. The strippers are generally from 1 in. to 2 in. larger in diameter than the workers, so we have them running worker and stripper 4 in. and 5 in., 5 in. and 6 in., 5 in. and 7 in., 7 in. and 8 in., 7 in. and 9 in., and so on. It is a point requiring much attention that, when new machines are ordered, full particulars should be given, so that the machines may be thoroughly adapted for the class of material and kind of work for which they are intended.

## Fine machine tows

In dealing with fine machine tows, the necessity of freeing from nap and opening up is the main point. Especially in soft mill-scutched Irish tow this difficulty is great. Tow coming from a brush and doffer hackling machine is very nappy if the brush is not set with great accuracy. These tows are mainly for good yarns. The naps in some tows may be opened up sufficiently by once carding, but, if very nappy, a great many of the naps will be drawn into hard knots, and require second carding to throw them out. In the finer tows the fibre generally is shorter, being machine and sorting tow from Irish, Flemish, Dutch, and Courtrai cut line,[2] and to work these the workers and strippers are lessened in diameter, say to 4 in. and 5 in. and 5 in. and 6 in. respectively, a greater number being put in, increasing to 8, 9, and 10 pair on a card. Particulars of a card, for 25 lea,[3] made from long line tows, are given at page 106, but this card must not be considered as a standard from which you get finer or coarser for finer or coarser yarn. Take, for example, one of our very coarsest tows, "re-scutched Irish," and we find that the finishing card cylinder will require to be covered with about 40 pins to the square inch, spinning say 14 to 20 lea.[4] This tow requires a great amount of carding to free it from dirt, open the lumps, knots, &c.

Owing to the great length and matted condition in which this tow comes from the scutchers, it requires a coarse shaker or teaser. Particulars of this machine will be found at page 106. The person spreading or feeding stands on a high platform, and the tow is discharged, well shaken or teased, below this platform. Some machines of this description discharge at the back, and consequently no platform for the feeder is required. Passing through a breaker similar to the one particulars of which are also given at page 106, and coming to the finisher, we require a card a great deal finer than would be supposed from the coarse nature of the material. In order to open the naps we must have the cylinder clothed nearly as follows: – Pins No. 20 wire, $^{3}/_{16}$ in. long, 17 rows in stave, 24 in. x 3 in., which equals 40 pins per square inch, for 14 to 30 lea. For heavier numbers, wet and dry spinning, coarser cards are used.

## Tow preparing[5]

Tow preparing is a more important operation even than flax preparing, owing to the very different state of the sliver coming from the card compared with the flax sliver from a spreadboard.[6] The remarks on flax preparing as to the proper relative speeds of the different parts of the machines apply equally to tow preparing. So also does the caution as to having the gills overloaded, &c. Owing to the short fibre in tow, naps, lumps, &c., it is an essential point to have the faller coming as close as possible to the nip of the roller, and so to hold the sliver, especially short fibres, naps, &c., until taken hold of by the rollers. With a long distance between the nip and fallers, naps, lumps, &c., are carried into the rove without being drawn. In order to prevent this we require smaller drawing rollers than in flax preparing; in some very lumpy or nappy tows, roving frame rollers being made as small as $1^1/_8$ to $1^1/_4$ in. diameter, to allow the faller to be brought close to the nip. It is also necessary to have as short a pin as possible consistent with the weight of the sliver, as this also tends to allow the faller to be close to the nip.

The conductors at the back of the drawing frames should be as wide as the gill will properly admit, especially at the back of the roving. The conductors at the front of the finishing drawing frame or delivering bosses should not contract the sliver much, but keep the sliver as wide as possible for the roving; and, at the drawing roller of the roving, contract the sliver suddenly, say to one-third of its width, in very nappy tows and those with a good quantity of short fibres.

In flax preparing the drafts run from say 10 to 15 on the drawing frames and roving, but in tow, owing to the much shorter fibre, &c., the drafts are much shorter, say 6 to 8. Working very short tows, rope tow, waste sliver, card waste, &c., for heavy dry spun yarns, does better with six of a draft; while fine and sometimes combed tow, for 60 to 100 lea, will do with eight or longer. In flax preparing, again, the speed of the roving is regulated by the speed of the spindles, or rather the spindle gearing; but in tow preparing the speed of the fallers regulates the speed at which we may drive. This is owing to the much shorter draft, and 200 fallers per minute is considered a high speed for screw gills, the pitch of screws being $^3/_8$, less or more, and thus we are prevented driving up to what the spindle gearing would permit. In the very fine tow trade frequently four drawing frames are used, and generally speaking, three drawing frames for all tows for wet and dry spinning are used. However, where two cards are used, and for coarse heavy yarns, such as 6 lbs. per spindle and upwards, and for wefts, where cheap production is the main point, two drawing frames only are used; and when 40 lbs. per spindle, made out of hemp, coarse rope tow, &c., is reached, a rotary gill roving is sometimes used (no spinning frames) running 300 to 400 fallers per minute, or the spindles of a frame with 9 x 4½ in. bobbins, running 1200 to 1500 revolutions per minute.

## Notes

1 Flax was cultivated in the Russian provinces of Archangel and Jaroslav. These names, as well as the district names Kama, Rjeff and many others, were given to the fibre. It was sold largely through the Baltic ports of Riga and St Petersburg.

2 'Cut line' designates flax of superior quality.

3 Lea was the historical unit for the count of linen yarn, indicating the number of 300-yard lengths per pound. 25 lea equals approximately 66 tex (the metric measure of grams per kilometre).

4 Around 118 to 82 tex. Note that the higher the lea, the finer the yarn, whereas a higher tex indicates coarser yarn.

5 Preparing is used here in the technical sense of gilling, a form of combing. The difference in sliver signalled is that between carded and combed fibre.

6 The flax spreadboard is a gilling machine. It has a feedboard marked with spaces to enable the worker to spread a given weight of flax over a given area. A travelling apron and feeding roller take the fibre to the gill bars that comb it, and beyond the drawing rollers at the far end is a plate that divides the strands and converges them into a sliver.

# Part 3

# THE ‘LOW WOOLS’

## Shoddy and mungo

*Fig. 7* Factory views of the rag sorting room and blending room at Joseph Auty and Co., Ltd., Clerk Green Mills, Batley. See Ch. 9 this volume.

*Source*: Beaumont, Roberts. *Wool Substitutes* (London: Sir Isaac Pitman & Sons, 1922), pp. 15, 35. Author’s collection.

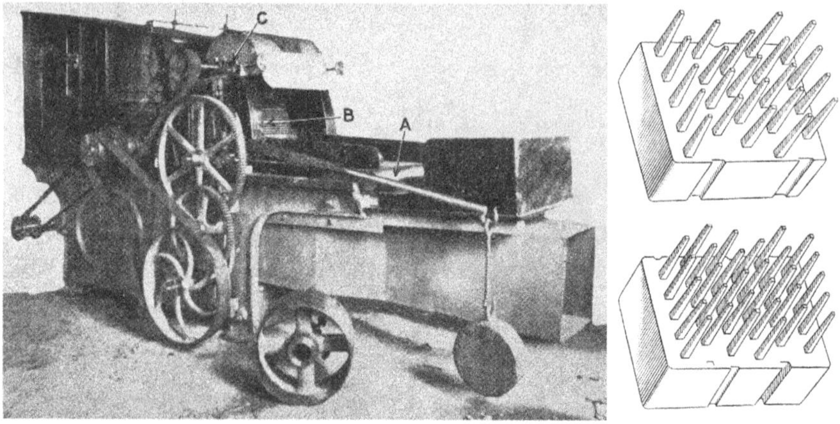


*Fig. 8* Rag-grinding machine, and lags used in covering the cylinder of the rag-grinding machine. See Ch. 9 this volume.

*Source*: Beaumont, Roberts. *Wool Substitutes* (London: Sir Isaac Pitman & Sons, 1922), pp. 27, 31. Author's collection.

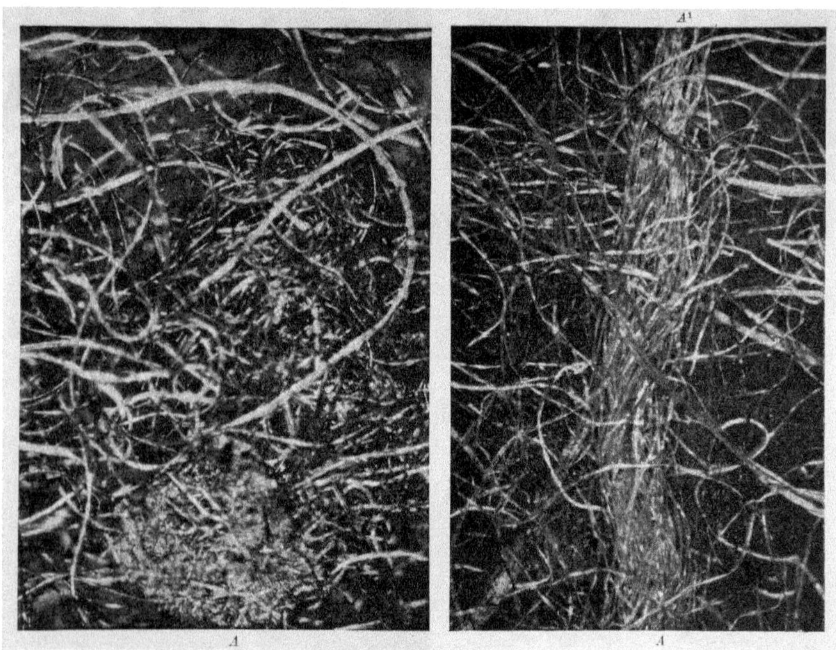

*Fig. 9* Microscopic views of faulty pulled wool rags: with matted bits, and with cotton strands. See Ch. 9 this volume.

*Source*: Beaumont, Roberts. *Wool Substitutes* (London: Sir Isaac Pitman & Sons, 1922), pp. 39, 43. Author's collection.

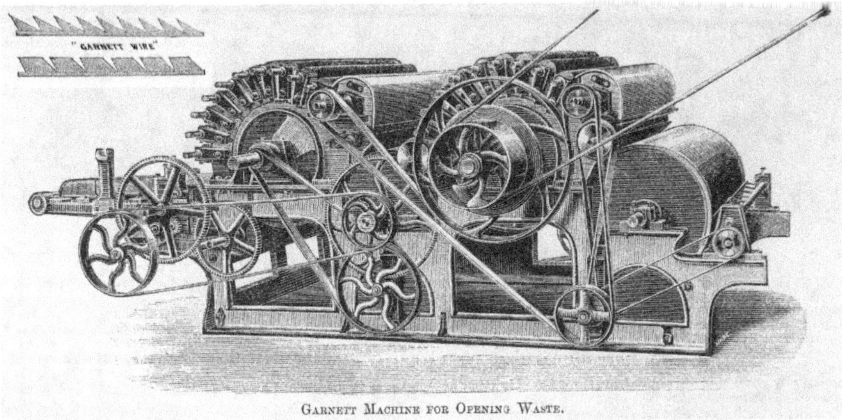


*Fig. 10* Garnett machine for opening wool waste, with profile of Garnett wire inset. See Ch. 10 this volume.

*Source*: *The Century's Progress: Yorkshire. Progress. Commerce 1893* (London: The London Printing & Engraving Co., 1893), p. 216. Author's collection.

## Editorial Headnote

### Head, George, Sir. 'Dewsbury', *A Home Tour through the various Manufacturing Districts of England, in the Summer of 1835* (London: John Murray, 1836), pp. 144–149.

Sir George Head (1782–1855) had a career in the provisioning side of the military, serving in Spain during the Peninsular Wars and in Canada afterward. He published on both experiences. However, he is best known for his *Home Tour*. Written in his characteristic style, with humour and a touch of eccentricity, Head avoids commonplace matters to focus on the remarkable and suggestive. A reviewer in London's *The News* wrote:

> It is a light sketchy descriptive tour, and has nothing whatever to do with the economy of our manufacturing interests. There are descriptions, and interesting ones too, of certain processes of manufacture; but the book is altogether graphic, without a bit of philosophy from the beginning to the end. It is written in so sprightly and pleasing a style that we heartily commend it to the general reader (22 May 1836, p. 6).

Released in mid-March 1836, it retailed at booksellers for 9s. 6d. *Home Tour* proved so popular that another printing was issued in August. Harper and Brothers of New York also published the book that year. Thus encouraged, Head undertook another tour, published in 1837 as a continuation volume. The next year a second edition of *Home Tour* was brought out. Finally, in 1840 Murray published a cheaper third edition with both tours offered as a set for 12s. A reprint of the second edition was published by A. M. Kelley in 1968.

In his preface, entitled 'Advertisement to the Reader', Head clarified his intention:

> Always a stranger, moving about from place to place at my leisure, seeing with my own eyes, neither troubling myself with the opinions nor prejudices of others, I took no indirect means to obtain information when not readily granted. . . . My chief aim, whether in description or narrative, has been – fidelity, – to render to others, instead of personal opinions, impressions, if possible, as I received them.

# 7

# HEAD, GEORGE, SIR. 'DEWSBURY'

## *Home Tour through the various Manufacturing Districts of England, in the Summer of 1835* (London: John Murray, 1836), pp. 144–149.

The town of Dewsbury is not only celebrated for its manufacture of blankets, but also for a novel business or trade which has sprung up in England, in addition to the arts and sciences, of late years, – namely, that of grinding old garments new; – literally tearing in pieces fusty old rags, collected from Scotland, Ireland, and the Continent, by a machine called a "devil," till a substance very like the original wool is reproduced: this, by the help of a small addition of new wool, is respun and manufactured into sundry useful coarse articles, such as the wadding which Messrs. Stultze and Co. introduce within the collars of their very fashionable coats,[1] and various descriptions of druggets, horse-sheeting, &c.

The trade or occupation of the late owner, his life and habits, or the filthiness and antiquity of the garment itself, oppose no bar to this wonderful process of regeneration; whether from the scare-crow or the gibbet, it makes no difference; so that, according to the transmutation of human affairs, it no doubt frequently does happen, without figure of speech or metaphor, that the identical garment to-day exposed to the sun and rain in a Kentish cherry-orchard, or saturated with tobacco-smoke on the back of a beggar in a pot-house, is doomed in its turn, "perfusus liquidis odoribus,"[2] to grace the swelling collar, or add dignified proportion to the chest of the dandy. Old flannel-petticoats, serge and bunting, are not only unravelled and brought to their original thread by the claws of the devil, but this machine, by the way, simply a series of cylinders armed with iron hooks, effectually, it is said, pulls to pieces and separates the pitch-mark of the sheep's back, – which latter operation really is a job worthy of the very devil himself. Those who delight in matters of speculation have here an ample field, provided they feel inclined to extend their researches on this doctrine of the transmigration of coats; for their imagination would have room to range in unfettered flight, even from the blazing galaxy of a regal drawing-room down to the night cellars and lowest haunts of London, Germany, Poland, Portugal, &c., as well as probably even to other countries visited by the plague. But as such considerations would only tend to put a man out of conceit with his own coat, or afflict some of my fair friends with an antipathy to flannel altogether, they are much better let alone:


DOI: 10.4324/9780429274190-11

nevertheless, the subject may serve as a hint to those whom a spirit of economy may urge to drive an over-hard bargain with their tailor, or good housewives, who inconsiderately chuckle at having been clever enough, as they imagine, to perform an impossibility, – that is to say, in times while the labourer is worthy of his hire, to buy a pair of blankets for less than the value of the wool. These economists may treasure up much useful information, by considering well the means by which materials may be combined to suit their purpose: for the "shoddy," as it is called, may be, as occasion requires, mixed with new wool in any proportion; so as to afford, by the help of various artists, in this free country, equal satisfaction to all parties, whether the latter be tidy or dirty by nature.

As I was anxious to see somewhat of the above process, I walked from Dewsbury to the village of Batley Carr,[3] on the river Calder, about a mile distant, where there are several rag-mills, and paid a visit to one of them. The rags were ground, as they term it, in the uppermost apartment of the building, by machines, in outward appearance like Cook's agricultural winnowing-machine,[4] and each attended by three or four boys and girls. The operation of the machinery was so thoroughly incased in wood, that nothing was to be seen, though it consisted, as has been before observed, of cylinders armed with hooks, which, being of different sizes, perform their office one set after another, till the rags put in at the top come out at the bottom, to all appearance like coarse short wool. A single glance at the ceremony going forward was quite sufficient to convey a tolerable idea of the business, – a single whiff of air from the interior of the apartment almost more than could be endured.

I will not undertake to render intelligible to the other senses what is an affair of the nose alone, – in other words, I will not attempt to describe an ill smell: first, because the subject is not agreeable, and next, because it is particularly difficult; indeed, I know not even whether it be a physical or a metaphysical question, whether or not a smell be, *de jure*,[5] a noun and the name of a thing, having substance and dimensions, or whether it be an ethereal essence void of material particles, – as it were the benediction of animal matter departing from the physical to the metaphysical world, and at that very critical moment of its existence, or non-existence, when it belongs to neither. But if the smell of the rag-grinding process can be estimated in any degree, and an inference drawn, by the quantity of dust produced, the quality of the latter at the same time not being forgotten, then some little notion may probably be given by stating, that the boys and girls who attend the mill are not only involved all the time it works in a thick cloud, so as to be hardly visible, but, whenever they emerge, appear covered from head to foot with downy particles that entirely obscure their features, and render them in appearance like so many brown moths.

It is really extraordinary to observe, on taking a portion of shoddy in the hand as it comes from the mill, the full extent of its transmutation, – how perfectly the disentanglement of the filament has been effected; although, notwithstanding its freshened appearance, time and temperature must have inevitably brought it nearer to the period of ultimate decay.

The shoddy thus prepared in the mill is afterwards subjected to the usual process of manufacture, and together with an admixture of new wool, and the help of large quantities of oil, it is passed through the discipline of the carding-machine, mules, &c., till a thread is formed, which latter is handed to the weavers. But, alas! there is no such thing as perfection in human nature, or the works of man; – notwithstanding all possible exertions, there are certain parts and particles appertaining to these fusty old rags that cannot be worked up into new coats, do what men will; and of which the shoddy, to do it justice, may be said to be wholly liberated and purified: such things, for instance, as the hides of ancient fleas that have lingered through a rainy season and died of rheumatism, – and so forth. Yet, in the present day, such is the enlightenment of man's understanding, that even all these, be they what they may, are scrupulously turned to account, being mixed up together with all the refuse and that part of the shoddy too short to spin, packed in bales, covered with coarse matting, and thus shipped off to Kent as manure for hops. In this state, called "tillage muck," it fetches about forty-seven shillings a ton. In a yard adjoining Raven's wharf, which, though a mile from the town of Dewsbury, and the road to it extremely hilly, is the usual place of shipment, I saw a large heap of this compost which very much resembled, "horresco referens,"[6] – "I have a crawling sensation as I write," – the stuffing I have occasionally seen, nay, slept upon, in inferior mattresses. Workmen were at the time employed in lading a cargo of these bales; as well as the compost that lay in bulk in the yard, they were then heating most violently. Impressed, on account of the vessel, with an apprehension of fire, for never did I see goods put on board in such a state, I asked the man at the crane whether he did not think there was danger. After looking at me for some seconds with attention, his reply was at least emphatic, – "I like, Sir," said he, "to see 'em sweat."

## Notes

1 George Stultz came from Germany and established his tailoring business at 10 Clifford Street, London, around 1809. He was known for his fashionable cut, excellence of materials and high prices. He is said to have retired to France a wealthy man and died in 1833. However, the London business was continued by John Stultz. John Jackson's *The Improved Tailors' Aera* (London: W. Smith, 1829) is dedicated to J. Stultz praising his systems for obtaining the correct position of the neck.

2 Drenched in perfume. From Horace 28 *Odes* 1.5: 'Quis multa gracilis te puer in rosa perfusus liquidis urget odoribus grato, Pyrrha, sub antro?', which may be translated: What slender youth drenched in liquid perfume, embraces you, Pyrrha, amongst the many roses in your pleasant grotto?

3 Spelled Battley Carr in the original.

4 John Cooch (1756–1828) patented a winnowing machine that was later improved by his son Joshua Cooch (1804–1865).

5 By right.

6 I shudder to say.

## Editorial Headnote

## Fenton, Farrar. 'Woollen Shoddy. Its Invention, History, and Manufacture', *Textile Manufacturer*, 7:76–82 (15 Apr–15 Oct 1881), pp. 131–132, 172–173, 208–209, 251–252, 287–289, 328–329, 365–367.

Farrar Fenton (c1832–1911) grew up in Lincolnshire, the son of Richard Fenton, clerk in orders. In 1851, he was living with his widowed mother and siblings at Mappleton. At that time, he was pursuing the scholarship of classical, oriental and modern languages, and in 1853, began a translation of the Bible into modern English. However, practical employment must have been necessary, and in 1861, Fenton was living with his uncle John Fenton in Fishguard, while he worked as printer and reporter for the press. He appears to have left this employment in 1862, finding a new interest in alternatives to cotton fibre.

By the mid-sixties, Fenton had moved to Dewsbury where he married Letitia Cleaver (c1836–1901) in 1866. There he set up with his younger brother Reginald Fenton (born around 1840) as rag merchant and broker. This partnership was dissolved in 1867, succeeded by another with James William Wood (1837–1903), styled Fenton and Wood, as shoddy and wool manure manufacturers. The following year, Wood left but Fenton continued under the same name until this firm was liquidated by arrangement with creditors in 1873. Meanwhile, by 1871, he had joined with the rag merchant Samuel Firth (born around 1828) under the firm Fenton and Firth. When Firth left in 1875, Fenton continued on his own, carrying on as a manure manufacturer into the early 1880s. In 1883, he changed his career to that of colonial and British land and share broker, under the style Ferrar Fenton and Co., and in 1889 removed from Batley to London. This business continued until 1892 when 'he attributed his failure to losses in connection with the Crystal Reef Gold Mining Company, which he considered he was persuaded into buying by fraudulent misrepresentation' (*Leeds Mercury*, 13 May 1892, p. 7). Fenton managed to revive his business as share broker until, in the last decade of his life, he supported himself through journalism while he returned to work on Bible translation.

Fenton appears to have attempted a less Yorkshire-centric account of the history of shoddy, with which locals found fault:

> It was believed he had given too much credence to the statements of persons, many of them living at a considerable distance from the West Riding, anxious to figure in the history of a trade which had become long before 1880 of more than national importance.
>
> (*Batley Reporter*, 8 Oct 1897, p. 10)

Edwin Law, grandson of Benjamin Law, pioneer of the shoddy industry, disputed the date for the introduction of shoddy cloth, placing this at 1809, but admitted

Fenton brought much valuable information to the subject (see *Textile Manufacturer*, 7:79, 15 Jul 1881, p. 248). The entirety of the series of articles was printed (nearly simultaneously) in the American monthly, *Designer and Weaver*, from June to December 1881. Sections were also reprinted in regional newspapers, and in the trade journal, *Clothier and Furnisher*.

# 8

# FENTON, FARRAR. 'WOOLLEN SHODDY. ITS INVENTION, HISTORY, AND MANUFACTURE'

## *Textile Manufacturer* (15 Apr–15 Oct 1881), pp. 131–132, 172–173, 208–209, 251–252, 287–289, 328–329, 365–367.

In the history of commerce, we often see that important results have sprung from trivial events, that at the time were regarded as unworthy of notice. I have no intention of referring to old illustrations of the above trite observation, as the history of shoddy, which I propose to give, is, in the field of modern invention, one of the most striking illustrations. The history of shoddy forms an important part of the history of the modern woollen trade, and just now, owing to the fierce battle of tariffs, a knowledge of its nature and extent is of great consequence to our industry at the present time, owing to the near negotiations of important treaties of commerce.

Shoddy has usually been written of with contempt, by men who have no practical knowledge of it or its history and use, and has been passed over by writers and statesmen as unworthy of serious attention; but from knowing its really vast extent and importance, for some years past I have carefully gathered the facts regarding its origin, development, and extent.

"But what is 'shoddy'?" a large portion of your readers will ask, for though the word has been made familiar enough, along with its sarcastic equivalent "Devil's-dust," invented by Mr. Busfeild Ferrand as a jewel of Parliamentary eloquence some years ago, yet the idea conveyed by it is quite indefinite to most people.[1] "Shoddy" has two distinct meanings when used by woollen workers. The first represents a particular kind of woollen material made by pulling into their original fibrous condition worsted fabrics of any sort, old blankets, flannels, old stockings, called in the technical language of the trade "softs," as distinguished from "mungo," which was of considerably later invention, and which is produced from pulling into the original state of wool old broadcloth rags and new snips, called technically "hards." But in its wider acceptance it is used as a family or generic name, for not only the two above-named varieties, but for all forms of recovered woollen or hair or mixed fabrics that can be used afresh to produce tissues of animal or combined fibres, and excludes "extract-wool," "linsey," and "flocks,"

DOI: 10.4324/9780429274190-12

the peculiar characteristics of each of which may be noted as follows: – Extract, or as it is sometimes called, carbonised wool, is made by first steeping in a bath of diluted corrosive acid, usually diluted vitriol, or its vapour, rags having cotton or other vegetable warps, so as to rot these while leaving the woollen weft but little injured, and after this, drying and pulling out by requisite machinery, the wool in its original length. Linsey shoddy, on the contrary, is produced by “grinding,” or “pulling,” – for both terms are used indifferently in the trade – rags of mixed vegetable and woollen fabric, without first destroying the cotton or other portion, in the same machinery that is used for grinding shoddy and mungo of all wool, thus making linsey-shoddy or linsey-mungo, as the case may be. Flocks are made of mixed fabrics or woollen, as above, as well as being a necessary product of various processes in the manufacture of cloth, such as the “milling,” “raising,” and “cropping,” or “shearing” the surfaces in preparing the fabrics for the market, and are put to a great variety of uses, both for spinning again, felting, and domestic purposes, as will be explained when the processes of the manufactures of the shoddy trades come to be spoken of. To the above articles must be added hair of all kinds, which has of late years become an important factor in the heavy woollen trade, used both in its raw state and as hair shoddy and flocks, and a long list of vegetable fibres used for admixtures and warps or wefts, that have from time to time been devised, and the history of which will be given hereafter.

Several years ago the writer was staying at an hotel in London, when someone remarking in the commercial room that he came from Yorkshire, the jesting talk turned on shoddy, and he was asked who invented it. He replied that it was attributed by one local report to a Benjamin Parr,[2] of Batley, and by another to a Benjamin Law.[3] “Eh, what is that you are saying about the invention of shoddy,” broke in an elderly Jewish gentleman; you’re quite mistaken – neither Law nor Parr invented it, they only adopted it. My father was the very first man who ever thought of or made it.” “How was it, and when?” was the general enquiry. “Well, I’ll tell you about it,” replied our Jewish friend, “exactly as my father used often to tell me. It arose thus: My father was an extensive dealer in second-hand clothes in Whitechapel here, and when the Peninsular War broke out, after old Bonaparte had overrun Spain, owing to the stoppage of the supply of Spanish wool and the brisk demand for army goods for the contemplated expedition to Spain of Sir John Moore and the rest,[4] Spanish wool, which was then used for making them, rose to a great price, and my father, who, as a ‘clothes-duffer,’[5] had been used to seeing the lot of woollen dust, or ‘mill-puff,’ as it was then called, brushed off the old clothes in preparing them afresh for the market, got a new idea in his head. It occurred to him,” he said, “that if he bought wool in London, opened the bales, and inserted amongst the fleeces 50 per cent. of old blankets or white flannels torn up with curry-combs into fibre again, it would be a paying speculation. He consequently flung aside his second-hand coats and trousers and covered his ‘duffing-cushions’ with old blankets, and set off a lot of ‘doctored’ bales, and realized full prices in Yorkshire. When my father first began to tear up the old blankets into shoddy he was able to buy them at fourpence each, but he had not been at work over a month before they rose to the price of one shilling. He kept at this work till wool fell in value, and then turned to making flocks for stuffing saddles and mattrasses[6] to replace wool, which had previously been used for those purposes. That, gentlemen was the origin of 'Shoddy,'" concluded our informant, putting his cigar into his mouth again, and casting a glance of triumph towards us. This gentleman gave no absolute date as being that on which his father began his shoddy pulling, but as between 1803 and 1805–6 wool rose on the average some 32 per cent. in price, it will be safe to place the genesis of his operations about the latter date. I have made considerable effort, and spent some time in researches, to acquire proof or otherwise of the above anecdote, as I did not at the time ask the narrator his name, and from various quarters both in London and Yorkshire have gained information corroborative of its general accuracy, and am led to believe that the narrator's name was a Mr. Davis, who then or afterwards carried on an extensive business as an outfitter and merchant tailor in Cheapside, under the style of Moses, Son, and Davis.[7] The name shoddy itself is also confirmatory, as it is of Persi-Arabic extraction apparently, being a modification of Shodjah, which signifies to the Semitic origin of the inventor of the article.

But though no doubt many Yorkshire clothworkers had been involuntary and unconscious spinners of shoddy delivered to them in mixture as Spanish wool, the invention of shoddy-cloth did not occur till the year 1813, according to the general report of the contemporaries and descendants of the inventors, and of local tradition for unfortunately no documentary evidence of the exact year is now known to be in existence.

The first idea of making shoddy-cloth belongs to Benjamin Law, a small farmer and weaver of what was then the little moorland village of Batley, in Yorkshire, lying between Leeds and Huddersfield, where it was the custom to fill up the spare hours from farm work with hand-loom weaving and spinning in the cottages. Law has been described by his contemporaries as a man of bright, quick eye, tall, handsome, and sharp in his bodily movements, altogether considerably different to the regular type of his neighbours. He was pushing and proud, it is said, and instead of being satisfied with selling the Leeds market, extended his ventures to London, and on one occasion in 1813, whilst seeking orders or hunting for payments there, he was amusing himself by looking into the shop windows, and at a saddler's caught sight of a material that looked like white wool, such as was then used for stuffing harness, but which yet appeared in some respects to differ from any he had been used to. He stepped in and asked to be allowed to examine it more closely, and the proprietor, whose name was Littlewood,[8] politely passed a handful to him. Law pulled it in the way a spinner would do to try its 'staple' (that is the length of its fibre), and then proceeded to twist it into a yarn or thread between his finger and thumb, and asked what it was used for and where it had been got from. Mr. Littlewood informed him, and Law thereupon proceeded to secure a quantity from its Jewish inventor and producer, Mr. Davis, which he took down to Batley to test for the manufacture of cloth. This first used parcel, as a relative of his informed us, was white, and made from old blankets. The stuff answered, and

Law kept his work a profound secret, admitting no one to its knowledge, except his brother-in-law, Benjamin Parr, who became his co-adjutor in the development, and ultimately his partner, as will be seen, in grinding rags locally and inventing plant for the work, but for the first year the supply of shoddy was obtained entirely from London, so as to keep it from rival manufacturers.

Such was the origin of shoddy and shoddy cloth, according to the best data. But some make a slight variation in the first introduction of shoddy to the notice of Benjamin Law, relating that he was himself attempting to sell flocks to the saddler, Littlewood, when that gentleman showed him shoddy as a cheaper article. However, I have been assured by relatives of Law that he never was a dealer in flocks, and that the version I give above is accurate.

The use of “opened,” or “pulled,” thrums (that is, waste yarn) must not be confused with the use or invention of shoddy, or even the mixing of flocks with wool previous to spinning, as a Yorkshire local writer seems to have done, for the use of both these articles was of old standing in Devonshire centuries before Mr. Davis, of London, invented, or Benjamin Law, of Batley, thought, the one of pulling old blankets again into fibre, or the other of adopting the article as a standard material for cloth manufacture. Complete evidence of the Devonshire men having extensively utilised flocks and thrums for re-spinning is furnished by an Act of Parliament passed in 1467, permitting the continued use of them in Devonshire cloths, but prohibiting them in any other of the woollen districts of the kingdom.[9]

The quantity of shoddy brought from London by Law would not appear on the first occasion to have been more than a few stones in weight, but from it sprang the new industry whose development and progress I propose to delineate in my next article.

Having stated the origin of woollen shoddy, we proceed to record its development after Benjamin Law had determined to apply it to the making of fabrics. His course was by no means one of plain sailing, for the difficulties to be overcome, as in all new manufactures, were innumerable. Law soon concluded that bringing the shoddy from London was a costly and troublesome operation in the then state of the carrying trade, and that it involved, as he feared, great risks of the discovery of his secret, for he is traditionally said to have been a man reticent and suspicious to an extraordinary degree. He and his brother-in-law, Benjamin Parr, therefore decided to try and produce it themselves; but haunted by the terror of discovery, they feared to buy rags for this purpose locally, and it was decided that Parr should proceed to Scotland to collect them, Law, it is said, entreating him before he started, “to let nobody, *not even the shirt on his back*, know the object of his journey!” or the secret would be out. There has been, and is, considerable controversy among local writers and in tradition as to the date when this expedition of Parr’s was undertaken; but from the information given us by Mr. B. Parr, a son of the inventor,[10] who recollects the event during his childhood, and by Mr. John Law,[11] a grandson of Benjamin Law, corroborated by Mr. R. Wade,[12] a retired manufacturer of this district, who remembers the period, we may safely fix it as being some time during 1815. When the rags arrived, Law was afraid to receive them into his premises, and as Parr lived at a house further removed from public observation, they were stored with him. As noted in our former article, Mr. Davis, the inventor of shoddy in London, had made it by means of tearing his blankets up with currycombs,[13] and when Parr and Law constructed a machine to work more efficiently, they resorted to the currycomb as its basis. No drawing of their early machine exists, nor has any description of it been published heretofore that we can discover, but from a minute one furnished to us verbally by a son of its contriver, and one or two other gentlemen who can remember it, the following was its construction: The framework was the same in form as that of a carding engine, but instead of the broad cylinder of that machine, the drum or "swift," as it is now called, was about a foot wide, and only two feet in diameter; or, to use the phrase of one of our informants, "not bigger than a grindstone." This drum was fluted across its face with flutes laid in the manner of saw-teeth, and on each of these indentations a strong steel currycomb blade was firmly screwed, so that one slightly overlapped the other. These worked against other combs set in the opposite direction on smaller fluted rollers. It was fed at both ends with rags, and as from the diagonal position of the combs on the drum, they soon choked a rapidly-revolving brush fixed below, which swept the shoddy out of them as a groom does the hair pulled off a horse when his currycomb is clogged.

There are fierce local disputes as to who was the machinist that built this machine for Parr and Law, and even as to whether it was the invention of Parr and Law at all, the disputes being rendered more involved and bitter by the fact that about the same date, or a little earlier, someone, whose name we have in vain endeavoured to ascertain, had started a machine for opening yarn waste on the old Devonshire plan at Brighouse, a neighbouring village; but from very careful enquiry and comparison of evidence amongst the few remaining contemporaries and their immediate descendants, we are fully satisfied that this first rag-grinding machine was constructed from Parr's instructions by a Mr. Joseph Archer, of Osset,[14] a village between Dewsbury and Wakefield. Indeed, Mr. B. Parr the younger, who still survives, the son of Benjamin Parr and nephew of Benjamin Law, the inventors, informs us that when a boy it was his special work to take the rollers to Mr. Joseph Archer's to get the frequently broken combs renewed, and as roads adapted to wheeled vehicles were rare in the district in 1815, and long after, the conveyance of machinery and goods was effected on men's shoulders or by pack-horses, so that he sweated under the load. Besides being defective in other respects, the constant liability to breakage was found a very expensive matter, so that Mr. Joseph Archer, and an apprentice of his, Jonas Haley,[15] who afterwards became an eminent machinist at Dewsbury, set their minds to work to improve on the combs, and contrived a drum armed with upright conical steel teeth, such as have been used ever since; but this improvement was not effected for some years. The machine was surnamed, with true Yorkshire wit, "The Devil," owing to the stifling vapour it produced, and the groaning and shrieks with which it tore up the rags consigned to its mouth. It was erected at the Old Mill, Batley, in a partitioned-off room, and if we are rightly informed, the late Mr. John Fenton,[16] who was employed confidentially by Parr, worked it with as much privacy as possible. This gentleman (Mr. John Fenton) afterwards became the founder of the eminent woollen manufacturing firm of John Fenton and Sons, of Batley Carr, Dewsbury.[17] In spite of precautions, however, the very thing Law had wished to avoid – the discovery of his secret of using shoddy – overtook him almost immediately. The secret escaped, and several other of the villagers, in a couple of years' time, entered vigorously into the trade, and in 1818, the late Mr. Joseph Jubb, John Fox, Phineas Fox, George Newsome, and John Burnley, all of Batley,[18] united to construct a rag machine, and as the model of one seems to have been matter of doubt, Joseph Jubb went to the "Thrum" Grinder of Brighouse, before referred to, with a mechanic named Gibson,[19] under pretence of buying pulled waste, but the party suspecting a "sell," refused to admit the blacksmith into his premises. However, Jubb was allowed entry to look at the prepared waste he wished to purchase, and took such note of the machine as to enable the smith to construct a workable copy, which was put up at a small and very old corn mill, called Howley Mill, and driven by water-power. The quaint old building still endures, and afterwards fell into the hands of our Benjamin Parr, in whose family we believe it continues to the present day. As will be seen, as we proceed, it is classic ground in the history of the shoddy trades, being connected with every step in their development.

But though the grinding or tearing of rags mechanically into a fibre capable of being spun again was thus accomplished by the genius of Davis, followed and developed by Parr and Law, the difficulties of its manufacture into cloth were only in a manner begun. Amongst others, the cards of that day, being all constructed for carding pure wool only, operated very imperfectly on shoddy; the greater part of it dropped below the swifts or cylinders, and could not be got to mix with the wool. This portion was swept up and applied as top dressing to a crop of potatoes. The plants were greatly benefited by the manure, and on digging up the crop in the autumn, Law and Parr observed that the action of the sun, rain, and wind had so softened and opened the hard portions of this apparently waste shoddy as to make it look capable of use again. They accordingly tried it, succeeded in making good yarn therefrom, and thereafter continued to make a crop of potatoes, manured with obdurate shoddy, one of the preparatory engines of the manufacture, till Archer and Haley's improved "devil" rendered it unnecessary. This curious fact we first learnt from Mr. W. H. Fenton,[20] who some forty years ago was engaged in business in this district, previous to his removal to the Cape, where he is now a prosperous sheep farmer; but always considered it as a joke till it was the other day confirmed to us by a son of Parr himself. The anecdote is useful, though reading like an incident from a child's fairy tale, as it shows how small a thing may decide the success or failure of a great invention, and showing to us moderns, further, how a constructive intellect of great power – as there is hardly a doubt those of Law and Parr were – often has to arrive at success by the lessons learnt from its failures.

Law, at this period, took a leap forward in his business and circumstances, and in that dark day of stagnation and ruin amongst the Yorkshire woollen manufacturers, caused by the operation of the celebrated "Berlin Decree" of Napoleon I, excluding English manufactures from the whole of the Continent,[21] the fact excited great wonder among his neighbours, and the village gossip soon reported that he was grown rich by old rags made by some secret process into wool again! Finding it useless to further attempt to hide the affair, Parr and Law offered the article, under the name of "Shoddy," to their townsmen, and we are told effected the first sale of it to Messrs. Jubb and Spedding,[22] and afterwards to Mr. John Burnley. This was inevitable, but it told on the profits of Law, and followed as it was by the prostration of trade, caused by the terrible famine following the loss of the harvest in 1816, and lasting to that of 1817, preceded in his case by the wasted outlay invariably attending attempts in a new field of manufacture, pressed hardly[23] on him and Parr. They had no wealthy capitalist at their back, like Arkwright had with his cotton machinery; but Law was not the man, with his restless and venturesome mind, to abandon the position without a struggle.

Finding no market for his goods in England at the moment, he determined to try the United States, and sent off his third son, John,[24] with a considerable consignment of cloth, to New York, according to the date given us by Mr. John Law, architect, of Batley, a nephew of the John we may call the American voyager, in 1816–17. The venture turned out highly profitable, and on the young man's return he was requested to stand on a bench at the Sunday school, that all might have a good view of the wonderful man who had crossed the Atlantic, a quaint proof of the different facilities and means of travel between then and now.

Other Batley men having now decided, at the cost of the ability and pockets of Law and Parr, that there was something in shoddy, determined, as stated above, to begin grinding it for themselves in 1818, and besides the machine set up at Hawley Mill, another was started in his barn by Mr. John Burnley, a farmer and weaver, and worked by a donkey – not like our modern ones acting by steam, but by such amount of power as might dwell in his four legs. This, added to the loss of customers for their shoddy to Law and Parr, in addition to increased rivalry in the cloths, entailed upon them the gloomy fate of pioneer inventors. Then came further bad times, and Law again tried to revive the position by sending his son a second time to New York, in 1820, with all the cloth he had. No report arriving from the young man, his father decided to follow him, and the result was discovered to be that after landing in New York his son seemed to have disappeared from sight, and the most diligent inquiry could obtain no trace of him or his consignment. Law, in despair, wrote to his partner, Parr, that they were ruined, and that he must make the best he could of affairs in England, for that, as for himself, he never intended to see him or Batley again. He, however, afterwards returned to England, and settled at Hyde, removing afterwards to Stockport, in Cheshire, where he died in 1837, but was buried in Batley churchyard. He was born at Great Gomersal, the 8th of November, 1772, a village near Batley, and so died a broken-hearted man at the age of 65, the originator of one of the most important modern industries, ruined by the fertility of his genius – a man worthy of a monument to record the benefits he conferred on millions, but who has only a broken headstone to mark his grave, and a name unknown to the mass of his countrymen.

The history of such men is the best argument for a patent law, rendering the production of their genius as easily, inexpensively, and safely defensible to themselves as the copyright of a book is to its author, as far as the nature of the case will admit.

The fate of Benjamin Law, and his partner, Benjamin Parr, was hard enough. When they began developing the idea of shoddy cloth both were, for the place and period, substantial men, and for the short time they could hide their work in darkness they rapidly progressed in trade; but by 1818–20, when their outlay and labour had brought it to practical success, others, fresh in funds and hope, stepped in, investing the whole available capital and commercial connection of the village in rivalry of the exhausted inventors, as stated above, and easily carried off the harvest they had sown.

In 1820 Joseph Jubb and his companions became perfectly satisfied, from the results of the rag-grinding at Hawley Mill, that shoddy was going to the fore, and suggested that all should unite and build a factory, where every man in the woollen trade in Batley could place what machinery he had, to be driven by steam power. The plan was accepted and a shed run up, in which was placed an old steam engine, and the building was opened in 1822, and named Hick Lane Mill – the first building ever designed for the sole manufacture of shoddy cloth. The partners in this company mill – as such associations which do not involve partnership or shares in the joint stock acceptation of the term are called locally – are given differently by various informants, but we believe the following list to be as accurate as possible: Messrs. Joseph Jubb, John Burnley, S. Spedding,[25] John and Phineas Fox, George Newsome, and Benjamin Parr, the inventor. Law was not in it, having wearied of the battle, and only from a distance heard of the success of those he left behind. In 1820 the late Mr. George Hall[26] began dealing in woollen rags for shoddy grinding – the first man who saw his way to make it the basis of a livelihood – at Clark Green, Batley, and afterwards also, by adding manufacturing to it at Dewsbury and elsewhere, became a leader in the blanket trade. In the same year (1820) the first manufacturer outside Batley tried shoddy – Mr. Halliley, of Aldam's Mill, Dewsbury;[27] but when he gave the order to Benjamin Parr, it is related by Parr's son, also Benjamin, Mr. Halliley was ashamed to use the word "shoddy," so requested "to be supplied with three packs of 'made wool' as a trial!" This shame about the new article was almost universal, and the late Mr. Joshua Walker, manager of the Dewsbury branch of the Huddersfield Banking Company,[28] who possessed many of the traditions of shoddy, used to relate amongst others the following, as illustrative of the terror under which some of the adopters of it laboured: "When old Mr. Gott, of Leeds,[29] the great cloth manufacturer of the West Riding of his day, decided to begin using shoddy, he was haunted by the fear that his neighbours should think him dishonest for so doing, and therefore bought his first year or two's supply with the proviso that it was to be packed to imitate wool bales, and as a further precaution had it carried to his works at midnight, and the loads only admitted by a confidential servant or himself." And he was by no means singular either among his contemporaries or since.

But shoddy was now (1822) fairly started, and, as we shall see when we come to its statistics year by year, told decisively on the volume of the British woollen industry, and by 1830 had become the King of Yorkshire; but for thirty years yet to come invention was busy before all its varieties and resources were developed, as we will proceed to show.

## Mungo, extract, and shorts

In our last we had intended to have included the history of the origin of all varieties of shoddy, but found the subject too extensive for such condensation, if we retained any wish to make the facts intelligible to our readers, consequently we now continue the narrative with a biography of the second species invented – mungo – which has, by its subsequent progress, proved to be a most important contribution to the raw materials of the great industry we are considering, and therefore worthy of a detailed statement of its development and uses.

As stated in our last, by 1830, shoddy, made from soft rags, had established itself as a staple material for Yorkshire manufacturers, and upon it villages were growing into large towns, and towns into cities, with the population of former provinces. And whilst this was developing, the active minds of Law and Parr had not been idle. To which of them the first conception of the thing was due we have not been able to learn, but at any rate the determination to try the grinding and subsequent spinning of hard cloth rags was made by them, and in consequence a quantity of tailors' snippings[30] of new broad cloths was procured from London. To make the mouths of the present generation of mungo-pullers water, we may mention that these "new clips" were then bought at ⅛d. per lb. weight, as a Kentish dealer, who could remember the age before mungo, told us, as at that period their only use was to manure hop-gardens. These clippings were as usual, for secrecy, brought to the house of Parr, who tried to grind them on the curry-comb machine, but failed to succeed after every effort, and therefore the clips were thrown on a dunghill and allowed to rot till carted away to the farm. In fact the job was a failure, and but for Archer & Haley's improvement of making rag devils with sharp conical teeth, as before related, would probably have remained so to this day. Our informant does not recollect the exact date of this attempt, but from his age at the time we estimate it was somewhere between 1824 and 1830.

But like many an inventor's failure, it became the germ of future success. The disappointment was, we are told, often discussed in the family circle, and loss on the speculation mourned, and these discussions were, no doubt, not lost on young George Parr,[31] the son of Benjamin, who afterwards became the successful solver of the invention. This youth was at the time apprenticed to Mr. S. Armitage, of Batley Carr,[32] but when he had "served his long seven years," according to the custom of the day, the best form of technical education, as at once teaching the pupil not only the scientific and practical basis of his manufacture, but enforcing a training to business habits and procedure as well, he was disinclined to follow the trade he has learned – that of a cloth-finisher – and he became a salesman of shoddy for his father. In his journeys seeking orders, he called at the Bridge Mill, Batley Carr, and at the works of Messrs. Porritt & Co. there,[33] who hired a small room with power to put a flock machine in, he observed some flocks of a kind new to him lying on the floor. He took up a handful, made a few inquiries, and was told that the firm were making a new kind of stuffing flocks by grinding up old coats. He at once perceived that he had now before him, in an imperfect shape, what his father had previously tried in vain to make from new clips. He offered to buy two bags and they were weighed off to him. George Parr was at this time in his twenty-first year, which brings our date to 1834.

When he tried to spin some of his purchase of flocks he found the Batley cards too coarse, so he took a sample to Mr. John Watson, of Morley, near Leeds,[34] where fine broad-cloths were produced. At his request, Mr. Watson tried to card and spin a little, and produced a yarn, but so mixed with cotton threads and linen linings torn up with flocks as to be useless. The disappointment was great, till Watson, looking closely at the yarn remarked, "If we could get rid of the cotton ends I might do with it," adding, "send up what you've got and I'll try." This was done, and Mr. Watson set some girls to pick out all bits of cotton thread and lining. He then spun and wove the rest. Mr. B. Parr, jun. went over or was sent for to see the resulting cloth, and was surprised and disappointed to find it standing in the loom a coarse, hard, knotty fabric, more like rough tow-spun hemp bagging than broad-cloth. It consequently speaks volumes to the honour of Watson's enterprise that, instead of flinging the fabric into the fire-hole and swearing "there was nothing in it," as most manufacturers would now-a-days, he determined, with the aid of the Parrs, to try the affair further. The great first defect of the article, its admixture with cotton and linen threads, was obviated by George Parr devising the plan of examining the cloth before grinding it. The length of staple was increased also by the suggestion of Benjamin Parr, the younger, to wet the rags with water before grinding, but which he afterwards abandoned for the use of oil, as oil produced still better results. With this improved mungo the experiment of producing cloth was continued by various manufacturers in the district as well as Watson, for the Parrs offered it freely, and the Jubb family, the Brearleys, the Sheards, Burnleys, Oldroyds, and Halls,[35] whose names have since been associated with the foundation of the largest firms of the British woollen trade, doggedly struggled to utilize the new fibre, encouraged by the good results previously obtained from shoddy. Mr. John Watson would appear to have come to despair over absolute success, however, for there is a local tradition that one day when George or Samuel Parr,[36] for the names of the two brothers are both given variously by narrators, called on him to enquire into the progress of the matter, Watson replied testily in the Yorkshire idiom, "It'll nivver goa." "Nivver goa?" retorted young Parr in hot passion at the decision so adverse to his hopes, "Nivver goa, did'st ta' say? But I'll tell thee, after all the brass we've spent on't *it mun go*," ("must go," to explain the words for foreign readers). But as Parr went back to his home at Hawley Mill, sore at heart at the asserted futility of his labours, his anger burst into a fit of sardonic laughter as it struck him that it would be a sweet piece of revenge on fate to force the invention forward, and name his article "mungo," as a record of his agony and ultimate triumph; his family consulted, and it is so called to this day.

But success was far off yet, as Mr. George Brearley, of Clark Green, Batley,[37] one of the first who tried mungo, has kindly informed us. After the cotton threads had been got rid of, the shortness of staple in it made the mungo almost impossible to work over the cards. It separated from the wool mixed with it and clotted up the teeth like dust, and even what passed to the end of the carder, then flew off from the doffer or fell down from the sliver-sheet, or made the sliver and roving so feeble in tenacity, even if got from the carder, that the operation of slubbing, that is drawing out the carded sliver into a soft roving for subsequent spinning, at the wheel or hand-jack then generally used – exceedingly difficult and precarious. Condensing was not yet:[38] in fact it was a development of carding woollen material invented to meet this very difficulty. Years were consumed, says Mr. G. Brearley, in endless experiments, but at last success arrived, and mungo, the second development of shoddy, was confessed to be of even greater value to the world's comfort than shoddy. Shoddy was followed by another branch of the family, which in our opinion is destined to surpass even it in utility, though hitherto it has made but comparatively little progress amongst English wool-workers – we refer to "extract" or "carbonised wool." As soon as the grinding and carding of mungo had been brought to a successful issue its use spread far more rapidly than that of shoddy had done, for it was found applicable to a more extended range of serviceable and handsome textures, from fine broad cloths to strong and impervious textures to warm the ploughman and the hardy sailor exposed to the hardships of life at sea. George Parr, however, made little out of his skill and ingenuity; some say, that losing heart in his struggle, he took to indulging in drink as a solace to his griefs, and finally left the district. But while the family of Benjamin Law, not one of whose descendants, though holding position as professional men in Batley, succeeded in reaping benefit from their ancestor's genius in manufacturing, Mr. James Parr,[39] the son of George Parr, retrieved by great energy the position, and is still largely engaged in the manufacture at Boothroyd Mills, Batley.

"Extract" sometimes, but very seldom called "carbonised-wool" by our modern trade dandies, who are too "refined" to speak of "shoddy," was the third step in extension of the utilisation of waste woollen substances, and the inventor was, by a freak of genius, quite ignorant of any branch of the woollen manufacture; he was a sea-captain, we have been informed, named Corbett,[40] residing at or near London, and like others was attracted to visit the Exhibition of 1851. There, where all the secrets of manufacturing in every trade were exposed for the benefit of mankind, a paper maker showed woollen stuff rags with cotton warps, such as are produced at Bradford and Norwich, in all stages of operation for paper making up to a printed journal. The process consisted of boiling rags of mixed wool and vegetable fabrics in a closed boiler or "keer,"[41] where they were subjected to caustic alkaline washes, boiled under a pressure of 50 lb. to 60 lb. of steam, which converted the woollen weft into gelatine, leaving the cotton warp extract. No doubt thousands looked and wondered but Captain Corbett looked and thought as well. He was a ship-captain and the things before him were worsted linsey rags, but something impressed him that they might be put to a more profitable use than paper making, by destroying the cotton warp and preserving the woollen weft. He therefore began to study in chemistry and mechanics, and after long investigation he discovered that a weak solution of sulphuric acid contained in a lead-lined vat, in which the rags were to be steeped for a short time, completely destroyed the cotton portion, whilst it inflicted little or no apparent damage on the wool. He had now attained his chief object, and the next question was how to separate the cotton thread from the wool, so as to preserve it in its full length of staple. He had seen shoddy and mungo machines at work in the Exhibition, and noticed how terribly (to his eyes) they broke up the staple, so determined to avoid this he looked round for assistance nearer home. Amongst paper makers in Kent and Surrey a machine, called a "pulp-shaker," was, and perhaps is now, in common use. He tried this, and found it to answer fairly for the experiment, but noted that certain modifications would be needed. These he made and thereupon opened works for the commercial production of extract shoddy, in the full confidence of an inventor that owing to its cleanness and length of fibre it would take the lead of all other; but his samples were looked coldly on by the heavy woollen manufacturers, who no doubt saw the defects for their class of goods in this shoddy far more clearly than he did himself; it would not mill or felt. In the West of England, in Somerset and Devon, it found a little favour, as the late Mr. G. C. Hacker,[42] to whom we are indebted for much of the history of this invention, told us he used it freely in the factory he was there connected with, though it never became popular. Disappointed in his expected success with the Yorkshire trade, the captain put his ship on another tack and went to London. There he did a good stroke of business with the higher class of carriage builders, army and hunting saddlers, and those who made furniture for the wealthier classes. For the use of these trades rag flocks, or flocks made from shoddy waste, had been found quite inapplicable, as when goods stuffed with them were exported to India or other warm climates, or placed in the heated rooms of the wealthy the paddings became a mass of loathsome vermin. Horse hair and fleece wool, which had been used in the old time for padding, had become too costly to use as a rule, and cow and goat hair which had been substituted in part had followed the same course, owing to the late Mr. Edwin Firth, of Heckmondwike,[43] having originated an all devouring use for them in his invention of spinning hair for the manufacture of railway rugs and artificial skin fabrics, in mixture with shoddy. The new extract shoddy was, however, discovered to be an admirable successor to the last articles, owing to its perfect disinfection and cleansing by immersion in an acid bath during its manufacture, and a demand was established for it that soon outran the inventor's means. A company was therefore formed, and the works sold to it, and for a while a very profitable business was carried on, the trade being extended to the United States, where an unlimited market was found, and also to Germany, where it was readily adapted to textile purposes. But in spite of success the works were before long broken up, from the directors quarrelling among themselves, and rushing into the High Court of Chancery to settle their disputes. The trade, however, was too profitable to let die, and, if we are rightly informed, Messrs. Bates and Co., of Bow Common, and Knight Rider-street, London, entered into it.[44] The period of the great civil war in the United States was approaching, and on its outbreak an insatiable demand was made for extract shoddy by the Governments of both North and South, presumably for making hospital beds and army saddlery, and Messrs. Bates met it energetically, whilst extract works sprung up over the London district almost as rapidly as armed men at the States' field of combat. The shoddy in finer qualities brought 2s. 6d. per lb. in London, and only very inferior varieties were sold at 1s. 6d. and 2s., so that fortunes were lost and won in the course of a few weeks by speculations in the rags and prepared shoddy.

But having given a sketch of the discovery and progress of "extract" at its birthplace, it is time that we should return to Yorkshire to relate its local history, so far as we have been able to trace. Our first authority for the facts is the late Mr. Henry Wildsmith, of Batley, who founded the eminent extracting firm of Wildsmith and Carter, of Bradford Road, in that town.[45]

In 1856, Mr. Henry Wildsmith was head cloth finisher to the late Mr. John Nussey, of Batley,[46] a very extensive producer of mungo fabrics, and who was also distinguished for his wide enterprise connected with manufactures and banking. Wildsmith in some way, probably by a sample being left at his employers, heard of extract shoddy, and that it was made by some application of vitriol to linsey rags. He at once determined to try, and succeeded in a basin, and then proceeded with locked doors to larger preparations, using for this purpose the domestic wash-tub, soon rotting the unlucky tub with his vitriol, but provided successors, and continued to devote all his spare time to experiments. At last he discovered the exact degree of acids that would rot the cotton warps, without reducing the woollen weft to a brittle tinder, a point attained by the middle of 1857. On the 5th of August in that year he took a quantity of linsey rags he had dipped and dried to Mr. Benjamin Parr, the younger, of the Hawley Mill, locally so celebrated in the history of shoddy, to be shaken and rough carded, to get the cotton dust out of them, according to the date given us by the kindness of Mr. B. Parr, who has searched back in his books to find the first entry. All turned out well, and he sold the result of his venture at a profit, and found a customer ready to take all he could produce by means of his wash-tubs. Discovering he had not means to develop the trade, he applied to his father-in-law, the late Mr. Carter, to join him. At that time Mr. Carter was a tollbar keeper, on the Carlinghow road,[47] and also dealt to a moderate extent in a low kind of wool, locally called "shirtings." It struck him that the extract shoddy would sell in the same quarters and for the same purposes as the kind of wool he dealt in, and he consented to a partnership. The article, however, was found to meet no favour in the Batley district, but went better in

Huddersfield, and a firm there, whose name we have not succeeded in discovering, offered to take it in the shape of yarn if Wildsmith and Carter would spin it. In May, 1859, they began to do so, employing Mr. B. Parr, the younger, as the executant of the work. He found the article obdurate, and the results obtained not very promising, but with commendable perseverance Wildsmith and Carter stuck to it till April, 1860. The outcome, however, was so poor that after that they abandoned the attempt, and by selling the article in bulk for export solely soon reached a princely trade, and with the outbreak of the American war a golden shower of profits burst over them as well as others, and extract works arose through the West Riding in regiments, for extract with a strong complement of jute bagging pulled into a vegetable shoddy formed the staple of the "U. S. blankets" and other army goods supplied to the unfortunate "Yank and Sesesh" soldiers,[48] so that the production of the article took a firm hold of the Yorkshire district, though it has never, except as above, been much used by our clothing manufacturers in other departments than in the Bradford stuff and Halifax wool trades. But we believe there is a great future reserved for it, for abroad it has been applied to a variety of textile uses. These we will refer to when considering the manufactures producible from shoddies.

The last variety of "shoddy" we have now to refer to is that called "croppings," "cuttings," or "shorts." These consist either of the short hairs or fibres shaved or cut from the face of broad-cloths in the operation of "finishing" for the market, or of flocks or portions of cloth or hair reduced to a fine meal or flour-like dust by sharp vermicular cutting blades arranged as a proper machine for the purpose. At first only the necessarily produced "shorts" from the finishers work were used, but observing these to run short for the demands of the manufacture, the present writer in 1873 designed the machine for producing them artificially from waste.

The credit of devising the application of the "croppers" dust to the remanufacture of cloth was not due to a Yorkshireman but to an American, of Danvers, in New England. He mixed up this short dust with a strong solution of soap and size, and by milling very loose woven fabrics in the mixture, he succeeded in producing a cloth peculiarly adapted for clothing in the bleak winters of New England and Canada. It is thick and close in the bottom, can be worked up to any weight per yard, and is almost as impervious to wind and rain as leather, whilst it is at the same time capable of being finished to a handsome surface, and properly made it is very lasting in wear as workmen's clothing, and also very cheap. The use of this process was first begun in Leeds, for England, and was brought over by a returning emigrant, and has becomes an extensive industry in Yorkshire.

Having now sketched the origin and development of the woollen shoddy trade with as much succinctness as possible, we propose to proceed in our next article to treat of its raw materials and the sources of their supply, which will show how our fathers, under trade depression severer than we now suffer from, built up by strong hope and patient work an industry amongst the first, if not indeed the largest in volume anywhere to be found.

## Sources of supply – rags

As we said in our first article, the original source of shoddy was old blankets collected and reduced to fibre in London; indeed they would be the most obvious material for a first trial, owing to being the most softly spun and woven of all textures, and by their freedom from sewn seams being most readily reduced by the old mode of hand currycombs to an imitation of fleece wool, for which object shoddy was first produced. This went on till 1815, in which year, as previously related, Law and Parr determined to begin making shoddy themselves, and Benjamin Parr went to Scotland to secretly buy the rags. It would appear from the facts that in the "land'o cakes"[49] he did not find old blankets over plentiful, for, as his son informs us, he brought back wholly or chiefly tartans, stockings, and Scotch (Kilmarnock) caps or "bonnets," of soft wool texture, along with carpets, all capable of being ground into shoddy proper, and from that date the South and East of Scotland had been our best fields for superior rags of this class. After this first importation the "rag bags" rapidly succeeded the "wool-pack" as the basis of Batley trade, and as heavy and fancy woollen fabrics took the place of plain broadcloths in the variations of fashion following the end of the French revolutionary wars, the field of rag collection extended. Scotland and England were first overspread by the army of rag-collectors, and old brass and iron dealers made fortunes by adding woollen rags to those (at that time) begging trades. By 1830, the demand out-stepping the supply, the peasantry of Ireland were invited to exchange their fifty-year-old garments (as consult Charles Lever)[50] for new shoddy-made frieze, it being common, as I recollect when a boy, for the wandering collectors to sell new cloth for old, as a bait to induce a more ready exchange. In England, when all snips of woollen the housewife thought worth offering had been cleared out, they would produce from pack or van "a waistcoat-piece," and offer it *gratis* for the privilege of being allowed to go and search the ash pit or dunghill for a further supply. This never failed to attain the object, and by the aid of a good steel fork, in the vigorous hands of the speculator, always richly repaid him. Of course, the fact that "the giniwine West o' Highland broadcloth" offered in exchange was only former collections of "woollens" returned to the villagers in a new form was carefully concealed, the ragman volubly explaining "that he wor' a-buying them owd woollens to smelt steel wi' i' Sheffield." These anecdotes may seem trivial waste of time to some readers, but on reflection all will perceive their use, as showing that great industries are not always the outcome of "heroic attitudes," as so many writers on our trade biographies lead their readers to imagine, but the result of obscure labourers, whose object was not to startle the world by their haughty brow, and suddenly become millionaires by one invention, but to earn daily bread by patiently doing their duty industriously hour by hour as it arose to their hands. The false picture of the heroic millionaire, born on a dunghill, absolutely illiterate, but yet surpassing in genius all that the most careful cultivation of special talents could effect, has, in our view, done much to produce that dead lethargy of commercial enterprise, and gross ignorance of and contempt for all that science can do in manufacturers, which so disgracefully distinguish the commercial world of Great Britain, as compared with its foreign rivals who are so fast out-stripping her in the race of industry. Whatever may be the case in art or literature, success in productive industry is only attained by hard and skilfully-trained work. It was so in the cases of Arkwright and Stephenson, as well as that of Law and Parr, though success brought wealth to the two first, and partly to the two last, and the sooner our youth learn it, despite the false literary atmosphere of late years thrown around Arkwright and Stephenson, the better.

The demand for woollen rags, both "softs" and "hards," after the invention of mungo, in 1834, by George Parr especially, became an ever-extending one but it is curious that so far as we can trace, it was not first met with from abroad in the shape of raw rag, but in the form of shoddy much superior to which its Yorkshire inventors could make, and it did not come from any of the centres where our trade lay, but from a remote village in Denmark! The origin of this curious fact has only been lately brought to light by a communication made to Mr. F. W. Reuss, of Dewsbury,[51] by the son of the original maker and shipper, Marcus Bech, of Aarhus, in Denmark.[52] Mr. Bech, by some unexplained means, became aware of the manufacture of shoddy in Yorkshire. As Mr. Bech would appear to have been a farmer, he learnt the then obscure fact probably when visiting Yorkshire to purchase horses, many Danes then being engaged in dealing in horses for the Russian market. Let this be how it may, in 1827 he secretly obtained and carried over to Denmark, the constituent parts of a rag-machine, and erected it in a barn at Aarhus, and turned it by horses. The resulting shoddy he shipped off to Hull to the firm of Messrs. Roberts and Trigg,[53] of High Street, who would appear not to have taken it in. It consequently lay there until, in 1830, during the excitement of Brougham's canvass of Yorkshire for a seat in Parliament,[54] three Batley men, whom we have before seen active in the new trade – Joseph Jubb, his son John Jubb[55] (who is our informant), and George Senior[56] – went to Hull to share in the fun of the election. Wandering over the docks, John Jubb was astonished to see a quantity of shoddy on a Danish ship. He examined it, and found it of very superior quality. He at once asked who it was consigned to, and on learning went to their office. Fourpence per lb. was asked for it, and he was told they had another cargo stored in the warehouse. He next mentioned the matter to Mr. Geo. Sykes[57] and his own father, and they three bought about 10,000 lb. weight at 3½d. per lb.; and then, only having about £10 loose cash left in their pockets, for they had not come to trade, so had left their cheque books behind, they agreed to take all the rest, and fixed the bargain with the cash saved in the ½d. per pound they had induced Roberts and Trigg to concede. This was the first drop of foreign supply, and Mr. Marcus Bech succeeded in keeping the secret of his manufacture for many years, and so monopolised the market, no rival appearing to him, either in Denmark or elsewhere, till 1851, when Mr. Gustav Köber, of Manheim, on the Rhein,[58] started both shoddy and mungo making there, but more especially devoting his care to mungo. He procured his machine teeth from Yorkshire, but constructed the rest of it himself, and is said to have improved on the English structure so as to be able to turn out better work; but be this as it may, for there is some dispute as to whether he or another German, named Johann Gross of Oberursal,[59] was the inventor of that appliance to rag-machines known in England as "Rhodes' Cover,"[60] he turned out a very superior mungo, and personally brought over to Batley, in 1851, a cargo of it. It sold rapidly and well, and he appointed Mr. Charles Fitton, of Huddersfield, his agent.[61] This displays a strange fact – that foreign rags reached us first, not as rags, but as very perfectly prepared shoddy and mungo, better than the home make, though in both cases the machinery was obtained from Yorkshire. But the knowledge of the manufacture having travelled to foreign lands faster than a knowledge of the paths leading to the Yorkshire markets, between 1845 and 1850 Continental rag merchants began to consign to British paper-makers parcels of woollen rags along with their former linen ones, with a request that the paper-makers would try to sell them for account in Yorkshire, and so many paper-makers came to add the branch to their own trade. The Parliamentary denunciations of "shoddy" and "devil's-dust," between 1840 and 1850, by the temporarily-noted Mr. Busfeild Ferrand, and the literary onslaught of the late Thomas Carlyle on them, served to bring in an avalanche of the denounced "rags" from all parts of the globe, and to supply the dogged rag-grinders with a bounteous supply of raw material from all parts of the world where English Parliamentary debates and English literature were read. By 1848 the consignment of woollen rags had fully set in from all parts, and has regularly increased, till in 1879–80 we imported of them, for the special purpose of re-manufacture, according to the Board of Trade Returns, a weight of 74,612,160 lb., and this is but a fraction of the total consumption of the trade, as we shall show when we come to estimate its present extent. At the present time France is the chief field of our foreign supply, where we obtain 10,155 tons per annum. Next comes Germany, with 9,435 tons; Belgium, 6,521 tons; Holland, 9,019 tons; Denmark, 1,684 tons; and from all other countries only 1,495 tons, thus proving that a wide field still exists for extension.

As a rule French mungo rags are of good quality, as well as those of Belgium, whilst the shoddy-rags (worsteds) of Holland, Germany, and Denmark are of the highest class, equalling the same kind collected from the populations of our fishing villages and seaports. The United States formerly sent us a large quantity of the best woollens in the market, but have of late years totally ceased, as they now consume all their own make in their rapidly-extending cloth trade, and in addition import from us some 7,000 to 8,000 tons of shoddy and rags yearly. Rags are also brought to us in considerable quantities from Italy, Spain, Austria, and even Turkey and Egypt, and we have had in our warehouse, when the article rose to high prices, old fabrics from the Tartar Steppes of Central Asia, and our Colonies also send us small lots, but of very good quality.

As in the opening of this very curious but now important trade the regular merchants would as soon have thought of forgery as [of] disgracing themselves by touching dirty woollen rags, the would-be exporters were in a difficulty to get their wares to Yorkshire. But a path was opened by the late Mr Pearson, a "bum-bailly"[62] (to use local diction), starting as a general agent for their sale by auction, first at the Canal Wharf of Ravensthorpe, near Dewsbury, and afterwards at Batley Railway Station, as soon as the London and North-Western line opened. The supply of home and foreign rags now increased, and Mr. George Rydill[63] followed, establishing, by personal visits to them, a large connection with continental rag merchants and grinders. Mr. B. Eastwood[64] followed next; and then came the late Mr. Henry Cullingworth, who founded the princely firm of rag and shoddy auctioneers of Henry Cullingworth and Sons,[65] which has become almost synonymous with Dewsbury as the centre of the trade. And Mr. F. W. Reuss should also be recorded as the representative of several of the best foreign firms as an auctioneer.

To go through these or any of our great warehouses or rag-grinderies would yield to reflective minds many lessons, and lead them to reverse not a few doctrines asserted by popular writers on social science. The old rags tell the condition of comfort or want of a population, or classes of it, as truly as a weather-glass records the state of the air. Those rags are Irish – they, along with the Glasgows and Manchesters, are the dirtiest, most worn and wretched, of all sent to us. The heaps of bales filled with thick and sooty rags, but yet not worn to the seams, are from the coal and iron districts. Those clean, large pieced, and moderately worn mungo and soft rags are from London and the agricultural districts, and hold a high place in the estimation of the rag-grinder. They also show that the masses of those parts are, as a rule, in better worldly circumstances then the bulk of the manufacturing workpeople, as proved by the fact of not being driven to wear their clothing so long. But the kings of British woollens are "seaports," as shown by those thick and unpatched stockings, Guernsey and flannel shirts, and indigo jackets and trousers, made to strike our sight by the intermixed scarlet neckties. They are mostly as clean as if washed before selling to the rag-collector, and prove an immense amount of evenly-distributed wealth among their populations, where none would seem very poor, or overloaded with excess of riches. Of foreign rags, Germany and Denmark send us the best; Dutch are also good, something like our "seaports." French woollens are much worn and well mended, showing the industry of the French women, and, but for their greater cleanliness, they apparently come from a population as deeply impoverished as those of Ireland or Glasgow. Turkish and Egyptians are wretched, but Italy tells fairly, and Spain not so bad. To record all varieties, and the sermons they preach, would require a volume.

In our next paper we propose to give a review of the statistics of the manufacture, showing its extent, and the bearing it has had on the commerce of the world, which will then be seen to have been, and to be, far more important than has ever been shown or imagined.

## Statistics. – Present extent of the trade

Having last month related the growth and sources of supply of the shoddy trade, we now proceed to explore the heretofore uninvestigated field of the statistics of the whole shoddy and woollen manufacturers of the United Kingdom, for it is impossible at the present day to separate the one from the other, as no man can tell where the use of shoddy, in some of its various forms, ends in connection with the production of animal fibre textures. The regular estimate of the volume of the British woollen industries is usually given as follows: That they consume, as a total of all kinds of material, 380,000,000 lb. per annum, employing 5,100,000 spindles, though some writers place the spindles at 1,000,000 more in number. But by permission of all previous writers on the subject, we beg to say that our researches into the animal fibrous trades brings us to the conclusion that the figures assigned to them above are absolutely wrong from beginning to end, and that the whole system of analysis by which [they] have been arrived at rests upon imperfect knowledge. The method adopted in handling both the cotton and woollen manufactures has been and is simply that of a school-boy "sum" in simple addition and subtraction – deducting the exports of the raw materials from the imports in either case; except that with wool a further great effort of intellect has been undergone – of adding a rough guess at the weight of British wools retained from exports of them, and supposed to be used at home for textile purposes.

Such a plan of investigation may be perfectly correct and accurate with respect to cotton, which, when once manufactured, ceases absolutely again to be usable by the spindle, and goes to the paper-maker,* and, 60 years ago, would have been equally correct when applied to wool; but since the invention of shoddy and mungo, and their development, it can only lead to most lamentable error; for, as the outcome of them, we have not only fleece wool to carry to account, but skin wool – hair of every variety, from the horse to the hog – and vegetable fibres of various kinds used in the production of mixed fabrics, unions, and warps, as well as shoddies of both home and foreign origin. As the Board of Trade returns give no direct figures bearing on most of these substances, and but very imperfect indirect ones, the research necessitates many tedious journeys through the whole returns of imports and exports and agricultural statistics, from "Living Animals," to "Wool Flocks;" and such extensive figuring and reductions of "yards" and "values" to pounds weight, by estimations arrived at by wearisome calculations from data often hard to find, that, as far as we are aware, no one has hitherto undertaken, whether private statistician or Government official. It is very doubtful, if they had, whether any of them would have possessed sufficient practical knowledge of the modern woollen industries to have enabled them to approach correctness.

Owing, then, to the novelty of the field, we shall be compelled to enter a little into detail to show the methods employed to arrive at our knowledge of its

* We would observe that this statement is not quite accurate. Various descriptions of waste are made in the preparation and spinning of cotton, and that which accrues from spinning one class of yarns is used as raw material for a lower grade, the very sweepings of the floors finally being used for "bump" yarns. In the weaving department the loose waste – such as hand-waste from winding, and "cop-bottoms" from both winding and weaving – are broken up and spun, and woven in to fabrics extensively known as waste cloths, and sometimes called handloom cloths. – Editor *Textile Manufacturer*

production. The period selected, a fair average one, will be the year 1879–80, not representing a time of inflation, but of severe depression in the woollen trades, and therefore not likely to lead to an exaggerated estimate of their extent. Starting with imports of fleece wool, we landed of all sorts and all countries, including sheep's, alpaca, lama, vicuña, and other kinds, 418,505,163 lb. Of British wool fleeces, from 32,237,958 living sheep and lambs in the United Kingdom there was shorn, at an average of 7 lb. each (the usual estimated weight adopted by writers on agriculture), 225,265,666 lb. We imported 9,402,911 sheep and lambs' skins, which at an average of 3 lb. per skin (which weight I adopt, to be under the mark rather than over, for the average weight of Australian sheep and lambs' fleeces is 4 lb. 7 oz., if the Board of Trade agricultural returns and the number of sheep in Australasia, compared with the wool exported thence, are correct), would supply of wool 28,208,733 lb. For slaughter, as food, we imported 944,889 sheep, and though being of European breeds for the most part, they would average, probably, as much wool per head as the British. We will only estimate them then at 3 lb. per fleece, which would give us 2,834,664 lb. in addition to which, the unenumerated skins, from various parts of the world, must be taken into account; but as only the gross money value is given in the returns of the Custom House, we have had to estimate the number by means of the average price of the counted skins, and thus find it to be 1,326,322, which, at 3 lb. each, yields 3,978,966 lb. of wool. In the Metropolitan Cattle Market there were slaughtered of British sheep 807,760, and we were at first somewhat puzzled to ascertain the number of sheep killed for the rest of the kingdom, as the Board of Trade agricultural reports give no information further than the Veterinary Department of the Privy Council's returns for London. At last it occurred to us to find what proportion the inhabitants of the metropolis bore to the total population of these islands, and discovering it to be about one-twelfth, we multiplied the above sheep by 12, and produced a slaughter of "gentle woollies" for food, of 9,693,120, which at the British average per head of 7 lb. of wool, supplies us with another 69,851,840 lb. of fleece wool.

To the above heavy weights of new fibre for our modern woollen manufactures and trades we have now to add hair of various kinds, which, during the last 40 years, has become a very important factor in the production of both heavy and light woollen fabrics. We then, in 1879, imported in bales hair of all kinds to the weight of 20,748,426 lb. Our foreign raw hides numbering 3,085,973, taking 3 lb. for each ox and horse hide (which we believe is under the mark), we received 9,107,499 lb.; of hair on goat and other skins (except sheep and lambs'), amounting to the number 11,288,499, at an average of 3 lb. per head, 33,865,497 lb. more were added to our stores. To these we must add the fibrous coating of British cattle slaughtered for food, whose numbers reached 2,402,520. Taking these at 3 lb. per hide, we obtain a weight of 7,207,560 lb., whilst from foreign bullocks killed for food in Great Britain, to the number of 247,768, there was a yield of 743,304 lb. of hair; and still yet, from horses killed or dying in these islands during that year, and which we will only average for hair at 3 lb. each, though we believe 5½ lb. is nearer the actual weight, there must be put to our sum 2,933,097 lb. further, from

977,699 animals. These, in total, bring us to the nice little weight of raw material, all new, adaptable to the woollen-shoddy trades, of 825,250,100 lb.! Or, to write it in full for stammering statisticians, eight hundred and twenty-five millions, two hundred and fifty thousand, one hundred pounds! Where we will stop and take breath, and take a retrospective glance over our progress thus far.

Having enumerated the list of new raw animal fibres, we now come to those constituting the shoddy family proper, in its various branches. These consist, the reader will excuse us from reminding him, of old or used fabrics restored again to a position for remanufacture. The first article that meets us is the hair-bagging or canvas made from camel, goat, cow, and horse hair, and which reaches us in the shape of wrappage or bags, containing various merchandise from Greece, Turkey, and several parts of Asia, where these materials are plentiful and hemp scarce. As a curious instance of how far the rippling waves of the shoddy trade have already reached, we may mention that we have seen in Dewsbury rag warehouses hand-spun horse hair blankets and worn out tent cloths from Central Tartary, such as Humboldt describes as being used by the Kirgheez.[66] It is not easy to arrive at an accurate estimate of the weight of this hair cloth, as no record of it is kept at the Custom House, it only appearing there as containing other goods; but seeing we import from the land of its origins some 260,000 tons of merchandise, much of which is wrapped in it, we cannot be far wrong in putting down the weight of it at 2,500,000 lb., all of which ultimately comes to the hungry teeth of the shoddy "devil," to be ground up again for various uses of human need or ornament, from hair ropes, to bind the legs of refractory cows during milking, up to sofa cushions, magnificent carpets, and camlet cloths and rugs, to please and adorn vanity, luxury, and beauty.

We have now fairly got again into the highway of rags or pure shoddy materials, along which we shall proceed, and first note 74,612,160 lb. of woollen rags destined for the making of mungo and shoddy, exclusive of those imported for other uses, according to the Customs House returns. And along with these comes another caravan, "creeping along like a giant caterpillar with a million legs" – to use the quaint metaphor of an American writer, the Hon. Mr. Everett[67] – bringing some articles that it may startle the reader to find us adding to the list of contributions to shoddy; but if he will have patience with us he will see in the end how all comes out right. In the van of the march we find an importation of woollen cloths, which we estimate at an average of one pound per yard all round, and so obtain 55,221,000 lb. Then comes woollen yarn, weighing 11,044,820 lb., followed by hair manufactures, to the weight of 1,290,980 lb., which brings us to the end of the foreign supply of animal fibres, as far as we venture to include, or can find any reliable data to ground an estimate upon. For though a large quantity of pigs' or swines' hair is imported, and much of it consumed in the making of rugs, blankets, and carpets, as well as human hair in some classes of goods, yet not being able to procure any data to distinguish bristles from the spinnable portion of the pig's coating, which is all massed together in the Customs' returns, we add no estimate of it to our list.

And now comes the question – What is the weight of British woollen rags entering into the volume of this mighty river of human industry? We asked information of, apparently, well-informed men, who all declared they had never thought of the matter, but furnished us with their "guesses" at the truth. The highest of these "guesses," however, we afterwards discovered was so far below the mark, that from confidential information subsequently given us from parties personally engaged in the woollen rag trade in Dewsbury themselves, it did not equal the weight sold per annum by more than one single firm there. This decidedly convinced us that "guessing" was totally useless, so we set to our old plan of collecting a mass of isolated facts, and by analytical calculations, trying to arrive at the general result of them. To begin with the metropolis of the trade, the parliamentary borough of Dewsbury, which includes that of Batley, the weight of rags brought in by the railways and canals yearly is 153,216,000 lb. as nearly as we can obtain grounds for an estimate, which we are obliged to do by ascertaining the number of loads passing out of the railways and wharves during a given time, and noting thereof woollen rags from other sorts of traffic. We were driven to this troublesome and imperfect method by the fact that the railway directorates, to all of whom we applied for definite statistics, which no doubt they could easily have supplied, one and all absolutely refused to give the slightest information, and also, it would appear, to have prohibited their local managers from furnishing even for their own district. As Dewsbury is only one amongst some 84 towns and villages in Yorkshire, avowedly engaged in the shoddy manufacture, and they are only one of the British districts engaged in the cloth trade, all of which, whether of the finest or coarsest qualities, are now mixed with shoddy, as also, as we shall show, are all woollen textures of foreign make as well, we concluded the business was larger as a total than even we had before estimated. Failing, then, to obtain a summarised view of the national trade in woollen rags by aid of the managers of the national carrying trades, we proceeded as follows: We collected together, from the Board of Trade returns, the whole of the woollen and mixed fabrics exported, as well as woollen and worsted yarns and raw wool and rags, and, reducing the whole to pounds weight, deducted them from the gross of all the raw materials, to discover what was retained for home consumption by our own population. We found the proximate weight of the above portion dealt with by the merchanting branches of the woollen-shoddy trades to reach 417,217,912 lb., whilst the gross weight of raw material dealt with by them, and the manufacturing branches was 2,182,666,886 lb., thus leaving 1,775,448,974 lb. for home consumption by the population of the United Kingdom every year.[†] Here it will be seen we have had to bring forward reference to our total result, before we have placed all the factors of it

† We suspect that a considerable allowance ought to be made here for dirt, short stuff, and other matters accruing from the reduction of the materials to a fibrous condition, and which material will be absolutely unusable excepting for manure. – Editor, *Textile Manufacturer*

before the reader; but for the purpose of necessary condensation in our limited space it is unavoidable. If of this weight we set aside 50 per cent. as absolutely destroyed in the wearing, or lost in the collection of rags (which is a very large allowance, considering how carefully every scrap of woollen is gathered up), and allow still further a weight of 82,710,905 lb., for metal buttons and linings on the collected rags, which is about 10 per cent., being the average we used to discover when in the woollen rag trade, we find the British woollens collected in a condition capable of making shoddies and mungoes of various kinds to be 805,013,582 lb.! And now to demonstrate how, we must return to our researches into the raw sources of these fabrics, so that our astounding figures may not seem to rest on mere assertion. As we before noted, in addition to the mass of new raw wools and hairs used in the woollen-shoddy manufacture, a large number of vegetable fibres had been adopted as mixtures, which are the pure offspring of shoddy.

I will take, first of these, China grass, or Rhea fibre,[68] in the introduction of which we ourselves had a considerable share between the years 1860 and 1864. It is used as a mixture with mohair, alpaca, worsted, and lustre fabrics, and with high-class blankets and flannels, to which it gives a snowy, pearly appearance. As near as we can ascertain, about 4,480,000 lb. are so consumed, but some authorities would place it much higher. Then cotton has to be accounted for, and on the authority of fully competent factory managers, acquainted not only with the Yorkshire working, but that of Scotland, Leicester, Lancashire, and the West of England, as well as the knowledge we ourselves possess of the proportions entering into the mixtures or blends for tweed and hosiery and dress yarns, and the weight as cotton warps, we cannot calculate it at less than one-third of the weight of the wool, hair, and shoddy consumed. One of our most experienced informants even lays his calculation at fully one-half all around; but we shall take the lower estimate, which gives us 390,314,544 lb. to be taken from the annual supply of the cotton and consumed by the woollen trades. Besides, we have to take jute used in combination with the animal fibre in the carpet and rug manufactures, and in warps for them. From the best data we can obtain, the weight is about 20,919,600 lb. of that and its cognate fibres, hemp and flax, also used for the same purpose, and the whole sum total of new and old animal and vegetable fibres used in the modern British woollen industry is found to reach the almost incredible weight of 2,182,666,866 lb. of raw material, from which must be deducted the weight of wool, hair, rags, and shoddy exported in the raw state, amounting to 270,468,232 lb., which leaves 1,922,197,206 lb. of fibre yearly for our wool spindles to lick up! Of this, 140,749,680 lb. are exported in the shape of fabrics and yarns, and 1,775,448,947 lb. are retained for home consumption.

Perhaps our readers will cry, "It is impossible!" but in spite of that we would this month give, what schoolboys call the "cross proof of the sum," but for want of space, as in spite of every effort at condensation, we cannot compress all the statistics into this article, but hope to do so in our next.

## Statistics (continued) and products

Our last article closed with a summary of the gross totals of the woollen and shoddy raw materials, making the weight dealt with by the British woollen industries in 1879–80 to approximate 2,182,666,886 lb., and showing that the weight retained at home for the production of yarn, fabrics, and other goods, into which woollen and hair fibres enter, was 1,922,197,206 lb. As these totals are so astonishingly different to those popularly current on this subject, we now proceed, as promised, to furnish corroborative evidence in support of their general accuracy. Our first step will be to examine them by the investigation of the number of spindles devoted to the manufactures, and the possible quantity of work they can turn off in a year, estimating nothing for what they might do if run overtime. According to our Government returns – which, however, are clearly not so accurate as we could wish, for a large number of mills engaged, to our personal knowledge, in the mixed woollen manufactures are placed in the "cotton spindles" list – there are 5,500,000 absolutely engaged in wool spinning. The reader will please to recollect in "wool" we include all animal fibres and their admixtures. For the reason just stated, this return is certainly far below the actual fact, but as we have no Minister of Commerce to attend to the accuracy of our industrial reports, and to see the facts properly marshalled, we must take the statement as we find it, for we can procure no better tool to dig up our "hidden treasure" than this broken shovel supplied by the Board of Trade. As we were not willing to trust to our own personal knowledge in the spinning of Angola, Leicester, and Scotch yarns, as a sufficiently wide basis to serve for a calculation of all the branches of the trade, we have availed ourselves of the assistance of widely-experienced men to reach a safe standing ground. Two of the best-informed factory managers in the Dewsbury district, men acquainted with other than our Yorkshire work, give the following as the average out-turn per 275 spindles for a week, taking the average size of yarns, from the finest to the coarsest, and the different sorts of material: Of shoddy yarns, about 10 packs per week: mungo yarns, 6 to 8 packs; hair mixtures, 10 packs; and pure fleece wool, 12 packs. A "pack" is a woollen spinner's weight of 240 lb. (English), and as the above figures are equivalent to 9½ packs of material a week for each set of 275 spindles, it gives us about 1 lb. 6$^1/_9$ oz. a day of yarn for every spindle's out-turn. Mr. John Jubb, J. P., of Lamplands House, Batley, one of the patriarchs and merchant princes of the woollen shoddy manufacture, as we have previously related, has confirmed to us the average accuracy of this amount of yarn per 275 spindles, and we could not have a more competent authority.

Taking this, then, as a starting point, we will, to avoid exaggeration, write off the 6$^1/_9$ oz. per spindle, to cover stoppages of all kinds, and assume 1 lb. per day as the possible product. In a year we must deduct 52 days for Sundays, and 13 for holidays devoted by our operatives to recreation, thus leaving 300 for work; and then multiplying the product of one day, 5,500,000 lb., by 300 we find 1,650,000,000 lb. of yarn as the outcome of the annual labour of our 5,500,000 wool spindles, which leaves of the total weight of raw materials to represent vegetable warps and woollen felted fabrics 272,197,206 lb., of which amount, on the best data we can procure, may be estimated 200,000,000 lb., goes for cotton, jute, flax, and hemp warps, and the remaining 72,197,206 lb. for felted goods, which latter class ranges from steam-pipe casings and hats to exquisite articles of ladies' dress.

Another gauge may be taken from the Government Factory Returns, which inform us that 5,079 operatives, male and female, are employed in "shoddy factories" – that is, in works for the production of mungo and shoddy, though we are not informed whether this includes hands employed at rag devils in mills devoted to the making of cloths and worsted goods, a large number of which have rag or waste machines on the premises to supply part of the shoddies they use. We will presume that this is the case, though the returns relating to our domestic industries, and especially to our woollen trades, are so confused, and so charily collected and edited by men not conversant with them, that we cannot be sure. However, as it requires three attendants to superintend two rag machines, 5,079 would represent 3,386 rag devils, each of which will produce on an average of pulled stuffs, shoddies, or mungoes, etc., 900 lb. per day, and taking 300 days as the working year, we arrive at 914,220,000 lb. of material, which is not far from the weight of 805,013,582 lb. that we had, by a perfectly independent line of investigation, been led in our last article to believe the British woollen rags collected for re-manufacture amounted to. When we add to it the 74,612,160 lb. of imported rags, the difference being no more than might be expected in estimating from such data as are alone procurable in so new and unexplored a field, especially as we have made no attempt to carry forward our different lines of research simultaneously, but have followed each one independent of the others, for fear of an unintentional "cooking of the account."

We had got so far when a thought occurred to us that the above technical analysis could only be fully understood as to accuracy or incorrectness by those engaged in the trades, and that the general public could only estimate by a rule being in every man's house. That rule, then, should be the comparative weights of cotton and woollen clothing each person carries at any moment. Strip and weigh, sir, if you would learn. After that, becoming an enthusiast for statistics, weigh all your carpets, rugs, mats, blankets, curtains, chair covers, coach linings, railway trimmings, linings, and paddings, against all the cotton goods about your premises, and you will find from your back to your cart saddle the average will be three of woollen or hair goods to one of cotton. Now we find, after deducting from the gross weight of raw cotton imported, which in 1879–80 was 1,469,338,464 lb., the weight of the raw staple and manufactured cotton goods exported, and the amount of cotton taken for subsidiary use by our woollen manufactures, there was left for consumption as cotton fabrics by the population of the United Kingdom 620,239,225 lb. At the period we are considering the people of Great Britain and Ireland were estimated by the Registrar-General to be 34,155,126. This would give an average consumption of cotton goods per head of 18 lb. 3 oz. per annum, whilst our estimate of the raw material of the woollen trades retained for home use, after deducting, as in cotton, all raw material and manufactured products or wool exported is, as above shown, 1,075,448,974 lb., which equals about 51 lb.

15¾ oz. of woollens per head of all sorts and for all uses, from bed-flocks to hats, from coats to carpets, and clothing for man, beast, and furniture; and if you made a "rule of three" sum for your boy out of the factory – cotton 18 lb. 3 oz., and woollens 51 lb. 15¾ oz – he will not be long in telling you it is about three of wool to one of cotton.

The conclusion, therefore, that is forced upon us by the above figures, defective in some points as they must unavoidably be, is that the woollen manufactures and trades are, at the present moment, by far the most extensive and important of British industries, and worthy of much more attention, both from statesmen and statisticians, than they have of late years been considered. During the period when shoddy was struggling into existence, from 1813 to 1825, the wool manufactures of England were diminishing, as proved by the statistics of that time as we shall hereafter show, and cotton weaving for the Lancashire spinners, who had not then adopted Cartwright's grand invention of the power-loom,[69] had become the prevailing industry of the West Riding. In 1825, as we have stated in a former article, the influence of shoddy began to appear in the volume of the woollen trades, and from then to 1840 the tide gradually turned, and Yorkshire and Scotland returned to their ancestral industry. The invention of mungo enabled manufactures to turn out cloths of a beauty of finish, effect, and style surpassing any that wool had ever before furnished to human skill, and at the same time those fabrics were warmer, cheaper, and as lasting as the less attractive ones formerly made from pure fleeces. This may be denied by some persons, but we have had the privilege of inspecting an ancient splendid gold-laced scarlet child's baptismal robe, of the time of Queen Anne, preserved carefully by one of our old county families, owing to a traditional connection of the robe with that monarch and an ancestor, and though doubtless made of the very best cloth then procurable, its finish and texture do not equal a mungoed broad-cloth of our ordinary draper's shop at 5s. per yard.

During the last forty years, from 1840, however, the woollen manufactures have, by dogged and silent progress, been advancing on cotton, till they again occupy the pre-eminent position in our commercial world that they did under the reigns of the Plantagenets and Tudors; and considering that the greater part of the raw material they consume is the produce of the three kingdoms, and nearly the whole of the remainder the growth of our colonial possessions, the trade, as a source of national and imperial wealth, must be very fruitful, for nearly every penny of the enormous value of its raw material, the working of it, and the finished goods, is or has been what we may call "spendable income" to our own people, whilst a manufacture whose raw material is mainly furnished from foreign sources would be only half as productive of the means of comfort and happiness to our fellow-countrymen.

## Productions of woollen shoddy

"What are the products of shoddy and mungo?" was a question once put to us in the presence of that great moral philosopher Smell Fungus.[70] Before we could reply he epitomised them in an epigram: "Productions, sir?" he exclaimed. "Nothing but nasty, rotten, stinking rubbish, that sticks to your fingers and falls to pieces as you handle the blotting-paper-like stuff that rascally manufacturers palm off on the gullible and swindled public as cloth – actually as cloth, sir! I wouldn't, myself, touch a bit of it (except with a pair of tongs, to fling the cloth on the fire back). Every inch of it stinks of the dunghill, so that it turns one sick – fact, sir!" But his belauding audience laughed on t'other side when he pointed out that the indignant philosopher was swathed from head to foot in superfine broad-cloth of mungo origin, and that everyone of themselves was wrapped – from flannel shirt to tweed trousers, or the latest variety of ulster – in shoddy products, and the whole of the elegantly-attired ladies and artistically-dressed children around them were clothed in various mixtures of shoddy (woollen and silken – for we have silken shoddy as well as woollen), with requisite proportions of new fibre, from hat to sleeve linings. "Not," cried Smell Fungus, "those who, to escape your rascally British fabrics, only use foreign ones!" "Pardon us," we replied; "but allow us to state a fact – that French, Spanish, Italian, German, American, and Belgian manufacturers now use shoddies and mungoes as extensively as our own, and not only use up the major portion of their own rags, but are becoming, especially the United States and France, very serious competitors for British ones at our regular rag auctions. Nay, more, species of shoddy and mungo, so poor that our Yorkshire and Scotch manufacturers consider unusable, are sent to France and Belgium, and return from Roubaix and Louvain to us in the form of cloths as fine as silk to the eye, and like velvet to the hand, the skill of their operatives in many departments far surpassing ours. We know these things," we added, "from having personally supplied the articles for export to these transmarine districts." Smell Fungus was silenced.

It would require a volume to go into details of the different fabrics into which shoddy and mungo enter, but as a general statement we may say that the whole of that extensive class called "long cloths" and "tweeds" were purely originated by and from them, as well as the modern styles of "costume cloths" for ladies' garments, and they enter, without exception, into every species of woollen or hair fabric made, in varying proportions, from all shoddy or mungo to small mixings, to secure a finer surface to the fabrics than raw wool used alone can give; for it is necessary to note that in soft woollen fabrics of the flannel and blanket kind shoddy gives a closer, warmer substance, and softer and more fleecy surface or "nap," as it is technically called, than wool alone does; and mungo mixed produces on broad-cloths and the tweed class of tissues a better and more beautiful face than all-fleece can be made to show, and at the same time the cloths, if properly milled and worked, are quite as lasting and strong, as any one can prove who will go to the Welsh hills and procure cottage-spun and woven all-fleece cloth, and wear it against a good English shoddy-made article, as we have done; and in addition, the English tweed will be handsome to the eye, and the Welsh cottage cloth, from its want of surface, will raise an idea of eccentricity in the wearer. Nay, the best kinds of shoddy and mungo rags actually fetch a higher price in the open market than fleece-wool of equal quality at the London public sales. The latest market quotation there for super woollen rags we have seen ranging from £120 to £150 per ton, which is more than the late figures of Australian wool fleeces, and we may be sure that shrewd men of business would not give more for the rag if it did not make a better fabric – improving the wool by admixture. And as a fact, in the shape of certain shoddies for the highest classes of costume and fancy fabrics of the Huddersfield and West of England makes, fully 50 per cent. more per pound is given for them than was given for the wool portion of the cloths. Still further, though we are afraid to state it for fear of disbelief, we have seen an exceedingly fine kind of mungo made in Germany which is sold in England for decorative purposes at 13s. per lb., and the maker of it told us it was now very extensively made and used in the United States for the same purposes. But we trust we have recorded sufficient to explode the literary cant heretofore current as to what shoddy and mungo (or devil's dust) are, and to show them as constituting the most important industry of the modern civilized world; and there only now remains for us to present to our readers "The Results of Shoddy on the Commerce of the World," which we propose to do as the conclusion of our sketch of its results on British industry. This portion of our task we shall follow on a strictly statistical method, displaying the expansion, through shoddy, of the wool growing and manufacturing trades of the globe from 1813 to 1880, and noting also the social and international outcome of it.

## Results of shoddy on the commerce of the world

During the course of our narrative very many of the results of the discovery of shoddy have been apparent to the reader on the surface of the recorded facts, but by no means all of them, for some of the widest and most permanent results are not standing at our doors in Batley and Dewsbury, or even in the United Kingdom itself, but are only disclosed by a wide study of contemporary history and a scientific investigation of the trade development of the past seventy years. In 1813 to 1820, when shoddy in the hands of Law and Parr was struggling for life, we have seen Dewsbury-Batley and the whole neighbourhood peopled by a few poor agricultural hand-spinners and weavers, whose looms were, even with the most wealthy of them, placed in the one-story cottages in which they dwelt, to be turned to when rain or the winter prevented working in the fields, and, in the case of the larger peasant-weavers, in the chambers, or "lofts" as they were locally called, above them. Few seem, as the old men still surviving have told us, to have possessed more than one hand-loom, and he was considered a "big man" who had more. To be able to turn out weekly as much cloth of any sort as the "maister" – that is, husband – could carry on his shoulder to Leeds market was considered a thriving business; and we have heard a gentleman, who before his death, not very long ago, had become the most extensive manufacturer in his line in the world, relate an anecdote of having carried his shoulder-load of druggets to Leeds; and the piece having especially pleased the merchant, he was asked, "Couldn't you make two pieces more like that against next week?" He was able triumphantly to reply, "Ay, lad, for I've gotten another at home that only wants 'fellin' (cutting out of the loom), so I'll be off at once and fetch it for ta-neet," and according to his word he did so, and returned with it into his merchant's warehouse at five o'clock in the evening. This was the first time, he used to add, that any Heckmondwike weaver had ever delivered two pieces in one week to his merchant, unless when bad times had forced him to accumulate stock. Tarry wool,[71] as we have been told by a gentleman of the Jubb family now deceased, was about the only sort used locally, and when a manufacturer wanted a supply he did not, as now, proceed to the "wool sales" to lay in a cargo or two, but the Wakefield carrier was waited on, and 50s., being the largest amount of capital the majority were able to dispose of at once, was handed to him with a request that he would bring "a pack o' tarry" (240 lb.) back from that agricultural centre. In Dewsbury-Batley only one small shed existed to spin for the weavers, not larger than the dimensions of a moderate-sized house of our luxurious days, and the power was chiefly supplied by mules or asses, aided by an old bucket steam engine of Savary's make[72] that had been once used at the coalpit. All the weaving was done by hand and the principal part of the carding and spinning also by hand-cards and spinning-wheels. And as it was in Yorkshire, so it was over the whole kingdom. But even poor as this state of the woollen trade was, it became yearly worse, and in Yorkshire and all the north cotton weaving was superseding it, the crowded poorhouses even being engaged in cotton work for Lancashire, as the demand for wool-weaving had practically ceased.

These illustrations will serve to show, as well as a hundred, the condition of the woollen trade when Law and Parr, in 1813 introduced shoddy as a constituent of woollen fabrics, and in a similarly depressed state they continued, though with gradually a brightening hope, till in 1825 the new material first began to tell sensibly on the volume of this industry, as revealed by public statistics. To them the invention was ultimate ruin – a tragical story; but the result of sixty-seven years' growth of their mental child has transformed Batley into a forest of factories to the aggregate of sixty, and collected in the bounds of the Parliamentary borough of Dewsbury, of which it forms a part, a population of nearly 100,000 depending on some 150 mills or blocks of manufacturing works containing spindles by the million, and driven by an aggregate of thousands of steam horse power, and turning out every five minutes of the day a greater quantity of work than all the place did in a month sixty years ago. Dewsbury, which now names the district, did not enter on the race till 1820, in which year the late Mr. Halliley first tried shoddy there, as we have previously shown, but has progressed so rapidly in it as to transform the then little agricultural-weaving village into being now one of the best-known manufacturing centres of the world, and the head of the modern British woollen trade – a result so astounding to the people of Dewsbury-Batley that they have not yet practically realised the fact that they are of as much importance to mankind as Manchester is, and have ceased to be villages. At the present moment, there are in that borough, as near as we can learn, 350 firms directly engaged in the woollen-shoddy trades, to say nothing of the number of subsidiary trades whose existence depends straight upon them. If we add to these the absolute offspring of shoddy and mungo, the whole of the Yorkshire trade, to say nothing of the rest of the country, we attain to about 2,500 firms, every one of which, in one form or other, uses mungo, shoddy, or their congeners as the basis of its prosperity; and extending our view through England, Scotland, and Wales, to omit for the present Ireland, we find on the best data that 3,948 firms are directly engaged as woollen manufacturers in the gigantic industry we are investigating, to set aside the dyers, machine-makers, and merchants, who reach to 1,430 firms, exclusive of yarn agents, whom we omit, as we are not able clearly to select the purely woollen from the cotton yarn agents by any of the returns we have consulted. We find, then, that 5,398 firms[73] in Great Britain alone are directly connected with the manufacture of woollen-shoddy in the branches of woollen, worsted, and mixed fabrics, as against 2,500 capitalists engaged in the cotton, which latter is the number given by the best Lancashire statisticians for that industry throughout the three kingdoms; and, adding 51 firms for Ireland, the woollen trades showed, in 1879–80, 5,449 firms immediately engaged in them in the British Isles, employing fully half a million of workpeople, 202,711 of whom are working in the West Riding alone, to count nothing for the subsidiary trades.

On the mass of the nation the effect has been as visible as that resulting, in a manufacturing point of view, in the woollen districts. We can remember, when boys, forty years ago, that the use of woollen clothing was almost totally confined to the adults of the propertied and professional classes, and was not by any means universal with them, except on stated occasions; and their sons, whilst in the school-boy stage, were dressed in cotton cords, fustian, or linen fabrics. The working classes were universally clothed in vegetable textures, and seldom had more woollen about them than their stockings at any time. A good broadcloth cost 30s. a yard, and for 20s. only inferior sorts could be bought retail, and were always suspected to have a mixture of “devil’s dust,” which was then beginning to make a noise in the worlds of trade, literature, and politics, as the curious may learn by reading Thomas Carlyle’s “Latter-day Pamphlets,”[74] Busfeild Ferrand’s “Speeches In and Out of Parliament,”[75] and the decision of the War Office not to allow “shoddy” to be used in Army goods, the consequence of which was that until that decision was rescinded the British soldier was habited in the very worst fabrics made, such as are now only equalled by those supplied to the Turkish forces from our looms; but now, by reason of good mungo and shoddy being admitted into them, our men are wrapped in the warmest, best, and strongest regimentals to be found on earth. In spite of opposition and a great amount of ridicule, and with the prospect of wealth and plenty before them, in place of poverty and want, our north-country lads went on, till we now see almost the whole of our population regularly clothed in woollen garments, and, to be so habited, has become to be considered the sign of civilisation throughout the world. That this revolution in fabrics has been a beneficent one there can be no doubt, for it is the general opinion of physicians that animal substances are far healthier than tissues made of vegetable material for clothing.

As we have remarked, shoddy first popularised the use of woollen fabrics in modern times, and, indeed, nothing else could have made it possible for wool to become the clothing of the masses in competition with cotton. It was invented, as before shown, in 1813; but to secure equal ten-year periods of statistics for noting its progress we will start with the state of the woollen trade in 1810. That year we imported from all quarters only 10,914,137 lb., about 6,000,000 lb. of which came from Spain, then our chief source; 900,000 lb. from Germany; whilst the Cape sent us but a handful of 29,717 lb., and Australia one single bag of 167 lb. weight, and our home production of fleeces being limited to 86,000,000 lb., or a total for the whole volume of the trade of 96,914,137 lb. But at the end of the decade the statistics prove, as we before related, that the British manufactures in this material were gradually dying out, and in consequence the imports of wool in 1820 had decreased by over one million pounds weight, falling to 9,775,605 lb., or over 10 per cent.; and our exports of manufactured articles, which in 1810 were to the value of £5,773,000, had declined to £5,586,000, and, notwithstanding the rapid increase of the national population, the home consumption also appears to have receded.

Law and Parr, during seven years of this period, had been fighting a losing battle in their unaided endeavour to carry out their invention of shoddy cloth. This was inevitable, for shoddy had to make its fields of supply before it could fully display its capacity of production by gradually cheapening cloths so as to promote their use, and so, by calling for larger supplies of new fleece wool for admixture, to induce the breeding of sheep for the sale of their fleeces alone,[76] and by a reflex action cause the existence of a larger yearly outcast of rags over the world as well, to be collected also for grinding into itself. This operation was necessarily slow. The material was unknown, except in the little village of Batley, and was there only a theme for rough satire; but in 1818 four of Law's neighbours – the late Joseph Jubb, J. and P. Fox, George Newsome, and John Burnley – united their resources to make and start a rag-devil, and being satisfied by the result that there was something in shoddy, in 1822, as before detailed, opened, in conjunction with others, Hick Lane Mill, Batley. Joseph Jubb was, I believe, the master-spirit of the enterprise, from the fact that his son John, who still survives, was the one who wove the first piece of cloth made in the mill and let down the first stock-foot (milling machine) that fell in the finishing department. That was the moment of the restoration of the British woollen manufacture, and shoddy was fairly afloat. The effect was a rapid development. By 1825 our importation of wool had run up nearly 500 per cent., being 43,816,966 lb., against 9,775,605 lb. in 1820; whilst our native growth of fleeces had increased by about 14,000,000 lb., and the import of wool from Australia had advanced from under 200 lb. in 1813 to 323,995 lb. in 1825, though the Cape had stood still. The revolt of the American colonies of Spain no doubt also aided in no small degree the development of the trade, as the loans they one and all raised on the London Stock Exchange were made in great part payable in manufactured goods, of which blankets and army cloths formed a large proportion; but the fact that exports did not increase in anything like the ratio of raw material shows that the benefit of a cheapened supply of warm clothing reached our own people first. The next ten years was a period of steady development, shoddy and mungo became recognised articles in the trade, and the price of articles into which they could enter gradually declined and the use extended. The altered character of Yorkshire cloths exported was quickly noted by our customers abroad, not, as the cynic may suppose, as being worse, but better than formerly, according to the opinion of our foreign customers. The cause of this was unknown to them, but the fabrics of certain firms were observed to be of a closer and thicker substance, warmer and less penetrable by atmospheric influences. Inquiries, as old men who remember this period have told us, were poured in upon our export merchants for "cloths close and thick in the milling, and well filled," as, said our transmarine correspondents, they could not sell the old open, spongy makes, "but must have a better kind, like the enclosed," the "enclosed" being a sample of shoddy or mungo mixed goods. Many makers, who, in spite of this, stuck tight to pure fleece wool, lost the trade; others, especially some leading firms in Leeds, only saved themselves at the last moment from destruction by an energetic resolve to let prejudice go by the board and to fall in with the new industry. The fame of the movement and its cause soon reached Europe, and in 1830 foreign shoddy was sent us first from Denmark, and in 1834 the ultimate triumph of the modern woollen manufactures was decided by the invention of mungo by the younger Parr, as before detailed. From that date till within the last three years or so the onward movement has been unchecked. By 1840 our wool imports had grown to 50,425,541 lb., and our home fleeces to an increase of 10,000,000 lb. over 1830, the weight of new wools dealt with by the trade in that year (1840) being 170,425,541 lb., or about twice the weight of 1810, exclusive of shoddy and mungo. But as mungo was then (1840) only just beginning to reach the practical stage, and as yet had made no observable impression on the volume of the trade, we may exclude it, and then can only estimate the shoddy worked up as equal to twice the weight of raw wool, or 340,851,082 lb., which makes the total turn-over for that year 511,276,623 lb., or a growth of more than 500 per cent. from 1810. Yet, great as that was, it is a fact that the whole of this increased production had quite been absorbed by the home consumption of our own population in the three kingdoms, for our average exports had been at a positive standstill, the Board of Trade returns for 1810 reaching, for exports of wool and woollen manufactures, £5,773,000, and for 1840 only £5,780,810. These extraordinary facts have never previously, we believe, been brought before the public.

In the next decade, from 1840–50, mungo began to tell heavily on the volume of the industry, and, as a consequence, the demand for Australian and Cape wools, which are especially adapted for admixture with it, enormously increased, the imports of the first having expanded from 9,721,248 lb. to 39,018,221 lb., and the latter from 751,741 lb. to 5,709,529 lb. – a rate of commercial progress unprecedented for any ten years in the history of the world of which we possess any record. The export trade now also, for the first time, showed decisive expansion, owing to the beautiful broadcloths and tweeds which mungo enabled our manufacturers to turn out. It doubled in value, and in 1850 the exports read £10,040,332, against the £5,780,810 of 1840. The great exhibition of 1851, by displaying to the world the immeasurable superiority of British woollen goods to all competitors, added a great impetus to the industry; and the addition of the discovery of spinning hair, made shortly before by the late Mr. Edwin Firth, of Heckmondwike,[77] brought in another element, which has been extending ever since, so that by 1860 the manufacture had at least doubled itself, as shown by the increased importations and home growth of wool, hair, rags, and foreign-made shoddies and mungos, which now began to be extensive. Australia and the Cape were no longer able to present sufficient fleeces for mixture, though the one added 50 per cent. to her production and the other 300 per cent. The River Plate, Peru, Chili, Patagonia, the deserts of North Africa, Egypt, Arabia, Syria, the Tartar Steppes of the Black Sea and the Caspian, the snow-clad hills of the Caucasus, Persia, India, Russia, far-off China, and New Zealand began to pour in an ever-increasing volume of wool, hair, rags, and fibres, from the softest lamb's wool to the pig's hair of the Celestial Empire, to supply a demand that grew by what it fed on. By 1870 the trade had again doubled, and in the next ten years (1879–80) had redoubled itself once more, or rather, to speak correctly, in the first eight of that ten, and then in 1877–8 came a check, from which we are still suffering, though this check, we believe, is rather one of a cessation of development than one of retrogression, though the transfer of our leading capitalists to Germany and the States is ominous.

But an increase of commercial wealth to Great Britain has not been the only result of shoddy and mungo: the distribution of mankind has been determined by their demand for animal fibres. The lands around the Mediterranean Sea – of old the seats of mighty and civilised empires, but which had all, both on its northern and southern shores, sunk into decay and barbarism – have by their demand been brought again within the area of civilization. The deserts of Southern Asia have been roused from their solitude, and their peoples wakened from mental and social death by the demand for wool, their sole produce. South Africa has been impelled to a continual extension of her territories, so as to supply more and more pasturage for her increasing flocks, till on the north she touches the Limpopo River, and will soon reach the Zambezi, and unfold the flag of Britain as the emblem of civilization, freedom, and Christianity for the dusky millions of Central Africa. On the advent of that right arm of civilisation, the modern British woollen trade, Australia was, by the mass of Englishmen, regarded as a land of mythic horrors, fit only for the dwellings of the most hardened criminals; but now, by the demands of mungo and shoddy for wool, Australia has become known to men as a noble land for the growth of empires, a vast extension of Anglo-Saxon faith and enterprise, whose fertile tracts are luxuriantly cultivated, and her seemingly waterless regions pierced with wells, and covered by flocks of the finest sheep on the face of the earth, and all this has been done without any accursed slave trade supplying its miserable cargoes of men as the instruments of this great advance of commerce. Unlike sugar and cotton, it has caused none of God's creatures to cower in dread "before the voice of the driver,"[78] and no "captive" has for it "wished for death to be free from his master." All it has done has been the work of the hands of free men, obeying the divine orders "to take up the fragments that nothing be lost," and "to replenish the earth and fill it,"[79] that its produce may make glad the hearts of themselves and their fellow-men in peace and plenty. "How has shoddy done this?" our readers may ask. "Is it not the work of colonisation?" Only as a secondary result; for had not shoddy and wool, like man and wife, been mutually reproducing each other in a continually-increasing ratio, and so made the settlement of sandy regions more profitable than cultivable ones, colonisation would never have flowed to them. But more even than this. To the shoddy manufactures were practically due the destruction of slavery in the United States by supplying clothing in substitution for cotton during their Civil War, and so keeping the civilised world from interfering to preserve slavery to supply its necessities and comfort; for had not the capacity of rapid extension possessed by it and mungo then clothed men and supplied work to labour, universal bankruptcy would have followed, and the European governments have been driven to crush the North by their starving multitudes.

Though our own Government and statisticians have been and are blind to the value of this great industry, foreign ones are clear-sighted enough as to see it, and Germany, France, but above all the United States, are making strenuous efforts to induce its removal to their territories by offering the bounties of high protective duties to our manufacturers who settle there, and, in fact, all our firms not absolutely pinned to the spot by mortgages are going, or preparing to go, to one or other of them. To give a list would be invidious, but if done it would be startling, and furnish matter for grave reflection as to the future of our manufactures.

## Notes

1 William Busfeild Ferrand (1809–1889), in a widely reported Parliamentary statement of 24 February 1842, denounced cheapened manufactures as a cause of decline in trade. He claimed that the term 'devil's dust' was one given by the Yorkshire workers themselves.

2 Benjamin Parr (1781–1829).

3 Benjamin Law (1772–1837), of Batley.

4 John Moore (1761–1809), British army general, took command of British forces in Portugal in October 1808 for the planned march to Spain.

5 More commonly known as a 'clobberer', this was the trade of reviving old clothing for re-sale.

6 Original spelling retained.

7 Moses, Son and Davis was formed by Samuel Moses (1810–1883) and Elias Davis (1809–1883). Each had married a sister of the other in 1832, so were closely bound by family as well as business ties. The firm was described as wholesale clothiers in 1846,

offering ready-made clothing. By 1854, they had expanded into production of rubber coated fabrics, and supplied waterproof blankets that year for soldiers in the Crimea. The partnership was dissolved and both men retired from business in 1878.

Elias Davis's father was Israel Davis (c1771–1831). From the birthplaces of his children, Davis appears to have moved from Swansea to Woolwich between 1806 and 1807. Elias Davis wrote a letter to the editor of the *Textile Manufacturer* in June 1881, denying that he was the anecdotist of the commercial room, but Fenton defended his claim that the elder Davis was involved in the origins of shoddy (*Textile Manufacturer*, 7:79, 15 Jul 1881, p. 249).

8 No London saddler named Littlewood has been located. An approximate match for the story is James Little, an upholsterer at 47 Mortimer Street near Cavendish Square, who was active between 1802 and 1839.

9 The previous parliament of 1463 had banned the mixing of flocks with wool, and the Devonshire clothiers sought exemption claiming that the wool they used required blending to obtain an acceptable quality of cloth.

10 Benjamin Parr the younger (1810–1898), wool manufacturer.

11 John Law (1820–1885), architect, son of George Law (1792–1864).

12 Reuben Wade (1806–1883), wool card dealer.

13 A hand-held device with saw-like teeth for grooming horses.

14 Joseph Archer (1767–1849), machine maker.

15 Jonas Haley (c1791–1864), machine maker.

16 John Fenton (1811–1873).

17 John Fenton founded the firm with his eldest son Thomas Wright Fenton (1832–1904).

18 Joseph Jubb (1784–1867); the brothers John Fox (1786–1850) and Phineas Fox (b. 1789); George Newsome (1803–1867), rag merchant; and John Burnley (c1779–1836).

19 Joseph Gibson (born around 1781) enumerated in the 1841 census of Cleckheaton as a machine maker.

20 William Henry Fenton (born around 1820), married in Waltham, Lincolnshire in 1841, and had a son Joseph Barnes Fenton (1843–1903) who died in South Africa.

21 The Berlin Decree of 21 November 1806 cut off Yorkshire's key markets in the North Sea and Baltic ports.

22 Joseph Jubb (1784–1867) and Michael Spedding (1786–1856).

23 Meaning pressed hard.

24 John Law (1801–1820).

25 This may be Samuel Spedding (1758–1844).

26 George Hall (c1798–1876).

27 John Halliley (1778–1837), of Halliley, Brooke and Halliley, which failed in 1834.

28 Joshua Walker (c1815–1875), banker. The Dewsbury branch of the Huddersfield Banking Company was established in 1857.

29 Benjamin Gott (1762–1840), wool manufacturer and merchant.

30 The off-cuts or clippings of garments were a perquisite of the tailor.

31 George Parr (born 1813). It seems that Parr became incapacitated in some way around 1850, possibly through drink as implied later in the article. His wife Martha née Dixon (1812–1879) ran the family business by 1851 when the census return shows her as head of household, although not widowed.

32 This was possibly Samuel Armitage, father of the Batley Carr flock dealer Joseph Armitage (c1818–1853).

33 Probably Day, Porritt and Co., scribbling millers, Batley Carr.

34 John Watson (c1791–1868), clothier. Watson ran into financial difficulty in 1837 and assigned his estates for the benefit of creditors. He was recorded in the 1841 census as a cloth manufacturer, but in 1851 as a weaver of woollen cloth.

35 The key members of these families are cited elsewhere in the article apart from the Oldroyds. Mark Oldroyd (1798–1875) and two of his sons, George Oldroyd (1824–1876) and John Oldroyd (1825–1883) built up a large multiple-site concern in Dewsbury.
36 Samuel Parr (born 1801).
37 George Brearley (c1826–1874), rag merchant.
38 Condensing relied on a mechanism that rubbed the carded fleece along its length to consolidate the fibres into ribbons able to withstand drawing and spinning.
39 James Alexander Parr (1843–1893).
40 It has not been possible to identify Captain Corbett. In a letter to the editor of the *Textile Manufacturer* (7:79, 15 Jul 1881, pp. 248–249), a London-based associate of the Bates Brothers firm claimed an earlier precedent for extract wool dating from 1848 in Rochdale. The idea was then taken up by the fent dealer William Crone (c1808–1875) of Manchester, and patented along with Richard Fenton, waste dealer of Prestwich and William Aldred, bleacher of Manchester, on 12 August 1853 (no. 1891). The patent was later voided (see *Morning Chronicle*, 21 Oct 1856, p. 3), probably based on prior claims. Julian Zipser cited a process invented by Höber in 1851–1852 (*see Textile Raw Materials and Their Conversion into Yarns* (London: Scott, Greenwood & Son, 1901), p. 81). Höber is probably a misrendering by the translator of Gustav Köber (see Note 58).
41 More usually, kier.
42 Possibly George C. Hacker (c1815–1874), of Kent origins, and a hop merchant toward the end of his life.
43 Edwin Firth (1799–1863), blanket merchant and manufacturer.
44 Bates and Sons specialised in cotton wadding. In 1848, the firm began marketing its 'Imperial coverlet' – made from thin fleeces of cotton wadding quilted together – as a substitute for blankets. By the 1870s, the firm had become Bates and Co., and in the 1880s this changed to Bates Bros., but it continued to produce cotton wool products, with its London warehouse at Little Knightrider Street.
45 Henry Wildsmith (1826–1870), extract wool and shoddy manufacturer. In 1859, Wildsmith and Carter established their extracting business. The following year, Wildsmith, along with his partners Joshua Carter (c1808–1880) and James Joshua Carter (1835–1908), patented their improved methods and machinery for extracting wool from cotton mixture cloth.
46 John Nussey (1785–1879), woollen manufacturer and merchant.
47 Carter's trade was recorded in the 1841 census as shoemaker, and in 1851 as cordwainer. This trade could have been combined with the other activities mentioned.
48 Slang terms for Unionist and Confederate (secessionist) soldiers.
49 Scotland, famed for its oatcakes.
50 Charles James Lever (1806–1872), Irish novelist.
51 Frederick William Reuss (1839–1922), rag and shoddy merchant.
52 Marcus Gottlieb Galthen Bech (1795–1863). His son Marcus Galthen Bech (1840–1918) later took over the business.
53 Henry Roberts, William Henry Trigg and Augustus Frederick Ohrt were partners in the firm of Roberts and Trigg as merchants and commission agents at Kingston-upon-Hull. The firm was established around 1830 and traded until December 1834.
54 Henry Peter Brougham (1778–1868). Brougham resigned from his seat as MP for Winchelsea to stand for election at Knaresborough in February 1830.
55 John Jubb (1807–1888).
56 George Senior has not been reliably identified.
57 Fenton appears to mean the same person, previously identified as George Senior, one of the party at Hull.

58 Gustav Köber was the director of the Badische Wollen Manufactur in Mannheim.
59 Johann Gross was a foreman rag grinder working for Mathias Stirn und Söhne, Niederursel, who, in 1857, added a cover to the rag machine that enabled unpulled pieces to be collected and returned to the feed sheet, producing a more uniform product. Oberursel is the modern spelling of the place name given.
60 Known after its English supplier, Joseph Rhodes and Son of Morley, who in 1862 purchased knowledge of Mathias Stirn and Sons' improvement through a third party, and then patented it in Britain.
61 Charles Fitton (c1795–1878), commission agent, and mungo and shoddy importer.
62 William Pearson (born around 1791) began rag sales around 1851, but retired by the 1860s. A bum-bailly is a bailiff.
63 George Rydill (c1830–1907) began rag sales around 1851. He married Suzette Elizabeth Rumpff on 16 February 1858, and employed her as bookkeeper and German correspondent (*Batley Reporter and Guardian*, 15 Mar 1907, p. 10).
64 Benjamin Eastwood (c1814–1897) commenced rag sales in 1857.
65 Henry Cullingworth (c1809–1864) commenced rag auctions by the late 1850s, and was advertising weekly auctions at the sale rooms of Henry Cullingworth and Son, South Street, Dewsbury by 1862.
66 Tartary refers to Central Asia. Alexander von Humboldt (1769–1859) undertook an expedition across the Russian empire in 1829. He wrote about the Kirghiz in his three-volume *Asie Centrale: recherches sur les chaînes des montagnes et la climotologie comparée* (Paris: Gide, 1843).
67 Edward Everett (1794–1865), American politician, who was ambassador to Great Britain from 1841 to 1845.
68 The two main sources of ramie fibre, China grass from China and Rhea from the Malay archipelago.
69 Edmund Cartwright (1743–1823) designed and patented power looms in 1786, 1787 and 1788. The power loom was not widely adopted until the end of the 1820s.
70 A faultfinder, first encountered as 'the learned Smelfungus' in Laurence Sterne's *A Sentimental Journey through France and Italy by Mr. Yorick* (Dublin: printed for G. Faulkner et al., 1768), vol. 1, pp. 54–55.
71 Sheep were treated with tar mixtures to prevent parasites before sheep dips became more common.
72 Thomas Savary (1650–1715) patented a steam powered pump in 1698.
73 The figures here are as printed in the original, but 1,450 is probably the number intended as the second addend.
74 Thomas Carlyle (1795–1881). His *Latter-Day Pamphlets* (London: Chapman and Hall, 1850) do not contain the reference alluded to here. This occurs in *Past and Present* (London: Chapman and Hall, 1843), pp. 121, 177.
75 This title has not been located.
76 Sheep bred for meat did not produce optimal wool.
77 Edwin Firth (1799–1863) established a blanket manufacturing business in Heckmondwike in 1822.
78 Possibly taken from a slave narrative. The *Life and Times of Frederick Douglass written by himself* contains a related line: 'slaves, accustomed from childhood to cower before a driver's lash' (Hartford CN: Park Publishing, 1881), p. 56.
79 John 6:12. 'Gather up the fragments that remain, that nothing be lost.' Genesis 1:28. 'Be fruitful and multiply, and replenish the earth.'

## Editorial Headnote

### Beaumont, Roberts. 'Wool Substitutes', *Woollen and Worsted Cloth Manufacture: Being a Practical Treatise for the Use of Persons Employed in the Manipulation of Textile Fabrics* (London: George Bell and Sons, 1888), pp. 16–21.

### Beaumont, Roberts. 'Mungo and Shoddy', *Wool Substitutes* (London: Sir Isaac Pitman & Sons, 1922), pp. 30–45.

Roberts Beaumont (1862–1922) was the son of Professor John Beaumont (1821–1889), and succeeded his father as Professor of Textile Industries at the Yorkshire College, Leeds in 1889. He spent the next thirty-four years dealing with a formidable lecturing, examination and publication schedule. Such unrelenting pressure evidently took its toll. The census year 1911 saw Beaumont in residence at the Leyfield Institute for Intemperance in West Kirby, undergoing treatment for alcoholism; this was a three-week residential therapy involving the use of gold chlorate. His early retirement in 1913 may have been prompted by continuing pressures; the College Council placed on record their high appreciation of his services and regret at the resignation. Even in retirement, Beaumont pursued a rigorous writing schedule. His two-volume treatise on *Woollen and Worsted* was announced in 1915 (*The Scotsman*, 6 April, p. 7). He completed *Union Textile Fabrication* in December 1919, and *Dress, Blouse and Costume Cloths* in July 1921.

Selected here are Beaumont's treatments of reclaimed wools in his first and last works on the subject. His first monograph was completed in September 1887, and issued by the publisher as part of a series of technological handbooks. By this time, Beaumont had modified his baptismal name 'Robert' to the pen name of 'Roberts', although retaining the former in daily life. When writing the 1888 treatise, Beaumont was a lecturer and demonstrator working under his father at the Yorkshire College. Viewed as a manual for the technical student, the book was praised for its clarity and conciseness. A reviewer for the *Yorkshire Post* asserted, 'he evidently understands how to bring out the essential points of any difficulty, and to make the way plain for a learner' (7 Dec 1887, p. 3). The *Leeds Mercury* commented, 'We are very glad to see such a book from the pen of a lecturer and demonstrator at the Yorkshire College, and are confident it will be very largely serviceable in the cause of technical education' (7 Dec 1887, p. 3). Selling at 6s. 3d., the book was pitched at an affordable level.

When the publisher brought out a revised second edition in 1890, Beaumont had taken his father's place as Professor of Textile Industries. A third edition, 'rewritten', was issued in June 1899, but there were no significant changes to the section extracted here; the price increased to 7s. 6d. Beaumont used this earlier book as the basis for a more extensive two-volume work *Woollen and Worsted* that was published in 1915. The section on 'wool substitutes' closely follows the early text, even in the description of machinery. *Wool Substitutes*, released in December 1921, was his last major work published while living. It sold for 10s. 6d., in a handsome black 'linen' bookcloth. Beaumont's insistence on 'substitutes' in the title emphasises his wish to free reclaimed wool from its association with spurious or adulterated material.

# 9

# BEAUMONT, ROBERTS. 'WOOL SUBSTITUTES' AND 'MUNGO AND SHODDY'

*Woollen and Worsted Cloth Manufacture: Being a Practical Treatise for the Use of Persons Employed in the Manipulation of Textile Fabrics* (London: George Bell and Sons, 1888), pp. 16–21; and *Wool Substitutes* (London: Sir Isaac Pitman & Sons, 1922), pp. 30–45.

## Wool substitutes

In the manufacture of so-called woollen and worsted goods, various materials are used as substitutes for wool proper. The employment of such fibres has tended to cheapen, to a very considerable extent, the productions of the loom, and made it feasible to weave an attractive article at a surprisingly low price. The trade generally has also been largely extended by the entrance of re-manufactured fibres into textile productions. The following are the most important and valuable wool substitutes now in use: noils, mungo, shoddy, extract, and flocks.

***Noils.*** – Noil is the short, curly fibre cast out as waste in combing wool for worsted yarns. Strictly speaking, it is the pure produce of the sheep. It does not, however, possess the same degree of elasticity and wavy fulness as the original fleece from which it is extracted. This arises from the preliminary processes of worsted yarn production to which the material is subjected previous to the noil being formed, tending to comb the curl out of the wool, or to straighten the fibres.

Noils are of four classes – Botany, English, Mohair, and Alpaca. The first class is the outcome of combing Australian and other fine wools. The second class is obtained from English wools of a Lincoln and Leicester type; while Mohair and Alpaca noils result from combing the produce of the Angora and Alpaca goats.

*Botany Noils* are the most valuable. The uses to which they are put are almost too numerous to mention. However, it may be stated that such noils occupy an important place in the materials used in the production of fancy woollen fabrics. They are blended with wool in making yarns for shawls, and are also suitable for mixing with cotton in spinning small twist threads.[1]

DOI: 10.4324/9780429274190-13

*English Noils* are of a coarser and broader quality, but are, nevertheless, used for similar purposes as Botany, only in lower classes of goods. Cheviot fabrics consume a large proportion of English noils, many cloths thus designated being made entirely of noil. Sometimes these noils, when used in the black, are mixed with black shoddy, or with shoddy and cotton, the latter fibre assisting the materials to spin to a greater length.

*Mohair and Alpaca Noils* are much brighter in appearance, as well as softer and more silky in the hand, than the two preceding kinds. They possess but little milling property, and are, therefore, not selected for cloths where felting is essential. In combination with shoddy and cotton they are occasionally spun into weft yarns for low goods; but the principal trade which absorbs these noils is that of the Scotch, or Kidder carpet manufacture. As the chief essentials in yarns intended for this class of goods are strength, brightness, and thickness, Alpaca and Mohair noils are highly adapted to their production.

***Mungo and Shoddy.*** – Although these materials are obtained from different sources, yet, as the mechanical operations to which the rags are subjected from which they are derived are practically the same, they may be treated of together. Both fibres are wool products, being obtained solely from wool garments. Mungo is the result of grinding into a soft, fibrous form rags of a hard character, such as milled cloths, whereas shoddy originates from soft rags of a blanket or comforter class, and also from knit goods. There are two descriptions of mungo – *new* and *old.* The former is produced from new rags, *i.e.*, tailors’ clippings, pattern clippings, &c., while old mungo is got from fragments of cloth that have, at one time, appeared in a made-up garment. The smallness of the cost of these materials, as well as the diversity of shades in which they can be obtained – for mungoes and shoddies can be purchased in the black, brown, blue, or almost any colour or mixture desired – causes them to be employed in almost all classes of woollen goods. The method of applying mungo or shoddy to the better qualities of fabrics with a warp face consists in blending them with wool in the formation of the weft thread. In other cloths mungo forms the bulk of the material used in the construction of the backing yarn, or the thread used in producing the underneath surface of the texture. The method of introducing this fibre into low goods is somewhat different to the preceding. Here it is the principal and most expensive material used in the composition of the fabric, the weft thread generally being mungo simply, and the warp cotton. Both warp and weft yarns used in medium-priced fabrics are usually a combination of wool and mungo, the proportions varying according to the quality of the texture produced.

*Difference between Wool and Mungo.* – The properties of a good wool are necessarily of a very superior character to those of mungo. Under the microscope there is not always a marked dissimilarity between the fibres, the filaments of some mungoes being in a far more perfect state of preservation than others. Sometimes the fibres are partially stripped of serrations, but probably others might be examined from the same handful of material possessing, when microscopically examined, the complete mechanical development of the wool fibre. Evidently the difference between mungo and wool does not arise in the main from any necessary dissimilarity in the structure of the fibres. Practically, mungo possesses no definite length of fibre – staple, as compared with wool, it has none – while in elasticity and strength it is also deficient. Doubtless some of these deficiencies are due to the mutilation of fibre occasioned in the grinding process to which the rags are submitted, and in which filament is forcibly torn from filament, causing, as a natural consequence, the material to be short, brittle, and wanting in elasticity.

Of course the milling power of mungo depends entirely on the nature of the wool used in making the cloth from which the fibre has been obtained. If the rags ground up were originally made from an excellent fulling wool, then the mungo will undoubtedly possess a certain degree of felting property. Shoddies, though longer in the fibre than mungoes, do not usually felt so well – the wools employed in the production of the rags from which they are recovered being principally of an inferior fulling power.

*Mungo Production.* – Rags intended for conversion into mungo pass through various processes before they assume the fibrous appearance of wool. *Dusting* is the first operation. It consists in shaking the dust and dirt out of the rags before they are transferred to the hands of the sorter, who classifies them according to quality and colour. Considerable care and judgment have to be exercised in this preliminary work in order to ensure the production of a regular and uniform stapled material.[2] Both old and new rags are submitted to this process. As many as from twenty to thirty varieties have been collected from one bale.

*Seaming* follows sorting. It applies solely to rags obtained from cast-off garments, and consists in removing all the cotton threads used in stitching. The rags are now oiled to soften the material and facilitate grinding. The machine in which this, the principal work in mungo production, is effected is shown in fig. 2. It consists of feed-sheet, fluted rollers, main cylinder, or swift, and funnel for conducting the mungo out of the machine. The swift *S*, which may be said to be the leading feature of the machine, is enclosed in the framework; it is about 18 inches long, 42 inches in diameter, has a surface space of 1,638 square inches, and contains from 12,000 to 14,000 strong iron teeth. The speed at which it runs varies from 640 to 800 revolutions per minute. The rags, having been spread on the feed-sheet *F*, are conveyed to the fluted rollers, on emerging from which they are seized by the teeth of the cylinder, which not only separates thread from thread, but literally tears fibre from fibre, and thus reduces the whole to a flossy, wool-like state. As the rags are ground up, the material is forced down the funnel *A*, and thus finds an exit from the machine. Any hard fragments of cloth only partially torn to pieces fall into the cage *C*, from whence they are replaced on the feed-sheet. The weights, *W*, allow the upper fluted roller to rise should the machine be overcharged, and by this means admit of the rags being conveyed without retention direct off the feed-table on to the cylinder, which continues to throw them into the cage until the machine gets properly cleared.

***Extract Wool.*** – This material is obtained from rags of which the threads are composed of cotton and wool respectively, as in stuff goods with a cotton warp and mohair or lustre worsted weft, or in low union fabrics which have a similar warp thread, but thick woollen weft. As the object in extracting is to recover the animal fibre, the vegetable thread is destroyed by a process of carbonizing. To effect this, the tissue is steeped in a solution of sulphuric acid and water, and then heated in an enclosed chamber. This drying process causes the water to evaporate, leaving the sulphuric acid in a very concentrated form upon the fabrics, in which state it has a very powerful action on the vegetable matter they contain, entirely transforming it, and reducing it to such a condition that it powders when friction is applied. Washing-off now takes place, to remove the acid from the reclaimed woollen thread. This effected, the material is run through a coarse, open carder, which gives it the required woolly appearance of a textile fibre.

As to the properties of extract – it is not a good milling wool-substitute, and is wanting in fullness, elasticity, and substantial feel. It can be obtained in a large variety of colours, and is used in the manufacture of low tweeds and, when blended with wool, medium-class fancies.[3]

***Flocks.*** – These are soft, fluffy fibres cast out of the different machines used in the various processes of cloth production. They are of three kinds, "milling," "cropping," and "raising." The first class, which is formed in the milling or fulling machine, is of more value to the textile producer than either cropping or raising flocks. White fulling flocks always command a high price, and are suitable for blending with wool in the production of a large variety of goods of a Cheviot class. As fulling flocks sometimes possess a bright colour and generally diffusiveness of character, they are largely used by sale yarn spinners.

*Cutting* or *cropping* flocks are the fibres removed from the cloth in what is termed the cutting operation. Such flocks are not frequently selected by manufacturers as a fit material for yarn making, being principally used in the production of what are called flock-papers[4] for decorative purposes.

*Raising* flocks are derived from the teazles of the "gig," which retain a certain quantity of the short fibre, drawn from the surface of the cloth in the raising process. Such fibres, when removed from the teazles, are designated raising flocks, and are similar in character to those formed in the fulling process, hence they are employed for like purposes in textile productions.

## Mungo and shoddy

The production of mungo and shoddy comprises rag sorting, blending and pulling. Women are employed in the sorting room, Fig. 3, which is well lighted and ventilated. The bales of rags, previously classified by the merchant (and with the quality and nature of which the manufacturer is fully acquainted), are picked in handfuls, which are spread on a sorting table having a wire-grid surface, through which some of the dusty matter passes. The operation is not particularly arduous but requires the exercise of judgment and discrimination in arriving at the "sorts" to which the rags belong. Handle or feel, as well as shade or colour, are the determining factors.

The number of sorts (about three) is fixed, and the sorter sets to work by clipping away the seamed bits, and by removing all pieces containing cotton or vegetable fibre, whether this be in the form of a thread or in the form of a union yarn, that is, composed of cotton and wool. Cotton-adulterated fabrics are immediately detected, an experienced sorter perceiving at once by the handle of the rags if they contain vegetable matter. Such rags possess a firmer and closer feel than rags made of wool. The rags containing cotton, in any form, are grouped into a class to themselves, for carbonization.

Prior to "bedding," the rags may be run through a "shaker," a machine which softens their texture, and removes the dirt, dust, etc. It consists of feed and delivery travelling lattice sheets, usually both, placed in the front of the machine, and of a large spiked cylinder or drum (enclosed in the framework) making from 350 to 400 revolutions per minute. For carrying off the dust a powerful fan is employed.

During the operation, the rags are not only freed of hard dirty matter, but they are rendered more pliable and brought into a suitable condition for oiling, blending and piling.

In "bedding" the rags are distributed in layers and sprinkled with oil to facilitate and accelerate grinding, applying some five gallons of oil to each pack (240 lbs.) of rags. The "bed" or "pile" may consist of several cwts. or of three or more tons, varying, in the weight of the rags, with the character and composition of the "bed," and with the class of goods for which the material is intended. The pile is vertically divided, securing the same mixed assortment of the rags being placed on the feed sheet of the grinding machine, as exists in the layers of the rags forming the pile.

The machine used in pulling or grinding is that illustrated in Fig. 4, and is termed the "rag picker." The rags are placed on the feed table *A*, which carries them to the fluted rollers, set at a distance from the cylinder *B* to agree with the average length of the rags being pulled. The "clothing" or covering of the cylinder is made up of lags studded with flat or round teeth, as shown in Figs. 5 and 5a. The lags have fifty-two teeth per row for hard goods, and twenty-eight teeth per row for soft goods, on a 36-inch diameter cylinder, having an 18-inch working space; and fifty-six teeth and thirty teeth per row for hard goods on a 24-inch diameter cylinder having a 20-inch working space. The average shoddy production in 10 hrs., on the machines with cylinders of these diameters, is stated below –

| *Diameter of Cylinder* | *Mungo from New-cloth Clippings.* | *Mungo from Old Rags.* | *Shoddy from Merinos.* | *Shoddy from Berlins.* | *Flannels.* | *Shoddy from Knitted Goods.* |
|---|---|---|---|---|---|---|
| 36" | 7 cwts. | 8 cwts. | 7 cwts. | 13 cwts. | 7 cwts. | 11–12 cwts. |
| 24" | 6–7 cwts. | 7 cwts. | 6–8 cwts. | 11–12 cwts. | 6–7 cwts. | 10 cwts. |

Production depends on the nature of the rags, and on the working efficiency of the cylinder, the speed of which is regulated by the kind of rags being torn. Machines having a 36-inch cylinder are adapted for treating hard rags, and machines having a 24-inch cylinder for soft rags, stockings, hosiery goods, serges and flannels. The cylinder speeds (revs. per min.) for acquiring a maximum output – 10 hrs. – on different materials are –

| *Diameter of Cylinder* | *Mungo from New-cloth Clippings.* | *Mungo from Old Rags.* | *Shoddy from Merinos.* | *Shoddy from Berlins.* | *Flannels.* | *Shoddy from Knitted Goods.* |
|---|---|---|---|---|---|---|
| 36" | 750 | 500 | 350–400 | 300–500 | 300–500 | 300–500 |
| 24" | 1000 | 800 | 750 | 800 | 800 | 800 |

The rags proceed from the feed sheet *A*, Fig. 4, to the fluted rollers, which grip them, when they are attacked by the teeth of the cylinder. The action of the teeth literally separates the fibres from each other into the individual threads of which the rags consist, and results in their being rapidly reduced to a fibrous, flossy substance or shoddy. Any bits of rag insufficiently torn come in contact with the blades of the "bitter" roller *C*, which automatically throws them back on to the feed table, to be repassed to the cylinder.

The pulled material may be delivered by suction and conveyed by zinc piping into bales or sheets for re-blending and carding, or it may be delivered from the front of the machine under the feed table. A fan is used for inducing a draught, and also for assisting the recovery of the shoddy in an even and open condition.

When the suction conveyor is used, it is that shown attached to the teazer in Fig. 6. In applying it to the rag grinder, the receiving end of the conveyor *T* is fixed underneath the machine. The fan *F* draws the treated material or shoddy into metal tubing, by which it is conveyed to another part of the mill or to any convenient destination. Thus, the plant may be designed to carry the shoddy from the "picker" to the blending or teazing room or to deliver it in sheets in the stock room. The system is economical and efficient and has advantages over the common practice of delivering the pulled material on the floor of the rag grinding department of the factory.

Ordinarily two types of machines are installed for the treatment of *soft* and *hard* cloths respectively, but a machine is constructed in which the cylinder may be changed according to the class of rag being dealt with. In using this type of machine, duplicate sets of feed rollers, driving pulleys and change wheels are necessary, a set for *soft* rags, in which the feed rollers are larger in diameter, and a set for the *hard* variety of rags.

The resultant material, as compared with fleece wool, is deficient in staple or lock.[5] The fibres in the shoddy are, however, in a freer and better separated relation than in wool, for, if examined, fibre can be readily picked from fibre, and the whole bulk product is equally lofty and open in texture. In raw or scoured wool, felted and entangled filaments occur in the staple, and the locks of the wool are also intermatted with each other, so that the wool, after scouring, requires to be mechanically worked before it is in so favourable a state for manufacturing as the material from pulled rags.

In one operation, rag grinding effects the reduction of odds and ends of cloths to a fibrous substance, and also the production of this substance in a condition suitable for carding, and this, though the filament constituents of shoddy may vary largely in length, fineness and character.

It should be understood that inefficient rag grinding is detrimental to carding, and to the preparation of a satisfactory yarn. Figs. 7 and 8 are microscopic views of two faulty pulled rags, the first on account of the matted or meshed groups of filament *A*, and the second on account of the cotton ends *A*, $A^1$. The composite nature of the average blend of pulled rags is illustrated in the first specimen. The fibres are not only seen to differ in length and in fineness, but in their blended relation. They do not present any definite order, but cluster and criss-cross with each other in every imaginable direction.

The variable thickness, coarseness and length of fibres are very apparent in certain sections of the specimen, while the masses of the fibres are shorter and finer, and more freely mingle with each other. The former indicate that a certain percentage of the rags were of a different quality from the bulk of the rags torn up, but the differentiations in filament sort, in portions of Fig. 7, are fairly typical of the average shoddy. The shorter clustered fibre in Fig. 8 is more typical of the average mungo. Such marked differentiations in filament quality as here observed, are not, however, consistent with pulled rags representative of either a good mungo or a good shoddy.

The admixture of rags so different in fibre composition as here indicated, does not tend to yield a material which would card evenly and spin into a thread of equal fibre consistency through its length. The shorter fibres would have a tendency to run into the core of the thread, and the longer fibres to twirl round them, and unless, in carding and sliver production, each grade of fibre, long and short, were uniformly distributed throughout the material, the result would be an unsound and "twitty" yarn.

Moreover, the setting of the carding machines, for the effective distribution and intermixture of fibres thus differing in length, would be rendered difficult. The specimens are, therefore, illustrative of points to be obviated in the rag sorts passed through the pulling machine together, namely, rags substantially differing (1) in make and fineness; (2) in fibre character; and (3) in the facility with which the rags may be reduced to filament.

Rag-grinding machinery cannot be suitably adjusted for dealing satisfactorily with rags varying to the extent described. For producing either an evenly mixed shoddy or mungo, the rags dealt with must correspond in fabric quality and structure, by which is meant not only a similarity in the class of wool of which they are composed, but also in their adaptability to be torn up and converted into a fibrous substance simultaneously. If, for example, the rags should be of the same grade of wool, but a portion of the fabrics comparatively loose in structure, and other portions of the fabrics of a firmer build, due to the weaving or milling practice, the setting and speed of the fluted rollers and the cylinder, while suitable for tearing up the former, would be less effective in tearing up the latter.

This feature emphasizes the importance of the work of sorting and of blending rags of a character which, in the grinding operation, will offer a similar quality of fabric, both as to fibre and as to make, to the action of the teeth of the cylinder. An ideal shoddy is one in which the fibres are of a proximate length and diameter, and in which they are so completely mixed as to make a material which, when opened out, shows the same nature and possesses the same handle throughout its composition.

The microscopic views of the "pulled" specimens in Figs. 7 and 8, suggest what takes place when, by any accident, or through lack of efficiency in sorting, bits of cotton are allowed to remain in the rags. The picker or grinding machine is not designed or constructed for the separation of fibres from each other in cotton or vegetable yarns, especially when these consist of isolated threads as in Fig. 8.

The thousands of teeth in the cylinder are equal to disintegrating woollen or worsted yarns. These they readily reduce to their fibrous units. But, while the cotton threads may be broken or torn on the surface, they remain more or less intact, and pass in this form on to the carding machine, where, if only fractions of such threads, they are liable to be carded with the wool filament and to enter into the sheet of carded material, and into the condensed sliver, in which case they would ultimately become part of the spun thread. Further, should cotton ends occur to any perceptible extent in the shoddy, they would form a substance that would, first, result in a defective yarn, and second, in a fabric which would be specked when piece-dyed. Both these microscopic views indicate the points to be obviated in rag-sorting and blending, as well as the general character of the shoddy, or recovered wool fibre, which results from the operation of rag grinding.

## Notes

1 Twist usually indicates doubled yarns of two or three plies. The implication of *small* twist is not certain, most likely small numbers in the yarn count system, thus coarser yarns.

2 Beaumont's previous statement that mungo possesses no definite length of fibre presumably means that mungo rags come from a wide range of wools of varied staple lengths; the potential staple length of the resulting mungo is determined in the sorting process.

3 The third edition added an image of a 'union' fabric (cotton warp and worsted weft) after the action of the acid bath, showing the weft hanging loosely together.

4 Flock wallpapers.

5 Staple and lock are closely related. *Staple* is most commonly used to refer to the length (and uniformity of length) of wool fibre, while *lock* includes the other characteristics of a group of fibres that have grown together on the sheep, such as waviness and density.

## Editorial Headnote

### Bercry, William A. and Ellis, Granville A. (eds.). *Waste Merchants from The Century's Progress: Yorkshire. Progress. Commerce 1893* (London: The London Printing & Engraving Co., 1893), pp. 106, 157, 198, 216.

The London Printing and Engraving Company was the project of the Americans William Augustus Bercry (1855–1926) and Granville Alden Ellis (1856–1921). The partners were to publish six commercial directories between 1892 and 1894, covering London and several industrial regions of Britain. Funded on a subscription basis, such directories could be highly profitable. In this case, subscribers paid around three pounds with an agreement to receive six copies, and the publishers undertook scriptwriting, typesetting and printed illustrations from the subscriber's existing print blocks. A descriptive essay headed each volume, and pages were set aside for additional advertising. The books were attractively presented in brown cloth with embossed borders and lettering, more like a literary magazine than a directory.

Bercry's father-in-law Richard Edwards (1828–1887) was a publisher of annual directories who pioneered a new illustrated style that combined the historical background of localities with brief sketches of local businesses. His *Industries of Philadelphia* of 1881 probably set the model for the later British titles. Bercry came to Britain with Edwards to assist with *Industries of London*, and when Edwards died in 1887, completed the work under the family firm, the Historical Publishing Company. It is not known how Bercry met Ellis but both were in London in 1891, the year Ellis married Anna Mai Bosler (c1860–1911), an American journalist who wrote under the nom de plume Max Eliot. The two men formed a partnership under the name London Printing and Engraving Company bringing out their first directory for Lancashire by September 1892. The Yorkshire volume, the second in the series, was probably in preparation along with Lancashire, but was not completed until 1893.

The uninhibited laudatory language bestowed on the firms in the commercial sketches by the American editors seems at odds with the traditional restraint of the Yorkshireman, and we can only guess at the wry humour this may have provoked, especially when elevating minor tradespeople to positions of eminence in their communities. The firms included were self-selected by subscription, leaving many prominent names unmentioned. In the case of the waste wool industry, only four firms were included, but they capture a range of types. Apart from P. & C. Garnett, whose machinery gave its name to a process, the directory brings into view some companies that might otherwise escape attention. Such company histories help to build a picture of the networks that shaped a prosperous trade.

# 10

# BERCRY, WILLIAM A. AND ELLIS, GRANVILLE A. (EDS.). WASTE MERCHANTS FROM *THE CENTURY'S PROGRESS: YORKSHIRE*

## (London: The London Printing & Engraving Co., 1893), pp. 106, 157, 198, 216.

**T. L. Ogden & Co., Wool, Noil, Yarn and Waste Merchants**, 44, Union Street, Bradford. Telegraphic address: "Wools, Bradford"; Telephone No. 765. – Projected in the year 1863 by the late Mr. Roberts Ogden, the business passed into the hands of his son, Mr. T. L. Ogden, in the year 1885,[1] and is now under the control of that gentleman and his partner, Mr. R. Pollard, trading under the style and title above designated.[2] The firm's premises are most eligibly situated in Union Street, and consist of a large and substantial three-storeyed warehouse, admirably appointed throughout with offices and ware-rooms and every facility for the rapid transaction of a very large home and export trade in all kinds of wools, yarns, noils, tops and waste, which are distributed to worsted spinners, manufacturers of dress goods, worsted coatings, heavy woollen goods, blankets, flannels and the like, not only throughout the United Kingdom, but very largely to America and the Continent of Europe. The firm, moreover, are manufacturers of Botany, English, Cheviot, mohair, &c., cardings on a large scale, their elaborately equipped, power-driven works, replete with carding and other machinery of the latest and most improved kind, being located in Longside Lane. The affairs of the house are administered with sound judgment and ability, and its whole career has been marked by sound principles and honourable methods, continuously in the ascendant, which have endowed it with a special claim to consideration among the representative mercantile institutions of Bradford.

***

**Henry Ellis, Waste Flock, Mungo, and Shoddy Merchant,** 1, Bishopgate Street, Leeds; and at Galashiels. Telephone No. 35; Telegraphic Address: "Ellis, Leeds." – The precise date of the inception of this business is 1871, when operations

 DOI: 10.4324/9780429274190-14

were begun by the present proprietor[3] with the object of supplying raw materials to woollen manufacturers. Being practically acquainted with the trade, and a man of indomitable energy and push, he soon laid the foundation of his business on sure and solid ground. During the whole of the time there has been no lack of enterprise and attention to every detail, with the consequence that every year he has added to the volume and importance of his transactions. The premises in Leeds are large and commodious, consisting of a substantial block three storeys high, and comprising a handsome suite of general and private offices, warehouses and packing-room on the ground floor, and stock-rooms on the upper floors. The works are at Holbeck and are known as the Manor Mills.[4] They are large in extent and equipped with the best class of plant and machinery for cleaning and preparing waste and flock. Employment is found in the mills for a force of no less than one hundred hands. Mr. Ellis controls a very large trade in mungo, shoddy, waste, and flock, and his commodities are known in the market as of reliable quality. From the amount of business done, together with the facilities of manufacture, the proprietor is in a position to fill the largest orders with promptness and to quote such prices as cannot be duplicated elsewhere. The trade extends to all the cloth-making towns in the United Kingdom. In consequence of the growth of the Scotch trade it has been found necessary to open a branch establishment at Galashiels,[5] where samples and stocks are kept as at the headquarters. Mr. Ellis gives the business his personal attention, and spares no efforts to satisfy his customers in quality, price, and despatch. As a straightforward and honourable business man he is held in great respect among the trading community, and in private life he is well known and esteemed for his generosity and personal worth.

***

**William Myers, Rag and Mungo Merchant**, Clough Street, Morley. – Though not by any means as old as many similar businesses in Morley, that of Mr. William Myers[6] is one of considerable repute and is being steadily developed. It was founded in 1886, originally in Commercial Street, by the present proprietor. These premises becoming too small for the requirements of the business, Mr. Myers in 1891 built and entered upon those now occupied, which comprise a well-built stone building of two storeys in height, having a frontage of sixty feet to the street. It is partly used as a warehouse and partly for manufacturing purposes, as mungo manufacture is conducted on the premises on a considerable scale. Machinery and appliances of improved modern type are used in this connection, steam power being used. The rags and mungo are supplied to rag merchants, woollen manufacturers, &c., of Morley and the neighbouring districts, a business of considerable importance being conducted. Mr. Myers personally superintends the business in all its varied features. He is a gentleman of large experience and much resource, and is developing a fine business, his influential business connections among cloth manufacturers being steadily on the increase.

***

**P. & C. Garnett** (Partners: Peter Garnett and I. Henry Leather),[7] **Machinists and Engineers**, Wharfe Works, Cleckheaton. Telegrams: "Garnett, Cleckheaton;" Telephone No. 1,309, Dewsbury Exchange. – Among those who by their ingenuity and skill in the invention of special machinery for facilitating and improving the processes employed in the manufacture of textiles, the firm of Messrs. P. & C. Garnett, of Wharfe Works, Cleckheaton, the well-known machinists and engineers, occupy a prominent position. Operations were commenced in 1850,[8] and, being conducted on sound business principles, a good start was soon effected, and a career of progress and prosperity entered upon, which has been maintained down to the present day. With large experience and matured and practical ability, the founders were not long in making a position in the local trade. From time to time they have introduced novel machinery of an admirable and efficient nature into this branch of industry, and have obtained a reputation which is not surpassed by that of any house in the same line of business. Repeated alterations and additions to the premises have been called for to meet the increasing demand, and eventually, in 1883, the works were enlarged to their present size. They now consist of an extensive block of two-storey buildings, erected in the shape of a hollow square, together with a continuous series of one-storey shops, running at right angles from one side, the whole covering an area of about two acres, and comprising foundry, casting-sheds, pattern-rooms, and fitting and finishing shops. The equipment is the result of the proprietors' long experience, and embraces all the latest and most improved apparatus, plant, and machinery known to the trade, as well as many special tools and appliances which have been introduced by the firm, and which are exclusively used by them. Seventy to eighty skilled hands are kept in constant employment, and every department is maintained in the most efficient condition for producing the best results. A large and valuable business is controlled as general machinists, but more particularly in the manufacture of improved double-action burring machines, burr rollers for carding-engines, lickers-in for cotton and wool, and similar apparatus.[9] In this branch the firm has long held an undisputed superiority. The material employed is of the best possible character, and all the work is finished with the nicest accuracy, while embodying many special and valuable improvements. The firm, however, are best known as the patentees and manufacturers of the famous Garnett machine for opening waste, which has now superseded every other mechanical means for opening hand-twisted woollen, worsted, silk, and cotton waste. The machine is something in the form of a carding-engine, consisting of a series of cylinders covered with the patent Garnett wire, having teeth like a saw, which, in revolving, tear out "the knotted and combined locks" of the waste. By its operations much of the waste which was formerly thrown aside, and before the invention of this machine was frequently used as manure, can now be employed, and a vast saving in material, as well as in time, is thus effected. Messrs. Garnett's invention is thoroughly efficacious, and by far the best of the kind yet known. During the last few years great improvements have been introduced into these machines in every detail. The most important of these is a new system, invented and patented by this firm, of applying double wires to the rollers,[10] which can now be clothed as fine as thirty rows per inch, whereas it was thought formerly that twelve rows per inch was as fine as could be satisfactorily accomplished. The immense advantage of this in opening very fine hand-twisted waste can very readily be understood. Another point to which Messrs. P. & C. Garnett have devoted a great deal of attention lately is the hardening and tempering of the teeth on the rollers. Formerly these were made of Swedish charcoal iron, but now they are made of cast steel, and by a special process just the tips of the teeth are hardened, so that they will keep a sharp point for several years. They have now brought this to a great state of perfection. The rapid increase in the demand for these machines shows unmistakably that manufacturers have become fully alive to their worth and superiority. All orders receive prompt and careful attention, and no effort is spared to give entire satisfaction to customers, not only in the character of the work turned out, but also in prices and despatch. The proprietors are eminently practical men, of acknowledged skill and sound experience, and their personal supervision is given to the business in its entirety. In their dealings they are strictly fair and honest, and by their liberal policy they command the respect of their patrons. Messrs. Garnett occupy a good position in trade circles, and in private life enjoy the esteem of all who know them for their many good personal qualities, their well-deserved success, and inflexible uprightness.

## Notes

1 Robert(s) Ogden (1827–1900), wool stapler and merchant, was the founder of this firm. The partnership became Roberts Ogden and Sons, probably in the mid-1870s when Thomas Lister Ogden (1850–1903) and his brother Feather Ogden (1854–1903) reached maturity. Feather Ogden left in October 1879. The firm faced bankruptcy in 1885, but after paying dividends to creditors, and a period of trusteeship, Thomas L. Ogden recommenced business in his own name in 1887.

2 Robert Pollard (c1841–1922). The partnership between Ogden and Pollard was dissolved 16 August 1893 (*London Gazette*, 13 Feb 1894, p. 934).

3 Henry Ellis (c1844–1919) was listed as a commercial traveller at the time of his marriage in October 1871. In census returns of 1881 to 1911, he is variously called a wool and flock merchant, wool merchant, and wool waste dealer.

4 A report of a fire refers to 'the premises of Mr. Henry Ellis, flock merchant, Manor-road, Holbeck' (*Leeds Mercury*, 22 May 1882, p. 5). The usage 'Manor Mills' seems to have been adopted by the 1890s.

5 Ellis had properties at Wilderhaugh and Albert Place in Galashiels.

6 William Myers (c1848–1900), woollen rag merchant. Myers's father died of cholera in 1849, age 33, leaving his mother with four young children. Although she remarried around 1852, the children began work at a young age. William was a 'wool piecer' by the time of the 1861 census. He married Ruth Gaunt (1847–1923) in 1866, and worked as a rag grinder for twenty years before setting up his own business.

7 Peter Garnett (1825–1900), with his brother Charles Garnett (1834–1862), were the founders of the firm. John Henry Leather (1842–1912), mechanical engineer, joined P. & C. Garnett in 1865.

8 The date of establishment is usually given as 1851.

9 The author is noting here a few of the specialist forms of toothed wire-covered rollers that were produced by the company. Burring machines that removed burrs from wool had rollers with flattened, rather than sharp-pointed teeth. Lickers-in are rollers with wire-teeth clothing that accept the waste material from the feed rollers and perform the first action of breaking up the waste into fibre.

10 The original Garnett wire was invented around 1851. John Henry Leather (1842–1912) patented in 1877 the improved method that allowed wire setting in double rows, and he was granted a patent for further improvements in 1888.

## Editorial Headnote

## Cook, Alexander S. *Old-Time Traders and Their Ways* (Aberdeen: William Smith, Bon-Accord Press, 1904), pp. 62–63.

In *Old-Time Traders*, Alexander Skene Cook (c1830–1912) reminisces about his apprenticeship as a draper's assistant in the Aberdeen of the 1840s. He recalls the sales banter of the day, and gently exposes the marketing ploys of that era. The sketches were first written for the weekly *Bon-Accord* magazine between 15 August 1901 and the end of that year, with the editor providing the title under which they are known. The collected volume was published in response to the request of readers. Although the preface was signed in February 1902, the book did not appear until the end of 1904. A reviewer for the *Aberdeen Press and Journal* praised the work, 'written with ease and without any affectation of style . . . calculated to recall the past in a very vivid form' (29 Dec 1904, p. 5).

By 1860, Cook had his own business as a clothier, and in the 1880s, he employed twenty tailors, three female tailors and three shirtmakers in his tailoring and outfitting business. Retired at the time of writing, these sketches were a diversion from a more serious work he wrote on the history of the temperance movement, published in 1901. The interest in this short extract – for our subject – is in the disdain expressed for suiting materials containing shoddy, and a mock test designed for their avoidance.

# 11

# COOK, ALEXANDER S. *OLD-TIME TRADERS AND THEIR WAYS*

## (Aberdeen: William Smith, Bon-Accord Press, 1904), pp. 62–63.

Furnishing Tailors, or Merchant Tailors, as they preferred to designate themselves, were those who had shops large or small, and who kept a stock of cloth and supplied customers direct with the clothing. The requirements of the largest number of inhabitants, however, were otherwise supplied with material from the woollen draper or clothier, and a tailor of their own selection was engaged to make it up for them. This was a mode which many preferred as being more economical. To secure a suitable article, and at a proper price, they arranged with a practical man to come with them to buy the cloth. This was readily done, and the purchaser, along with his advisor, went to the clothiers to inspect his stock. The tailor was the spokesman, and invariably gave an opinion as to the quality of what was shown, and when the price was quoted he would not infrequently hazard an opinion as to the value offered. Some were more troublesome than others, but as a rule there was little difficulty in completing the transaction. The tailor looked wise and hesitated before advising, and generally took the cloth between his thumb and forefinger, and, doubling it, he gave it a smart jerk, which yielded a sharp sound, and doing the same with other pieces by way of comparison he gave his preference to the one with the loudest report, as this, he said, was an evidence of the purity of the wool and the absence of shoddy. The man for whom the purchase was being made looked on in silent admiration at the acumen and skill of the tailor, whose judgment was fully relied upon, and was considered very much preferable to that of the salesman. The cloth was cut off, parcelled up. and paid for, and they left together, apparently mutually well pleased with the transaction. Within a quarter-of-an-hour or so, or in a very short time after, the tailor returned with a trifling order for buttons or thread, making sure to secure the services of the salesman who had supplied his friend. His return was to receive the commission which was allowed on such sales, and which was an understanding in the trade, but of which the real purchaser was entirely ignorant. The discount would have been the buyer's had he not brought an assessor with him, whose time was taken up in being the intermediary between the salesman and himself, and for which service he never thought of compensating the tradesman, simply paying him for the trimming and making-up of the garments. Some of the small master and journeymen tailors did very well in this way by using their influence to secure customers to the woollen draper.


DOI: 10.4324/9780429274190-15

## Editorial Headnote

### Priestman, Howard. '"Pulled" Wool or Shoddy', *Waste Trade World*, 2:12 (18 Jan 1913), pp. 16–17; 2:18 (1 Mar 1913), p. 19.

Howard Priestman (1865–1931) was born in Bradford into a Quaker family. His grandfather, John Priestman (1805–1866), was a miller whose temperance principles deterred him from the profitable malt trade, leading him in 1844 to begin manufacturing worsted cloth in a small way at Ashfield Mills. The firm of John Priestman and Co. prospered, and under his sons Frederick Priestman (1836–1934) and Edward Priestman (1838–1920), the business expanded greatly in both worsted spinning and manufacture, and was incorporated as a limited company 24 March 1892. Edward Priestman, Howard's father, retired from the business around 1900, but Howard's elder brother, George Edward Priestman (1863–1942), who had become a partner in 1893, became managing director.

Howard Priestman was destined to join the family firm, beginning work by 1884, and rising to manager of the spinning department of the factory. He had an inventive mind, and had already co-patented an improvement to Noble's combing machine, 9 August 1883. In 1901, he began further education and was a Clothworkers' medallist in 1903 at the University of Leeds. The next year his *Principles of Wool Combing* (London: George Bell & Sons) was published, soon followed by *Principles of Worsted Spinning* in 1906 and *Principles of Woollen Spinning*, with a chapter on shoddy, in 1908 (both published in London by Longmans and Co.). In the latter year, Priestman left the family firm to set up as an independent textile consultant, developing a large practice. He became advisor to the War Office on army clothing in 1914, and technical advisor to the British Research Association in 1919 (Marwick, 1962: 28). Toward the end of his career, Priestman received the 'compliment' of being mocked in *Punch* concerning a purported study concluding that we would be warmer without clothes ('The Clothing Question Again', 31 Jul 1929, pp. 116–117). This demonstrates that his work not only had an impact on industry, government and academia, but also in the public sphere.

Priestman was drawn to the shoddy trade as 'a marvel of ingenuity', as a trade which required 'individual thinking on the part of the manager' because processes were not fully codified. He drew attention to the importance of the detailed pre-sorting of rags, and astute blending of the pulled wool product to achieve the desired shade, lustre and uniformity of yarn.

# 12

# PRIESTMAN, HOWARD. ' "PULLED" WOOL OR SHODDY'

*Waste Trade World* (18 Jan 1913), pp. 16–17; (1 Mar 1913), p. 19.

It has been well said by a distinguished economist that the trades in which there is most vitality are those which are most flexible in their methods, and the woollen rag trade would appear to be an excellent example of this.

In 1860, 16 million pounds weight of woollen rags were imported into this country; in 1870 the weight was 38 million pounds; in 1880 it was 92 million pounds; to-day, (that is to say, in 1911) we took from other countries no less than 56,338 tons.[1] This is an amount largely in excess of all the wool grown in these Islands, and it is a fact that is easy of proof, that the proportion of rag wool to raw wool, imported from all parts of the world, has been a steadily increasing ratio during the past decades.

How much weight of rags actually goes every year to the pulling machines (or "devils" as they are called) in the neighbourhood of Dewsbury there are no figures to show, but there is little doubt that the amount must be well over 200 million pounds weight per year. Contrary to the theory which is usually accepted, that raw materials lose considerably in weight in the manufacturing process, rags gain in weight in their conversion into shoddy. This is due to the large amount of oil that is added to them in the process, and if we leave the increase in weight out of account, we find that about four pounds is produced each year, for every man, woman and child in the British Islands. That is to say that every man may have a complete suit of shoddy every year if he chooses, and some must have more than one.

It must be clear to any thinking mind that the use of waste as compared with the destruction of waste is economically advantageous; such a point needs no argument, and economic laws have a way of working in spite of all petty opposition. Indeed the early opposition to the use of shoddy can hardly be described as petty, in anything but the spirit in which it was conceived. It was fierce and long continued. Shoddy was long known as "Devil's Dust." The name was invented by a Mr. Ferrand,[2] an individual who laboured with much zeal, much ignorance, and with entire futility to destroy the growing trade of Batley and its neighbourhood. But economic laws were working then as they are now, and in obedience to those laws, the Dewsbury and Batley district is now attracting to itself rags from every part of the civilised world, and from some parts that we regard as uncivilised.


DOI: 10.4324/9780429274190-16

Before describing the present requirements of the trade, it is necessary that all those who have rags to dispose of should realise that, whatever may have been the case in the past, rags to-day are divided into a vast number of classes. Everything is done and must be done to save unnecessary expense, particularly the expense of redyeing and carbonising, therefore cotton must be separated from wool, and part cotton from them both, because part cotton rags must be carbonised. All black must go by itself to make a black yarn without being dyed again, and all navy by itself for a like purpose. Soft spun goods must not be mixed with hard, long fibred with short, if the best results are to be obtained.

Let us see what these facts mean to the trade. They have, from very simple beginnings ended in the construction of a complex business system.

Prior to the year 1830 it was the custom of nearly all manufacturers to make what shoddy they required from such rags as they could pick up from the wandering rag and bone man, or as they are called in text books itinerant rag gatherers. It followed as a matter of course that each manufacturer had to deal with all manner of colours and qualities, many of which were of no use to him, and as the trade increased by leaps and bounds a class of small merchants arose in Batley, who bought from the rag men, and did a little sorting and exporting from their native town to places then distant, as Halifax and Huddersfield were before the advent of railways. These middlemen, who really were merchants, began by sorting the rags they bought, but as the demand increased and became more complex, as more and more qualities and shades were required, there appeared room for yet another type of trader between the user, [and] the rag gatherer proper, who goes round from house to house, so that now in addition to that humble and often despised but independent man of business, we have the professional rag dealer, still known as a "marine store dealer" (though he deals in nothing but rags); and again the rag sorter, who in turn sells to the puller or the manufacturer.

In most of the countries from which we import the trade is now organised on somewhat similar lines, and merchants in the heavy woollen district probably buy from some one equivalent to our shoddy or rag dealer. On the other hand some big pullers[3] buy direct from foreign merchants, and although they usually pull them (that is, reduce the rags to fibre) themselves, there is no trade etiquette to prevent their selling any stocks they may hold, just as they come to hand, either to other pullers, or to merchants who are for the moment short of stock, or in need of some special type.

There is no hard and fast distinction as to who is buyer and who is seller, a state of affairs which admirably illustrates the meaning of the economist's term of "elasticity," and furthermore, there is a curious resemblance on a much larger scale to be seen when we examine the relations of international markets.

Dewsbury also has its "sales," and just as London is the Mecca of the wool buyer, so is Dewsbury the Mecca for him who deals in rags.

The Dewsbury sales are held by several firms of brokers, whose primary duty it is to sell by auction for a foreign or country client to a home consumer (manufacturer or puller), or to a local merchant. This is done for a small commission.

In one other respect is this trade widely different from the kindred trade in wool. There is little trade on "commission." It may be that the great cost of stocking a worsted factory has broken that trade into small sections, and made owners (large and small) into commission combers, commission spinners, or commission weavers, as the case may be, who comb, spin, and weave the materials sent to them by others, which they never own themselves.

In Batley, firms who exist to do work in this way are few and far between. It is true that some large pulling houses will do pulling on commission for others in the trade, if they happen to be slack. They may carbonize on commission, or even card; but such incidents should be regarded rather as amenities undertaken through mutual convenience, than as trade institutions, as such [these] require no further exposition.

Why pulling differs from other branches it is hard to say, for whilst there are only two firms that regularly advertise themselves as pulling on commission and doing nothing else, there are well-known firms who have carbonizing plants, who never own the material that they treat, just as there are firms in Bradford who carbonize wool for others.

In spite of the fact that the destruction of any type of waste product or by-product must be economic loss to the community, there are still people to be found who object to the use of shoddy for any purpose, and anyone with ears to hear may hear the word shoddy used as a term of reproach, even in Yorkshire to-day.

Now, as far as this country is concerned, Yorkshire, or to be more particular the district of which Batley is the centre, has almost a monopoly in the transformation of woollen rags into shoddy, and it is therefore the more curious that a trade which brings such an immense amount of money to the country should still be regarded there with any signs of disfavour. This is of course not only a sign of ignorance, but it is the result of ignorance as well, and it really looks as if the inhabitants of neighbouring districts who love to speak contemptuously of Batley and all its work, remain in ignorance by choice.

Let it be said at the outset that the writer was born and bred in a worsted district,[4] and brought up to the worsted trade. Nevertheless, he regards the shoddy trade as a marvel of ingenuity, a trade in which each pound of yarn requires more individual thinking on the part of the manager, than is the case in the worsted trade itself.

The shoddy trade is in fact a clever as well as a very "elastic" trade, and there is no better way to make this clear than to make oneself acquainted with the uses and destiny of woollen rags. First let us get our terms in order.

Shoddy is the fibrous material which results when unmilled cloths such as serge, cashmeres, hosiery, the like are "pulled," that is to say, when they are beaten so hard by the pegs in the "Devil" that they break up into their constituent fibres. This must not be understood that fibres after they are pulled are like they were soon after they came from the sheep's back. In the first place, most of them are dyed, in the second many of them are broken, and therefore much shorter than they were originally, thirdly they are worn. The natural roughness of the surface is not always in its original condition, and where the serrations have been badly damaged in the process, spinning power is very often again diminished thereby.

Mungo, as opposed to shoddy, is the product of cloths which were milled in their first existence. In other words, it is made from old dress cloths,[5] old dress uniforms, waiters' clothes and any other dress (woollen) face fabrics.[6] Mungo is shorter than shoddy for two excellent reasons. In the first place there are few exceptions to the rule that woollen cloths are milled and worsted cloths are not. Woollen also consists of shorter fibred material than worsted. The reasons for its shortness of staple are therefore two-fold, firstly, because the cloths from which it is made were themselves made originally from short wool, secondly, because the fibres are so tightly bound or felted together in the milling process that most of them are badly broken before they can be separated again.

Extract is a third class of pulled or disintegrated rags. It is made from fabrics, either milled or unmilled, that have originally consisted of both cotton and wool. These rags have all their cotton "extracted" from them by any of the various carbonizing processes. They are sold in a condition of absolute freedom from cotton, but the acid and the heat of this process leave their mark on the fibres, and it is seldom that they are passed off in the same category as products of pure wool cloths.

The term extract was one which I heard frequently when I was in Huddersfield and Ossett, that is to say, it was a term in regular use by those who dealt in it. Shoddy and mungo, on the contrary, were words that were seldom if ever heard. It may be some deference to old time prejudice that made the woollen trade adopt terms that conveyed more meaning to the initiated. Be that as it may, shoddy made from worsted is not now sold in Batley as shoddy but as "worsted," and other terms, such as serge, flannel, Cheviot, and merino are some of those which bear a very different meaning in adjacent towns. In the West Riding merino is the one remaining term that should perhaps be explained, because it may or may not be carbonized. There should be no cotton in the cloth from which merino rags are made, but at times it is carbonized to destroy the cotton thread used in sewing the garments of which it is composed.

Having arrived at a superficial knowledge of the terms in daily use, we may now turn back and pick up the thread of the narrative. We have seen how rags are bought and sorted and re-sold. It would be confusing to follow them through all their complicated wanderings, but we may collect a list of the various sorting processes through which rags go without bothering where each sorting takes place. In the very first place they are classed in three sorts: (1) Those containing wool and silk (animal fibres); (2) those of cotton, linen, hemp, etc. (vegetable materials chiefly used in paper trade); and (3) rags of mixed animal and vegetable fibres which must be carbonized or treated with sulphuric acid to destroy the cotton.

In a second sorting wool is separated from silk and from wool with which silk is mixed. Thirdly, the wool rags must be divided into milled and unmilled varieties, each of which in its turn is sorted into clean and dirty sorts.

It may be said that [it is] at this point that sorting really begins, for as a fifth operation the milled rags will be divided into fine, medium, and coarse qualities, in each of which there may be many shades which are divided in the sixth selection.

In the case of unmilled rags, things are even more complicated. It must be remembered that milled fabrics all consist of wool that is fairly uniform in length, but that the serges, costume cloths, flag bunting, and cashmeres forming the other group may contain coarse Lincoln wool full 12 in. long as well as fine Cape merino of less than 3 in. There are, of course, all types of intermediate growths: some yarns are hard twisted and some so soft that they will scarcely hang together. It is therefore necessary and natural that an almost endless variety of qualities and colours should result. Let us take but four examples. Most worsteds made for men's wear are known as worsted when they are pulled. Materials made from the longer and lower qualities of wool which contain old flags and floor cloths make what is known as serge. Flannels, though unmilled, are woollen fabrics composed of fine short-fibred wool. They are kept to themselves, blacks and whites apart, and are known in the trade as flannels. Likewise, as a reminder of its origin, the shoddy which results from dress goods and fine hosiery is known as "merino." And whilst we are discussing names it may be as well to insert here a reference to the material that is known as shoddy in Bradford. As a matter of fact it is not shoddy at all, for it is not a pulled product; it never has been manufactured. It is a by-product of the carding process. It consists of the short fibres that gather in the teeth of the carding engines. These fibres have to be removed in the form of a wide felted sheet whenever the teeth become so full that the work of the teeth is impeded. This material must not be confused with any of the shoddies that result from the pulling of fabrics.

Turning again to the question of sorting, it must not be supposed that the six or seven sorting processes take place in all cases or in the order named, it may be that many of them are done at one and the same time. A manager in this trade must be a man of expediency and resource. He must know how to adapt himself and his staff to any need that may arise, for he has to sell to shade as well as to quality, and if a black that he is making should begin to take on a flatter tone when the lot has run a day or two, he must know what other sort to introduce to make it bright again. If the requisite shade is not to be found at the moment, some other batch must be dyed and added to give the needful tone.

Again, let us suppose that a batch of sorted rags are being dyed some shade of brown before being pulled. They will not all come out alike if they are allowed to go haphazard to the rag grinder; the resulting shoddy will vary in shade from day to day. The manager must be ever on the alert to see that various shades go in the proper proportions. It may be that even so variation will take place, and he may be forced to dye some proportion to a deeper or lighter colour and mix it in to ensure that the final blend shall be exactly correct throughout.

In Bradford we find at times men of small mind, or, shall we say, small business grasp, who think it is not their business and not worth their while to trouble their heads as to the uses to which a buyer will put their wool. They neither know nor care whether the spinner makes fine counts or thick, dull finished cloths or bright. They seem to be concerned only with the immediate present, to sell one lot of wool quite heedless of the fact that if they persuade a spinner to buy a good looking but unsuitable parcel, they are likely to close an open door on their own trade.

There are analogous positions in the rag trade. Few big businesses are built up on anything but a large insight both as to their own and their customer's needs, and the rag merchant small or large, who has a few reliable well sorted lots to sell, will save his customer trouble and earn for himself a reputation and a connection. There are few walks in life where a sound connection does not pay and pay well. In nearly all it is one of the soundest assets a man can have, and the rag trade, with its infinite possibilities for making or saving a big lot of trouble, is never likely to prove an exception.

There is also another point of note that is well worth the retailer's notice. It is the great variety in the price of qualities resulting from different qualities in the same lot of rags. With French imperial black, for example, when carded the price may vary from 3½d. up to 5½d. per pound or more. A mixed London merino would vary more than this, and as it is proverbially difficult to assess the value of a lot in which different values are blended in unknown quantities, the buyer of which sorts will always leave himself a margin in such lots. The lesson is too obvious to need any insistence. It is a difficult lesson to apply to a trade that is so little standardized; but the principle embodied in it is undoubtedly one that is considered by the big progressive houses in the trade, and in these days of stress and hurry the one who will save a big trader trouble is one who will always find an open door.

## Notes

1 Roughly 127 million pounds.
2 William Busfeild Ferrand (1809–1889) used the term 'devil's dust' in a speech of 1842. It is more correct to say Ferrand popularised than invented the term.
3 Rag pullers, that is, those who make shoddy fibre from rags.
4 Bradford.
5 Wool cloth for dress wear, such as suitings.
6 Wool cloth finished by raising and shearing the fibres on one surface, to create a smooth face.

# Part 4

# THE WASTE OF ONE IS THE RAW MATERIAL OF THE NEXT

## Cotton waste

*Fig. 11* A mechanic depicted with his emblematic oil can and engine waste. See Ch. 13 this volume.

*Source*: *Concerning Cotton: a brief account of the aims and achievements of the Amalgamated Cotton Mills Trust Limited and its component companies* (Manchester: ACMT Ltd, 1920), n.p. Manchester Metropolitan University Library.

*Fig. 12* Sponge cloth loom. Framed by the batten are seen the two rows of needles, one pointing up and one pointing down, that hold the warp for gauze weaving.

*Source*: *Some of our Specialities*. Bury: Robert Hall and Sons, c1910. Manchester Metropolitan University Library.

*Fig. 13* Machinery for waste cotton processing: breaker card and Derby doubler by Platt Brothers and Co., Ltd, Oldham. See Ch. 19 this volume.

*Source*: *Textile Mercury*, 1, Jun–Dec 1889, pp. 628–629. Manchester Libraries and Archives.

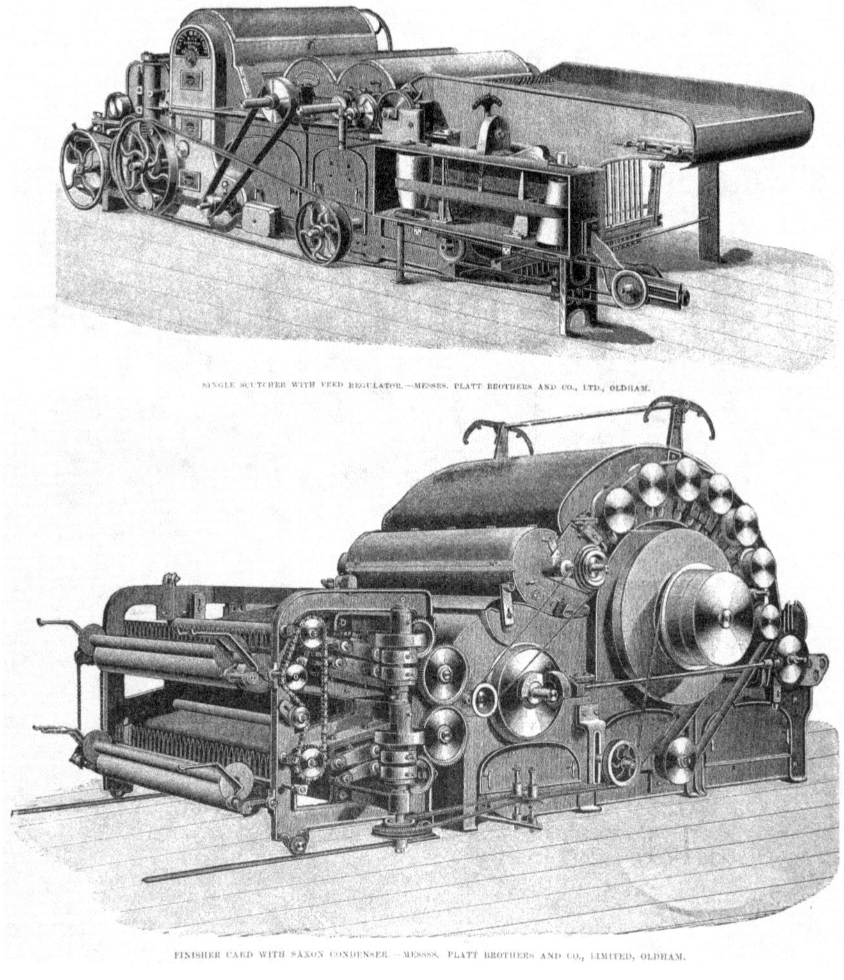


*Fig. 14* Machinery for waste cotton processing: scutcher and finisher card with Saxon condenser, by Platt Brothers and Co. Ltd, Oldham. See Ch. 19 this volume.

*Source*: *Textile Mercury*, 1, Jun–Dec 1889, pp. 178, 646. Manchester Libraries and Archives.

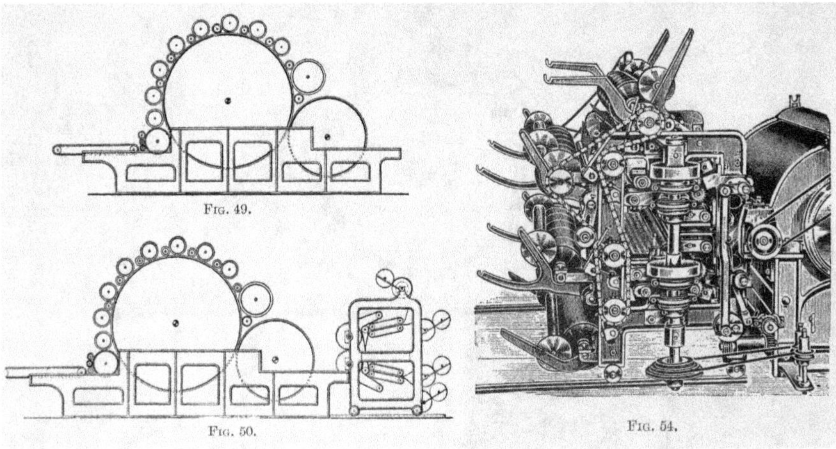


*Fig. 15* Diagrammatic views of the breaker and finisher waste cards as made by Hetherington (left). A condenser arrangement attached to a finisher card; the condenser divides the carded web into narrow strips, which are rubbed into strands, then wound onto a bobbin (right). See Ch. 20 this volume.

*Source*: Thornley, Thomas. *Cotton Spinning (Honours, or Third Year)*, 2nd ed. (London: Scott, Greenwood & Son, 1907), pp. 206, 210. Author's collection.

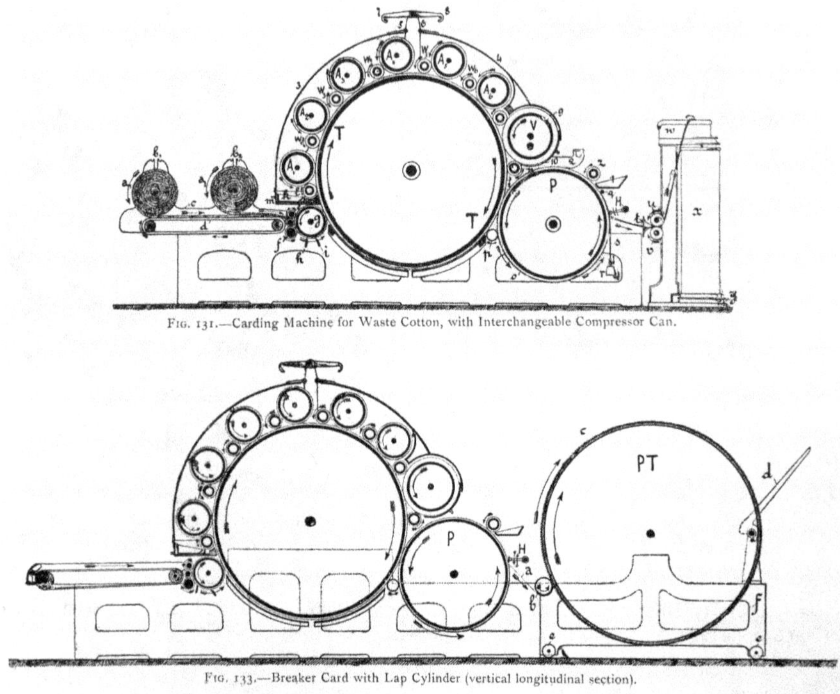


*Fig. 16* Diagrammatic views of carding machines representing two modes of feeding. Multiple rolls of lapped fibre can be layered before entering the finishing card (top); or a single lap can be wound on a large roller which is then cut through to form layered sheets to feed into the finisher card. See Ch. 20 this volume.

*Source*: Zipser, Julius. *Textile Raw Materials and Their Conversion into Yarns*. Translated from the German by Charles Salter (London: Scott, Greenwood and Co., 1901), pp. 231, 234. Author's collection.

*Fig. 17* View of Redmayne and Isherwood's hard waste store at School Street Shed, Blackburn.

*Source*: *Concerning Cotton: a brief account of the aims and achievements of the Amalgamated Cotton Mills Trust Limited and its component companies* (Manchester: ACMT Ltd, 1920), n.p. Manchester Metropolitan University Library.

*Fig. 18* Cotton waste workers at Collyhurst Waste Mills, in photographs by Alvin Langdon Coburn. See Ch. 25 this volume.

*Source*: William C. Jones Ltd. *Cotton Waste: A Study of a Great Lancashire Industry* (Manchester: Charles W. Hobson, 1920). John Rylands Library, R233501. The University of Manchester.

## Editorial Headnote

### 'About Cotton Waste. Specially Contributed', *The Waste Trade World: An International Organ of the Waste and Old Material Trades and for Articles of General Collection*, 1:1 (4 May 1912), p. 13.

### 'The Disposal of Shoddy Dirt: A Boon to Cotton Waste Willowers', *The Waste Trade World*, 2:6 (7 Dec 1912), p. 8.

The *Waste Trade World* began publication in London on 4 May 1912 as a journal of the metal, cotton, woollen, paper and other waste trades. A weekly of twenty-four pages (including covers), the journal's motto was 'Wealth in waste'. The editor introduced the first issue:

> The waste and old material trades, so varied in their nature and extensive in their scope, have up to the present been–at least so far as this country is concerned–totally unrepresented from a journalistic point of view. Our attempt to remedy this state of matters is embodied in the production now before the reader. . . . A trade journal requires to be built up bit by bit, adding new feature after new feature as the occasion allows and the demands arises, gradually gathering contributors and correspondents around it until it attains its full measure of usefulness. . . . [T]he originality of the venture necessarily involves the absence of any ready-made machinery for collecting information and news such as we could avail ourselves of in many other trades. The erection of this "machinery"–that is to say, the organization of the necessary market and news services–has already occupied a considerable time, and its perfection will continue to engage our attention for a further period to come.
>
> (p. 3)

The proprietor of the journal was MacLaren and Sons, a partnership between William Frederick de Bois Maclaren (1856–1921) and Frank Copeman (1862–1927), publishers of industrial books and technical magazines. By the time the journal was launched both men were heavily involved in the rubber trade in Indonesia. Direction of the publishing arm of the business was taken by Joseph Hancock Macadam (1864–1951). The son of an Edinburgh baker, he became a journalist by 1901, and likely brought the bakery and confectionery trade journals into the company portfolio. Copeman's eldest son, Cecil Bertram Copeman (1887–1961) was involved in the sales side of the firm.

The young journal took its share of jokes about there being 'a great demand for rubbish', but it served a real need, evidenced by its survival – with a couple changes of title – to the present day, as *Materials Recycling World*. The first article reproduced here acts as an introduction to the industrial range and relevance of cotton waste at the start of the twentieth century. The second demonstrates the economic necessity to make full use of even the residue of the waste evolved in waste cotton production.

13

# 'ABOUT COTTON WASTE. SPECIALLY CONTRIBUTED' AND 'THE DISPOSAL OF SHODDY DIRT: A BOON TO COTTON WASTE WILLOWERS'

*The Waste Trade World: An International Organ of the Waste and Old Material Trades and for Articles of General Collection* (4 May 1912), p. 13; (7 Dec 1912), p. 8.

## About cotton waste. [Specially contributed.]

Of late years reference to cotton waste in quite a few novels and short stories, especially since the advent of the motor car, has been frequent. If, as the story is told, one shouted "Mac" down into the engine room of any steamer one would be sure of a reply, be sure that if "Mac" came in answer to your call, he would have a wad of cotton waste in his hand. This, however, is only one kind of waste – engine-cleaning waste – in which is utilized thrums, doubler's waste, winder's waste, picked loom shed sweepings, and soiled thread waste generally.[1] Wherever the locomotive heralds the approach of western civilization the engine-man has his wad of waste. The river steamer of the Niger or the Congo has its waste also, and sponge cloths, "sweat rag," entirely made of cotton waste, probably round the neck of the fireman. Indeed, it is found all over the world, whether it be called engine waste in Great Britain, wiping waste in America, known as putzwolle in Germany or dechets d'essuyage in France. This is only one of the uses of waste.

If you have a Bolton bleached counterpane on your bed, the weft of it is waste. If you like a substantial bed sheet, the weft is also waste. If you use candle, the wick is waste. Your lamp wick is waste. The beautiful cotton tapestries woven in France have a proportion of threads spun from waste. Medicated absorbent cotton is generally waste. The wadding in your coat is waste. The little tuft of cotton you see on bananas at times is waste, being part of the wadding in which it has been packed. The basis of the cordite used by our Army and Navy is waste.[2] The cotton flock in cheap bedding and upholstery is waste. Celluloid is made from a fine quality of waste. Some methods of making artificial silk have waste as their basis.

 DOI: 10.4324/9780429274190-18

In the United States and Canada the mattresses are made from cotton waste and linters, a use for the article not current in Europe. An enormous quantity is also consumed there for the production of "bats," i.e., carded sheets for inner lining of wadded quilts or comforters, as they are named there, as well as for carpet linings, which make a very soft tread compared with the felt lining we use. Very large quantities of waste go into consumption for mixing with wool in Yorkshire. On the Continent much waste is used for Vigogne yarn, being dyed raw and spun on woollen machinery.[3]

We do not propose to enlarge on all these various uses of waste at present, but hope to treat upon some of them in greater detail on some future occasion. We trust sufficient has been pointed out to enable our readers not closely identified with this branch of waste products to appreciate how important cotton waste is as an article in the world's commerce.

## The disposal of shoddy dirt: a boon to cotton waste willowers

Hitherto an important question when considering the advisability of putting down a cotton waste willowing plant, has been how to dispose of the dirt or residue from the waste.[4] In willowing, the waste is first of all fed into the willows, which clean the waste fairly well from stick, seed, and sand, and while delivering cleaned waste, force this stick, seed, and sand through the grids into a scroll arrangement which carries it and feeds it automatically into another willower, called the flocker. The flocker is filled with a much closer grid, and separates the flocks from the sand. This sand – or shoddy dirt, as it is called – is really composed of sand, broken cotton seed, shell, a certain amount of leaf, and a small amount of fibre (for it is practically impossible to profitably recover all the fibre in the first process).

A few figures may be quoted to show the importance of the dirt question. In willowing low or medium droppings, the production of willowed droppings may be 20 per cent., and the flocks 5 or 6 per cent – the rest is shoddy dirt. A day's work on a four waste willows and a flocker may produce about 4000 lb. of willowed drops, and perhaps 1000 lb. of flocks, which means that 10 to 16,000 lb. of shoddy dirt has gone into the dirt hole, if on low material. Until very recently the chief – indeed practically the only – outlet for shoddy dirt was the farmers in the vicinity, who would take it away and use it in the first place for bedding down their cattle and afterwards as a fertiliser. It was discovered that the heavy dirt would quickly rot, and well mixed with dung formed a wonderful ground fertiliser.

During the winter months when the cattle are housed at night there was little difficulty in disposing of the dirt at a charge of, say, 1s. to 3s. per load. In some districts where the farmers are more numerous or keener, somewhat better prices may have been obtained. On the other hand, when the summer months came round no shoddy was required by the farmers, and then the trouble commenced. Perhaps you were making five or six loads of shoddy a day, and disposing of one or two loads a week. From drawing 3s. a load it came to paying 3s. or 4s. a load to the farmers to take it away. Perhaps these figures were not generally paid (though instances are known of), but it was certainly a case of paying to get the stuff carted away. A man (often two men) had to be kept continually in the shoddy dirt hole shovelling away and stacking up as well as he could until an occasional cart came along to give relief.

All sorts of ideas were tried to alleviate the trouble. One company used this shoddy dirt for the manufacture of gas, with a certain amount of success, but for some reason this was discontinued. Many willowers attempted to burn it in their boiler fires, but only a small quantity could be disposed of in this way, and even with the installation of forced draught, great care had to be exercised to prevent "banking" the fires. Moreover, it made dirty fires, and raking out was too frequently required.

Happily these difficulties now seem to have been overcome – permanently, we may hope. Some new use has sprung up for the dirt, and better prices are being obtained. Particulars are not available at present, but one rumour is to the effect that it is being used in cattle food!

A correspondent, however, states it as his belief that the shoddy is treated by special machines which separate three classes of production. The fibre and flocks are thoroughly taken out, and then the seed is separated from the stick and sand. Without a question, there must be oil in the seed for it is the real cotton seed even if broken into shell. The flocks recovered are presumably disposed of in the usual way for upholstery, and the sand and stick will still have a value to the farmers. The use of the seed must be guessed at.

There is, adds our correspondent, sufficient attraction in the scheme to have induced three or four firms to try it, although it may be attended with its own difficulties. A great amount of storage room will be required, for it seems to have its off seasons for despatch. Quite irrespective of monetary value, the fact of their being able to dispose of their shoddy dirt will be a great boon to willowers.

## Notes

1 All these are forms of spun yarn as opposed to raw cotton fibre, distinguished as hard and soft waste respectively.

2 Cordite was the common name given to a propellant introduced in 1889 as a replacement for gunpowder; nitrocellulose in the form of guncotton was a major ingredient.

3 Vigogne yarn can indicate a blend of cotton and wool; or cotton spun to look like wool.

4 Willowing was a preliminary process of opening and preparing fibre for carding. The equipment was similar to the machines used for the later processes, but built for a coarser level of treatment.

## Editorial Headnote

### Crankshaw, W. P. 'Famous Bolton Cotton Fabrics', *in* 'Industrial Bolton: the Crompton Centenary Supplement', *Textile Manufacturer*, 53 (Jun 1927), pp. 29–41.

William Percy Crankshaw (1867–1946) had a career as a cotton mill manager before entering teaching. Starting at the Ramsbottom Technical School in July 1894, he was also appointed teacher of the cotton weaving class of the Walkden Technical Classes that September. From 1898, he taught at Bury Technical School, also taking on the Worsley Technical Classes from 1903. In 1907, the *Cotton Factory Times* announced his leaving Bury 'having been appointed head of the Textile Department in the Royal Technical School, Salford' (13 Sep, p. 5). Crankshaw also left the Worsley Classes to focus on the Salford school, and on publishing teaching materials, such as *Weaving Questions for Class and Home Work* (Manchester: Marsden & Co., 1912), and *Weaving* (London: Isaac Pitman & Sons, 1924). By 1925, after three decades of teaching, Crankshaw withdrew from the headmastership at Salford to begin consultancy work on a survey of the Welsh textile industry commissioned by the University of Wales.

Crankshaw had a deep interest in the early history of the cotton industry in his native Bolton, and was working on the history of a Bolton firm at the time of his death; it was edited by Alfred Blackburn and published posthumously: *A Century and a Half of Cotton Spinning, 1797–1947: the History of Knowles Limited of Bolton* (Bolton: Knowles, 1947). Lord Leverhulme's foreword remarks how Crankshaw confronted the paucity of known sources: 'By diligent and persistent labour Mr. Crankshaw supplemented this meagre information from contemporary newspaper articles, books, and the personal recollections of old employees and others'.

In the work extracted here, the author acknowledged his indebtedness to (George) Archibald Sparke (1871–1970), Borough Librarian, for assistance in preparing the article for publication. Sparke was born in Cardiff and began his library career there as an assistant in 1883, moving on to become librarian at Kidderminster around 1893, then city librarian at Carlisle in 1898. He was appointed librarian at Bury in March 1901, and began a position at Bolton as chief librarian and art curator in July 1904, retiring in 1931. He built a strong reputation as a bibliographer and antiquarian, and would have provided the medieval and early modern references for this article.

Crankshaw's interpretation of the introduction of fustian weaving may be questioned. More important here, the article highlights several important Bolton fabric types that use thick cotton yarns for the design (caddows), and for padding (quiltings); these yarns could make use of the ample cotton refuse of fine spinning. Also, Bolton sheetings are specified as using waste yarns. The development of these weaves side by side with Bolton's fine spinning industry suggests a symbiosis between the greater wastage necessitated by finer cottons, and the means to make use of such waste.

# 14

# CRANKSHAW, W. P. 'FAMOUS BOLTON COTTON FABRICS'

## 'Industrial Bolton: the Crompton Centenary Supplement', *Textile Manufacturer* (Jun 1927), pp. 29–41.

To-day Bolton is chiefly famous as being the centre of the fine cotton spinning industry. But in former times it was equally famous for its production of woven fabrics, and even to-day, within a radius of three miles from the Bolton Town Hall, there is a greater variety of fancy cotton fabrics produced than in any area of similar size elsewhere in the world. The textile history of the town is said to date back to the year 1160, and a century-old directory states that it was considered to be the original seat of the cotton industry in Lancashire. It is related that the first batch of Flemish clothiers who came over to England in the year 1337, on the invitation of Edward III,[1] and who were promised, amongst other things, "good beds and better bedfellows," settled in the neighbourhood of Bolton and introduced the manufacturer of "cottons." There is, however, little doubt that there was already in existence a textile industry which had probably been established by an earlier influx of weavers during the inundations in Flanders some two centuries earlier. There is a statement that woollens were manufactured in the town as early as 1160, and apparently what the settlers of 1337 did was to consolidate and improve that industry, and also introduce new fabrics, particularly the "cottons" above mentioned.

The religious persecutions in the Low Countries and France during the sixteenth century caused a large number of textile workers to pour into England – this time without any kind of inducement from the English Sovereign, – and many of them settled in Bolton and the neighbourhood. From this time the town definitely emerged as a prominent textile centre. Leland, about 1538, writes: "Bolton-upon-Moore market stondeth most by cottons and course yarn," and "divers villages in the mores about Bolton do make cottons."[2]

Probably these cottons were the same as those mentioned in connection with the settlers of 1337, which are usually described as having been woollen goods in reality. But from Leland's time increasing mention is made of another class of cottons, which, instead of being made from wool, had a cotton weft and a linen warp, and which eventually became described as "fustians."

It is conjectured that the name "fustian" was derived from Fostat, a suburb of Cairo, where the cloth was first manufactured. It found its way to Italy, which left

 DOI: 10.4324/9780429274190-19

its mark upon the fabric in the term "Genoa back," applied to one variety of fustian, and was carried by the Moors to Spain, from whence it travelled to England by way of the Netherlands. It is interesting to surmise whether the original fustian was composed wholly of cotton, or whether, like the Flemish make, the weft only was cotton. Possibly it was wholly of cotton, as Eastern spinners had acquired the art of producing a thread from cotton which was sufficiently strong to be used for warp. But the Flemings had been skilful workers in flax from the tenth century, or earlier; hence the use of a linen warp for the new fabric would appear to be natural. Were the "cottons" brought over in 1337 really woollen goods as commonly described, or were they not "fustians," and, at least partially, correctly described as cottons? The frequent references to fustian in the literature and documents of the period indicate that the material, both as a fabric and as a synonym for anything which claimed pretensions not warranted by its quality, was in general use in England from the thirteenth century onwards.[3] And when it is remembered that cotton as a textile fibre was well known at the time – there is a reference to its use for candlewicks in 1290, – and that the Flemings of the 1337 settlement could hardly have failed to be acquainted with the manufacture and virtues of linen for warp, there would appear to be reasonable grounds for the assumption that the "cottons" then brought over were not wool fabrics at all, but were, after all, if only partially, correctly described as "cottons."

By the end of the sixteenth century the manufacture of fustians was well established in Bolton. It had a market for these goods long before its larger and more blatant neighbour, Manchester, had a market for textiles of any kind. In 1566 the industry had become important enough to warrant the appointment of a deputy alnager for the town, which, up to that time, had been under the control of the officer who was responsible for the whole of the county of Lancaster. In 1626, Humphrey Chetham, the founder of Chetham's Hospital, Manchester, bought fustians in Bolton market for sale in London. In 1641 the town is described by Lewis Roberts as being the principal seat of the manufacture of fustians, vermilions and dimities.[4]

It would appear that in these early times the name fustian was applied to every kind of cloth which contained cotton, as the records of the period referred to its use for outer clothing, linings, and domestic purposes, including bedding. Fuller, in his "Worthies of England," says that fustian was "creditable wearing for persons of primest quality," and that "it served mean people for their outsides and their betters for the linings of their garments."[5] There are references in 1460 and 1494 to the use of fustians for bed-covers, and in 1554 to "a paier of fustian blankets."[6] In 1696 "dimetty" is said to have been called "pillow fustian," and "to be of great use to put feathers in for pillows."[7]

To-day fustians are generally understood to be heavily wefted, hard-wearing fabrics chiefly used for workmen's clothing and upholstery in the heavier makes, and for ladies' wear and linings in the lighter and finer qualities. Two distinct types are produced, one having on either or both sides, a "nap" or fibre pile, produced by a raising process subsequent to weaving, and the other a thread pile formed by flushing or floating weft threads on the surface of a closely woven ground cloth, so as to form "races" or rows of floats, which can afterwards be cut by a finely pointed knife to form a face pile.

To the first type belong "cantoons" or "diagonals," which have pronounced left twills on the surface, and are used for riding-breeches; "imperials," which are heavily wefted sateens, and used, according to their weight, for linings or for men's wear; "lambskins" and "swansdowns," which are heavily raised on one or both sides, and used for children's and women's underwear. "Moleskins," "beaverteens," and "bullhides" are thick, heavy fabrics, used by workmen engaged in laborious occupations, as their leatherlike character makes them impervious to water and insensible to the splashes of molten metal in the foundry and the thorns of the Australian bush.

To the second type belong velveteens and corduroys, the first of which has the pile uniformly covering the surface like velvet, whilst in corduroys it runs in straight lines along the length of the cloth to form ribs or cords. According to the size and roundness of these cords, the cloth is known as "thickset," as "cable," "bang-up," "constitutional," "King's cord," "Queen's cord," etc.

In common with others, the fustian trade has suffered severely from the remarkable change which has taken place in fashions and modern ideas regarding clothing. Nowadays the whole of a lady's clothing, under- and over-wear together, weighs little, if any, more than a single yard of some of the heavier fustians, and the navvy and gamekeeper have forsaken their moleskins and velveteens for more showy woollens, often enough shoddy to a degree which would have rendered the old-time detractors of honest fustian inarticulate.

Reference has been made to the use of linen yarn for warps. The original source of such yarn is not recorded, but there is a statement that in 1626 Humphrey Cheetham was importing Irish yarn and Cypress wool. It is also recorded that Richard Percival, of Gorton, a captain in the Parliamentary Army, and said to have been the first person to be killed in the Civil Wars, was a cotton-linen manufacturer.[8] Doubtless the fustian industry continued to depend upon imported yarn, but it would appear that eventually a flax-spinning industry was developed in the neighbourhood of Bolton, as somewhere about the year 1825 a factory, which is still in existence, and is known as the "linn" or linen mill, was built on the banks of the river in the centre of the town, for flax spinning. Richard Cobden – of the Corn Laws – was at one time connected with this mill, and it was the scene of a disastrous boiler explosion in the year 1844, when three persons were killed.[9] A group of houses in the vicinity of the factory is still called "Flax Place."

The next fabrics for which Bolton was (and in this case still is) famous are counterpanes and bed-quilts. These are used for the outer coverings of beds, and are generally of a figured character. Out of the many varieties of fabrics used for the purpose, two were almost exclusively manufactured in Bolton and the neighbourhood. These were the caddow or knotted counterpane, and the quilting fabrics known as the toilet and the Marseilles quilt.

The word "caddow" appears to have been originally used to denote a rough woollen covering, apparently of Irish manufacture. But the Bolton caddow is a cotton fabric, and bears more resemblance to the "mockado" or "mocadow" brought to England by the refugees during the Spanish persecutions. This material is frequently mentioned in the literature of the sixteenth and seventeenth centuries, and was composed of silk and wool, linen or cotton, either self-coloured or variegated. It had a design woven in tufts which were cut in imitation of figured velvet. In the caddow counterpane, however, the tufts were left uncut. Probably the Bolton caddow dates from the same period, and it appears to have been carried to Canada by French emigrants. At any rate, examples woven by French Canadians were exhibited in London in 1907.[10]

The outstanding feature of the caddow is the formation of knops or loops from weft. It is essentially a hand-loom product, and is one of the few fabrics which the power-loom has failed to produce, although many attempts have been made to adapt the power-loom for the purpose. The structure of the fabric, and the loom also, are of a very simple character. The fabric is practically plain or tabby, and the loom identical with the ordinary hand-loom for weaving plain cloth, with the exception that the warp beam is provided with a ratchet-wheel to hold it rigid during weaving, this being necessary on account of the weight of the cloth. The reed contained 18 to 22 dents per inch, and had one end per dent of 12's to 16's cotton, although earlier makes had linen warps, which establishes a connection with the early fustian period. Two shuttles were used, one a wheeled "fly" shuttle, containing a "binding" weft of two to four hanks per pound; the other a hand-thrown shuttle containing "double" or folded yarn equivalent to about half of a hank to the pound.

In weaving, two plain picks of "binding" were first inserted. The second shed was then left open and retained by thrusting one of the treadles beneath a T-shaped holder for the passage of the "double" shuttle, which was thrown by hand and allowed to remain on the race-board at the opposite side. Next, the sley was pushed away from the cloth and held back by a short prop, whilst the weaver picked up the "double" into short loops or knops by means of a slightly hooked "piker," to form the pattern. On the completion of the row of loops, the "double" shuttle was removed and placed on the cloth, whilst another pair of binding picks were inserted, following which the "double" shuttle was thrown through the open shed to the opposite side. In the best qualities knops were picked up on every double pick, in "full" or medium qualities on alternate picks, and in low or "radical" qualities on every fourth double pick.

It will thus be observed that the actual process of weaving was a comparatively simple matter, but a very considerable amount of skill was required to place the successive rows of knops in the correct positions in order that the desired pattern might result; it was comparable to the skill which a designer would require to build up a design by marking out the interlacings pick by pick without any outline to guide him. Beginners were, of course, provided with designs for their guidance, but the expert weaver quickly memorised these, and was able to produce the most intricate patterns without such assistance. The last of the master weavers was able to make a dozen caddows, one after another, each different in pattern, and without a design of any kind to aid him. And he used to say, "Ah! but you should have seen what the old weavers could do: they were real weavers; they could not only make their own warps and put them into the loom, but they could also design their own patterns." It is related that one of these old weavers went to church one Sunday, and apparently became more interested in the designs of the stained-glass windows than in the minister's sermon, for on his return home he proceeded to design a pattern which became famous as "Deane Church window's pattern." Another famous pattern, known as the "Cemetery Wall" design, resulted from the attendance of another old weaver at a funeral, during which his eye was caught by the peculiar contour of the wall surrounding the sloping side of the cemetery.

As will be seen from the illustrations, the patterns are of a highly conventionalised character, and the standard patterns, of which three point-paper designs are shown, by passage through the hands of successive generations of weavers, have become practically perfect. Space does not permit more than a passing mention of the "crooked stick," "simnel," "cow pap," and "Duke of Brunswick's star" middles; the "bed-stocks," "hanging firs," and "spectacles" borders; and the "cat-step" and "peltering-iron" edgings. Or of the caddows with the Jubilee portrait of the late Queen Victoria; one with the Lord's Prayer woven in; and another, woven before the days of registrars of births and marriages, containing the names and dates of birth of the weaver and his family.

Apart from the design and the manner in which it is developed, the outstanding feature of the caddow was its strength and durability. It was a common practice to include among wedding presents a caddow with the names of the happy couple and the date of their marriage woven in – a kind of wedding certificate, – and this was expected to outlast their married life. Numerous examples are still to be found which have withstood the use of two generations. On page 31 is shown the caddow quilt presented in 1846 by the Counterpane Weavers' Association to "Mine Host" of the "Horse Shoe," Bolton, where the executive committee of the Association – which was founded in 1843 – held its meetings.[11] The caddow was indeed a weighty token of esteem; it measures 3¼ yds. by 4 yds., and weighs 20 lb. A similar caddow, now in the Bolton Museum, was presented in the same year to the Borough Coroner, also "as a token of esteem"; and both are still in excellent condition. Moreover, there are still in existence at least two caddows which reach back to Crompton's time. The Museum holds one inscribed "Thomas Leaf, Esqr., Feby 2, 1795," with the Royal Arms and "May the King live for ever" in the centre.[12] This caddow is also interesting because of its "purled edges" – *i.e.*, long loops of "double" weft surrounding the border design and the edges of the cloth. Another illustrated in the advertisement on page 28, was woven to commemorate the building of St. George's Church, Bolton, in the year 1805.

In 1833 there were 1000 caddow counterpane looms at work in Bolton, and the number increased until in 1862 there were 1700. From that time the demand for caddows began to decrease, due, it has been said, to the loss of a large trade with Russia consequent upon the Crimean War, and especially to the competition of power-loom quilts, particularly the alhambra and the honeycomb. Repeated attempts to produce caddows by the power-loom had met with complete failure. A considerable trade still continued, however, with public institutions, such as hospitals and work houses, until eventually the weavers died out, and the two looms illustrated herewith – probably the last hand-looms in Lancashire to produce cotton goods for the regular market – ceased to work in 1925. With them ceased also a fine race of craftsmen who are worthy of the admiration and respect of the Lancashire cotton industry, and the connection between the Bolton, Lancs., of to-day and the Bolton-in-the-Mores of ancient time.

## Toilet and Marseilles quilts

Toilet and Marseilles quilts possess the features and characteristics of the quilted fabrics produced by sewing together two pieces of cloth between which a layer of wadding of fibrous or other soft material has been placed, the wadding or lining being retained in its place by the stitches, which can also be made to develop pattern.

TOILET QUILTS. – In the toilet or Marcella quilt illustrated a pattern of an embossed character was produced by stitching heavily tensioned warp threads through a plain woven cloth of fine texture which had a lightly tensioned warp. In low qualities of the cloth the effect depended entirely upon the difference in the tension on the two sets of warp threads, but in the better qualities it was emphasised, and the bulk of the cloth also increased, by a series of special "wadding" picks which were inserted between the face cloth and the underlying "back" or stitching warp threads. In "loose backs" these stitching threads were floated loosely on the underside from one stitch to another, but in "fast backs" they were interlaced by special "back picks" from the same shuttle as the face weft, wadding picks being from the same shuttle, or from a second shuttle, according to the quality and the extent to which it was desired to raise the figure. In weaving the cloth, a compound harness consisting of heald-shafts for the face cloth and a jacquard harness for the stitching warp were used. For the "fast-back" qualities two cumberboards were used, one to receive all odd-numbered cords,[13] and the other all even-numbered ones, and both were connected to treadles whereby they could be lifted alternately. As the harness cords were knotted immediately above the boards, the arrangement enabled the stitching ends to be lifted in plain order for the back picks independently of the jacquard – after the manner of "split" or "bannister-harness" weaving, – the design being so arranged that the ends lifted by the jacquard were all odd-numbered for one shed and all even-numbered for the next.[14] According to the quality of the cloth and the kind of back – *i.e.*, "loose" or "fast," – from two to five or six picks were inserted for each card or stitch, the jacquard griffe[15] remaining lifted while the appropriate sheds for the several picks were formed by healds and cumberboards or "pressers."

THE MARSEILLES QUILT chiefly differed from the toilet quilt in having plain cloths of equal texture for both sides, so that it was perfectly reversible, also it was usually bulkier and heavier owing to the use of coarser wadding weft. A compound harness was also used in its production, but in this case the whole of the face and half of the back warp threads were controlled by healds, and the remaining half of the back threads by the jacquard. Also, each hook of the jacquard governed two adjacent back threads, which were, however, split over two "pressers" to enable the back weave to be kept perfect. For each card or stitch there were four face, four back, and one wadding pick – nine in all, – and the jacquard griffe was raised for two of the face picks only. The arrangement was a good example of the economical use of the jacquard machine, since the number of hooks required was only one-eighth of the number of warp threads in one repeat of the design, and the number of cards only one-ninth of the number of picks. The capacity of the jacquard was also further increased by the use of the centred or vandyke system of harness tie.[16]

QUILTINGS were narrow width piece-goods of a structure similar to that of the loose-back toilet quilt, but generally finer in texture and lighter in weight, and including designs of a simpler character, such as piqué cords or "welts," diamonds and others which came within the capacity of a shaft harness, in addition to jacquard designs. They included some exceedingly fine textures, and were used for ladies' and children's outer wear, vestings, neckwear, and table coverings. Some of the figured vestings produced eighty years ago were probably the most beautiful examples of cotton fabrics ever produced. They were made on the toilet structure, and the embossed effects so developed were elaborated by the addition of extra warp threads of one or more colours, each dent of the reed often having three or four "extras" in addition to the three ends required for the toilet effect. Four examples of these old fine quiltings are illustrated. The cloths are reproduced exact size as woven, and two of them are of special interest in showing how the wearer in the old days often indicated his favourite sport or pastime on his vest.

But fabrics, like time and fashions, are ever changing, and the toilet and Marseilles quilts and the fine quiltings have given place to other styles, usually of a cheaper or a more showy character. For the purposes of this article a brief mention of the present-day quilts will suffice. They include the Mitcheline or patent satin quilt, which has a raised figure formed by coarse weft; the alhambra quilt, in which pattern is produced by an extra coloured warp upon a plain ground, produced by a fine white warp and a very coarse white weft; the honeycomb quilt, with one series of warp and one series of weft threads, either single or folded, and pattern developed upon a honeycomb weave ground; and the Grecian quilt, with folded yarns and pattern developed by twill or satin weaves.[17] The down quilt has become a great competitor of the woven quilt, largely because of its lightness, for which reason a good deal of attention is being given to light-weight bed-covers, into the composition of which artificial-silk yarn is largely entering.

There is a statement that the manufacture of quiltings was introduced into Bolton in the year 1763 by Joseph Shaw.[18] Possibly the statement is correct, as an earlier date would take us to the fustian period of linen warps and comparatively coarse cotton wefts, such as would hardly be likely to give satisfactory results in a quilting fabric. It may, however, be significant that the manufacture of toilet quilts was carried on in Belgium up to recent years, and that a certain variety of Marseilles quilt was called a Belgian.

Up to the middle of the nineteenth century the handloom was still largely in use in the quilting trade, and, of course, before the advent of the jacquard machine the draw-loom was used for figured designs. Although the obvious advantages of the jacquard caused it to be speedily adopted in other branches of the industry, the draw-loom continued to be used for quilt weaving for a considerable time afterwards. Up to a very short time ago there were to be seen old men who began life as draw boys, and who could sing the songs they used to sing to assist them to draw the simple cords in unison with the treadling of the healds and the picking of the shuttle by the weaver, and also [tell] of the weaver's skilful use of a lam-rod when the unfortunate boy allowed his attention to wander.

The accompanying reproduction of the membership card of the Marseille Quilt Weavers' Society, of about the year 1825, shows the application of the draw-loom to quilt weaving.

MUSLINS. – Next to fustians, perhaps the most famous of Bolton fabrics were muslins, which are also interesting in connection with the present celebrations, because they were the direct outcome of Crompton's invention, which was first called "the muslin wheel."

Successive Acts of Parliament passed in 1700, 1721, and 1736, in the interests of the wool industry, prohibited the wearing and manufacture of cloth composed entirely of cotton, and these Acts were not repealed until the year 1774. But before the latter date attempts had been made to produce calico and muslin in imitation of the East Indian fabrics which, during the wars of the middle eighteenth century, had ceased to be imported. It is stated that in 1764 Joseph Shaw, of Anderton, near Bolton, commenced to manufacture coarse muslins from specially hard-twisted yarn, spun on the single-spindle handwheel, and had made some progress with the experiment when he was compelled to abandon it through the flooding of the market with cheap Indian goods on the peace which shortly ensued.

But when Arkwright's throstle frame began to provide a supply of cotton yarn which was not only suitable for warp yarn, but was also finer in counts than any previously produced, attention was again turned to the production of whole cotton fabrics. Thomas Ainsworth, of Bolton,[19] is said to have recommenced the muslin manufacture in 1779 when he produced a piece of "36-reed jaconet," which he succeeded in finishing to imitate the real Indian product.

Then came Crompton's invention, which provided a supply of yarn of a fineness hitherto undreamed of, and enabled the local manufacturers to excel the choicest Indian goods. The result was that by 1782 there commenced in the town a period of unexampled prosperity, which has been called "the Golden Age of the Muslin Weavers," and which lasted almost to the end of the century.

For our present purposes it will be sufficient to state that muslins include a wide variety of light, flimsy fabrics which are woven from medium to fine count yarns. They include plain cloths of the finer makes, such as jaconets, cambrics, mulls and nainsooks, and figured effects as stripes, both crammed and corded; checks, spots, lappets, and lenos, all of which are well known to-day, and were made in the early days referred to. It is recorded that Samuel Oldknow,[20] who was regarded as the leading muslin manufacturer of the Golden Age, employed the draw-loom for some of his designs, and also produced patterns which are called "clip spots" to-day, from the fact that loosely floating threads on the underside of the cloth were clipped or cut away after weaving.

One other type of Bolton fabric calls for brief mention – namely, "Bolton sheetings." Whilst these possibly originated in the town and are still manufactured therein, they are now chiefly made in other districts. They are twill cloths chiefly woven from waste weft, and are sold in the grey or in the unbleached state for bedding purposes.

Bolton is recognised as the centre of the fine-cotton spinning industry. But it can also still claim to be the "chief seat" of the manufacture of fine and figured cotton goods.

Many specialties are produced, as well as fabrics for all purposes of dress, domestic use, and furnishing. These include shirtings, cambrics, muslins, poplins, voiles, lenos, cellulars, brocades, handkerchiefs, tablecovers, sheetings, towels, Bedford cords, coloured stripe shirtings, twills, satins, flannelettes, khaki and white drills, swansdowns, moleskins, cords, etc. Many of the Bolton manufacturers are now producing artificial-silk dress goods of the highest class, and it is of interest to note that Bolton firms were amongst the first to manufacture cotton goods with guaranteed non-fading colours.

## Notes

1 Edward III (1312–1377), reigned 1327–1377.

2 John Leland (c1503–1552) undertook one Welsh and five English itineraries between 1538 and 1543, keeping extensive notes on his travels that were first published in the eighteenth century: *The Itinerary of John Leland the Antiquary*, 3rd ed. (Oxford: James Fletcher, 1769), vol. 7, p. 49.

3 The earliest reference to this usage appears to be 1589: Greene, Robert. *Menaphon Camillas alarum to slumbering Euphues, in his melancholie cell at Silexedra* (London: Thomas Orwin for Sampson Clarke, 1589).

4 Roberts, Lewes (1596–1641). *The Treasure of Traffike, or, a Discourse of Forraigne Trade. . .* (London: printed by E. P. for Nicholas Bourne, 1641), p. 32–33:

> The towne of *Manchester* . . . buy Cotton wooll, in *London*, that comes first from *Cyprus*, and *Smyrna*, and at home worke the same, and perfit it into Fustians, Vermilions, Dymities, and other such Stuffes; and then returne it to *London*, where the same is vented and sold.

5 Fuller, Thomas (1608–1661) *The History of the Worthies of England. . .* (London: printed by J. G. W. L. and W. G. for Thomas Williams, 1662), vol. 2, p. 106. Fuller also notes of fustian: '*Bolton* is the *staple-place* for this commodity, being brought thither from all parts of the County'.

6 These references have not been located. However, Andrew Boorde (1490?–1549) refers to a fustian bed cover in his *Compendyous Regyment of a Dyetary of Helth made in Mountpyllyer. . .* (London: Wyllyam Powell, 1547), n.p.:

> I do aduertyse you for to cause to be made a good thycke quylt of cotton, or els of pure flockes or of clene wooll, and let the couerynge of it be of whyte fustyan, and laye it on the fether bed that you do lye on.

7 J. F. *The Merchant's Ware-House Laid Open. . .* (London: John Sprint and Geo. Conyers, 1696), p. 8.
8 Richard Percivall (1595–1642) was shot 15 July 1642 in a skirmish with Royalists.
9 The fatal explosion occurred on 1 July 1884 at the manufactory of Butterworth and Brooks, Bridge Street, Bolton. James Swift (aged forty-nine) and James MacDonald (aged twenty-seven) were killed on the spot; and Bridget Hart (aged twenty-seven) died the next day from her injuries. There were nineteen wounded (*Manchester and Salford Advertiser*, 6 Jul 1844, p. 8).
10 Probably shown at the Franco-British Exhibition of Science, Arts and Industries, 14 May–31 October 1908, Shepherd's Bush, London.
11 Presented to Hugh Gillibrand, Bolton innkeeper (c1804–1880).
12 Neither Leaf nor the occasion has been identified.
13 Also comberboard, a board positioned between the jacquard machine and the loom below, drilled with rows of holes to guide each harness thread.
14 In the split harness, two or more harness cords are connected to each neck cord that is controlled by the hooks of the jacquard. A full explanation with diagrams can be found in W. Watson, *Advanced Textile Design* (London: Longmans, Green and Co., 1925), pp. 164–167.
15 The griffe is the part of the jacquard mechanism which raises the hooks that lift the threads of the warp.
16 This tie system can be used with bisymmetrical patterns to give a repeat on twice as many threads as there are hooks in the jacquard, because the cords are tied in both straight and reverse order. A detailed, illustrated explanation can be found in W. Watson, *Textile Design and Colour* (London: Longmans, Green and Co., 1912), pp. 232–233.
17 The Mitcheline is a jacquard-woven double cloth in which a fine warp and weft form the ground, and a coarse warp and weft form the figure at the points where the cloths intersect. The Alhambra was the cheapest of the woven quilting structures. The honeycomb quilt employed bold designs in keeping with the cellular cloth texture. The Grecian quilt had a reversible structure.
'Folded yarns' indicates two or more yarns plied together.
18 This attribution is given by John Britton in *The Beauties of England and Wales. . .* (London: Vernor Hood and Sharpe, 1807), vol. 9, p. 295. Britton stated that his information was supplied by Samuel Oldknow.
19 Thomas Ainsworth (1758–1831), muslin manufacturer.
20 Samuel Oldknow (1756–1828), muslin manufacturer.

## Editorial Headnote

### Nodal, John Howard (ed.). 'The Shoddy Exchange, Manchester', *The Sphinx*, 1:6 (29 Aug 1868), p. 49.

### Hitchman, James F. (ed.). 'Cotton Waste Dealers' Exchange', *Manchester Courier and Lancashire General Advertiser* (11 Mar 1869), p. 4.

John Howard Nodal (1831–1909) came from a Quaker family of Manchester, and attended Ackworth School in Yorkshire from 1841–1845. An early influence was the Christian socialist Frederick Denison Maurice (1805–1872), founder of the Working Men's College, where Nodal worked as secretary for three years in his youth. From the time he became sub-editor on the *Manchester Courier* in January 1864, Nodal steadily gained in reputation as an editor and journalist until his retirement in 1904. He was instrumental in the launch of *The Sphinx* on 24 July 1868 as 'a journal of humour and criticism'. The dedicatory prologue declares the journal's aim to be a popular instructor and guide that blends seriousness with entertainment. This short article on the 'Shoddy Exchange' is of the serious character. While beginning in light tone, it moves toward its moralistic purpose to separate modern trade practice from the old custom of conducting business at a local hostelry – with its implied drunkenness and shady dealing. Nodal left a notebook recording payments made to contributors to the first volume of the *Sphinx* but as no contributor was paid for this article, it can be presumed to come from the pen of Nodal himself.

The article attempts reform by shaming 'the character of the men' willing to engage in their trade in a public house. It apparently succeeded, as in March the following year a meeting was held to establish Manchester's new Cotton Waste Dealers' Exchange, documented in the article from the *Manchester Courier*. From about 1839, Robert Scarr Sowler (1815–1871) was editor of the *Manchester Courier*, but he was a practising barrister with an expanding professional career. When the *Courier* became a daily paper, James Francis Hitchman (1839–1890), previously with the *Western Morning News*, was brought in to help; Sowler's continuing professional commitments finally led him to withdraw as editor in 1867. Hitchman then assumed editorial control. He moved to Manchester, marrying Jessie Blair in 1868 at the parish church of Birch in Rusholme, and the couple had five children while residing in the North West. In 1874, they returned to London where Hitchman became assistant editor and leader writer of the *Standard*.

Although this news article reporting the meeting of cotton waste dealers is straightforward in nature, it can be noted that the conservative values of the newspaper were supported by the chairman's opening speech, and backed up by names of upstanding members of the trading community. These men were mostly from a generation born around 1830, who grew up in times when business was unbridled, and now valued a sober and temperate reputation. The article was reprinted in the *Preston Chronicle*, on 13 March 1869 (p. 5).

# 15

# NODAL, JOHN HOWARD (ED.). 'THE SHODDY EXCHANGE, MANCHESTER' AND HITCHMAN, JAMES F. (ED.). 'COTTON WASTE DEALERS' EXCHANGE'

*The Sphinx* (29 Aug 1868), p. 49; *Manchester Courier and Lancashire General Advertiser* (11 Mar 1869), p. 4.

## The shoddy exchange, Manchester

The cotton trade has its shoddy branch as well as the woollen trade. The woollen shoddy trade is occupied in reducing woollen rags to their primitive state of wool, which it remanufactures into shoddy cloth. The cotton shoddy trade is occupied in manufacturing cotton waste into shoddy sheets, twill calicoes, quilts, counterpanes, towels, and a variety of cotton productions, all of which are for the most part made to sell and not to wear. Cotton shoddy moves in a circle of its own. It has favoured localities for its mills. Thus at Stockport and New Mills lamp and candlewick spinners congregate; Bolton is home of the quilt weavers; Ramsbottom, and northwards to Bacup, waste yarn is devilled into cotton again, and worked up into sheets and twills. Shoddy has its own machinery and process for spinning, which is an abbreviation of the ordinary cotton process. It has its own middlemen, its own practises, and its own Exchange.

Like the rest of the cotton trade, shoddy has gone up and down in recent years. During the cotton famine it became a highly palpable trade. High prices forced demand upon the cheapest productions. When Surat cotton took the place of American, shoddy, yarns and fabrics, as far as they would go, took the place of those made from raw cotton. The shoddy trade suddenly expanded. Those who were in it found themselves suddenly growing rich. Many new mills sprang up, and many old mills were filled with machinery for shoddy. Waste, that was before considered worthless, or fit only for the paper maker, became valuable for spinning purposes. As cotton fell, shoddy lost ground where it had taken the place of raw cotton. It has kept on losing ground, though far from returning to its dimensions previous to the famine. Within the last two years shoddy has had numerous representatives in the list of bankrupts.

DOI: 10.4324/9780429274190-20

The reason why shoddy separated itself from the rest of the cotton trade in its Exchange operations, arise to some extent out of the nature of the trade, but chiefly out of the character of those who are in it. The Manchester Shoddy Exchange is to be found towards the Shudehill end of High Street, within and upon the pavement in front of the Corn Stack public house. On Tuesdays, from noon till two o'clock, it is High'Change. There is something significant of the character of the men engaged in the shoddy trade in the place of its Exchange. A few years ago an attempt was made to rescue the trade from this place. A few aspiring members took rooms in Market Street, and attempted to found there a new Cotton Waste Exchange. The experiment failed. Shoddy gravitated back to the Corn Stack. There is a custom almost universal in the trade, a custom by no means monopolised by it, of settling accounts and negotiating sales, over a glass of something more or less strong, at the expense of the seller or the payee. Rooms in Market Street are not favourable to this custom; the Corn Stack is. Besides a tolerable dinner, as town dinners go, is to be had at the Corn Stack at a low price, – and shoddy is not particular about appearances. It is lamentable that an important branch of the cotton trade should hold its Exchange within and about a public house.

## Cotton waste dealers' exchange

A preliminary meeting of cotton waste dealers, convened by circular, was held on Tuesday last in the sample-room of the Royal Exchange. The meeting was numerously attended. Mr. Councillor LANCASTER, of Burnley,[1] presided. – The CHAIRMAN stated that for years he had considered their present place of business to be a very inconvenient, disadvantageous, and disgraceful one. It was very unhealthy, inasmuch as they had to be exposed to the inclemency of the weather, and they could not deny but that their meeting in High-street led them to become a very great nuisance to the neighbourhood. The practice of transacting business regularly in a public-house he looked upon as being very disreputable and humiliating. Through such their sons who were being brought up in the trade were exposed to fearful temptations, whilst those who were older were to be found sometimes in such a state that they were incapable of transacting business properly. He hoped that they would unitedly determine to remove at once, and thus put an end to such as state of things. – Mr. T. GRUNDY of Chorley,[2] secretary *pro tem.*, concurred in the views expressed by the chairman. He said a few persons engaged in the trade, who were dissatisfied with their present place of business, had resolved to try and bring about a change. They had considered that it would be best to call a meeting of representatives from the various towns in Lancashire, with the view of commending an agitation in favour of the object for which they had met. A few circulars had accordingly been issued calling that meeting. He was glad to find that the feeling in favour of a change was so strong as to bring together such a large meeting, which was far more numerously and influentially attended than they had expected. He hoped they would not only resolve to change their place of business, but that they would persevere in the endeavour until their effort was crowned with success. He moved: "That this meeting considers it to be highly desirable to remove the Cotton Waste Dealers' Exchange from High-street to some more convenient place." – Mr. H. SOWERBUTTS, of Preston,[3] seconded the motion, which was carried unanimously. – Messrs. R. BUCKLEY, of Heywood,[4] and Mr. MILLS, of Oldham,[5] moved: "That a committee be appointed for the purpose of enquiring after a suitable room for a Cotton Waste Dealers' Exchange; said room to be submitted for approval to general meeting of the trade, called by the committee for that purpose." A committee was afterwards appointed, consisting of Messrs. H. Sowerbutts, Preston; W. H. Buckley, Ashton;[6] – Isherwood, Heywood;[7] B. Whittingham, Bolton;[8] W. Lancaster, Burnley; W. Baron, Rochdale;[9] R. Harrop, Oldham;[10] G. Parkinson, Blackburn;[11] B. Bottomley, Stalybridge;[12] and J. Hodgson, Manchester.[13] Mr. J. Law, Rochdale,[14] treasurer; and Mr. T. Grundy, Chorley, secretary *pro tem.* – On the motion of Mr. B. WHITTINGHAM, of Bolton, a vote of thanks was accorded to the chairman.

## Notes

1 William Lancaster (1813–1902), cotton waste merchant, Burnley town councillor and Wesleyan lay preacher.

2 Thomas Grundy (c1844–1918) was a cotton waste dealer for a period of time in the 1860s and 1870s. He was in partnership with Thomas Noon (c1823–1903) until 1869, both men having started out in shoemaking. Thomas's brother James Grundy (c1853–1915) worked for Noon as a young man, and then made his career in the cotton waste trade.

3 Henry Eli Sowerbutts (1839–1900).

4 This is probably the Robert Buckley who had a near-bankruptcy at Luzley Brook in 1858, and went into debt again in 1864. Luzley Brook is about five miles from Heywood. Robert Buckley (c1809–1870), a cotton waste dealer of the 1850s and 1860s, father of William Henry Buckley (see Note 6), is usually associated with Ashton-under-Lyne.

5 In 1867, James Mills of Oldham, cotton waste dealer, was mentioned as a trustee for assignees in debt, and he was to find himself in the same position as debtor in October 1879. His lifetime dates have not been ascertained with certainty.

6 William Henry Buckley (c1839–1900) entered the spinning and cotton waste business of his father, Robert Buckley (c1809–1870), in the early 1850s, and became a partner in 1865. He inherited the business with his brother but they split in 1873, each to trade on his own account.

7 Thomas Isherwood (1830–1899) of Manchester Street, Heywood and Irk Mills, Manchester. He was the first mayor of Heywood when the borough was incorporated.

8 Benjamin Whittingham (1829–1893) was the manager of a muslin manufactory in 1861 before entering the cotton waste trade later in the decade.

9 William Baron (c1828–1902) began working in the family firm of James Baron and Sons, Rochdale, in 1856, becoming a partner in 1858. He took charge of the Rochdale arm of the firm after the death of his father James Baron (c1795–1867), founder of the firm.

10 Robert Franklin Harrop (c1832–1912).

11 Giles Parkinson (1827–1880) was the son of a weaver. He began work by the age of thirteen as the feeder of a carding machine. When he married in 1853, he was working as a bookkeeper, but by the time of the 1861 census, he had become a waste dealer.

12 There were two firms of cotton waste dealers in Stalybridge: Bottomley and Hyde at Wakefield Road, and Bottomley Brothers at Harrop Street. Neither firm appears to have had a principal whose first name began with B.

13 This is possibly John Charles Hodgson (c1844–1920) who became established as a cotton waste dealer in Pollard Street, Blackburn, by 1871. In 1893, the waste shed he formerly occupied was sold, and it was probably at that time Hodgson became a barrel and tub dealer.

14 Joseph Law (c1831–1883) set up as a waste dealer in Rochdale by 1861, first at Gibraltar Rock, and by 1863 in Victoria Street, Whitworth Road. For a brief summary of his career, see 'Death of Mr. Joseph Law', *Rochdale Observer*, 20 October 1883, p. 5.

## Editorial Headnote

### Sowerbutts, Eli. *The Cotton Waste Dealers' Directory, being a Complete List of Waste Dealers, and of all Other Trades Connected Therewith. Arranged in Alphabetical Order, and in Towns for Ready Reference* (Manchester: Abel Heywood & Son, 1882), pp. 3–35.

Eli Sowerbutts (1834–1904) was born in Chorley, son of Thomas Sowerbutts (1809–1897) and his wife Ruth (c1806–1837). Young Eli was apprenticed in the printing office of Manchester stationer Benjamin Love (1811–1869). Concurrently, he improved his education at the Mechanics' Institution and later the Working Men's College in the city. In April 1859, he married Emma Casson (c1831–1916) and the couple moved to London where Sowerbutts worked for Robert Barclay, Bucklersbury stationer and printer, rising to foreman at a salary of £130 a year. However, at the end of 1862, Sowerbutts was accused of the theft of blank engraved bank notes. He appears not to have been convicted, but left to start his own stationery business in Huddersfield in April 1863. This business failed in 1866, and Sowerbutts returned to Manchester where he set up as an accountant, a profession he continued to practise alongside his more passionate involvement in geography which came about in the late 1870s. In 1879, Sowerbutts attempted to establish a geographical society in Manchester, and although he could not secure support at that time, he continued in this pursuit until the Manchester Geographical Society was launched 15 October 1884.

The *Waste Dealers' Directory* was a project that occupied a couple of the intervening years, allowing some interplay of his accounting and geographical skills. By 1876, Sowerbutts had become secretary of the Manchester Cotton Waste Dealers' Exchange Company, and acted as its auditor. His *Directory* did not list only members, but tried to give a full and accurate picture of regional activity, while his 'town lists' map the geographical spread of the trade. The *Directory* came out in December 1882 in a simple, wire-stitched paper cover. This is the only edition known, and it is thought that the copy held in John Rylands Library is the sole surviving example (R232842).

Once the Geographical Society began, Sowerbutts devoted his whole activity there. His obituary in the *Geographical Journal* recognised:

> It is impossible to exaggerate the amount of time and labour which Mr. Sowerbutts gave to the Society; he was constantly at the rooms, ever ready to give information to callers; he was in correspondence with societies all over the world; he arranged the regular meetings, securing the services of travellers and explorers; he edited the Journal, and prepared himself to deliver addresses which never failed to interest and instruct his audiences.
>
> (23:6, Jun 1904, pp. 792–793)

John Mortimer affectionately wrote,

> the purpose of his life, seemed to be attained when, having helped to found a geographic society in our city, he became, as secretary, its guiding and controlling spirt, well content for such slender salary as could be afforded from its finances.
>
> ('Our Geographer: A Vignette', *The Manchester Quarterly: A Journal of Literature and Art*, 24, 1905, pp. 1–6)

# 16

# SOWERBUTTS, ELI. *THE COTTON WASTE DEALERS' DIRECTORY, BEING A COMPLETE LIST OF WASTE DEALERS, AND OF ALL OTHER TRADES CONNECTED THEREWITH*

(Manchester: Abel Heywood & Son, 1882), pp. 3–35. Courtesy of the University of Manchester.

## Preface

A complete Directory of the Cotton Waste Trade, and of the kindred Trades, has been a long felt want, and the present is the first attempt to supply that want in a form handy of reference and full in information.

Every effort has been made to have the information given accurate, and as full as it has been possible to obtain it. It is hoped that this Directory will meet the wants of the Trade, and of Trades having business with them.

The Town Lists will be of great service.

Notice of any errors in addresses or in description, or any omissions will be thankfully received, as it may be useful to publish from time to time a correcting sheet to keep the directory as full and as accurate as a book of this kind ought to be. E.S., Christmas, 1882

## Key to trades

N.B. – The following list contains all the various trades referred to in the Directory. Each one is prefaced by a number, and that number will be found after the name in the alphabetical list, thus indicating the trade or trades carried on by the firms whose names appear in that list.

1 Cotton Waste Dealers or Merchants
2 Flock Dealers or Makers
3 Bag Dealers or Makers
4 Rag Dealers
5 Candlewick Makers or Dealers

DOI: 10.4324/9780429274190-21

6 Bump Spinners
7 Paper Makers
8 Paper Waste Dealers or Merchants
9 Engine Waste do. do.
10 Woollen Waste Dealers
11 Spinners
12 Yarn Agents
13 Machine Brokers
14 Wadding Manufacturers
15 Oil and Tallow Dealers
16 Rope and Twine Manufacturers
17 Fent Dealers
18 Millowners
19 Waste Bleachers
20 Machinists

N.B. – Members of the Manchester Cotton Waste Dealers' Exchange are set back in the alphabetical list, and a reference is made to the firms they represent. Where no name is placed opposite a name set back, the firm named immediately preceding is represented by those persons. Members of the Oldham Cotton Waste Exchange are marked by a star.

## Alphabetical list of waste dealers, &c., &c

| *A* | | | |
|---|---|---|---|
| Adams & Co. | 1 2 9 | Cable Mills, Livesey Street | Manchester |
| John Godbert | | | |
| J. J. Neale | | | |
| Allen, J. & Sons | 1 | Albert Mills, Cook Street | Bury |
| John Allen, junr. | | | |
| Allen, John, junr. | | See: J. Allen & Sons | |
| Allen, Peter | 1 | 1, Back Princess Street | Bury |
| P. Allen | | | |
| Allen, William | 1 3 | Walker's Croft, Hunt's Bank | Manchester |
| Allott, J. F. | 1 | 48, Charles Street | Ashton-under-Lyne |
| Almond, Wm. & Co. | 7 | South Belgrave | Over Darwen |
| Ambler, Timothy & Son | 7 | Ingrow Mills | Keighley |
| Andrew, J. & J. F. | 1 | 9, Bower St., and 11, Castle Mill St. | Oldham |
| Ashton, Henry | 1 | George Street | Chorley |
| Ashton, William | 1 2 | 23, Back Mayes Street | Manchester |
| Ashworth & Co., Ltd. | 7 | Brookside Mill | Church |
| Ashworth, J. & Bros. | 10 | Livesey Street | Rochdale |
| Ashworth, James Hy. | 1 | Albert Works | Cloughfold |
| J. H. Ashworth | | | |

| A | | | |
|---|---|---|---|
| Ashworth, John | 1 | 12, Walshaw Road | Bury |
| Ashworth, Miles<br>M. Ashworth | 1 | Falinge Road | Rochdale |
| Atkinson, John | 1 | Paradise Lane | Blackburn |
| Atlas Paper Mill Co. | 7 | Ecclesfield Mills | Sheffield |
| Austin, C. E. | | See: C. E. Austin Bros. | |
| Austin, C. E. & Bro.<br>C. E. Austin<br>J. H. Leach | 1 5 9 | Marlboro' Mills, Union Street | Manchester |
| Ayland, Samuel & Co. | 5 | 26, Cannon Street | Manchester |

| B | | | |
|---|---|---|---|
| Baerlien & Co.<br>Hy. Gabbott | | 12, Blackfriars Street | Manchester |
| Bailey, Robert | 1 | 165, Blackburn Road | Haslingden |
| Baker, William | 1 | Upper Vauxhall Street | Manchester |
| Bannister, J. | 1 | ----- | Bolton |
| Barber, Joshua<br>J. B. Lomax | 1 | Salop Street | Bolton |
| Bardsley, C. T. | 1 | Wright Street | Oldham |
| Bardsley, G. W. & Son<br>W. E. Bardsley | 1 | Breightmet Street | Bolton |
| Bardsley, W. E. | | See: G. W. Bardsley & Son | |
| Barlow, Charles | | See: Thomas Barlow | |
| Barlow, Charles | 1 | 20, Back Hope Street | Oldham |
| Barlow, George | 1 | 28, Back Hope Street | Oldham |
| Barlow, H. | 1 | Pilling Street | Burnley |
| Barlow, James | 1 | 122, Manchester Road | Heywood |
| Barlow, John | 9 | 7, Crowcroft View, Stockport Road., Levenshulme | Manchester |
| Barlow, Thomas<br>Charles Barlow | 1 | Falinge Road | Rochdale |
| Barnes & Buckley | 9 | Roe Street Mill, Livesey St., Oldham Road. | Manchester |
| Barnes, E. S. | | See: Tatham & Co. | |
| Barnes, Henry | 1 | ----- | Cloughfold |
| Barnes, John | 1 9 | 1, William St., Rochdale Road. | Manchester |
| Barnes, Smith<br>Smith Barnes | 1 | Taylor Street, Oxford Street | Accrington |
| Baron, Arthur | | See: James Baron & Sons | |
| Baron, George<br>George Baron | 1 | 17, Canal Street | Stockport |
| Baron, James | | See: James Baron & Sons | |

(Continued)

(Continued)

| *B* | | | |
|---|---|---|---|
| Baron, James, & Sons<br>John Baron<br>Arthur Baron<br>Wm. Sutcliffe | 1 | Finsley Gate | Burnley |
| Baron, James & Sons<br>James Baron<br>William Baron<br>John W. Baron | 1 | Castle Hill | Rochdale |
| Baron, John | | See: James Baron & Sons | |
| Baron, John, W. | | See: James Baron & Sons | |
| Baron, Wm. | | See: James Baron & Sons | |
| Barraclough, Benjn | 1 | 50, Tutbury Street, Ancoats | Manchester |
| Barrett, John<br>John Barrett | 1 | 97, Bradford St., and Platt St. Mills, Bridgeman St. | Bolton |
| *Barroclough, E. | 1 | 1, Castle Mill Street | Oldham |
| Barton, Francis<br>F. Barton | 1 | ----- | Blackburn |
| Barton, Henry<br>H. Barton | 1 | Randall Street | Blackburn |
| Bateman, James | 1 | Lower Wharf St. | Ashton-under-Lyne |
| Bateson, Roger | 7 | Matshead Mill | near Garston |
| Baxter & Son | 1 | 12, Mayes Street | Manchester |
| Bayley, Wake & Co | 5 | 4, Balloon Street | Manchester |
| Beard, John | 5 | 60, High Street | Manchester |
| Beaumont, Jas. & Geo. | 4 | Albert Mills, Pump Street | Manchester |
| Beaumont, W. | 1 | Foundry, Salmon Street | Preston |
| Bell, James<br>James Bell | 1 | ----- | Heywood |
| Bell, John | 1 | ----- | Heywood |
| Bell, Richard | 1 | 30, Derby Street | Heywood |
| Belshaw, James A.<br>J. A. Belshaw | 1 | 11, Back York Street | Heywood |
| Benson, Thomas | | See: Abraham Milnes, Preston | |
| Beswick, Samuel | 1 | Breightmet Street | Bolton |
| Bibby, James<br>Jas. Bibby | 1 | ----- | Burnley |
| Bibby, Thomas | 1 | Crook Street, Ribbleton Lane | Preston |
| Birtwistle, Thos. | 1 | Syke Street | Accrington |
| Blunt, Thos. & Sons | | ----- | Bury |
| Boardman Bros. | 1 9 | Ludgate St. Mill, Rochdale Road. | Manchester |
| Bolton, Thomas | 1 | 29, Union Street | Oswaldtwistle |
| Bolton, William | | See: William Bolton & Sons | |

*B*

| | | | |
|---|---|---|---|
| Bolton, William & Sons<br>William Bolton | 1 | ------ | Bury |
| Bonsor, Barthrop | 7 | Higher Mills | Staleybridge |
| Boodle, F. A. & Co. | 2 | 79, Charter Street | Manchester |
| Booth, Alfred | 1 | Whitehead Street | Oldham |
| Booth, William | | See: Cotton W.D. Fire Insurance Co. | |
| Bottom & Lord | 1 | 10, Garden Street | Oldham |
| Bottomley & Hyde<br>James Bottomley | 1 | Wakefield Road | Staleybridge |
| Bottomley Bros.<br>William Bottomley | 1 | Harrop Street | Staleybridge |
| *Bottomley, James | | See: Bottomley & Hyde | |
| Bottomley, John<br>John Bottomley<br>M.L. Bottomley | 1 | 88, Wellington Street | Ashton-under-Lyne |
| Bottomley, M. L. | | See: John Bottomley | |
| *Bottomley, William | | See: Bottomley Bros. | |
| *Bowdon, Geo. | | See: R. Gilliatt | |
| Boyle, Daniel | 2 | 2, Stevenson Square | Manchester |
| Bracken, T. H. & Co. | 7 | Bradley Mills<br>Hunslet<br>Stainland | near Halifax<br>near Leeds<br>near Halifax |
| Bracken, Jonathan & Sons | 7 | Dean Mills | Luddenden |
| Bradbury, Robert<br>Robert Bradbury | 1 | 9, Medlock Street | Oldham |
| Bradley, Isaac | 4 | 76, Lower Moss Lane, Hulme | [Manchester] |
| Brear, William | | See: John Crossley & Sons | |
| *Brelsford, James | 4 | Castle Mill | Oldham |
| *Brewer, James | | ----- Royton | Oldham |
| *Bridge, John | 1 | 1 Court, Medlock Street | Oldham |
| Brierley & Wilson | 6 | Turner's New Mill, Smallbridge | near Rochdale |
| Brierley, James | 4 | 4, Lloyd Street, Albert Square | Manchester |
| Brierley, Luke | 1 | 42, Back Turner Street | Manchester |
| Brierley, R. | 1 | 16, Johnson St., & 10, Back King St. | Bolton |
| Brindle, Alfred | | See: C.H. Brindle & Sons | |
| Brindle, C. H. | | See: C.H. Brindle & Sons | |
| Brindle, C. H. & Sons<br>C. H. Brindle<br>Alfred Brindle | 1 8 | Short Street<br>30, Ward's Buildings | Blackburn<br>Manchester |
| Brindle, G.<br>G. Brindle | 1 | Union Street | Darwen |
| Broadbent, Samuel | | See: James Stott | |

*(Continued)*

(Continued)

| *B* | | | |
|---|---|---|---|
| Broadbent, Wm. & Sons Ltd. | 7 | Cream's Mill, Little Lever | near Bolton |
| Brooks, Robert B.<br>R. B. Brooks<br>J. H. Brooks | 1 | Stamford Road | Mossley |
| Brown, J. | 1 | Bolton Street | Chorley |
| Brown, J. H. | 1 | Cheapside | Chorley |
| Brown, J. W. | | See: Thomas Brown & Son | |
| Brown, Thos. & Son<br>J. W. Brown | 1 | Bath Place, & Lower Bridgeman St. | Bolton |
| Brown, W. H. | 12 | Barrowford | Colne |
| Buckley, B. | 11 | ----- | Heywood |
| Buckley, C. | 1 | 18, Beever Street | Oldham |
| *Buckley, Fred. | | | |
| *Buckley, Henry | 1 | 13, Cross Street | Oldham |
| *Buckley, James | 1 | ----- | Ashton-under-Lyne |
| *Buckley, John<br>J. Buckley | 1 | 63, Bell Street | Oldham |
| *Buckley, Philip | 1 | 16, Lamb Street | Oldham |
| *Buckley, Robert | | | |
| Buckley, T. L.<br>T. L. Buckley | 1 | Stamford Road | Mossley |
| Buckley, W. | 1 | 85, Huddersfield Road | Oldham |
| Buckley, William | 1 | 45, Church Street | Ashton-under-Lyne |
| *Buckley, W. Hy.<br>W. Hy. Buckley | 1 | Bentinck Street | Ashton-under-Lyne |
| Burgess, James | 5 | 13 & 15, Bradshaw St., Shudehill | Manchester |
| Burnley Paper Works Co., Ltd. | 7 | Calder Vale Mill | Burnley |
| Burrows, A | | See: E. Burrows | |
| Burrows, E.<br>A. Burrows | 1 | Tame Valley | Dukinfield |
| Burrows, Thos.<br>Thos. Burrows | 1 | King Street East | Stockport |
| Bury Paper Making Co., Ltd. | 7 | Gigg Mills | Bury |
| Butterworth, E. & Co.<br>D. Goodill | 1 8 9 | 52, Ward's Buildings, Deansgate | Manchester |
| Butterworth, J. & Co. | 1 | Molesworth Street | Rochdale |
| Butterworth, John<br>J. Butterworth | 1 | ----- | Rawtenstall |
| Butterworth, Moses | 1 | Brunswick Street | Oldham |

*C*

| | | | |
|---|---|---|---|
| Cain, Joseph | 1 | 53, Goulden St., Rochdale Road. | Manchester |
| Caldwell, John | 1 4 | 49 to 57, Bengal Street | Manchester |
| Caldwell, John, junr. | 4 | 14, Dyche St., Rochdale Road. | Manchester |
| Card, Nathaniel & Co. | 5 | Richardson St., Rochdale Road. | Manchester |
| Carlisle, Sons & Co. | 7 | Primrose Mills | Clitheroe |
| Cartwright, John | 4 | 1, Dean St., Clayton St., Newton | Manchester |
| Carver, Thos. | 1 | Station Street | Oldham |
| Cawtherly, John | 1 | 11, Blackburn Street | Burnley |
| Chadwick & Taylor<br>I. Gaskill | 1 | Factory Yard, Miller Street | Manchester |
| Chadwick & Taylor | 7 | Ordsall Hall Mills | Salford |
| Chadwick, Charles | 1 | 58, Henshawe Street | Oldham |
| Chadwick, John | 13 | Well Street | Heywood |
| Chadwick, S. & J.<br>T. Gaskill | 1 | Irk Mills, Long Millgate | Manchester |
| Chadwick, T. | 1 | Heap Riding Mill | Stockport |
| Chadwick, Walter | 13 | 4, Wellington Street | Heywood |
| Chadwick, William & Sons | 7 | Broughton Grove Paper Works, and Agecroft Hall Paper Works, Pendleton | Manchester |
| Cheetham, Elisha | 1 | Willow Street | Oldham |
| Clark & Luke | 7 | Ripponden | near Halifax |
| Clayton & Whitehead<br>Hy. Clayton | 1 | Grimeshaw Street | Preston |
| Clayton, James | 1 | Hope's Carr | Stockport |
| Clayton, James | 6 | Carr Mills, Waterloo Road | Stockport |
| Clayton, Henry | | See: Clayton & Whitehead | |
| Cleasby, A. & Co. | 1 2 | 3, Hood Street, Ancoats | Manchester |
| Clegg, Ann | 2 | Walker's Croft, Hunt's Bank | Manchester |
| Clegg, James | 1 | Vale Street | Heywood |
| Clegg, J. E.<br>J. E. Clegg | 1 | Heap Riding Mill | Stockport |
| Clegg, J. T. | 1 | 52, Wellington Street | Heywood |
| Clegg, John | 1 | 4, McDonald's Bldgs, Market-place | Manchester |
| Clegg, R. | | See: R. Clegg & Sons | |
| Clegg, R. & Sons<br>R. Clegg | 1 | Todd Street | Rochdale |
| *Clegg, Samuel | | ----- | Oldham |
| *Cohen, Eli | | ----- | Manchester |
| Collinge, John | 5 | 1 Peel Street, Duke Street | Manchester |
| *Collinge, Robt. D. | | | |
| Collins Paper Mill Co. | 7 | Collins Mill | Over Darwen |
| Conroy, Catherine | 4 | 32, George Leigh Street | Manchester |
| Cooke & Greenhalgh<br>W. H. Cooke | 1 | ----- | Farnworth |
| Cooke, Henry & Co. | 7 | Whitcliffe & Castle Mills | Richmond [Yorkshire] |

*(Continued)*

(Continued)

| *C* | | | |
|---|---|---|---|
| Cooke, Leonard | 7 | Vale Mills, Horwich | near Bolton |
| Cooke, W. H. | | See Cooke and Greenhalgh | |
| Cookson, James | 1 | 3, Great Egerton Street, Heaton Norris & Higher Hillgate | Stockport |
| Cookson, Joseph | 1 5 9 | 21, New Cannon Street | Manchester |
| Coop & Co. | 1 | School Common Mill | Wigan |
| Cooper, James | 1 | Mill Street, Long Millgate | Manchester |
| Cooper, John | 1 | 1, Hutchinson Street, Queen Street | Salford |
| Cooper, Joseph | 1 | 10, Victoria Street | Oldham |
| Cooper, Samuel | 1 | 22, Bell Street | Oldham |
| Cotton Waste Dealers' Mutual Fire Insurance Co.<br>Wm. Booth | | Argyle Buildings | Heywood |
| *Cowell, R. H.<br>R. H. Cowell | 1 | 1, Court, Medlock Street | Oldham |
| Crabtree & Hardman | 1 | 63, Bell Street | Oldham |
| Crabtree, Charles | 7 | Tube Mills | Bingley [Yorkshire] |
| Crabtree, Edwin<br>E. Crabtree<br>R. Duckworth | 1 | 23, Aspinall St. | Heywood |
| Crabtree, Henry | | See: Thos. Crabtree | |
| Crabtree, James | 1 | Hooley Brow | Heywood |
| Crabtree, J. | 1 10 | 14, The Baum | Rochdale |
| Crabtree, Thomas<br>Hy. Crabtree<br>John Whitehead | 1 | 6, Bamford Road | Heywood |
| Crawshaw, Richard | 1 | 34, Tile Street | Bury |
| Crawshaw, Thomas<br>Thomas Crawshaw | 1 | | Bury |
| Crompton, Jas. R. | 7 | Elton Paper Mills | near Bury |
| Crompton, John & Thos. B. | 7 | Farnworth Mills<br>Standish Mills | Bolton<br>Wigan |
| Cronkshaw, James | 1 | ----- | Rawtenstall |
| Cronkshaw, William | 1 | Hoyle Bottom Mill | Oswaldtwistle |
| Crook, James | 1 | St. Mark's Street | Bolton |
| Cropper, A. | | See: Cropper Bros. | |
| Cropper Bros.<br>Wm. Cropper<br>A. Cropper | 1 | Piercy Mill | near Newchurch |
| Cropper, William | | See: Cropper Bros. | |
| Cross, John | 1 4 | Cuple Gate | Halifax |
| Crossland, Fred. | | See: J. Fletcher & Co. | |
| Crossley, John & Son<br>William Brear | | Dean Clough Mill | Halifax |
| Crossley, Peter | 1 6 | Carr Mills, Hope's Carr | Stockport |
| Cunliffe, George | 1 | 99, Deardengate | Haslingden |

*D*

| | | | |
|---|---|---|---|
| Dacca Twist Co.<br>Chas. Wilde | 14 | Portland Street | Manchester |
| Darwen Paper Mill Co., Ld. | 7 | Spring Vale | Darwen |
| Darwen Paper Mill Co., Ld. | 7 | Lower Darwen Mills | Darwen |
| Davies & Pennington | 1 | 5, Bower Street | Oldham |
| *Davies, William | | | |
| Dawson, C. A. | | See: T. Isherwood | |
| *Dawson, James | | | |
| Dawson, John Thomas<br>J. T. Dawson | 1 | Fir Street | Heywood |
| Dean Brook Waste<br>Bleaching Co.<br>H. K. Wooler | | Dean Brook Works | Moston |
| Dearden, Jonathan & Co. | 1 | Little Bridge Mill, Chorley Street | Little Bolton |
| Dearden, John<br>J. Dearden | 1 | 70, Manchester Road | Heywood |
| Dearden, W.<br>W. Dearden | 1 | Waterloo Street & Mowbray Street | Oldham |
| Deeply Vale Paper<br>Manufacturing Co.<br>Limited | 7 | Walmersley | near Bury |
| Devine, John | 4 | Henry's Court, Henry Street, Oldham Road | Manchester |
| *Devonport, James<br>J. Devonport | 1 | ----- | Oldham |
| Devonport, William | 6 | Brinksway | Stockport |
| Dimmock, Jas. & Co. | 7 | Darwen Paper Mills | Darwen |
| Dineley, William | 1 2 8 9 | 19 & 22, Mayes Street | Manchester |
| Dixon, Peter & Son | 7 | Spring Grove Mills, Oughty Bridge | near Sheffield |
| Dodge, S. | 6 | ----- | Stockport |
| Dodgon, Robt. | | New Line | Bacup |
| Dorran, Matthew & Son | 1 | Garden Street, Mumps | Oldham |
| Downs & Robert | 1 | 5, North Street | Manchester |
| Duckworth, R. | | See: E. Crabtree | |
| Duckworth, Robt.<br>Robt. Hy. Duckworth | 1 | ----- | Ramsbottom |
| Duckworth, R. H. | | See: R. Duckworth | |
| Dumville, Joseph | 4 | 82, Rochdale Road | Manchester |
| Dunkerley, E. J. & Co. | 2 9 | 33, Spring Gardens | Manchester |
| *Dunkerley, Joseph | 1 | 26, Whitehead Street | Oldham |
| *Dunkerley, Herbert | | | |
| Duxbury, Yates & Son | 7 | Hall-i'th-wood | near Bolton |
| Dyson, Benjamin | 1 | 30, Medlock Street | Oldham |
| *Dyson, Eli<br>Eli Dyson | 1 | Cromwell Street & Medlock Street | Oldham |

*(Continued)*

(Continued)

| *E* | | | |
|---|---|---|---|
| Eagley Paper Mill Co. | 7 | Eagley Bridge | Bolton |
| East Lancashire Paper Co. Ltd. | 7 | ----- | Radcliffe |
| Eastwood, Abraham<br>A. Eastwood | 1 | 25, Back York Street | Heywood |
| Eastwood, James | 1 | 52, Lees Road | Oldham |
| Eastwood, William | 1 | 65, Bolton Street | Ramsbottom |
| Eccles, John | | See: N. & J. Eccles | |
| Eccles, Nathaniel | 1 | ----- | Over Darwen |
| Eccles, N. & J.<br>John Eccles | 1 | Shifnall Street | Bolton |
| Emmet, John & Co. | 7 | Springfield Works | Bolton |
| Entwistle, A. | | See: J. & A. Entwistle | |
| Entwistle, J. & A.<br>A. Entwistle | 1 | Foundry Street | Bury |
| Entwistle, John<br>J. Entwistle | 1 | Back Dutton Street | Accrington |
| Entwistle, O.<br>O. Entwistle | | ----- | Bury |

| *F* | | | |
|---|---|---|---|
| Fairham, F. G. | | See: William Fairham | |
| *Fairham, William<br>W. Fairham<br>F. G. Fairham | 1 | 106, Molesworth Street | Rochdale |
| Fauthorp, James | 1 | Greetland | near Halifax |
| Fazakerley, Thos. | 1 | 26, Mayes Street | Manchester |
| Fearnley, Joseph | 1 | 1, Albert Street, Lower Broughton | Manchester |
| Featherstone, Charles | 4 8 | 26, Newton Street | Manchester |
| Fenton, Thos. | | See: Thos. Fenton & Co. | |
| Fenton, Thos. & Co,<br>Thos. Fenton | 1 | 45, Church Street | Heywood |
| Fenton, William | 1 9 | 7, Bilberry Street, Ashley Lane | Manchester |
| Fernley, Joseph | 1 | Storey Street | Salford |
| Field, Charles | 1 | Willow Street | Oldham |
| Fielden St. Mill Co.<br>J. H. Riley | 1 | Weir Street | Blackburn |
| Fletcher, James | | See: J. Fletcher & Co. | |
| Fletcher, James & Co.<br>James Fletcher<br>Fred Crossland | 1 | 21, Johnson Street | Bolton |
| Fletcher, J. H.<br>J. H. Fletcher | 1 | ----- | Oldham |

| *F* | | | |
|---|---|---|---|
| Fletcher, John<br>John Fletcher | 1 | Molesworth Street | Rochdale |
| Fletcher, Robert & Son | 7 | Kersley Works | Stoneclough |
| *Flitcroft, Wm. | 1 | Bolling's Mill, Bradshawgate | Bolton |
| W. Flitcroft | | Bell Street | Oldham |
| *Freeman, John | 1 | Castle Mill Street | Oldham |
| Froggatt, Joseph | 6 | ----- | New Mills |

| *G* | | | |
|---|---|---|---|
| Gabbott, Henry | | See: Baerlien & Co. | |
| Garnett, Peter & Son | 7 | Wharfe Side | Otley [Yorkshire] |
| Garside, R. | 1 2 5 9 | 111, George Leigh Street | Manchester |
| *Gartside, John<br>John Gartside | 1 | 12, Slack Street | Rochdale |
| Gartside, Joseph | 1 | Glodwick Street | Oldham |
| Gaskell, Isaac | | See: Chadwick & Taylor | |
| Gaskell, Thomas | | See: S. & J. Chadwick | |
| Gent, George | | See: Haworth & Gent | |
| Gillespie & Mason | 7 | | Newton-le-Willows |
| Gilliatt, Robert<br>R. Gilliatt<br>J. W. Gilliatt<br>Geo. Bowden | 1 | 6, 8 & 17, Shaw Road | Oldham |
| Glazebrook, John | 1 | Boodle Street | Ashton-under-Lyne |
| Godbert, John | | See: Adams & Co. | |
| Goodill, D. | | See: E. Butterworth & Co. | |
| *Greaves, Benjamin | 1 | Waste Street | Oldham |
| Greaves, James, Exors of | 1 | Hall Street | Oldham |
| Greaves, W. C. | 15 | Grimshaw Street | Burnley |
| Green, George<br>Daniel Hilton | 1 | 26, Bell Street, Mumps | Oldham |
| Green, James | | See: Healey Wood Mill Co. | |
| Greenhalgh, H. | | See: T. Isherwood | |
| Greenhalgh, J. & Co. | 1 | Back Hope Street | Oldham |
| Greenwood, John | 1 | Back Burnley Road | Accrington |
| Grime, Thos. & Co. | 7 | Knot Mills | Over Darwen |
| Grimshaw, Selina | 1 | 5, Dean Street, Port Street | Manchester |
| Grove Mill Paper Co. Limited | 7 | Grove Mill | New Mills |
| Grundy, James | | See: Thos. Noon | |
| Guerin, J. & T. | 1 9 | 67, Addington St., Oldham Road. | Manchester |

*(Continued)*

(Continued)

| *H* | | | |
|---|---|---|---|
| Hadfield | 6 | ----- | Stockport |
| Hague, Joseph<br>Thomas Hague | 1 | Eagle Mill, Tame Street<br>Vale House | Staleybridge<br>Mossley |
| Halkyard & Hyde | 1 | 16, Bell Street | Oldham |
| Hall, E. & Sons | 1 | Station Street | Oldham |
| *Hall, Edward | | | |
| Hall, James | | Turf Street | Bury |
| Hall, Wm. & Sons | 7 | Diggle Mill | Dobcross, Yorkshire |
| Halliwell, J. H.<br>J. H. Halliwell | 1 | Twyford Mills | Stockport |
| Halstead, James | 4 8 | 85, Long Millgate | Manchester |
| Hamilton, Robert<br>R. Hamilton | 1 | Birchin Lee Mill, Royton | Oldham |
| Hamnett, R. H. | 1 | Egerton Mill, Great Egerton St., Heaton Norris | Stockport |
| Hamner, Samuel | | Park Mill, Dale Street, Elton | Bury |
| Hannan, Thos. | 1 | Brook Street | Oldham |
| Hanson, Buckley | 1 | Lees Road | Oldham |
| *Hanson, George | | | |
| Hanson, Scott, & Co. | 16 | Twincroft-lane | Stockport |
| Hanson, W. & G. | 1 | 14, Beever Street | Oldham |
| Hardman, A. and K. | 1 | 35, Russell Street | Heywood |
| Hardman, Joseph<br>Jos. Hardman | 1 | 62, Bell Street | Oldham |
| Hargreaves, George<br>Geo. Hargreaves | 1 | ----- | Cloughfold |
| Hargreaves, James<br>Robert Hargreaves | 1 | Pippin Bank | Bacup |
| Hargreaves, John & Sons<br>J. Stansfield | 1 | ----- | Rawtenstall |
| Hargreaves, Moses<br>Moses Hargreaves | 1 | Grimshaw St., & Aqueduct St. | Burnley |
| Hargreaves, Robert | | See: James Hargreaves | |
| Hargreaves, S. | 1 | 41, Aspinall Street | Heywood |
| *Harrison, Ralph | | See: R. Harrison & Sons | |
| Harrison, Ralph & Sons | 1 | Springfield Works, Springfield | Manchester |
| Harrop, George | 1 | 53, Bell Street | Oldham |
| Harrop, John | 1 | Bell Street | Oldham |
| *Harrop, Robert F.<br>R. F. Harrop | 1 | Bell Street | Oldham |
| Harter, John<br>John Harter | 1 | Ridgeway Lane | Stockport |
| Hartley, John<br>John Hartley | 1 | ----- | Settle |

*H*

| | | | |
|---|---|---|---|
| Hartley, Matthew<br>M. Hartley | 1 | Water | Newchurch |
| Hartley, Robert<br>R. Hartley | 1 | ----- | Burnley |
| Harwood, John | | See: J. Harwood & Co. | |
| Harwood, J. and Co.<br>John Harwood | 1 | Union Street | Darwen |
| Harwood, Lawrence | 7 | Spring Vale Mill, Turton | near Bolton |
| Hastings, Edward | 7 | Morton Mills, Morton | near Bingley, Yorkshire |
| Haswell, J. C. | 1 | Bell Street | Oldham |
| Haworth & Gent<br>Geo. Gent<br>H. Parkinson | 1 | ----- | Blackburn |
| Haworth, Thos. | 1 | Carlisle Mill, Bradshawgate | Bolton |
| Hayes, Johnstone | 1 | 23, Back Acres | Bolton |
| Hazelgrove & Nephew | 1 2 5 9 | Robert Street Mill, Cheetham | Manchester |
| Healey Wood Mill Co.<br>J. Green | 1 | Healey Wood Road | Burnley |
| Heap, David | 1 | ----- | Crawshawbooth |
| Heap, R. | | See: Shackleton & Co. | |
| Heap, W. T.<br>W. T. Heap | 1 | ----- | Rochdale |
| Hebblethwaite Bros.<br>G. H. Hebblethwaite | 1 | ----- | Huddersfield |
| Hebblethwaite, G. H. | | See: Hebblethwaite Bros. | |
| Henthorn & Buckley | 1 | 14, Bell St. & 20, Back Hope St. | Oldham |
| Hesselgrove & Marsden | 1 | 1, Court, Medlock Street | Oldham |
| Hey, John & Co.<br>Stephen Hey | 1 | Derby Street | Colne |
| Hey, Stephen | | See: John Hey & Co. | |
| Heywood, E. | 1 | Roscoe Street | Oldham |
| Hibbard, P. & S.<br>S. Hibbard | 1 | 7, Beever Street | Oldham |
| *Hibbard, S. | | See: P. & S. Hibbard | |
| Hibbert, Thos. | 4 | Walker's Croft | Manchester |
| Higginbottom, Jas.<br>F. Livingstone | 1 | Longstone Buildings, 21, Cannon Street | Manchester |
| Hill, James | 6 | ----- | New Mills |
| Hill, Joseph | 1 | St. James's Pool, Whitworth Road | Rochdale |
| Hill, W. F. | 6 | ----- | New Mills |
| Hilton, Daniel | | See: George Green | |

*(Continued)*

(Continued)

| *H* | | | |
|---|---|---|---|
| *Hilton, John | 1 | 24, Whitehead Street, Mumps | Oldham |
| Hindle, A. & J. James Hindle | 1 | 13, Blackburn Street | Haslingden |
| Hindle, James | | See: A. & J. Hindle | |
| Hindley, James Jas. Hindley | 1 | ----- | Blackburn |
| Hodgson, J. C. | 1 | Pollard Street | Blackburn |
| Holden, George | 1 | Medlock Street | Oldham |
| Holden, J. W. J. W. Holden | 1 | 13, 15, & 17, Taylor Street | Darwen near Burnley |
| Holden, John (Exors the late) | 7 | Simonstone Mill | Padiham |
| *Holden, Ralph | | | |
| Holden, Simeon Simeon Holden | 1 | 6 & 8, Roscoe Street | Oldham |
| Holden, William | 1 | 16, Back Hope Street | Oldham |
| Holker, Samuel | 7 | Lumb Mill, Edenfield | Bury |
| Holland, James William Whittaker | 1 | 82, Manchester Road | Burnley |
| Holland, William | 6 | ----- | Stockport |
| *Holroyd, John | 1 | 8, Victoria Street, Mumps | Oldham |
| *Holroyd, J. N. | | See: John Holroyd | |
| Holt, Edmund E. Holt | 1 | 163, Bradshawgate | Bolton |
| Holt, Henry John Holt | 1 | 1, New Street | Haslingden |
| Holt, Isaac Isaac Holt | 1 | Salop Street | Bolton |
| Holt, James | 1 | Spring Side Mill, Lees | Oldham |
| Holt, John | | See: Henry Holt | |
| Holt, Thomas | 1 | 143, Green Lane | Heywood |
| *Holt, W. H. W. H. Holt | 1 | Back Hope Street | Oldham |
| Hopwood, T. | 6 | ----- | Stockport |
| Horrocks, Henry H. Horrocks | 1 | ----- | Bury |
| Horrocks, J. & W. W. Horrocks | 1 | Old Bowling Green Mill | Darwen |
| Horrocks, W. | | See: J. & W. Horrocks | |
| Horsfall, W. | 1 | Birchcliffe | Hebden Bridge |
| Howarth, James | 1 | 41, Lord Street | Rochdale |
| Howard, Joseph Jos. Howard | 1 | 14, Alexandra Grove, Trafford Road | Salford |
| Howard, M. A. & Sons | 4 | 23, Hilton Street and Springfield Lane | Manchester Salford |

| *H* | | | |
|---|---|---|---|
| Howard, Thos. | 1 | Roger Street, Red Bank | Manchester |
| Howe, James L. | 1 | Turner Street | Ashton-under-Lyne |
| Howe, J. W. | | See: J. L. Howe | |
| Hoyle, R.<br>R. Hoyle | 1 | Cannon Street | Oldham |
| Hughes, John Robert | 1 9 | 2, Bagshaw's Court, Shudehill | Manchester |
| Hulme, Wm. | 6 | Carr Mills, Waterloo Road | Stockport |
| Hyde, James Hy. | | See: John Hyde and Sons | |
| Hyde, John | | See: John Hyde and Sons | |
| Hyde, John & Sons<br>John Hyde<br>Jas, Hy. Hyde | 1 | ----- | Stalybridge |
| Hyde, R. | 1 | Britannia Mill, Bell Street | Oldham |
| Hyde, S. R. | 6 | Ludworth | Marple |

| *I* | | | |
|---|---|---|---|
| Ingham & Broadbent | 1 | Crow Nest | Hebden Bridge |
| Ingham, James B. & Sons | 7 | Shuttleworth Mill, Shuttleworth | near Bury |
| Isherwood & Brindle | 7 | Salmesbury Mills | near Preston |
| Isherwood, E. | | 5, New Street, Hanover Street | Manchester |
| Isherwood, James | 1 | 15, George Street | Haslingden |
| Isherwood, John<br>John Isherwood | 1 | Salmesbury | near Preston |
| Isherwood, Thomas<br>T. Isherwood<br>C. A. Dawson<br>H. Greenhalgh | 1 | Ormerod Street<br>and Irk Mills, Long Millgate | Heywood<br>Manchester |

| *J* | | | |
|---|---|---|---|
| Jackson, Eli | 1 | Fleet Street | Ashton-under-Lyne |
| Jackson, J. | 1 | 20, Whitehead Street | Oldham |
| Jackson, James | 1 | Bradshawgate Mill | Accrington |
| Jackson, James | 7 | Oaken Clough | near Garstang |
| Jackson, John<br>J. Jackson | 1 | 67, Primrose Street, Ancoats | Manchester |

*(Continued)*

(Continued)

| *J* | | | |
|---|---|---|---|
| Johnson, James<br>J. Johnson | 1 | 15, Wright Street | Oldham |
| Johnson, William | 1 | 16, Gloucester Street, Haulgh | Bolton |
| Jones Bros. | 4 | Queen's Road, West Gorton | Manchester |
| Jones, Robert | 1 | Starrcliffe, Moses Gate | Bolton |
| Jones, Wm. Chas.<br>W. C. Jones<br>James Taylor | 1 9 | Appleton Street, Collyhurst Street | Manchester |
| Joy, Seth | 2 4 | Little Peter Street | Manchester |

| *K* | | | |
|---|---|---|---|
| Kay, A. H.<br>A. H. Kay | 1 | Bradshaw Street | Bolton |
| Kay, James | | See: Wm. Kay & Sons | |
| Kay, John<br>J. Kay | 1 | ----- | Bury |
| Kay, Levi<br>L. Kay | 1 | 36, Clayton Street | Blackburn |
| Kay, William | 1 | ----- Royton | Oldham |
| Kay, William | 1 | Stamford Road | Mossley |
| Kay, William, junr. | | See: W. Kay & Sons | |
| Kay, William & Sons<br>Wm. Kay, junr.<br>James Kay | 1 | 11, Johnston Street | Blackburn |
| Kellett, Edward | 2 9 | 8 & 9, Green Street, Tib Street | Manchester |
| Kellett, Moses | 1 | Wellbeck | Ashton |
| Kelly, James | 4 | 57, Pump St., Rochdale Road. | Manchester |
| *Kershaw, James | 1 | Regent Street | Oldham |
| Kershaw, James<br>Jas. Kershaw | 1 | Wimpole Street Mill | Ashton-under-Lyne |
| Kershaw, William<br>Wm. Kershaw | 1 | 20, Back Hope Street | Oldham |
| King, William & Co. | 7 | Mulberry Mill | Sheffield |
| Kirk, Abraham | 4 8 | 31, Wharf Road, Church Bank | Bolton |

| *L* | | | |
|---|---|---|---|
| Lancaster, James | | See: W. Lancaster | |
| Lancaster, William<br>William Lancaster<br>James Lancaster | 1 | Bank Parade | Burnley |
| *Law, Edward<br>Edward Law<br>James Law | 1 | Bellfield | Oldham |

| L | | | |
|---|---|---|---|
| Law, Frank | | See: Joseph Law | |
| *Law, James | | See: Edward Law | |
| *Law, Joseph | 9 | Little Dale Street | Rochdale |
| Joseph Law | | | |
| Robert L. Law | | | |
| Frank Law | | | |
| *Law, Robert L. | | See: Joseph Law | |
| Lawton, A. H. | 1 | 2, Wilkinson Street | Oldham |
| A. H. Lawton | | | |
| *Lawton, Albert | | | |
| Lawton, F. | 1 | Station Street | Oldham |
| Laycock & Nephew | 5 | 4, Union Street, Church Street | Manchester |
| Laycock, Joseph | 1 | Weir Street | Blackburn |
| Joseph Laycock | | | |
| Leach, John | 1 | ----- | Rochdale |
| Leach, J. H. | | See: C. E. Austin & Bros. | |
| Lee, David | 1 | Back Foundry Street | Bury |
| Lee, Lawrence | 1 | Wheatly-lane | Colne |
| Lee Valley Mill Co. | 1 | 2, St. Ann's Place | Manchester |
| | | and Charlesworth, King Street | Oldham |
| Lees, E. | | King Street | Oldham |
| Lees, James | 1 | 8, 9 & 13, Castle Mill Street | Oldham |
| Lees, John | 1 | 14, Lamb Street | Oldham |
| *Leigh, John | 1 | 11 & 12, Brook St., 1 Bower St. & 10, Birch St. | Oldham |
| John Leigh | | | |
| *Leigh, Wm | | See: John Leigh | |
| Lingard, Joseph | 14 | | Chapel-en-le-Frith |
| Livingstone, F. | | See: James Higginbottom | |
| Lomax, James | 1 | ----- | Stockport |
| Lomax, Joshua B. | | See: Joshua Barber | |
| Lomax, William | 1 | Ainsworth Vale | near Bolton |
| Longworth, John | 1 | 1, Bury Street | Darwen |
| Lonsdale, James | 1 | Commercial Street | Church |
| Lonsdale, James | | See: R. Lonsdale & Son | |
| Lonsdale, R. & Son | 1 | 32 & 38, Taylor St., Oxford St. | Accrington |
| Jas. Lonsdale | | | |
| *Lord, Abraham | 1 | 9 & 11, Shaw Road | Oldham |
| A. Lord | | | |
| Lord, Edward | 1 | Salford Mill | Todmorden |
| E. Lord | | | |
| *Lord, James | 1 | Grove Street | Oldham |
| Jas. Lord | | | |
| *Lord, Levi | | | |
| Lowe, E. | 1 | Bell Street | Oldham |
| Lowther, J. W. & Co. | 1 9 | Nightingale St., Strangeways | Manchester |
| Lynch, Daniel | 4 | 17, Charles Street | Manchester |
| Lyne, W. H. & Sons | 1 | Simmondley | Glossop |
| Lyons, William | 4 | 36, Mason Street | Manchester |

*(Continued)*

(Continued)

| *M* | | | |
|---|---|---|---|
| McKee, Samuel | 1 4 | 10 & 14, Sutton St., Bradford St. | Manchester |
| Maden, William<br>W. Maden | 1 | Walker Street | Rochdale |
| Mallalieu & Buckley | 1 | 5, Waste Street, Mumps | Oldham |
| *Mallalieu, Benjamin | | | |
| *Manchester & County Bank | | | |
| Marland & Howe<br>John Marland | 1 | Turner Lane | Ashton-under-Lyne |
| Marland, John | | See: Marland & Howe | |
| Marsden, Charles & Son | 7 | Rivelin Mills<br>Dearne Mill<br>Calder Grove Mills<br>Frank Mills | near Sheffield<br>Barnsley<br>near Wakefield<br>Sheffield |
| Marsden, Thomas | 7 | Valley Paper Works, Smithies | Barnsley |
| Maudsley, James | 1 | 32, Grove Street | Oldham |
| Mayall, R. | 1 | Glodwick Road | Oldham |
| *Mayall, Thomas | 1 | 16, Garden Street, Mumps and Mount Pleasant | Oldham |
| Meadowcroft, R. & Co. | 1 | Bradshaw Street | Heywood |
| Meadowcroft, W. | 1 | Garden Street, Mumps | Oldham |
| *Megee, Peter | 1 | 9, Hall Street | Oldham |
| Megson, Thos. | 4 | 20a, Cross St., Hanover St. | Manchester |
| Mellalieu, Holden<br>H. Mellalieu | 1 | Scaitcliffe Old Mill | Accrington |
| Mellodew, John | 1 | 17, Wright Street | Oldham |
| Mellodew, Thomas | 1 | 20, Bell Street | Oldham |
| Mellor, John | 1 | 38a, Deansgate | Manchester |
| Mellor, John | 1 2 | 2, Back Mayes Street | Manchester |
| Millett, R. | 1 | 18, Knowsley Street | Bury |
| Mills, James | 1 | 38, Grove Street | Oldham |
| Mills, John<br>John Mills | 1 | ----- | Rochdale |
| Mills, Thomas | 1 | Rose Mill, Wigan Road | Bolton |
| Millward, S. & Co. | 4 8 | 56, Princess Street | Manchester |
| Milnes, Abraham<br>T. Benson | 1 | Sydney Place, Moor Lane | Preston |
| Milnes & Co.<br>W. F. Milnes | 1 | Trinity Works, Blackfriars St. | Salford |
| Milnes, W. F. | | See: Milnes & Co. | |
| Mitchell, J. W. | | See: Wm. Mitchell | |
| Mitchell, John & Sons | 7 | Primrose Mills | Clitheroe |
| Mitchell, Wm.<br>W. Mitchell<br>J. W. Mitchell | 1 | ----- | Rawtenstall |

| *M* | | | |
|---|---|---|---|
| Moorby, John<br>John Moorby | 1 | Narrowgates Mill, Barley | near Burnley |
| Moore, J. | 1 | Allen's Buildings, 32, Victoria Street | Manchester |
| Moorhouse, John | 1 | | Whitewell<br>Bolton<br>Newchurch |
| Morgan, Joseph & Sons | 1 5 9 | Ducie Works, Corporation St. | Manchester |
| Morris, William | 1 4 8 | 11, Johnson Street | Bolton |

| *N* | | | |
|---|---|---|---|
| Neale, J. J. | | See: Adams & Co. | |
| Neill, John & Co. | 7 | Dock Street | Leeds |
| *Nicholls, Thos.<br>Thos. Nicholls | 1 | 2, Dawson Street, Greengate | Salford |
| Nicholls, S. S. & Co. | 7 | Grimshaw Bridge Mills | Darwen |
| *Noall, E. R. | 1 | 18, Bell Street, Mumps | Oldham |
| Noon, Thomas<br>T. Noon<br>J. Grundy | 1 | Edward Street | Chorley |
| Norton, S. | 4 | 48, Temperance Street | Manchester |

| *O* | | | |
|---|---|---|---|
| Ockleston, Robt | 7 | Millbank | near Warrington |
| Ogden, Joseph | 1 | 18, 20 & 22, Greenacres Street | Oldham |
| *Oldham, Robert | 1 | | |
| Olive Bros. | 7 | Woolfold Mill | Bury |
| Olive & Partington | 7 | Turnlee Mills | Glossop |
| Ormerod, George | 1 | ----- | Bury |
| Ormerod, Geo. Wm. | 1 | ----- | Newchurch |
| Orrell, John<br>John Orrell | 1 | Leighton Street | Preston |
| Owen, James | 1 | 10, Castle Mill Street | Oldham |
| Oxley, William | 6 | 97, Ancoats Street | Manchester<br>Stockport |

*(Continued)*

(Continued)

| *P* | | | |
|---|---|---|---|
| Parke, Thos. B. | 7 | Withnell Fold | near Chorley |
| Parkinson, John | 1 | Silverwell Lane | Bolton |
| Parkinson, H. | | See: Haworth & Gent | |
| Partington & Hodgson<br>Robert Partington | 1 | Shiffnal Street | Bolton |
| Partington, John<br>John Partington<br>M. G. Partington | 1 | Mount St.<br>& Irk Mills, Long Millgate | Heywood<br>Manchester |
| Partington, Moses G. | | See: John Partington | |
| Partington, Robert | | See: Partington & Hodgson | |
| Partington, Samuel<br>S. Partington | 1 | Rock Street | Heywood |
| Patchett, William<br>Wm. Patchett | 1 | 61, Miller Street | Manchester |
| Patrick, William | | See: Wm. Patrick & Son | |
| Patrick, William & Son<br>Wm. Patrick | 1 | Commercial Street | Stacksteads |
| Pattison, Robert | 1 4 | Pump St., Oldham Road. | Manchester |
| Peake, John | 17 | 7 & 9, Manor Street | Bolton |
| Pearson, George | 1 | 12, Mayes Street | Manchester |
| Peebles & Son | 7 | Rishton Mills, Rishton | near Blackburn |
| Pemberton, J. E. | 1 | 3, Bower Street | Oldham |
| *Pennington, John | 1 | | |
| Pettit, E. S. & Co. | 1 2 5 9 | North St., Miller St. | Manchester |
| Philbin, John | 4 | 12a, Back Old Mount Street | Manchester |
| Philbin, Michael John | 4 8 | 33, Jackson's Row | Manchester |
| Pilling, A. & Sons | 4 8 | Proctor Street | Rochdale |
| Pilling, James<br>James Pilling | 1 | 166, Rochdale Road | Bacup |
| Pomfret, W. & F. | 1 | Lord Street | Preston |
| Posnett, James | 18 | Junction Mills, Bridge St., Portwood | Stockport |
| Potter & Co. | 7 | Hollin's Mills | Over Darwen |
| *Potter, James | 1 | See: Robert Stott | |
| *Potter, Thos. | 1 | | |
| Priestly, David | 1 | ----- | Rawtenstall |

| *R* | | | |
|---|---|---|---|
| Ramsbottom Paper Mill Co. Ltd. | 7 | ----- | Ramsbottom |
| Ramscar, James | 1 | Hope's Carr | Stockport |
| Ramscar, William | 6 | Carr Mill, Waterloo Road | Stockport |
| Ratcliffe, S. & Bros. | 6 | ----- | Marple |
| Ratcliffe, Thos. | 1 | Mellor | Marple |
| Ravenscroft, Thos. | | 12, Redfern St., Miller St. | Manchester |

| *R* | | | |
|---|---|---|---|
| Read, Ashworth<br>A. Read | 1 | 6, Elizabeth Street | Burnley |
| Read, Edward & Son | 4 | Hilton Street | Manchester |
| Reason, George | 1 | Seymour Road, Astley Bridge | Bolton |
| Redmayne, E. B. | 1 | Weir Street | Blackburn |
| Redmayne, Leonard<br>L. Redmayne | 1 | Walpole Street | Blackburn |
| Rendtorff & Co. | 1 | 7, South Parade, St. Mary's | Manchester |
| Rhodes, James<br>James Rhodes | 1 | Dawson Street, Moss Side | Heywood |
| Richardson, John | 1 | Bell Street | Oldham |
| Rigby, J. O. & S. | 1 | Short Street, Heaton Norris | Stockport |
| Rigby, Josiah & Co. | 1 5 9 | 59, 61, & 72, Temple St., Chorlton-on-Medlock, & Wellington Mill, Ancoats | Manchester and at London |
| Riley, J. H. | | See: Fielden Street Mill Co. | |
| Rishton, W. H. | 1 | Ratcliffe Fold | Haslingden |
| Roach Bridge Paper Co., Ltd. | 7 | Roach Bridge, Salmesbury | near Preston |
| Roberts, James<br>Jas. Roberts | 1 | Union Square | Bacup |
| Robertshaw, Henry | 18 | 63a, Caldervale Road | Burnley |
| Robertshaw, John<br>John Robertshaw | 1 | | Hebden Bridge |
| Robinson Bros.<br>E. Robinson | 1 | Starkie Street | Blackburn |
| Robinson, E. | | See: Robinson Bros. | |
| *Robinson, James | 1 | 12, Lamb Street | Oldham |
| *Robinson, Samuel | 1 | 12, Lamb Street | Oldham |
| Robinson, William | 1 | Enfield | Blackburn |
| Robinson, William | 4 | Pump Street, Oldham Road | Manchester |
| Rosson, E.<br>E. Rosson | 1 | Mark-lane, Withy Grove | Manchester |
| Rothwell, T. & W. | 1 | Croston's Road | Bury |
| Rourke, E. M. | | See: Martin Rourke & Co. | |
| Rourke, Martin & Co.<br>E. M. Rourke | | Trentham Street Mills, Chester Road | Manchester |
| Rowbottom, James | 16 | ----- | Charlesworth |
| Rowbottom, Samuel | 16 | ----- | Glossop |
| Rowe, [Thomas][1] | 1 | 50, Lees Road | Oldham |
| *Roye, Mark | 1 | ----- | Middleton |
| Royle, Edward | 1 | 26, Mayes Street | Manchester |
| Russell, Alex. | 1 | Burnley Road | Bacup |
| Ryan, John | 4 | 96, George Leigh Street | Manchester |

*(Continued)*

(Continued)

| *S* | | | |
|---|---|---|---|
| Sargentson, James, jun. James Sargentson, jun. | 1 | Padfield | Glossop |
| Sargentson, William W. Sargentson | 1 | Bank Bottom, Padfield | Glossop |
| Savage, James | 4 | Causeway | Halifax |
| Schloesser, C. R. F. | 7 | Rock Mills | New Mills |
| Schofield, E. | 1 | 615, Manchester Road | Failsworth |
| Schofield, E. C. | 1 | Vernon Street | Oldham |
| Schofield, Ed. | 1 | Castle Mill Street | Oldham |
| Schofield, James | 1 | Duckworth Place | Rochdale |
| *Schofield, James | 1 | 25, Regent Street | Oldham |
| *Schofield, John | 1 | 1, Waste Street | Oldham |
| Schofield, Peter | 1 | Higher Carr Mill, Hope's Carr | Stockport |
| Schofield, Robert | 1 | Medlock Street | Oldham |
| Schofield, William | 1 | Nunnery Street | Oldham |
| Scotshaw Brook Paper Co. Ltd. | 7 | ----- | Lower Darwen |
| Seddon, Henry | 4 | 24, Canal Street | Manchester |
| Sefton, R. | 1 | 46 & 48, Charles Street | Bolton |
| Selby, James | 1 | | |
| Shackleton & Co. R. Heap | 1 | ----- | Colne |
| Shackleton, J. & Sons | 7 | Borough Paper Mills, North Wing | Bradford, Yorkshire |
| *Shaw, Charles Charles Shaw | 1 | 13, Shaw Road | Oldham |
| Shaw, Giles | 1 | Bell Street | Oldham |
| Shaw, John | 1 | Willow Street | Oldham |
| Shaw, J. W. | 1 | Bell Street | Oldham |
| Shaw, Joseph | 1 | Stamford Street | Ashton-under-Lyne |
| *Shaw, Robert | | See: Thos. Shaw | |
| *Shaw, Thos. | 1 | 28, Grove Street | Oldham |
| Shawcross, John | 1 6 | Newbridge Lane | Stockport |
| Shawcross, John & Co. | 5 | Junction Street, Store Street | Manchester |
| Shepherd, J. | 1 | Birtle | Bury |
| Shepherd, Richard R. Shepherd | 1 | ----- | New Church |
| Shepherd, Robert | 10 | 35, Baron Street | Rochdale |
| Sherran & Co. M. Sherran | 1 3 | Sharp Street, Rochdale Road | Manchester |
| Sherran, M. | | See: Sherran & Co. | |
| Shorrocks, C. A. C. A. Shorrocks | 1 | Weir St., & 41, Bicknell St. | Blackburn |
| *Siddall, Richard | | See: W. & R. Walker | |
| *Sidebottom, Isaac | | See: Samuel Sidebottom | |
| Sidebottom, John John Sidebottom | 3 9 | 23, Wharf Street, Ancoats | Manchester |

| S | | | |
|---|---|---|---|
| Sidebottom, Samuel | 1 | Bardsley | Ashton-under-Lyne |
| Sidebottom, Samuel | 1 | 90, King St., & 12, Bell St. | Oldham |
| Sidebottom, Samuel | 1 | Woodbine Street | Rochdale |
| Simons & Pickard | 7 | Dunsley Mill & Masson Mill, Matlock | Bath |
| Simpole, Geo. W. | 1 4 | 16, Sutton St., New Islington | Manchester |
| Simpson, John | 1 | Willow Street | Oldham |
| Sinkinson, J. & R. | 1 | Grove St. & Castle Mill St. | Oldham |
| *Sixsmith, J. | 1 | Jackson Street | Oldham |
| Slack, John | 7 | Bank Vale Mills | Hayfield |
| Slack, John & Co. | 7 | Whitebow Mills | Chapel-en-le-Frith |
| Slater, Ralph | | See: R. Stott | |
| Smart, Arthur & Co. | 1 2 5 9 | Robert Street, Cheetham | Manchester and at Bury and London |
| Smethurst, James | 1 | 32, Medlock Street | Oldham |
| Smethurst, J.<br>J. Smethurst | | ----- | Manchester |
| Smith, Charles | 1 | Garden Street | Oldham |
| Smith, John<br>John Smith | 1 | ----- | Halifax |
| Smith, Samuel<br>S. Smith | 1 | ----- | Nelson |
| Smith, Thomas | 1 | Scout | Mossley |
| Smith, Thomas | 1 | Old Cock Yard | Halifax |
| Smith, William | 1 | Square Road | Halifax |
| Smithies, Levi | | See: W. & L. Smithies | |
| Smithies, W. | | See: W. & L. Smithies | |
| Smithies, W. & L.<br>L. Smithies<br>W. Smithies | 1 | Saville Street | Bolton |
| Southworth, W. & J. | 1 | Longsight | Clitheroe |
| Sparling & Co. | 1 | Salop Street | Bolton |
| Speak, Wm. | | See: Wm. Speak & Co. | |
| Speak, Wm. & Co.<br>Wm. Speak | 1 | Wood Mill, Eastwood | near Todmorden |
| Spencer & Cuerdale<br>James Spencer | 1 | Bury Ground Works | Bury |
| Spencer, J. & Co. | 1 | New York Mill | Heywood |
| Spencer, James | | See: Spencer & Cuerdale | |
| *Spitz, J. | | See: Staub, Guyer & Spitz | |
| Stafford, Joseph | 1 | Arundel Street | Glossop |
| Stanley, Edward | 4 | 2, Frederick Place, Pilling St. | Manchester |
| Stansfield, James | | See: John Hargreaves & Son | |
| *Stansfield, Samuel | 1 | | |
| *Stansfield, Squire | 1 | ----- | Oldham |
| Stanyer, Ann | 4 | 166, Rochdale Road | Manchester |

*(Continued)*

(Continued)

| *S* | | | |
|---|---|---|---|
| Star Paper Mill Co. Ltd. | 7 | Feniscowle | near Blackburn |
| Staub, Guyer & Spitz | 1 | 22, Dutton St., Park St., Cheetham | Manchester |
| Stocks, John | 1 | 16, Beever Street | Oldham |
| Stott, James<br>Samuel Broadbent | 1 | Bell Street | Oldham |
| Stott, R.<br>R. Slater | 1 | Blanche Street | Oldham |
| Stott, Stephen | | 16, St. George Street | Little Bolton |
| Sucksmith, A. | 1 | Royton | Oldham |
| Summerfield, W. & Co. | 7 | Collyhurst Paper Mills, Collyhurst | Manchester |
| Sumner, James C.<br>J. C. Sumner | 1 | 59, Sackville St., Portland St. | Manchester |
| Sutcliffe, Robert<br>R. Sutcliffe | 1 | | Hebden Bridge |
| Sutcliffe, William | | See: James Baron & Sons | |
| *Sutcliffe, William | 1 | Nunnery Street | Oldham |
| Swallow, George & Co. | 1 | Mansfield Chambers, St. Ann's Square | Manchester |
| Swallow, George H. | 5 | Charles Street, Oldham Road | Manchester |
| Swallow, John T. | 1 | 2, St. Mary's Parsonage | Manchester |
| *Swindells, George | 1 | ----- | Liverpool |
| Sykes Bros. | 19 | Well Bridge, Dukinfield Hall | Dukinfield |

| *T* | | | |
|---|---|---|---|
| Tasker, R. & Son | 1 | Union Street | Accrington |
| Tatham, W. & Co.<br>E. S. Barnes | 20 | Vulcan Works | Rochdale |
| Tattersall, George<br>G. Tattersall | 1 | Walker Street | Rochdale |
| Taylor, C. & Co. | 1 | 15, Market Street | Manchester |
| *Taylor, Ellis<br>E. Taylor | 1 | 3, Waste Street | Oldham |
| *Taylor, G. B. | 1 | ----- | Oldham |
| Taylor, Hugh | 1 | Back York Street | Heywood |
| Taylor, J. | 1 | Castle Mill Street | Oldham |
| Taylor, James<br>J. Taylor | 1 | Walker Street | Rochdale |
| Taylor, James | | See: W. C. Jones | |
| Taylor, J. & Bros. | | 1 Britannia Street | Oldham |
| Taylor, John | 4 | 20, Dych St., Rochdale Road. | Manchester |

| *T* | | | |
|---|---|---|---|
| Taylor, Joseph | 1 | Lower Carr Mill, Hope's Carr | Stockport |
| J. Taylor | | | |
| *Taylor, J. W. | | See: J. W. Taylor & Bros. | |
| Taylor, J. W. & Bros. | 1 | Bellfield | Oldham |
| J. W. Taylor | | | |
| Taylor, Samuel | 1 | Fir Street | Heywood |
| Tempest & Son | 7 | Little Eaton | near Derby |
| Thatcher, John H. | | See: R. Thatcher | |
| Thatcher, R. | 1 | 6, Victoria Street, Mumps | Oldham |
| John H. Thatcher | | | |
| Thatcher, Robert | 1 | 5, Elbow Street, Turner Street | Manchester |
| Thornby, Marianna | 1 6 | ----- | New Mills |
| Thornton, John | 1 | 59, Hindle Street | Accrington |
| Thwaite Bros. | 1 | High Mill, Bridge Street | Bury |
| Tither, John | 1 | Blanche Street | Oldham |
| Tobin, W. | | Hall Street, Moston | Manchester |
| W. Tobin | | | |
| Toothill, A. | 7 | Wood Mill, Horsforth | near Leeds |
| Town, Joseph & Son | 7 | Turkey Mill | Keighley |
| Turner, Chas. & Co. | 7 | Spring side, Sharples | near Bolton |
| Turner, James | 1 3 | 30 & 32, Sheriff Street | Rochdale |
| Turner, John | 1 | Fir Street | Heywood |
| Turner, J. W. A. | 7 | Albert Mills, Newtown | New Mills |
| Turner, Thomas | 1 | Back York Street | Heywood |
| Thos. Turner | | | |
| Turner, Wright & Son | 5 | Kingston Mills, Cobden Street, Brindle Heath | Salford |
| Tweedale, B. | | See: E. Tweedale & Sons | |
| Tweedale, E. & Sons | 1 3 | Irk Mill, Long Millgate | Manchester |
| B. Tweedale | | | |
| Tweedale, James | 1 3 | 7, Ancoats Street | Manchester |

| *U* | | | |
|---|---|---|---|
| Underwood, M. A. & Son | 1 | 12, Lever Street | Manchester |
| Union Paper Works, Limited | 7 | Bellfield | Rochdale |
| Unsworth, Jeremiah | 1 | Brook Mill | Adlington |
| J. Unsworth | | | |

| *V* | | | |
|---|---|---|---|
| Vickers, Joseph | 1 | 47, Ancoats Street | Manchester |
| Voss & Deluis | 1 | Phoenix Street | Oldham |

*(Continued)*

(Continued)

| *W* | | | |
|---|---|---|---|
| Waddington, Jas. Haigh | 7 | Crown Works, Beighton | near Sheffield |
| Walcott, J. F. | 1 | Salop Street & Shifnall Street | Bolton |
| Walker, J. A, | 1 | Bradford Buildings, Mawdaley St. | Bolton |
| Walker, R. | | See: W. & R. Walker | |
| Walker, W. & R.<br>R. Walker<br>R. Siddall | 1 | Sheriff Street | Rochdale |
| Waller, Ralph & Co., Limited | 5 | 45, Dale Street | Manchester |
| Waller, W.<br>W. Waller | 1 | ----- | Brighouse |
| Walley, George | 1 | ----- | Brighouse |
| Walley, George | | See: G. Walley & Son | |
| Walley, George & Son<br>G. Walley<br>H. Walley | 1 9 | 25, Mayes Street | Manchester |
| Wallwork, J. W. & Bros. | 1 9 | Dawson Street, Greengate | Salford |
| Wallwork, J. W & R. T. | 1 | Brinksway Mill, Brinksway | Stockport |
| Walton, James<br>James Walton | 1 3 | 8, Anderton Street | Chorley |
| Warburton, A.<br>A. Warburton | | Flash Mills | Haslingden |
| Warburton, Elizabeth | 1 | 102, Bury Street | Salford |
| Ward, John | 4 | Holt Town | Manchester |
| Ward, Peter & Son | 1 | Saville Street & Shifnal Street | Bolton |
| Wareing, J. Booth<br>J. B. Wareing | 1 | 15, Medlock Street | Oldham |
| Warhurst, Josiah | 1 | Padfield | Glossop |
| Waterhouse, James | 1 | New Road | Marple |
| Waterhouse, Joseph | 1 | Boodle | Ashton-under-Lyne |
| Waterhouse, Thomas | 1 | 2, Longshut Lane West | Stockport |
| Watson, Cleophas | 1 | Waterloo Road | Stockport |
| Watson, James | 1 | Sunny Bank Mill | Darwen |
| Webb, John | 1 8 9 | 21, Friday St., Spear St. | Manchester |
| Whalley, J. & T. | 1 | Rhodes Bank Mill | Oldham |
| Whalley, Joseph | | See: J. & T. Whalley | |
| Whalley, Richard<br>R. Whalley | 1 | ----- | Burnley |
| Whalley, Thos. | | See: J. & T. Whalley | |
| Wheeler, Thomas<br>T. Wheeler | 1 | Brunswick Street | Oldham |
| White, John<br>J. White | 1 | ----- | Wigan |
| Whitehead, Abraham<br>A. Whitehead | 1 | Glodwick St., & Exchange St. | Oldham |
| Whitehead, John | | See: Thos. Crabtree | |

| *W* | | | |
|---|---|---|---|
| Whiteley Bros. | 7 | Slitheroe Mill | Rishworth |
| Whiteley, William & Son | 7 | Skyreholme Mill | Skipton |
| Whittaker, J. C.<br>J. C. Whittaker<br>R. Whittaker | 1 | 31, King Street | Haslingden |
| Whittaker, R. | 1 | Breightmet Street | Bolton |
| Whittaker, Rostron | | See: J. C. Whittaker | |
| Whittaker, William | 1 | 13, Henry St., Manchester Rd. | Bolton |
| Whittaker, William | | See: James Holland | |
| Whittingham, Benjamin<br>B. Whittingham | 1 | Cunliffe Street | Bolton |
| Whittle, James | 1 | 2, Back Mayes Street | Manchester |
| Whitworth, John | 1 | Greetland | near Halifax |
| Wigglesworth, John | | See: John Wigglesworth & Bros. | |
| Wigglesworth, John & Bros.<br>J. Wigglesworth | 1 | Massey Street | Burnley |
| Wild, Isaac | 1 | Brighton Mills | Oldham |
| Wild, John | 1 | Brighton Mills | Oldham |
| Wild, John | 1 | Egerton Street | Oldham |
| Wild, John & Sons | 1 | 11, Brown Street, Mumps | Oldham |
| Wild, John & Sons | 7 | Broad Damers & New Bridge Mills | Radcliffe |
| Wild, John C. | 1 | | |
| Wild, John F. | 1 | Brighton Mills | Oldham |
| Wild, Joseph<br>J. Wild | 1 | ----- | Bolton |
| Wild, Leonard | 1 | 22 & 26, Folds Road | Little Bolton |
| Wild, Thomas | 5 | Ten Acre Lane, Newton Heath | Manchester |
| Wild, William<br>W. Wild | 1 | ----- | Heywood |
| Wilde, Charles | | See: Dacca Twist Co. | |
| Wilde, James & Thomas | 1 | Wilde's Buildings, Medlock Street | Oldham |
| Wilde, Thomas | 1 2 4 8 | 55, Ancoats Street | Manchester |
| Wilkinson, Fred. | 1 | 8, Medlock Street | Oldham |
| Wilkinson, Thomas | 1 | 32, Lower Bridgeman Street | Bolton |
| Wilkinson, Thomas | 7 | Lomax Bank, Little Lever | Bolton |
| Wilkinson, W. H. | 1 | ------ | Mirfield |
| Williams, Robert | 1 | 22, Mayes Street | Manchester |
| Williams, William<br>W. Williams | 1 | Hamer Street, Crawford Street | Rochdale |
| Wilson, George | 6 | Carr Mill, Waterloo Road | Stockport |
| Wilson, J. | 6 | New Mill, Smallbridge | near Rochdale |

*(Continued)*

(Continued)

| *W* | | | |
|---|---|---|---|
| Wilson, Thomas<br>T. Wilson | 1 | Barnes Street | Accrington |
| Winder, D. | 1 | 22, Ashbourne Street | Bolton |
| Winterbottom, Wm. | 1 | Union Street | Oldham |
| Wolstenholme, Robt.<br>R. Wolstenholme | 1 | Chapel Street & Miller Street | Heywood |
| Wood, Daniel | 6 | ------ | Stockport |
| Wood, G. E.<br>G. E. Wood | 1 | Spa Mill | Bolton |
| Wood, John | 6 | California Road | Stockport |
| Wood Street Mill Co., Limited | 1 | Wood Street, Elton | Bury |
| Wood, Walter C.<br>W. C. Wood | | Byng Street East | Bolton |
| Woodward, Wm. King | 7 | Olive Mills, Loxley, Stannington | Sheffield |
| Wooller, H. K. | | See: Dean Brook Waste Bleaching Co. | |
| Woollerton, Edward | 4 | 29, Bengal Street | Manchester |
| Worsley Bros. | 1 9 | Park Street, Red Bank | Manchester |
| Wright & Batty | 1 | Slate Lane | Audenshaw |
| Wright, H. & J. W. | 7 | Freedom Mills, Morton | near Bingley |
| Wrigley, Jas. & Son | 7 | Bridge Hall Mills | Bury |
| Wrigley, J. & Robert | 1 | Spring Bank | Mossley |
| Wrigley, Samuel | 1 | 15, Cross Street | Oldham |
| Wroe, Thomas<br>T. Wroe | 1 | 50, Lees Road | Oldham |

| *Y* | | | |
|---|---|---|---|
| Yarker, William | 1 | 14, Bright Street, Freetown | Bury |
| Yates Bros. | 7 | Woodhill Paper Mill, Elton | Bury |
| Yates, Edward | | See: H. Yates & Sons | |
| Yates, H. & Sons<br>Edward Yates | 1 | 50, Railway Road | Over Darwen |
| Yates, Robert<br>Robert Yates | 1 | Carlisle Mill, Bradshawgate | Bolton |
| Yates, William | 7 | Pool Mills | near Otley |
| Young, Henry | 3 4 8 | 24, Mayes Street | Manchester |
| Young, John | 1 4 8 | 63a, Dantzic Street | Manchester |

## Note

1 See under Wroe.

## Editorial Headnote

### Edwards, Richard and Bercry, William A. (eds.). *Waste Manufacturers and Merchants from Manchester of To-day. An Epitome of Results. Business Men and Commercial Interests. Wealth and Growth. Historical, Statistical, Biographical* (London: Historical Publishing Company, 1888), pp. 120, 137, 142, 157, 168, 172.

Richard Edwards (1828–1887) was an American publisher of annual directories who pioneered a new illustrated style that combined the historical background of localities with brief sketches of local businesses. His *Industries of Philadelphia* of 1881 probably set the model for the later British titles. Edwards came to Britain with his son-in-law, William Augustus Bercry, in the mid-1880s to work on new-style city directories for London and other British cities, to be published by his Philadelphia-based Historical Publishing Company. When Edwards died in 1887, Bercry completed *Industries of London* that year and similarly titled directories of Glasgow, Manchester, and Bristol in 1888. Afterward, he undertook directories of Tyneside in 1889, Yorkshire and Scotland in 1890 and Ireland in 1891. The following year the company was replaced by a new partnership, The London Printing and Engraving Company.

The earlier volumes were of some merit, but the quality quickly subsided into formulaic descriptions of an inflated character, as Bercry's energy focused on salesmanship to gain the lucrative pre-publication subscriptions from participant firms, rather than on the finished product. A commentator for the *Hudderfield Chronicle* found many entries 'so grotesque as only to excite amusement':

> The firms given are either "eminent," "influential," "noted," "important," or "typical," and their principals, in many cases, are reported . . . as representing all the public and private virtues involved in good citizenship. . . . We give the Historic Publishing Company, of 90, Chancery-lane, London, credit for having hit upon an ingenious method of administering flattery to the limited number who will pay for it, but the trade and commerce of Yorkshire will not benefit by such extraneous puffing as is shown in these pages.
>
> (30 Aug 1890, p. 5)

Manchester profited from the more careful coverage of the early works begun by Edwards. Its directory appeared in October 1888, retailing at 3s. 6d., although merchants probably presented copies free to customers. Despite the limited merit of the descriptions, they highlight firms that would be otherwise be largely unremembered.

# 17

# EDWARDS, RICHARD AND BERCRY, WILLIAM. A. (EDS.). *WASTE MANUFACTURERS AND MERCHANTS FROM MANCHESTER OF TO-DAY.*

## (London: Historical Publishing Company, 1888), pp. 120, 137, 142, 157, 168, 172.

***Boardman Bros.***, Manufacturers of Engine-cleaning Cotton Waste, Sponge and Carriage Cloths, Lamp Cottons, Engine Packing, &c., Sharp Street Mills, Rochdale Road. – Few industries have made more rapid strides than the manufacturers of these articles. What was formerly waste in reality, is now passed through machines which tease and cleanse it, and render it fit for cleaning the most delicate machinery, and also for packing the same and other goods for export. Sponge cloths are also used for cleansing machinery, and have the advantage of being capable of being washed five or six times and re-used. Engine packings, lamp and candle wicks, torch wicks, are accessories of this trade, and in this connection mention should be made of the old-established and well-known firm of Boardman Bros., proprietors of the Sharp Street Mills. They are also manufacturers of plaited and twisted blind-cords, and all kinds of superior plain and polished cotton ropes, and cotton and hemp fishing lines, twines, and yarns, as well as mops, thrums, &c. Their goods are suitable for both home and shipping to all parts of the world. Their mills are equipped with the most modern machinery, employment being given to a large force of skilled hands. The goods made by this firm have a standard reputation in the trade, being made from the best materials in the most skilful manner. The facilities at their command enable the firm to offer special advantages to customers, and to execute all orders with great promptitude. The head of the firm, Mr. Joseph Boardman,[1] is an enterprising and


DOI: 10.4324/9780429274190-22

thoroughly reliable business man, and enjoys the esteem and respect of the commercial community.

***

***John Mellor, Cotton and Cotton Waste Merchant***, 38 Deansgate. – The cotton and cotton waste trade is one of the great businesses for which Manchester has a world-wide reputation; it represents many millions of money, and is in many hands. A well-known firm in this line is that of Mr. John Mellor,[2] which has a reputation of upwards of half a century, and is conducted by his son. The premises occupied consist of a spacious building of five stories,[3] which affords excellent offices and great storage capacity, and is fitted with a large engine, and special facilities for packing cotton and cotton waste for all markets. Mr. Mellor carries a very heavy stock of cotton and cotton waste, the cotton being of the finest staples imported. Mr. Mellor has special facilities for obtaining superior cotton and cotton waste, and during his fifty years he has always borne the highest name for reliability. He carries on a very heavy trade, having a splendid connection among the leading Lancashire spinners and manufacturers. He has also representatives in all the known markets in Europe, as well as agents in America, and does a large export trade. An ample staff is employed, and the organisation of the business is such that the largest orders are executed with dispatch. Mr. Mellor is well known all over Lancashire in the leading business circles, and he is highly esteemed for his admirable qualities, whilst he ranks among the chief cotton and cotton waste merchants of Manchester.

***

***Mr. Joseph Lingard***, Patent and Sheet Wadding and Cotton Wool Manufacturer, 6, Church Street. – In the historical review of the manufactures and industries of Manchester and its vicinity, written with the object of presenting in a short and concise form the origin and history of the leading houses engaged therein, it is incumbent upon us to give special prominence to those firms which have for many years been identified with some particular branch of commerce or manufacture. For more than thirty years the well-known name of Mr. Joseph Lingard,[4] patent and sheet wadding and cotton wool manufacturer, has been most intimately associated with the commerce of this city. This firm has very extensive works at Chapel-en-le-Frith, known as Milton Mills, where the manufacture of the patent and sheet wadding, also the cotton wool, is carried on. These mills rank amongst the largest of their kind in the United Kingdom; they are replete with the best and most improved machinery and appliances, and turn out these goods in large quantities and of first class quality, and give employment to an efficient staff of workpeople. This firm is in every way a representative establishment, being not simply dealers, but manufacturers of their own goods. They send out travellers covering the whole of Great Britain and Ireland, and also do an extensive shipping trade, these goods finding a ready sale in all the markets of the world. The business in all its branches is conducted in a most spirited and enterprising manner, and is well recognised as one of the oldest and most extensive in the trade. Mr. Joseph Lingard has been long and honourably connected with this business, and has contributed in no small degree, by his energy and enterprise, to the development of this branch of commerce, and the prosperity of the neighbourhood where his works are situated. The firm occupies a high position in commercial circles, and is fully deserving of the success which it has attained.

***

**Thomas Isherwood, Spinner, Cotton Waste, &c.**, Irk Mills. – One of the best-known and most successful establishments connected with the cotton waste industry in Manchester and Heywood is that of which Mr. Thomas Isherwood is the proprietor.[5] This concern was established about thirty years since. The Manchester branch, which is located at the Irk Mills, in Long Millgate, presents at all times a scene of business activity. The Irk Mills are large and commodious, and a numerous staff is employed. The waste warehouses at Heywood are situate in Ormerod Street and Schofield Street Mills. The Foundry Street and Railway Street Mills cover a very large space, and are replete with every mechanical appliance for spinning. Mr. Isherwood is well known in commercial circles and on 'Change as a gentleman of long experience and thorough business integrity.

***

***Wm. Flanagan***, Wadding Manufacturer; Warehouse, 14, Union Street, Church Street. – The commodious warehouse of Mr. W. Flanagan,[6] wadding manufacturer, forms the central depot of a business which has now been established for several years, and has in that time attained to very large proportions indeed. As an indication of this, the amount of work in Mr. Flanagan's warehouse necessitates the employment of nearly a score of hands. The manufactory in connection with this warehouse, and known by the name of "West End Mill," is situated at Mottram, and is likewise the scene of a large degree of business and activity. A very considerable number of hands are employed at West End Mill, which is fitted up with the best modern machinery and appliances devised for the manufacture and preparation of wadding for the infinite variety of purposes for which that article of commerce is now used. Mr. Flanagan's trade extends over a wide area, both at home and in many markets, to which his goods are consigned in very considerable bulk. His straightforwardness, combined with his consideration for the claims and interests of others, has secured Mr. Flanagan the esteem of his patrons and connections.

***

***Sillitoe & Seares***, packers of cotton waste, Mary Street, Strangeways. – The cotton industry is divided into a great many branches, that of cotton waste packing, &c.,

being of no small importance. Among the Manchester establishments so engaged the foremost place is held by that of Messrs. Sillitoe & Seares, which was founded by the present proprietors twenty-one years ago. This firm were the introducers of the present system of packing. The premises occupied are large and commodious, being built especially for the business. The spacious warehouse is well stocked with cotton waste, cleaning waste, &c., and the appliances and presses used in the packing operations are powerful and of the latest improvement. The work is carried out with promptness and efficiency, and the business done is heavy and rapidly increasing. The firm stands in high favour with the chief shippers and dealers in the city and its vicinity, and the management throughout is able and energetic. The partners are Messrs. James H. Sillitoe and Henry Seares,[7] men of ability, integrity, and courtesy, and highly esteemed.

## Notes

1 Joseph Boardman (b. 1841) began employment as a cotton weaver. By 1881 he was a small manufacturer and merchant employing eight women and four men. The Boardman Brothers firm was based at Sharp Street around 1884 to 1894. It had moved to Knott Mill by March 1896 when Boardman retired due to ill health. The Boardman family was involved in the firm at least until 1929 when Nathan Higginson Boardman (1871–1931) retired.

2 John Mellor is listed in Sowerbutt's 1882 *Cotton Waste Dealers' Directory*, but biographical information has not been traced. A fire sale of 1894 confirms the involvement of the firm in the American trade, as several thousand pounds of American and Sea Island classes of cotton were advertised (*Manchester Courier*, 20 Dec 1894, p. 3).

3 The basement storey appears to have been counted here, as accounts of the fire of 1894 report the building being four storeys tall (*Manchester Evening News*, 12 Dec 1894, p. 4).

4 Joseph Lingard (1831–1907) began the partnership of Lingard and Redfern at Milton Mill in Chapel-en-le-Frith before 1856, taking it over on his own account in 1859. His sons Joshua Lingard (1865–1911) and Walter Lingard (1866–1937) succeeded him in the business, the latter retiring in 1933.

5 Thomas Isherwood (1830–1899) was born the son of a miner. In 1843 he was apprenticed to a shoemaker and began his working career as a clogger. In 1864, he commenced as a waste dealer, at first continuing his shoemaking alongside. With success in the waste trade, he expanded into spinning in the 1880s. See 'Notes on Men and Things: The Late Mr. Thomas Isherwood, J.P.', *Heywood Advertiser*, 2 Jan 1903, p. 8.

6 William Flanagan (c1840–1915), born in Ireland, came with his family to Manchester as a boy and entered the trade of warehousing as did his father. He progressed from clerk to salesman and cashier before commencing business on his own as a wadding manufacturer in the 1880s. His son, William Henry Flanagan (1871–1944) succeeded him in the wadding business.

7 James Hill Sillitoe (c1836–1897) began employment as an advertising agent, but moved into the packing trade by 1866. In 1858, he married Emma Mary Seares (1831–1912), and her brother, Henry Seares (c1846–1921) was to join him in business. By 1881, the census recorded the firm employing seventeen men, eight women and nine boys. The Strangeways warehouse was acquired by 1883.

## Editorial Headnote

## Nasmith, Joseph. 'Chapter XI. Waste Spinning', *The Student's Cotton Spinning* (Manchester: Joseph Nasmith and John Heywood, 1892), pp. 377–387.

Joseph Nasmith (1850–1904) was the son of machine maker John Nasmith (1822–1892), and was to follow the paternal path to become a consulting mechanical engineer. At the time of writing *The Student's Cotton Spinning*, Nasmith was already known for his *Modern Cotton Spinning Machinery* published in 1890. In that work, he stressed the need for using a plain manner when writing about practical work, and advised making suggestions rather than imparting dogmatic rules. The new book was based upon eight lectures given at the Manchester Technical School, delivered (probably weekly) from 5 January 1892, and then amplified for publication. Conversion to book form transpired quickly; it was ready at the start of May, and was reviewed in the *Textile Manufacturer* that month. There it received the highest praise as 'a work which we can unhesitatingly recommend, not only to students as unquestionably the best work extant, but also to all interested in the cotton spinning industry' (18:209, May 1892, pp. 205–206). Unfortunately for us, the reviewer saw no need for 'special remark' of the chapter on waste spinning, in any case implying that inclusion of waste spinning was expected rather than exceptional. The book was priced at 6s., but was advertised by D. W. Bardsley, a technical book seller in Oldham, at the discount rate of 5s. (*Cotton Factory Times*, 17 Jun 1892).

A second edition was produced in 1893, and an enlarged third addition in 1896. The book remained in print until about 1920, proudly displaying on the cover the number of thousands of copies printed, eventually reaching 18,000.

18

# NASMITH, JOSEPH. 'WASTE SPINNING'

## *The Student's Cotton Spinning* (Manchester: Joseph Nasmith and John Heywood, 1892), pp. 377–387.

In the series of processes which have thus been described there is necessarily a large quantity of waste produced. The amount varies naturally with the quality of the cotton and the skill of the workpeople, but it is always large. Over the whole series of operations the amount varies from 12 to 20 per cent, but some of this is the dust and similar impurities deposited in scutching and opening. While there is always a certain part of the waste made in the two stages named which consists of fibres of more or less value, on the whole, the usable waste – if the phrase may be employed – is principally that which is made in the carding engine and subsequent processes. Waste is defined as being "hard" or "soft," the former including all cotton into which twist has been put, and the latter, untwisted or partially twisted material. These are the broad distinctions made, and are sufficient for practical purposes. At present the trade in yarns spun from waste is principally a Continental one, and in England it is the exception to produce this class of yarn. The reason for this is probably that to spin it requires a special plant, which is different in many cases from that usually found in the spinning-mill. It is, however, an undoubted fact that waste spinning is an operation which repays the trouble entailed, and a brief treatment of the method usually pursued is likely to prove interesting.

Much of the waste which it is possible to spin into yarn is of a greasy nature, and this partially facilitates and partially retards the performance of the operation. It is obviously the first thing to do, when dealing with hard waste, to restore the material to its fleecy condition and detach the fibres from each other. For this purpose it is obvious that the machines employed to deal with cotton in its ordinary open condition are absolutely useless, and that the treatment given to it must be quite different. Accordingly waste is first treated in the Oldham willow, which has already been referred to.[1] The willow is constructed with a drum or cylinder, having its surface covered with spikes or teeth. It is surrounded for the greater part of its circumference with a grid also fitted with projections on its inner side. By the rotation of the cylinder, the twisted cotton is rapidly broken up, as it is called, and reduced to a soft fleecy mass. The form of machine employed varies a little in its details. In one type, which is constructed for dealing with hard waste, more especially in the form of cop bottoms,[2] there are several cylinders used one after

DOI: 10.4324/9780429274190-23

the other, each provided with round taper teeth, and revolving at a rapid rate. The cylinder shafts are made long enough to project beyond each side of the machine, so as to receive the necessary pair of driving pulleys. This construction is adopted in order to enable the cylinders to be reversed after the teeth have become bent out of their true position, which sometimes happens. When they become too much inclined, the reversal of the cylinder is necessary, in order that they will be fully effective. Machines on this principle are made with three, four, or six cylinders, and the hardest waste is speedily reduced into a condition resembling raw cotton. The length of staple obtained depends largely upon the character of the cotton broken up, and it must, of course, be understood that the fibres have lost part of their strength by their repeated manipulation. Still, an excellent product can be obtained from clean hard waste, and it is worth noting that for this class it is found that a treatment by six cylinders gives the best result. Soft waste – such as that made in the processes of scutching, carding, and drawing – obviously does not need the same severe treatment as that described, only requiring to be dealt with so as to remove any dirt or other extraneous matter which may be mixed with it. Two courses may be pursued with the waste opened in the willow or breaker. It may be passed through a Crighton opener[3] or a scutching machine, fitted with a lap attachment, and fed to a breaker carding engine. In the former case, a modification in the details of the machine is necessary, in order to allow of the effective treatment of the material. An extra picker or breaker cylinder is provided, and the cotton is fed by means of a lattice apron, it being, of course, essential that this operation is conducted with care, so as to produce a good and even lap. A pedal motion being fitted, the latter object is naturally considerably aided. To all machines for cleaning and opening waste it is advisable to apply fans to carry away the dust, of which there is a considerable quantity.

When the opened or broken-up cotton is thus obtained, it is carded, and in this operation we meet with a distinct departure from the methods previously described in connection with the carding of cotton. It was shown in Chapter IV that the cotton was fed to the carding engine ordinarily in the form of a single lap, the regularity and evenness of which was obtained by the mode of producing it on the scutching machines. In proceeding to card waste, a different course is followed. If the cotton has been formed into a lap on the scutching machine, two of these are placed on a lattice apron fitted to the end of the machine, so that a certain amount of doubling takes place at this point. For reasons which will be detailed later, it is desirable to obtain an even weight in the sliver at the earliest possible time. If the cotton is in the open or loose condition, the practice is to weigh a certain portion and spread it upon the feed lattice, thus pursuing a similar course to that which is followed in carding wool. Sometimes, but not often, weighing is resorted to as in dealing with wool. In many respects the manipulation of cotton waste resembles that of wool, and it is found that, like the latter material, the carding is better performed if the waste is a little greasy. When the material is too dry, it is therefore the custom to use a lubricant to increase its working qualities. The object aimed at in feeding the breaker card is to get a regular and uniform supply delivered to the action of the machine. So far as the construction of the latter is concerned, that described in paragraph 112, Chapter IV, is closely followed, except that the number of worker and clearer rollers is greater. There are also in some cases extra or "fancy" rollers fitted, these being practically similar in construction to the workers, by which the cotton is raised from the surface of the cylinder, and is more effectively delivered to the doffer than it otherwise would be. The material is doffed from the cylinder in the usual way, and the web taken from the doffer is variously treated. There are three ways of dealing with it, but the object in each case is the same, and a few words may be expended in explaining it. As there is not any very effective separation possible of the various grades of waste produced, it is at once obvious that there will be a great variation in the component parts of the opened mass, so far as quality and length of staple is concerned. This is especially the case when waste spinning is conducted as a special business, and the raw material is bought from dealers in it, or from several mills. To produce really satisfactory results, it is therefore of the highest importance that the mixture of the various elements in the broken waste shall be as intimately made as possible. When a six-cylinder breaking machine, such as was described, is used, this object is to a large extent attained, but it is absolutely necessary not to neglect it, and no precautions are too great to ensure its full attainment. It is therefore the practice so to deal with the web, as taken off the breaker carding engine, as to ensure the fibres within it receiving this intimate mixture, and the four principal methods of doing this will now be described.

The first plan of which notice need be taken is to form the web into a sliver, and coil it into a can in the same way as if cotton were being carded. If this course is pursued, it is necessary to take special precautions to prevent the sliver being broken, as it is very liable to rupture owing to the short staple and the weakness of the cotton fibres within it. It is obvious that if a fibre has been twisted on its axis as described, the separation of it from its fellows in the severe manner which is requisite must weaken it, and there is every reason to suppose that the effect of its natural convolutions is largely destroyed. After slivers have been obtained, however, they are drawn from the cans, and passed through a machine known as a Derby Doubler. This machine, although at one time extensively employed in the preparation of cotton for spinning, has not hitherto been described, because the methods of spinning used at the present day in this country have largely rendered it obsolete. A number of cans are placed so that the slivers can be readily drawn from them and traversed along a polished plate alongside each other, after which they are combined and passed through a pair of compression rollers, and are afterwards rolled into a lap of about 25 inches wide. The lap is by these means made very solid, and is usually about 15 lbs. to 20 lbs. in weight. As the various slivers are possibly composed of different qualities of fibre, a combination is thus obtained, which, when treated by the finishing carding machine, results in their intimate mixture. The second method of dealing with the web is to wind it upon a large drum constructed of wood, and of such a size that a bulky web is obtained. When the required thickness is thus wound, the web is taken off the drum by being cut across at one point, the sheet thus produced being fed to the finishing carding engine. As there are several layers in this sheet – which resembles wadding – it is evident that when it is treated by the teeth of the licker-in, the fibres will be laid upon the cylinder promiscuously, and will be intimately mixed, but they will not be crossed. The third plan pursued is to use what is known as Blamires' feed.[4] This consists of an apron or lattice of the same width as the cylinder, fitted immediately behind the doffer upon which the web is deposited. The lattice in turn delivers the web to a transverse lattice, placed below, and running at right angles to it. The delivery is made by rollers, in such a way that the fleece or web is laid all over the surface of the second lattice in folds. As this formation takes place the second lattice slowly traverses and delivers the web to a lap roll, by which it is rolled up into a lap of the requisite width. It is important to note that the direction of the fibres on the first lattice and in the lap is necessarily different, they being disposed at right angles to their former direction when in the lap. This, although at first sight a defect, is not really so, as the fibres are laid in every direction within the delivered web, and further, this peculiar arrangement, when the lap is afterwards carded, greatly aids the proper mixture, the importance of which has been described. When the laps are formed, they are fed to the finishing carding machine, and, as in the first mode of dealing with the material which was described, two laps are placed on the lattice, so that they are doubled and presented simultaneously to the action of the licker-in. In the Scotch feed the plan pursued is to take the web as it leaves the doffer of the first carding engine, and form it into a band three or four inches wide, which is taken upwards by a duplex feed tape or apron, and carried to the feed lattice of the finishing carding machine. Here the web is laid across the feed apron in successive layers, which overlap each other for about half their width, and is carried to the cylinder, so that the fibres are presented to the latter with their length running across its face.

Whatever form the cotton is given it is carded a second time on a machine which is of similar construction to the one used for breaking, so far as the carding part of the machine is concerned. The object of the second or finishing carding is to complete the blending of the fibres, so as to obtain a better and more uniform thread than is otherwise possible. As the web leaves the doffer it is dealt with by a device known as a "condenser." This is an arrangement by which the web is cut or divided into narrow strips which are rolled up into the form of a round strand. The number of divisions made depends upon circumstances, but the range is from about 40 to 120. There are two chief forms of condenser, the Bolette steel tape[5] and Saxon or leather tape. In each case the operating instrument is a narrow tape which, in combination with rollers consisting of alternate rings and grooves, divides the web into a number of separate filaments or ends. The Saxon condenser, however, divides the web after it is taken from the doffer. The web is first compressed by a pair of calender rollers over which the tapers pass. The rollers are grooved, and are so set relatively, that the grooves of one are opposite the raised part of the other, the leather tape resting in the grooves. They are, therefore, alternately placed, and by guiding the lower set upwards and the upper set downwards, a division of the web is obtained in accordance with the number of tapes used. The exact number employed depends, of course, upon requirements, but this can be arranged as desired. Opinions differ as to the merits of the two systems of division; but, in late years, the steel tape condenser has met with great favour. It is desirable, in using the machines, that the dividing mechanism is kept in good order, as it is requisite to get a clean, sharp division of the web and thus avoid any unevenness in the roving produced. After the slivers – as they may be called – leave the dividing tapes they are passed between broad bands of leather, very smooth on their surface, and stretched over rollers to which a rotative motion is given. The leather bands are being constantly traversed longitudinally, so that the strips of carded material placed between them will be carried forward and delivered at the point where the leathers pass round their respective rollers. The surface velocity of each band must, therefore, be identical, and it is highly desirable that the bands shall be quite free from any unevenness or roughness. In addition to the longitudinal motion, the bands are given a transverse reciprocal movement in opposite directions by means of eccentrics fixed on an upright shaft driven from the cylinder shaft. Thus the strips are rubbed up between the leathers, and are formed into a roving which, while acquiring a large amount of cohesion, has no twist, in the proper sense of the word, but is very cylindrical. The pressure exercised upon it is sufficient for all practical purposes and is considerable, so that the roving, when it emerges, has strength enough to enable it to be wound on to specially constructed bobbins, and to be unwound from them with equal facility. The name of the apparatus is, therefore, evidently derived from the method of treating the material, the strips formed from the web being literally condensed by the action of the "rubbing leathers." The bobbins upon which the rovings are wound are light barrels of metal or wood, with light flanges at each end, and mounted so that they can be readily and freely rotated. From twenty to thirty ends are ordinarily wound on each bobbin, which thus is capable of containing a considerable length of material. It is sometimes the practice to provide each of the finishing cards with two sets of rubbers, this entailing two rollers for removing the web from the doffer. It is, on the whole, preferable, if this arrangement be used, to spin the bobbins produced on the upper and lower condenser separately, as it is difficult to get the doffing quite equal in each case. The whole of the arrangements of the condenser require care and watchfulness, and the leathers used should neither be too rough nor too dry. It is also necessary to keep them clean, as any adhesiveness would speedily result in a defective roving. In some cases an ordinary doffer is applied to the machine, and by the removal of part of its clothing at intervals the web is divided into several parts which can be taken off in the form of long strips. This does not give so good a result as the condenser. The operation of carding waste, generally speaking, is not a difficult one to effect, but it naturally possesses several points of difference to the carding of raw cotton.

Having obtained the rovings in the shape named – viz., on bobbins from 24 to 30 inches long – it is necessary to spin them. The twisting of waste varies from that of ordinary cotton, mainly because the character of the material has been so changed that it will not permit of any draft being put into it until it is partially twisted.[6] It is this fact which necessitates the great care to which we have referred as being essential in the preparation of the roving. There is no chance of rectifying by means of a draft exercised on a combined sliver any unevenness which may be found in it, and it becomes the more requisite therefore to obtain from the finishing carding machine a web as even in weight and thickness over its whole area as it is possible to make. The intimate mixture of the fibres to which reference has been made has this object, and the formation of laps or the weighing of the cotton fed to the carding engines are directed towards the same end. Whatever unevenness exists in the roving when formed will be found in the twisted thread, with such reductions as follow upon the operation of spinning. This factor affects the construction of the spinning machine, because it is necessary to provide means by which, subsequently to the introduction of twist, a little draft can be exercised. Waste spinning is therefore generally conducted on a mule of a construction which, in its main features, resembles that employed for spinning woollen threads. It deals with the thread in an entirely different way to that in which ordinary yarn is formed, and the characteristics of the thread correspondingly vary. It was shown that the twisting of cotton yarn, although completed in some cases after the draft had ceased, was, to a large extent, put in simultaneously with the reduction of the roving by the rollers. Further, the draft of the carriage takes place at the same time as the twisting, and thus the attenuation and spinning of the material are effected during one period of the cycle of movements. In consequence of these factors, a thread is produced which is remarkably level, but the counts which can be spun are naturally limited. In some cases an attempt is made to get a little draft by means of rollers, but, on the whole, the best results are obtained by the employment of mules in which this element is absent. Accordingly only one line of rollers is used, and it is principally in the arrangement of the parts affecting these that the difference between a waste spinning and ordinary mule is found. The condenser bobbins are placed in a creel, and the various ends are taken from them and guided to the rollers. These are made 1¼ inch diameter, and the top rollers are self-weighted. The rollers may be made with two bottom lines, on which the top rollers rest, the roving being passed between the rollers, and being thus nipped twice. The cops are formed in the usual way, the turns per inch depending upon the same conditions as those ordinarily existing. At first the carriage runs out at its highest speed, and the rollers deliver the roving at the same or a little quicker speed than the travel of the carriage. The exact amount of the excess of roller speed depends, of course, upon the strength of the roving, which is determined by the character of the mixing made. When the carriage has made a certain portion of its outward run the rollers are disengaged and the delivery of the roving entirely ceases, but the traverse of the carriage continues at a slower velocity. In this way the twisted yarn is drawn, and for the reasons explained in Chapter VIII, this results in a certain reduction of the thick places owing to the hardening of the thinner ones by the twist. This, it will be noticed, is a somewhat similar procedure to that adopted with fine yarns, being a species of "jacking," but it differs from it because it is the only draft which is exercised on the yarn throughout. There is a wheel provided on which figures are stamped, and by setting a finger to the required figure the detachment of the rollers takes place at the right moment. A draft of a few inches is given, and instead of calculating this, and making elaborate wheel changes, the adjustment of the setting finger is all that is needed. If required, a drawback motion can be fitted. As the cops spun are naturally large the gauge of the spindles is great, varying from 1¾ inch to 2½ inches, and from 300 to 500 spindles are usually fitted in one mule. Productions vary naturally with the counts being spun, but 7½ lbs. per spindle per week of 56 hours is a common production when producing No. 4's yarn. The strength of waste yarn depends upon two factors – the quality of cotton used in the waste from which it is spun, and the twist introduced – but is in some cases considerable. As was said, it is possible to spin waste yarn from condenser bobbins on continuous flyer or ring spinning machines, but, generally speaking, the method described is that adopted.

Although soft waste may be dealt with by a set of machines such as those described, it is a common practice to use it up in the mill in which it is spun by mixing it – judiciously, of course – with the cotton as it is passing through. For some classes of yarns a mixture of two-thirds soft waste and one-third cotton can be advantageously used, and it must not be forgotten that waste in this condition consists of fibres which have not been twisted, and are not, therefore, so liable to damage in opening them. Of course the drafts of the rollers must be arranged to suit this special mixing, and the resultant yarn is sure to be weaker than one spun from cotton solely, but by careful arrangement the whole of the soft waste can be easily utilised in the ordinary work of the mill. A certain loss is inevitable, however great the precautions taken, but the utilisation of the waste in the best manner is a most important thing in the economy of a mill. It is recommended by some persons that soft waste of all kinds should be made a mixing of by themselves, and spun in the ordinary manner, but this is an objectionable and expensive course. It is much preferable to use this class of material along with cop bottom waste, and spin it by the series of machines previously described. On the Continent Vigogne and Barchant yarns,[7] which are the specific names given to waste spun material, are produced on machines of this character, and as the principal seat of the manufacture is found in Germany and Italy it may be taken for granted that the system described is the best and most economical.

## Notes

1 Oldham, a centre for processing waste cotton, gave its name to the willow which remained in use largely in the waste sector of the industry. The willow dashes the cotton with the spikes of a revolving cylinder against spikes that are fixed on a surrounding casing, thereby loosening matted fibres and freeing them from dirt. The shape and density of the spikes are the distinguishing features of such willows.

2 In mule spinning, yarn is wound in a package called a cop; this is built upon a spindle in the shape of a cylinder with conical ends; the lower cone where winding commences is

the cop bottom. Cop bottoms became a term applied generally to waste yarn formed in the processes of winding spun yarn onto spindles.

3 In openers, the cotton is subjected to beater arms that fling it against prepared surfaces. Openers are distinguished by the construction and position of the cylinder holding the beaters. The Crighton opener has the cylinder oriented vertically and the beaters describing a conical shape. Crighton and Sons, machine makers of Manchester, were established in 1814. William Crighton (1814–1895) was the senior partner at the date of Nasmith's writing, when the firm was located at Castlefield Iron Works.

4 Invented by 1867, and improved in the early 1870s, by Thomas Howard Blamires (c1830–1896) and Harry Marsden (c1816–1888), both of Huddersfield.

5 This device was invented around 1870 by the Belgian engineer Jean Sebastien Bolette (1837–1894), of Pepinster.

6 Draft is the amount the roving is stretched in length by the spinning machine rollers.

7 Vigogne usually indicates cotton spun to look like wool (and sometimes mixed with wool), while Barchant sometimes indicates a cotton yarn spun from a mixture of hard and soft waste. Nasmith suggests here a simpler distinction with Vigogne yarn being spun from mainly soft waste and Barchant from mainly hard waste.

## Editorial Headnote

## Marsden, Richard (ed.). 'The preparation and spinning of Barchant or waste yarns', *Textile Mercury*, 1:10 (29 Jun 1889), pp. 178–179; 1:35 (21 Dec 1889), pp. 628–629; 1:36 (28 Dec 1889), pp. 646–647.

The *Textile Mercury* was launched 27 April 1889 as Britain's first textile trades weekly. With around eighteen pages, it sold at 3d. per issue. As an advocate for the extended interests of the textile industries, the journal became the 'vigorous mouthpiece' of textile employers under the leadership of the editor, Richard Marsden (1837–1903).

Marsden's obituarist traced his early career:

> He commenced his industrial life in 1848 at the age of eleven as "utility boy" in a printing and bookselling establishment at Blackburn, the staff of which consisted of the master and one apprentice. Afterwards he entered a cotton factory, and subsequently became manager. Quitting the productive branch, Mr. Marsden entered the grey cloth trade in partnership with another Blackburn man.
>
> (*Northern Whig*, 26 May 1903, p. 9)

When he left after fifteen years to become editor of *The Textile Manufacturer* in 1878, his practical experience of cotton spinning and weaving, alongside selling, gave him a thorough understanding of the needs of his trade readership. Marsden was soon to complete the textile articles for *Spons' Encyclopaedia of the Industrial Arts, Manufactures, and Commercial Products* (1879–1882), which became a standard reference work. He went on to author two volumes in the George Bell & Sons technical series – *Cotton Spinning* (1886), and *Cotton Weaving* (1895).

The bound copies of the first volume of the journal held by Manchester Central Library include one issue, No. 31 of 23 November 1889, inscribed in blue pencil with names (or initials) of contributors: R.M. [Richard Marsden], E.E.M. [Edward Ellis Marsden], Beatty, [S. William] Beck, Marcroft, W. J. Smith and A. Williams. This points to a small editorial team, with Marsden and his son Edward Ellis Marsden (1866–1915) taking a large share in the writing, and also evidences shared authorship in some instances. Samuel William Beck (1852–1906) probably contributed articles of historical interest, with others those of a technical nature.

# 19

# MARSDEN, RICHARD (ED.). 'THE PREPARATION AND SPINNING OF BARCHANT OR WASTE YARNS'

*Textile Mercury* (29 Jun 1889), pp. 178–179; (21 Dec 1889), pp. 628–629; (28 Dec 1889), pp. 646–647.

One great feature of our modern industrial systems and which distinguishes them from the crude methods of manufacturing in olden times is the rigid economy on which they are conducted. In early days this was not the case, as the aim and end was principally to secure a good article irrespective of the cost of production. Profits then were very different from those that can be obtained now, and this was one cause of the prevailing disregard of the cost of production. But the rapidity with which money was made soon put an end to this wasteful method, as the lucky fortune coiners of early manufacturing times, not knowing what better to do with the money they made, re-invested it in extending their means of production in that which had already yielded them their wealth. Hence arose competition which every year from the early part of the present century until to-day has been growing keener, and largely from the operation of the same causes. Diminishing profits induced increased attention to the means of economical production, machinery was improved and rendered increasingly automatic thus reducing the labour cost. The cost of power driving was successively reduced to dimensions that would surprise the manufacturers of half a century ago. Correspondingly with this, increased attention was given to the waste or by-products of the various processes. Many men who cannot yet be called old, will remember how, in close proximity to the cotton mills of forty years ago, great stacks of waste from the openers and scutchers of the mills were formed. These consisting of the dust, droppings, and other matters, including some of the best fibre, were carried out wholesale and stacked in the manner alluded to in order that their contents might decompose before being carted away upon the land as manure. Many a fortune has been thus disposed of for want of better knowledge of the means of extracting the valuable material, and its application to useful purposes when obtained. But those days are gone by never to return. Most of the cotton waste of the time to which we refer found its way to the vat of the paper maker. Gradually, however, it dawned upon various people that a better use could be found for most of it and

 DOI: 10.4324/9780429274190-24

attempts were made to work it up into useful fabrics, necessarily of a lower character than those to which the material it had been abstracted from was devoted. Such is a brief sketch of the conditions and causes which led to the development of an interesting though subordinate branch of the cotton trade, that of the production of waste yarns and cloth.

With the enormous growth of the cotton trade, there has been, in spite of the most rigid economy and the use of the best appliances, a considerable increase in the production of inevitable waste. Since the discovery of means of rendering it useful this has not been as before all loss. Its manufacture has been steadily growing in importance, so much so that it has been deemed quite great enough to engage the attention of our leading machinists and has led them to endeavour to make machinery for the special use of this branch, of equal excellence to that employed in the manufacture of pure cotton.

Amongst the firms who have taken up this matter is that of Messrs. Platt Brothers and Company, Limited, of Oldham.[1] Their installation of Barchant or waste yarn machinery[2] is the most interesting and complete that we have had the privilege of inspecting. It is especially designed for working up waste cotton of almost every kind, such as blowings, cardroom sweepings, roller, flat and mule waste, damaged cottons and cottons of very short staple. For a long time the English cotton trade has paid, and even now pays far too little regard to these materials, and it is usually, at least to a large extent, bought for export and shipped abroad to Belgium, Germany, and Holland, where it constitutes the raw material, out of which a great variety of cheap and useful goods are manufactured.

The low prices which articles produced from this class of material fetch in the market makes it essential that only a minimum amount should be spent on the cost of production. This renders it necessary that the machinery employed should turn off a large production with the least possible attendant labour or attention. Messrs. Platt Brothers have taken all these matters into consideration in the construction of their system of waste manufacturing machinery. The series of machines include the following, all of which are especially modified to serve their particular purposes. First, the Oldham Willow; second, improved scutcher with pedal regulator; breaker card; Derby doubler, finishing card with condenser attachment, with the improved Bollette steel tape, or if preferred, the improved Sachsische leather tape systems, and a specially constructed mule. These machines complete this remarkable installation, a description of which we propose to lay before our readers.

THE OLDHAM WILLOW. This is a machine about which it is not necessary to say much. It is the mechanical substitute for the old process of beating cotton with willow wands upon a netting in order to shake off the dust and dirt which fell through the meshes of the net, or the closely set grate bars originally used. Possibly, judging from its name, it may have originally been invented and introduced in the town from which it derives its name. The mechanical Willow usually consists of a cylinder about 40 inches diameter, and 40 inches wide across the face. In the case of this machine it is thus mounted on a shaft, furnished with driving pulleys and rests in bearings in the framework. Fitted on and extending across its periphery are several rows of strong teeth or blunt spikes. A semi-circular casing internally furnished with rows of similar spikes covers the upper part of this cylinder. The lower portion is enclosed with a wire grid constructed in two parts and hinged together. The back portion of this grid is fixed to the frame and the front is free to move up and down in an opening in the front of the machine. It is also furnished with an exhaust fan. The material, on being fed to the machine, is dashed against the fixed spikes on the internal face of the casing, by which its matted fibres are loosened, sand, dust, and foreign matters are freed from it and fall through the grid into a cavity below, or are drawn away by the fan and discharged into the air. The material is left in this machine until it is judged to be sufficiently opened and cleansed.

IMPROVED SCUTCHER WITH PIANO FEED REGULATOR. Cotton waste sweepings, and so on, owing to the grease and dirt with which they are often loaded, are not as tractable to deal with as pure cottons. Much more difficulty is experienced in forming them into a level lap,[3] and this has necessitated special modifications of the scutcher with a view to overcoming the difficulty. It is hardly necessary to go into the details of these alterations, as it would render our description too lengthy. It may suffice to say that the principles of the scutcher remain substantially unchanged and that the modifications consist of alterations in details. An improved pedal feed regulator, as shown in our illustration, conduces very considerably to the production of an even lap. An improved picker cylinder, specially designed for this machine, thoroughly separates all the fibres composing the raw material, and greatly facilitates its thorough cleansing. Our readers familiar with cotton machinery will be able to gather a very full and accurate conception of the merits of this machine from the excellent illustration given herewith. This will obviate the necessity of any lengthened description. . . .[4]

The next machine calling for attention is the BREAKER CARD (shewn in fig. 1). The economical production of waste yarns imperatively requires that the number of processes, or passages of the material through machines, should be reduced to as few as possible. This fact, in turn requires that the construction and arrangement of every machine should be such as will advance the object in view as much as possible, namely, the attaining of regularity in the disposition of the material, whether in the lap, the breaker card sliver, or at subsequent stages. Keeping this object in view and remembering the nature of the material, the makers have provided the breaker cards with an extended creel and lattice for the reception of two laps to run off together, so that by commencing the doubling process at this early stage the object sought may be attained all the earlier, the inequalities of one tending to correct those of the other. This feature is prominently shewn in our illustration. Passing from the lattice, the material is received by a pair of feed rollers covered by a patent metallic wire and delivered to the taker-in, which is also covered by a similar wire and supplied with two knives. These in their combined action extract a great amount of dirt. The material next passes to the cylinder, which is 50in. in diameter and 50in. across the face. Another noticeable feature of this card is the increased number of clearers and workers[5] that are brought into operation, besides the usual dirt roller, the fancy, and the fancy stripper.[6] This has been accomplished by a special construction of the framing. As will be obvious the improved arrangement increases the carding power and the productive capacity of the machine. There are two ways of dealing with the material as it leaves the doffer, from which it is stripped in the ordinary manner. The ordinary method would be to coil it in a can, and form it into a lap on the Derby doubler, but an alternative is offered, if desired, which dispenses with the latter machine and process, and this is to wind it on a lap drum, from which it may be cut when it has attained the proper thickness, and be taken straight to the finisher card. When it is preferred to doff in the can and retain the Derby doubler, an ingenious appliance is introduced to prevent the breakage of the web as it leaves the doffer. This greatly diminishes the amount of waste that would otherwise occur. Experience has demonstrated that the retention of the Derby doubler in the system is decidedly the best, as by its use greater regularity can be attained.

THE DERBY DOUBLER. This machine is a well-known one, and the particular type forming part of this system does not differ from the ordinary construction beyond in a few small details, to suit it better for its special purpose in this case. We give an illustration of this machine in fig. 2.

The cans of sliver from the breaker card are brought and passed through this machine, making the whole into laps half the width of the finisher card. Knowles'[7] powerful compression rollers are used, and by their means a very solid lap is made, weighing from 15 to 20 lb. each.

THE FINISHER CARD. We now come to a point where the system diverges greatly from the methods usually followed in the manipulation of cotton, and passes over to that of woollen. This is seen in the finisher card, which, instead of doffing its product in the ordinary manner in a sliver, is fitted with a condenser, as will be seen in our illustrations. The condenser, it may not be superfluous to remark to those of our readers who are only acquainted with the cotton system, divides the sheet of carded material, as it leaves the cylinder, into a large number of ribbons or strips, rolls each into the form of a slub or rove and winds them upon two, three, or four bobbins as may be arranged, after which they are ready for the mule.[8] It will be seen, therefore, that this attachment to the card dispenses with the drawing[9] and all the flyer frames, thus saving quite a number of processes.

The finisher card can be supplied with one or other of two condensers, namely, the Saxon or the Bolette condenser, according to the option of the purchaser, who will be governed in his choice by the nature of the material he is going to use. The Saxon condenser is of the latest and most improved form, having leather tapes. The Bolette has steel tapes.[10] Every provision is made to ensure the perfect and continuous division of the web into threads of uniform thickness. The weight turned off the finisher card is 30 lb. per hour of cotton counts No. 3. The observer, whether inexperienced or an expert, will be struck by the regularity of the work, and the quality of the results achieved, and more than all, by the little supervision needed by the machines. We illustrate the finisher card with the Saxon condenser applied.

THE SPINNING PROCESS. The spinning process in the production of Barchant and waste yarns is performed either on the cotton mule or the woollen mule, according to the purpose for which the yarn is to be used. The cotton mule in its construction differs only in being arranged to spin from condenser bobbins, and having several special appliances to suit the requirements of the article being produced.[11] The first of these is a special motion to disengage the delivering rollers at a distance of from 1in. to 3in. before the carriage completes its outward run. The carriage then continues its course, the effect being that thick uneven places that have not taken any twist are drawn out, rendered even with the rest, and receive their complement of twist. Others are: a patent rope tightening apparatus for the taking-in; a scroll-band tightening frame; a patent clip for fastening the check-scroll band; a click-locking motion; a patent automatic nosing motion; a backing-off chain tightening motion; a long copping rail with loose front automatic incline for regulating the locking of the faller; patent step covers; special arrangements in connection with the drawing-out and taking-in of the carriage, which causes it to stop in cases of obstruction during the drawing-out, and by which the spinning operations will cease automatically, should the cam shaft by accident make its change before the proper time; an arrangement by which the mule can be suddenly stopped during the going in of the carriage to prevent accidents; a safety catch to keep the mule stopped; special arrangements to disengage the taking-in friction by the going in of the carriage. These various patents are the same as are applied by the makers to their cotton mule. To the woollen and waste mule is applied a stop motion for stopping the mule when the carriage is close up to the roller beam, by which the attendant can stop it from any part of the whole length of the mule when requisite to replace empty condenser bobbins with full ones, or any other purpose, without having to run the headstock.

THE SELF-ACTING WASTE MULE. The self-acting mule is often constructed on the woollen mule type of headstock for spinning the finer counts of waste and Barchant yarns, say 8's to 12's. This is usually fitted with the following motions, in addition to those used in the cotton headstock, as already described, viz.: – A spindle stop motion, a single and double speed, a drawback motion, variable drawing out scrolls in lieu of the "back-shafts." These mules can be made with rim shafts at right angles to the rollers or parallel with them according to requirement, to suit any position of main driving shaft in the building in which they have to be placed. They are made to contain from 300 to 500 spindles, 2in. distance, or can be made 1⅝in. to 3in. distance. They are constructed on three different systems in the roller parts as follows: – 1. With three lines of bottom fluted rollers at small diameters, the front and middle top rollers covered with cloth and leather, and weighted with lever and saddle; the back top roller is solid, 1¾in. diameter, polished and self-weighted. All three lines of top and bottom rollers are adjustable so that the distances of front and middle, and middle and back lines can be altered very easily, and adjusted to requirement. When draught is not required in the rollers the front and middle top rollers can be removed and the back solid top roller placed upon and between the front and middle bottom rollers thus being self-weighted. 2. With one line of top and bottom rollers, the top roller of 2¼in. diameter, and self-weighted same as the ordinary woollen mule roller parts. 3. With two lines of bottom rollers and only one line of top rollers, all polished and plain, the top roller resting upon and between the two bottom rollers, the top rollers having no end pivots. This style is growing in favour very much, especially when the engines and condensers are of the best construction.

These mules are made to spin direct from the condenser. The numbers spun range from 2's spun condensed to 10's cotton counts, either soft or hard twisted yarns. To those who have been accustomed to regard a level yarn as only capable of being made upon the ordinary cotton system, the uniformity in that respect of those produced on this plan will be a great surprise.

The production of yarn is very large; the stretch of mules is generally 72in., and when spinning 4's and upwards they run 5 draws per minute, producing 7½ lb. per spindle per week of 56½ hours, of 22 hanks from pin cops and 27 hanks from twist.

In very large cotton spinning and manufacturing establishments, and especially in those isolated from the great centres of industry, where waste spinning has become a separate branch of industry, it might be worth considering whether introduction of this system of machinery, and the working up of all the waste made in the establishment, would not be an economical arrangement. To those with whom it is an independent business, and whose machinery may not be up to date, we commend an inspection of the system, for which the makers give every facility, as the most complete that has come under our notice.

## Notes

1 Henry Platt (1793–1842) established the business as manufacturers of cotton spinning machinery in Oldham around 1821, soon forming a partnership with Elijah Hibbert (1801–1846), and building the Hartford Works around 1829. When joined by Platt's sons Joseph Platt (1815–1845) and John Platt (1817–1872) in 1837, the firm became Hibbert, Platt and Sons. With the death of the others, John Platt became the senior partner. In 1854, the Hibbert interest was bought out, and the firm became Platt Brothers and Co., incorporated as a limited company in 1868. Samuel Radcliffe Platt (1845–1902) became the Chairman after the death of his grandfather John Platt. He took the company through a crisis in 1898 when it was wound up temporarily and registered as a new company with the same name. Platt Brothers was known for being at the forefront of textile machinery design.

2 At this time, the distinction between barchant and waste cotton yarn in general was that barchant usually indicated cotton yarn spun from hard waste.

3 In other words, a sheet of uniform thickness.

4 A continuity paragraph beginning the second instalment of the article has been omitted.

5 Smaller rollers working in conjunction with the large central cylinder that catch and pull open clumps of fibre and return the material to the cylinder.

6 The fancy roller had fine long teeth positioned to come into touch with the teeth of the central cylinder, and lift the fibres toward the surface of the cylinder ready for doffing from the machine. The fancy stripper kept the fancy roller clean.

7 Wilson Knowles and Sons, Chapel Lane, Heckmondwike, machine makers, established in 1861.
8 The spinning mule.
9 Drawing is the process of stretching out the rove before spinning, but cannot be performed on the more delicate waste cotton roves.
10 The tapes are raised leather or steel sections on a roller that fit into corresponding depressions on a roller opposite, and these have a scissor action that cuts the sheet web into strips.
11 The precise nature of these specifications is not explained here, the important point being the accumulation of numerous small improvements built into the new machinery.

## Editorial Headnote

### Thornley, Thomas. 'Waste and Waste Spinning', *Cotton Spinning (Honours, or Third Year)* (London: Scott, Greenwood & Son, 1901 [2nd ed., 1907]), pp. 200–211.

### Thornley, Thomas. 'The Use of Cotton-Waste Yarns in Weaving', *Cotton Waste: Its Production, Manipulation and Uses* (London: Scott, Greenwood & Son, 1912), pp. 232–240.

The official syllabus for the third year course in Cotton Spinning reflected the intergration of waste cotton into industrial production by the end of the century. The syllabus required a thorough foundation, spanning:

> The character and quantity of waste produced at each stage in the preparation and spinning of cotton and its utilisation; the preparation of waste for spinning; spinning waste; the machinery used for this purpose; the character of the yarns produced, and the purposes for which they are suitable.
>
> (p. 1)

Similar terrain had been treated in other textbooks, but Thornley's volumes particularly addressed the student preparing for examinations, the schema for which had been revised and expanded around 1897 leaving a gap in coverage. His approach was distinctive:

> The system on which the writer has worked has put the books more in the form of a textile catechism, for after stating the ground required to be covered by the student, the principal questions asked in recent examinations are inserted, and answered in a terse, yet full, manner.
>
> (*Textile Manufacturer*, 27:322, 15 Oct 1901, p. 338)

Thornley's Honours course volume was published in October 1901, the final one in a set covering the three stages of the City and Guilds of London Institute syllabus for cotton spinning. Those undertaking the Honours course aimed to obtain posts as managers, foremen or other positions of responsibility in the cotton industry. Suitably priced for the student at 5s., demand led to a reprint edition issued in April 1907 without any update to the examination questions.

Another selection from Thornley's writings is from his definitive monograph on *Cotton Waste* that came out in October 1912 at 7s. 6d. The reviewer for the *Textile Manufacturer* thought the book dealt 'in an exhaustive manner with the whole process of converting cotton waste into yarn' (38:455, 15 Nov 1912, p. 376). While most of the chapters require a familiarity with materials and machinery for full comprehension, that on cotton waste yarns is accessible to the general reader. In the preface, Thornley warned his target readership of masters, managers and foremen that 'no one can afford to neglect the question of waste, whether it be in the direction of reducing its amount, or applying it more and more to useful and profitable purposes'. The selection here details the main uses to which waste was put. A second edition of the book was issued in May 1921; it had few revisions but added five new chapters.

Thomas Thornley (c1861–1935) was born at Chisworth, near Glossop, in humble circumstances. Self-educated, he began his working life early as a piecer in a cotton mill, eventually rising to mill manager. Thornley commenced teaching about 1885 in Glossop. In 1896 he became lecturer in cotton spinning, weaving and applied mechanics at Bolton Technical College where he taught for over two decades. From 13 December 1895, he was also known as 'Lectus' in articles on spinning contributed to the *Cotton Factory Times*.

# 20

# THORNLEY, THOMAS. 'WASTE AND WASTE SPINNING' AND 'THE USE OF COTTON-WASTE YARNS IN WEAVING'

*Cotton Spinning (Honours, or Third Year)*, (London: Scott, Greenwood & Son, 1901 [2nd ed., 1907]), pp. 200–211; *Cotton Waste: Its Production, Manipulation and Uses* (London: Scott, Greenwood & Son, 1912), pp. 232–240.

**Q.** 1898. You are assumed to be dealing with a mixing of low middling American and Dhollera cotton[1] in the proportion of two to one. What proportion of waste would you expect to find (a) at the opener, (b) at the scutcher, (c) below the undercasings at the carding engine, and (d) as strippings?

**A.** It is probable that the opener would make about 4 to 5 per cent. of waste, very little indeed of which would be of much use to anyone. We might reckon the waste at the first scutcher at about 2 per cent., and that at the second scutcher at about 1¼ per cent. The total waste at an ordinary revolving flat carding engine is usually somewhere about 5 per cent., and it is probable that this total does not vary a great deal whether the card be using low, medium or good American cotton, or even Egyptian cotton. Furthermore, the percentage in some cases may be more for the better cottons than for the worst, or the opposite may hold good, according to the general conditions of the card and the manner in which the various parts are adjusted to each other. The author has personally known the waste to vary at the card between 4 and 7 per cent. Taking 5 per cent. as the basis for the descriptions of cotton under notice, it is probable that about 3.2 of this 5 would be due to the strips from the flats, cylinder and doffer, leaving about 1.8 to be due to the undercasings of the taker-in and cylinder and from below the doffer and lap and sliver waste.

**Q.** 1897. Describe briefly the method of preparing and spinning waste yarns suitable for wefts and flannelettes.

**A.** The machines used in waste spinning properly so-called differ very considerably in character from those used in ordinary cotton spinning. They vary

DOI: 10.4324/9780429274190-25 

somewhat in style and arrangement, but a good modern arrangement may be taken as follows: First, cop bottom machine, or hard waste breaker, or Oldham willow, these differing in construction from one another, but in all cases being arranged to subject the cotton to considerable breaking up. Secondly, a scutcher may be used, differing somewhat from the ordinary type of scutcher as used for cotton spinning. Thirdly, a breaker roller card, which is more suitable for waste spinning than the revolving flat, as the latter tends to take too much waste out, and to give the fibres a disposition more approximating to the parallel than the roller card; neither of these properties being wanted in waste spinning. After the breaker card may be used the Derby doubler, in order to make a lap suitable for placing behind the finisher roller card, the latter being generally used in waste spinning. This card should be fitted with a condenser at the front, in order to wind the cotton into suitable form for the waste spinning mule or billey. This last-named machine differs from a spinning mule in having no drawing rollers, as it gives the slight attenuation necessary to the cotton by the principle of "ratching" or "jacking."[2] The processes of waste spinning are distinguished from cotton spinning by the absence of drawing rollers in the former, the two chief objects of drawing rollers being unrequired, *viz*., attenuation of material to a very fine degree, and making the fibres parallel, and also making the yarn very uniform. As much attention as possible should be bestowed upon the cotton in the earlier processes in order to secure an approximately even thread. Yarn spun in the manner indicated would suit flannelettes or the wefts of similar goods.

**Q.** 1897. What should be the weight of waste made per week in a scutching machine through which is passed 15,000 lb. of Orleans middling cotton, and in a revolving flat card producing 800 lb. of slivers from the same cotton? Does the character of the waste vary at different parts of either machine, and, if so, how? Give the percentage of waste made at each point.

**A.** The total waste made by the scutcher may be taken at approximately 1½ per cent., and for the card at approximately 5 per cent. These percentages would in the cases under discussion give the total waste of the scutcher at 225 lb., and that of the card at 40 lb., reckoning on the above total weights of 15,000 lb. and 800 lb. respectively. The waste of a breaker scutcher would be greater than that of a finisher, and might reach 2½ per cent. To be strictly accurate on the card the waste would be, say, 42 lb.

As regards the distribution and character of the waste, it may be said at once that it differs very materially in both respects at different parts of either machine. In the scutcher the greater portions of the waste and impurities are found below the beater bars. The very numerous and powerful blows of the beater have the effect of causing the comparatively heavy seed, leaf, shell, dirt, etc., with some proportion of fibre to fall through the grate bars; the first of which is frequently set some distance – say half an inch or so – from the feed roller, in order to allow of the heavier impurities falling through. The droppings here are usually quite black looking, with leaf, shell, etc., as compared with those elsewhere.

In the cavity underneath the cage bars is found a much less proportion of droppings, and it is whiter, with shorter fibre than the preceding, and the leaf is smaller. The grate bars, however, for this cavity have been more subject to differences in shape than the beater grate bars, and at the present time we have them laid at right angles to the sides of the machine, or parallel thereto, or in a herring-bone style, just as the case may be. Crighton's[3] employ a travelling lattice called the leaf extractor at this point, the same idea being lately adopted by another machinist.

From the insides of the cages, and more especially from the upright box ends of the cages, and out of the exit trunks is gathered at times a smaller proportion of very heavy black dirt, consisting largely of very short and broken fibres which have passed through the interstices of the cages, along with fine dust and sand, the latter being the weighting part of this waste.

At the card the great bulk of the waste is formed either below the licker-in or as strips from the flats of the cylinder and doffer. The licker-in and its mote knives[4] and undercasings play practically the same part on the card as the beater plays upon a scutcher, and from beneath are taken out all the heavier impurities which have escaped the previous processes, such as seed, motes, leaf, etc. There should not be much short fibre or fly taken out at this point, and especially is this the case with modern metallic takers-in and the dish feed. The short fibre and fly are largely taken out by the flats, and, passing to the front of the card, are there stripped out by the stripping comb and stripping brush, and fall down upon the doffer cover. A fair amount of strippings are embedded in the teeth of the cylinder and doffer, and are at intervals removed by the stripping brush used by the strippers and grinders. A comparatively small percentage of waste is gathered from beneath the doffer and the cylinder, but nothing near as much as was the case before the very general adoption of improved undercasings.

**Q.** Specify the proportions of waste usually made in the different processes of a cotton spinning mill.

**A.** An approximately correct list would be somewhat as below: –

| | |
|---|---|
| Opener | say 4 per cent. |
| Breaker scutcher | say 2 per cent. |
| Finisher scutcher | say 1½ per cent. |
| Card | say 5 per cent. |
| Drawframes | say 1 per cent. |
| Fly frames | say 1¾ per cent. |
| Spinning | say 2 per cent. |
| Total, | 17 per cent. |

With good clean cotton the total waste may come out as low as 14 per cent., while with dirty, wasty cottons the per cent. of waste is increased.

When combers are used the average loss per cent. in waste for the comber alone may be taken at about 17 per cent.

**Q.** In some mills the waste made in the different processes is brought back to the mixing to be worked over again. If too much is put into the mixing at once, what is the effect on the lap, as well as upon the yarn?

**A.** The addition of waste to a mixing tends strongly to give lap-licking, because of its soft character. In proportion to the amount of waste put in with the good cotton the yarn becomes weaker, more irregular and less compact, while the waste is very liable to again come out as waste at the various machines. The most common practice is to take bobbin waste back to the mixing, and a certain amount of this is often permissible, except in very good yarns.

With a large proportion of waste it is very difficult to keep "nep" and "slubs" out.[5]

**Q.** Name and shortly describe the various kinds of waste made in Oldham spinning mills.

**A.** (a) From the openers and scutchers: droppings from below the beater bars and cage bars, and dust and dirt from inside the cages and dust flues. Little of this can be used again.

(b) From the cards: strippings from the flats, cylinder and doffer; strippings from rollers and clearers, and from the ends of these rollers, if such are used; licker-in fly and fly from beneath the doffer and cylinder; sliver waste and lap ends.

(c) From the frames: sliver waste and bobbin waste, top and bottom clearer waste, waste from roller laps and broken rovings.

(d) Spinning waste, crow waste,[6] top clearer waste, waste from roller laps, bad ends, waste from picking saddles[7] and roller ends, bobbin waste, piecing-up waste.

In addition to the foregoing we might specify the following: cleaning waste or oily waste, sweepings up, old banding.

**Q.** 1900. Describe the methods of preparing the various kinds of waste for re-spinning. How are they prepared for carding, how treated, and how delivered by the card? Is it possible to draw waste yarns? If so, to what extent, and where is it effected?

**A.** Broadly speaking, there are two principal classes of waste used in waste spinning: (1) Soft waste, which includes all waste made before the cotton has received the final twist at the mule or ring frame. (2) Hard waste, which comprises all waste made after the cotton has been twisted at the final spinning process. The various kinds of waste are subdivided according to cleanliness, etc. For some purposes it is better that the waste should be of a greasy character, and to impart this to the cotton there is occasionally used a "soaper," which is an appliance fitted to the opener. In the blowing-room various kinds of openers are more or less in use containing anything from one cylinder, or beater, up to six or more. For very soft waste a one-cylinder machine is often used, while for hard waste the six-cylinder machine is a favourite. After the opener a wide scutcher is usually employed to make a lap for the card. These machines are shown in previous sketches.

In waste spinning it is customary to double card the cotton and to use the roller and clearer card. To secure uniformity often two laps are fed together behind the breaker card. Sometimes the cotton is transferred from the breaker to the finisher by the Scotch or cross-feed arrangement, while in other cases the slivers from the breaker are converted into narrow laps on the Derby doubler, and two of these are placed end to end behind the finisher card.

It is sought to deliver the fibres finally in a crossed and intermingled condition – as distinct from the parallel arrangement – hence the use of the roller and clearer card.

The cotton is taken from the finisher card by a condenser, which divides the doffer web into a number of narrow strips, which are rubbed into strands and wound side by side on the long condenser bobbin. A condenser arrangement is shown in fig. 54.

The number of divisions or strands varies greatly according to the counts to be spun.

It is not often that drawing rollers are used in waste spinning, the usual practice being to take the long condenser bobbins and place them behind the waste spinning mule, in which only one pair of rollers are used. The only "draft," therefore, is between the spindle points and these rollers, and it seldom exceeds more than about 40 to 50 inches pulled into about 70 inches. Diagrammatic views of the breaker and finisher waste cards as made by Hetherington are shown in Figs. 49 and 50.

**Q.** 1899. Assume that you are dealing with a mill producing 30,000 lb. weight of twist yarn per week from American cotton, what quantity of waste would you expect to get? How much cotton would you need? Distinguish between the various kinds of waste, and say how you would dispose of each. Does the amount of waste vary from year to year?

**A.** The total loss over all might be, say, 16 or 17 per cent. Some of this would be invisible loss, and some would be visible, in the shape of fly, droppings, rovings, etc. In many cases students and others work this calculation as follows: Taking the total loss to equal 17 per cent., then to get 30,000 lb. weight of yarn warm from the spindles, we should want 30,000 lb. of cotton plus 30,000 x $^{17}/_{100}$ = 5,100 lb. According to this we should therefore require 35,100 lb. of raw cotton. The more correct method is as follows: – 30,000 x $^{100}/_{83}$ = 36,144.5 lb. of raw cotton required. By this latter method the waste is allowed for on the added quantity. Waste from the blowing-room and sweepings up are of very little use except for making into manure, or flocks, or candlewick yarn. The strips and fly from the card and the clearer waste may be used up in waste spinning and mixed with Bengals in the production of coarse quilting, weft, etc. Roving waste is often used up again in the spinning mill, and comber waste also is often used for the ordinary processes of cotton spinning.

**Q.** 1899. In carding waste yarns how is the material fed? State fully the different methods pursued, what position the fibres occupy relatively to the card teeth, and what advantages are claimed for each method.

**A.** In some cases the material may be fed in loose state behind the breaker card, while in others two laps from the scutcher may be placed behind the breaker. To feed the finisher card there are mainly two methods. (1) The slivers from the breakers are made into laps for the finisher by the Derby doubler. (2) In the second case the Scotch or cross feed takes the cotton in the form of a ribbon from the breaker and spreads [it] across the back of the finisher as it were in layers so as to form a continuous sheet.

The fibres are crossed and mixed a great deal in relation to the card teeth, as it is not desired to make the fibres parallel. The Scotch or cross feed probably presents the fibres in a more crossed manner to the finisher card teeth than does the sliver lap machine. The condenser is an apparatus placed at the delivery end of the finisher card, by which the web or fleece is divided into individual strands or ends, which are then wound on the condenser bobbins ready for the creel of the mule.

Various methods of feeding are shown diagrammatically in Figs. 51, 52 and 53.

Fig. 51, at left hand, shows [a bank] feed; Fig. 52, at the left hand, shows the lap drum; and Fig. 53 shows the Scotch or cross feed method of conveying the cotton from breaker to finisher.

**Q.** 1900. For what purposes are waste yarns employed? For what kinds of fabrics are they most useful, and why?

**A.** The worst waste spun yarns are used for a large assortment of coarse purposes, such as candlewick, lamp wick and cleaning cloths. It is probable that the better classes are of the greatest service in the production of cheap goods which are intended to be raised, and are required to be soft to the feel, such as flannelette and cotton blankets. A good deal of waste spun yarn is used for the weft of plain and fancy quiltings and goods of that character as to material used.

**Q.** 1898. Describe generally the mode of spinning the slubbings produced on a condenser carding engine from waste yarn. How are they drawn?

**A.** It must be remembered in considering this question that in this case none of the machines used would contain drawing rollers, so that the pertinence of the examiner's query – How are the slivers drawn? – will in this connection be made very clear. On a condenser carding engine the fleece from the doffer is divided up into a number of parts, say, for instance, in this case about 22. Each part is rubbed or condensed and wound upon a long condenser bobbin nearly the full width of the card. Fig. 54 shows the delivery end of a finisher waste card fitted with Bolette's steel tape condenser. The condenser bobbin thus formed is taken directly to the specially formed creel of the "Billey," or waste spinning mule. Such machines as the drawframes and the bobbin and fly frames are omitted altogether. In the waste spinning mule, or "Billey," there are [no] drawing rollers, but simply a pair of large diameter rollers through which the slubbings pass, very much after the style of the rollers of a ring doubling frame, with the important difference that the top rollers are much longer.

The term "mule" is to some extent a misnomer when applied to the Billey, since a "spinning mule," properly so called, ought to possess both drawing rollers and the principles of "ratch" and "gain."[8] In the Billey the comparatively soft slubbings being passed through the rollers and attached to the twisting spindles, the carriage and rollers may both move for something more than one half of the usual stretch of 72 inches. Then the rollers may stop while the carriages finish the stretch and the requisite amount of twist is put in the yarn. It is quite obvious that only the coarsest numbers can be spun in this manner, owing to the limited amount of drawing power possessed by the machines used. A soft, thick yarn is produced, admirably suited for some descriptions of goods.

## Chapter VI. The use of cotton-waste yarns in weaving

*The Weaving of Cotton-Waste Yarns.* In considering the adaptability of cotton-waste yarns to woven fabrics, it is necessary to remember that compared with yarns spun on the ordinary cotton system of equal counts they are deficient in strength and elasticity, but are of greater softness and fullness, and of an oozy fibrous nature.

In the majority of cases their weakness precludes their use in the form of warp, since they are unable to withstand the strain of shedding, the friction of the healds, reed, and shuttle in all but exceptional instances.

*Woven Goods in which Yarns Spun from Cotton Waste may be Used.* Cotton-waste yarns are as a rule soft twisted and are very bulky. They are largely used in the manufacture of such goods as the following: Table covers, carpets, quilts, cotton sheetings, cotton blankets, flannelettes, curtains, cheap shirtings, cheap suitings, bath sheets and towels, cheap dress goods, cheap overcoatings, upholstery for all classes of furniture, cheap towels, cleaning cloths, sponge cloths, grey twills for such purposes as working drawers or overalls for spinners, miners, stokers, and other classes of workmen. The wide range of fabrics may be either plain or fancy, plain or coloured.

Improvements continue to be made whereby finer yarns are spun and this increases the range of fabrics for which cotton-waste yarns may be adapted.

In the weaving of cotton-waste yarns into fabrics of any kind it must always be remembered that in proportion to bulk these yarns are weak, and partly for this reason they are generally used as wefts, and the only strain therefore that is put upon the yarn is that of drawing from the shuttle and carrying through the shed that is formed by the warp.

Speaking generally the mechanisms of the looms used for weaving fabrics into which cotton-waste yarns enter, are very much of the ordinary kind. If there is any modification at all in any of the mechanism it is very often in connexion with the shuttle and shuttle boxes.

For example, the shuttle might be of increased size to take a larger cop,[9] and this would also compel a larger shed to be made to permit the shuttle to pass through with sufficient freedom.

Frequently it happens that trouble is caused by these cops slipping from the shuttle tongue,[10] thus causing excessive waste and other damage. With ordinary shuttles this might be remedied by opening the shuttle tongue to give a better inside grip of the cop. Possibly a remedy might be found by the spinner starting to build higher up the spindle, which would reduce the size of aperture in the cop but would give shorter cops unless there was previously some unused length of spindle above the apex of the full cop. In some cases it is considered advisable to re-wind the coarser counts into solid cops, which are very tightly wound, so that for equal dimensions a cop will last longer in the shuttle.

In the quiltings, suitings, and other cloths of this class the cotton-waste yarn is often used as backing weft in which there is a face warp while the backing weft shows only on the back. To put this in other words we may say there would be two wefts and one warp, but the waste weft remains at the back of the cloth, being stitched in by allowing some definite number of warp threads to interweave with same. The object of such cloth is to give warmth, weight and body and yet to keep the price comparatively low.[11]

In regard to cotton sheetings these are generally of a coarse twill weave, and they can be produced very cheaply by using coarse or cotton-waste yarns, so that such sheetings are in extensive use at home and are also exported.

A large amount of this kind of cloth is produced and used in the United States.

Referring now to cotton blankets, these have a distinctly different feel and appearance from the cheap sheetings, the difference being largely due to the fact that the cotton blankets have a nap or finish raised upon them to imitate woollen goods. As regards weave this may be either of a plain or twill character.

The cheap shirtings in which cotton-waste yarns may be used may be of a satin weave, resulting in a fine warp face and a waste weft back.

Sponge or cleaning cloths represent a very different type from the foregoing, and may be regarded as among the very cheapest, and lowest classes of goods woven from cotton yarns of any description. Sponge or cleaning cloths are as a rule composed entirely of coarse shoddy or waste yarns – both warp and weft – and are very open in the weave, partly to obtain an enhanced porous effect. As a rule the weave is of a plain character, or possibly a gauze weave may sometimes be adopted.

Large quantities of cotton-waste yarns are now being used in the upholstery trade, being woven into tapestry cloths, with good patterns, and really good effects produced by rich and tasteful dyeing.

From the nature of the cotton waste it is not practicable to spin any but yarns of low counts, which are therefore sold at a low price per pound, and are mostly used in fabrics of a bulky, heavy character but moderate price. The price of cotton-waste carded on the roller and clearer principle, using double cards, often with the Derby doubler interposed,[12] together with other circumstances, often leads to good condenser yarns[13] of the finer counts commanding a higher price than yarns of equal counts spun on the ordinary system, and the cloths containing the better and finer condenser yarns are often of superior appearance and finish.

A few of the leading cloths in which cotton-waste yarns are used may be more fully explained.

*Cotton Blankets*. – Ordinary qualities of this cloth such as are exported in large quantities to the Eastern markets, Africa and South America, are made with the plain weave, the warp being relatively fine in counts, say 20's to 24's. The weft ranges from 50's to 130's bump counts,[14] i.e. 50 to 130 yards per ounce, this being a common method of numbering cotton-waste yarns of the coarsest nature up to three or four hanks per pound. . . . Better qualities for the home trade, sometimes sold as "charity" blankets, are made in heavier weights with twill weaves and with strong warps, say 12's to 18's, and perhaps with more picks per inch of coarse weft than if for export. The weft is from cotton waste of moderate quality such as "wash" waste and "clearers," taking a medium mixing for blanket weft and better qualities being obtained by adding cop waste.[15]

Headings or stripes of coloured weft are usually inserted near each end of a blanket, the heading consisting of solid black or red bars or variegated stripes according to the market for the cloth. . . .

*Raising Process*. After weaving, cotton blankets are passed through a raising machine which produces a dense woolly surface upon the cloth by partially scratching or dragging fibres out of the weft threads, the softness of the latter and the arrangement of the fibres being particularly suitable to this process. The raising machine in common use for cotton fabrics consists of a number of small rollers, each covered with fine teeth, and supported in bearings at the end of arms which are attached to a central shaft. The cloth is stretched tightly round the rollers, and when the central shaft is revolved, and the cloth drawn forward, the rollers also are revolved. Meanwhile the wire teeth have penetrated the soft spun weft threads and as they leave the cloth they drag the ends of fibres with them, thus giving a fine nap or pile to the surface of the cloth. Originally the nap or pile was obtained by scratching the surface of the cloth by card filleting, but while giving the desired effect this process dragged a considerable number of fibres out of the cloth. With the newer machines there is very little loss of fibre and weight, and a better nap is obtained with fewer passages through the machine.

For some markets blankets are dyed, scarlet being a common colour; in other cases the cloth is printed with variously coloured floral designs; animal figures are also printed upon the cloth for markets, the lion, tiger, elephant, etc., being represented in large sizes.[16] The printing is usually done by hand by the aid of blocks, this being one of the few remaining cases in which the old-fashioned method of cloth printing still survives.

Sheetings are lighter in weight, and made from finer yarns of better quality than blankets, the weft ranging from 3's to 8's cotton counts and the twist up to 32's.[17] The weave is generally two up and two down or sheeting twill, but the plain or calico twill is also used. Same type of loom, but of lighter construction . . . is used for sheetings, and the cloth is sold both in the raised and non-raised condition.

*Cleaning Cloths*. These are an exception to the general rule in that they have both warp and weft composed of coarse waste yarns. The softness of the latter, together with their low price and open structure arising from the method of interweaving them, giving a fabric which by reason of bulk and absorbent properties is specially suitable for cleaning purposes. This cloth is also very easily cleaned for using again, and when used for cleaning oily machinery the absorbed oil can be reclaimed. Two styles of cleaning cloth are in use. In the first kind the warp and weft are interwoven in the plain or calico order by looms of ordinary construction, but the second kind, commonly known as sponge cloth, is woven by the gauze or leno principle of weaving, in which the warp threads are twisted partly round each other, with the result that increased strength is obtained without losing the required open structure. For ordinary gauze or leno weaving, specially constructed healds known as "doups" are employed; but the coarseness and strength of the warp yarn, together with the strain arising from the necessary deep shed, or division in the warp to be formed for the passage of the shuttle, causes rapid wear and destruction of such doup healds. Sponge cloths are therefore woven by specially constructed looms in which two rows of needles take the place of doups and healds, one row pointing upwards, and the other row pointing downwards, while the warp threads are alternately drawn through the needle eyes. The needles are secured in bars which are controlled by tappets and levers in such a manner that, besides rising and falling to form a shed, they can also be moved sideways for the crossing of the warp threads.

At each end of the piece a few picks of fine weft are usually put in and woven in plain order more closely than the coarser picks of the body. In these picks the needles are moved up and down in plain order only, and the speed of the take-up motion is automatically reduced. A few picks of coloured weft are also thrown in at the ends and a drop-box is provided at one end of the sley for this purpose.[18]

*Double Cloth Weave with Waste Cotton Weft*. It is sometimes the case that double-cloth weaves are constructed with either the weft or the warp of wadding or cotton waste yarn, the use of weft in this connexion being much more prevalent than that of warp.

This practice adds both weight and bulk to the woven cloths, and it is possible to do it in double cloths without the waste yarn showing on either the face or the back of the cloth. Take a specific instance with the face and the back of cassimere twill with one face, one back in the warp, and one face, one back, one cotton waste yarn in the filling.

The cotton waste or wadding yarn is of course a bulky, moderately twisted and cheap yarn, and this is picked into the cloth, the face warp ends are lifted and the back warp ends are held down so that the weft waste yarn is put in the centre of the cloth without showing and without interlacing with either face or back warp ends. Weight and bulk are thus durably imparted to the cloth without deteriorating the appearance. In some cases of cotton-waste warp the waste yarns are raised over every backing pick and depressed over every face pick so as to be put into the centre of the cloth.

One reason for cheap thick yarns from cotton waste spun on the condenser principle being more used for weft than warp, is that warp yarns are subjected to more strain than the weft, and are liable to be rubbed by the healds and reeds and shuttle.

Tapestry carpet is a simple figured warp-pile fabric, containing loops of uncut pile-warp and all the surface of the fabric covered with the pile in a uniform manner. The pattern is formed by printing the design on the pile-warp and formed on the surface of the cloth by the pile. It is convenient to print a certain length of pile warp a desired colour, so that this colour is reproduced in the cloth for a certain distance, after which an alternative colour may obtain for a space.

In a tapestry cloth there may be a centre warp possibly of cotton-waste yarn which passes between the ground picks without interlacing after the manner obtaining with the cotton-waste warp yarn in a double or backed cloth.

Although the structure of a Brussels carpet is quite different from that of a tapestry, yet it is quite possible for some of the pile threads that are disposed in the body of the cloth to consist of cheap thick yarns, although the main body of the fabric may be of as good yarn as the face.

*Waste in Weaving Sheds*. In a weaving mill the control of the waste to the best advantage is one of the most difficult duties of the overlookers and manager.

Although the waste of a spinning mill may be much greater in amount it is probably more easily checked and supervised. It is fairly easy, for example, to check the amount of waste made in the blowing-room,[19] or at the cards or combers.

Suppose, however, a certain number of skips of yarn are delivered at a weaving mill and pass into the winding room, each winder may be required to bring back or give up in some way the waste she makes; but the full bobbins are probably taken directly to the warper, and no one knows what the half-full bobbins contain in weight of yarn, so it is awkward to check. At the end of the week the overlooker may weigh his waste and compare with yarn given to winders, but percentages are not easy to check, partly on account of yarn on the bobbins.

Naturally at the six months' stock-taking it is possible to say how much yarn entered the winding and warping room, how much waste came out, how much yarn has left the room on the full beams, and an estimation can be made of weight on the bobbins. In this way the waste per cent can be estimated, and if too much the overlooker talks severely to the operatives and says they must bring less waste in. They will do this, but it is common knowledge that in many cases it has been only because they have taken some of the waste home, and so the master now has a double loss.

It may be easy at stock-taking to find out that a considerable weight of yarn has entered the winding room that has never been accounted for, but it is not so easy to pick out the culprits and bring them to book.

Much the same remarks apply to the weavers in many cases, and especially in places in which the moral and religious characters of the operatives have not been developed and maintained. Often the weavers simply fetch skips or boxes of weft, bring the waste back with the empty skip, are rebuked or fined if too much waste is brought in, with the result that next time some of the waste is taken home, and probably nothing is said to the weaver. All this kind of thing puts a premium on the unscrupulous weaver, and the thing is manifestly wrong in principle.

## Notes

1 Dhollera was an Indian cotton sourced from the Bombay Presidency.
2 These terms are explained more fully in the final question and answer.
3 Crighton and Sons, machine makers, Manchester.
4 Motes are fragmentary or immature seeds with tufts of attached cotton fibre. A blade positioned near the licker-in cylinder can prevent such impurities entering the carding process.
5 A nep is a small tangled mass; a slub is an irregular thickened part on a yarn.
6 Crow waste is the Lancashire term for the waste picked up by the underclearer rollers of spinning mules.
7 The picking or cop-bottom machine was characterised by 'a very large number of very fine teeth'. See Thornley's *Cotton Waste*, p. 117.
8 Ratch is the stretching of the cotton roving that takes place in the mule when the drawing rollers are stopped, whereas gain is the stretching that occurs when the carriage of the mule is travelling faster than delivery of cotton from the drawing rollers.
9 A cop is a torpedo-shaped package of wound yarn on a spindle.
10 The shuttle tongue receives the hollow spindle at the central axis of the wound yarn forming the cop, allowing it to rotate and unwind smoothly.
11 A binding warp of matching colour could also be employed, paired for example with every fourth warp, weaving tabby on the verso with a padding weft. Whether tied in with the main warp or a binding warp, the backing part of the weave gives the fabric its weight and draping quality, while making it feel soft to the wearer, acting somewhat as built-in lining.
12 Double cards means two carding assemblies, the Derby doubler being a device to carry the carded strips from the doffer of the first carder to the intake of the second.
13 The condenser device rubbed the carded strips to consolidate them sufficiently to withstand machine spinning. Thornley's second edition adds a chapter on condenser spinning, a site for innovation in the 1910s decade.

14 Bump count was a measure of yards per ounce as opposed to the standard count of the number of 840-yard hanks per pound. Thus the bump count is 52.5 times the usual cotton count.
15 Cop waste would have a longer staple, hence increasing strength and quality of the resultant yarn.
16 Eastern markets is probably intended here.
17 Twist is the warp yarn.
18 The drop-box allowed rotation between different shuttles, enabling weft colour to be changed easily.
19 Blower is another term for a scutching machine used to open the cotton before carding. In scutching machines, the cotton was often driven through by means of fans, hence *blowing.*

## Editorial Headnote

### Heylin, Henry Brougham. 'Examples of Trading', *Buyers and Sellers in the Cotton Trade, being a Handbook for Merchants, Shippers, Manufacturers, and Others who are Interested as Producers or Distributors* (London: Charles Griffin & Co., 1913), pp. 143–145.

Henry Brougham Heylin (1870–1956) was brought up in the textile districts of Lancashire where pursuit of a textile career was an easy choice, but he evidently had innate aptitude. Beginning his career as a woven cotton designer, he became a teacher at the Salford Technical Institute in 1893. This experience is reflected in his first publication, a manual for students: *The Cotton Weavers' Handbook* (London: C. Griffin & Co., 1908). In 1905, Heylin became a weaving mill manager, and this practical experience appears to have influenced the content of *Buyers and Sellers*. It was 'in press' in 1912, the preface signed in February 1913, and the published volume advertised in the *Spectator* in April for 8s. 6d.

Apart from the practical examples of trading methods and terms, Heylin's analysis did not satisfy the academic standards of Dr Melvin T. Copeland of the Harvard Business School. On balance nevertheless, Copeland concluded, 'the collection of these facts about the English cotton goods trade, however fragmentary, will be of assistance to students of commercial organisation' (*American Economic Review*, 4:1, Mar 1914, p. 143). More pertinent here is the remark of the reviewer for the *Textile Manufacturer* that the chapter 'which deals with examples of trading, is a very faithful reflection of every-day occurrences in the business life of Lancashire cotton manufacturers and their confreres' (39:463, 15 Jul 1914, p. 232). In the year of publication, Heylin was appointed Inspector of Textiles for the Army Ordnance Department, having become known as an expert buyer and judge of materials.

# 21

# HEYLIN, HENRY BROUGHAM. 'EXAMPLES OF TRADING'

*Buyers and Sellers in the Cotton Trade* (London: Charles Griffin & Co., 1913), pp. 143–145.

### Damp cotton waste

Most of the spinning and weaving mills in the cotton industry usually contract with a waste dealer to take their waste and sweepings for a period of twelve months at an agreed price. The opportunity for quoting is given to a few competitors in the trade, and as a rule the firm that quotes the best average price for the whole assortment obtains the contract. There are records of dealers having had a contract for several years consecutively and then being beaten in price by a competitor, but if the sellers have wanted to continue business as before, a kindly hint has been the means of getting the offer raised to the level of the competitors, thereby enabling them to retain the business. Instances, too, are known of some would-be competitor not quoting prices, but stating verbally that he would be willing to offer a certain percentage above the highest price quoted by any of the competitors!

It is customary for those firms who are invited to quote to pay a visit to the mill and casually inspect the different kinds of waste, in order to form an opinion regarding their true value. They like to see how the different kinds of waste are separated, and, with respect to the sweepings, how much matter other than lint cotton appears to be mixed with the bulk. They also like to know the conditions under which it is stored, and to see its place of storage. Assuming a waste dealer to have obtained the contract for the first time, he sometimes finds the first delivery proves very disappointing. Through some unaccountable reason the bulk of the waste seems excessively damp, the bags are coated with mud and dirt, and are much heavier than the tare indicated on the ticket attached to the bag. The "sweepings" contain a large amount of ground dirt, chips, leather, in many cases bits of iron and occasionally broken brick-bats, which suggest a rubbish heap rather than cotton sweepings. He might make a mild protest to the sender, but in a large number of cases he would be told that he had seen the quality of waste before accepting the contract, and, so far as they knew, no deviation had been made from the ordinary custom in filling up the bags. Some of the waste dealers make the "best of it" under the circumstances, but suggest that a little more care might be exercised in future deliveries.

DOI: 10.4324/9780429274190-26

## Sorting and storing waste

A number of the larger firms have already realised that it pays not only to keep the various kinds of waste well stored in a dry place, but also see that proper care is bestowed on the sorting of the same. In some of the smaller concerns, unless the boys or "sweepers-up" are properly instructed, they will put everything from the floor into the sweeping-bag, under the impression that it will "help to weigh"! The place of storage also in the case of such firms is likely to be of a questionable character. So long as the weather remains fine and dry, very little harm may be done to the stored waste; but when wet weather comes the water drips through the store shed roof on to the bags and waste. In many cases, too, the water gets into the earth below the waste bags inside the waste shed, and then gets absorbed by the bags and waste. As the water will be absorbed much quicker than it will be again lost, even if there is no rain, we may take it that in the weighing of the waste this extra weight will be registered to the credit of the seller and to the detriment of the waste dealer. Some conscientious men have made allowances for this excess dampness when weighing, but the complaint of many waste dealers is that such instances are few and far between. Not long ago a certain waste dealer had to carry out from his storage a very large number of full waste bags because of their tending to fire owing to being damp and stored with his ordinary stock of waste. In another case a delivery of waste sent by rail weighed from 6–10 lbs. per bag lighter when received than appeared on the invoiced weight.

Those to blame are mostly weaving firms, but owing to competition and the low esteem (as it seems to the waste dealer) in which the manufacturer holds him, the former must "grin and abide" by the usual custom of the trade. A number of them, however, are beginning to inquire whether some organised standard cannot be arrived at, and are of the opinion that some steps should be taken for obtaining an improvement in this direction. They are, however, entirely separate bodies, appear to lack cohesion, and probably will have to make the best of the situation till a better understanding is then arrived at. There appears, however, to be reason in their complaints.

## Editorial Headnote

### Nasmith, Frank. 'The Utilization of Soft Cotton Waste', *Journal of the British Association of Managers of Textile Works (Lancashire Section)*, 7 (1916), pp. 49–60.

Frank Nasmith (1879–1948) was born in Manchester into an engineering family; he was the son of mechanical engineer Joseph Nasmith (1850–1904), and grandson of machine maker John Nasmith (1822–1892). In an obituary, Hugh L. Robinson narrated Frank Nasmith's background in textiles:

> His technical training was obtained at the old Mechanics' Institute in Manchester and later at the Manchester College of Technology when it was started about 1900. At these two institutions he was thoroughly trained in cotton spinning and manufacturing, also mill management and mill designing. He "served his time" during this period at the Daisyfold Mill, Pendleton, going right through the mill. He then joined his father, Joseph Nasmith, who was in business in Manchester as a consulting engineer, and completed the necessary qualifications to become a registered patent agent. His father was also editor of the *Textile Recorder* – Frank was made assistant editor. Upon the death of his father in 1903, he took over the editorship and also the patent side of the business, and continued in that capacity until the outbreak of the 1914–1918 War.
>
> (Journal of Textile Institute Proceedings, 40:2, 1949, pp. 177–179).

After the war, Nasmith returned to editorship of the *Recorder*, and also launched the *Silk Journal and Rayon World* in 1928.

This lecture was delivered on 8 January 1916. It was read by William Greenwood of Oldham. It is probable that then Lieutenant Frank Nasmith of the Royal Engineers was on active military duty. An earlier version of Nasmith's lecture had been delivered at the Meeting of the National Association of Cotton Manufacturers, 28–29 April 1915 in Boston, titled 'Utilization of Cotton Waste by German and Austrian Methods', and printed in *Textile World Record* (49:2, May 1915, pp. 259–263).

# 22

# NASMITH, FRANK. 'THE UTILIZATION OF SOFT COTTON WASTE'

## *Journal of the British Association of Managers of Textile Works (Lancashire Section)* (1916), pp. 49–60.

In practically every manufacturing process waste is produced which in a great many cases is put to some definite profitable use. In the cotton spinning industry, although a certain amount of the waste produced is mixed with the fresh cotton and combined in the yarn forming the staple product of the mill, there is always a comparatively large amount which the spinner cannot use in this way and which he sells to the waste merchant or waste spinner. You will remember the varied and, in many ways, remarkable collection of fabric samples made in Germany and Austria which were displayed in Manchester last year,[1] examples of which were analysed and described by Professor Fox and Mr. Hübner to the Textile Institute.[2] Although many of these fabrics were made from what we may, for the purposes of this paper, term legitimate raw material, some of them were composed of mixtures of raw material and waste and in some cases wholly waste. It is in the production of materials and fabrics from what we consider the lowest class waste trade that the Germans and Austrians have excelled. Although these fabrics are in many cases manufactured to act as substitutes for all cotton or all wool material, there is a large market for them which at the moment cannot be completely supplied owing to the stoppage of exportations from Germany and Austria.

Before going further it will be necessary to draw a distinct line between hard and soft waste. In Lancashire the former class of waste is thoroughly understood and its treatment has been developed to produce such good results that foreign competition is not felt. As a matter of fact, Germany used to export hard waste to be treated in Lancashire just as Lancashire used to export soft waste to Germany. Hard waste, comprising chiefly cop bottoms,[3] is dealt with by a range of machines comprising hard waste breaking machine, scutcher, breaker carding engine, derby doubler, finisher card with condenser, and mule or ring frame.

It is not intended to say anything further about hard waste in the present paper, but to direct your attention, firstly, to the treatment of low quality soft waste – sweepings droppings, card strips,[4] comber waste, etc., as employed in the German and Austrian mills. Whatever reason may be forthcoming in regard to the treatment or non-treatment of soft waste in England the fact remains that in the

 DOI: 10.4324/9780429274190-27

past the Germans and Austrians have carried out experimental and research work until they have developed a very considerable and profitable industry. Their waste utilisation industry has been brought to a high state of economical and productive effectiveness, and it is absolutely impossible for us to immediately compete with them in the production of the wide range of yarns and fabrics they turn out. Only after years of endeavour will it be possible to compete on equal terms, for one must recognise the value of specialised effort, and the knowledge that is the outcome of practical development. At the same time it is possible to immediately produce with machinery at our disposal certain ranges of yarns and fabrics hitherto produced in Germany and Austria and shipped to England and the United States. It must be recognised that the extreme cheapness of the material dealt with and the low priced goods into which it is eventually manufactured make it imperative that the cost of the treatment would be small. In dealing with low soft waste made up into yarns for carpet backings, sponge cloths, cheap hosiery, candle-wicks, and the like, if these are to be produced cheaply, then the output must be considerable, and bulk lots will have to be handled. Particularly is this the case in regard to black hosiery yarns, and in place of the comparatively small parcels usually dyed at one time, lots of 2,200 pounds are commonly dealt with in Continental mills.

Before briefly describing a type of apparatus suitable for dyeing bulk lots, it can be said that the old objection to the trade as being an extremely dirty and dusty one has been largely removed by the introduction and employment of dust extraction devices, which not only clear the atmosphere of the room, but also remove the dust from the various machines immediately after it is created.

One form of Continental dyeing apparatus comprises a central perforated column or shaft and outer segmental plates. An inner and outer ring of plates are employed, these being built up round the central column. Between the inner plates and the column, the material – to the amount of 2,200 pounds – is packed, after which the outer plates are secured in position, a cover fastened on and the material washed, then dyed, and finally washed by circulating the liquors through the central column, through the material, through the inner set of plates and back to the pump. A batch of 2,200 pounds can be dyed and washed in a maximum time of ninety-six minutes. When completely treated the plates are removed, the stack of material broken down and delivered to a hydro-extractor, after which it is passed through an opening and loosening machine which will treat the wet material. Hitherto the material used pass direct to the drying machine from the hydro-extractor, but a great deal more steam is required for drying purposes when this is the case. After drying, the material passes forward to the first machine of the series it has been decided to use. Apparatus of this character has decided advantages over that dealing with comparatively small quantities. In the first place a saving of from 60 to 70 per cent. in the steam used may be effected, and a savings of 70 per cent. in the labour involved.

. . .

Coming to the machinery necessary for the production of yarns, it is proposed merely to give the names of these with a few details of special machines. The first is the opening machine, known as the willow which in the ordinary way has to deal with matted material in an extremely dirty state. Dust exhaust devices have now been applied to willows which have very materially improved the conditions existing in opening rooms. On the Continent, fresh broad cotton of short staple – chiefly Asiatic cotton – is mixed with the waste, and [the] Crighton opener becomes a necessary unit of the plant.[5]

A great deal of the soft waste made in both mule and ring mills is found to contain hard threads which may form a comparatively small percentage of the total weight, but nevertheless have to be separated out before the waste can be returned to the mixing. Machines, termed thread extractors, are employed to remove these hard threads, and they comprise: a feeding funnel, three spiked rollers which are made to revolve at a high speed to thoroughly loosen the material so that the "soft" waste is separated from the "thread" waste, [and] a fan to draw away the soft material the threads wrapping round and being retained by the spiked roller.

A machine that has given excellent results in the direction of improving the mixing is termed the Pickering machine, made with either one or two cylinders.[6] The scutcher and lap machine employed does not differ very materially from the type used in the ordinary mill. The foregoing machines are well known and are common to the trade.

It is when we come to carding that a difference in methods and machines between Continental and English spinners is to be noted. For yarns from 1's to 6's[7] a comparatively simple plant is advocated in England with a set of machines comprising a single breaking carding engine fed by scutcher laps, and connected by a Scotch feeder[8] to a single finisher carding engine with ring doffer. It is claimed that a ring doffer condenser makes the best quality of yarn, besides which it is simple in construction and easy to work. Leather tape condensers are also employed and several improvements have recently been made in this class of apparatus.[9] The advent of condensers with four to six pairs of rubbing leathers has rendered it possible to produce the maximum number of threads (up to 240 in the case of machines 72 inches wide) without risk of their coming in contact whilst being rubbed, and the output of a set of carding engines is thereby materially increased.

As has been previously pointed out, one of the chief objects of the Continental waste spinner has been to secure large production in short periods of time, and to this end the machinists have developed a form of card – on the woollen principle – which certainly achieves the desired result. Compared with the machines advocated by English makers, the Continental cards are complicated and demand a higher class operative to tend them. The difficulties in relation to stripping and grinding have in the past proved a deterrent to their large adoption outside Germany and Austria, but it certainly cannot be denied that their production is very considerable. The waste trade can be divided as follows: waste yarns, 1's to 4's; imitation vigogne yarn, 4's to 8's; vigogne, 8's to 20's;[10] and modifications in the carding sets are made for each section. . . .

It is impossible to draw a comparison between the soft cotton waste industry of England and the Continent, because in the latter case we have a highly developed specialised trade built up gradually over a number of years, and in the former, up to the present we have had have only a small industry not to any great extent endeavouring to produce high class waste fabrics which will act as substitutes for the real article.

On the Continent good raw material is often mixed with the waste material, and cases of spinning Egyptian cotton on the waste principle to produce a certain result are well known. I am credibly informed that in Lancashire one firm for a number of years has adopted the same principle in relation to Sea Island cotton,[11] but the custom is not common, and the point remains that on the Continent it is a common practise to mix waste with good raw material of short staple. The resultant yarn has naturally more life and will raise and finish better than the ordinary waste yarn.

Quite a considerable market is open to the manufacturer who will lay himself out to compete with the Continental mills. It must be clearly understood that cost is important in the success or non-success of the undertaking, and in certain qualities it is only by treating the material in large quantities that the first costs can be kept at a figure at which competition is possible. Black hosiery yarns, for example, are sold at a very low figure.

## Notes

1 The samples were exhibited at the Textile Institute in Manchester, 4–8 October 1915. Cotton fabric samples collected by the Board of Trade, and samples of German dress goods obtained by the Bradford Technical College, were exhibited together with analytical details. See also 'Foreign Fabrics', *Journal of the Textile Institute*, 6:2 (Nov 1915), pp. 212–220; 'Analyses of Fabrics of Foreign Origin Collected and Exhibited by the Board of Trade, *Journal of the Textile Institute*, 6:1 (Oct 1915), pp. 51–88.

2 Thomas William Fox (c1856–1917), head of the Spinning and Weaving department, and Julius Hübner (or Huebner, 1866–1942), head of the Bleaching, Dyeing, Printing and Finishing department, of the Manchester School of Technology.

3 Hard waste designates fibres that have been spun into yarn or thread. Cop bottoms is a term applied to waste yarn formed in the processes of winding spun yarn onto spindles in the form of cops; the cop bottom itself is the cone of yarn formed in the initial stage of winding the cop.

4 Short fibres clinging to wire card clothing and stripped off by brushes.

5 The Crighton opener, made by Crighton and Sons, machine makers of Manchester, had a cylinder oriented vertically holding beaters that described a conical shape. The beaters opened the cotton by flinging it against the sides of the machine.

6 The Pickering machine was a variation on other devices for opening and cleaning waste. It featured a central cylinder covered with hardwood lags studded with steel teeth. The machine could be extended by a second cylinder.

7 These low counts indicate coarse yarns.

8 The Scotch feeder formed the fleece from the breaker cards into a loose ribbon for transfer to the finisher cards.

9 The action of the condenser was to split up the wide cotton fleece deposited by the cylinder onto the doffer into the required number of individual strands, and then to rub each strand to give sufficient consistency to wind on and off a bobbin without breaking. In the ring doffer, the card clothing was divided by rings, with about one-quarter the surface given over to these divisions that acted to separate the fleece into strands. In the leather tape condenser, the whole surface of the doffer was covered with card clothing, and the cotton stripped from the doffer in a continuous fleece. It then passed through feed rollers to a pair of *space rollers*. The space rollers had leather tapes spaced across their surface such that where there was leather on one roller, there was smooth metal on its opposite; the action of these tapes split the fleece into the required strands.

10 Vigogne was a name given to a type of waste cotton yarn, largely spun on the Continent, that imitated wool. Nasmith sets out three classes here based on yarn counts that might be considered very coarse, coarse and average.

11 Sea Island cotton is a long-staple, high quality cotton. The post-lecture discussion mentioned that the firm concerned was based in Bolton.

## Editorial Headnote

### Wakefield, Sam. 'Waste and Production, Cost and Organisation in the Doubling Mill', *Cotton Doubling and Twisting* (Manchester: Marsden & Co., 1917), pp. 6–15.

Samuel Wakefield (1861–1935) was born in Heaton Norris, son of a baker and provision dealer. In 1886, he married Jane Balfe (1859–1900), daughter of George Balfe (1835–1918), a partner in the cotton doubling firm, John Balfe and Co. of Heaton Norris. This assured his career in the cotton industry, and Wakefield became a manager for his father-in-law's firm. From 1891 to 1895, he was often a correspondent in the 'questions' columns of the *Cotton Factory Times*, where he proudly displayed his experience-based knowledge, on occasion mocking the cotton teachers from the technical schools. A colleague recalled,

> He was a great friend of mine when I was engineer and millwright for Messrs. McConnell and Co., fine cotton spinners, Ancoats, Manchester, and Mr. Wakefield was manager over the doubling, winding, warping, and reeling. He was also manager for Balfe and Co., of Stockport, at West Gorton Mills, where we spent many happy hours together.
>
> (*Cotton Factory Times*, 7 May 1920, p. 4)

By 1911, Wakefield appears to have become independent, working as a yarn agent, and later spending some time in the United States as a consultant.

Wakefield began contributing a series of articles to the *Textile Mercury*, which became the core of the four-volume set of books on *Cotton Doubling and Twisting*, released individually between January 1916 and the end of 1917. In a review of the final volume containing the section on waste, it was noted that Wakefield advocates more precise systems of costings as a means for achieving success: 'doublers are really indebted to him for putting at their disposal such a well-written and valuable treatise' (*Textile Manufacturer*, 44:521, 15 May 1918, p. 134). The set sold for 25s., but separate sections were obtainable in paperback, priced from 2s. 6d. to 7s. 6d. Wakefield's texts became the standard works on the subject, and eventually a new edition was demanded. The updated volumes were released between September 1929 and July 1930, priced at 30s. the set. In reviewing the final volume, the *Manchester Guardian* took interest in the definition of waste: 'The waste he refers to, it should be noted, is material in process which is in part lost, and in part rendered unusable for the regular processes and deteriorated in value' (14 Jul 1930, p. 17). Wakefield was keen to quantify waste and use this awareness to reduce waste.

# 23

# WAKEFIELD, SAM. 'WASTE AND PRODUCTION, COST AND ORGANISATION IN THE DOUBLING MILL'

*Cotton Doubling and Twisting* (Manchester: Marsden & Co., 1917), pp. 6–15.

### Cost of losses

The effect of waste of material on cost has several bearings; the primary loss of material and its increase in cost of raw material, which is its exact effect on cost, and can be readily calculated; the effect of waste on production, that is, the reduction of labour and machinery resulting in proportion to the amount of wastage of the material experienced, which is difficult of expression in currency terms; and the still more elusive one, the moral effect of unnecessary waste.

In most, if not all, the costings I have seen it is customary to add an estimated cost per cent. of loss on the cost of the single. In a cost sheet I have before me, the following is given: –

| *FOR 2/80 GASSED* | | *FOR 2/80 PLAIN* | |
|---|---|---|---|
| Single cost 74's | 12.75d. | Single cost 80's | 13.75d. |
| Wage cost | 2.78d. | Wage cost | 2.29d. |
| Expenses | 1.69d. | Expenses | 1.20d. |
| Waste, 10 per cent. | *1.27d.* | Waste, 2 per cent. | *0.28d.* |
| | 5.74d. | | 3.77d. |

But it is obvious that this is not correct, for the further the yarn gets in process the more costly it becomes.

Taking the same cost sheet, it will be instructive to approximate the waste to each department: –



DOI: 10.4324/9780429274190-28

| SINGLE COST AND WAGE | | WASTE COST | |
|---|---|---|---|
| Single cost per lb. | 12.75d. | 2 per cent. in cop winding | 0.2550d. |
| Winding wage | *0.59d.* | | |
| | 13.34d. | | |
| Doubling wage | *0.60d.* | 2 per cent. in doubling<br>1 per cent. in clearing | 0.4182d. |
| | 13.94d. | | |
| Clearing wage | *0.49d.* | | |
| | 14.43d. | | |
| Half cost of trading, | *0.84d.* | | |
| etc., expenses | 15.27d. | 5 per cent. in gassing | 0.7635d. |
| | | | 1.4367d. |

It may be well to explain that the waste made in cop winding should not bear the winding wage, unless the winders are paid per pad of cops. If this principle is adopted, however, the cost of the waste is still further increased by the amount of the winder's wage, and the loss in cop winding amounts to 0.2668 pence.

The waste made in doubling will bear the cost of cop winding and doubling if the oily and four-fold yarn is wound off the bobbin onto the doubling spindle, but should not incur clearing wage unless the defective yarn is sent to that department to deal with. Under the latter arrangement 1 per cent. will bear doubler's wage only, as roller laps, etc., and 1 per cent. will bear clearer's wage in addition. The 1 per cent. clearer's waste represents hand waste in that department, which should not incur winding expenses.

The allowance for waste made in the cost sheet is per pound of yarn 1.275; the actual cost of the same percentage of loss is really 1.4367 at the lower estimate. This is an unaccounted for loss of 0.162d. per pound of yarn produced. If we take the production of a 20,000 spindle mill on 2/80 26 turns gassed at 20,000 lb. for 65 hours' running, this unaccounted loss amounts to £13 10s. per week.

It is to be noted that all the calculations are based on a price of 12¾d. for single, and monetary loss will increase with higher single prices, and increased wages cost.

## Value of waste

A further point worth emphasis is the value of small saving in waste; 10 per cent. loss at a cost of 1.427 per pound on the above production is equal to £120 per week. The 5 per cent. loss in gassing can scarcely be dealt with in this respect, so that the figures we have to deal with so far as savings goes are restricted to the winding, doubling, and clearing room waste. These waste losses of 5 per cent. amounting to 0.6732d. per pound, on the same production show a loss of £57 per week. Therefore, a saving of ½ per cent. in the processes is an increase in profits of £5 10s. per week.

This loss may be considered also from another point of view: the recoverable and irrecoverable. Taking the losses as they occur in process, it will be found that about 1 per cent. of the loss in cop winding is due to the paper tubes, and this is not recoverable. Some proportion of the loss in cop winding, twisting (partially dry) and clearing consists of moisture, and is usually compensated for in the warehouse. The loss of material is partly recoverable in the selling price of the waste. The loss in weight in gassing is in part recoverable in conditioning, but the major part is entirely lost, except that the yarn is enhanced in value resulting from the raised counts. The hand waste made in the reeling is compensated for by the tie-yarn used.

There is still a trifling savings to be made on the waste account, which I'm afraid does not receive so much attention as it deserves. I refer to the care taken of the waste after it has been made. Most of the work people have little consideration for it, and the waste is dropped on the floor, dirtied under foot, and it eventually finds its way into the sweepings bag. A moment's consideration shows the importance of care being taken of all waste made, but to put the saving in actual figures brings the difference more forcibly to mind. The main divisions of doublers' waste may be taken as follows: (The prices are assumed, the proportions are fairly accurate):

| | |
|---|---|
| Cop bottoms (entirely without paper tubes) | $3\frac{3}{4}$d. per lb. |
| Cop waste, hand waste | $3\frac{1}{2}$d. per lb. |
| Doublers' waste | 2d. per lb. |
| Reelers' waste | 2d. per lb. |
| Sweepings | 1/- per score |

Every pound of waste *swept up* in the cop winding room loses $3\frac{1}{8}$d. per pound. Every pound of waste *swept up* in the doubling, clearing, or reeling room loses $1\frac{7}{8}$d. per pound. The losses we have under consideration, 5 per cent. on 20,000 lb. equals 1000 lb. which we can divide: –

| | |
|---|---|
| 1 per cent. cop tubes | 200 lbs. |
| 1 per cent. cop winding | 200 lbs. |
| 2 per cent. doubling | 400 lbs. |
| 1 per cent. clearing | 200 lbs. |

If only 5 per cent. of the waste goes permanently into the sweepings there is another an additional or unnecessary loss of 7s. 6d. per week, but the percentage of waste so treated is nearer 20 per cent. of the total, and means a saving or loss of 30s. weekly, according to its treatment.

The workpeople as a body are absolutely ignorant of the enormous cost of this waste item to a mill, and if they are, how can one expect them to take an intelligent interest in its reduction? I have found foremen even, equally as oblivious to the fact that the waste bill alone (in gassed yarns) is equal to the general expenses put together, and amounts to more than half the wage cost.

## Editorial Headnote

### U. S. Dept of Commerce: Bureau of Foreign and Domestic Commerce. *Foreign Markets for Cotton Linters, Batting, and Waste*. Special Consular Reports – No. 80 (Washington: Government Printing Office, 1918), pp. 39–46.

Burwell Smith Cutler (1876–1958), Chief of the Bureau, compiled this report which was submitted 15 March 1918. The letter that heads the account explains its purpose:

> There is submitted herewith a compilation of reports on foreign markets for cotton linters, cotton batting, and cotton waste, which were prepared by American consuls in various trading centers throughout the world and transmitted to this Bureau during 1915 and 1916. . . . The dearth of information available in the past with regard to this important branch of the cotton industry has doubtless handicapped its development along export lines. It is hoped that the present report will supply the preliminary data that are necessary for the expansion of the trade in the foreign field.

Extracted here is the United Kingdom section of the work, assembling information gathered from thirteen American consular agents stationed in British cities:

| *City* | *Consular Agent* | *Dates of appointment* |
|---|---|---|
| Belfast | Hunter Sharp (1861–1923) | Dec 1910–May 1920 |
| Bradford | Augustus Eugenio Ingram (1867–1937) | Jun 1909–1920 |
| Bristol | Lorin Andrews Lathrop (1858–1929) | Aug 1907–May 1919 |
| Cork | Wesley Frost (1884–1968) | 1914–May 1917 |
| Dublin | Edward Le Grand Adams (1851–1928) | Mar 1909–1919 |
| Edinburgh | Rufus Fleming (1852–1920) | Oct 1897–Apr 1920 |
| Gibraltar | Richard Louis Sprague (1871–1934) | Jul 1901–Oct 1934 |
| Leeds | Homer Morrison Byington (1879–1966) | 1913–1917 |
| Liverpool | Horace Lee Washington (1864–1938) | May 1909–Aug 1924 |
| London | Robert Peet Skinner (1866–1960) | Jun 1914–Oct 1924 |
| Manchester | Ross Edgar Holaday (1869–1929) | Jul 1915–Nov 1929 |
| Nottingham | Calvin Milton Hitch (1869–1944) | May 1915–1923 |
| Sheffield | John Marbacher Savage (1864–1938) | Jul 1914–Jun 1919 |

The capacity of the American Bureau to bring minor contributions together under specialist headings to create impressive assemblies of evidence is clearly demonstrated. Manchester emerges as the centre for purchase and manufacturing of waste cotton materials. Only Gibraltar is so distant, that it becomes cheaper to purchase from Barcelona. Nevertheless, the report identifies the Scottish cities of Dunfermline, Dundee and Glasgow as potential markets.

The report was priced at ten cents, sold through the American Superintendent of Documents, and remained available until 1931.

# 24

# U. S. DEPT OF COMMERCE: BUREAU OF FOREIGN AND DOMESTIC COMMERCE. *FOREIGN MARKETS FOR COTTON LINTERS, BATTING, AND WASTE*

## (Washington: Government Printing Office, 1918), pp. 39–46.

### BELFAST. Consul Hunter Sharp

Cotton spinning in this consular district is almost negligible, and according to the returns of the Belfast Harbor Commissioners, there were no exports of cotton batting (locally termed wadding) during the five years 1910 to 1914. Neither do cotton linters appear in the trade returns. Exports of cotton waste amounted to 27 and 18 tons, respectively, in 1910 and 1911, but dropped to 1 and 2 tons in the three following years. These small shipments were principally, if not entirely, cotton thrums exported to the Manchester district of England.

Cotton batting and cotton waste imported during the five years ended in 1914 were as follows:

| *Articles.* | *1910* | *1911* | *1912* | *1913* | *1914* |
|---|---|---|---|---|---|
| | *Tons* | *Tons* | *Tons* | *Tons* | *Tons* |
| Cotton batting | 23 | 10 | 11 | 17 | 24 |
| Cotton waste | 431 | 470 | 484 | 428 | 410 |

Cotton waste is imported from England and Scotland in bales of 112 pounds, containing approximately 100 pounds net. The cheaper grades are stated to have more or less jute mixed with the cotton. Practically the entire local demand for cotton waste is for machine wiping. It is imported by mill furnishers, who sell to railways, factories, tractor-engine owners, and similar firms. There are no factories here using cotton waste for manufacturing purposes. Except for the small quantities that may at times be found mixed with flax waste no cotton waste is exported from this district to the United States.

DOI: 10.4324/9780429274190-29

Nearly all the cotton wadding sold here is bought in Manchester. It comes in sheets measuring about 36 by 20 inches, one dozen sheets to the packet. It is sold also in 12-yard rolls, but there is very little demand for it in this form in Belfast. About half of the total quantity imported is black and of the remainder two-thirds is gray and one-third bleached.

### Bradford. Consul Augustus E. Ingram

So far as can be learned there had been no imports of cotton linters, batting, and waste into this consular district during the five years preceding the war. One large firm of carpet manufacturers uses certain low grades of soft cotton waste, but it buys its supplies in this country.

No linters or batting is produced here, but the weaving sheds where cotton warps are used with wool or worsted weft produce thread waste. Most of this is bought by Lancashire firms, which send their buyers direct to the mills. A certain quantity, however, has been shipped to the United States for several years, the maximum being reached in 1903, when these exports were valued at $10,072. In 1914 the shipments amounted to 141,383 pounds, valued at $7,096. The declared values of such shipments to the United States during the five years ended in 1914 have been as follows: 1910, $8,644; 1911, $5,952; 1912, $8,318; 1913, $8,212; 1914, $7,096.

The usual Bradford terms are payment in 14 days, but for export shipments, if a firm is satisfied as to the purchaser's financial standing, any reasonable terms are extended. There are apparently no importers in this district, and only two firms export cotton waste. For export the bales are usually packed by hydraulic press and weigh from 600 to 700 pounds each.

Instead of wiping waste, the mills in this district are using an increasingly large quantity of wiping cloths, or sponge cloths, as they are called locally, made from a rough thick count of yarn that is in turn made of soft cotton waste. Formerly these wiping cloths were made of a silk noil yarn, but because of the price cotton has now been substituted. The advantage of the cloths over ordinary wiping waste is that the cloths are easily washed and the oil with which they become saturated is recovered. One firm states that its production of these cloths has increased several fold during the last few years, until now it is turning out 500 gross each week. The cloths are sold with a contract to wash and mend them when needed during a specified period, and by this means last year, washing approximately 250,000 cloths a week, the firm referred to recovered about 300 tons of oil. Some firms, however, especially in the engineering trade, purchase the cloths outright and attend to the washing themselves in order to benefit by the recovery of the oil. Wiping cloths are now being exported to the United States, where it is understood that the same practice of recovering the oil is being followed.

Another advantage that the cloths have over ordinary wiping waste is said to be their freedom from dust or grit that is injurious to machinery parts.

### CARDIFF. Consul Lorin A. Lathrop

Cotton waste is largely used in South Wales, but the sale of cotton linters and cotton batting is very limited. Gray waste, long, clean, and free from such whitening mixtures as china clay, is the product in demand. It is used for cleaning the machinery of the coal mines and of the great fleet of steamships trading from South Wales ports. It comes from Manchester. There are no statistics, but large dealers estimate the annual consumption as fully 25,000 tons. None of this is exported, but probably half goes into vessels in the form of engineers' stores.

An obstacle in the way of shipments direct from the United States to South Wales is to be found in the lack of wholesale merchants and jobbers. Manchester firms deal directly with the consumer or with the firms that sell to the consumer. There is, for instance, no intermediary between Manchester and a large coal mine, and the ship chandlers and marine-store dealers that supply ships also buy direct. Many of the firms, however, do so considerable a business as to justify their importing direct.

### CORK. Consul Wesley Frost

The trade in linters, batting, and cotton waste in Cork[1] is decidedly small, the total consumption being estimated at less than $75,000 per annum.

For cushions and furniture upholstery, as well as for wadding in cheap saddlery, the common article here is kapok, which is slightly less expensive than linters and is said not to mat so quickly. For filling bedquilts, feathers are much more frequently used than in the United States, but the principal kind of cheap bedding is wadded with woolen flock produced by macerating rags. These flock quilts are not washable, in general.

Rag flock is produced by a firm in Leixlip, County Dublin, from which Cork dealers in bedding obtain a good share of their stock.

Cotton batting is mainly purchased from Manchester, which also supplies absorbent cotton. Cotton linters have occasionally been taken here in trial orders, but none very recently.

### DUBLIN. Consul Edward L. Adams

According to statistics for the port of Dublin, Ireland, the number of pounds of cotton wadding imported was 58,760 in 1910, 26,880 in 1911, 29,120 in 1912, 26,880 in 1913, and 35,840 in 1914. Of cotton waste for the same years the imports were 716,800 pounds, 795,200 pounds, 712,320 pounds, 564,480 pounds, and 739,200 pounds, respectively. Values and countries of origin are not officially given, but dealers state that they buy practically all their waste from England, the Manchester district being the main source. As far as could be ascertained, no linters are made or imported in this district, nor are waste and batting manufactured here. Waste is usually bought in packages of 112 pounds. Limited quantities of flax waste and bleached mutton cloths are imported.[2] Waste is used for yachts, power stations, and all kinds of machinery. Dealers generally will pay cash on delivery, with varying discounts, and desire c.i.f. Dublin[3] quotations in English currency. One firm pays quarterly with 2½ per cent discount.

### EDINBURGH. Consul Rufus Fleming

East Scotland is not an important market for cotton or cotton materials. In the fishing-net industry, which is not a large one here, raw cotton is used to a limited extent. It is American cotton, purchased from Manchester importers.

Linters are neither imported nor manufactured and are practically unknown in the district. The cotton seed, principally Egyptian, worked by the local cottonseed oil and cake mills – about *20,000* long tons per annum – is neither ginned nor decorticated here, but passes through the mills in the condition in which it is received.

The consumption of cotton batting is small. The principal users are dressmakers, tailors, and firms or individuals engaged in various kinds of fancy needlework. The product is sold by the principal dry-goods houses and comes to this market almost exclusively from Manchester.

A considerable quantity of hard cotton waste is used in machine shops and shipbuilding and engineering establishments, and also by railway and shipping companies. The product is handled in this district by middlemen only, who buy from Manchester and Glasgow cotton mills. Local ship chandlers and oil merchants sell cotton waste. The usual terms of credit are 30 days, with discount according to quantity.

### GIBRALTAR. Consul R. L. Sprague

Cotton linters and batting are not sold here at all. Cotton waste, however, is imported by ship chandlers, hardware dealers, and barge owners. Before the war it came solely from England, but owing to the high rates of freight and the unavoidable delay in delivery, importers have been compelled to place most of their orders in Barcelona, the center of the Spanish cotton industry. There are no official statistics of the imports of this colony, but it is estimated that the quantity received yearly does not exceed 40 tons. The largest consumers are the Government dockyard, ship chandlers, and barge owners. Considerable quantities are now in demand by the large number of steamers calling at this port. Spanish waste is slightly cheaper than English, but the quality is somewhat inferior. American waste will always find a market provided it can equal the English product in price and quality.

### LEEDS. Consul Homer M. Byington[4]

The Leeds consular district is inland, and no statistics are obtainable as to the quantities of cotton linters, cotton batting, and cotton waste imported or exported. Extended inquiries, however, have secured the following data:

Soft cotton waste is used here in the making of the lower-grade cloths, and supplies are obtained on contract from the adjoining county of Lancashire. The soft wastes are blended with the mungo shoddies and spun into woolen yarn. None is exported. Goods are delivered packed in a kind of bag (locally known as "sheets"), of dimensions about 3 by 1½ yards.

Hard waste (locally known as "thrums") from the factories using cotton warps is produced within the district and is exported at the rate (estimated) of 100 tons per week. No hard waste is imported.

Cotton linters are of small account and when brought in appear to be used in the same manner as the soft wastes. One firm of bedding manufacturers reports that it buys linters in Liverpool and uses them for making batting (wadding). Other similar firms state that they use no linters but use kapok for their waddings.

Hard wastes are contracted for at the mills, the dealer taking the waste as made. Hard wastes are generally opened and then are used for cleaning purposes. They are sold within the district and have been exported to Germany and Canada. Terms have been cash against documents. The wastes are packed in square-ended bales, with iron hoops, holding 7 hundredweight (784 pounds).

### LIVERPOOL. Consul Horace Lee Washington

Liverpool's importance in the trade in cotton linters, batting, and waste is that of a seaport and distributing center. One firm uses a relatively small quantity of linters in the manufacture of lint. Manchester and other manufacturing cities nearby consume all three of these cotton products in large quantities.

The official statistics do not show the trade in linters or batting, but according to a leading importer and merchant, during the 12 months from September 1, 1913, to August 31, 1914, 3,000 bales of linters were imported from the United States, 750 bales from Brazil, and 660 bales from Peru and Chile. The average weight of the bales of American linters is 450 to 550 pounds. American exporters generally draw at 60 days sight on Liverpool banks with documents attached. Frequently cash is paid against shipping documents.

Cotton waste is imported from the United States principally, but also in small quantities from Brazil, Peru, Japan, China, and India. The imports and exports at Liverpool of "cotton waste from worked cotton" during the years 1909 to 1914 were as follows:

| *Years* | *Imports* | | *Exports* | |
|---|---|---|---|---|
| | Pounds. | Value. | Pounds. | Value. |
| 1909 | 2,937,700 | $97,660 | 16,216,000 | $923,734 |
| 1910 | 5,185,435 | 350,207 | 21,298,200 | 1,352,940 |
| 1911 | 3,281,851 | 245,570 | 22,890,000 | 1,518,065 |
| 1912 | 6,337,471 | 393,188 | 21,752,200 | 1,340,009 |
| 1913 | 6,908,267 | 467,343 | 23,717,100 | 1,475,424 |

The imports of cotton waste from the United States during the years 1909 to 1914 were as follows:

| *Years.* | *Pounds.* | *Value.* | *Years.* | *Pounds.* | *Value.* |
|---|---|---|---|---|---|
| 1909 | 420,634 | $25,242 | 1912 | 3,392,589 | $184,479 |
| 1910 | 1,993,902 | 156,754 | 1913 | 2,268,460 | 166,551 |
| 1911 | 709,664 | 64,801 | 1914 | 2,162,299 | 112,707 |

The usual terms of purchase are cash against documents. There is no uniformity in the weight of cotton baled waste, which varies from 150 to 800 pounds per bale. The average weight of American bales is about 500 pounds and of Indian bales 400 pounds. Cotton waste is almost invariably purchased and sold on bulk sample.

### London. Consul General Robert P. Skinner

The table that follows shows the quantity and value of imports and exports of "cotton waste from worked cotton" for the United Kingdom during the years 1910, 1911, 1912, 1913, and 1914.

The term "cotton waste," as used in the official statistics, includes American super strips, American best strips, American ordinary strips, willowing strips, Egyptian best strips, American knur laps, American ring laps, peeler comber, American droppings, cardroom sweeps, spinner sweeps, No. 1 cop waste, ring cop waste, and engine-cleaning waste.[5] Statistics of linters and batting imports and exports are not compiled.

| *Years* | *Imports* | | *Exports* | |
|---|---|---|---|---|
| | Pounds. | Value. | Pounds. | Value. |
| 1910 | 37,710,333 | $3,173,566 | 87,042,400 | $6,007,903 |
| 1911 | 31,086,976 | 2,448,390 | 97,614,700 | 7,107,504 |
| 1912 | 40,065,608 | 2,628,898 | 99,660,700 | 6,764,002 |
| 1913 | 34,839,252 | 2,510,467 | 110,737,900 | 7,596,056 |
| 1914 | 34,363,451 | 2,574,130 | 69,979,700 | 4,781,949 |

Many firms in this district gather cuttings, rags, old curtains, cotton rope, etc., out of which cotton waste is made, but no manufacture of waste, linters, or batting is carried on in the vicinity of London. Cuttings, rags, etc., are baled and shipped to Manchester, to be pulled or otherwise treated. There are no importers in this district.

### MANCHESTER. Consul Ross E. Holaday

The principal use of cotton linters is for the manufacture of absorbent cotton wool, the material being cleaned by willowing, then bleached and carded and put in rolls ready for sale. On the Continent of Europe, it is reported, linters are also extensively used for spinning into coarse counts, such as carpet and bump yarns.

Batting or wadding is largely manufactured in the Manchester district, and in consequence only very small quantities are imported. It is used by tailors, upholsterers, etc., and the very low qualities are now used extensively for banana packing. The gray or black batting used by local tailors is made up in 12-yard pieces.

Cotton waste is both produced and used extensively in the cotton mills of this district. Sheetings, flannelettes, quilts, bedcovers, cotton blankets, sponge cloths, towels, and cretonnes are among the goods manufactured from waste, which also is bundled into hanks and used in making ropes and twines. Sized waste, doubled waste, and other waste not suitable for respinning is made up for cleaning.

The foreign trade of Manchester in "cotton waste from worked cotton" during the five years 1909 to 1913, inclusive, is shown in the following table:

| *Years* | *Imports* | | *Exports* | |
|---|---|---|---|---|
| | Pounds. | Value. | Pounds. | Value. |
| 1909 | 18,430,629 | $1,278,166 | 55,413,000 | 3,130,901 |
| 1910 | 27,726,048 | 2,568,733 | 51,936,300 | 3,731,607 |
| 1911 | 21,857,070 | 1,865,324 | 55,548,500 | 4,099,023 |
| 1912 | 28,326,484 | 1,956,250 | 60,043,300 | 4,192,134 |
| 1913 | 21,780,981 | 1,690,013 | 63,826,700 | 4,479,501 |

### NOTTINGHAM. Consul Calvin M. Hitch

Only one firm of importance in this district is engaged in the manufacture of cotton waste. It makes engine waste only, and does a comparatively small business handling the waste of the lace and hosiery manufacturers located in this district. According to the information at hand, their output, which is practically the total output of the district, amounted during five recent years to approximately 20,000 tons. While statistics are not available, it is believed that the greater portion of this was sold to British concerns, both domestic and colonial, and the balance to various South American railways through their agencies in this country.

Waste is usually put up in 5-hundredweight (560-pound) bales. Terms vary according to the quantity purchased by the customer. In foreign business they are usually cash against documents, except when sold to the foreign concerns having agencies in this country. To these the usual terms of cash in one month are allowed.

### Sheffield. Consul John M. Savage

A considerable quantity of cotton waste is used by the numerous manufacturing plants in this consular district, but statistics as to the amount are not available. As there are no local cotton mills, the waste comes from Manchester, the center of the cotton industry of Great Britain, which is only 40 miles distant. The trade, as a rule, is supplied by local dealers, except in the case of large users, who buy direct. Terms are 2½ per cent, 30 to 90 days, according to the financial reliability of the purchaser.

### Other Centers

Bristol, Huddersfield, Hull, Plymouth, Southampton, and Newcastle-on-Tyne are markets of some consequence for cotton waste, linters, and batting. They are to be reached either direct or through the larger centers, such as Liverpool, Manchester, Leeds, and Nottingham. Dunfermline, Dundee, and Glasgow are potential markets for these products. Malta is an inappreciable market, owing to the fact that the demand is confined to waste for cleaning machinery of vessels. The island's supply comes from Great Britain.

### Notes

1 Then known as Queenstown, since 1920 as Cobh (pronounced like *cove*).
2 Mutton cloth was an absorbent cloth used to wrap meat, and also as a wiping cloth. The term, judging by its appearance in British newspapers, was introduced around 1900. By the 1920s, it had come to indicate cotton stockinette.
3 Cost, insurance and freight to Dublin.
4 The published report erroneously printed the name as Homer W. Byington.
5 'Strips' would be strippings from opening or carding cylinders, often removed by special cylindrical brushes. Lap implies a fleece in sheet form that could be collected on a screen; this is probably the equivalent of the British *fly* waste. Combing was performed on long-stapled cottons, with rejected fibre periodically removed from the needles of the comb. Droppings and sweeps imply fibre that has fallen to the bottom of machinery or the floor.

## Editorial Headnote

### William C. Jones Ltd. *Cotton Waste: A Study of a Great Lancashire Industry.* (Manchester: Charles W. Hobson, 1920), pp. 8–14.

This article heads a promotional booklet conceived by the advertising agent Charles W. Hobson to lift the important international waste business of W. C. Jones Ltd. from its uncultured associations. Tastefully presented in the form of an art publication, it features images by the renowned photographer, Alvin Langdon Coburn (1882–1966), known for his moody and soft-textured style. Both text and images provide an evocative glance intended more to intrigue than fully inform the reader. Coburn posed the workpeople, but they retain a feeling of candidness through the natural attitudes of their everyday activity.

The waste cotton company was established in 1871 by William Charles Jones (1851–1903), born in Manchester of Welsh parentage. He enlisted the help of his brother John Levinus Jones (1846–1886), a yarn agent, but in March 1878 the elder brother withdrew, and William C. Jones continued on his own account. This was a time of expansion in the cotton waste field, and the business prospered. In 1894, it was incorporated as a limited company, which enabled it to continue after the death of its founder. Jones's estate, valued around £31,000 with a personalty of nearly £30,000, is a measure of his business success. The company was based at Collyhurst Waste Mills, 203–219 Collyhurst Road; Thomas Smith Deakin (c1862–1934), Paul Carl Miller (c1876–1918) and William Charles Jones (1887–1962) were directors in 1914. Hit by the global depression, in 1931, the company decided to wind up voluntarily to allow a restructure that enabled the firm to survive into the post-war era.

The publisher of the promotional volume, Charles William Hobson (1887–1968), began work as a warehouseman, then entered the merchant marine in 1907. After the First World War, he left the sea to set up the Cloister Press. An article in the *Yorkshire Post* explains, 'He later began, in collaboration with the late Mr. Haslam Mills, to devote his attention to advertising, in which he speedily made a name for himself' (7 Jan 1931, p. 14). In 1924, Hobson wrote *The Manchester Guardian Advertising Review: a Brief Notice of Some of the Theories & Principles of Advertisement and of the Contributory Arts*. Hobson's obituary writer in *The Guardian* paints a colourful picture of his career:

> Soon after the end of the First World War a young man, with red hair flowing like a comet's tail (and a first mate's ticket earned in sail) started in Manchester an advertising agency, now known as Charles Hobson and Grey. This was Charles William Hobson, and he became at that time the century's most important influence in British advertising. Almost immediately he introduced such innovations as literate writing, illustrations by artists of standing instead of hacks, and well-chosen typography sensitively laid out instead of a slapdash assembly of newspaper type. . . .

> He was a brilliant innovator, far ahead of his time and, for what he did to raise advertising towards his own exacting standards from its previous crude approach, he should be remembered.
>
> (14 Mar 1968, p. 6)

The author of this text, William Haslam Mills (1874–1930), had a distinguished career as a reporter for the *Manchester Guardian* from 1904 to 1919 before joining Hobson in advertising.

> He brought to this task a touch of precision and delicacy which enabled him to say much in little . . . he was the most patient seeker after the precise word and phrase to express the quality as well as the semblance of things.
>
> ('Mr. Haslam Mills' *Manchester Guardian*, 23 June 1930, p. 18)

Mills wrote several books on Lancashire subjects, with a keen ability to find grandeur in the everyday.

# 25

# WILLIAM C. JONES LTD. *COTTON WASTE: A STUDY OF A GREAT LANCASHIRE INDUSTRY*

## (Manchester: Charles W. Hobson, 1920), pp. 8–14.

The Lancashire cotton trade is one of the rare romances, and one of the many puzzles of the Economist. Lancashire is a Colossus with a foot in each hemisphere. She buys in America and sells in Asia. From the plant as it is grown to the garment as it is worn, cotton travels practically the width of the world, and the trade is not only one of the giants of commerce but in a way one of its freaks. The prosperity of Lancashire is based entirely on its successful manipulation of a fibre which is grown mainly in the Far West and used mainly in the Far East; a fibre which the vast majority of Lancashire's vast population have never even seen in its native state, and which in its finished state is too flimsy to be worn by itself in the climate most suited to its manufacture.

THE WORLD PLAN~There is room for wonder here. If the globe had been laid out on strictly logical lines, if the Garden of Eden and the wastes beyond had only a modern town-plan, things might have been different. With the cotton field, the gin, the spinning-mill, and the weaving-shed arranged in different blocks on one lot there would have been a vast saving in freights and journeyings to and fro. If it only had! But the spirit bloweth where it listeth.[1] And perhaps the world is all the better, a little brighter, and a little less monotonous in consequence. After all, the world is rather too big for a town-planning scheme, and perhaps the very promiscuousness of its fruits, necessitating as it does the more frequent communing of the gatherers, produces a valuable social result.

LANCASHIRE IN THE SCALE OF NATIONS~Anyhow, whatever the causes may be – and they are not far to seek – Lancashire is the world centre of cotton manufacture, and Manchester its capital city. Lancashire lives, moves and has its being in cotton. There are more people in Lancashire than there are in Scotland or in Australia. Manchester itself with its neighbouring borough of Salford, from which it is indistinguishable, has a population of about a million, and "Greater Manchester" is considerably more populous than the Dominion of New Zealand. "Greater Manchester" consists of a constellation of stars in the form of the Lancashire towns which cluster around Manchester, and of stardust in the shape of semi-rural, semi-urban districts in which manufacturing goes on. "Greater Manchester" is about the busiest and the densest industrial population in the world. Its population

DOI: 10.4324/9780429274190-30

may be reckoned at something around three millions, and the number grows enormously with every mile that is added to the circumference about Manchester.

PIONEERING~The Lancashire cotton trade again is historically the most interesting of all the modern trades, because it is the one in which the new world of steam and the factory system came to birth. It was in 1785 that steam was first used in a Manchester cotton-mill, and in the whole of English history there is no date which counts for more than that. At the present time, with an export trade of £127,000,000 and a huge home trade, Lancashire is one of the great supporting rafters of the edifice of English commerce. The English cotton trade, which, allowing for a little spilling over into adjoining counties, means really the Lancashire cotton trade, stands second to agriculture in the list of national trades.

ALWAYS RAINING~And why has Lancashire become the greatest cotton centre in the world? Why was it ever the place for spinning and weaving a fibre which is too delicate to be grown anywhere on English soil? Historians explain the matter by a reference to the special suitability of the Lancashire climate to the industry and to the topographical and geological peculiarities of the county. The Lancashire climate is habitually reviled, but nobody ever doubted its suitability for cotton spinning. The Atlantic breezes, discharging their moisture on sloping hills with their faces to the west, give the necessary degree of humidity, and in the old days a series of rivers and rivulets provided a sufficiency of water power. The water-mill has gone, but a rich coalfield has supplied and continues to supply its modern successors with steam and electric power. But the beginnings of the trade go back long before either water or steam had been harnessed by industry and so these beginnings must be attributed to climate and atmosphere alone.

COTTON WHICH WAS REALLY WOOL~The beginning is rather difficult to fix, though one cannot fob it off with the usual phrase of the historian in a difficulty – it is not "lost in the mists of antiquity." Manchester was known in the days of the Roman occupation of Britain as a fortified station, but neither then nor for many centuries afterwards did it spin or weave cotton. The actual date of the beginning of the industry is a little more difficult to find by reason of an old nomenclature which confused cottons with woollens. It seems incredible in these days when the direction of the deceit has been exactly reversed, but still there is authority for the belief that in some sixteenth century references to Manchester "cottons," the fabric meant was really woollen imitation of continental fustians. At any rate, a petition of "Merchants and citizens of London," which asked for a continuance of a grant for reforming frauds committed in the manufacture of bombazine cotton, "such as groweth in the land of Persia being no kind of wools," seems authentic evidence that for twenty years before 1621, the date of its presentation, "diverse people in the Kingdom, but chiefly in the County of Lancaster," had been engaged in the making of fustians.[2] Roberts' "Treasure of Traffic," in 1641, affords corroborative evidence,[3] and in 1727, according to Daniel Defoe, cotton had become more important in Manchester than wool, the city's old staple. "The grand manufacture which has so much raised this town," wrote Defoe, "is that of cotton in all its varieties," and there is evidence that Defoe used the word cotton in the sense in which we know it now.[4]

GROWTH AND GROWING PAINS~But these were only the beginnings giving little promise of the vast importance which the Lancashire cotton trade was to attain afterwards in the economy of the Empire. In 1774 the population of Manchester was about forty thousand; in 1801 it had risen to over one hundred thousand, and in 1821 to nearly two hundred thousand. In 1700 Lancashire found no place among the five most populous counties in England; a hundred years later it was second only to Middlesex (London's county), and in the twenty years after 1801 Lancashire grew faster than Middlesex itself, from about six hundred and seventy thousand to well over a million. It cannot be said that this growth of population was accompanied by an increase of popular contentment. At this time large masses of Lancashire people were at active war with the introduction of machinery, and the factory system springing up suddenly in a world which was not prepared for it, introduced child labour, and kept it at work for a span of hours which a generation later had to shorten in the interests of humanity. But the new world of the machine and the factory happened suddenly to mankind in this the Lancashire cotton trade, and the new departure was almost bound to cause much suffering and discontent. The industrial revolution, stimulated by a line of able native inventors, had set in; the factory system had been established, and with the opening of new methods of communication the world's demand had grown.

SPINNING AND WEAVING~It has been growing ever since. The supply of raw cotton has never quite kept pace with the Lancashire demand for it. The trade has carried specialisation further than almost any other trade. One part of Lancashire, the South-East, mainly spins, and the other part, the North-East, mainly weaves. Of the towns which spin, some like Oldham spin medium counts, and others like Bolton fine counts; and the weaving towns are marked by a traditional fidelity to their own markets, those of India or China, or the West Coast of Africa. And the trade has a record of almost continuous progress. In cotton, Lancashire is still emphatically the predominant power. Great Britain, which in this sense really means Lancashire, possesses about forty per cent. of the world's spindles (ten per cent. more than all the other countries of Europe put together), and consumes about twenty per cent. of the world's cotton supply. The disparity which is apparent here is accounted for by the fine counts which form a branch of Lancashire specialisation as against the coarse yarns spun in some other countries, notably India and Japan.

IN LATER YEARS~It can reasonably be claimed that the growth of the trade has been fostered not only by the specialised skill of a body of operatives whose forbears have followed the same occupation for generations, but also by the enterprise, amounting almost to adventurousness, which is part of the Lancashire character. In the eighteenth century the Duke of Bridgewater, who has been described as "the first Manchester man," stinted his personal expenses to £400 a year in order to construct a system of canals which did much to cheapen transit between the Lancashire towns and to bring the cotton trade into actual contact with the coal supply.

AN INLAND PORT~The more recent history of the city is fully in keeping with these great commercial and scientific traditions. About the eighties the steady growth of Lancashire and Lancashire trade seemed to have been arrested. The community appeared to be becalmed and Manchester men began to be afraid that Lancashire was becoming stationary. So far from folding its hands in the presence of this threat, the county answered it by undertaking almost the greatest engineering project the world had then seen. This was the construction of the Manchester Ship Canal. It was opened in 1894, after costing seven years in time, millions in money, and about the severest strain that was ever put on human courage and resolution. It has brought the sea to the gates of the city. Manchester had long had a great advantage in its nearness to the great world port of Liverpool, but that advantage has been tremendously increased by the inland waterway which brings ocean liners to the very steps of the Royal Exchange, and gives the city direct access to all the principal cotton fields. The original shareholders of the Canal had to wait some twenty years before they received any return for the faith which was in them. Manchester itself has the largest financial stake in the Canal, and an enterprising and even daring use of municipal credit, extended at a time when the proposition seemed to have proved too great for voluntary effort, has been abundantly justified by the increased life which the new artery has brought to the province of which Manchester is the capital.

THE MAIN SUBSIDIARY – "WASTE"~And where there is cotton there must necessarily be cotton-waste. Once upon a time, under looser and more slovenly methods of manufacture, waste may have been more plentiful than it is to-day. An economy in machinery and greater carefulness in handling, dictated by the narrow world margin on which the Lancashire manufacturer works, has produced an increased salvage. The modern mill manager would see red ruin in the waste bags which his forerunner of half a century ago filled with equanimity. But what it has lost in quantity – and, of course, the shrinkage is only a matter of percentages – waste has more than gained in preciousness. In the early days of cotton industry it was a despised by-product sold for an old song, and of which the domestic economy of the mill was too lordly to take account. Now it is not only the main subsidiary of the cotton industry. But it rivals the sound fibre itself in its importance as a raw material. For some purposes the proper grade of cotton-waste commands a price equal to that of the bale of which it originally formed part, for there are some effects which can only be got from waste – effects which cotton, no matter how expensive, cannot give.

A MISNOMER~The magnitude of the cotton-waste business is in keeping with the magnitude of British Textile interests in general. "Waste," except in the relative sense – is, of course, a pure misnomer. Trade usage has given the word a convenience for description, but apart from that there is only one thing that cotton-waste is *not*, and that is waste in the sense in which the dictionary writers define it. No by-product is so indispensable, or so versatile in its adaptability. You can do anything with waste except perhaps eat it. Its range spreads from a candlewick to the most powerful explosive, from a bed-sheet to an easy chair, or a surgeon's dressing and, in between and beyond both, it forms the basis of multifarious fabrics in which one-half of the world either dresses or sleeps. It will clean the engines of a "Dreadnought"[5] or conceivably it may dress a lady for afternoon tea. And there is plenty of waste in Lancashire of all sorts and all grades. According to the latest estimates Great Britain, which again, let it be understood, for this purpose virtually means Lancashire, has 1,951 cotton mills, with 57,685,841 spindles, 787,697 looms, and over 600,000 operatives. And as it is the world centre of the cotton industry, so Manchester is the world centre of the cotton-waste industry. The two necessarily go together.

THE WAR AND NEW TRADE CHANNELS~Gigantic strides have been made in the utilisation of waste during the last half century, and the progress of the industry has by no means reached its limit. But already the world's trade in cotton-waste amounts to several hundred million pounds sterling a year. New uses are being discovered year by year, even day by day. The world cataclysm has probably had a powerful effect too in changing accustomed channels of the trade.

OF WILLIAM C. JONES LIMITED~Many firms, large and small, are engaged in the Waste Trade. It is perhaps a sufficient indication of the relative position of William C. Jones Limited to mention that this little book, intended for circulation among the firm's customers, needs be printed in five different languages.[6] This is greatly significant, because established reputation perhaps counts for more in the cotton-waste industry than in any other. The nature of the trade itself necessarily leaves much to the honour and the judgement of the manufacturer and merchant, and confidence in these matters is the root basis of a vast number of transactions. It is therefore relevant in the highest degree to say that after an experience of nearly half a century of its course of dealing, the cotton-waste industry recognises the firm of William C. Jones Limited as one of the largest of its kind in the world. As a Government contractor the firm envisages more than half the globe. It is a contractor for the British Admiralty, the British War Office, all the Colonial Governments, the principal European Governments, and to most of the principal railway companies and public authorities at home and abroad. As a buyer it handles all the waste of some of the tallest giants of the cotton trade, such as The Fine Cotton Spinners' and Doublers' Association Ltd.,[7] J. & P. Coats Limited of Paisley,[8] the English Sewing Cotton Company Ltd.,[9] and half a score of great firms on the Continent. This means, of course, that it has the pick of whatever is best in the markets of the world.

TWO SIDES~The business has two branches. As a merchant, the Company specialises in cotton and cotton waste for re-spinning and for the manufacture of surgical wadding and medicated cotton-wool and for explosives; as a manufacturer, it is a large exporter of engine-cleaning waste to all parts of the world. The firm was founded in 1871 by the late William C. Jones, and incorporated as a limited company in 1894. Sir A. Herbert Dixon, Bart.,[10] is the Chairman, and the members of the present executive Directorate are Messrs. T. S. Deakin, Wm. C. Jones, E.

H. Smith, and W. Mather.[11] For the home trade, orders are booked and executed direct from the headquarters, the Collyhurst Waste Mills, Manchester. The firm has advanced with the times, and every mechanical improvement known to the trade has been successively utilised at the Collyhurst Waste Mills. Electricity has completely superseded steam. The firm has adopted all the modern methods of safeguarding the health and welfare of its workers, and wherever dust is caused by the working of a machine, it is removed by a vacuum dust extractor. A London office, at Sussex Place House, Leadenhall Street, keeps the Company in touch with buyers in the metropolitan area, whilst numerous branches, and a network of agents, cover every district in the world where cotton waste is produced or used. The warehouses of the firm at Lille in which the waste of the French cotton trade was collected and stored were under bombardment in October, 1914, were destroyed. Since the conclusion of the armistice larger premises have been secured, and the firm have at Lille a very fine mill equipped with the most modern plant. A separate French Company has been formed under the style of the Société Anonyme William C. Jones.[12] This Company, in addition to its activities at Lille, has acquired warehouses at Blainville[13] and taken over as a going concern an old-established business at Colmar in Alsace. Altogether, the output of two million French spindles is thus assured. Italy is also an important gathering ground. Large stocks of waste are kept on hand in this country, and the volume of the business transacted is indicated by the fact that here the firm is represented by a resident Agent-General, Mr. John W. Vernon,[14] who is established at Via Principe Umberto, 10, Milan.

THE AMERICAN COUNTERPART~In the United States the firm works in close association with the William C. Jones Company of Boston and New Bedford, Mass.[15] New Bedford is the principal centre of the high-grade spinning industry in the United States, and as the largest exporter of cotton-waste in that country the William C. Jones Company of Boston and New Bedford may be regarded as the American counterpart of the parent Company in England. The New Bedford Mill is a very important one. It covers four acres of ground and is equipped with the most modern machinery. The output of such important firms as The American Thread Company, The Spool Cotton Company, and The Canadian Spool Cotton Company is assigned to the American branch,[16] a lusty offspring of the old stock. Altogether it may be said that William C. Jones Limited covers the whole world. There is much evidence that it covers it to the complete satisfaction of its clients.

## Notes

1 After John 3:8 'The wind bloweth where it listeth'.

2 *To the honourable knights, citizens, and burgesses, of the Commons House of Parliament the humble petition as well, of divers merchants and citizens of London that use buying and selling of fustians made in England, as of the makers of the same fustians* (London, 1621). This reference was first highlighted by W. H. Price, 'On the beginning of the cotton industry in England', *Quarterly Journal of Economics*, 20, 1906, p. 610.

3 Roberts, Lewes (1596–1641). *The Treasure of Traffike, or, a Discourse of Forraigne Trade*. . . (London: printed by E. P. for Nicholas Bourne, 1641), pp. 32–33:

> The towne of *Manchester* . . . buy Cotton wooll, in *London*, that comes first from *Cyprus*, and *Smyrna*, and at home worke the same, and perfit it into Fustians, Vermilions, Dymities, and other such Stuffes; and then returne it to *London*, where the same is vented and sold.

4 The quote is said to come from Defoe's *Tour Thro' the Whole Island of Great Britain*, published 1724–1727. However, it appears to be from a paraphrase of Defoe (vol. 3, pp. 210–211, p. 216) first published in Adam Anderson's *Historical and Chronological Deduction of the Origin of Commerce* (London: printed for A. Millar, J. and R. Tonson, J. Rivington. . ., 1764), vol. 2, pp. 314–315.

5 British battleship of a steam-turbine powered type introduced in 1906.

6 Copies survive in English, German, French and Italian:

Baumwollabfall: eine Studie einer grossen Industrie der Grafschaft Lancashires.
Déchets de coton: étude d'une grande industrie du comté de Lancashire.
Scarti di Cotone: uno Studio di una Importante Industria della Contea di Lancashire.
The fifth language was likely Spanish or Portuguese.

7 The Fine Cotton Spinners' and Doublers' Association Ltd. was a large conglomerate constituted in 1898, with headquarters in Manchester. Scott Lings (1855–1917) played a large role in the negotiations for the floatation of the company.

8 J. and P. Coats Ltd. was incorporated in 1890, from predecessor partnership firms. In 1895, the company joined with J. and J. Clark to form what was known as the 'Coats combine'.

9 The English Sewing Cotton Company Ltd. was a conglomerate constituted in 1897, with headquarters in Manchester. It was intended to create a strong rival to the Coats combine.

10 Alfred Herbert Dixon (1857–1920) was a founder of Fine Cotton Spinners and Doublers. See Dictionary of National Biography.

11 Thomas Smith Deakin (c1862–1934); William Charles Jones (1887–1962), son of the founder; E. H. Smith [not identified]; and W. Mather, company secretary.

12 Based at 19–19 bis, rue d'Avesnes, Lille.

13 Probably Blainville-Crevon, near Rouen.

14 Possibly John William Vernon (c1866–1949).

15 William C. Jones Inc. had its headquarters in Boston and mill in New Bedford, Massachusetts.

16 The American Thread Company had its headquarters in New York City, and its main mill in Dalton, Georgia. The Spool Cotton Company had its headquarters in New York. The Canadian Spool Cotton Company was established in 1901, with its headquarters in Montreal.

# Part 5

# AN 'UNINVITING AGGREGATION OF RUBBISH'

## Spun silk

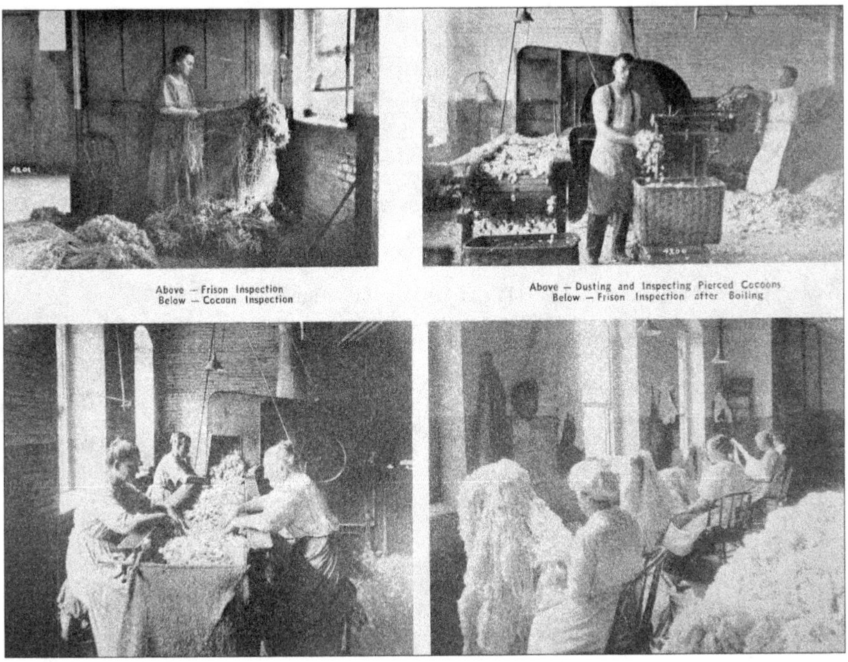


*Fig. 19* Preparing waste silk (clockwise from top left): Frison inspection. Dusting and inspecting pierced cocoons. Frison inspection after boiling. Cocoon inspection.

*Source*: N. D. White, 'Spun Silk', *American Dyestuff Reporter*, 25:2 (27 Jan 1936), p. 29. Courtesy of AATCC.

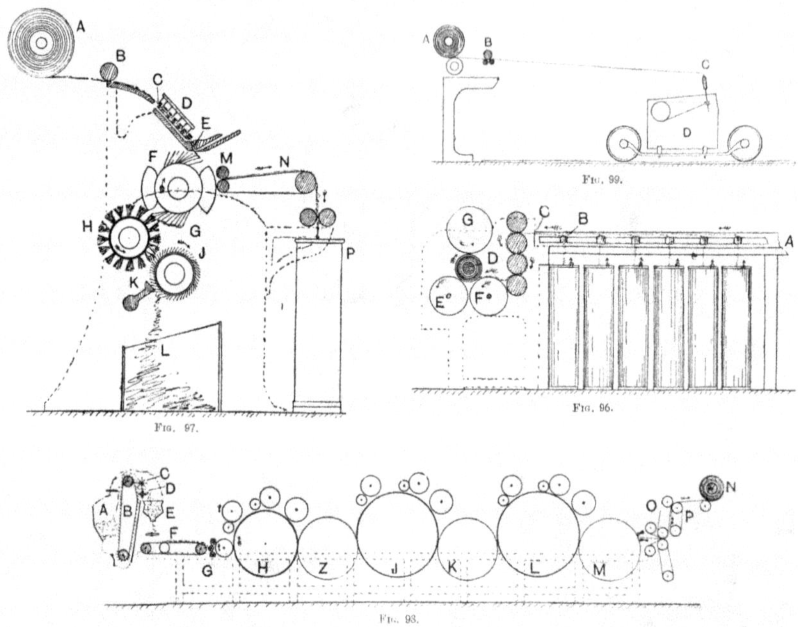


*Fig. 20* Diagrams of machinery used in waste silk spinning: Derby doubler combining carded slivers (fig. 96); Combing silk on the Heilmann principle (fig. 97); Garnetting machine used for carding silk (fig. 98); and, Mule spinning of condensed silk rovings (fig. 99). See Ch. 30 this volume.

*Source*: *Textile Manufacturer*, 29:340 (15 Apr 1903), p. 119. Author's collection.

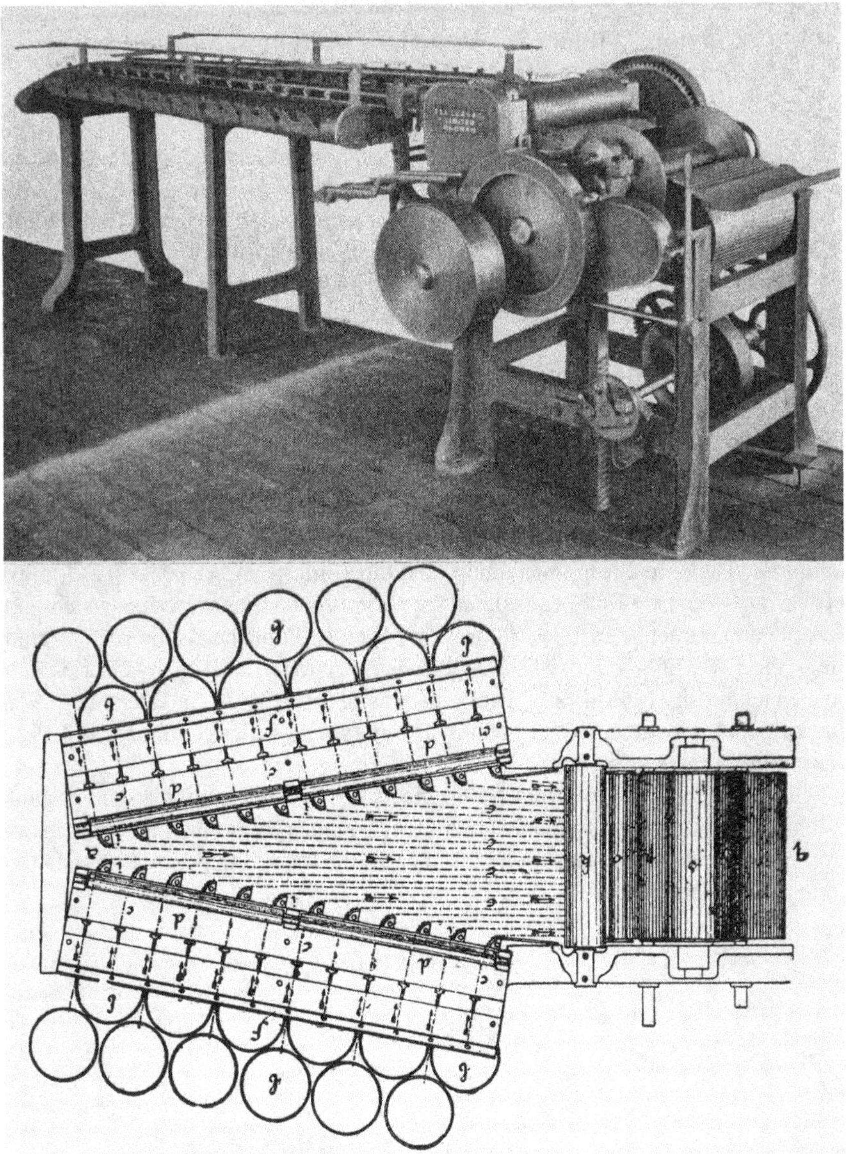

*Fig. 21* Derby doubler by Asa Rees and Co. Ltd, Oldham (top); and a plan view showing the multiple canisters of sliver being fed into the doubler to form a lap (bottom). See Ch. 30 this volume.

*Source*: Rayner, Hollins. Silk Throwing and Waste Silk Spinning (Scott, Greenwood and Son, 1903); Zipser, Julius. *Textile Raw Materials and Their Conversion into Yarns*. Translated from the German by Charles Salter (London: Scott, Greenwood and Co., 1901), p. 153. Author's collection.

## Editorial Headnote

### Claxton, William J. 'Waste not, want not', *Silk and the Silk Worker*. Rambles in Our Industries series (London & Glasgow: Blackie & Son, 1913), pp. 57–62.

William John Claxton (1877–1950) was an educational author for children, writing largely on nature and industry subjects, and producing over fifty titles between 1910 and 1949. He had attended a technical school in Barking before becoming assistant schoolmaster in a north London primary school, where he worked at the time of writing *Silk and the Silk Worker*. It was among the first three books in a series released in June 1913. The expanding series was announced in *The Scotsman*, 'From Messrs Blackie & Sons, London, come six separate volumes (each 9d.) of a novel and attractively illustrated series of reading books for schools that describe "Rambles Among Our Industries" ' (16 Oct 1913, p. 2). The books satisfied a gap, and Claxton was to contribute three more volumes by April 1914. A reviewer for *Belper News* praised their bright style: 'not a prosaic compilation of facts, but . . . really the romance of work in the mine and the mill. . . . Parents should not hesitate to place these books in the hands of their children. They are cheap, interesting, and most informing' (15 May 1914, p. 6). The *Cotton Factory Times* considered the various industries 'described in a bright, simple and attractive manner' (8 May 1914, p. 7). Published in limp cloth bindings, the cover of *Silk and the Silk Worker* was printed in a design by Charles Rennie Mackintosh (1868–1928). The price was dropped to 7d. in December 1916, making the series attractive gift books. The *Industries* series continued until 1922, reaching fourteen volumes.

Claxton's inclusion of waste silk reflects the secure position it had attained within the silk industry. While his narrative promotes the myth of the great inventor, more importantly, it allowed him to carry the moral injunction to 'waste not' into the industrial sphere.

# 26

# CLAXTON, WILLIAM J. 'WASTE NOT, WANT NOT'

## *Silk and the Silk Worker* (London & Glasgow: Blackie & Son, 1913), pp. 57–62.

All the silk with which we have been dealing up till now has been known as "raw silk". This, as we have seen, was originally spun by the caterpillar kept in captivity on some silk farm.

But there are millions and millions of cocoons made by wild silkworms, or *tussehs* as they are called, which are quite unreelable; that is to say, the threads are simply a gummy stuff so closely matted that no reeler can unwind them. Even in the case of the domestic silkworm, only about one-third of the fibre can be reeled, because of the extreme softness of the threads and the hardness of the gum. Another drawback to reeling is that there are many "freak" cocoons, such as two cocoons in one, or a "double" cocoon, cocoons formed of broken fibres; and so on.

It has been said that: "Precious as silk is, no textile fibre incurs a larger proportion of waste in the process of production". Put into simple language this means that there is more waste and loss in the silk manufacture than in any other textile industry. Not only has there been great loss of wild silk cocoons, but, as we have seen, in the floss, or rough silky coverings to the cultivated cocoons. For years and years this was cast away, although it was real silk fibre, coarser perhaps than that in the middle of the cocoon, but silk all the same. The inner layers of the cocoons were also cast aside as unreelable owing to their thick coating of gum and their extreme fineness. You remember, too, that we said some of the cocoons had to be laid aside so that the pupae might develop into moths, and that when the moths emerged from the cocoons they burst the fibres and made them unreelable. In the silk factory there must also be a certain amount of waste. In nearly all other factories they use the "waste" in some other form, but for a very long time the waste silk was quite useless.

You must have heard the old proverb: "Waste not, want not", and no doubt you have seen this written up in many places. Here was a very bad case of waste. Fancy, beautiful and precious fibre being thrown away, or sold at a halfpenny a pound, for this is all that was paid for the waste of Indian raw silks. Surely some clever man would find out a way of avoiding this waste! At last a clever inventor, who was also a great worsted manufacturer, thought that if all the unreelable silk fibre could be spun like the fibres of wool, cotton, flax, and other textiles, it could

DOI: 10.4324/9780429274190-32

be made ready for the weaver to work with. This gentleman was Mr. Samuel Lister, of Bradford, afterwards made Lord Masham.

Mr. Lister first bought a quantity of wild silk from a London chemist. After experimenting with it for a long time, he boiled it, and so the natural gum was made quite soft. He then had a mass of tangled fibres, and the difficulty was to unravel them and make one long thread, for the silk manufacturers always require a continuous thread for weaving. In his worsted mill he had a combing machine which was used to comb out the tangled masses of wool, and he thought that by certain alterations in this machine he could make one which would comb out the more delicate silk. After many failures he was quite successful, and he managed to obtain a fine sliver, or soft silk rope, in which the fibres had been laid parallel and smoothed out, when they could be quite easily spun into thread.

This was only the beginning of the new industry. It was thought that knubs, broken cocoons, floss, factory waste, &c., could all be brought into similar slivers, and if this were possible, then silk goods would be much cheaper. As years went by, new combing machines were made which would work on all these "wastes" so that they were brought to fibres all of which were as near alike as possible.

Do not think that all this took place without great labour and expense. It is said that the new inventions and the new machines cost over £300,000, but they well repaid in the end. Waste silk, which commanded a halfpenny a pound, now sold at three shillings; *useless* refuse, which had been cast aside, was now made into yarn which would fetch over £1, 1s. a pound.

It must be said, though, that spun silk is never so good as raw silk, either in brightness or strength. The manufacturers cannot quite account for the great difference between the two fibres. It is thought, though, that it is due to the breaking and pulling of the fibres in the spinning process. By passing the fibres through the gassing machine, whereby the fine hairs and rough frayed pieces are singed off, the silk may be made to look almost like raw silk for a time, but when it is worn the fibres soon fray out.

## Editorial Headnote

### Burnley, James. 'Fortunes Made in Business. XXII. Mr. S. C. Lister', *London Society: An Illustrated Magazine of Light and Amusing Literature for the Hours of Relaxation*, 39:230 (Feb 1881), pp. 171–184.

In January 1879, *London Society* launched a new series called 'Fortunes Made in Business' catering to the public fascination with men of fabulous wealth. The series quickly became 'one of the most notable features' of the serial (*Yorkshire Gazette*, 14 Feb 1880, p. 8). It eventually encompassed thirty-six numbered articles issued at irregular intervals up to June 1886, with unnumbered additions in January and March 1887. In the preface to a collected volume selected from the series in 1891, the magazine's editor, James Hogg (1829–1910) acknowledged 'the energy, patience, and technical skill of those whose co-operation helped to reduce to order the scattered recollections and tangled facts. . . . Chief amongst these contributors is Mr. James Burnley'.

James Burnley (1842–1919) was known for his sketches on Yorkshire subjects while on the staff of the *Bradford Observer* in 1871, and for similar contributions to *All the Year Round*. In the late 1880s, he moved to London, where he published largely on British industrial enterprise, in later years shifting his focus to American millionaires. On the title page of *Yorkshire Stories Re-told* (Leeds: Richard Jackson, 1885), he identified himself as the author of *Fortunes Made in Business*, signifying the extent of his input to the series. It can safely be assumed that Burnley was the originator of all the articles relating to Yorkshire, and this article matches in style and phrasing the chapter on Lister in Burnley's *History of Wool and Woolcombing* (London: Sampson, Low, Marston, Searle and Rivington, 1889). James Hogg inserted paragraphs believed to enhance the literary style or increase the entertainment value, but not grounded in experience like Burnley's work. Burnley, well-known in the West Riding under his own name and his pen-name 'Saunterer', later gained greater renown as the editor of *Pears' Annual*.

The Lister essay was included in both the 1884 and 1891 collections edited by James Hogg and published as *Fortunes Made in Business: A Series of Original Sketches, Biographical and Anecdotic, from the Recent History of Industry and Commerce*. There it was retitled 'Mr. S. C. Lister and the Story of "Silk Waste" '. Burnley did not depart significantly from the mythology surrounding Lister's inventions, but the focus is on the economic wonder of wealth from waste.

# 27

# BURNLEY, JAMES. 'FORTUNES MADE IN BUSINESS. XXII. MR. S. C. LISTER'

*London Society* (Feb 1881), pp. 171–184.

Mr. Lister's[1] life has been spent amongst inventions. He has registered more patents than any other man in England, and in carrying out improvements in machinery, of one kind and another, has spent fortune upon fortune; always, however, holding on until success has been won, when his outlay has come back to him fourfold. His career has been marked by two leading episodes. The first portion of his history is prominently associated with the perfecting and bringing into operation of the woolcombing-machine, at which he laboured with unswerving devotion for many years; the second period of his commercial life has been concerned in the invention of machinery for the manipulation of silk waste, theretofore treated as refuse, but now made the basis of many beautiful fabrics in velvets, silks, plush, and other kindred materials. Several hundred thousand pounds were expended by Mr. Lister in respect of the woolcombing-machine before it yielded him a penny; but when once it reached a practicable shape and came to be accepted by the trade, the return he obtained for his labour was on a scale so princely as to put the gains of all previous inventors into the shade. Mr. Lister received as much as 1000*l.* per machine as patent right. Then, in regard to the silk-waste manufacture, his experience has been much the same. Mr. Lister was 360,000*l.* out of pocket by his operations in this direction; indeed, he wrote off a quarter of a million as entirely lost before he began to make up his books again. Still, in 1865, he found himself sole master of the position – possessed of a valuable invention and without a competitor, English or foreign.

To tell the story of Mr. Lister's life from the time when, while yet a mere youth, he entered upon a commercial existence, to the period when, at the last general election, he was prevailed upon to come before one of the great county constituencies as a parliamentary candidate still in commercial harness, would be to tell the history of two important branches of our textile industries. We cannot attempt to do more than give the rough outlines of such a career.

Mr. Lister was born in the Waterloo year at Calverley Hall, near Leeds, being descended from one of the old county families, the Listers of Manningham. When Mr. Lister was some two or three years old, his father, Mr. Ellis Cunliffe Lister,[2] removed to the family mansion of the Listers, Manningham Hall, and at this seat Mr. S. C. Lister continued to reside for nearly half a century. When Bradford


DOI: 10.4324/9780429274190-33

became a parliamentary borough in 1832, Mr. Ellis Cunliffe Lister, in conjunction with Mr. John Hardy, father of the present Viscount Cranbrook,[3] was elected M.P. The position of the family was such that, although Mr. S. C. Lister was but a fifth son, it was never imagined he would adopt a commercial career. In fact, a very different destiny had been marked out for him. From his boyhood he had been taught to regard the Church as his future field of labour, and he was educated with this view. To make this course still more definite, his grandmother bequeathed him the Rectory of Addingham,[4] on the express condition that he should take holy orders.

It was not to be, however. The world was just then full of 'mighty workings:' the steam-god was revolutionising the industrial world, the picturesque valleys of the West Riding were fast becoming dotted with towering factory chimneys, the spirit of invention was everywhere abroad, and the heart of young Lister throbbed with strong yearnings as he saw all these signs of activity spreading around him, and he longed to make one of the great army of workers. It must have been a source of infinite sorrow to the family to find that their efforts to train up a pillar of the Church from one of their number were doomed to failure, and that he had determined to 'soil his hands with trade.' But, conscious of what was within him, S. C. Lister made his resolve and stuck to it; and the result has been, not that he has tarnished the lustre of an ancient name, but that he has given a brightness to it that centuries of simple county magnates could not have equalled.

Mr. Lister was educated at a school on Clapham Common, and then, instead of passing forward to the University, as it was at first intended he should have done, he obtained a position in the counting-house of Messrs. Sands, Turner, & Co., Liverpool.[5] While holding this appointment, Mr. Lister made several voyages to the United States, where he made himself well acquainted with what was going on in the shape of invention and enterprise. Those were the days of sailing vessels, and trips across the Atlantic were looked upon as something extraordinary; so Mr. Lister got some little fame for his knowledge of American affairs, his friends alluding to him generally as 'American Sam.'

[The section on Lister's invention of a woolcombing machine is left out here.]

Mr. Lister, however, was not content to rest upon his laurels, and to remain satisfied with the ample fortune that his machine had brought him; he had the true inventor's instincts, and no sooner had he solved one mechanical difficulty than he longed for others to attack. Accident showed him a new world that was waiting to be conquered. Going one day into a London warehouse, he came upon a pile of rubbish which strongly attracted his attention. He had never seen anything like it before. He inquired what it was, and was told that it was silk waste. 'What do you do with it?' he asked. 'Sell it for rubbish, that is all,' was the answer; 'it is impossible to do anything else with it.' Mr. Lister felt it, poked his nose into it, and pulled it about in a manner that astonished the London warehousemen. It was neither agreeable to the feel, the smell, nor the touch; but simply a mass of knotty, dirty, impure stuff, full of bits of stick and dead mulberry-leaves. In the end Mr. Lister made the offer of a halfpenny a pound for the 'rubbish,' and the sale was there and then concluded, the vendor being especially pleased to get rid of it on such advantageous terms.

When Mr. Lister got this 'rubbish' down to Manningham, he spent a good deal of time in analysing and dissecting it, and he came to the conclusion that there was something to be done with it. He now set himself to inquire into the exact position of the silk manufacture at home and abroad, making the fullest possible investigation. The result of this was that he found silk waste was treated all the world over as he had seen it treated in the London warehouse – as 'rubbish.' Mr. Lister now set his heart upon inventing machinery that should be able to manipulate this waste and imperfect product of the silkworm into fabrics that should vie in appearance with materials manufactured from the perfect cocoon. In this venture he was not beset by rivals, as he had been in the days when he strove to conquer the difficulties of the woolcombing-machine; he had taken a thing in hand now in which no one but himself felt the shadow of an interest, and he could work on without being haunted by the fear of some one stepping in between him and success. He engaged a number of skilled workmen from foreign countries – men well acquainted with the manufacture of silk in all its branches – and although at first they viewed their master's experiments on silk waste with suspicion and distrust, they eventually came to think with him that there was 'something in it.' Mr. Lister now ceased to take the strong interest which he had hitherto done in woolcombing; he allowed the work to fall into other hands and to spread generally over the worsted district, he preserving to himself, however, the full rights and royalties of his patents. For the next ten years he applied himself heart and soul to the solving of the new problem which he had set before him, and early and late he worked at it, getting nearer and nearer to success every day. Few men would have held on as Mr. Lister did to this idea, in spite of commercial panic and weary and prolonged effort. In the crisis of 1857 loss upon loss was sustained by him; but he faced the brunt of the battle and carried himself gallantly through, not only bearing up against all this weight of misfortune, but against the enormously heavy expenditure which he was put to in regard to his silk inventions. There was much secret toil indulged in, in those days, at the Manningham Mills; the outside world knew little of what mighty schemes were there being matured. As before stated, Mr. Lister spent 360,000*l.* in perfecting machinery for the manufacture of silk waste before he ever made a single shilling by it.

By the year 1865 Mr. Lister had accomplished his task; he had subjected silk waste to so many intricate and delicate operations, that he was able to manufacture from it velvet fabrics of great beauty. Many machines had to be invented – machines on a very gigantic scale – before the preparatory processes could be successfully mastered; and when this had been done, there was the velvet loom to bring into operation. This loom – which is the invention of Mr. Reixach, a Spaniard – gradually grew into a tangible fact, however, and it is considered to be a *magnum opus* as an invention. Mr. Lister bought this patent, and engaged the inventor's son[6] to superintend its carrying out. It was some years after the loom got into Mr. Lister's hands, however, that it was made perfect. A power-loom for weaving velvet had been thought of before, it is true, Heilmann[7] himself having in the early days of his inventive career brought out a loom for weaving two pieces of velvet simultaneously. It is curious to note how the lives of Heilmann and Lister have, in the matter of mechanical invention, run largely in the same groove: in the one case, however, the inventor had a wealth of original ideas, but was wanting in the practical application necessary to insure complete success; in the other case there was not only much real inventive power, but a super-abundance of energy and practical knowledge.

From a very remote period the manufacture of silk had been carried on with more or less success, but until Mr. Lister came upon that heap of rubbish in the London warehouse no one had ever been able to do anything with silk waste. From the earliest ages silk had been recognised as the most beautiful material that the eye of man had seen; the poets were never tired of singing its praises; it had a foremost place in all the pageantry and magnificence of the past; and its associations were those of rank, wealth, and beauty. The Romans of the second century esteemed a pound of silk 'not inferior in value to a pound of gold,' Gibbon tells us;[8] and for centuries this exquisite material was only to be found as an adornment of the rich. Aristotle makes allusion to the silkworm,[9] and Pliny records the fact that silk came from Assyria, and was worked by the Greek women.[10] In those far-back days China and Persia had the monopoly of the raw material; but in the time of Justinian silkworms were brought to Constantinople by two Nestorian monks,[11] and by this means the silk manufacture was introduced to Justinian's subjects. The manufacture subsequently spread into Sicily, Italy, Spain, and France, and James I. made the attempt to acclimatise the silkworm in England; but neither then nor later was it possible to establish it in our humid atmosphere, and to this day we have to rely solely on foreign countries for the supply of the raw product. So, up to the seventeenth century, England only knew silk as it was imported by the mercers who used to congregate in Cheapside. Lydgate's *London Lackpenny*[12] says:

'Then to the Chepe I began me drawn,
Where much people I saw for to stand;
One offered me velvet, silk, and lawn:
Another he taketh me by the hand.'

Evidence is plentifully scattered through our early literature of the extreme favour in which silk was regarded as an article of costume. The much-enduring Grissell of the old ballad,[13] when she married her brutal husband, exchanged her country russet for silk and velvet, and in the first stage of her subsequent debasement

'Her velvet gown
Most patiently she stripped off.
Her kirtle of silk with the same.'

The Lady Greensleeves of the Elizabethan ballad, too, has her

'Smock of silk both fair and white,
With gold embroidered gorgeously.'

So far back as 1286 silk mantles were worn 'by some noblemen's ladies at a ball at Kenilworth Castle;' and in 1534 the fabric had grown so much in favour, that the clergy began to array themselves in it. Whittington, the nursery hero, was a dealer in silks. Silk was held in the highest regard in England all through the Plantagenet and Tudor periods, and under the rule of the Stuarts something was done in the way of introducing the manufacture of this class of goods into this country. At last, when the Edict of Nantes forced a band of exiles, who had been engaged in the silk manufacture at home, to England, and they took up their abode in Spitalfields, the manufacture of silk was perfected and established there.[14] In course of time the trade came to hold a not unimportant place amongst the national industries. Mechanical invention was brought to its aid, as to all other textile manufactures, and the trade was considered down to 1857 to have made all the advancement that could be expected of it.

It is not a little surprising, therefore, that an entirely new development of the silk trade should have been hit upon by one who had had no connection with that manufacture. And when Mr. Lister came to take this matter in hand, the difficulties in the way of success seemed to all but himself altogether insurmountable. The silk waste which he had set his heart upon converting into attractive fabrics, and which everybody had discarded as worthless since silk had been known, was the most uninviting aggregation of rubbish it was possible to conceive. It consisted of the waste made from the manufacture of neat silk[15] and pierced cocoons; and, as it came to Mr. Lister, looked like mutilated ropes, dirty flocks, or mucilaginous hemp, and was knotted and sticky and choked with sticks and leaves and dead silkworms. There were many who shook their heads discouragingly when they saw the heaps of dirty stuff which Mr. Lister had gathered round him; they thought the investment a bad one even at so low a price as a halfpenny a pound. It was not one machine simply that Mr. Lister had to invent before he could bring this rough material into subjection; he must invent a whole series of machines, if the thing had to be dealt with at all. So he began at the beginning, and invented machine after machine, and process after process, until the silk waste was in the end transformed into rich and beautiful fabrics. He had discovered a use and created a market for the much-despised rubbish, and from all the corners of the earth it now found its way to the Manningham Mills – from Persia, China, Japan, India, Italy, and elsewhere. Mr. Lister also made extensive arrangements for producing the raw material in its perfect form on an estate of his own; he accordingly purchased an estate of 1000 acres in Assam.[16] It was found, however, that the difficulty of obtaining labour in that part of our Eastern dependency was so great that the idea of producing raw silk there had to be abandoned, and the estate was transformed into a tea plantation, and has been used as such ever since. More recently

Mr. Lister has become possessed of extensive estates in the Punjab and Dehra Dun,[17] where the Assamese worm has been introduced with considerable success, and where also the Italian and Japanese worms are being largely cultivated. There are great filatures at one of these places, where it is intended to reel neat silk. The Assamese worm,[18] it may be mentioned, does not feed upon the mulberry-tree, but upon the castor-oil plant, and produces five crops a year, the leaves of the plant remaining fresh all the year round.

It may be interesting at this point to attempt a brief description of the various processes which silk waste undergoes at Manningham Mills. Allusion has already been made to the condition in which the waste arrives at Mr. Lister's works, and the dirty unkempt appearance it has at that stage. To begin with, groups of boys are to be seen in a large room, sitting upon their haunches 'sorting' the waste, freeing it from the bulkier descriptions of impedimenta, and shaking it into more manageable form. From this department it is taken to the wash-house, where it is put into huge tanks, and washed and shaken with astonishing force and vigour. After this experience of soap and water, the fibre is transferred to a drying-room, in which place it lies in limp helplessness until the wet evaporates and it assumes an aspect of comparative cleanliness. It has now to make the acquaintance of Mr. Lister's machinery, being hurried away to the drums and preparers, where it is dragged and twisted and racked in a most terrible way. At each successive stage it becomes cleaner and softer and silkier; for the ponderous drums, belts, pulleys, and teeth it has to encounter are not accustomed to work without making a marked impression. Many of the machines are exceedingly formidable monsters, and grind their teeth and roar in the most terrific manner. The preliminary processes are naturally very numerous; but at length the fibre reaches the combing-machines, and emerges from the latter a beautifully soft flossy filament. There is no doubt now as to its being convertible into lovely fabrics. It is altogether impossible to recognise in it the uncouth ill-looking stuff which was lying in heaps in the warehouse just as it came in. After the silk has left the combing-machines, it enters upon a more refined state of existence, passing successively through the hands of drawers, rovers, doublers, spinners, gassers, reelers, warpers, spoolers, and others, until it assumes the more recognisable shapes of warp and weft.

The weaving departments at the Manningham Mills are full of interest. One shed, covering an area of about 7000 yards – the Beamsley Shed – is entirely given up to the weaving of pieces. What an army of operatives one sees assembled here! They are all weaving velvet or plush, and the looms go through their operations with unerring exactitude, the shuttles flying to and fro with great speed. It is here that we see Mr. Lister's wonderful velvet-loom in active operation. Two pieces – one above the other – are woven in the same loom; and a mysterious knife glides across at each motion and effectually separates the twin pieces. There are looms of marvellously intricate formation engaged in weaving velvet ribbons; and others are employed in weaving the coarser kinds of silk into sacking, carpets, machine-cloths, &c. Everything that enters within the gates of Manningham Mills is utilised in some shape or other, a surprising variety of articles being produced in all from silk waste. The following may be enumerated by way of example: silk velvets, velvets with a silk pile and a cotton back, silk carpets, imitation sealskin, plush, velvet ribbons, corded ribbons, sewing silks, Japanese silks,[19] poplins, silk cleaning-cloths for machinery, bath-towels, floor-cloths, dish-cloths, and so forth. And all these from the once-despised silk waste! Such a revolution in one branch of manufacture was never accomplished before by any one. The consequence has been that silks have been greatly cheapened, and that a material which was regarded as worthless has come to have a value in the market, the price obtained for silk waste being now very greatly in excess of the original price paid by Mr. Lister.

It was no easy matter, at first, to get Mr. Lister's newly-invented silk machinery into proper working order. The 'hands' had to be taught over again. Each weaver cost the firm many pounds sterling before she had mastered the loom she had under her control. Meanwhile, Mr. Lister and a skilful staff of inventors were day by day engaged in perfecting and inventing machinery; and to this day this work of improvement goes on at Manningham Mills, each year seeing a marked advance upon the preceding one. Mr. Lister seems to be for ever on the point of bringing out another improved machine, of which the world will talk when it comes to have passed the Rubicon of the Patent Office.

The sewing-silk department at Manningham Mills is well worth inspecting. There is a very large quantity of the silk spun at these works converted into sewing-silk, and to watch the delicate threads coiling round the bobbins, under the guidance of a number of girls, is to be deeply interested. Thousands of bobbins of silk thread for the sewing-machine are here produced every week, black and white being the prevailing colours, although there is a good sprinkling of silk threads of warmer and more attractive colours.

In connection with the works there are dye-houses, mechanics' shops, finishing-rooms, &c., all the processes connected with the manufacture of silk being begun and completed on the premises.

. . .

Mr. Lister's latest success in manufactures has been the production of plush goods, of which the world of fashion has recently become so deeply enamoured. During the last two years many thousand pieces of plush, ranging in colour through all the hues of the rainbow, have been made at the Manningham Mills. Indeed, the principal portion of the supply of this class of goods in England has been despatched from Mr. Lister's establishment, although both in Yorkshire and Lancashire several manufacturers have lately entered into rivalry to some extent with Mr. Lister in this branch of industry.

. . .

It is as an inventor and promoter of English manufactures that Mr. Lister will be remembered, and the work that he has done in those directions will always preserve his name prominent amongst the industrial annals of the nineteenth century.

## Notes

1 Samuel Cunliffe Lister, 1st Baron Masham (1815–1906).

2 Ellis Cunliffe Lister-Kay (1774–1853), MP for Bradford from 1832–1841. He took the name Lister under the will of his first wife's uncle, and Kay under the will of his second wife's father.

3 John Hardy (1773–1855) was MP for Bradford from 1832 to 1837 and 1841 to 1847. His son, Gathorne Gathorne-Hardy, Viscount Cranbrook (1814–1906), was a Conservative politician.

4 Addingham is a village near Ilkley in West Yorkshire.

5 Sands, Turner and Co., merchants and commission agents of Liverpool was named after its principals Thomas Sands (1790–1867) and Charles Turner (1803–1875). In 1840, Turner left; by this time, Joseph Sands had joined his brother in the Liverpool firm. The partners also ran the New York firm Sands, Turner, Fox and Co. The several firms failed in 1847.

6 José Reixach y Gispert (c1842–1918), son of Ferdinand Reixach, manufacturer.

7 Josué Heilmann (1796–1848), Alsatian inventor of textile machinery.

8 Gibbon, Edward. *The Decline and Fall of the Roman Empire* (1776–1788), vol. 1, ch. 2.

9 Book 5, Ch. 17.

> A certain great worm, which has as it were horns, and differs from others, at its first metamorphosis produces a campe, afterwards a bombylius, and lastly a necydalus. It passes through all these forms in six months. From this animal women unroll and separate the bombycina (cocoons), and afterwards weave them.
>
> (*Aristotle's History of Animals in Ten Books*. Translated by Richard Cresswell, London: Henry G. Bohn, 1862, p. 124.)

10 This repeats an error. The *Natural History* of Pliny does not give such a provenance. William T. M. Forbes attributed the confusion with Assyria to the Pauly-Wissowa article 'Bombyx' in volume 3 of the *Realencyclopädie der classischen Altertumwissenschaft* (see 'The silkworm of Aristotle', *Classical Philology*, 25, Jan 1930, p. 22 of pp. 22–26). The Pauly-Wissowa volume was not published until 1897 (too late for the reference here), but it is a revision by Georg Wissowa of an older version of the encyclopaedia begun by August Pauly and completed by Christian Waltz and Wilhelm Siegmund Teuffel in 1852.

11 Followers of Nestorius, whose teachings on the separate human and divine persons of Christ were condemned as heretical in 431.

12 The author seems to have consulted Bell, Robert (ed.). *Early Ballads Illustrative of History, Traditions and Customs* (London: J. W. Parker and Sons, 1856), for this and the following quotation. At that time, *London Lackpenny* was ascribed to John Lydgate (c1370–1451).

13 Deloney, Thomas (attrib.). *An excellent ballad of the noble marquis and patient Grissel* (London, 1635). Robert Bell (see Note 12) writes, 'The story upon which the ballad is founded was first related by Boccaccio. . . . The earliest English version of it is in the *Canterbury Tales*. See: https://babel.hathitrust.org/cgi/pt?id=hvd.hwpady&view=1up&seq=81&skin=2021 Chaucer, Ann Ed., II. 126' (p. 73).

14 The author has relied here upon Joseph Haydn's *Dictionary of Dates, or Universal Reference Relating to all Ages and Nations*. . . . First published in 1841, the 8th edition's entry for 'Silk' reads,

> In England, silk mantles were worn by some noblemen's ladies at a ball at Kenilworth Castle, 1286. Silk was worn by the English clergy in 1534.

> Manufactured in England in 1604; and broad silk wove from raw silk in 1620. Brought to perfection by the French refugees in London at Spitalfields, 1688.
>
> (London: Edward Moxon, 1857, p. 598)

15 Neat silk is cultivated cocoon silk.
16 State in northeastern India.
17 Dehradun, capital of Uttarakhand, the neighbouring state of Punjab in northern India.
18 The Assamese worm often designates *Antheraea assamensis*, known as the muga silkworm. However, it is *Samia cynthia ricini*, the eri silkworm that feeds on the leaves of the castor oil plant which is referred to here.
19 Evidently not made in Japan, but imitating silks of Japanese manufacture, that is, plain-weave silks of soft handle.

## Editorial Headnote

### Lister, Samuel Cunliffe. 'The Silk Comb', *Lord Masham's Inventions. Written by Himself* (Bradford: The 'Argus' Printing Works; and London: Percy Lund, Humphries & Co., 1905), pp. 52–62.

This book appeared on 1 January 1906, Lord Masham's ninety-first birthday. It was well-received. The *Leeds Mercury* wrote:

> 'In it the veteran Peer tells the story of his achievements, and the Bradford reader will find in it the echoes of many famous controversies in which "Sam Lister" – as they still call him – has figured. The firm of J. and S. C. Lister made its appearance in Manningham so far back as 1838. Mr. Sam Lister – as he was then – had just returned from a long stay in America. His first invention was an ingenious device for inserting ornamental designs in plain cloths, and this was followed shortly afterwards by a patent for fringing shawls, in which the firm at that time did an immense trade with America. But the most remarkable of all Lord Masham's inventions was the designing of a wonderful patent by which silk waste could be converted into fabrics' (2 Jan 1906, p. 6).

In 1886, the Society of Arts had awarded Lister (1815–1906) the Albert Medal 'for the services he has rendered to the textile industries especially by the substitution of mechanical woolcombing for hand-combing, and by the introduction and development of a new industry – the utilisation of silk waste'. Although use of silk waste was not new, its industrialisation was, and Lister's inventions enabled a greater range of waste silk to be spun to greater perfection, suited to a wider array of products.

Lister disputed the storcy of his inventions with others that had rival claims, and the book set out his version of events from a favoured position. A contemporary observed,

> 'he might not improbably have ended his days in a workhouse, and have been referred to, if referred to at all, as a hair-brained dreamer, who wasted his life in following phantoms. But making some splendid hits, his costly failures were not only balanced, but he accumulated vast wealth, obtained national distinction, and enriched his country and the world' ('Our Inventor', *Northern Daily Telegraph*, 29 Jan 1906, p. 2).

# 28

# LISTER, SAMUEL CUNLIFFE. 'THE SILK COMB'

## *Lord Masham's Inventions* (Bradford: The 'Argus' Printing Works; and London: Percy Lund, Humphries & Co., 1905), pp. 52–62.

It was in the year 1855 that a Mr. Spensly,[1] a London waste silk broker, who had heard of my great success in wool-combing, sent me a small sample of what he called "native Indian Chassum," being the waste produced by the natives in reeling their cocoons. At that time I had never seen any silk waste, and knew nothing about it. The first look of it was not very inviting, nor very encouraging, as it looked to me to be nothing but rubbish. In fact it was nothing else, as no silk spinner had made or could make anything of it. He said that there were five or six hundred bales in the London Docks, and that no one would buy it, and in order to get quit of it they had tried to use it as manure, but they found that it would not rot, and so what to do with it they did not know. It was not inviting, as it was largely composed of dead silk worms, and the smell and odour from them was anything but pleasant. Leaves and straw and all kinds of extraneous matter were mixed and bound together by a certain amount of dirty looking fibres. Altogether it was not a very tempting material to experiment with. The only inducement was the price, as it was offered to me at practically nothing – at a halfpenny per pound. I bought a few sample bales at that price.

The first thing was, by boiling it in soap and water, to cleanse it to some extent from gum and dirt. This at once disclosed that there was a certain amount of beautiful fibre, of a rich golden colour, but so matted and mixed with rubbish that it looked impossible to make anything of it. However, as I was then full of experiments with other fibres, I thought that I would try what I could do. But I was almost like the savage who sees in vain the rich golden thread in the virgin rock, in the virgin ore, but has no idea how to extract it. And what made it vastly more difficult for me was that I had never before seen any silk waste, and knew nothing whatever how to treat it, as I had never been in a silk mill. In fact I have never since been in one that I can remember. It is quite certain that if I had I should have thrown it aside as worthless and unworkable, as the trade did. My very ignorance was the cause of my doing what I otherwise should not have done. A practical silk spinner would at once have said, "There is plenty of good waste; why bother with this rubbish? It will never pay even if you have it for nothing." And he would have


DOI: 10.4324/9780429274190-34

been quite right, for there was no machinery upon which it could be worked to pay. But not being a practical silk spinner and knowing little or nothing about silk or silk waste, I thought I would try and see what could be done with it.

As might be expected, after boiling, washing, and cleansing it as much as possible, it was worked upon such machinery as I had. It was first put through some drums covered with teeth which had been used for preparing China grass. This was done several times, which opened it and straightened the fibres and cleared it a good deal from extraneous matter. Then it was gilled[2] to prepare it for combing. So far it looked very well and promising, but when it came to be combed (and I had all kinds of combs) it was a regular fiasco, a complete and hopeless failure with such machinery as I then had. During 1856 I did little or nothing beyond experimenting with a few pounds.

It is very curious and remarkable that my complete ignorance of everything relating to silk and silk waste was what now caused me to try to do what no one knowing anything about the trade would. It was just the same with wool-combing. The past history, the disastrous story of all that had been done from the time of Cartwright's first great invention[3] was altogether unknown to me. I thought that the machine that stood before me was entirely new, entirely Mr. Donisthorpe's invention.[4] It is very surprising how he could think of putting such a machine before the public, as he must have known (indeed he did know, for he mentions him in his specification) that Cartwright's machine was public property, and had been for long, as the patent had lapsed many years before, and that his machine must either be better, or it would be useless to try to sell it. But he had the luck to find in me an ignorant purchaser, who very ignorantly purchased a bad machine when he might have had a much better for nothing.[5] So it was with Mr. Spensly. He found in me an ignorant buyer for his rubbish. At one time I had lost a fortune in attempting to make a silk purse, so to speak, out of a sow's ear in trying this waste. Being prosperous, and having nothing specially requiring my personal attention, and always being fond of all kind of sport – although for long years I worked hard, I always would have and did have my share of what for me was health, and I may say life itself (for I am very sure that without it this brief history would never have been written by me) – I took the Moy Hall shootings, near Inverness.[6] I had a large family shooting party, and we enjoyed ourselves immensely. It was, I think, the pleasantest three months I ever spent, to be followed by years of toil and trouble, for on my return I heard the first sound of the coming storm. But to be brief – for it is not a pleasant subject – I was informed that the Halifax concern was in difficulties, and wanted help.[7] Then I found that Mr. Brown, the managing partner,[8] had accepted bills to a large amount that had nothing to do with the business, but as they were accepted in the name of the firm I was responsible for them and had them to pay. This I could not do at the moment, so the concern had temporarily to suspend payment to give me time to find the money. It was then, or rather a short time after, that I sold the French combing concern to Sir Isaac,[9] as I had great difficulty in finding the necessary funds, so that one partner profited by the wrong-doing of the other.

But all this might have been avoided had I been wise and not foolishly proud, for the Governor of the Bank of England most thoughtfully and considerately sent for me. That meeting I shall never forget. In a large gas-lighted underground room (it appeared to me), I was introduced to the Governor and three or four Bank Directors. He sat with a big book before him and received me very pleasantly, but soon showed that he meant business, and asked me some very searching questions, every answer being carefully entered in the big book. At last he asked me the very plain question, "Did I think I could pay my way?" He said that he was aware that I had a number of concerns doing a large business, and if they should stop payment it might and would greatly increase the panic that was then prevailing. This at once raised my pride, that I should be asked such a question, for I had hitherto considered myself one of the richest and most prosperous men in the country. In a rash moment, I remember so well, I coloured up and said, I thought I could.

The big book was immediately closed. He rose from his seat, and with a bland smile said: "We are delighted to hear it. Good morning, Mr. Lister," and so I was bowed out of the bank. But when in the street, too late I saw my folly. It is as true to-day as it has been for all time, "Nemo mortalium omnibus horis sapit" – "that no man is wise at all times," and I never did a more foolish thing, for it would have saved me a world of trouble and an immense loss if I had only pocketed my pride and asked for assistance. The Bank of England deserves well of the country, for it has often assisted others in similar difficulties, and I mention this little incident in grateful memory of its thoughtful consideration for myself.

The Halifax concern remained under the supervision of the creditors for some time, and made about ten thousand pounds, which, to my great indignation, the Income Tax people assessed, claiming that it was creditors' money and not mine, and we had a great wrangle about it. But I beat them. It was no easy thing for all the other concerns to pay their way, and that, too, without any assistance – and I am always proud of it – and if I had only allowed the Bank of England to have given me a bit of help my loss would have been comparatively trifling. But pride stood in the way.

So ended the year 1857, which had opened so full of promise, but closed in gloom and disaster. My loss, direct cash loss, besides what I suffered from having to sell stocks and other things at ruinous prices, was a hundred and fifty thousand pounds. This, together with my serious loss on silk-combing, so crippled me that for years I was more or less always in pecuniary difficulties.

In 1858 I did nothing. I had quite enough to do to attend to finance, and gave up my experiments with the velvet wire loom, and I made no further attempts at velvet weaving for the next ten years.

In 1859 we succeeded – that is, I and my partner, Mr. James Warburton[10] – in making the first silk-comb, which was patented in our joint names,[11] and it gave great promise of future success, but like Cartwright's wool-comb, it was just good enough to lose money on. From the beginning it made a first-rate sliver and fairly clean work, but its great fault – a fatal one – was that it produced so little top and made so much noil that it did not pay.[12] So far as the machine was concerned the mechanical arrangement was admirable, and it did what had never been done before. It produced a splendid, regular and even sliver, just what was wanted in the spun silk trade. We had got something of immense value, but did not know it, as Mr. Warburton knew no more about the silk trade than I did. If we had known, I have a strong opinion that the comb would have paid almost from the first, but we did not know the then value of the yarn it produced.

Nett silk,[13] Italian, was at that time worth over forty shillings a pound, and was anything but level and free from lumps, and other imperfections, whereas our Manningham spun silk yarn was in many respects superior, and was used as a substitute. So far as the machine itself, the invention of the machine, that is the comb, is concerned, I was greatly helped by my partner, Mr. Warburton, who was joint patentee, but he had little or no part in working it, that is, trying to make it a success. He lived at the mill at Addingham, and his time and attention were mainly directed to the spinning, in which he was clever, and we were then experimenting with wool, flax and silk spinning, for which he took out several patents.[14] The best thing he did was to invent the intersecting screw gill, which may be said to work two sets of fallers or gills, one up and the other down, but intersecting each other.[15] I have no copy of the patent, nor do I remember where it was invented, but in after years I had good reason to know something about it. At first, and for many years, the English spinners would not look at it, but after a time Messrs. Greenwood & Batley, of Leeds,[16] took it in hand, and being always first-class in their work, made it work so admirably that the foreign spinners adopted it, and with such success as to make nearly as good yarn out of hand-dressed silk as I could do with the comb, which they had never been able to do before, as with the ordinary preparing machinery they could never make it so level and free from thick and thin places. It is very remarkable, but absolutely true, that this very machine in that way was the means of killing the silk-comb, which for some years was immensely profitable.

At one time, especially for velvets, Lister and Co. could command almost any price for their yarns, but the intersecting gill changed this, as the yarn made from the hand-dressed silk was nearly as level and good as the machine-combed yarn. This after a time became so serious that we had, much against my will, to adopt the old system of hand-dressing, and we have some now. The hand-dresser could always beat the comb in the yield, that is in the production of top to noil, so that it could always produce a cheaper yarn; and when by improvements in preparing and drawing it they succeeded in getting a level yarn, the comb became obsolete and worthless except for some special purposes, especially making a very superior sliver for mixing with mohair. We had not many hand-dressing machines, and when one day walking round and looking at them with vexation and disdain, as I thought it a terrible humiliation that I (of all men) should be obliged to adopt them, it suddenly occurred to me that I could make a self-acting dressing frame. I was not long in doing it, for this time I was well trained, and had a great practical experience. My years of experiment with the silk-comb were not lost.

In due course – a short time in fact – to my great delight, and I may say also to my great surprise, my self-acting frame went to work, so far as I remember, without a single alteration, and is, I believe, at work to-day. But it did not at first make a sliver (it made a lap). The sliver was an improvement that was made afterwards. It is an immense and costly machine, and requires a great deal of room and power. The first twenty cost us considerably over a thousand pounds each, but we made them a little cheaper afterwards. They were all made at Manningham. When I gave up my personal attendance at the mill I had great fears that they would not be worked successfully, as they require experience, knowledge, and good management, but I am pleased to say that Mr. W. Watson, who is now managing director of the company,[17] has not only worked them successfully, but considerably improved them, for which he has taken several patents. It was the first self-acting dressing frame that was ever made (and also the only one that ever made a sliver), and so far as I know there is only another now, a foreign machine, but it is not used in England, and only to a limited extent on the Continent.

## Notes

1 William Spensley (c1799–1869) was born in Grinton, Yorkshire. He became a silk merchant in London by the 1830s; he had moved into dealing in waste silk by 1844 when he ended a partnership in Little Winchester Street, London. Although Spensley was declared bankrupt in March 1864, this was annulled in January 1865, and he left effects valued in the region of £10,000 when he died 21 September 1869.

2 A gill is a set of comb-like needles, and gilling was a coarser version of the combing process, using rollers in combination with the gills to draw out and align the fibres.

3 Edmund Cartwright (1743–1823) took out patents for wool-combing machines in 1790 (no. 1747 and no. 1787), and 1792 (no. 1876).

4 George Edmond Donisthorpe (1811–1875) obtained patents in 1842 (no. 9404) and 1843 (no. 9780) for wool-combing machines.

5 Lister and Donisthorpe took out joint patents for combing apparatus in 1849 (no. 12712) and 1850 (no. 13309), so the two men evidently worked more profitably together than Lister admits here.

6 Moy Hall was a seat of the Mackintosh clan, situated in Moy, south of Inverness in the Scottish Highlands. It was renowned for its grouse shooting.

7 Lister's worsted spinning mill, Wellington Mill, in Halifax. Payments were suspended in December 1857. At a meeting of creditors that month, Lister's proposal to pay full liabilities in instalments over the course of two years was accepted.

8 Henry Brown was the resident managing partner from the time the Wellington Mill was built and equipped in 1853. The partnership between Lister and Brown was dissolved 16 January 1858 (*London Gazette*, 19 Jan 1858, p. 289).

9 Isaac Holden (1807–1897) joined in partnership with Lister in 1848. He had set up factories at St Denis, Lille and Reims. When he bought out Lister in 1857, his firm was renamed Isaac Holden et fils.

10 James Warburton (born 1815), machine maker. The partnership between Warburton and Lister was dissolved from 1 January 1864 (*London Gazette*, 31 Jan 1865, p. 472).

11 Patent no. 2832 of 13 December 1859.

12 *Top* refers to the usable fibre and *noil* the rejected fibre.

13 Nett silk is yarn produced by combining filaments unwound from the silk cocoon, known as thrown silk, as opposed to spun silk.

14 One of these, Lister and Warburton's joint patent no. 222 of 28 January 1862, was for improvements in preparing cotton for spinning,

15 Lister patented an intersecting screw gill for preparing fine wool, no. 3834 of 16 December 1868.

16 The machine-making firm of Greenwood and Batley was established in 1856 out of a former partnership. The principals were Thomas Greenwood (1807–1873) and John Batley (c1823–1891). It was incorporated as a limited company in 1888.

17 William Watson jun. (1846–1925) came to Manningham Mills in 1886 to manage the spinning department before becoming a managing director.

## Editorial Headnote

### Boden, Joseph. 'The Spun Silk Industry of England', *XXXIII Annual Report of the Silk Association of America*, 1905, pp. 95–100.

Joseph Boden (1850–1910) began his career before the age of twenty as a salesman for a silk broker. Later, in the 1870s, he joined the firm of Francis Kidd and Co., linen merchants. There he successfully initiated silk into the firm's range of business, and was made a partner in the 1880s. Francis Kidd (1845–1888), of Irish birth, worked in Manchester in the linen trade, and began trading in his own name in 1867. Following Kidd's sudden and unexpected death, Boden married his widow in 1889, taking responsibility for Kidd's six children, and seeing the two boys into merchant careers. Boden was chairman, then president of the Silk Club, and became the second president of the closely allied Silk Association from 1909 until his death.

Boden read this paper at the Annual Meeting of the Silk Association of Great Britain and Ireland, held in London on the 15th February, 1905. The *Manchester Courier* reported that 'The meeting warmly thanked Mr. Boden for his paper, and obtained that gentleman's consent to its publication' (*Manchester Courier*, 16 Feb 1905, p. 9). This suggests it was printed in the British Association's annual report, although the American Association's March publication date probably preceded any British appearance.

Boden's paper is important for correcting the notion that Samuel Cunliffe Lister was the first to spin waste silk in Great Britain. Others at the meeting concurred: 'Several speakers expressed satisfaction that the statement had been corrected, though they did not wish to rob Lord Masham of the honour of having invented machinery for dealing with silk waste' (*Manchester Courier*, 16 Feb 1905, p. 6). Importantly, Boden highlighted the precarious nature of the spun silk trade due to the rapid and wide fluctuation in the price of both raw material and finished product; he also provided comparative information about the wages of workpeople in the industry.

# 29

# BODEN, JOSEPH. 'THE SPUN SILK INDUSTRY OF ENGLAND'

## *XXXIII Annual Report of the Silk Association of America*, 1905, pp. 95–100.

The following very interesting paper, by Mr. Joseph Boden (Messrs, Kidd, Boden & Co., Manchester),[1] was read at the Annual Meeting of the Silk Association of Great Britain and Ireland, held in London, England, on the 15th of February, 1905. Its luminous treatment of an important branch of the silk industry entitles it to a wide publicity among progressive silk manufacturers everywhere, and the Silk Association of America therefore reproduces it in its annual report, expressing at the same time the Association's appreciation of Mr. Boden's admirable monograph, which he entitles:

### Some observations on the rise and progress of the Spun silk industry

The spun silk industry cannot, like woolen, cotton and flax, lay claim to any great antiquity, for so far as I have been able to discover, the first mill for spinning silk yarns from waste silk[2] was that of Messrs. Wm. Thompson & Co., at Galgate, near Lancaster, which was established in the year 1792, when Messrs. Armstrong, Noble & Thompson bought a corn mill called "Ellel Mill," which then occupied the site of the present silk mill. This firm was converted into a limited liability company in 1869, and two of the gentlemen who were then directors are connected with the concern to-day.[3] The first silk spinning firm established on the Continent, that of Messrs. J. S. Alioth & Co., commenced operations in Bale in 1822, was transferred to Arlesheim in 1824, and existed till 1872, afterwards being amalgamated with others and becoming Chançel, Veillon, Alioth & Co.[4] This firm was subsequently turned into a limited liability company as the Société Industrielle pour la Schappe, and is now the largest producer in the world of silk yarns, Mr. W. Alioth, grandson of the founder, being one of the chief directors.[5]

### More pioneers

It would appear that at first the demand for spun silk was not a very extensive one, for within the next forty years the only other firms in the trade here were seven,

DOI: 10.4324/9780429274190-35

viz., Reade & Co., Congleton;[6] Hinde & Co., Lancaster (failed);[7] John Hadwen & Sons, Kebroyd (failed);[8] J. Holdforth & Sons, Leeds and Congleton (failed);[9] J. and T. Brocklehurst & Sons, Macclesfield;[10] E. Fisher & Co., Huddersfield;[11] and Lister & Co., Manningham, three of whom are still in active operation. There is a very common but erroneous impression that Mr. S. C. Lister, now Lord Masham, was the pioneer of the spun silk industry in this country, and possibly this has arisen from a paragraph in a book entitled "Fortunes Made in Business."

Mr. Lister was not born until about a quarter of a century after the establishment of Messrs. Thompson's business. Waste silk was shipped to England and the Continent long before the period referred to in the paragraph above mentioned, for you will see by the catalogue (produced) of the East India Company's sales of raw silk in 1802, there were large quantities of raw silk arriving in this country at that time, whilst waste silk was obviously being largely produced at the same period, and must have been commonly in use. This was a common article of import in the year 1835, as shown in the catalogue produced of that date, and it must also have been imported at a much earlier period.[12]

## A fluctuating and speculative trade

The business in this country appears to have taken its rise about the time of the French Revolution, and no doubt the disturbances there induced the commencement of operations on this side. The trade for many years seems to have been of a fluctuating and speculative character, arising no doubt from the fact that in former times silk worms were subject to diseases, for which cures and remedies have since to a large extent been found, but the consequences were, in those days, that the crops varied very greatly in quantity, and prices therefore were irregular, especially in the period from about 1862 onwards,[13] during which time China raw silk approximately varied in value from 13s. to 28s. per lb., whilst the variation of Italian and other fine silks was even greater. Naturally, when raw silk was at these high prices, which existed for a number of years, it created a great demand for spun silk yarns, more or less to take the place of trams and organzines[14] for weaving purposes. I am told on the best authority that in 1793 the price of waste silk suitable for making cops was then about 5s. per lb., whilst the silk yarn on cops sold from about 17s. to 17s. 6d. per lb., upon which obviously there must have been, even in those days, a very large margin of profit, but about 1870–76, 2–60's boiled off long spun yarn was sold from 27s. to 31s. per lb.,[15] and as good a yarn as that sold at 27s. has within the past three years been obtainable at 6s. 3d. per lb. It must be borne in mind, however, that during the former period the production of yarn in England was not nearly so great as it is at present, because in those days the spinners were fewer in number and the production not so large, partly because the speed at which they were running the spinning frames was probably not more than an average of 2–3,000 revolutions per minute, whilst to-day it is as much as 7–9,000.

## A booming period

During this period, 1870–6, which appears to have been one of the most prosperous in the history of the trade, I have given buyers 10s. per lb. clear profit upon their purchase of a year before, and made a profit myself on each occasion by the buying and selling. Whilst I do not know what spinners at that time were making per lb., I have a very good idea that it must have been, for those who were favorably situated and not heavily under contract, as much as 15s. per lb. The demand which caused prices to advance in the manner described was largely for yarns for the lace and fancy dress goods trades, the latter taking heavy warps of 2–60's blued,[16] the weft being made from black polished cotton. These dress goods, which were light and fashionable, went to the United States in great quantities for many years, but owing to the institution of heavy tariffs there, the trade was completely ruined, nearly every one connected with it having either retired or gone into other branches of business, so that this demand for spun silk yarns has probably gone for ever.

## Unprofitable industry on the whole

On the whole the silk spinning industry has not been a profitable one, as there are now only 25 firms left in England, which, with the exception of the six mentioned earlier in my paper,[17] have all been established within the past 40 or 50 years, whilst in that period 16 firms have failed and five have retired from business, three because they saw no prospect of making a current profit. During the past 40 years the prices of waste silk have varied enormously, China waste between 2s. and 10s. 6d., mixed French between 1s. 10d. and 9s. 6d., China tussah waste between 5½d. and 3s. 1d., and other wastes in proportion. There is, therefore, room for a great deal of discretion on the part of a producer as to when he should purchase his raw material, and when retire from the market, so that a successful spinner has many things to follow in the way of fashions, fluctuations of raw material, etc., besides managing the production of his yarns. One advantage of the adversity which has existed in this trade to a considerable extent, and with few exceptions during the past 15 years, has been to improve the methods of dressing, preparing and spinning, so that there never has been a period when yarn has been spun in such a satisfactory manner as is the case at present. I cannot help thinking that if the world's production of silk, and consequently silk waste, continues to increase as it has done during the past generation, the raw material may ultimately overtake the spindles, and thus induce a lower range of values, a better demand, and an improved margin of profit to everyone connected with the industry, for I think, compared with other branches of trade, the spun silk business is not on an average reasonably remunerative, taking into consideration the skill and capital required to conduct it.

## Foreign spinners successful

On the whole, during the last generation, the Continental silk spinners appear to have been more successful than those at home, judging from the profits made by the limited companies and other private concerns of which one has knowledge. During the last year, however, I have every reason to believe that results there were no better than here, or even so good, because Continental spinners and dressers had much larger stocks of raw material in proportion to their production than was the case with home spinners, the consequence being that they must have suffered much more heavily from depreciation than was the case at home, the fall in values in eighteen months being about 30 to 35 per cent.

## The world's production of silk yarns

It may interest you to know that an approximate estimate of the spun silk spindles in the whole of the world puts them at about 660,000, spread over France, Switzerland, Italy, Germany, Austria, England, America, China, Japan, and India, though the three last are of little consequence. I make it that the world's production of silk yarns is about 15½ million lbs. per annum, say 11 million lbs. on the Continent, 3 million lbs. in England, and 1½ million lbs. in China, Japan, America and India. Of the world's production some 20 per cent. is English, whilst about one-third of the world's production is produced by two of the 29 spinning and dressing firms on the Continent. As you may take it that on an average 3 lbs. waste are required for every 1 lb. of yarn produced (taking into consideration all qualities, of which a very large proportion is very common), the total amount of waste silk consumed during a year must be some 45 million lbs., whilst the value of the world's production of yarns at an average price say of 6s. 6d. per lb. would be about £5,000,000. In addition, there are, of course, the by-products, such as noils, of which at least some 10 or 12 million lbs. per annum must be produced, the price of which is as fluctuating as any other article connected with spun silk. For example, three years ago qualities of Schappe noils were selling at 1¼d.[18] per lb. to 1½d. per lb., which are now worth 8d. per lb., and other qualities of white noils, which were then about 2d. per lb., have been recently bought at as much as 1s. 5½d. per lb. It is an interesting matter for consideration how it arises, as before mentioned, that the Continental spinners have been so much more successful than their competitors here, and I will endeavor to give the reason so far as I am able to account for it. In the first place they largely produce yarn called Schappe, from which the gum is not totally discharged in macerating before dressing, and consequently it gives the fibre a resistance which enables them to dress upon a different system, viz., upon the circular frame, which economizes in the dressing to the extent of about on an average 4d. per lb., the labor cost of dressing in this country being about 8d. per lb., and that on the Continent about half for a similar class of material.

## Wages abroad

The workpeople there are about as well paid as at home, but they work 66 hours per week, against 54½ hours here. In Switzerland women and girl workers get about fcs. 2.50,[19] or equal to about 2s. per day, and men dressers and mechanics from fcs. 3.50 to fcs. 5, or equal to about 2s. 9d. to 4s. per day, so that practically there is no difference between these wages and those earned by our workpeople. Our spinners' and doublers' (women) wages range from 8s. to 12s., and dressers 21s. per week on an average.

I am therefore led to believe that one of the principal economies that they make abroad in the production of yarn is in the dressing, for a difference of 4d. per lb. in that respect on the average cost of yarn will be equal to about 5 per cent. I have no doubt also that in working the material in the Schappe state they obtain better yields from a given material, which will, of course, make a further saving, besides which a good many mills on the Continent are turned by water, which also supplies the power for electric lighting. In France also it must not be forgotten that they have an advantage, inasmuch as when we send yarns into their markets they charge us a duty of fcs. 0.85 to fcs. 1.40 per kilo., but when they ship yarns to England to compete with our productions they are admitted duty free, which makes a difference of 5 to 7½ per cent. against our English producer. In the United States, as most of you are aware, the duty is still more excessive, having been adjusted with the object of keeping out the English spun silk yarns as much as possible, and amounting as it does to some 35 per cent. of the value of the yarns. This object, however, has not been accomplished, because I find the total shipments of yarn to America from the Continent and England are:

| | |
|---|---|
| 1903. Schappe yarn | 1,634,986 lbs. |
| 1903. English yarn | 360,026 lbs. |

I cannot give the particulars for 1904, as they are not yet published.[20]

## Silk spinning in the United States

Before the year 1899 English spinners monopolized the bulk of the American trade in silk yarns to the extent of 60 to 75 per cent., but afterwards the Continental spinners seem to have been more successful in catering for the demand, insomuch as they are able to produce Schappe at a lower price than English yarns, therefore it enters that market under a lower rate of duty. The duty in America is graduated according to the price, the higher the price the higher the duty, ranging as it does from 20 cents per lb. and 15 per cent. on yarn worth $1 per lb., to 60 cents and 15 per cent. on yarn worth $2.50 and upwards. No doubt the import duty in the States was originally intended to foster the spun silk industry there, which it has done to some extent, for although there are only four spinners in that country, these could not have existed at all unless there had been heavy import duties. I have been told there are other people quite ready to embark in silk spinning on that side, and supply all the wants of their manufacturers, but they are never sure that some alteration might not be made in the tariffs, and in such case they are well aware that the machinery, which is mostly imported, and upon which high duties will have been paid, would be almost valueless. A silk spinning concern of any size requires a large capital, especially when such high prices through freight and duty have to be paid for machinery, therefore people in the States hesitate to embark in what becomes under such circumstances a speculative business, even though the possibilities of profit are so large. In alluding to these fiscal tariffs I wish it to be distinctly understood that it is not with any political intention, but simply with the object of trying to arrive at the reason of the spun silk industry being in such an unsatisfactory state, as has been the case for some time, and in order, if possible, to find a remedy.

## Some difficulties

I am quite aware that it would be a somewhat difficult matter to macerate, dress, and produce Schappe yarn in this country, as is done on the Continent, partly owing to the unpleasant odor which is raised by the acid used in contact with the silk waste in the macerating process, which our sanitary inspectors and river conservators might not be disposed to allow, although this difficulty might not be altogether insurmountable with energy and enterprise on the part of spinners. But I fear another of the difficulties is that in this country, as macerating has only been carried on to a very small extent, it is only understood by very few people, though this might be obviated by importing workpeople from the Continent who are accustomed to the process, and who would be obtainable. Of course, this would entail both enterprise and expense, and I am afraid, when spinners are not making a fair return on their capital, that they very often naturally hesitate to go to any expense for which they cannot see some immediate result in the shape of profit. I do not find, so far as my researches have gone, that the Continental mills are superior to well-equipped mills at home in the preparing and spinning departments, nor in the speed at which the spindles are turned, neither do I find that the yarns that they can produce from a given material are better in quality than those produced at home by spinners with similar equipments. As regards the dressing to which I have before alluded, a new frame has just been completed by the joint efforts of an English and French patentee, which it is expected will work either boiled off or Schappe materials at a price which has never been possible hitherto, either by English flat frames or the circular frames used abroad: these machines will have a very large productive capacity, and are expected to improve the yields. This should be a great advantage, especially to home producers, in removing one of the principal causes of the extra cost of production compared with Continental dressers.

## English combine impracticable

On the Continent several of the leading firms consist of combinations and amalgamations which have taken place at different times. These seem to work satisfactorily, and during the past two years fresh combinations have taken place, three firms being merged into one company of dressers and spinners, and four other firms into two companies, with the object, I suppose, of cheapening production and preventing competition. It does not, however, appear possible to arrange a combination here amongst silk spinning firms, the extent of which vary so materially, and the amalgamation of which would present such serious difficulties in valuations, etc., these difficulties in other branches of business having led in many cases to disastrous results after the combinations have been made.

## Notes

1 The partnership between Francis Kidd (1845–1888) and Joseph Boden (1850–1910), silk and linen merchants at Manchester, Dundee and Belfast, was dissolved as of 30 November 1893, reflecting the death of Kidd some years earlier. The name of the firm was retained even after Boden's death in 1910, until its closure in 1966.

2 Arthur Young, in his *Six Months' Tour through the North of England* (1770), described a spun silk yarn mill in Kendal:

> They receive the waste silk from London, boil it in soap, which they call scowering, then it is combed by women (there are about 30 or 40 of them) and spun, which article employs about 100 hands; after this it is doubled and dressed, and sent back again to London. This branch is upon the increase.
>
> (vol. 3, p. 173)

3 Of the original partners of the firm, James Noble sold his share to William Thompson in 1807. William Thompson was succeeded by his son Thomas Thompson, who sold out in 1840. John Armstrong (1749–1829) had been succeeded by his third son John Armstrong jun. (1786–1858) who then became the owner. Upon the younger Armstrong's death, his brother Richard Baynes Armstrong (1789–1867), a barrister, took charge of the business. The death of this last successor to the original partners led to the firm's acquisition and incorporation as a limited company in 1869. In 1957, the company became a subsidiary of Patons and Baldwins, and it was closed in 1971.

4 Johann Siegmund Alioth (1788–1850) was the founder. The precise date of establishment and the move to Arlesheim vary in different accounts. It became Chancel, Veillon, Alioth et Cie from 1873 to 1881, but financial difficulties forced liquidation of the family partnership and incorporation as a company, Industrie-Gesellschaft für Schappe. The Arlesheim business was finally closed in 1977.

5 The son of founder Johann Sigmund Alioth was Daniel Auguste Alioth (1816–1889), who became a partner in the company in 1838, and after the death of his father, became principal manager around 1851. His son, (Sigmund) Wilhelm Alioth (1845–1916), remained connected with the business after its change to a limited company.

6 George Reade (1760–1838) built Stonehouse Green Mill for cotton spinning in 1784. He moved into silk throwing early in the nineteenth century, then into waste silk spinning by 1829. He was joined in the business by his sons. The eldest, John Fielder Reade (1799–1843) was head from the death of his father until 1842. In 1852, the name

of the firm changed from George Reade and Sons to Reade and Co., reflecting the withdrawal of the other Reade brothers. Arthur Isaac Solly (1829–1905), son-in-law of John Fielder Reade was principal partner from 1851 to 1890, followed by his son Arthur John Solly (1857–1926). The firm became a limited company in 1907.

7 Walter Alan Hinde (1801–1864), a worsted spinner, became a proprietor in the Ridge Lane Mill in 1840 and from that time the firm was known as Hinde and Co. The firm was continued after his death by his partner Edward Mason (1813–1882) who failed in 1877. See 'The Ridge Lane Silk Mill', *Lancaster Gazette*, 17 Jun 1876, p. 8.

8 Founded in 1800 by John Hadwen (1773–1852) as a cotton spinning mill, silk spinning was probably introduced in the 1830s, and became the primary activity of the mill by the 1840s. The firm passed to the founder's sons, Thomas Wilson Hadwen (1803–1855), John Wilson Hadwen (1805–1862), Sidney Hadwen (1807–1889) and George Burgess Hadwen (c1816–1895). Thomas died in 1855, Sidney withdrew in 1858, and John Wilson died in 1862, leaving the remaining brother, George, as head. He retired in 1892 and the business passed to his sons George Arthur Hadwen (1849–1894) and Frederick Walter Hadwen (1850–1921). The latter was a principal partner at the time of the firm's failure in 1901.

9 James Holdforth (1778–1861), started as a worsted spinner, but in 1807 began spinning silk waste. His sons Joseph Dempsey Holdforth (1816–1864) and James Holdforth jun. (born 1820) entered the business by the 1840s, with James managing the Congleton branch. A couple years after Joseph's accidental death from being thrown by his pony, James gave up the Congleton mill to run the main business in Leeds. However, in 1876, the firm petitioned for liquidation by arrangement.

10 The origins of this firm date back to 1745 as button manufacturers. It was the sons of button-maker John Brocklehurst (1754–1839), John Brocklehurst jun. (1788–1870) and Thomas Brocklehurst (1791–1870), who made the change to silk weaving, inaugurating the firm of J. and T. Brocklehurst. John's sons, William Coare Brocklehurst (1818–1900) and Henry Brocklehurst (1819–1870), as well as Thomas's sons Thomas Unett Brocklehurst (1824–1886) and Charles Brocklehurst (c1827–1884) joined the partnership which became J. and T. Brocklehurst and Sons. William Coare's sons William B. Brocklehurst (1851–1929) and Arthur J. P. Brocklehurst (1852–1926) took the firm into the next century, when it became a limited company in 1912.

11 The firm was established by John Fisher (1767–1840) as John Fisher and Co. His son Edward Fisher (1804–1888) entered the family business which became Edward Fisher and Brothers in 1839. By 1851, when the firm was Edward Fisher and Co., it employed ninety-nine men, sixty-two women, forty boys and fifty-nine girls in silk spinning. Of the next generation, Charles Edward Gregg Fisher (1840–1928) and Sharples Fisher (1845–1921) entered the partnership. The elder brother probably retired when he was made a baronet in 1887. Sharples Fisher remained until the business was closed and sales of equipment took place in 1897.

12 A newspaper account of the lecture provides further detail of these exhibits:

> he produced a catalogue of the East India Company's sales of waste in 1802, and read a placard announcing a public sale by auction on the 9th September, 1835, at the warehouse of Messrs. Barnby, Faulkner, and Co., Dale-street, Manchester, of 60 bales of silk waste from St. Petersburg and Riga, partially damaged. It was evident, therefore, that waste silk was a common article of import in 1835, as it must also have been at a very much earlier period.
>
> (*Manchester Courier*, 16 Feb 1905, p. 6)

13 Pebrine, a disease of the silkworm, caused the eventual collapse of the French and Italian silk industry in 1865, making supplies scarce.

14 Wefts and warps, respectively.

15 The '2' in front of the yarn count number (60s) indicates two yarns twisted together. Such doubled yarns were normally used for warps. In the silk system, two 120s singles doubled together make a 60s 2-fold yarn. The count, like cotton, is based on the number of 840-yard hanks in a pound. At first waste silk spinners used the *short spinning* system whereby the waste was combed in its natural gum, then chopped it into short equal lengths of one or two inches before degumming, carding and spinning. Long spinning boiled the waste first to take out the gum, then used gilling machines to comb the silk, thus preserving the fibre length as well as increased lustre and strength in the spun fibre.

16 Blueing is tinting with indigo dye to neutralise natural yellowish tone of the fibre and make the silk appear whiter.

17 Seven firms are mentioned earlier; this may be an indication that Boden's paper had a prior version, the addition of a seventh firm being an amendment.

18 Noils are the short-stapled residues of cocoon silk processing. Schappe silk is partially degummed by a fermentation process that leaves about 10–12 percent gum.

19 Swiss francs.

20 See page 94 of this Annual Report. Franklin Allen, Secretary. (The total imports of spun silk in the United States for the fiscal year 1904 is given on that page as 2,053,274 pounds [ed.].)

## Editorial Headnote

### Rayner, Hollins, aka *Filsoie* (pseud.). 'Silk Spinning: I. Introduction', *Textile Manufacturer*, 27:317 (15 May 1901), pp. 147–149; 'VII. Silk wastes', 27:322 (15 Oct 1901), pp. 335–337; 'VIII. Silk wastes (continued)', 27:323 (15 Nov 1901), pp. 367–368; 'XXV. Waste Products', 29:340 (15 Apr 1903), pp. 119–120.

These articles were first published under the pseudonym 'Filsoie'. Not long after their serialised appearance in the *Textile Manufacturer*, the collected articles were revised as a technical monograph, *Silk Throwing and Waste Silk Spinning*, released by Scott, Greenwood and Son in December 1903, and priced at 5s. The author is given as Hollins Rayner, who cites in the preface his many years in the silk trade. Despite all this experience, he seems to have left little record. Neither did he write anything else under this name. Hence, there is a suspicion that Hollins Rayner is also a pseudonym. The preface is signed with initials only, and gives no place of writing. If the author was concealing his identity, it is possible his merchant career included a venture that he wished to obscure. However, given his knowledge of Eastern markets, it seems more likely that the author was part of the Rayner family who established the merchant firm Rayner, Heusser and Co. in Shanghai around 1914. Charles Ernest Rayner (1859–1953), one of the principals of the firm, is a candidate. In 1896, he had been admitted a partner to Carlowitz and Co., a Hamburg-based firm active in the Chinese market. 'Hollins' might be a Chinese misrendering of Charles that was adopted as a nickname.

Another possibility is that authorship was a collaboration with principals of the company William Hollins and Co. Ltd., cotton, merino and silk spinners of Nottingham. The founder died in 1890 and, at the time, the firm was in the hands of his son William Hollins (c1863–1918), and nephews Robert Arthur Hollins (1837–1919) and Henry Ernest Hollins (1842–1920).

The *Textile Manufacturer*, as might be expected, had warm praise for the book: 'To most of our readers this book will come as an old friend under a new title, for it comprises the series of articles on "Silk Spinning," by Filsoie, which first appeared in *The Textile Manufacturer*'. The writer

> shows he is [as] thoroughly at home in the operations, tricks, and customs of the different silk-producing countries, as in the ways in which silk is merchanted and bought in manufacturing centres. . . . [L]ater chapters show that the author is as well acquainted with the mechanical side of the matter as with the silk classing and buying department.
>
> (29:348, 15 Dec 1903, p. 409)

The book sold well on both sides of the Atlantic, and the publisher issued a second edition in January 1921, but it is not clear if Rayner was personally involved in this version as the older preface was repeated. In 1947, when Frederick Oliver

Howitt (born 1903) published his *Bibliography of the Technical Literature on Silk* (London: Hutchinson's Scientific and Technical Publications), Rayner's text remained the most comprehensive on the subject of spun silk.

Where the 1903 text provides additional clarification to the earlier serialised version, the amendment has been included here in square brackets.

# 30

# RAYNER, HOLLINS, AKA *FILSOIE* (PSEUD.). 'SILK SPINNING, SILK WASTES, AND WASTE PRODUCTS'

*Textile Manufacturer*, (15 May 1901), pp. 147–149; (15 Oct 1901), pp. 335–337; (15 Nov 1901), pp. 367–368; (15 Apr 1903), pp. 119–120.

## Introduction

Although much information is obtainable in this country regarding the weaving of silk goods, very little seems to be understood about the earlier processes of silk working. The terms raw, waste, thrown, spun, or schappe silk are very vague even to the ordinary manufacturer, though he may use silk in conjunction with his cotton or worsted goods, and by others the terms are still less understood. The English silk industry has long been in a declining condition, although anyone looking in the principal drapers' windows cannot but be impressed by the growing popularity of the fibre. It is lamentable to have to admit that instead of progressing, as is the case with most of our other textile fabrics, silk has become less and less an English industry, and unless something is done, and done quickly, there appears the chance of it being entirely overshadowed by Continental competitors. A few years ago silk manufacturing was a most profitable industry in this country; but unfortunately, when import tariffs were removed and foreign competition began to be felt, there was a singular lack of energy displayed, and little attempt was made to keep abreast of the times. No trade has suffered more from conservatism; machines have not been modernised, and many in use at the present time have been in existence for a generation. Some manufacturers are still clamouring for protection as the only means of saving the industry, although the possibility of combating foreign competition is demonstrated by the very few energetic firms who have proved themselves capable of competing against all comers in the open market.

Of late years some cotton and worsted manufacturers have turned their attention to silk, and instead of looking to Macclesfield and Spitalfields as the centres of the British silk industry, we now turn to Bradford and district, or to Glasgow,

 DOI: 10.4324/9780429274190-36

whilst Manchester and the neighbouring East Lancashire towns get through a fair amount of spun silk for shirtings, zephyrs, striped goods, etc.; and although there probably never were fewer who could strictly call themselves "silk manufacturers," it is likely there never were more users of silk, even in the palmy days of the trade. This new life tends to bring the trade into line with other textile industries, and as cotton and worsted manufacturers find there are no great difficulties in the manipulation of silk, the number is likely to increase rather than diminish.

Of the two branches, spinning and throwing,[1] the former, as applied to the treatment and preparation of so-called waste silk, is by far the more important in this country, for while the latter has been a declining trade for the last fifteen years or more, there is to-day in England waste silk machinery capable of turning out more spun silk yarn than ever before; so in the gloomy picture of the decline of the silk trade it is pleasant to be able to record one branch which has managed to hold its own. Throwing, as one of the three distinct sections into which the English silk industry is divided, – viz, throwing, spinning, and manufacturing, – seems to be the branch in which we, as a nation, have failed altogether to keep pace with Continental throwsters. Our throwsters complain of the cheapness of labour abroad, which no doubt is a very important factor; but here again there has been lack of energy, with plenty of hard-headed conservatism, and a marked disinclination to do away with old-fashioned slow-running machinery, which ought to have been displaced long ago by speedier drums and spindles. In many mills the same old slow-running machines which have done service for fifty or more years still exist, though they are now only fit for the scrap heap, and would not be tolerated in any up-to-date Continental or American mill. Improvements in machinery can be traced to American and Continental sources, but they have not been generally adopted by English throwsters.

There is a large field open for our manufacturers, if they could and would cater better for the home market. At one time silk was looked upon as a luxury, but now, owing principally to the fact that a use has been found for waste silk which formerly was of little commercial value, its use as an article of adornment is practically universal. When it is borne in mind that for every 1 lb. of raw silk produced there is about 1½ lb. of unreelable silk remaining, and which, prior to the invention of silk spinning, was almost valueless, it will be at once recognised that there was a great possibility before an industry which would be able to use up this vast accumulation of waste. It is to this, then, that attention will be more particularly called, being far more elaborate and more interesting than throwing, although there will be a few notes on this as well, but more with a view to paving the way to spinning than with any attempt to give an exhaustive treatise on the manipulation of the raw silks in the process of making trams and organzines.[2]

## Silk Wastes

The term "silk waste" covers all classes of the raw silk which are unwindable and altogether unsuited for the throwing process. The term "waste," understood in the general sense as conveying the idea of something worthless or of no use, is quite a misnomer now. But, before the introduction of silk waste spinning, the refuse from the reeling and winding mills was indeed waste, there being at that time no use for it whatever, except for what could be combed and spun by distaff and spinning wheel, as still practised by peasantry in India and other Eastern countries. Considering that of all the silk spun by the silkworm more than half is useless for the throwster, it will readily be understood that there must have been a large accumulation of this material, and therefore a great future before an industry which could use up this so-called rubbish. Although there are a great many different grades and different classes of waste silk, there are really few distinct ways in which they are all produced, most, if not all, varieties being the waste from one or more of the following seven processes: –

1 The silkworm commences to spin its cocoon by first fastening itself to the twig of a tree or between two leaves. Where the worm is reared by the peasants in their cottages, the peasants use straws, to which the worms attach themselves. All this silk is unwindable, and too coarse and uneven to be of any use for the throwster, even if reelable. Naturally this first waste is very much mixed with straw and leaves, and is of a dull, coarse nature.
2 The cocoons are made up of layers of silk, and the outside ones, or the first spun by the worm, are too coarse and uneven for reeling, so the outer coating is stripped off and cast aside as waste.
3 As the silkworm nears the completion of its cocoon, the thread becomes finer and finer, insomuch that several of the last layers are made up of silk too fine to be strong enough to unwind, so that after the better or middle layers are reeled from the cocoon, the remaining part is discarded as useless for further reeling.
4 Among the cocoons there are some which are altogether unsuitable for reeling, included among which are the pierced cocoons. Although of no use for reeling, they are very acceptable to the silk-waste spinner.
5 During the process of reeling from the cocoon into hanks or skeins, the silk sometimes breaks, and in consequence there is waste made by the attendant in finding the true and sound thread.
6 Waste is produced in rereeling tsatlees into re-reels.[3]
7 All the waste produced in the throwster's mill, as described fully under the heading "Throwing."

Practically speaking, the various wastes are divided into two general classes – gum wastes and ordinary wastes. Gum wastes, whether home, European, or Eastern, are really all throwsters' wastes, and are especially adapted for the making of special yarns.[4]

*Steam Waste.* – The best known and most widely used silk waste in England is Canton filature waste, better known as steam waste. It is not a gum waste. There are two varieties, and several grades of each. The one which has generally found most favour with spinners is the "opened" waste, but owing to its lending itself so easily to adulteration, spinners are now paying more attention to the unopened quality. Opened steam waste is the unopened waste pulled out by the natives, who work among it with their fingers and teeth, opening out the hard knubs which have been formed when the wet waste has been thrown down by the reeler, and allowed to dry and mat together, on account of the natural gum [having hardened] which had [previously] been softened by the hot water in the basin attached to the reeling machine. Owing to the labour difficulty in China it is becoming more and more important that spinners accustom themselves to the use of unopened steam waste. There are really three grades of steam waste, which some years ago were known as "Selected," No. 1, and No. 2. But year by year the Chinaman seems to have got the better of the European silk inspector, and has let down the quality. In the "selected" he would leave a certain amount of No. 1, and in No. 1 he would put the No. 2, until at length the admixture of 1's and 2's was so much that No. 2 as a separate grade disappeared, all being mixed up with the No. 1, and passed as all No. 1. Naturally, the so-called "selected" got a greater percentage of No. 1, so that in time the European shippers decided to work up a better grade and call it "Extra selected." This latter came forward very nicely for a time; but gradually the Chinaman's cunning[5] got the better of the inspector, with the result that he again lowered the quality of the so-called "extra selected," and therefore the "selected." This process was again repeated, and there came a grade known as "Extra extra selected" steam waste, but this was likewise doomed to the fate of the former changes, and to-day there is known what is called the "Extra extra extra selected" steam waste, which in point of fact is to-day not so good as the old well-known "selected," and the "extra extra selected" is a mixture of the old 1's and 2's. The deterioration goes on year after year, each succeeding year being worse than the preceding one, and each season showing a gradual falling away from the standard established at the commencement of the season. It is a lamentable state of affairs, but so far the cunning Chinaman seems to have always managed to get the better of all the European inspectors, and so long as the present system of buying and passing of the waste is in vogue at Canton,[6] so long will the Chinaman be able to hoodwink the inspectors.

*Frisons* are cocoons with varying quantities of silk upon them which has been slightly pulled loose. Some qualities are full of wormy matter, but all are well liked by Continental spinners for schapping.[7] Wadding, or blaze, [which] is also used almost exclusively on the Continent, is the first silk spun by the worm – that is, the silk which is wrapped around the twigs or straws and leaves, and is in consequence full of such vegetable matters when sold to the spinner. The nature of the silk is dull, lustreless, and coarse. It is very heavily charged with gum, and consequently loses much when boiled off, and even then it is very inferior stuff. Wadding is a term also applied to silk which has been used as a packing inside the Chinaman's coat as a lining, and it may be of long fibre or otherwise. Frisons and cocoons are types which may come from all silk-producing countries.

Steam waste – that is, waste produced in the filature establishments in the Canton district – is the most widely used waste in England. Good waste is of a fair white colour, and in the gum state feels long and strong in staple, but is much subject to adulterations of a rotten nature, and brown in colour.

*Tussah Waste,* exported from [Shanghai], is of a dark brown colour. Usually known as Newchwang waste [and filature Tussah waste], it is nearly all spun in England, and used either for plush purposes or for dress goods. It is marketed in the waste in two grades, known as No. 1 and No. 2, which are packed quite separate in bales, and parcels are generally offered as 60 per cent. of No. 1 and 40 per cent. of No. 2, or 50 per cent. of each, written usually 60/40 and 50/50 respectively.[8]

*Nankin Buttons* is a gum waste from the interior of China, of exceptionally good white colour and lustre. The bulk of it is long in staple, but it is always mixed with so-called buttons, which are really small portions of silk slightly matted together, and, a worse fault still, cut into half-an-inch to one-and-a-half-inch lengths. This waste is exported from Shanghai.

*China Wastes* are from various sources, chiefly from English, French, and Italian throwsters. They are all long in staple. China soaped waste is from English and Scotch throwing mills. It feels soft, and its lustre has been hidden in the washing. French China is always bright, and not being weighted with soap often fetches a little more per pound than English silk. Italian and Swiss wastes are of the same nature.

*Shanghai Waste* is all gum waste, not quite so white as European silk, and harsher in feel. It is classed as fine white, fine yellow, coarse white, and coarse yellow. In the fine white are three well-known grades: Chintzah, which is the whitest and longest in staple; Hangchow, which is really a second picking or sorting over of the Chintzah grade, rather inferior in colour, not so long in staple, and more subject to twist waste and foreign matter; and the ordinary fine white, which is variable in colour, but good sound waste. The yellow varieties are produced in much smaller quantities, of similar qualities, but usually more mixed together, which really makes an inferior sort of article. Every sort is sold on its own merits; some spinners use only coarse varieties, and others only fine.

*Shanghai Szechuen* (or seychuen or sechuen) is a yellow waste, and the prefix Shanghai is to distinguish it from Canton waste of similar nature, sold as Canton szechuen. All Shanghai wastes were formerly offered as 1's, 2's, and 3's. Some shippers now continue this, but the No. 3 being very small in quantity and low in quality, parcels are often offered now as 1's and 2's. As the No. 3 is, however, still produced in the East, spinners are suspicious that in many cases it is judiciously mixed with the No. 2 portion by the expert Chinese packers. However that may be, proportions are generally 75% – No. 1, 25% – No. 2; or 70% – No. 1, 30% – No. 2; or 60% – No. 1, 30% – No. 2, 10% – No. 3. All these grades are always packed separately.

*Indian Waste.* – Of all the wastes used by spinners, the Indian wastes are the most mixed and unreliable. The colour varies from grey to yellow, but there is by far the larger proportion of yellow. The fibre of some is as fine and clean as the best China and Japan silks, whilst others are coarser than the punjum waste.[9] It is always subject to [an admixture of bits of] cotton, twist, black hairs, string, paper, etc. They are all gum wastes.

*Canton Gum Waste* is very similar in appearance to the re-reel waste, but is not so reliable, and is very often more mixed with black hairs, cotton, hemp, etc. No. 2

gum is now a very scarce article in this country, spinners finding it too much mixed with rubbish, and hence too costly in picking, etc.

*Re-reel* waste is a Canton gum waste produced in the mills where the Canton raws are re-reeled, just in the same manner as Shanghai gum in the more northern districts; but the former is of a softer nature, and has more lustre – in fact, Cantons are the most lustrous of all silks, but are of a creamy shade. The silk of Canton gum and steam waste is spun by the same genus of worm.

*Canton Szechuen Waste* is a yellow gum waste with a good, bright colour, but apt to be greasy. The production is very limited, and it comes forward in little lots of 5, 10, or 15 bales. It yields fairly well.

*Steam Punjums* are allied to both punjum waste and to steam waste. They are said to possess the virtues of both – i.e. they yield well and have the colour of steam,[10] and they combine the lustre of punjum.

*Punjum* has peculiar characteristics of its own, and is supposed by many people to be the most lustrous of all silks. It is a stringy waste in appearance, and loses very heavily in boiling off – something like 50 per cent. It is reeled from cocoons, a number of ends together, and put into book form very similar to the tsatlees, as described under the heading "Tsatlee Reel" in "Raw Silk"; but owing to the admixture of rice water, or some such substance, the threads mat together, and are consequently unwindable. In this form the waste is known as punjum books, which are divided into grades 1's, 2's, 3's, and 4's – 3's and 4's being the general run for English spinners, generally half-and-half. The waste is produced in exactly the same manner, except that no attempt is made to run it into a moss;[11] but, as an end breaks or runs off [during reeling], the waste is thrown.

*China Curlies* are a well-known waste shipped from Shanghai, and the quality and appearance are more allied to steam waste than to any other variety shipped from Canton. It is a greyish-white waste, somewhat harsh to the feel. The name "curly" is given to this waste on account of its being so full of little patches of material matted together, which have a certain resemblance to a curl of hair. The waste is much in favour both in this country and on the Continent, and as the crop is somewhat limited, many times the whole of the output is contracted for at the opening of the season. It is a commodity many speculators like to gamble with, the result being that many times, when the whole crop has been cornered, the price is many pence per pound over and above its value as compared with other classes of waste. Like most Shanghai wastes, curlies are to be had in three grades, but the No. 3 is so very inferior that few English spinners can afford to buy it on account of the extra expense necessary in picking out the sticks, string, and refuse, to say nothing of the trouble caused by some of these objects getting through the dressing, etc., having escaped the pickers in the first instance. Generally speaking, English spinners buy only the No. 1's, finding even the No. 2's too much trouble in working; but there are shippers who import the proportions 60 per cent. No. 1, 30 per cent. No. 2, and 10 per cent. No. 3, written 60/30/10. Curlies are generally shipped under a chop mark, the favourite being the "Yellow Pony" (or Peony), whilst such chops as the "Double Fighting Cock" and the "Gold Lion" are fairly well known. It must not be taken that *all* curlies are shipped under a chop mark, nor even that the best curlies have a particular name or trade mark. Some arrivals with no chop mark whatever are quite equal to any of the "Yellow Pony" chop shipped this season; but, as a general rule, spinners buying "to arrive"[12] wish to have the chop stipulated at the time of purchase, as a kind of semi-guarantee of quality, as the various wastes from the different filatures have a certain reputation.

*Shanghai Long Wastes* are the most expensive wastes shipped from that port. They are to be had from various inland districts, and are known under the different names of such places, though there is a great similarity in appearance and not much difference in their qualities and yields. They have very much the appearance of knubs, but are tapey and very long. They yield exceedingly well, and are of a good light colour. The annual production is comparatively small, and very few spinners can use them to advantage, on account of their high price. For particular special yarns where strength and evenness of thread are absolutely essential, Shanghai long waste is seen to advantage.

*Japan wastes.* – The best-known waste shipped from Yokohama is the Kikai Kibizzo, or Japan curlies. In appearance there is not much difference between this waste and China curlies, except that the former is generally of a better colour, and contains curls of larger size, longer staple, and consequently yields better. Japan wastes are more in request for Continental spinners than for England, being well suited for the schapping in vogue there. Just like the China curlies, Kikai Kibizzo is shipped in three grades, but the principal buying for this country is for No. 1's alone, although at times parcels 60/30/10 are freely offered.

*Iwashiro Noshi* is another waste which is fairly well known here by the spinners who use the very best class of wastes. What the Shanghai long waste is to Shanghai, so is Iwashiro Noshi to Japan. They are very similar, except that the latter is a better colour, and just as Kikai Kibizzo will fetch a better price than China curlies, so is Iwashiro Noshi more valuable than Shanghai long waste. The production is very limited.

*Noshito Joshiu* or Tamas is practically the lowest class of Japan waste which is shipped for consumption in England for the ordinary spinner, but there are many lower varieties from Japan which are well suited for continental schappe spinners. The reason why the latter can spin lower class wastes will be dealt with in a later article. Tamas are a stringy waste, not very good colour, and are subject to a certain amount of refuse. They are generally shipped in proportion 60/30/10.

## Silk Wastes (Continued)

Before passing on to European wastes, some details of the buying, inspecting, shipping, and landing of wastes from the East will not be without interest.

*Buying.* – As in most textile trades, so in the silk-spinning industry, spinners must anticipate their requirements to a certain extent, and buy "to arrive," or "futures." This latter term is, however, seldom made use of in the silk trade. Comparatively speaking, very little waste is sent over here on account of the shippers, most of them preferring to buy against orders;[13] and on this account, when some spinners had refrained from buying much "to arrive" last season, they found themselves short of material and with nothing much to be had on spot except at exorbitant prices. This was caused more especially, however, by the actual short crop, or possibly the holding back by the natives of all they could afford to do without selling. The buying "to arrive" is done by the spinners through merchants, who transmit the offers to Shanghai, Canton, or Yokohama, according to the kind of waste required, and the matter of quality is either fixed on certain standards which the merchant shows, or the spinner stipulates that it be equal to a certain shipment already had. In the absence of standards, the merchant undertakes to deliver the "season's average" – or, in other words, he contracts that his waste will be as good as the season affords, all due care being taken at the embarkation port that inferior waste is not shipped.

*Terms.* – The spinner buys on the "East India Company's Terms" – [generally written "Company's Terms."] It is understood, unless otherwise stipulated at the time of purchase, that the waste will be shipped from the port within four or six weeks after the placing of the order.

*Inspecting.* – The systems in vogue for inspecting at Canton, Shanghai, and Yokohama are very different, and much could be done in this respect to ensure better qualities and more uniformity in shipment, particularly so from Canton. In this latter place the shipper buys, say, a parcel of 50 bales of waste from a native dealer, who comes forward and tenders 50 bales already made up. The European inspector then picks out of the lot, wherever he may think fit, 3, 4, or 5 bales, and has them opened, and after examining them passes or rejects the parcel. If the lot is rejected, the Chinaman brings a further 50, which are subject to the same process, and so on until he has satisfied the inspector. It will be at once seen by one in the trade that this is a very lax method, for John Chinaman has these bales to sell, and sell them he will. If they are rejected by one inspector, he will tender them to another, in the hope that he may be lucky or unlucky enough to cause good bales out of the run to be opened, and so pass the lot. There is also another objection to this mode of procedure, for it is generally supposed that at all tricks of deceit and cunning the Chinaman stands in the first rank,[14] and he is certainly very clever in making up bales in such a way that the outer coating of the layers of which the bales are made up are composed of really good silk, whilst the inside is cunningly made up of inferior waste. This is a common fault of Canton wastes of all descriptions. The only remedy seems to be that the waste be delivered in bulk to the shippers' go-downs, to be inspected by them in bulk, and packed by them just as is done in Shanghai and Yokohama, from which ports the waste is far more uniform and more reliable. The majority of the shippers at Canton say that it is impossible to do this in the case of Canton wastes; but latterly, on account of the many serious complaints of inferiority sent over from this side, one well-known shipper has adopted this course, with the result that he is the most reliable shipper of steam wastes at the present time. It has only been done so far by way of an experiment, and it remains to be seen if it pays, so compelling other shippers to do likewise. Competitors, of course, report that it is not a success; but anything which would have the effect of raising the present standard of wastes from that market would be welcomed by the trade.

*Packing and Shipping*. – At Canton the wastes are all packed in small bales of one picul each (a picul is 133$^1/_3$ lb.), without press-packing, but they are well bound with cane, and the wrapping is matting. Shanghai wastes, which are packed under European supervision, and in the shippers' own go-downs, are made up in three-picul bales, and are press-packed. The Japan bales are very cumbersome, being packed similar to the Canton bales, except that instead of one-picul bales they come over in three-picul bales. Some Japan bales are, however, press-packed like the Shanghai bales. The shipping is, of course, undertaken by the European shippers out in the East, and, generally speaking, the documents covering the shipments are passed through the Eastern banks with a bill at four, five, or six months' sight, to be accepted here by the merchant and returned to the bank, which holds the waste until the bill is retired, when the merchant gets the necessary release order.

*Landing*. – On arrival in London the waste is at once taken in hand by the Dock Company or wharfingers, and, immediately it is landed, the gross weights of each bale are carefully taken, and a certain number of each parcel tared, and the average tare of those taken is reckoned on the whole parcel. No ¼ or ½ lb. are reckoned: supposing the average tare is 8¼, 8½, or 8¾ lb., the tare allowed is 9 lb. per bale, and any bale weighing, say, 129¾ lb. gross, even though the average tare were 8¼ lb., would only be chargeable 120 lb. net. When the bales have been landed, lotted, and examined for damage, dock samples are drawn from every fifth or tenth bale according to request, and sent down to the buyer, and on receipt of these he must decide whether the quality is up to the standard on which he bought. Once having passed these impartial dock samples, he is held to have passed the waste, and has no claim for inferiority should he be disappointed with the waste when the bulk is delivered at his mill, unless he can prove some very flagrant case of false packing, and even then he must trust to the merchant from whom he bought. Naturally it will often be in the latter's interest to meet his client when possible, and do as well for him as he can.

*European Wastes*. – Little need be said about the various qualities of these wastes, as all have very similar characteristics, and are, practically, with the exception of the French and Italian knubs, the products of the silk-throwing mills, as described under the heading "Throwing." Knubs, however, are the long wastes produced in the filatures where the raw silk is wound from the cocoon, and have the same appearance and characteristics as the Shanghai long waste and Iwashiro Noshi, except that they are finer and of a more "classical" nature. These knubs are particularly in request by the Continental spinners.

Of the many varieties of European wastes, the following are the best known: – French China, Swiss China, Italian China, French mixed, Piedmont, and Spanish waste. *French China*, as its name implies, is the waste produced in the French throwing mills working China raw silk. *Swiss China* is the same produced in Switzerland; *Italian China* the same produced in Italy. *French mixed* is grey and yellow waste from the throwing mills, and is composed of Bengal, Canton, and

Japan, as well as Italian and French wastes. It is somewhat subject to cotton, but is quite a favourite gum waste. *Piedmont waste*, as the name implies, is the fine Italian yellow waste made in the throwing mills producing organzines and trams from Piedmont raw silk. It is one of the most expensive yellow wastes, yielding very well, and producing a strong, lustrous yarn [of a very elastic nature].

These European wastes are not bought on what are known as "Company's Terms," but in the ordinary way of trade, the spinner getting credit, or at least getting the silk delivered before he pays for it, contrary to the custom with Eastern wastes. In this way he can ascertain, on the arrival of the bulk, whether it is up to sample or not. There are faults, however, which cannot easily be detected until the waste has been boiled or otherwise treated, so if he has any doubts about it at all, the spinner, immediately on arrival, takes steps to ascertain if it is free from twist or crape – i.e. hard twisted threads.

Given these brief notes on a few of the many varieties of silk waste, from which it will have been noted that the colour, the diameter of thread, and the packing are so varied as delivered to the spinner, and being also a much tangled mass of all lengths of fibre, some bales hard press-packed and other qualities loosely packed, it will be understood that preparatory to boiling or schapping – i.e. degumming – a certain amount of opening, sorting, and mixing will be absolutely necessary.

. . .

## Waste Products

Having particularised all the processes through which dressed silk, long drafts and short drafts, are passed to convert into yarn, we have now only to follow the course of the waste products of a silk-spinning establishment. These are: silk noils, the production of the dressing frame; fly, the very short fibres thrown out in the cards; roller and leather laps in the drawing machinery; roving waste in the roving frames; soft waste in the spinning frames; singles and double waste in winding and twisting; burnt fibre in the gassing process.

Burnt fibre is sold as waste, and used for artificial manure purposes.

Roving waste and soft spinning waste can be washed to free it from grease and dirt, and be then dressed, so converting it again into drafts and noils.

Hard single and folded waste can be dressed on hand machines, or put through a garnett machine.[15]

The longest kind of roller and leather lap waste can be fed into the spreading machine, converted into sliver, and mixed with the lowest quality going through the machinery, putting one or two ends up in the first head of the drawing. The short fibre can be mixed with roving waste and dressed.

The longest-fibred fly waste is recarded, thus being made into a sliver and mixed in the drawing frames. The shortest-fibred fly can be put through the same machinery as exhaust noil.

*Noils* are first opened by a scutching machine and then carded. The carded slivers are afterwards taken to a Derby doubler.

*Derby doubling.* – This process is carried out for the purpose of winding a certain number of carded slivers together on to a wooden core or drum. From 12 to 80 cans of sliver can be placed side by side on either side of a slanting table A, Fig. 96, and the sliver is passed over the spoon levers B, thence through the guide plates C to the wooden drum D. This latter is revolved by means of fluted rollers E, F, and the slivers all wound into one mass called a lap, and compressed by the pressure roller G, which, being mounted in slot bearings, rises as the slivers on the drum D increase in diameter. If a can becomes empty or an end breaks between the can and the receiving rollers, the spoon lever is arranged to drop and automatically stop the machine, so ensuring an equal number of ends of sliver throughout the length of the lap. The laps are next mounted behind a combing machine, which may be of the Noble, Lister, or Heilmann type.

*Combing.* A comb is for the purpose of removing from the silk all nops, dirt, straws, for eliminating fibres below a pre-determined length, and delivering the combed material in the form of a sliver. The Heilmann principle is a very good one for silk fibres, and is illustrated in Fig. 97. The lap is placed at A, and is revolved slowly by rollers under it, the sliver passing to the pressure roller B and thence to the feed grid C. This latter consists of two smooth brass grids into which fit the pins of the overhead comb D. When the nip E is closed, the feed comb D being lifted, the grid moves back for a portion of sliver; then the comb D descends, penetrating the sliver. Then, the lower hinge of the nip being opened, the silk is traversed through the mouth of the nip, which closes and so holds fast a tuft of silk projecting so that the teeth of the comb F, on the comb revolving, can comb or dress the fibres. The short fibres (exhaust noils) G which collect on the teeth of the comb are removed by a quickly revolving brush H, which deposits the combings on to a doffer roller J, from which they are stripped as a broad fleece by the doffer comb K and drop into the box L. When the tuft of silk is sufficiently combed the rollers M are operated in such a manner as to lay hold of the combed portion, and so draw the other, or uncombed, end of the tuft through the revolving teeth of the cylinder, which clears the silk as described for the first end. The combed tuft is delivered to the creeper N, formed into a sliver, and delivered to the can P.

The proportion of combed sliver to combings (exhaust noil) can be varied by adjusting the closeness of comb to nip, so that all fibres below $^{2}/_{3}$, $1^{2}/_{3}$, etc., of an inch, pass into noils. The more fibre taken out, the cleaner the resulting combed sliver, and the greater the production of noil. The combed sliver is used by short spinners, being either made into a combed yarn, or more often a certain number of the slivers are put in the drawings and so amalgamated with some other carded quality of shorts.

*Garnetting.* – Exhaust noils are made into coarse yarns on the woollen principle. The first process is designed to open or loosen the silk, and is much the same as scutching. Next, the silk is carded or garnetted on the machine shown in Fig. 98. It is fed by hand to the feed-box A, then carried up the pin-studded creeper B in a certain regular quantity, and delivered by means of the rollers C and D to the weigh box E, which opens automatically when it has received a predetermined weight of silk. It drops the silk on to the feeder F, which delivers to the taker-in rollers G, which in turn take it to the breaker card H. The doffer cylinder Z transfers the carded silk to the intermediate cylinder J and doffer K, which in turn delivers to the finisher card L and doffer M, and thence to the condenser bobbin N. The object of condensing is to convert the full width fleece of silk on the cylinder L into a number of thin, loose slivers. One or two doffer cylinders M (one only is shown) are used to strip the swift L. These are covered with card rings an inch wide,[16] with an inch blank space between each card ring, the blank of the top roller being above the card of the bottom roller, thus ensuring an entire stripping of the surface of the swift. The ends on the strips of card on the doffer M are then conveyed to the rubbing leathers O, P. These are endless leather belts carrying forward the thin ribbon of silk between them, but at the same time a sidewise motion is imparted which rubs the silk into a loose, round, pith-like roving without any twist in it. On leaving the leathers, the ends are conveyed to the bobbin N, on to which they are wound ready for spinning.

*Mule spinning.* – The condenser bobbins are placed behind the machine shown in Fig. 99, and the ends of silk conveyed to the rollers B. These rollers correspond to the back rollers of the spinning machines previously described, for they do not draft the roving. The roving being delivered by the rollers B, is wrapped round the spindles C fixed in the carriage D. This carriage is close up to the rollers at the commencement of the draw; but as soon as the rollers revolve, delivering roving, the carriage traverses away from the rollers at such a speed as to keep the roving stretched, but without drafting it. The spindles are meantime turning slowly, thus putting a little twist in the roving. When the carriage has gone half its journey, the rollers B cease to revolve, but the carriage travels on, thus stretching out the roving from 1 yd. to 2 yds. in length; while, as the spindles are still revolving, more twist is still going into the thread. When the carriage stops, the spindles revolve still more quickly until sufficient twist is put into the yarn, and the carriage is then traversed back to the rollers, while the spun thread is wound on to the spindles during this backward journey.

The count of the yarn is regulated chiefly by the size of the rovings delivered by the condenser, which in turn is regulated by the amount fed into the cards at the commencement. After spinning, the silk noil yarn is often sold in the singles, but if required two-fold it can be doubled on any class of doubling or twisting machinery.

## Notes

1 Throwing is the process of assembling and twisting together the long silk brins unwound directly from cocoons, while spinning is applied to yarns formed from silk that cannot be unwound, necessarily used in shorter lengths.

2 Trams and organzines are respectively weft and warp yarns made with reeled cocoon silk.

3 Tsatlee is a reeled China silk that was of varying thickness because the reelers did not efficiently keep the same number of ends throughout the whole length of yarn, and also with poor piecings of broken ends. In the re-reeling, faulty areas were removed and hanks sorted for greater uniformity.
4 The special purposes are clarified in the 1903 book as 'for lace, sewings, and weft purposes'.
5 Quite evidently, this tactic should not be linked to any nationality or culture. Although dishonesty is implied, there also seems here a sense of admiration expressed for the foreign trader able to manipulate the system to advantage.
6 Present-day Guangzhou.
7 Schapping is a partial degumming process using fermentation.
8 The 1903 book adds, 'Besides the two qualities named above, there are other qualities of tussah waste shipped from China, but these two represent by far the bulk'.
9 See later.
10 Described previously as a 'fair white' colour.
11 The moss is a measure of reeled silk, twelve mosses making a book, and twelve books making a bale of 100 to 104 lbs.
12 Explained in the following text.
13 Orders from brokers and merchants.
14 Rayner's characterisation of Chinese business prowess as deceitful seeks to absolve the lax British inspection process of its contributory role.
15 The garnetting machine is described in the final section.
16 The intersecting rings and blank spaces of the cylinders divide the lap fleece into ribbon-like strips.

# Part 6

# 'COMPLETE METAMORPHOSIS OF THE RAG'

## Rag flock

*Fig. 22* The Washington Lyon steam disinfector. See Ch. 31 this volume.

*Source*: Robertson, William and Charles Porter. *Sanitary Law and Practice*; 2nd ed. (London: Sanitary Publishing Co., 1909), p. 274. Author's collection.

*Fig. 23* A hair teaser showing the principal working parts, notably the conical tooth-studded lags that were characteristic of the early 'devils'. See Ch. 35 this volume.

*Source*: *Cabinet Maker*, 13 Dec 1924, p. 525. Manchester Libraries and Archives.

*Fig. 24* From rag flock to mattress: (1) Rag washing plant. (2) Part of rag drying department. (3) Curling and dusting. (4) Blending department. (5) Dispatch department. (6) Mattress making. See Ch. 35 this volume.

*Source*: *Cabinet Maker*, 10 Jan 1925, p. 53. Manchester Libraries and Archives.

*Rag Washing Machine by Hudson, Lyles & Co., Batley*

*Another view of the machine showing Lifting-out Gear for Rags and Swift Cover Removed*

*Fig. 25* Rag washing machine by Hudson, Lyles and Co., Batley. See Ch. 35 this volume.
*Source*: *Cabinet Maker*, 14 Feb 1925, p. 408. Manchester Libraries and Archives.

*Fig. 26* Rag tearing machine by Wm. Tatham Ltd., Rochdale. See Ch. 35 this volume.
*Source*: *Cabinet Maker*, 14 Mar 1925, p. 657. Manchester Libraries and Archives.

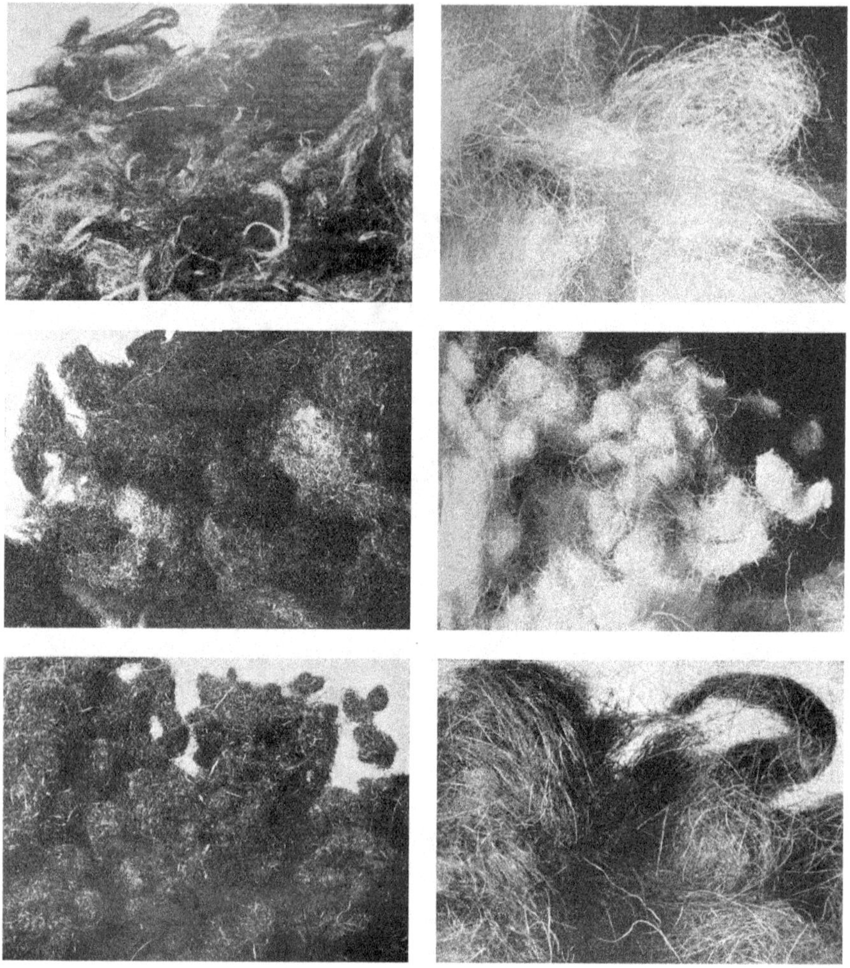

*Fig. 27* Some flock types: (left column, top to bottom) pulled washed rag flock, fine gig flock, fine gig flock curled; (right column, top to bottom) blanket flock, blanket flock curled, and best rugging flock. See Ch. 35 this volume.

*Source*: *Cabinet Maker*, 11 Apr, 9 May and 13 Jun 1925, pp. 47, 265, 522. Manchester Libraries and Archives.

## Editorial Headnote

**Parsons, Henry Franklin. 'Manufacture of Rag Flock and the Dissemination of Disease', *Textile Manufacturer*, 13:149 (15 Jun 1887), pp. 256–257.**

**Parsons, Henry Franklin. 'On the Manufacture of Rag Flock in Reference to the Possible Dissemination of Infectious Disease by this and other Products of Woollen Rags', *Fifteenth Annual Report of the Local Government Board, 1885–86: Supplement containing the Report of the Medical Officer for 1885* (London: HMSO, 1886), Appendix A, no. 7, pp. 61–72 [C.4844-I].**

Henry Franklin Parsons (1846–1913), author of these papers, was the eldest son of a Somerset surgeon who, from a boy, developed a keen interest in geology. He studied medicine at the University of London, obtaining his M.D. in 1870, and engaged for a few years in his father's medical practice. His obituarist in the *British Medical Journal* traced his subsequent career:

> in 1874 he was appointed Medical Officer of Health for the combined districts of Goole and Selby. Here he commenced that sustained study of public health which ceased only with his death. The character of his work in Yorkshire, and of his annual reports on matters affecting the health of his district there, attracted the attention of the central health authority, and five years later he was appointed a medical inspector of the Local Government Board. . . . His connexion with the State medical department only ceased, after thirty-two years' service, in 1911, when he retired under the age-limit regulation of the Civil Service.
>
> (2:1263, 8 Nov 1913, pp. 1263–1264)

The same author avowed Parson's 1884 report on 'disinfection by heat' a landmark in the subject. The obituary ends with regret that Parsons was passed by for promotion, and notwithstanding his distinguished work, received no state honours in keeping with a high-grade civil servant who served with distinction.

Parsons appears to have become quickly attached to Yorkshire, and was active in the local Naturalists Society as well as the county Medical Association. In 1879, he married Louisa Anne Wells (1846–1912), the daughter of a local land agent, further cementing his bond to the region. Parsons inevitably took an interest in the welfare of those in the rag flock trade so closely associated with the county. His report for the Local Government Board was written in 1885, and came into the public domain on publication in the *Annual Report* of 1886. When the *Textile Manufacturer* claims that its version was 'just issued from the Government press', this must refer to the sixteen-page reprint extract published in 1887. In an editorial, the journal drew the attention of readers to the appearance of the first instalment, but the intention to continue the article was either overtaken by the massive editorial demands of preparing the special issue for the Jubilee exhibition, or it may have been suppressed because it was deemed to reflect negatively on the textile industry. The missing section is restored here. Parsons' report was also quoted at some length in the *Leeds Mercury*, 15 February 1887, under the title 'The Rag Trade and Infectious Disease'.

# 31

# PARSONS, HENRY FRANKLIN. 'MANUFACTURE OF RAG FLOCK AND THE DISSEMINATION OF DISEASE' AND 'ON THE MANUFACTURE OF RAG FLOCK IN REFERENCE TO THE POSSIBLE DISSEMINATION OF INFECTIOUS DISEASE BY THIS AND OTHER PRODUCTS OF WOOLLEN RAGS'

*Textile Manufacturer* (15 Jun 1887), pp. 256–257; *Fifteenth Annual Report of the Local Government Board, 1885–86: Supplement containing the Report of the Medical Officer for 1885* (London: HMSO, 1886), Appendix A, no. 7, pp. 61–72 [C.4844-I].

The manufacture of rag flock consists in the tearing up of rags into a fibrous material used for the stuffing of beds and articles of furniture. The object of the present inquiry is to learn whether this manufacture involves any risk of infectious disease to persons engaged in it, or to those who use the manufactured article, and, if so, how such risks may be obviated.

Any such risk, if it exists, depends upon the nature and antecedents of the rags which form the raw material of the manufacture, rather than upon the processes to which they are subjected in their conversion into flock. It will therefore be necessary to consider what these rags are, and where they come from. For the same reason – viz, that danger of infection attaches to rags, *quâ* rags, rather than through the uses to which they are subsequently put – it will be convenient to consider briefly at the same time from this point of view the other industries besides flock making in which rags or their products are employed.

DOI: 10.4324/9780429274190-38

Cotton and linen rags are the province of the papermaker, and I need not here describe the processes of manufacture to which they are subjected, as I have already treated of these and the attendant dangers to the health of the workpeople in a report published as an appendix to the Annual Report of the Medical Officer of the Local Government Board for 1881.[1]

In the present report I shall therefore treat of the risks of infection attaching to the use of woollen and partly-woollen rags in the various industries in which they are employed.*

Rags are imported into this country from almost every part of the world in which people are sufficiently civilised to wear clothing. I am informed, however, that at the present time the imports of foreign rags are comparatively small, as the low prices which they now fetch will not pay for freight. Those coming into the English market are principally from the Continent of Europe. They are imported in largest quantities at the ports of Goole, Hull, London and Liverpool. Foreign rags ordinarily are compressed by hydraulic presses into hard and compact bales before shipment. Other rags are collected in this country, along with waste substances of other kinds, by people commonly called "marine store dealers," from whom they pass, through the hands of rag merchants and brokers, into those of the manufacturers. A very dirty class of rags is collected from the dust hills on which the refuse of London and other large towns is tipped. Rags of different primary classes, as cotton and woollen, are collected separately, and those of each class often undergo one or more sortings before they come into the hands of the manufacturers.

Paper mills are found in most parts of England, and the consumption of cotton rags is therefore distributed over the country. On the other hand, woollen rags are re-manufactured in the West Riding of Yorkshire, in the district around Dewsbury, at which town large sales of rags by auction take place twice a week; also in Gloucestershire and adjoining counties in the West of England, and in the neighbourhood of London.

Woollen rags go to the shoddy manufacturer, by whom they are torn up into an artificial wool, to be used again, with or without the addition of a proportion of new wool, for weaving into cloth, or into fabrics with a cotton warp, called "linseys." The rags are first dusted in a machine. The seams and linings, which contain cotton, are then removed by women, who at the same time sort the rags into different qualities. They are then placed in the machine called a "rag breaker" or "devil," in which they are passed between rollers and presented to a rapidly revolving drum set with numerous sharp iron teeth, by which they are torn up into fibre, a considerable amount of dust being set free at the same time, which is carried off by a fan and collected. The fibre is then "scribbled" in a machine, in which it is repeatedly combed out by a series of wire covered rollers, and is converted into a soft homogeneous wool, fit for the cloth manufacturer's use. Sometimes,

* Silk rags do not appear to be utilised, except as manure.

but not always, the rags after being torn up are dyed; if not dyed "pure" wool rags do not undergo any process of which it could be affirmed that it would with certainty destroy infectious matter, though it is probable that any such matter which they might contain, being attached to the surface as dirt, would be removed with the dust, or lose its activity by exposure to the air.

Rags of mixed wool and cotton, if containing sufficient wool to make it worth while, are subjected to a process called "carbonising" for the purpose of extracting the wool. There are two ways of doing this. In the wet way the rags are steeped in sulphuric acid somewhat diluted, at a temperature of 169–190° F., then rinsed in water and dried in a stove. In the dry way the rags, spread out on racks, are heated for some hours in a stove in an atmosphere of hydrochloric acid gas, evolved by pouring sulphuric acid on common salt in an iron retort, or by heating the crude hydrochloric acid obtained as a by-product in alkali works. By one or other of these processes the cotton fibre is destroyed, being converted into a powdery matter, probably glucose, which flies off as dust when the rags are beaten, but the wool, being unaffected by the acid, remains, and undergoes further processes for conversion into shoddy. Either the wet or the dry process of wool-extracting would eventually destroy any infectious matter that might be present.

Woollen rags are also used as manure, especially for hops; those rags which are too old, rotten, and dirty for shoddy making being used for this purpose, as is also the dust collected from the rag machines.

Flock making is carried out on the largest scale in the West Riding of Yorkshire, but there are mills also in Surrey, Gloucestershire, Lancashire, and other counties. The rags of which the commoner qualities of flock are made are the refuse of the shoddy trade – viz., what are called "heavy linseys," – *i.e.*, materials of mixed wool and cotton not containing enough wool to be worth extracting, such as "shallies" – *i.e.*, old dresses,[2] seams of woollen garments (ripped off by the sorters at the shoddy mills) and other articles of a character so miscellaneous as to defy description. Old carpets, consisting of wool on a backing of hemp or other vegetable fibre, are used for making a better kind of flock. The above materials may come from any part of the world, but principally, I was told, from England and France; but by the time they reach the flock manufacturers' hands they have commonly been so mixed and sorted that it is impossible to trace their origin. The rags from which the flocks are made are often far from clean, but their character in this respect will depend upon the quality and price of the flock, which vary greatly. Thus at Mr. Robb's factory at Ossett Spa,[3] a superior kind of flock, made of new wool from the combings of blankets, curled, was sold at 1s. ½d. per lb. On the other hand, the cheapest kind of flock made by Messrs. Sanderson, of Batley,[4] was sold at 6s. 6d. per cwt; this was made of rags of the coarsest and most dirty description.

The process of manufacture is as follows: – The rags on being taken out of the bale are carried by hand to the rag-grinding machine and placed on an endless band which carries them into the grip of fluted rollers, and the latter hold them to be torn by the teeth of a rapidly revolving cylinder, similar to that by which rags are torn into shoddy, except that the teeth are shorter and not so sharp – in fact, the cylinders of which the teeth are worn out for shoddy making are used for making flock. This machine is boxed in, and the dust is drawn out by a fan. The flock falls to the bottom, and is gathered in armfuls and packed in bags; or, in some cases, the flock is shot through a flue by the current of air produced by the rapid revolution of the cylinder, into another machine, in which it undergoes the process of dusting. The amount of dust in unwashed rags is considerable, from 25 to 50 per cent. of the rags used, according to their quality; dirty rags, of course, give more dust than clean ones, and wool gives more than cotton. The dust is inflammable, and occasionally fires and explosions have been caused by the heat generated by the friction of the revolving cylinder, especially if rags have been put in hot. To avoid this danger the rags are sometimes damped by sprinkling water over them before tearing up. The dust is conveyed to a dust-chamber, and is collected from time to time and sent up to the hop-growing districts for manure.

The above description applies to the manufacture of rag flock as carried on in Yorkshire. In Gloucestershire a different process is in common use. The rags are first chopped by hand on a block. They are then pulped in a machine similar to that used in paper mills; this consists of an elliptical iron tank containing a revolving drum set with angular iron ribs, which works against a plate similarly armed. The rags, immersed in water, rotate in the tank, and are brought in turn under the drum, by which they are broken up. The process occupies an hour and a half, a stream of water running through the tank all the time. The flock is then dried, first in a centrifugal wringing machine, and then in a stove; and finally is curled in a machine with revolving blades.

Flock is also made in the Gloucestershire mills by the Yorkshire method, but the rags usually undergo a preliminary washing, passing under a paddle-wheel in a tank similar to that above described, and being afterwards dried. At the Wandsworth Flock Mills, Surrey,[5] another washing process is in use, in addition to that last mentioned; the rags are placed under heavy wooden hammers, similar to the "stocks" used for fulling cloth, by which they are beaten for an hour under a stream of tepid water. This process, unlike the tank, does not require the rags to be first cut by hand; it is used for carpets – the tank process for flannel.

In Yorkshire the adoption of any process for the cleansing or purification of the rags before they are torn up appears to be exceptional, at any rate as regards the cheaper qualities of flock. The most frequent process appears to be washing, which is done when specially ordered. Messrs. Sanderson, of Batley, stated that washing with the subsequent drying would add 4*s*. per cwt to the cost of the flock; they said that they had not had occasion to use their washing machine this year, and the appearance of the machine certainly bore out this statement.

In the West of England, on the other hand, where water is plentiful, and a better class of flock is made, a large proportion of the flock is washed; at some mills, as those of the several Messrs. Grist, near Stroud,[6] none but washed flocks are made. Some of the West of England manufacturers, however, have felt themselves, as they say, reluctantly compelled in these days of low prices and keen competition to manufacture unwashed flocks, in order to hold their ground against the Yorkshire makers.

At the factories where the cheapest quality of flocks are made some of the rags were seen to be very dirty, and all were ground up together. At some factories, however, exceptionally filthy rags are rejected. Rags are sometimes met with which are soiled with blood or excrement, but I did not hear of poultices being observed, or anything which would lead to the inference that the rags had been used by sick persons. Such things would be more likely to be met with among calico than linsey rags. The rags are often infested with fleas and moths, but other vermin are said not to be often met with.

Washed flock is said to be less liable to be damaged by moths than that which contains the dirt.

Two Yorkshire manufacturers, Messrs. Robb, of Osset, and Illingworth, of Batley,[7] use in the case of inferior flocks a solution of permanganate[8] for damping the rags before tearing up. This is cheap, and would help to remove any offensive odour that might be present, but is not likely in the quantity used to have much effect in the way of disinfection properly so called.

Mr. Illingworth has also patented a machine for the disinfection of rags for flock making by heat and sulphurous acid gas.[9] His machine consists of an iron cylinder with a door at one end, and with double walls forming a steam jacket. Inside this cylinder is a revolving cylindrical cage with prongs which catch the rags and, lifting them, turn them over and over. A charge of rags is from 1 to 1½ cwt. At one end of the machine is a small iron furnace with a flue communicating with the interior of the chamber. In this chamber 4 oz. of sulphur are burnt with each charge of rags. Each charge remains in the machine 35 minutes. The steam in the jacket stands at 70 lb. pressure = 316° F., but steam does not enter the interior of the chamber.

In order to test the action of the machine a registering thermometer was embedded in a groove in a long wooden bar with perforations opposite the bulb. This arrangement was necessary to prevent the thermometer being broken, or its index displaced, by the motion of the cylinder. A piece of iodide of starch paper was wrapped up in a rag, and both it and the thermometer in the bar were placed in the machine in the middle of a charge of rags and allowed to remain 40 minutes, the cage, turned by an engine, revolving all the time. At the end of the period a thermometer on the bottom in the space between the cage and the steam-jacket registered 273° F., but that in the bar only 169° F. The iodide of starch paper was bleached by the sulphurous acid gas except in the folds where it retained its colour. In other experiments, after 50 minutes, the thermometer in the bar reached 177° F., after 1½ hours 217° F.

In my report on Disinfection by Heat (Annual Report of the Medical Officer of the Local Government Board, 1884)[10] are recorded experiments tending to show that the penetration of heat into textile materials exposed to hot air is greatly aided by moistening the air. At my suggestion, in view of these experiments, Mr. Illingworth had a ³/₈ in. steam pipe connected with his machine, so that a jet of steam could be admitted into the interior, at the same time omitting the sulphur vapour. The result was that, although the steam pressure in the steam-jacket fell to 65 lb. = 312° F., at the end of 35 minutes the thermometer in the bar recorded a temperature of 216° F.; so that when steam was used a temperature which can be considered sufficient for disinfection was attained in little more than a third of the time necessary with dry heat. The rags, after being removed from the chamber and allowed to cool, were not appreciably damp; indeed Mr. Illingworth finds that rags lose weight in the chamber even when steam is used.

Mr. Illingworth has invented another machine for disinfecting rags in the bale, but I regret that it was not in use at the time of my visit. It is a steam-jacketed chamber, but the special principle is that he displaces the cold air from the interstices of the bale by exhausting the chamber with an air-pump, and allows its place to be taken by chlorine and sulfurous acid gas let in by opening a valve.

Cheap as the inferior qualities of flock are, they are yet liable to be adulterated. The fibrous dust shaken out of woollen materials, as stockings, by the shoddy manufacturers is used for this purpose. The residue of the oily waste from the clothweavers, after the oil has been as far as possible recovered by hot pressing, is sometimes used to mix with flock, but this practise is scarcely considered by the trade as legitimate, and one manufacturer, not very particular about cleanliness, told me that he had given it up, as he found that the greasiness and bad smell which it gave to the flock caused much dissatisfaction among his customers. Still this oily waste is not likely to convey infection.

At one factory I saw an iron tank containing liquid with a thick, black putrid scum, like that which collects on the surface of a sewage tank, but more fibrous. I was told that the contents of this tank were the refuse and sweepings of the yard and workshops, and that once in six months or so they were washed and dried in a stove, and then were considered to make good flock, being sold at more than twice the price of the lowest quality.[11]

As regards the possibility of the transmission of infectious diseases by flock made from infected rags, I have made inquiries of a number of medical officers of health in the rag-working district of the West Riding of Yorkshire and elsewhere, and of flock manufacturers, rag merchants, and upholsterers; also, in respect of the dust, of medical officers of health and manure merchants in the hop-growing counties. The result of these inquiries has been to show that while workpeople engaged in the manufacture of flock suffer from certain symptoms produced by the irritation of inhaled dust, instances in which infectious disease had been contracted by them were scarcely to be met with. Indeed, many medical officers and manufacturers of large experience had never known any instance of an outbreak of infectious disease which could be attributed to rag-infection. A few cases were heard of in which persons who had been handling woollen rags for shoddy making had contracted small-pox or other infectious disorder, but the only case at a flock factory was attributed, not to infected rags, but to the re-making of a flock bed on which a small-pox patient had died.

In a report already mentioned, made in 1881, I quoted a number of outbreaks of small-pox among rag-sorters at paper mills; and since that date a good many others have been reported, some of them being at mills at which previous outbreaks were recorded in my report, some at other mills in different parts of the country. There is a common belief that woollen articles are more apt to retain infection than cotton or linen ones; but, so far as my inquiries go, workers among woollen or partly-woollen rags are exposed to less danger of infection than workers among calico rags. The explanation I believe to be that the latter consist largely of articles which come into close contact with the body such as underclothing and sheets, and are therefore more likely to be infected by a sick person, at any rate by one lying in bed, than woollen articles are. In corroboration of this view it is to be noted that the paper mills at which outbreaks of small-pox have occurred have been with few exceptions mills at which the best class of writing papers, made from white rags, are manufactured; sorters of coloured rags being seldom attacked. Probably also woollen rags undergo less handling than the rags at a paper mill do, as those for the best writing papers are cut up small by hand.†

The following are the instances of which I have been able to hear, in which infectious disease has been suspected to have been contracted from woollen rags or flock: –

Mr. Thomas Robb, flock manufacturer, Spa Mill, Ossett, Yorkshire, says: –

"My old workman, who says that it is over 17 years since he left me, says that the following case occurred before he left: –

"A bed was sent to my place to be re-dressed, but he refused to do it, or allow it to be unloaded from the dray at all. He stated then (and repeated last week) that a bed had been sent about a month before to Etchell's flock factory at Horbury[12] to be redressed; the man, named Smith, who fed the machine, took small-pox and died. His fellow-workman, who 'shook' it, was also taken ill of the same disease, but recovered. It was afterwards ascertained that the bed sent to Etchell's had been lain on by a person who died of small-pox. He says that the bed, although a flock one, was not a rag-flock bed. I have been 21 years in the trade here, and the above is the only instance I have known, or rather heard of, of a workman having caught an infectious disease from the material he was using.

" Etchell and Co. failed and left Horbury about six or eight years ago.

" I have always refused to re-dress a bed since."

† The explanation of the fact, if fact it be, that outbreaks of infectious disease are more frequent among workers in cotton and linen than among workers in woollen rags, does not seem to be that there are more rags of the former class in circulation. In the five years 1880–1884, the amount of woollen rags imported into the United Kingdom was 180,831 tons; of other rags, 142,391.

I made further inquiries at Horbury and neighbourhood, but could not learn anything more of this case.

Mr. Butterfield,[13] then medical officer of health for Bradford, Yorks, in his annual report for 1879, mentions the case of an unvaccinated girl aged 15 who was taken ill with small-pox. There had been no case in the borough for many months, and the patient had not left the neighbourhood of her home. On inquiry, it was found that she had been temporarily employed at a wool-extracting establishment sorting rags, a large proportion of which had come from London, where small-pox had been very prevalent. In a few days another young woman employed on the same work exhibited symptoms of the disease. A few more cases, difficult to trace, but probably springing from the same source, occurred.

Mr. Greenwood,[14] medical officer of health, Ossett, states that in 1880 a young woman working as ragsorter at a rag warehouse in Ossett was taken ill of small-pox. She had been working on "skirtings" – mixed cotton and wool for "extracting." She lodged at a mangle-house, and the case was at first concealed and proved the starting-point of a local epidemic, the district having been previously free.

Mr. Greenwood has met with other cases, produced apparently in a similar manner, but not recently. He also stated that people who work among rags are liable to contract itch. (Tardieu, *Dictionnaire d'Hygiène*, Art. *Chiffonniers*,[15] makes a similar statement.)

Mr. Francis Wood,[16] medical officer of health, Wakefield rural district, has met with several cases of small-pox originating among ragsorters, but more at paper mills than among sorters of woollen rags. In a case occurring in June 1881, the patient, who resided in the district of the Sandal Magna Local Board, had been working up to the time of her illness in sorting rags at a shoddy mill in Wakefield.

In April 1885 he reports that a woman living at East Ardsley was attacked with small-pox. She had been working at a rag mill in the neighbourhood; but she had visited at Leeds, in the neighbourhood of which town there had been cases of small-pox. The rags which she had been working at were "shallies," *i.e.*, old dresses (women's) from London; they were for carbonizing to extract the wool, not for flock making.

Dr. Wade,[17] medical officer of health for the borough of Wakefield, also states that all the cases of small-pox which have occurred in that borough during recent years have had their origin among workers in rag factories; but he was unable to give further particulars.

Dr. Goldie,[18] medical officer of health for Leeds, has sent me a report on some cases of small-pox which occurred among ragsorters in that borough in 1878. Of these cases, 1 and 2, girls living in adjoining streets, and working in the same mills, and at the same rags, were taken ill, the one on April 1st, the other about four days later. Case 3, sister of case 1, living and sleeping with her sister, and also working at the same bench with her in the mill, was taken ill on April 11th. (The dates seem to show that it is at least as probable that she took the disease directly from her sister as that she was infected by the rags on which they had both worked.) Two other cases of small-pox subsequently arose through personal communication with the above. There had been no previous cases in that part of the borough. The suspected rags, and all likely to have been in contact with them, were at once disinfected by chemical means and dry heat; their previous history was not ascertained.

Mr. Steele,[19] late medical officer of health, Morley, says in letters: –

> "I only remember one case of infectious fever presumably due to infected rags. This was a lad in the year 1880, who died of typhus fever. He was a ragsorter, and at the same time some cases of typhus had occurred in Leeds which were supposed to have been due to infected rags. No other case occurred either amongst the other men who worked with the deceased or amongst his own family. Typhus fever is practically unknown in this district, and the lad was not at all in destitute circumstances. I do not know where the rags came from; they were woollen rags used in the manufacture of cloth."

Mr. Partridge,[20] medical officer of health for Stroud and adjoining districts, says: –

> "I have not met with any cases of small-pox in the Bisley district, which includes the shoddy mills in Chalford and Brimscombe, since 1875. At that time we had several arising from the effects of opening bales of infected rags, as the women complained of a sickening smell at the time, and were taken ill with a severe form of the disease."

In 1871 an outbreak of small-pox occurred among ragsorters at the Toadmore mills, near Stroud.[21] In that year it will be remembered there was a widespread epidemic of the disease in this and other countries, and infected rags were therefore likely to be in circulation; but it is said that there had been no previous cases in the neighbourhood of Stroud. The particulars, as given me by the mother of one of the patients and the sister of another – the statements of the two women agreeing together – are as follows: In one room four women were at work sorting rags; they worked at two bags, two women at each bag. Of the four, three were taken with small-pox, C. (æt, 15), and D. (æt, 16), who worked at one bag, on the same day; B., a young married woman, who worked next them at the other bag, a day or two later. The other woman escaped, as did also the sorters in another room. The rags on which those who took small-pox were working were "shallies," *i.e.*, old dresses, of mixed wool and cotton, for carbonizing; but it was not known whence they came. C. and D. died, and a baby five weeks old, in C.'s family, was taken with small-pox a fortnight after her and died. Mrs. B. recovered, but her husband took the disease and died.

The "woolsorters' disease" which occurs in Bradford and neighbourhood among men engaged in handling the fleeces of animals which have died of anthrax has been described by Mr. Spear in the Annual Report of the Medical Officer of the Local Government Board for 1880.[22]

I have not been able to hear of any cases of infectious disease among upholsterers, or the public their customers, traceable to the use of infected rag flock. Doubtless the risk of infection to which these classes are exposed is much less even than that of the flock manufacturers, both because any infectious matter which the rags may have contained has in large part been got rid of in the form of dust, and also because any that may remain will be older and thus likely to have had its activity diminished or lost. Cases, however, of infectious disease among the general public from the use of infected flock, if such occurred, would probably be very difficult to trace and are not likely to be recorded.

I learn that large upholsterers and firms of repute use, as a rule, wool or flock made of new or washed material, and that the coarser qualities are chiefly used by small and obscure tradesmen, among whom also the still more objectionable practice is sometimes adopted of using the flock out of old beds and furniture for the stuffing of new. The cheapest sort of flock is said to be used for stuffing mattresses for emigrant ships, being thrown overboard at the end of the voyage.

The greater part of the materials used by upholsterers of repute for stuffing beds and furniture are not likely to be infected. Feathers are purified by steam heat. Horsehair, being purified by washing, is curled at a very high temperature, about 300° F. "Millpuff" is the woolly waste beaten out in the process of fulling which cloth undergoes in the course of manufacture.‡ Cotton flock, a cheap material largely used, is the refuse of raw cotton. Other materials of a vegetable nature are straw, chaff, cocoa-nut fibre, a kind of coarse wiry grass resembling the mat-grass of our sandy coasts, and a kind of seaweed (apparently a Zostera), said to be imported from Russia, and called in the trade "ulva."[23] Such materials, unless taken out of old furniture, have not previously been used. The better classes of flocks are made of new or comparatively clean material, so that it is only the inferior classes which are at all likely to be infected.

The dust which flock retains as received from the manufacturers is further removed by a process of beating and carding at the hands of the upholsterer before the flock is used for stuffing.

The following instances are all those which I have been able to hear of in which disease has been attributed to the handling of infected waste used for manure: –

Dr. Robinson,[24] medical officer of health for East Kent, writes: –

> "I have a record made on April 29, 1877, of four cases of blood-poisoning derived apparently from infected wool waste (I believe shoddy). They occurred at separate cottages some distance from each other, but the sufferers had all been at work engaged in carrying wool waste. One man whom I saw had erysipelatous inflammation[25] on the hands and at the back of one ear, and was much prostrated. He informed me that on

‡ The short flock used by paper-stainers in the manufacture of flock wall-papers consists of the superfluous 'nap' from the surface of cloth, sheared off in the process of manufacture.

account of the land being heavy it was difficult to distribute the manure by cart and shovel, and in consequence the manure was carried in a basket and cast on the land by hand in the same way as wheat is hand sown. Further, he told me that he had a habit of scratching the back of the ear, the spot which had evidently been inoculated.

"The other three men suffered from sickness, diarrhoea, and febrile disturbance.[26] The symptoms were obscure, but more like septic poisoning than anthrax. No fatal case occurred, but one of the latter three men was very ill, viz., the one who carted the wool waste from the station.

"I do not remember any cases of small-pox arising from infected wool waste. In some other instances of illness occurring among persons who attributed their attacks to poisonous wool waste the evidence on the subject was not very clear."

Dr. E. F. Fussell,[27] medical officer of health for East Sussex, mentions a case in which a lad who had for a week or more been employed in spreading with his hands "fur waste" manure over a field, was taken ill of scarlet fever which was attributed to infection in the manure, as there had been no previous cases in the neighbourhood, and the lad had been nowhere away from home except to his work. The "fur waste" is described as the refuse of fur and felt manufactories; it would not appear *a priori* to be a material very likely to be infected, and it hardly comes within the scope of this report.

Workers in flock factories, on commencing to work among the dust, suffer from a malady known among them as "flock fever." Mr. Illingworth, a large manufacturer, says that he has never known anyone escape it. The symptoms are described as those of a severe catarrh of the bronchial passages, viz., shivering, difficulty of breathing, cough, soreness of the chest, and expectoration of mucus charged with dust. In about a week's time, if the man continues at work, a tolerance of dust is established, the symptoms subside, and do not recur so long as he keeps at the same work: but on leaving it off the tolerance for dust is soon lost, and on returning, after a week or two's absence, a man suffers again as at first. I am even told that the men will not empty the dust-chamber on a Monday, as they would suffer more from the dust then than if they had been at work the day before.

Men who can eat well are said to be comparatively little affected by the dust, but those whose appetite fails are apt to break down. Heavy drinkers, on the other hand, cannot stand the dust well, and men are said to cough much at their work if they have been drunk the night before. A "cold," with catarrh of the air-passages, also causes the irritative effects of the dust to be felt.

When men have got used to the dust the work is not considered unhealthy. Among some 25 men constantly employed by him about the rag machines, Mr. Illingworth says that only one has died in the past 12 years; he was a man who drank heavily, and the dust used to punish him much. He had a bad cough and died of inflammation of the lungs.

This so-called "flock fever" does not appear to come under medical observation, but is treated by domestic remedies, as for a common cold. In fact the only way is to continue at work, for if the sufferer gives up he has to go through it all again. The condition of the workshops has been much improved of late years through the operation of the Factory Acts by boxing in the rag machines and drawing off the dust by fans; and the men are said to suffer much less from dust than they formerly did. If the rags have been washed before tearing up, much less dust is evolved, and what there is is less irritating than that from dirty rags.[§]

Upholsterers' men, when working among flock, are said also to suffer in some degree from the effects of inhaling a dusty atmosphere.

As regards the precautionary measures which may be taken against the spread of infectious diseases by rag flock, I find that three classes of measures may be recommended; the first two being specially for the protection of the work-people; the third for that also of the public at large: –

A. *Vaccination.* – Against small-pox, which is the disease most likely to be propagated by infection contained in rags, vaccination, with re-vaccination on arriving at adult age, is, when properly performed, a very efficient, if it be not an absolutely certain, prophylactic; and rag merchants and manufacturers should make it a condition of their service that every rag worker should have been efficiently vaccinated and revaccinated.

B. *Avoidance of Dust.* – Much has been done in this direction, and it would seem with beneficial results as regards the general health of the workpeople. Any further steps in the same direction that may be practicable should be taken. The general cleanliness and ventilation of the premises should be looked after, and facilities afforded for habits of personal cleanliness on the part of the workpeople.

C. *Cleansing and Disinfecting of Rags.*

   (a.) Washing of the rags, thoroughly performed, as by one of the processes already described, would in all probability remove any infectious matter adhering to the rags. It is not, however, any protection to the workpeople. On the contrary, the additional handling required in the early stages would tend in the opposite direction. The principal danger appears to be in the first opening of the bales, and therefore any measures of disinfection, to be effective, must be applied to the rags while still in the bales.

   (b.) Chemical disinfectants, as permanganate of potash, sulphurous acid, or chlorine gas, may be of use as deodorants and for destroying vermin with which the rags may be infested, but the result of recent experiments has been to show that the efficacy of such agents for the destruction

§ This advantage, it may be remarked, is gained at the cost of a certain amount of river pollution; the streams carrying off the organic matter, which would otherwise find its way to the land as manure.

of morbid poisons has been greatly overrated, and that they cannot be depended upon for that purpose unless they are in a comparatively high degree of concentration, and allowed to act for a considerable period, in which case they may injure the fabrics to be disinfected. Their disinfecting power is, however, increased at high temperatures.

(c.) On the other hand it has been shown that heat, especially moist heat, readily destroys the activity of morbid poisons. In my report on Disinfection by Heat, before quoted, it is shown that the spores of the bacillus anthracis (the minute parasitic organism which produces wool-sorter's disease),[28] the most refractory of known infective materials, were destroyed by an exposure of five minutes to 212° F. in steam or boiling water; and by one of four hours to 220° F., or of one hour to 245° F. in hot air, dry or moist, while infective organisms devoid of spores were destroyed by one hour's exposure to 220° F., in air. Steam was found to penetrate into badly-conducting materials, such as bales of rags, much more rapidly than hot air; in the case of hot air the penetration of heat was found to be aided by moistening it. Moist heat is the best agent for disinfecting rags, since it will penetrate them in the bale and thus avoid the necessity for unpacking and the consequent handling of the undisinfected rags, and the most effectual way of applying heat with moisture is in the form of what is called "dry" or superheated steam. In Lyon's patent steam disinfector[29] a temperature of 206° F. was attained in the centre of a press-packed bale of rags weighing 5 cwt. in three hours, and one of 252° F. in four hours. In the latter experiment the increase of weight of the bale due to moisture condensed from the steam was only four per cent. It is stated that in an American apparatus in which superheated steam is injected into the centre of the bale through hollow screws, effective disinfection can be carried out in considerably shorter time even than that mentioned above.[¶] Of Mr. Illingworth's machines for disinfecting rags I have spoken in an earlier part of this report, and I have no doubt that loose rags can be effectually disinfected in the one that I saw in action. Whether a press-packed bale could be heated through in a reasonable time I do not know.

¶ I am informed by Messrs. Cohen & Co., rag merchants, of Great Dover Street, London, who send many rags to the United States of America, in which country the importation of undisinfected rags is prohibited, that they prefer to expose the rags, hung on racks, to the fumes of burning sulphur before shipment, rather than allow them to be subjected by the American authorities to the steam process above mentioned, which is considered by manufacturers to injure the rags. This injury, if real, is likely to be the result of the very high temperature (330° F.) of the steam employed; a temperature quite unnecessary, judging by the results of the experiments to which I have referred above. [Aaron Cohen and Co., rag and metal dealers. The principals at the time of Parsons's report were Samuel Aaron Cohen (c1824–1895), Edward Aaron Cohen (d. 1921) and John Aaron Cohen (d. 1924).]

In my report on rag infection in the paper trade it was shown that desirable as it might be for the safety of the workpeople, that all rags should be disinfected before being sorted, it was difficult to recommend that such disinfection should be made compulsory, for the following reasons: –

The law already forbids under penalty the selling, transmission, or exposure of infected articles, so that if infected rags pass into the market, it is through a breach of the law on the part of the original vendor, and it would hardly be just to require manufacturers to guard against such a possible breach on the part of other persons by disinfecting all rags which passed through their hands; while in the absence of any character by which infected rags could be recognised – and there is no such character, – it would be impossible to discriminate between the few cases in which disinfection was required and the many in which it might safely be omitted.

These considerations apply also to the case of rags used for flock making, but there are some differences in the two cases.

(a.) In the case of paper-making, the question is only that of danger to those who sort the rags, and not to the public who buy and use the paper, for the rags after sorting undergo processes by which any contagium which they may contain is certain to be destroyed. Flock, on the other hand, does not necessarily undergo any process of purification beyond the removal of the dust before coming into the hands of the public.

(b.) In the case of paper-making, any preliminary disinfection of the rags would not improve the quality of the finished paper; it is even feared by paper-makers that the paper would be injured thereby. In the case of flock, a disinfected article would presumably be worth more, certainly it would not be worth less, then a crude one. Disinfection would at all events destroy any insects, such as moths.

(c.) On the other hand, there appears to be more danger of infection connected with the rags used in paper-making than with those from which flock is made. Possibly, however, the result of attention being called to the subject may be to show that instances of infection being conveyed by woollen rags are not so rare as at present appears.

Thus, in the case of flock making, the manufacturer does not obtain the same degree of security against the operation of infection contained in the original rags as is obtained by the paper maker; and though it may not be practicable to enforce upon the flock maker a general disinfection of all rags used in his business, yet there must be variety of means by which he can reduce the danger of infection being conveyed with his rags. To that end, it is to be desired that the attention of manufacturers, upholsterers, and the public should be drawn to the risk of such infection, and to the advantage of a preliminary disinfection of materials.

The advantage of a washed flock over one "in the dirt," as it is called, is already recognised in the trade; only, it is alleged, many of the public will not pay the necessary price for the better and safer article.

## Recapitulation

1. Rag flock is a material used for stuffing articles of bedding and furniture.

It is made by tearing up rags, usually of mixed cotton and woollen nature.

The rags from which the inferior qualities of flock are made are commonly very dirty, and do not, as a rule, undergo any process of purification beyond the removal of the dust.

2. Flock makers and others exposed to rag dust suffer, especially at first, from symptoms produced by the inhalation of dust. They do not, however, appear often to contract infectious disease.

A few cases were heard of in which persons working among woollen rags, or handling rag dust used as manure, had contracted small-pox or other infectious disease, possibly from infectious matter contained therein.

No cases of infectious disease, attributed to the use of infected rag flock, were heard of among upholsterers or the general public.

Workers among woollen rags appear to incur less danger than cutters of cotton and linen rags at paper mills, probably owing to the fact that woollen rags consist mainly of articles which do not come into close contact with the body.

3. The following precautionary measures are available: –

A. Vaccination and re-vaccination of rag workers.
B. Ventilation, cleanliness, and avoidance of dust in rag factories.
C. Disinfection or purification of rags; preferably in the bale. The best disinfectant for the purpose is heat in the form of superheated steam, or hot moist air.

In conclusion, I have to express my obligations to the various medical officers of health, manufacturers, and others who have kindly furnished me with information for the purpose of this report.

## Notes

1 H. F. Parsons, 'On an Outbreak of Small-pox among Rag-sorters at the St Mary Cray Paper Mills, and on the Precautions which can be taken for Preventing the Spread of Infection by Rags', *Eleventh Annual Report of the Local Government Board 1881–82: Supplement Containing the Report of the Medical Officer for 1881* (London: HMSO, 1882), App. A, no. 15, pp. 106–125 [C.3337-I].

2 Probably a local rendering of *challis*. Challis was originally a lightweight all-wool dress fabric, but cheaper imitations with cotton warp and worsted weft – or using blended cotton and wool yarns – were introduced and sold as challis.

3 Edinburgh-born Thomas Robb (1827–1912) apprenticed as a clothier. He moved to England by the time of his marriage in 1850, settled in Leeds the following year, and became a flock dealer at Ossett by 1870. His eldest son, Henry Verity Robb (1851–1911) joined him in partnership as Thomas Robb and Son. The partnership was dissolved in 1905 with the retirement of Thomas Robb, but carried on by Henry V. Robb until his sudden death 27 September 1911.

4 William Sanderson (1835–1907) was the stepson of a flock dealer. He had become a flock merchant in his own right by the time of his marriage in 1862. By 1870, his mill was at Bradford Road, Batley. He went into debt in 1880, surviving liquidation only to become bankrupt in 1887. He moved to Bethnal Green and continued in business again, at least until 1901.

5 The Wandsworth Flock Company began around 1868, established by the brothers Charles Henry Pike (1854–1889) and Seymour James Pike (c1859–1930). The mills were located at Garratt Lane, Wandsworth. After Charles's death, the partnership was continued by his widow Harriet Helen Pike (née Smith, c1858–1927) until 1915 when she withdrew, leaving Seymour Pike the sole proprietor.

6 In the 1820s, Matthew Grist (1803–1852) took over the flock trade probably commenced by his father who came to Stroud about 1790. The business, situated at Capel's Mill, was continued by Grist's widow, Elizabeth Grist (c1804–1858) with her sons Richard Grist (c1828–1891) and Samuel Grist (1831–1896) under the firm Grist, Sons and Co. Younger sons William Charles Grist (c1834–1899) and John Jabez Grist (c1836–1903) later entered the partnership. Another son, Matthew Henry Grist (1829–1917), ran his own flock business at Merrett's Mills. In 1872, the group of four brothers dissolved their partnership, with Richard Grist taking control of the firm; it passed to his sons on his death. In 1908, Richard Grist and Co. was made a limited company. Also in the trade was Matthew Grist's elder brother Henry Grist (1798–1867), whose sons William Charles Grist (1820–1867), John Grist (1824–1876) and Samuel Grist (1828–1882) later carried on in the trade from a mill at Rooksmoor.

7 John Illingworth and Son of White Lee was founded in 1865 by John Illingworth (c1845–1918). Born in Heckmondwike of humble origins, he commenced work as a pit boy. 'At the age of nineteen, he was employed as a firer at a Batley mill, but later began business as a flock maker, first at Mirfield and then at Gomersal' (*Leeds Mercury*, 9 Feb 1918, p. 5). By 1881, he was installed at Ridings Mill, White Lee, and in the 1890s his son Arthur Illingworth (1868–1937) became a partner in the firm.

8 Potassium permanganate ($KMnO_4$) solution, a mild antiseptic.

9 'Improvements in the method of and apparatus for disinfecting rags and other fibrous substances', no. 2415, 12 May 1883.

10 Parsons, H. F. 'Report on Disinfection by Heat', *Fourteenth Annual Report of the Local Government Board: Supplement Containing the Report of the Medical Officer for 1884* (London: Eyre and Spottiswoode, 1885), App. B, no. 10, pp. 218–303 [C.-4516].

11 The extract from the *Textile Manufacturer* ends here.

12 Wesley Guilleaume Etchells (1825–1905) of Horbury Bridge went into liquidation in 1878 (*London Gazette*, 25 June 1878, p. 3804).

13 Harris Butterfield (1835–1895), M.R.C.S., L.S.A.

14 John William Greenwood (1833–1904), M.R.C.S.

15 Tardieu, Ambroise (1818–1879). *Dictionnaire d'hygiène publique et de salubrité, ou Répertoire de toutes les questions relatives à la santé publique*, 2nd ed. (Paris: J.-B. Ballière et Fils, 1862), vol. 1, pp. 445–446.

16 Francis Henry Wood (1854–1920), M.R.C.S.

17 William Swift Wade (1829–1911) was Medical Officer of Health for Wakefield from 1866 to 1903.

18 George Goldie (1839–1908), M.R.C.S.

19 Sidney Thomas Steele (1850–1929), M.R.C.S.
20 Thomas Partridge (1830–1906), M.R.C.P.I.
21 Toadsmoor Mills was in the hands of A. B. Woolaston and Co. The principal of the firm was Alfred Buchanan Woolaston (1818–1901); in 1871, he employed fifteen men and forty-five women and young persons.
22 Spear, John. 'On the So-called "Woolsorters' Disease" as Observed at Bradford and in Neighbouring Districts in the West Riding of Yorkshire', *Tenth Annual Report of the Local Government Board 1880–81. Supplement Containing the Report of the Medical Officer for 1880* (London: Eyre and Spottiswoode, 1881), App. A, no. 8., pp. 66–135 [C.-3048.].
23 A genus of seaweed with ribbon-like leaves, commonly known as eelgrass. Peter Lund Simmonds, in his *Dictionary of Trade Products, Commercial Manufacturing, and Technical Terms* (London: G. Routledge &Co, 1858) cites: 'ALVA-MARINA, a commercial name for certain dried sea-weeds used for stuffing beds, &c.' (p. 9).
24 Major Kirkby Robinson (1832–1916) was appointed Medical Officer of Health for East Kent in 1872, previously holding the post at Leeds.
25 Localised inflammation caused by bacterial infection.
26 Feverish convulsion.
27 Edward Francis Fussell (1826–1896) of Brighton.
28 Another name for anthrax.
29 Washington Lyon (c1891–1901), bleacher. The patent machine was manufactured by Manlove, Alliott and Co, Nottingham, and was described on pages 293–294 of Parson's report on heat disinfection.

## Editorial Headnote

### Fyfe, Peter. 'What the People Sleep Upon', *Various Lectures – 1892–1904* (Glasgow: Corporation of Glasgow, 1908), Lecture 9: pp. 1–11.

Peter Fyfe, the Chief Sanitary Inspector for Glasgow, brought the problem of unhygienic rag flock mattresses to the attention of the public through this seminal lecture of 1904 which was widely reported in the press. The paper was delivered at the 22nd Congress of the Sanitary Institute, held at Glasgow University, 25–30 July of that year. It was soon issued as a pamphlet of eleven pages printed and circulated for the Committee on Health of the Corporation of Glasgow. Its preservation within a collected edition of nine lectures in 1908 further ensured its survival.

Peter Fyfe (1854–1940) was born in Glasgow. His father died while he was young, and he began work at age fourteen in his uncle's iron foundry. Starting in 1870, he followed a six-year apprenticeship as engineer at the London Road Iron Works of Duncan Stewart and Co., and afterward became chief draughtsman to a firm of crane-makers. It was in 1879 that he joined Glasgow Corporation as engineer to the Cleansing Department, taking part in the planning for a new 'refuse despatch' works to treat the city's refuse on a large scale. When the Chief Sanitary Inspector died in 1885, Fyfe was the successful applicant for the post. In the post of Sanitary Chief until 1919, and as Director of Housing until 1923, Fyfe was devoted to improvement of housing for the poor and working classes of Glasgow, wielding wide influence through his lectures. In 'What the People Sleep Upon', we can see Fyfe's command of argument and persuasive ability when he took up a cause. The lecture was often cited by others in the lead up to the Rag Flock Act of 1911.

# 32

# FYFE, PETER. 'WHAT THE PEOPLE SLEEP UPON'

## *Various Lectures – 1892–1904* (Glasgow: Corporation of Glasgow, 1908), Lecture 9: pp. 1–11.

It has been said that "there are combinations of evil, against which no human energies can make a stand."[1] Combinations of evil, at all events in a sanitary sense, seem peculiarly attachable to a certain class of the people. It is this class I had in my mind when I put down the word "people" in the title of the present paper. The major part of the people in this city are composed of those who nightly sleep in houses of one or two apartments. The most of them dwell in this limited space because they cannot afford to pay for more. Poverty compels them. The combinations of evil which dog the heels of poverty anywhere, but especially in the welter of city life, are only really known by those who day by day go down among it; and even *they* would need a microscopic eye to see the causes of the evils there. We see diseases the origin of which we cannot trace; they spring up here and there in apparently unconnected series, and, science baffled, labels them sporadic. They linger persistently in the poorer quarters of the town, and the prescription of preventive medicine – cleanse the house, flush the drains, hose-wash the courts, limewash the ashpits, and all the other hygienic formulæ – appear to fail as a panacea for them. Enteric, dysentery, diarrhœa – autumn after autumn seem as busy as ever among the people. To me it has always appeared unaccountable that, with a wet climate, an irreproachable water supply, daily supplies of uncontaminated milk, a closely guarded meat and food supply, a reasonably perfect sewage system, and gigantic cleansing operations continually proceeding – we should still witness the sufferings of the people from obviously preventable diseases such as I have named, and others I have not named. It may be that every weapon which bacteriology and chemistry can arm us with will fail to bring our elusive enemies within striking distance, but it appears to me one of the duties of sanitary inspectors to be also sanitary "suspectors," and leave no covert unsearched and unbeaten in which these enemies may be lurking.

It was in such a frame of mind I happened to be, when, in the company of friends fully a year ago, one of them, who was in the bed-making trade, began to speak of some new pine-fibre material he was introducing to this country, which would be cheaper and healthier than hair to sleep upon. The conversation soon turned upon the whole question of bedding material, and this expert's opinion was that much of the material of which beds were made, and particularly wool-flock, with which also chairs, sofas, and cushions were stuffed, was of a most objectionable

DOI: 10.4324/9780429274190-39

kind. I determined, when time would permit, and upon a suitable occasion, to make some investigation into the subject. This Congress of The Sanitary Institute seemed to offer the chance of a wider publicity for its consideration than any local meeting could; so, in view of to-day, I proceeded to collect some special information on what the poorer of our people sleep upon. I called to my aid some makers of common wool-flock, wholesale vendors of this material, some of the sanitary staff (male and female), and, finally, the Corporation Chemist, Mr. Harris,[2] and the City Bacteriologist, Dr. Buchanan;[3] and to all I have been much indebted for their hearty co-operation. Let me now present you with a brief statement of the proceedings which were taken, and the facts which have been brought to light.

I think you will agree with me that the existing state of affairs is most deplorable, and that this conference of sanitary inspectors from the four corners of the United Kingdom and Ireland would be wanting in appreciation of the magnitude of the evil, if it did not unanimously call upon the Council of the Institute to earnestly press upon the Government, the need for immediate reform.

The first proceeding was to discover the truth with regard to the exact nature of this wool-flock. I accordingly visited the works of several makers of it in this city. There, in the middle of February, I witnessed in each place a conglomeration of filthy rags – the offcast of every class of the population, from the wealthy of the West-end to the tramp and vagrant of the East. I examined certain individual parts of material, which was to be made by the "Devil" into bedding for the people. (I may explain that this is the appropriate name given to the machine which performs the laniary[4] process.)

To explain to you, in Parliamentary language, what I observed on some of the torn garments would be impossible. It is better left to the imagination. Only those pieces, soaking wet or too damp for the "Devil" to tear into shreds, were cast aside to be stoved, either beside the steam boiler or in a special drying chamber heated by steam. Nothing in the nature of cleansing or disinfection is attempted. All goes into the machine if sufficiently dry. At the other end it comes out as "flock," shredded so finely by the spikes or teeth on the periphery of the drums as to appear as fluffy wool of a dark grey, black, or brown hue, depending on the colour of the rags passing through the machine.

I show you here, in a glazed wooden case, the various kinds of flock used as bedding, 12 in number, and the wholesale prices of each class. I will refer to the contents of the case later on.

The great mass of dust and finely-powdered filth which is set free by the "Devil" is blown by a fan attached to it, into a dust chamber, out of which much of it finds its way into the surrounding atmosphere.

From one of the factories I secured in February last fully a pound of the flock as it came from the machine. At the sanitary office I weighed off half-a-pound. The Corporation Chemist gave me two Winchester jars of cold distilled water, in which I twice rinsed this quantity. The first rinsing was in 2.09 litres, or .45 of a gallon, for ten minutes; and the second rinsing in the distilled water of the second jar, containing 2.5 litres, or .55 of a gallon, for an equal time. These two samples

*Table I.* CHEMICAL ANALYSES OF RINSINGS FROM ½-LB. OF WOOL FLOCK (expressed in grains per gallon).

| | *Free and Saline Ammonia.* | *Albuminoid Ammonia.* | *Oxygen absorbed in 4 hours at 27°C.* | *Oxygen absorbed in 15 minutes at 27°C.* | *Chlorine* | *Solids in Solution.* | | | *Colour of Solution. (Loch Katrine Water = 10).* |
|---|---|---|---|---|---|---|---|---|---|
| | | | | | | *Mineral.* | *Volatile.* | *Total.* | |
| 1st Rinsing | 1.336 | 1.330 | 9.560 | 5.104 | 18.2 | 66.92 | 57.54 | 124.46 | 454 |
| 2nd Rinsing | 0.588 | 0.672 | 4.280 | 2.793 | 4.2 | 19.04 | 21.00 | 40.04 | 333 |
| | | | | | | Suspended Solids contained in Crude Sewage. | | | |
| Quarterly Average Composition of SEWAGE for Quarter ending 29th February, 1904 | 0.816 | 0.236 | 3.811 | --- | 12.6 | 10.56 | 13.84 | 24.40 | --- |

1-lb. of WOOL FLOCK (made from rags) was obtained immediately after passing through the Flockmaking Machine in one of our East-end Manufactories. ½-lb. of this Flock was twice rinsed in 2.25 litres or thereby (= 0.5 of a gallon) of Distilled Water for a period of 10 minutes. The dirty water from both rinsings was put into two Winchester Jars and sent to Mr. Harris, the Corporation Chemist, for Analysis, on 25th February, 1904.

AMOUNT AND NATURE OF SUSPENDED SOLIDS.

| | *Amount of Suspended Solids in grains per gallon.* | | *Actual Weight of Suspended Solids in ½-lb. of Flock.* | | *Weight of Suspended Solids in percentage of Weight of Flock rinsed.* | | *Actual Weight of Total Suspended Matter extracted.* | *Weight of Suspended Solids in percentage of Weight of Flock rinsed.* |
|---|---|---|---|---|---|---|---|---|
| | *1st Rinsing.* | *2nd Rinsing.* | *1st Rinsing.* | *2nd Rinsing.* | *1st Rinsing.* | *2nd Rinsing.* | | |
| | *Grains.* | *Grains.* | *Grains.* | *Grains.* | *Per cent.* | *Per cent.* | *Grains.* | *Per cent.* |
| Volatile or Organic Matter | 82.40 | 36.78 | 37.784 | 20.469 | 1.08 | 0.58 | 58.253 | 1.66 |
| Greasy or Oily Matter (Ether Extract) | 28.90 | 13.30 | 13.253 | 7.04 | 0.36 | 0.20 | 20.657 | 0.58 |
| Mineral Matter | 47.24 | 18.45 | 21.663 | 10.274 | 0.62 | 0.30 | 31.937 | 0.88 |
| TOTAL SUSPENDED SOLIDS | 158.54 | 68.53 | 72.700 | 38.147 | 2.06 | 1.08 | 110.847 | 3.12 |

(Amount of Water – 2.09 litres (0.45 gallon), 1st Rinsing; and 2.5 litres (0.55 gallon), 2nd Rinsing.)

of defiled water were then handed to the Corporation Chemist for analysis. His report to me is contained in the table (Table I).

In order that you may be able to grasp the extent of the filthiness of this bedding, the chemist, at my request, has placed underneath, on the third row, his corresponding analysis of average Glasgow crude sewage for the quarter ending 29th February. Under every heading the bedding shows very badly, as compared with the sewage. Expressed in grains per gallon, the sewage contained .816 of free and saline ammonia, against 1.924 grains in the rinsings from half-a-pound of the flock. Of albuminoid ammonia, against .236 for the sewage, we have 2.002 for the flock. The oxygen absorbed in four hours at 27° Centigrade by the sewage was 3.811 grains, against 13.840 grains for the bedding. Of chlorine, 12.6 for the sewage, against 22.4 for the bedding.

Now look at the total suspended solids in the crude sewage, as compared with that found in the two rinsings of this half-pound of flock. For the average sewage we note it is 24.4 grains per gallon, while in the bedding rinsings it reached the alarming figure of 227.07 grains per gallon. You will observe that, even the second ten minutes' rinsing of the flock contained almost three times more suspended solids than had been found in the sewage.

I will not weary you with further comparisons (the tables tell their own dreadful story), but I finally direct your attention to the last column, in which you will see that the suspended solids rinsed during twenty minutes from the flock formed 3.12 per cent, of the whole.

In case it might be urged in criticism that the material I secured at this flock-making factory might have been of a specially filthy character, I caused a new flock bed, bolster, and two pillows to be purchased on the 10th of May from one of our largest city house furnishers. I first shook and beat the bed on a clean dust-free floor, in order to ascertain if the dried dust and filth could come through the ticking. I found it did so, showing that the tick permits a considerable quantity to escape whenever the bed is shaken or made.

I then sent the whole up to the Sanitary Wash-house at Ruchill, with instructions to the manager to clean out one of the machines thoroughly, weigh the wool-flock very carefully, and then rinse it for half-an-hour in pure cold water. He did so, and sent me the result as follows: –

The two pillows contained 4 lbs. 10 oz. of flock; the bolster, 5 lbs. 4 oz.; the bed, 32 lbs. 3 oz.; or 42 lbs. 1 oz. in all. After half-an-hour's rinsing in the machine, the flock was taken out and dried. It was again weighed most carefully, coming out at 40 lbs. 2 oz.; thus showing a loss of 31 oz., or almost 2 lbs. avoirdupois, or a loss of 4.86 per cent. of the total weight.

The contents of this new bed were, therefore, found to contain a greater percentage of solid matter than was found by the Chemist in his half-pound of selected flock.

In order to present you with an ocular demonstration of the filth which was rinsed out of it, I asked the manager to slowly evaporate the rinsings until they could be contained in a Winchester bottle. The bottle is before you. This black, dirty-looking mass I pour out into a receiver on the table, so that any one may examine it for himself.

You see here a second bottle full of a clear brownish liquor. It contains some of the rinsing passed through filter paper, in order to show the amount of colour which is due to dye alone.

The third bottle shows you part of this filtration distilled, by which, it will be observed, a perfectly clear liquid is again obtained.

Having now satisfied myself as to the extremely obnoxious character of this description of bedding, I asked some of the male and female inspectors to make enquiries in the homes of the lower classes, for the purpose of ascertaining the kinds of bedding the majority sleep upon. About 2,300 houses in all were visited, in which special investigation was made into the composition of 3,163 beds. The following is the result: – Hair beds, 22; feather beds, 115; clean flock, 37; cotton clippings, 103; straw, 371; chaff, 39; shavings, 4; old clothes, 1; and common flock, 2,471.

Hence we find that 78 per cent. of the beds the common people nightly seek their repose upon are stuffed with that most pernicious material. How is this abominable material chosen? There can only be one answer: because it is cheap, and the people are ignorant of its real nature.

The glazed case you see here contains twelve samples of flocks kindly furnished me by a well-known English firm who manufacture all kinds. Under each sample the price is clearly marked. I need only direct your special attention to the common unwashed flock (No. 3), sold at 4s. 6d. per cwt. all over the country; and the better class, which is free from filth and is sold against it, namely, No. 7, called "grey millpuff,"[5] at 9s. 3d. per cwt. I am informed by the makers that the millpuff is ground almost to a pulp, which is kept in a moving stream of pure water for three-quarters of an hour.

Now, assuming a complete bed and pillows contain 42 lbs. of material, the whole difference to the public between that clean-looking grey millpuff and the dirty unwashed wool flock so much in use is only 1s. 9¼d. per bed; while, if we take the washed woollen millpuff at 10s. per cwt., the difference is not over 2s. per bed. Beds are not purchased so often by the people as to make a difference of 2s. felt, even by the humblest, and in any event it is clearly against the public interest that this vile material should be dispersed broadcast over the country. Even the makers of this stuff have conscience enough to reprobate its use. The owner of the factory from which I took the sample called upon me the following day, and in the conversation which followed he stated that he had often wondered that its manufacture and sale were not put a stop to. He admitted it was a filthy and dangerous material, but he had to make it in self-defence, and even as it was he was under-cut in price in the Glasgow market by manufacturers in Yorkshire. In conversation since with several bedding manufacturers, cushion makers, and chair and sofa furnishers, I found all were of one mind about it, but none dare decline to sell it for fear of losing business.

If anyone can still be found to support its continued sale, let me tell him what Dr. Buchanan, our City Bacteriologist, has written me about it. I give you the report in his own words: –

> "Seven specimens of 'flock' were received from you for bacteriological examination on the 17th of February last. The specimens comprised seven different qualities of flock, as sent out by manufacturers for use in upholstering and mattress-making.
>
> "In view of the fact – which has been demonstrated in our presence – that this material is frequently made from rags and cast-off clothing gathered from ash-pits, the bacteriological examination was undertaken to determine, from the number and kind of bacteria present, the amount of cleansing or disinfection to which the materials had been subjected in the course of manufacture.
>
> "Cultures were made as follows: – A definite quantity by weight of each sample of flock – namely, $^1/_{10}$ gramme – was thoroughly washed in 100 cc. of sterilised water. A definite volume (1 cc.) of the washing was diluted, so that the quantity ultimately added to the culture media represented the washings of $^1/_{10,000}$ gramme of flock. The results are computed as the number of bacteria in the washings of 1 gramme of flock. The figures can only be taken as an approximate indication of the numbers present, as the simple process of washing could only set free bacteria approximately representing the whole number in the material.
>
> "Two culture media (agar and gelatine) were used, in order to determine growth at blood heat and the temperature of the air.
>
> "The samples were examined on two occasions, at an interval of about three months; and, while the results of the second examination show a tendency to diminution of the bacteria, they at the same time show a general agreement with those of the first examination.
>
> "The experiments very clearly show that the different lots varied either in original cleanliness or in the processes through which they had been passed. The results obtained with 'common unwashed flock' are what might be expected from material gathered from such a source as that already mentioned. They indicate an amount of uncleanliness in the form of *live potential dirt* that is shocking to contemplate, when one considers the purpose for which the material is used. In the other samples of the first set, A, there is evidence of insufficient cleansing, and certainly no indication that any process of disinfection has been carried out. In the samples of set B there is evidence, in the relatively small number of bacteria, of marked improvement.* Taking sample B1, which may be

* It was afterwards admitted by the manufacturer of the samples B. that he had subjected them to a high temperature in a stove.

*Table II.* BACTERIOLOGICAL EXAMINATION OF "FLOCKS." BY DR. BUCHANAN.

| *Sample (Laboratory Mark).* | *Mark affixed by Manufacturers.* | *Condition.* | *Structure.* | *Value per Ton.* | FIRST EXAMINATION, *17th February, 1904.* | | SECOND EXAMINATION, *26th May, 1904* | |
|---|---|---|---|---|---|---|---|---|
| | | | | | *Bacteria in 1 gramme of Flock.* | | *Bacteria in 1 gramme of Flock.* | |
| | | | | | *At Blood Heat.* | *At Temp. of Air.* | *At Blood Heat.* | *At Temp. of Air.* |
| A1 | Common | Unwashed | Common Wool | £8 | 4,500,000 | 18,900,000 | 2,600,000 | 4,800,000 |
| A2 | No. 1½ | Supposed to be washed | Light Wool | £12 | 2,170,000 | 4,390,000 | 1,800,000 | 3,800,000 |
| A3 | No. 3 | Ditto | Grey Wool | £8 10s. | 700,000 | 350,000 | 530,000 | 540,000 |
| A4 | No. 4 | Ditto | White Wool | £14 10s. | 2,000,000 | 2,300,000 | 1,400,000 | 1,920,000 |
| B1 | 1½ | Not stated | Common Wool | --- | 10,000 | 90,000 | 20,000 | 20,000 |
| B2 | 2¾ | Ditto | Carpet Wool | --- | 140,000 | 100,000 | 60,000 | 130,000 |
| B3 | 3 | Ditto | Wool and Cotton | --- | 210,000 | 230,000 | 200,000 | 250,000 |

> compared with A1, there is such a wholesome difference in the numbers – 10,000, say, as compared with 4,500,000 – as to indicate, if not thorough washing, at least some attempt at disinfection. (It may be mentioned by way of comparison that the average number of bacteria in the same quantity of Loch Katrine water for the year 1903 was 75, and that the average of 32 examinations of Glasgow crude sewage was no more than 197,500.)
>
> "The results of the examination reveal a state of matters calling for remedial action."

When we consider this expert opinion, and look at the figures on the bacteriological table (Table II), which confirm those of our Corporation Chemist, it is with difficulty that we are restrained from giving vent to feelings of indignation that, as executive sanitary officials, we have been for so long powerless to cope with a widespread evil in every way calculated to bring disease into the closest proximity with our labouring population. It would be manifestly safer to sleep on a bed filled with sewage than on this material,[6] upon which, as I have shown, 78 per cent. of our humbler fellow-citizens are nightly reposing.

The figures can only be suitably described as *appalling* in their suggestiveness, for again, remember that it is not only the 78 per cent. of our humbler classes who are in danger from this material in their homes, but every West-end lady who, with severe and unthinking economy, purchases one of these "cheap and nasty" beds for her servant, takes into her otherwise well-appointed home a centre of disease potentiality. Filth in or about the servant may mean disease in her household.

Finally, let me express the hope that, now the facts are known, the Government will lose as little time as possible in passing a measure which will enable all Local Authorities to *sample* bedding both in the premises of flock manufacturers and in those who *sell* beds, sofas, couches, and cushions, and that punishment may follow every sale of any such material which does not conform to a certain standard of cleanliness and freedom from microbial impurity. What that standard may be I leave to the judgment of biological experts, but I trust we shall all be unanimous in the desire to see, at the very earliest date, a severe restriction put on the manufacture and sale of such material as I have had the honour to draw your attention to.

## Notes

1 Samuel Warren's *Passages from the Diary of a Late Physician* (Edinburgh: William Blackwood, 1832), vol. 2, p. 246.

2 Frederick William Harris (born around 1862) was City Analyst and Chemist to Glasgow Corporation from 1899 to 1935.

3 Robert MacNeil Buchanan (1861–1931) was the first City Bacteriologist for Glasgow, appointed in 1899 and retiring in 1930. A detailed obituary can be found in the *British Medical Journal*, 2:3686 (29 Aug 1931), pp. 401–402.

4 Lacerating and tearing.

5 Technically, millpuff is the woolly residue from the process of fulling (also known as milling) cloth. Here, however, it may be used to describe a type of pulled rag flock. Paul Hasluck described millpuff as a cotton mill residue, or a cotton/worsted mixture (see Article 33 this volume).

6 Fyfe allows his rhetoric to gain precedence over his science here by, in effect, treating all bacteria as equal in potential harm to humans, and judging only by comparative numbers of bacteria.

## Editorial Headnote

### Hasluck, Paul N. 'Upholsterers' Materials', *Upholstery, with Numerous Engravings and Diagrams* (Philadelphia: David McKay, 1904), pp. 15–17.

In March 1904, Paul Nooncree Hasluck (1854–1931) signed the preface of his book at La Belle Sauvage, London, the building of Cassell and Company's publishing house, where he worked. The book rearranged articles originally contributed to the weekly journal *Work: an Illustrated Magazine of Practice and Theory for all Workmen, Professional and Amateur*. Hasluck explained that it 'consists substantially of matter contributed by a working upholsterer'. The book was first issued as part of Cassell's 'Work' Handbooks series priced at 1s. The *St. James's Gazette* noted,

> The "Work" Handbooks make a useful series of technical manuals of a variety of crafts and industries. They are arranged in a form convenient for everyday use, and under the editorship of Mr. P. N. Hasluck a vast amount of information has been compressed into a small compass.
> (17 Sep 1904, p. 19)

Upholstery was introduced to the series alongside saddlery, leather working and harness making. The volume was brought out concurrently by David McKay in Philadelphia, and a pocket-sized version was issued by 1908. A second edition was released in 1915 by both publishers. Cassell offered a paperback version of this edition for 1s. 6d., priced for the amateur market.

Hasluck was born near Adelaide, South Australia, but moved to England as a child. He showed an early talent for mechanical subjects and was granted patent no. 2606 in 1868 for a device for 'registering the distance traversed by hackney carriages'. He began practice as a watchmaker at 254 Tottenham Court Road, setting up in co-partnership with Chapman Bower Bridge (1845–1876), trading as Hasluck and Bridge, jewellers and watchmakers. However, the firm went into liquidation by arrangement with its creditors at the start of 1876 (*London Gazette*, 11 Jan 1876, p. 132). In great anxiety about his embarrassed circumstances, Bridge committed suicide by swallowing prussic acid outside Kilburn police station on the 4th May (*Nottingham Journal*, 15 May 1876, p. 4). Hasluck fortunately changed his career path to become an author and editor. The 1881 census recorded him as an 'author of mechanical works', and from 1883 to 1884, he edited *Amateur Mechanics*. In 1889, the journal *Work* was begun with Francis Chilton-Young (1828–1898); Hasluck was editor from 1892 to 1909. He had truly found his metier. Known for his skill in translating technicalities into everyday language, he was to write numerous technical manuals adapted for the use of amateurs as well as professionals.

# 33

# HASLUCK, PAUL N. 'UPHOLSTERERS' MATERIALS'

## *Upholstery* (Philadelphia: David McKay, 1904), pp. 15–17.

For stuffing, curled horse-hair is the best material to use, but it has one disadvantage in that it is rather expensive. Several substitutes are sold, the following being the most important: Cocoanut fibre[1] is a splendid material for getting firm edges: it should be of the clean, long-stapled variety, and not powdered. Algerian grass,[2] dyed black, has much the same appearance as horse-hair, but is harsh and brittle. New Orleans moss[3] and wild pineapple fibre[4] are also used as horse-hair substitutes. When horse-hair is burnt it leaves a black ash, whilst vegetable fibres burn to a light grey ash.[5]

Alva, a seaweed[6] from the shores of southern Russia, the Baltic, and other places, is used in large quantities in the upholstering trade. It should be dry, as the damp green portions often seen in a bale of alva are liable to breed vermin. German alva is inferior to French, which is crisper and has more spring in it. The Dutch alva is the cleanest and most free from lumps. None of the vegetable fibres, however, is to be compared with hair, as they do not present the same amount of elasticity. Take a handful of each material and compress it; good hair will expand again on pressure being removed, while the others will do so only to a very limited extent. In use, seats stuffed with them become hard and lumpy very soon, while hair retains its spring for a considerable time, though, of course, it eventually becomes matted.

Cotton and woollen flocks were, until recently, almost exclusively used in the north of England for stuffing cheap furniture and beds. Flocks – short stapled, fluffy fibres – are the waste and fallings from the various machines used in preparing the threads for the looms and in finishing the cloth. There are several qualities and varieties of flocks, the best being those made in the operation of raising or fulling fine woollen cloth. The cheapest are the screenings from the cotton-cleaning machines. There are also mixtures of cotton and wool, dyed and in natural colour. Flock makes a nice warm stuffing, but is inferior to the fibres mentioned above for making good edges.[7]

Raising flocks are the short fibres torn from the surface of woollen cloth in the process of raising the nap or pile.

Cutting flocks are thrown off in the operation of cutting or clipping the face of certain kinds of cloth; these are cheap, usually very short in staple, and enter into the composition of flock wall-papers.


DOI: 10.4324/9780429274190-40

Milling flocks are formed in the operation of milling the surface of woollen fabrics.

Noils are the short fibres of wool removed in the process of wool-combing. Noils and millings are almost pure wool, and command a good price; they are chiefly used for woollen flock beds.

Mill puff is cotton or a mixture of cotton and worsted waste,[8] and is much used in stuffing cheap furniture. It is mostly the screenings or fallings from cotton, etc., thrown down during cleaning and burring.

Mungo is prepared from woollen rags torn into short fibres. Wool extract is very similar to mungo, but has all the vegetable matter extracted by a chemical process. In preparing flocks for the market, they are mixed or blended to produce the different qualities and colours. Cotton flocks, such as teazed or mill puff, are usually packed in bags of 56 lb., whilst woollen flocks are put up in 50-lb. bags.

Flock manufacture is usually carried on as an adjunct to a woollen mill, the woollen waste being sorted on large wire grids, which allow the dust and powdered material to fall through. The better qualities are dyed, dried by heat, and passed into a "willowing" machine, which beats and opens all the fibres. They are then passed into a curling machine, and blown out by compressed air, and afterwards packed in 50-lb. bags for the market.

The machine used by upholsterers for dressing flocks is known as a teazer or willey. Teazed wools are a pure wool flock, but are a bad colour, with no curl, and are manufactured from the fluff and sweepings of the mills; they are very cheap and warm.

Black wool flocks are in many different qualities and colours, and are chiefly made by the combing machines used in wool carding; they are of medium curl, are much used for mattress stuffings, and are often blended with coloured flocks and sold as "red spot fancy," mottled mixture, brown mixture, etc., the name denoting what colour has been blended with the black. White wools are a pure wool flock with a full curl and soft elastic feel, which in ordinary circumstances last for years without matting.

In addition to the fillings already mentioned, there are special materials for hot climates, the principal of these being paper shavings, wood wool,[9] manna,[10] aloes,[11] etc., the object being to get a loose texture which will admit of more perfect ventilation.

Wadding is cotton or cotton-waste very finely carded to give it a soft, fluffy appearance. It is gummed to tissue paper. The grey wadding is the kind mostly used by upholsterers.

## Notes

1 Coconut fibre, or coir, is extracted from the outer husk of the coconut, fruit of the coconut palm, *Cocos nucifera*.

2 Algerian grass is more commonly known as esparto, a fibre extracted from a perennial grass, *Stipa tenacissima*.

3 New Orleans moss is now known as Spanish moss, *Tillandsia usneoides*, an epiphytic plant that grows on large trees in tropical and subtropical regions. It is from the pineapple family, the bromeliads.
4 Wild pineapple probably refers to *Bromelia pinguin*, a perennial with long spiky fronds from which fibre can be extracted.
5 Burn tests were a readily available and common method for distinguishing fibre groups.
6 Alva is commonly known as sea grass, *Zostera marina*.
7 That is, horsehair and coconut fibre.
8 This differs from mill puff of woollen origin, here designated as 'milling flocks', but both consist of new fibre material.
9 Wood wool, also known as excelsior, consists of long slivers of wood, often cut from softwood evergreens.
10 It is likely that manila is meant here. Manila fibre is obtained from the leaf sheaths of the abaca plant, *Musa textilis*.
11 Fibre can be extracted from the succulent leaves of *Aloe barbadensis*.

## Editorial Headnote

**Wakley, Thomas (ed.).** ***Articles on 'Loathsome Bed Stuffing' from The Lancet: a Journal of British and Foreign Medicine, Surgery, Obstetrics, Physiology, Chemistry, Pharmacology, Public Health, and News.***

1 **'Loathsome Bed "Stuffing"', *The Lancet*, 167:4306 (10 Mar 1906), p. 690.**
2 **'Loathsome Bed-Stuffing', *The Lancet*, 168:4345 (8 Dec 1906), p. 1638.**
3 **'Loathsome Bed-Stuffing', *The Lancet*, 168:4348 (29 Dec 1906), p. 1834.**
4 **'Loathsome Bed-Stuffing', *The Lancet*, 169:4352 (26 Jan 1907), p. 265.**
5 **'Filthy Wool-Flock Beds', *The Lancet*, 169:4353 (2 Feb 1907), p. 309.**
6 **'Loathsome Bed Stuffing', *The Lancet*, 169:4366 (4 May 1907), p. 1241.**
7 **'Loathsome Bed-Stuffing', *The Lancet*, 169:4368 (18 May 1907), p. 1406.**
8 **'Loathsome Bed-Stuffing', *The Lancet*, 169:4371 (8 Jun 1907), pp. 1584–1585.**
9 **'"Loathsome Bed Stuffing"', *The Lancet*, 170:4384 (7 Sep 1907), pp. 727–728.**
10 **'Loathsome Bed Stuffing', *The Lancet*, 170:4385 (14 Sep 1907), p. 812.**
11 **'"Loathsome Bed-Stuffing"', *The Lancet*, 170:4387 (28 Sep 1907), p. 941.**
12 **'The Bacteriology of "Loathsome Bed-Stuffing"', *The Lancet*, 170:4391 (26 Oct 1907), p. 1173.**

From March 1906 to October 1907, the medical journal *The Lancet* carried a succession of short articles and correspondence, nearly all under the title 'Loathsome Bed Stuffing'. These texts incidentally reveal details of the processes of rag trading, rag preparation, flock production and rag-flock usage while they call for tighter regulation of rag flock production and use. As a set, they show the evolution of the campaign against insanitary bedding, and the difficulty of rousing the government to action. It was to be five more years before legislation took effect to ban the practice of using unwashed flock for bedding.

The agitation of 1907 led to the Local Government Board commissioning an investigation by Dr Reginald Farrer (1861–1921) in 1908, published as 'Report on the manufacture and sale of unwashed rag flock' with several related scientific analyses under the title *Reports on Rag Flock* (London: HMSO, 1910). Although no definitely proved instances of people contracting disease from sleeping on rag flock mattresses were found, the report found agreement that it was not safe 'to assume that disease never arises in this way'. It was the establishment of a reliable analytic test to distinguish washed from unwashed flock that enabled the institution of legislation, known as the Rag Flock Act 1911, that banned the sale of unwashed rag flock products.

The editor-in-chief of *The Lancet* at this time was Thomas Wakley (1851–1909). He had previously filled the role jointly with his father who died in 1907. Wakley was a scrupulous editor and careful to remain impartial. But he was trained in journalism under his uncle James Goodchild Wakley (1825–1886) who was particularly concerned with public health issues stemming from unsanitary conditions. Retaining the dramatic and memorable 'loathsome' keyword in the titles of these contributions loosely spread over time, helped to retain the issue in the memory and create a sense of accumulating evidence.

# 34

# WAKLEY, THOMAS (ED.). ARTICLES ON 'LOATHSOME BED "STUFFING" ', FROM *THE LANCET*

## *The Lancet* (10 Mar 1906), p. 690; (8 Dec 1906), p. 1638; (29 Dec 1906), p. 1834; (26 Jan 1907), p. 265; (2 Feb 1907), p. 309; (4 May 1907), p. 1241; (18 May 1907), p. 1406; (8 Jun 1907), pp. 1584–1585; (7 Sep 1907), pp. 727–728; (14 Sep 1907), p. 812; (28 Sep 1907), p. 941; (26 Oct 1907), p. 1173.

### Loathsome bed "stuffing." [10 March 1906]

The following story has quite recently reached us from a correspondent: A fairly large manufacturer, he writes, told me (and made no secret of the fact) that at his mills, they took in a large quantity of old clothes. These had the buttons, &c., removed and were at once turned into "flock" without any washing or disinfecting whatever, and used in that state to make cheap new mattresses. For higher price mattresses they wash this "flock" under heavy rollers, and all made with this "stuffing" are stamped "guaranteed washed filling." We are quite prepared to credit this story, for two years ago we referred to a paper read before the Congress of the Sanitary Institute in Glasgow by Mr. Peter Fyfe, entitled "What People Sleep On,"[1] in which the writer showed that a certain section of the bed-making trade made mattresses from a mass of rags rejected by every class of the population. There was no attempt to disinfect these rags or even to clean them. In 1905 the Home Secretary[2] was asked a question on this subject and his astounding reply was: "The compulsory cleaning of the materials referred to could not be generally secured under the existing law. The point has been noted for consideration but I cannot at present hold out any prospect of legislation on the subject." If ever an opportunity presented itself to our new legislators of convincing the country of their concern for the public health this is surely one. So far as we can discover, no steps have been taken and the filthy practice goes on unchecked and sanitary officers are powerless to interfere. The horse in the stable is much better looked after, for at least it is provided with clean straw or a clean cork litter. This scandal



DOI: 10.4324/9780429274190-41

demands instant suppression and we commend to the Government the desirability of prosecuting an immediate inquiry into this disgraceful breach of common hygienic principles. Little wonder that the dissemination of disease is so often obscure and that it is frequently found in the poorer districts that the bed of the patient emits a foul and sickly smell.

## Loathsome bed-stuffing. [8 December 1906]

We notice with regret the reply of the President of the Local Government Board[3] to a question asked by Mr. Lyulph Stanley[4] in the House of Commons last week as to whether it was the intention of his department, either by legislation or otherwise, to prohibit the use of rag-flock in the making of bedding without first subjecting it to some cleansing and disinfecting process. Mr. Burns said that the compulsory cleansing of rag-flock could not be generally secured under the existing law. He was not at present in a position, he added, to promise legislation on the subject but the point has been noted for consideration when a suitable opportunity offers. We have frequently called attention to this matter, and it seems to us extraordinary that there is no section of our administration which is able at once to deal with this evil. That the evil exists there cannot be the shadow of a doubt and we have referred to evidence on this point which we believe to be true. Quite recently we received a communication from Mr. J. O. Neumann[5] on this subject who has had abundant ocular demonstration of the filthiness of the flock used for stuffing beds, not the slightest attempt having been made to cleanse, not to say to disinfect, it. "These rags," he writes, "come from the dustbin, the ragshops, the gutters, and the corners of dilapidated buildings all over England. In going through a factory one sees floor after floor packed with bundles of garments, so dirty that even the ragpickers themselves will not touch them except with the end of a long pole. The stench arising from them is so bad that one proprietor admitted that he would be unable to keep a sufficient number of workmen were it not for the occasional finds of coin which are made even in these well-searched refuse heaps. I saw heaps of rags torn from the floors of railway carriages full of indescribable filth. In another corner were some 20 tons of old corsets which had just emerged from the process of being stripped from the whalebone, and were now ready to be made into bedding. Near by lay old greasy fragments of cotton and satin. Another floor was given up to children's garments, old caps and bonnets, curtains and carpets. All these odds and ends are torn into a fine fluffy material by machinery that is so coarse as to allow all but the heaviest atoms of dust and grit to remain in it. Washing would cost £2 per ton extra, and one-third of the dearly-bought rubbish would disappear in the process." And this is the stuff which people take their repose upon, its evil smell disguised by the application of an oil and its dirt and filth held together by the same agency. It is hardly possible to understand why, with our admirably equipped sanitary administration, this evil and menace to health should escape scotching.

## Loathsome bed-stuffing. [29 December 1906]

*To the Editors of* THE LANCET.

SIRS, – Having had 20 years' experience in the manufacture of bedding and rag flock I have read with great interest your remarks under the heading of "Loathsome Bed-stuffing" and am greatly surprised at the indifference with which the President of the Local Government Board has treated the subject. If he could but spare time to visit a flock factory he would be so disgusted at seeing the filthy rubbish which is made up into bed fillings, without the slightest attempt at washing or sterilising, that I feel confident he would take immediate steps to make the cleansing compulsory. I congratulate your correspondent, Mr. J. O. Neumann, on his knowledge of the trade; he does not in any way exaggerate the case. We have to buy the commonest and dirtiest rags obtainable from the marine-store dealer and he in turn collects from our vilest slums and ash-heaps; in fact, they are discarded garments of all descriptions which are too old and disreputable for our poorest poor, and who knows what disease is lurking in them. These rags are simply passed through a machine and torn into shreds without the slightest attempt to wash and sterilise, and owing to keen competition the art of the manufacturer is to keep in as much of the filth and dirt as possible, so that he can make a small margin of profit. But it is quite unnecessary to reject the material because it has been in contact with filth, and my contention is that there is nothing more hygienic, resilient, or better suited for bedding than these rags after they have been thoroughly washed and all dirt taken from them, and afterwards properly sterilised by heat. Apologising for having taken up so much of your valuable space,

I am, Sirs, yours faithfully, W. T. ELLERY.[6] Bath, Dec. 19th, 1906.

## Loathsome bed-stuffing. [26 January 1907]

*To the Editors of* THE LANCET.

SIRS, – My attention has been called to a letter appearing in your paper on "Loathsome Bed-stuffing," and I am pleased to note that Mr. W. T. Ellery has had the courage to speak up to his conviction. Would that other manufacturers did the same.

Writing from an outside point of view, I do not think the manufacturers are altogether to blame, but I consider the makers of the beds and mattresses are at fault; they buy a common class shoddy – in fact, made from what Mr. Ellery describes to be "the commonest and dirtiest rags obtainable"; this they stuff the bedding with and label it with such words as "sanitary" or "purified." Such words as these are misleading and beguile the public into buying a cheap article, leading them to think it is perfectly hygienic.

I am, Sirs, yours faithfully, SANITAS, Jan. 19th, 1907

## Filthy wool-flock beds. [2 Feb 1907]

Mr. Peter Fyfe has contributed to the *Journal of the Royal Sanitary Institute* for January[7] further evidence of the danger of common bedding to the public health. Four new wool-flock beds were bought in Bristol and Glasgow, at prices ranging from 7s. 6d. to 10s. 6d. each, and portions of the flock have been examined bacteriologically by Dr. R. M. Buchanan[8] and chemically by Mr. F. W. Harris.[9] The flock of the four beds contained respectively 3, 10½, ½, and 22 million organisms per gramme, comparing very badly with crude Glasgow sewage which contained about 197,000 organisms per gramme. A high proportion of soluble matter was present, the flock of one of the beds, weighing 36 pounds, losing 5½ pounds in weight when washed with 40 gallons of water. In all cases the washings on analysis compared unfavourably with crude Glasgow sewage. The latter absorbed 3.095 grains of oxygen per gallon in three minutes; the minimum corresponding figure for the washings from the flock bedding was 4.24 grains. The corresponding figure for each of the other three washings was more than double this amount. In each case the amount of albuminoid ammonia in the washings exceeded that present in crude sewage. Experiments were carried out to determine the effect on the atmosphere of a room of making an ordinary flock bed in a number of clean dwelling-houses. Agar culture plates were exposed in the rooms before and after the beds were made by the housewives in the usual way. Dr. Buchanan found an increase in the number of bacteria in the air of each apartment as the result of making the beds, the number being increased 30 times in the case of the cheapest bed and 230 times in the case of a bed which had been bought at second hand, while the atmosphere was rendered disagreeable in both apartments. The making of a number of more expensive beds produced only a relatively small increase in the number of organisms in the atmosphere and there was no perceptible odour or dust. As Mr. Fyfe points out, hundreds of thousands of persons in this country are constantly sleeping upon stuff which, after rinsing in a large volume of water, yields a liquid containing more putrescible organic matter than ordinary sewage, and more total solids, to say nothing of colour, than are allowed in effluents into rivers. Further, the presence of such filthy bedding in houses is a constant menace to the purity of foodstuffs, especially to milk, meat, and soup, for the storage of which there is seldom proper accommodation in those houses in which cheap bedding is to be found. The bacteriological examination of the flocks has not yet been completed but sufficient evidence has been produced to demonstrate again the pressing urgency of legislative measures to prevent the continued sale of loathsome bed-stuffing.

## Loathsome bed stuffing. [4 May 1907]

We make no apology for returning to this subject, as in our opinion the attitude of the Government in regard to it is very unsatisfactory, while a distinct menace to the public health is being allowed to exist with no organised attempt whatever to suppress the evil. We have received from many quarters complete endorsement of the remarks which we have made from time to time and we have abundant reason for believing that the information supplied to us is absolutely correct. The latest communication is convincing and contains singularly unwholesome facts. "The awful filth that finds its way into beds and mattresses is," says our correspondent, "appalling; rags of the most filthy kind and old carpets stinking with dirt are torn up by a machine known as 'the devil.'" After the heavy grit is shaken out the so-called wool is sent to the bedding manufacturer to be put into beds and mattresses and in many instances these are labelled and sold as "sanitary bedding." There cannot, of course, be the least objection to the use of such material for this purpose provided that it is thoroughly washed and sterilised. We understand, however, that this desirable process would add to the cost by about 2s. for each bed and rather than pay this extra amount for a sanitary and clean mattress a stupid section of the public would sooner run the risk of having an offensive bed to lie upon if not one which may very possibly reward their pigheadedness with disease. And manufacturers sell these mattresses realising full well the penalties which the buyer is likely to incur and yet they are powerless to stop it because if they insisted upon an extra charge of 2s. for a cleaned mattress their business and custom would be threatened with extinction. "20 years ago," writes our correspondent, "I made no flock but what was washed and sterilised, but to-day, I am sorry to admit, I am compelled to do as others do and make the filthy stuff to compete and hold my own, for there are many manufacturers who have no washing plant, and probably 80 per cent. of all beds and mattresses are made from the rags torn up and used as filling in their dirty state." This evil trade does not only apply to bedding, for there are reasons for believing that what is the most magnificent upholstery on the surface in the shape of velvets, sateen, and tapestry may, after all, be sheltering a loathsome stuffing. The public, or that section of it which cares for these things, would do well to regard this matter seriously, and it is easy enough to ascertain by a simple test whether the character of this material is objectionable or not. If a portion of the material be taken out of the case and placed in a basin containing some boiling water and stirred up there will be an unmistakeably offensive smell evolved if the material is unscoured and unfit for bedding, while the water will become dirty-coloured. Often, however, the stuffing is so palpably bad that such a test is quite superfluous. Surely some system of control should be established by the Government without any delay which will put an effectual end to this infamous disregard for cleanly dealing and common hygienic demand.

## Loathsome bed-stuffing. [18 May 1907]

*To the Editors of* THE LANCET.

SIRS, – We were glad to notice extract from your issue regarding impure bedding. We enclose a copy of our senior partner's little publication; second issue (six or eight years ago); see page 44 *et seq.* on same subject. We question very much if some who use the word sterilised know what it means. We think prosecution under the Merchandise Act should follow false advertising.

We are, Sirs, yours faithfully, MARTIN AND SON.[10] Edinburgh, May 8th, 1907.

P.S. – Old clothes from Scotland go over to Ireland and after Pat has worn and patched them they come back to Greenock in bales to be torn up, unwashed, and sold for bedding!

*The publication referred to is entitled "About Beds and Bedding," and it contains a good deal of practical and historical information on the subject. In regard to loathsome bedding the writer rather aptly, we think, quotes Dickens's story of the "Celebrated Sausage Shop"[11] in the "Pickwick Papers." Halves of buttons had been found in the sausages, and buttons have also been found, it is stated, in bed-mattresses. – ED. L.

## Loathsome bed-stuffing [8 Jun 1907]

Our attitude on the above subject, as explained in several articles in recent numbers of THE LANCET, continues to attract the attention of the trade and it is gratifying to us to find so many representatives of the bed-furnishing industry giving hearty support to our views. We have consistently urged that the evil can be suppressed by a simple system of inspection of the factories where bed stuffing is made and handled. We are convinced that no respectable firm would resent this plan should it become part of a Government scheme for preventing this scandal. On the contrary, the great furnishing houses, we feel sure, would welcome such an innovation and the plan of control could be conducted without needlessly submitting their business to inconvenience. This, at any rate, is the opinion of one great furnishing house – namely, Messrs. Maple and Co.[12] We understand from the representations made to us by this firm that the root of the mischief is simply and solely the disgusting policy of raking up the cheapest possible raw material. Any offensive rags, left off clothes, and so on, can be torn to shreds and converted into flock by the machine appropriately known as "the devil." The resulting mass, of course, should be thoroughly washed and scoured but that process obviously makes it more costly and so sanitary procedure is ignored and all sorts of abominations are mercilessly stuffed into the mattress. By the courtesy of Messrs. Maple and Co. we had the opportunity of inspecting their bedding factories and of watching the processes or series of processes which bed-stuffing of varying qualities goes through before it is considered fit for the purpose of stuffing mattresses. The raw material comprises hair, feathers, torn up carpets, rags, and so forth, all of which are carefully submitted not only to a cleaning process but to a dust-extracting process also. During the teasing out of this material the operation is conducted within the field of an exhaust fan or cyclone, so that all irritating and easily scattered dust is effectually removed. Is it unreasonable to demand that all raw material destined ultimately to be used for filling bedding should be treated on the scrupulous sanitary lines indicated? We not only think not but maintain that some form of Government machinery should enforce such treatment.

## "Loathsome bed stuffing." [7 Sep 1907]

Numerous paragraphs have appeared in THE LANCET under the above heading and we continue to receive a number of letters from manufacturers of rag flock and others in which we are very generally commended for the attitude which we have taken in regard to this subject. That attitude is simply an expression of concern that an obviously insanitary and filthy proceeding in connexion with the manufacture of rag flock for bedding purposes should be allowed to exist in these days of high hygienic standards. It is hard to imagine anything more offensive than the filthy rags, the offal of clothes, the worn-out dust-laden carpets which form the raw material out of which flock mattresses and many upholstered goods are made, and without the slightest attempt to submit them to a process of scientific cleaning. We write "scientific cleaning" advisedly, for it must be obvious that such material may and does contain pestiferous filth which no ordinary cleaning process can destroy. Such material should be absolutely sterilised in addition to washing before it should be allowed to fill the mattress or the cushion. It must be cleansed both macroscopically and microscopically. We enjoin such measures in the light of a full and practical knowledge recently gained on this subject.

A representative of THE LANCET has recently visited flock factories; he has seen for himself how offensive and disgusting this trade can be and at the same time how inoffensive it can be made, or how little exception can be taken to it on sanitary grounds, when the simple procedure of washing and sterilisation is adopted. Yet it is no exaggeration to say that the bulk of the flock made from cast-off clothing, old carpets, &c., receives no such cleansing treatment at all. It is merely worried into a flocculent material by the "devil." The fluffy substance after it leaves this powerful tearing up machine bears, of course, no sort of resemblance to the old coats, hats, dresses, carpets from which it is made and is more or less presentable to the eye when ocular examination is confined to the surface. Deeper inspection it will not bear; it is often loaded with dust and frequently has an offensive smell. Dormant as this filth may be in ordinary circumstances, it is unpleasant to think what a stimulus may be given to its disease-dealing potentialities when it is brought to the temperature of incubation and to a condition of moistness by the person who sleeps upon it. We have met not a few manufacturers who frankly acknowledge the evil, yet who are bound to confess that they are powerless to stop it because the demon of cheapness is deaf to sanitary considerations. The mattress that costs a shilling or so more because it has been thoroughly cleansed and sterilised is not regarded as better value for the money by an ignorant section of the public. If only disease entities were as obvious to the eye as, say, cockroaches, that view might be modified, and in this case a general agreement might possibly be arrived at that what was cheap was also decidedly nasty. The production of unwashed, unsterilised flock is thus thrust upon the flock manufacturer whether his views be clean and wholesome or not. He must meet a stupid, ignorant demand or lose a large part of his business.

But much to their credit there are manufacturers who detest this traffic and who, in spite of the risk of reducing the volume of their trade, have established at their factories cleanly methods and have gone so far as to provide for the complete sterilisation of the materials in an efficient steam sterilising apparatus prior to their conversion into flock in the "devil."[13] They have gone farther and have even placed the method under the control of a bacteriologist and have not been satisfied until the evidence was convincing that the material came through the process absolutely sterile as disclosed by bacteriological experiment.*

Of course such treatment adds to the cost of the material, but surely such a regard for sanitary considerations should be recognised and should never be allowed to be severely handicapped by the unchecked and unrestricted output of "wools" which are loathsome and filthy. Not long ago a question was put to the President of the Local Government Board in the House of Commons as to whether it was the intention of his department either by legislation or otherwise to prohibit the use of rag flock in the making of bedding without first subjecting it to some cleansing and disinfecting process. Mr. Burns replied that the compulsory cleansing of rag-flock could not be generally secured under the existing law. He was not in a position, he added, to promise legislation on the subject but "the point has been noted for consideration when a suitable opportunity offers."

It should be pointed out that the evil was well known to the Local Government Board more than 25 years ago. In the annual report of the medical officer of the Local Government Board, for example, for 1885 appears a report by Dr. H. F. Parsons "On the Manufacture of Rag Flock in Reference to the Possible Dissemination of Infectious Disease by this and other Products of Woollen Rags."[14] Dr. Parsons states that rags are imported into this country from almost every part of the world in which people are sufficiently civilised to wear clothing. There are large consignments from the continent, while other rags are collected in this country by "marine store dealers." A very dirty class of rags is collected from the dust hills on which the refuse of London and other large towns is tipped. Woollen rags, it appears, are also used as manure, especially for hops. Rags are sometimes met with, we learn from this report, which are soiled with blood or excrement, but Dr. Parsons "did not hear of poultices being observed or anything which would lead to the inference that the rags had been used by sick persons." In recapitulating the results of his inquiry Dr. Parsons states that the rags from which the

* We may, mention the names of two firms at least who communicated with us and who adopt the sanitary measures indicated and we are prepared to publish the names of any others who employ similar hygienic methods. The Wandsworth Flock Company, of Dunt's Hill Mills, Garratt-lane, Wandsworth, not only thoroughly wash the raw materials but afterwards place them in a well-known type of high-pressure steam steriliser. A well-known bacteriologist found that "the rags had been efficiently sterilised." Mr. T. R. Freeman, again, of Monkton Combe Mills, near Bath, has submitted to us samples of medium and cheap mattress wools "thoroughly washed and sterilised." "The rags are beaten by machinery specially adapted for the purpose," after which "the material is placed on stoves and dried at a germ-destroying temperature."

inferior qualities of flock are made are commonly very dirty and do not, as a rule, undergo any process of purification beyond the removal of dust. He recommends the disinfection or purification of rags, adding that the best disinfectant for the purpose is heat in the form of superheated steam or hot, moist air.

It is true that the law forbids under penalty the selling, transmission, or exposure, of infected articles, and that if infected rags pass into the market it is through a breach of the law on the part of the original vendor. The position that some manufacturers take, therefore, is that they are not responsible for any breach of the law which others may commit. It is pretty safe to assert that this attitude affords no security whatever to the public. The fact remains that material that may be no better than manure is being used for making bedding without any attempt being made to render it clean and wholesome by the scientific process of sterilisation by steam. There must be a number of filthy beds in the land and it is not improbable that this fact accounts for some mysterious outbreaks of disease.

We repeat that these circumstances demand immediate legislation and the application of an obvious and simple remedy – a remedy which some manufacturers already apply on their own initiative, though seriously handicapped by the silly demand for the cheaper, because untreated, material. It is also desirable that the public should not be beguiled into buying cheap bedding which is falsely described as "sanitary" or "purified" when the material has undergone absolutely no such cleansing process as is implied by the above terms. This species of fraudulent trading should, of course, be dealt with under the Merchandise Marks Act, which exists to suppress false trade description.

## Loathsome bed-stuffing. [14 Sep 1907]

*To the Editors of* THE LANCET.

SIRS, – May I draw your attention to the urgent necessity that exists for the establishment of some system of inspection of the places where bedding is made or re-made and cleansed? That such work is sometimes carried out at present under the most insanitary and odious conditions is an undoubted fact, one, indeed, of which I have an ocular demonstration almost daily. My windows overlook the little backyard of an upholsterer's shop in a respectable street in a fashionable quarter of London and there I see bedding "cleaned" in the following manner. The hair, flock, or wool contents of the beds or mattresses are emptied out either on an old door, an inadequate and dirty piece of canvas, or on the bare ground and beaten with rods by a lad or two, the stuff naturally flying hither and thither during the operation. The yard is unpaved, generally wet, always dirty; it is the playground of a family of children of unclean and disgusting habits, and in it are situated the water-closet, which is, I have reason to think, *seldom*, if ever, cleaned out, and the dust-bin. When the "cleaning" is finished the stray bedding stuff is swept up from the muddy yard and *from out of the closet* – this is the truth – and carried in ready to be packed into its new tick and returned to its blissfully ignorant owner.

The shop itself is quite tidy and clean, its tenant has every appearance of a respectable trustworthy tradesman, and no one who has not had the opportunity of getting a glimpse behind the scenes would suspect the real state of things. I fear that the case I am describing is not unique and the very idea that it is not so is disquieting.

I am, Sirs, yours faithfully, R.B.K., Sept. 9th, 1907.

## "Loathsome bed-stuffing." [28 Sep 1907]

*To the Editors of* THE LANCET.

SIRS, – Your article on Sept. 7th, p. 727, on the above subject is a very opportune one in view of the diseases we are having imported into this country and which the authorities profess they do not know the origin of. This being a free trade country we do not have the easy means of knowing where goods originally come from [that] they have in a protected country. Rags come to this country from Russia through Germany, and we know that cerebro-spinal meningitis has had for generations a habitat there. What more likely than that this is the medium of transit? We know that during the late war these rags could not be had; they are again on the market. Why, I have often been asked, if the rags were infected, have no troubles been traced to the factory where they were being torn up? Simply because in the process of teasing there is a natural disinfectant given off. This, however, is absent when one is lying on a bed, and the human system is also more susceptible to disease at night than through the day. Also, and this is important, you may not inhale sufficient microbes in one night to be deadly, but continue the process and see the result. Your correspondent "R. B. K." describes the process of making a new bed (?) and it is certainly bad enough, but he is apparently not aware of a worse evil in the trade – viz., brokers buy at sales old beds and simply put new cases on and sell them for new. In Glasgow recently all the old bedding from a disused poorhouse was sold by auction. Fleas are quite common amongst unwashed flocks, but I must speak respectfully of them as they do not bite me, but I cannot say that they would not carry infection to me on their feet (see THE LANCET, July 27th, p. 216, and Sept. 14th, p. 779).[15] If ever there was a case calling for Parliamentary intervention in the interests of public health surely this is it.

I am Sirs, your faithfully, A. B. Dewar.[16] Sept. 16th, 1907.

## The bacteriology of "loathsome bed-stuffing." [26 Oct 1907]

A recent bacteriological report on specimens of rags and examples of flock used for stuffing bed mattresses, cushions, and so forth has reached us and affords singularly unpleasant reading. In untreated rags as purchased the number of bacteria living and capable of developing in suitable nutrient media varied from upwards of 10,000,000,000 per gramme to over 9,000,000,000. The number of bacillus coli[17] and allied organisms of excremental origin was at least 10,000,000 per gramme, while the bacillus enteritidis sporogenes[18] was found in the same material. The report further shows that by the adoption of an efficient pressure steam steriliser this flock can be reduced to a state of bacteriological purity. These results completely confirm the expressions of opinion contained in an editorial article published in THE LANCET of Sept. 7th last. The Government, through the President of the Local Government Board, has declared that "the point has been noted for consideration when a suitable opportunity offers." Meantime the distribution of pathogenic entities proceeds in this way uninterrupted and on a wholesale scale and many a mattress containing this unsterilised flock must literally be a hotbed of disease.

## Notes

1 Peter Fyfe (1854–1940) read his paper, 'What the People Sleep Upon', at the 22nd Congress of the Sanitary Institute, held at Glasgow University, 25–30 July 1904.

2 Aretas Akers-Douglas MP (1851–1926) was Home Secretary from 1902 to 5 December 1905.

3 John Elliot Burns (1858–1943), President of the Local Government Board 1905–1914.

4 Arthur Lyulph Stanley (1875–1931), MP for Eddisbury 1906–1910.

5 Neumann had an interest in sanitation; he spoke to the Institute of Sanitary Engineers in December 1912 on 'The Collection of House and Trade Refuse' (*The Globe*, 14 Dec 1912, p. 8). This might be Joseph Oscar Neumann (born around 1861), son of Emil Neumann M.D.

6 William Thomas Ellery (1869–1948) was a mill manager for T. R. Freeman and Sons, flock mattress manufacturers, Monkton Combe near Bath. The company was founded by Charles William Freeman (c1824–1883). His son Thomas Richard Freeman (c1860–1920) took over the business. On his death, it passed to his sons Thomas Leonard Freeman (1892–1947) and Charles Henry Freeman (1889–1947) under whom it was incorporated as a limited company; Ellery became a managing director. The company was wound up in 1966.

7 'Common Flock Beds in relation to the Public Health', *Journal of the Royal Sanitary Institute*, 27:12 (Jan 1907), pp. 714–722. A paper delivered at the Conference of Sanitary Inspectors, Bristol.

8 Robert MacNeil Buchanan (1861–1931) was the first City Bacteriologist for Glasgow, appointed in 1899 and retiring in 1930.

9 Frederick William Harris (born around 1862) was City Analyst and Chemist to Glasgow Corporation from 1899 to 1935.

10 Established in 1895 by William Martin (1837–1910) at 121 George Street, Edinburgh, with his son Robert Kay Martin (1877–1955).

11 The story of the sausage shop is told in Chapter 30 of *The Pickwick Papers* (London: Chapman and Hall, 1837), pp. 320–321.

12 Maple and Co. Ltd., Tottenham Court Road, London. Established by John Maple (1815–1900) in 1840; his son John Blundell Maple (1845–1903), made a partner in 1867, oversaw the subsequent large growth of the business.

13 The Wandsworth Flock Company, referred to in the note as one of the companies adopting sanitary methods, was established by 1870 at the Duntshill site by the brothers Charles Henry Pike (c1844–1879) and Seymour James Pike (c1858–1930). The latter was the principal partner at the time of the article.

14 Henry Franklin Parsons (1846–1913) in *Fifteenth Annual Report of the Local Government Board, 1885–86: Supplement Containing the Report of the Medical Officer for 1885* (London: HMSO, 1886), App. A., no. 7, pp. 61–72.
15 Buchanan, R. M. 'The carriage of infection by flies', pp. 216–218; and 'Flies as carriers of disease', pp. 779–780.
16 Possibly Alexander Brechin Dewar (c1857–1924), flax and jute cloth merchant.
17 Probably *Escherichia coli*, commonly found in the lower intestine, and associated with faeces.
18 Historical name for the bacteria associated with diarrhoea.

## Editorial Headnote

### Ludlam, Albert J. (attrib.). 'The Inside of a Mattress. Rag Flock Production. Modern Methods and Machinery Reviewed', *The Cabinet Maker and Complete House Furnisher*, (13 Dec 1924), pp. 524–525; (10 Jan 1925), pp. 52–53; (14 Feb 1925), pp. 408–409; (14 Mar 1925), pp. 656–657; (11 Apr 1925), pp. 46–47; (9 May 1925), pp. 264–265; (13 Jun 1925), pp. 522–523.

From its start, the weekly trade journal the *Cabinet Maker* covered the furnishing textile and upholstery sector. The journal's proprietor was Ernest Benn (1875–1954), who took over the Benn Brothers firm from his father in 1892, and in 1923, incorporated the company under his own name. His editor was Henry Percival Shapland (1879–1968), the son of a cabinet maker, with interests in antique furniture and decorative furniture techniques. Mattress-making was an unexplored subject, and the journal seems to have sensed in these articles a rare opportunity, evidenced by the extended serialisation in forty-nine parts, which appeared on a monthly basis across no less than four years from December 1924 to December 1928. In the light of continuing debate about the cleanliness of mattress fillings, the editor noted at the end of the fifth instalment, 'we have ample evidence that these articles, which endeavour to let the light of publicity into the inside of mattresses, are welcomed by the trade'.

The articles almost certainly originated with Albert James Ludlam (1899–1997). Ludlam began working for the bedding and flock manufacturer William Rhodes Ltd., in 1923, taking control of its new Nottingham branch as manager from 1924 until 1949, after which he emigrated to South Africa. Toward the end of his career in 1947, he wrote *The Craft of Mattress and Bedding Production* (London: The Furniture Record Ltd.). Its text bears stylistic similarities to the *Cabinet Maker* articles, although apart from the 'filling material' section, it covers different ground. Ludlam was a keen promoter of both hand and machine-made mattresses. Speaking in 1939, he noted: 'A straw bed for a horse costs £10 a year. Why should we kick at paying £10 for a mattress which will last ten years?' (*Nottingham Journal*, 20 Jun 1939, p. 3).

Ludlam's employer, William Rhodes Ltd., featuring in the articles, claimed a history going back to 1840, summarised in its centenary year by the managing director William Rhodes (1906–1958), of the fourth generation in the family firm:

> the founder was really a poet, but began dealing in flocks. In 1860 his son, Joseph Rhodes, who was an engineer by trade, assisted in the business, and it was about this time that they first began to make mattresses from flocks. In 1910, the first "Somnus" mattress was made, and in 1912 the firm was made into a private company.
>
> (*Yorkshire Post and Leeds Intelligencer*, 6 Jan 1940, p. 7)

The early dates may be somewhat mythologised. The founder, William Rhodes (1810–1894) is listed in the 1871 census as a farmer and his son, Joseph Rhodes (1845–1918), was at that time still a mechanic. Not until the following decade is William shown as a flock dealer and Joseph a cabinet maker, suggesting that entry into the bedding field in a substantial way did not occur until the 1870s.

# 35

# LUDLAM, ALBERT J. (ATTRIB.). 'THE INSIDE OF A MATTRESS'

*The Cabinet Maker*, (13 Dec 1924), pp. 524–525; (10 Jan 1925), pp. 52–53; (14 Feb 1925), pp. 408–409; (14 Mar 1925), pp. 656–657; (11 Apr 1925), pp. 46–47; (9 May 1925), pp. 264–265; (13 Jun 1925), pp. 522–523.

## I. – Rag flock standards and a preliminary glance at the trade

Rag flock for bedding and upholstery, although a well-recognised part of the furnisher's stock-in-trade, has in the past varied much in quality. Readers will doubtless recall the Press agitation of fourteen or fifteen years ago when such headlines as "What the People Sleep On" were followed by lurid details of the filthy materials which were to be found in *some* of the mattresses which were manufactured at the time.

We italicise the word "some," because the manufacturers who came into an unenviable notoriety in this respect were distinctly in a minority. For the most part the members of the bedding industry held a sufficiently conscientious view of their responsibilities to ensure a high standard of flock production. In the early part of the present century, however, those who were trying to maintain a high standard were seriously handicapped by the tactics of certain manufacturers who seemed determined to market inferior flock at cut prices.

It is not to be supposed, of course, that the public ever desired to sleep on dirty mattresses. There is a good deal in a mattress that does not meet the eye; hence the ease with which unscrupulous people could impose upon buyers.

### *The Rag Flock Act secured*

At the end of 1910 there was an unpleasant surprise in store for the dirty flock maker and his fellow misdemeanant, the don't-care-what-I-buy-if-it's-cheap-enough retailer of mattresses. As a result of earnest representations by a few leaders of the trade (THE CABINET MAKER bolstered up the movement from its


DOI: 10.4324/9780429274190-42

inception) the Rag Flock Act of 1911 was brought into being, providing definite penalties for the use, sale or possession of unclean flock manufactured from rags.

Section 1 provided that it should not be lawful for any person to sell or have in his possession for sale, flock manufactured from rags, or to use for the purpose of making any article of upholstery, cushions or bedding, flock manufactured from rags, or to have in his possession flock manufactured from rags intended to be used for any such purpose, unless the flock conformed to a standard of cleanliness prescribed by the Local Government Board. Any person selling, using or having in his possession flock in contravention to the Act made himself liable, on summary conviction, to a fine not exceeding, in the case of a first offence, ten pounds, or in the case of a second or subsequent offence, fifty pounds.

The Act included a provision by which a person purchasing flock under a warranty could pass on the responsibility for dirty flock to the person giving the warranty.

### *A definite standard of cleanliness provided*

The Local Government Board lost no time in prescribing a definite standard of cleanliness and a few months after the passing of the Act laid down "The Rag Flock Regulations. 1912." Under these rules, flock is deemed to conform to the standard of cleanliness for the purpose of the Act when the amount of soluble chlorine, in the form of chlorides, removed by thorough washing with distilled water at a temperature not exceeding 25 degrees Centigrade from not less than 40 grammes of a well-mixed sample of flock does not exceed 30 parts of chlorine in 100,000 parts of the flock.

The Act, although freely criticised in regard to its administration, does at any rate provide a standard and gives the manufacturers something definite to work upon. If any question arises as to the purity of rag flock it can be submitted to the touchstone of the Act, and the conviction of offenders is narrowed down to a question of fact established in the laboratory of the analyst.

### *A question of modern plant*

The standard is not a difficult one to adhere to and with the aid of the appliances and machinery which have been invented and improved for the production of hygienic rag flock manufacturers can proceed with confidence upon well-established lines.

In this article and the series which will follow it in our soft goods issues, the production of rag flock under modern conditions will be considered from the raw material to the finished product. Specifically the series will deal with rag flock machinery, and we shall also discuss machinery for the production of flock from materials other than rags, and bed opening machinery suitable for the retailer.

### *The complete metamorphosis of the rag*

The manufacture of rag flock has at various times had to encounter a good deal of prejudice and there are people who will assert that rags ought never to be used as a basis of bedding material at all. The same people raise no objection to paper (when they can get it) made from rags.

The objection in the case of properly made flock cannot be maintained. The metamorphosis which the rag undergoes in the maw of modern machinery is complete and absolute. The rag goes to the mill in every shape and form and is loaded with varying weights of dirt. It emerges disintegrated, cleansed, purified and carded – standard rag flock – an entirely new product.

### *An allied trade – the shoddy industry*

In our review of rag flock machinery we shall be brought into direct contact with the Yorkshire shoddy industry, which runs on parallel lines with it. The rag flock industry may even be said to depend largely upon the brains of the shoddy industry. In the Spen Valley,[1] which produces such a large quota of the necessary machinery, as well as the shoddy, there is no commoner sight in the main roads than bags of rags loaded upon trucks and trolleys, carts or drays. Steam-drawn or horse-drawn these vehicles are carrying rags from all parts of the country (and Europe) for conversion into shoddy or, it may be, rag flock.

The rag flock trade owes a good deal to the shoddy trade and the machinery makers who supply the one also meet the requirements of the other. "Devils," as they are commonly called, for tearing up old cotton and woollen material, are so strongly made that they last for many years, but the spiked swift and other working members of these machines, in both trades, constantly require repair and renewal. The wear and tear on the teeth is very heavy and there is a constant wearing down which calls for periodical renewals and a careful overhauling of the lags. The work of the rag tearing machines used in Yorkshire is greatly facilitated by the nearness of the manufacturers, who are thus able to give prompt personal attention to repair and renewal matters as they arise.

Apart from the very careful manufacture which is called for in the construction of these machines, a certain amount of specialisation is called for in connection with the spacing of the teeth on the swift. This varies in accordance with the operations to be undertaken. The teeth vary from small nails to heavy spikes, and the spacing of the teeth on the cylinder is a matter which has to be worked out with accuracy and precision. This aspect of the machinery will be dealt with in a later article.

### *Consumption of rags in the United Kingdom*

According to the latest records the consumption of rags in the United Kingdom is normally from 1,800 to 2,000 tons per week. It is anticipated that this figure will be reached again in the near future, as there is not sufficient output of wool to clothe the world, rags will be required to augment wool supplies.

### *An infinitude of grades*

Shoddy, as Frank Ormerod points out in his work on *Wool*,[2] has an almost infinitude of grades and constitutes a big cloth manufacturing industry which has grown up chiefly in and around the towns of Dewsbury, Batley, Heckmondwike, Ossett and Morley in Yorkshire. It employs between 4,000 and 5,000 persons and involves an average consumption of rag wool of 200,000,000 lb. per annum. At the Rag Exchange in Dewsbury come rags and waste from all parts of the earth. The rags are carefully graded – mungo, shoddy, extract, flocks and wastes. Mungo and shoddy undergo, according to the *Wool Year Book*,[3] the processes of dusting, sorting, seaming, oiling and grinding.

Dusting is largely a hygienic process. Sorting is in accordance with either quality or colour, or both. Seaming refers to the taking out of every bit of cotton thread, which otherwise would cause a bad spin or a "flecked" piece. Without injuring the wool the cotton is burned out of a mixture cloth by means of sulphuric acid or other chemical process. Oiling is to cause a gliding of the fibres on one another rather than rupture, which would mean a poor quality of spinning material. Grinding refers to the teasing out – the violently dragging apart – of the fibres, so that as much of the original length of the raw material as possible shall be retained.

Analogous processes are followed in the rag flock industry. We are considering here a class of ingenious machinery which turns the most unpromising material into a commodity of practical utility. It has always been so. The tale goes in Yorkshire that there was once a hard-pushed Yorkshireman who was told by his spinner that it was impossible to make thread from the poor material given him. "It mun go; it mun go," said the manufacturer, and go it did. In fact we have had mungo ever since.

### *The triumph of teeth*

Rag which is to be turned into flock presents its own set of problems. We shall follow the rags from their reception in sacks through the various operations which are required to cleanse them, to tear them to pieces (or grind them), free them from dust and curl them.

The key to the entire business, it will be shown, is the rag flock machine, which during recent years has undergone considerable improvement. These machines will be described in some detail. Special photographs will indicate that terrific tearing action to which the rags are subjected by the combined operation of thousands of teeth, which quickly reduce the rags to their constituent fibres. We shall have occasion to review the available machines and to show how their "swifts," "workers," "strippers," etc., act and react upon one another. The extraordinary pains taken by the manufacturers in the production of the teeth, and in the prolonged seasoning of the wooden lags on which they are mounted, will call for comment.

From these machines the treatment of the material will be followed until it becomes rag flock fit for bedding and upholstery. The latest machinery suitable for bedding manufacturers in a large way of business will be described and illustrated and we shall have something to say about the machinery employed in connexion with hair for the bedding and upholstery trade. By way of preliminary we illustrate below the interior of a modern hair teaser by John Halstead & Son, of Ossett.[4] In addition to the machinery which is offered for the purposes of rag flock production by the various manufacturers, the various grades of the product will be considered and the purposes for which these are especially suitable will be discussed. . . .

## II. – Rag flock production described

The collection, sorting and merchanting of rags is in itself a big business, and if we may judge from the fortunes left by individuals, it is by no means an unremunerative one. As shown in our last article the shoddy industry absorbs a large proportion of the collected rags, but many thousands of tons are needed by the rag flock maker in the course of the year, and to a great extent rags form his raw material.

The extraordinary transformation which takes place in the processes of a rag flock mill will be better appreciated if we visit works which are actually engaged in this important industry. On a recent occasion the writer had the privilege of inspecting the manufacture of rag flock in some extensive mills (William Rhodes, Ltd., Carlton Cross Mills, Leeds), which will serve our purpose admirably, for the conversion of cotton and woollen rags into flock can be followed in all its stages, while in another large range of buildings devoted by the firm to mattress making, we shall see what happens to the flock when it finally reaches the finished stage.

The premises referred to are modern, well lighted and completely organised for rapid production. There is no evidence anywhere favouring the notion that rag flock manufacture is an essentially dirty or unpleasant business. It is not even malodorous; and there are probably few industries which are conducted with such a small accompaniment of smell and noise; hence the possibility of carrying on such works in the centre of a big city where labour is readily accessible and every facility exists for prompt delivery.

### *Treatment in the washing department*

The rags employed in this business embrace all kinds and colours. They are received in bags and bales and are unloaded as required direct into the washing department. Here the rags are deftly handled and fed into the rag washing machines shown in Fig. 1. The fact that some of the rags are very dirty does not delay the process at all. They are made to swirl rapidly to and fro in water, and in the course of 35 minutes' washing pass through three changes of water.

As we shall see in a future article the effective cleansing of the rags presents a set of problems which have been tackled by engineers upon more or less divergent lines. In any case the effect produced is much the same. Although the process of cleaning does not end with the washing machines a very large proportion of dirt is removed in the department leaving comparatively little in the shape of dust to be eliminated in the dry. Behind the rag washers and not shown in the photograph are a number of hydro-extractors, and the rags, after the washing process is completed, are passed through these and divested of about 70 per cent. of the contained moisture.

### *How the rags are dried*

Visiting next the rag drying department (Fig. 2) we are reminded somewhat of the conditions which obtain in the stokehold of a vessel, for the men engaged on this work are stripped to the waist. There are three large enclosed drying tables or ovens in the department, and when the rags have been spread evenly over the grids by hand, the doors of the drying ovens are closed and by means of a powerful fan, hot air is drawn over them until they are completely dry. The process occupies about two hours, and the plant is capable of drying about 30 tons of rags per week. Our photograph shows a section of the drying plant only, with the doors closed.

### *The art and mystery of "rag grinding"*

After this the rags go literally to "the devil," and appropriately they go downwards through the floor. "The devil," or rag grinding machine, when in use in the mill has a singularly harmless appearance, owing to the fact that it is everywhere enclosed. A number of these machines will be described in a future article. The principal member is a fast-running cylinder or "swift" set with thousands of round and tapered steel points projecting about 1 in. from the wooden lagging. This, in association with the fast running beater rollers and adjustable plates, does the bulk of the work. The swift when divested of its casing is seen to possess the most formidable array of teeth which could well be imagined, and these, acting in conjunction with the spiked rollers (or "workers") and strippers, quickly reduce the rags to their component fibres.

The rags are fed into the machine by hand, being spread upon a feed lattice, and from thence presented to the cylinder by a pair of slow-moving fluted rollers. The fragments and fibres are torn away with incredible speed and by an ingenious arrangement any unduly large pieces which pass the swift are caught by a fast-moving beater and conveyed back to the feed-table or else are accumulated in the "bit box," whence they are brought back and fed into the machine again by hand.

### *Curling and dust removal*

The material yielded up by the "devil" is drawn by means of a powerful fan into a shaker, which curls and prepares the flock (Fig. 3), while the fan above takes out the dust – for in spite of the prolonged washing process already described, there still remains a big percentage of extraneous matter, and this has to be got rid of.

### *An interesting by-product*

It would appear that the rag flock industry like the pork packing business suffers nothing to be lost. In the next department visited we find all the necessary arrangements for dealing with the dust as a by-product. The dust is carried from the shakers through pipes to the floor below, where it is delivered through conical funnels bi-furcated at the bottom, and is packed in sacks. It will not be disclosing any trade secret if we add that the dust enters into the composition of manure and is used in its final form by the agriculturalist and grower of hops.

### *Grading*

The rag flock is now complete so far as manufacturer is concerned, but there is still much to be done in the way of grading, mixing with other grades of flock and so forth, before it becomes an integral part of a mattress. For this purpose special machinery is employed.

### *Quota from the mills*

The works now under consideration are by no means confined to the production of rag flock, for much of the flock produced in the mills draws its raw material from the woollen manufacturer, and in the woollen flock department next visited we are introduced to his machine (known as a "willey"), which opens up flock, hair and fibres. It is also employed as a mixer of flocks, and by its aid uniform colour is secured in the product and the flock maker is able to obtain uniformity of quality. The "willey" is primarily a machine concerned with new material – blanket combings, the residue from processes of cloth making and so on – the blanket flock yields white and red colours, while from the wool flock dark colours, greys, etc., are chiefly derived.

### *Curling wool flock for shake-up beds*

Passing quickly through the kapok[5] department (where machines are engaged in opening up this difficult material while at the same time expelling the seeds which drop down through grids, leaving the material commonly employed for the stuffing of pillows and cushions), we arrive at a series of machines whose sole province it is to curl the wool flock for filling shake-up beds.[6] As in the other machines, a large revolving "swift" is the main element, and the flock is curled by a combination of speed in the swift and the friction created by the flock when projected violently against the sides of the machine.

### *The finished mattress*

The practical uses of these materials in mattress making and their conversion into the finished product may be studied in the adjacent mills. In the stores here tickings and mattress coverings in endless variety lie ready for use. Another department is entirely given up to the storage of springs, the production of Somnus[7] mattresses and box springs.

One of our photographs shows the department devoted to the blending of stuffing materials. In another we see the final touches being given to the latest batch of mattresses.

## III. – Machinery for washing and drying the rags

As was shown in a previous article, the regulations made by the Local Government Board under the Rag Flock Act of 1911 laid down a definite standard of cleanliness, and, under the rules formulated in 1912, flock is deemed to conform to the Act when the amount of soluble chlorine, in the form of chlorides, removed by thorough washing with distilled water at a temperature not exceeding 25 degrees centigrade from not less than 40 grammes of a well-mixed sample of flock, does not exceed 30 parts of chlorine in 100,000 parts of the flock.

The rags which form the raw material for the business come from "everywhere" and it may readily be imagined that they are all more or less dirty. The first business is, therefore, effective washing.

A general idea of the washing process was given in our second article. We watched the reception of the rags at a big mill and saw them fed into rag-washing machines wherein they received three changes of water and were made to swirl rapidly to and fro for 35 minutes, passing from thence to the hydro extractors and so to the drying department.

The temperature of water usually employed for washing rags varies, but most firms use cold water. If warm water is used it is generally obtained from subsidiary processes, such as condensing steam from engines, etc. Where warm water obtained in this way is not available, only cold water is used.

Some of the machinery which has been designed by leading makers for washing and drying the rags will now be considered.

### *Typical examples of rag-washing machinery*

Rags washed in the machine shown in Figs. 1 and 2 are guaranteed by the makers – Hudson, Lyles and Co., Grange Road, Batley[8] – to pass all tests necessary under the Rag Flock Act. As shown in Fig. 1, the swift is carefully enclosed, the cover containing a channel which removes the dirtiest water as it is thrown up by the swift. Fig. 2 shows the machine with swift cover removed and brings the lifting-out gear for rags into prominence.

The swift is entirely constructed of metal in one piece and the machine is fitted with Hoffmann dirt and waterproof roller bearings,[9] carried upon heavy castings which extend to the tank bottom, and are bolted to a concrete foundation, thus taking all the weight of the swift off the tank sides. The lifting-out brattice is self-sustaining in any position, and can be raised or lowered and set in motion without the operator moving his position.

In operation the swift is set in motion and water allowed to run into the machine. The rags are then thrown into the tank and with the action of the swift are taken round the tank, under the swift and between the latter and a bridge where they are squeezed. This process is continued until the rags are sufficiently washed, when the lifting gear is lowered into the tank and the rags are brought out to be put into a hydro-extractor before being dried on a drying machine.

Figs. 3 and 4 illustrate the rag-washing machine developed by Petrie and McNaught, Ltd., Rochdale.[10] These machines consist, according to requirements, of two or four drums, and they are capable of dealing with 300 lb. per hour, dry weight, per drum. The labour required for working employs two men for a four-drum machine. Only clean water is used; about 800 gallons per hour per drum being needed.

The rags are placed in the drums, which are specially designed to ensure thorough washing of the rags, and a continuous flow of clean water enters at the end of the machine, passes through the drums, and is then run into the drains. The drums are automatically reversed after revolving five or six times in each direction, and consume about 3 h.p. each. The space occupied by a four-drum machine is approximately 36 ft. by 8 ft.

For drying the rags, Petrie and McNaught, Ltd., supply the "Chamber" drying machine, which is essentially the same machine as is extensively used for drying wool and other fibres. The rags are dried by means of hot air, which passes through the machine in the same direction as the material. As this hot air is brought into contact with the rags when in their wettest condition, and the consequent rapid evaporation of moisture immediately reduces the temperature of the air very considerably, it is possible to use air of a higher temperature in this machine than would be safe to use if the hottest air came into contact with the dried rags. The high initial temperature gives great efficiency, while the comparatively low final temperature prevents risk of injury or fire.

The fall in temperature is not nearly sufficient to reach dew point and consequently no moisture is condensed. On the other hand, by this method the speed of drying, high at first, is progressively retarded, so that the rags are finally delivered in a mellow condition without the fibres being rendered harsh or brittle.

Below the body of the machine through which the rags are conveyed (or if it is inconvenient to place it below, at the side) is placed a large and powerful blast fan. This fan is connected to a steam-heated tubular heater, through which it blows a large volume of air, which is thus heated up to the temperature required for drying. On leaving the heater this warm air travels up the duct or funnel at the feed end of the machine to the top tray, where it comes into contact with the rags fed into the machine by the feed rollers.

### *Ingenious feed method*

The feed brattice is an endless band of the same width as the machine and arranged to carry the rags from a point about 3 ft. above the floor level to the top of the machine, where the rags are passed through a pair of feed rollers driven by a special gear, ensuring that however thickly the rags are placed on the brattices the rollers cannot choke.

The rags after passing through the rollers are deposited upon the top tray, of which there are three or five, according to the size of the machine. By the action of the tray the rags are gradually carried to the other end of the machine, fall on to the tray below, travel the length of machine, fall to the next tray, and so on until delivered.

The construction of these trays is an important feature of the machine, which gives freedom from the many faults and troubles consequent upon travelling brattices and similar arrangements. Each tray or table consists of a row of alternately fixed and moving bars.

At the beginning of the stroke the material lies stationary upon the table of fixed bars, the moving bars being below them. The moving bars now rise up between the stationary ones, lifting the material bodily off them, and then, still above the fixed bars move forward about seven inches, carrying the rags forward with them. Having made this forward stroke, they fall down again between the fixed bars upon which the rags are once more deposited, and return below them to the starting-point, to repeat the operation. The trays are balanced one with another so that there is a minimum of power required.

What few wearing parts there are lie entirely on the outside of the machine, the inside being entirely free of frictional parts and therefore of the necessity for lubrication. This simple construction together with the very easy and slow motion of the machine render upkeep costs a negligible factor.

## IV. – Rag tearing and cleaning machines

In the previous articles we have traced the progress of rags used in flock manufacture through the preliminary operations connected with their collection and purification. We shall now proceed to illustrate and describe the principal machines which have been evolved by various makers in order to effect the disintegration of the rags.

To what has already been stated in regard to washing processes it may be added that while it is customary to employ water only, some firms use certain disinfectants and other chemicals, but we understand that these are in the minority.

### *General features of design*

Coming now to the design of the machinery which is employed in the work of rag conversion it is to be noted in the first place that the flock-making machine is necessarily enclosed. The various machines in their general features present points of strong similarity. A "devil" as a rule, to quote the *Wool Year Book*, consists of an enclosed swift 36 in. in diameter, and 14 in. to 18 in. wide, with straight hardened steel pins. The rags in being pulled from the feed rollers by the swift undergo a certain degree of opening, but if the amount of opening be not sufficient they are removed from the swift by a revolving fan or "biter" roller fixed above it and returned to the feed sheet. Above the swift is a baffle plate over which all small pieces sufficiently open are allowed to pass. By centrifugal force the heavier of these are thrown down a sliding board into a bin placed behind the swift from which they are periodically taken to be reground. The lightest material – really waste – is deposited into a chute arranged below the swift and is also carried into the storage bin. Walker and Smith, Ltd., Batley,[11] whose name we shall probably refer to rather freely in these articles as they cater very extensively for the bedding trade and have been engaged in the production of this class of machinery for 70 years, have perfected a "two-in-one" machine, forming a complete flock-production plant. In other words, the rags go in at one end and the clean flock comes out at the other. As the accompanying illustration (Fig. 1) shows, the plant consists of a rag-grinding machine or picker and a flock willey, the space required over all being 15 ft. by 9 ft. while the weight represents about 3 tons.

The rags are fed into the left hand machine being firmly handled at the point of entry by two fluted rollers. From thence they pass to the swift with its thousands of steel teeth, and this revolving at 750 r.p.m. promptly reduces them to a fibrous condition. The product is blown out under the feed apron and passes through a connecting pipe direct to the willey. Here the operation of another swift is brought into play subjecting the material to powerful friction and putting a curl on the flock. A further extraction of dust is effected and the material is cleaned and finished ready for market.

### *Improving bearing for bit roller*

Both the machines have been brought to a high state of efficiency and the rag machine has an improved design of bearing for the "bit roller" which prevents the wrapping of the shaft by such awkward things as fragments of stockings. These in the case of ordinary bearings are apt to prove extremely troublesome. The rag machines illustrated are extensively used, not only in this country but abroad, and four have just been sent to New Zealand. The plant illustrated in Fig. 2 is by another old-established firm, Wilson Knowles and Sons, Heckmondwike, Yorks.,[12] who cater very extensively for the bedding trade and to whose manufactures we shall frequently have occasion to refer in subsequent articles. The combined machines illustrated perform the entire work of converting rags into flock and work generally on the lines already described. The rags are fed in by hand and the feed lattice carries them forward until they are seized by two fluted steel rollers which hold them while they are operated upon by the swift, which is provided with extra strong patent flat teeth. The swift carries away the torn or pulled up fibres and any small bits that the swift has omitted are thrown back on the feeder by the bit roller in front of the cover, to be put through again, or conveyed by the tipper in the cover to the bit receiving box at the back when periodically they have to be emptied back on the feeder along with the bigger pieces which holds them until the swift pulls them up.

It will be noted that in these machines, bit roller fan and feed gear are all driven direct from the cylinder shaft. The "Tatham Rag Tearing Machine," illustrated in Fig. 3, and made by Wm. Tatham, Ltd., Vulcan Works, Rochdale,[13] opens and reduces to fibre all kinds of cotton and woollen rags. As in the machine already mentioned the rags are placed on a travelling feeder which conveys them to a pair of fluted feed rollers. The rags are held by the feed rollers and presented to the cylinder on the machine. The cylinder, 36 in. diameter, is covered with wood lagging fitted with thousands of fine steel pins or teeth, the action of which combs out or breaks up the fabric of the rags and reduces it to a fibrous condition. The opened material passes behind and under the cylinder and is delivered by means of piping in front of the machine, or into a suitable chamber. The machine has an ingenious bit roller by means of which any unopened pieces of rag are thrown back on the feeder automatically and again pass through the feed rollers to the cylinders.

### *The rag tearing machine as an engineering problem*

The machine illustrated in Fig. 3 contains many features which are claimed to be superior to the ordinary type of machine. Special attention has been paid in the design in order to give strength to the working parts, accessibility, ease in the setting of the feed rollers, bit roller and movable plates, and efficient lubrication. Care has been taken to cover all dangerous wheels with guards and to see that all revolving parts are well balanced. The various parts have been carefully machined to templates and standard gauges. In the result it is claimed that the opened or pulled material is superior to that produced on any other machine. The initial price is necessarily higher but it is claimed that the machine is well worth the extra cost entailed in the method of its construction.

The patent cylinder is made with the shell, arms and bosses entirely of wrought-iron and welded, i.e., it is made of wrought-iron with the shell in a continuous sheet welded together. The shaft is of Bessemer steel and is specially hardened. The self-oiling cylinder pedestals are of an improved type, and are fitted with best brass steps. The oil, after lubricating the shaft by means of a loose ring, runs back into the reservoir, thus preventing waste. The covers over the cylinder and bit roller are of sheet metal throughout, and are thus rigid, and comparatively light in weight.

A variable speed feed motion of special design gives five changes in the rate of feeding by simply moving a friction disc on shaft. Where different grades of material are to be treated the advantages connected with this arrangement are very obvious. Mark Lister and Sons, Croft Works, High Street, Heckmondwike,[14] furnish machinery covering a wide range in connection with bedding manufacture and their number 9 plant is a complete unit for manufacturing flock from new and old rags for bedding and upholstering. The rag machine runs at 650 to 700 r.p.m. and the willey (connected with it by a tube) at 350 to 400 r.p.m. The cylinder of the former machine is of 3 ft. diameter and is carded with lags fitted with thousands of steel pins made by the firm.

The flock shaker performs the double office of cleaning away the dust and curling the flock. All the working parts are carefully protected by iron coverings. This machinery, like other products of the firm of Mark Lister and Sons, is based upon long experience. Their plant is extensive and includes everything necessary for the production of the lags and steel pins which are so largely employed in the industry. We shall return to these later.

An improved rag machine made by Asquith Bros., Staincliffe, Dewsbury,[15] has several points of interest (Fig. 4). In tearing the rags, small pieces frequently pass through the cylinder insufficiently torn. Asquith's machine has a patent bit roller motion to prevent this. It is in the shape of a roller with teeth, above the cylinder of the machine, and it catches the untorn pieces and throws them back automatically upon the feed table to be re-passed through the cylinder. The torn material is delivered from the front of the machine under the feed-table. A fan is also included at the back of the machine which assists the draught and delivers the material regularly and evenly as it is torn up. The machines are very simply made, without any unnecessary gearing, and are of great strength.

A strong and durable machine for converting rags into flock is offered by George Thornes and Sons, rag and woollen machine makers, Bradford Road, Batley.[16] The machine is the outcome of many years' experience and has been evolved as the result of long and continued efforts to meet the special requirements of the trade.

From the description of the rag machines already given it will be realised that they are subjected to heavy strains. Only seasoned wood must be used for the lags which clothe the swift or the latter would quickly fail and fall to pieces. A constant wearing process is going on and the steel teeth, though specially made for the purpose, get slowly but surely ground down to a point where renewal of the lags becomes necessary. The teeth quite commonly become worn down in the space of from four to six months, according to the quality of material being treated. It happens consequently that in the Spen Valley a big business is done in refitting swifts periodically with new lags.

At the works of Wilson Knowles and Son, Heckmondwike, teeth for rag machines may be seen in all stages of their evolution, and the separate process associated with the grinding, cutting off, flattening and heading, hardening and tempering may be followed up. This, however, is only part of the story. The beech wood employed for the lags is of a specially hard kind grown in the North of England and the visitor will see an enormous stock of this timber which is kept at an even temperature for several years before use, the fires under the storage and drying rooms never being allowed to go out. Reference to Fig. 5 will indicate the large number of teeth required for a single lag.

At the works of Mark Lister and Sons may be seen the specialised arrangements which have been devised for drilling the lags. The drilling necessary to accommodate the teeth is effected by a special multiple drill which works with an almost uncanny precision, eighteen automatic spindles drilling two lags at a time. The arrangement of teeth and their frequency per inch is determined, of course, by the work which has to be done. There are lags for all purposes, and the selection of the most suitable lags for rag flock production is a matter upon which few, if any, are better fitted to give advice than the manufacturers who produce rag flock machinery in the Spen Valley.

## V. – Various kinds of flock described and illustrated

To the uninitiated flock as used in mattress making is a generic term, and even many of those who use the material are insufficiently versed in the nature and characteristics of the many varieties of flock. The passing of the Rag Flock Act 14 years ago gave considerable prominence to the question of cleanliness in bedding, more particularly in connection with flock made from old, worn and dirty rags of all kinds. Those who had first-hand knowledge of the rag trade could not do other than view with alarm and disgust the using of such material in its dirty state for the making of bedding. The Rag Flock Act of 1911 was an attempt to remedy that really shocking state of affairs. Since that time there has been a great deal of controversy, both legal and general, as to what actually constitutes rag flock. In the view of the writer of these articles, who has had opportunities for following the matter closely for many years past, rag flock must necessarily be produced from woven materials. Such materials or fabrics may have been woven or felted from cotton, wool or jute, such as old gunny bags. It is very difficult to believe that the by-products of woollen textile factories from new cloths or blankets were intended to be brought within the scope of the Act, but this is a personal opinion set down subject to correction.

It is astonishing that no attempt has been made hitherto to illustrate and describe in detail the various kinds of flock in order that those who use it may have, in a convenient form, first hand information as to the raw material of their particular industry. The illustrations which accompany this article are from untouched photographs, and the material in each instance is enlarged to exactly double its natural size in order that its nature may be clearly seen.

### *Unwashed rags*

. . . The reader is asked to consider for a moment what becomes of his own clothes. Let us say a suit of really high class material made by a West End tailor. When he has discarded it, it may be sold through a wardrobe dealer and worn for some time by someone else, and when he, in his turn, has finished with it it may be sold to a rag merchant or given away to a tramp, in any case little by little it becomes too ragged for use, is torn to pieces, and cleaned by processes which will be well understood by reference to previous articles of this series, and then the probability is that it will be re-manufactured into shoddy, and yet another suit will ultimately be made of it. But the unwashed rags which ultimately become flock are all of a discarded grade which is not good enough for re-manufacture into shoddy. As mentioned above, the rags may contain cotton, wool, or jute, but only such rags fall to the flock manufacturer as are quite useless for any re-manufacturing process or blending with wool for the making of cheap cloths or blankets. It was, in the main, this discarded and, on occasion, very filthy material gathered from various sources by rag merchants and marine store dealers, which was the subject of the outcry which resulted in the passing of the Rag Flock Bill. A great deal has been said decrying the use of rag flock, but really as it stands at the moment it is the only mattress filling material for which a standard of cleanliness is prescribed by law.

### *Washed rags*

These are merely the same rags washed by processes, some of which have already been described. The means adopted to wash the article to the Government standard are many, and manufacturers have of recent years discovered that that standard can be obtained if the rags are steeped or soaked. It is somewhat difficult to imagine that this was the intention of the Act, as this method does not eliminate dust or grit. Rag flocks ordinarily washed lose anything from 25 per cent. to 33½ per cent. *in weight*, while those which are steeped would not lose more than from, say, 10 per cent. to 15 per cent. Washed rag flock is largely used for upholstery and mattress making, and can be supplied in dark, medium grey or light grey, but the light grey being in the main of cotton, from the nature of its composition does not retain its resilience to the same extent as the dark. The dark, which contains more woollen, bulks better and is of greater resilience. As the quality of the filling really depends upon the proportion of wool contained in it, linsey rags are stated to make the most satisfactory rag flock filling.

### *Rag flock and woollen flock*

It should be noted in passing that the supply of linsey rags depends upon the state of the woollen trade, because if the woollen trade is flourishing and there is a demand for such rags for that trade, prices will become prohibitive for the flock manufacturer. There is also a distinct line of demarcation between rag flock and woollen flock. Woollen flock comprises (*a*) fine gig flocks, (*b*) dark cloth or milling flock, (*c*) blanket flock and rugging made from new cloth or blankets during the process of finishing. There are differences of opinion as to whether this new woollen flock in its various grades comes under the provisions of the Rag Flock Act.

### *Methods of packing*

The average price for washed woollen rag flock to-day varies considerably with the quality. It may be purchased as low as £22 or £23 per ton, while better qualities fetch £26 to £30 per ton. Rag flock is usually packed in 42 lb., 56 lb. and 1 cwt. bales. The greatest demand is for the 42 lb. bale as this is about the average amount required for a full size mattress, and it is thus convenient to handle. Woollen flock is mostly sold in the North of England – Lancashire, Yorkshire; and the Midlands also buy fairly large quantities.

### *Pulled washed rags*

Illustration No. 3 is of pulled washed rags after they have been through the tearing machines.

### *Fine gig flock*

Illustration No. 4 is of a fine gig flock. It is the woollen flock produced by a gig machine in the finishing stage of the manufacture of cloths. This flock is short and as pure as the cloth from which is it is obtained, and is particularly adapted for curling. When it is curled it is very suitable for the old-fashioned shake-up flock beds. . . . Illustration No. 5 shows fine gig flock in its curled state.

## VI. – Various kinds of flock described and illustrated

Included under the generic term flock there are mattress fillings composed wholly or in great part of jute fibre obtained from tearing and teasing old sacking, bagging or gunny as it is sometimes called. The bagging may have been used for the wrapping or packing of a great variety of substances – salt, sugar, bacon, coal, grain, flour, bone meal, fish meal, guano, activated sludge (which has sewage base), chemicals and chemical manures such as sulphate of ammonia and other manures and fertilisers, and a great number of other unsavoury substances; it would therefore appear to be very necessary that such materials should be adequately cleansed before being used as mattress fillings. Old sacking is particularly liable to attract a good deal of filth before it is ultimately discarded as worthless, and when it has been used for the packing of chemical substances it frequently becomes saturated with salts or acids of various kinds, and unless these are eliminated from the material it is very prone to absorb moisture from the atmosphere. It must also be obvious, even to the casual observer, that a jute fibre when compared with a wool fibre, such as the blanket flock which we also illustrate, is not from its very nature characterised by the same resilience and filling properties as blanket flock and dark cloth flock, or flocks which are mixtures in various ratios of wool and cotton fibres.

Gunny, or pulled old bagging, is composed entirely of jute or jute waste, and in its raw state is unattractive in colour, and it is therefore usually dyed a reddish tone to give it a more uniform and attractive appearance. Being rather brittle by nature, it tends to become dusty in use, and therefore to lose a percentage of its bulk in remaking.

Illustrations Nos. 8, 9 and 10 are respectively blanket flock, and this material is carded and curled. Blanket flock is a by-product obtained in the making of new blankets, and the best qualities are composed entirely of wool, but as there are many different grades of flock this material is often blended with similar by-products obtained from the manufacture of wool and cotton blankets. Blanket flock is a high-grade form of mattress filling, which varies in quality and price according to the percentage of wool which it contains. In its curled state, as shown in Fig. 10, it is employed in the manufacture of the old-fashioned shake-up beds.

## VII. – Further varieties of flock described and illustrated

It is not surprising that folk so well versed in fine distinctions as lawyers should have been bewildered by the intricacies of Rag Flock Legislation. We have in previous articles already described some nine or ten different kinds of flock, and the illustrations which we now publish add to that number. Fig. 11 is a photograph of rugging. This is a blanket wool generally coloured red and is made from new blankets which may be woven of all wool or a mixture of wool and cotton. In its open or carded form, it makes splendid mattress wool and when curled it is equally good for a shake-up bed.

## Notes

1 In West Yorkshire, the region of the valley of the River Spen which arises north of Cleckheaton and runs into the Calder south of Dewsbury. This was also a Parliamentary constituency in the region 1885–1950.

2 Ormerod, Frank. *Wool* (London: Constable and Co. Ltd., 1918), pp. 149–152.

3 The *Wool Year Book* was a trade annual published from 1909 in conjunction with the *Textile Mercury*, by Marsden and Co., Manchester.

4 John Halstead (1842–1918), machine maker of Highfield Works in Ossett, began his own firm in 1882 after the dissolution of a former partnership. He was later joined by his son James Edward Halstead (c1869–1926).

5 Kapok is a fibre from the inner wall of the fruit pod of trees in the *Bombaceae* family: Java kapok from *Eriodendron anfractuosum* (formerly *Ceiba petandra*), and Indian kapok from *Bombax malabaricum*.

6 A shake-up bed was an unstructured mattress, similar in form to a modern duvet, shaken after use to redistribute and fluff up the contents.

7 Somnus was a brand of William Rhodes bedding introduced in 1910, and made at the Lotus Street factory in Nottingham from about 1925. The Nottingham branch employed eighty-six workpeople in 1930, and turned out six hundred beds, three hundred feather pillows and twenty–thirty box springs per week (*Nottingham Journal*, 1 Jan 1930, p. 73).

8 Hudson, Lyles and Co., engineers, machine-makers and millwrights, was a partnership between Albert Hudson and Victor Sam Lyles (1892–1970). Hudson withdrew on 31 December 1923, with Lyles continuing under the same firm.

9 Named after Ernst Gustav Hoffmann (born around 1864, Dresden), mechanical engineer who helped set up the Hoffmann Manufacturing Company in 1898, with works located in Chelmsford. The company began producing roller bearings in 1908.

10 Petrie and McNaught Ltd., engineers and textile machinists, was formed in 1920 by the merger of John Petrie Junior Ltd. (incorporated 1888) of River Street Ironworks, and J. & W. McNaught of St George's Foundry, Crawford Street, Rochdale. The firm specialised in wool washing and carbonising machinery.

11 The firm of Walker and Smith, machine makers of Bradford Road, Batley, was established around 1860 as a partnership between Abraham Walker (c1816–1890) and Joseph Smith (c1830–1904). It was incorporated as a limited company in 1900. The directors were Smith's sons, including John Fox Smith (1862–1924).

12 Wilson Knowles (1840–1928), machine maker, Chapel Lane, Heckmondwike, set up on his own in 1866 following a previous partnership begun in 1861. He was later joined by his sons Pearson Newsome Knowles (1867–1933), Herbert Ernest Knowles (1869–1951) and Arthur Knowles (1871–1955). In 1946, the business passed to the next generation. It continues to trade as a family company, W. Knowles Ltd.

13 William Tatham (1826–1900), machine maker, separated from his brother Roger Tatham (1829–1870) to set up on his own in 1850. He patented numerous improvements to textile machinery from the 1850s to the 1870s, some of these with William Tweedale Heap (c1833–1917). In 1895, Tatham retired from the business which continued under Ellis Schofield Howarth Barnes (c1852–1913) and Louis Alfred Porritt (c1865–1927). Barnes left in 1907, and the firm was incorporated as William Tatham Ltd. in 1912 with Porritt as one of the first directors.

14 Mark Lister (1834–1900) established his machine-making business by the early 1860s, specialising in rag-processing machines. His sons John William Lister (c1863–1936) and Lawrence Lister (1865–1941) joined the firm to become Mark Lister and Sons. After Lawrence's death, the firm was continued by his widow Adelaide (née Lockwood) Lister (1879–1955).

15 The machine making firm of Asquith Brothers was established in the early 1880s by Walter Asquith (c1855–1901) and his brother Philemon Asquith (1856–1900), specialising in rag machines. The firm was carried on by Walter's sons Rupert Asquith (1882–1949) and Booth Asquith (c1885–1954).

16 The machine-making business established by George Thornes (c1849–1929) was joined by his sons John William Thornes (c1870–1910), Charles Henry Thornes (c1874–1958) and James Leadbeater Thornes (1879–1936) becoming George Thornes and Son(s) in the early 1900s.

# Part 7

# DOLLY SHOPS AND 'THINGS DONE WITH'

*Fig. 28* A rare image of a dolly shop with its doll. Hood's cartoon renders the well-dressed African visitor sympathetically, but its robust humour strays into uncomfortable territory. On the dolly shop, see Ch. 36 this volume.

*Source*: Designed and drawn by Thomas Hood (1799–1845) for *The Comic Annual* (London, A. H. Baily and Co., 1839). Author's collection.

*Fig. 29* Young women scraping lint by machine in a small workshop in Islington, London, while an outworker enters to deliver and pick up material. See Ch. 36 this volume.

*Source*: *Illustrated London News*, 17 Mar 1855, p. 4. Wood engraving by Charles William Sheeres (c1819–1899). Author's collection.

THE DUST-HEAPS, SOMERS TOWN, IN 1836.

*Fig. 30* Male and female workers at the dust-heaps, Somers Town, in 1836. See Ch. 39 this volume.

*Source*: Wellcome Images. Wood engraving signed WP, from Walford, Edward. *Old and New London: a Narrative of its History, its People, and its Places. Vol. 5: The Western and Northern Suburbs* (London: Cassell Petter and Galpin, 1878) p. 372. 

## Editorial Headnote

## Smith, Charles Manby. 'Lint', *Chambers's Journal of Popular Literature, Science and Arts*, 23:59 (17 Feb 1855), pp. 104–106.

Chambers's 'authors ledger' identifies Charles Manby Smith (1804–1880) as the contributor of this article. Smith's early life is known from his own account: *The Working Man's Way in the World: being the Autobiography of a Journeyman Printer*, first published in *Tait's Edinburgh Magazine* in monthly instalments from March 1851 to May 1852. The 1851 census records his occupation as a *printer's reader* – in modern parlance, a proof-reader, employment which Smith's autobiography richly records with pathos and humour. He writes there of the habit formed by his profession to see the 'faulty side of everything', taking more delight in the discovery of imperfection than its absence. Wandering about London in his dinner hour provided subjects for sketches of working-class life. In the preface to a collection of his vignettes, published as *The Little World of London; or, Pictures in Little of London Life* (London: Arthur Hall, Virtue and Co., 1857), Smith explains,

> The surface-view and the undercurrent of London life . . . both are well worthy of attentive regard . . . but in this case, as in most others, that which coyly shrinks from the light of day and the prying eye of the investigator, best rewards the trouble of the search.

Likewise, this article deftly exposes the hidden view, that of an occupation mainly performed by women in private, and serving the brutal but distant realities of war with its toll of wounded.

James Rawlings Elliott (1905–1958), in his *Short History of Surgical Dressings*, explained that during the 1850s, the surgical use of fluff scraped from linen (soft lint), or from unravelled threads of linen (charpie), gave way to the use of scraped linen cloth (sheet lint) – the *lint* described in this article. William Garnett Taylor (1798–1871) of Manchester patented a hand-operated linting machine in 1849, which was probably the device used by the outworkers described in the article. A new development just hinted at here was the first power-driven linting machine devised by William Robinson (1826–1911) of Robinson and Son, druggists' suppliers of Chesterfield, from experiments begun around July 1854. By 1867, when Joseph Lister introduced his antiseptic methods, sheet lint was the main form of surgical dressing used, but the composition could vary from linen to cotton-linen mixtures and pure cotton. Eventually cotton was found to have superior absorbency, but the changeover to cotton was probably driven more by economic factors than medical ones.

# 36

# SMITH, CHARLES MANBY. 'LINT'

*Chambers's Journal* (17 Feb 1855), pp. 104–106.

At the commencement of the present war,[1] and before a drop of blood had been shed in strife, or a single life had fallen a sacrifice to fever, malaria, or cholera, the government gave an order to a well-known London house for a thousand poundweights of lint, as a part of the medical stores to be shipped for the service of the army bound for the shores of the Euxine.[2] The *Times* newspaper, in an able and suggestive article,[3] called the attention of its readers to that significant fact, and admonished us to temper our warlike enthusiasm, by the melancholy associations which that single item in the tremendous list of preparations then urging forward was calculated to present to the imagination. If our mighty armaments were sent forth to conquer and to slay, they went forth also to bleed, to suffer, and to die: the blast of the spirit-stirring trumpet had to be echoed by the groans of the wounded warriors; and if provident care and forethought were needed to secure victory, they were needed no less to assuage the agony of the victor. It is to be feared that the thousand poundweights of lint supplied by the Messrs Savory and Moore,[4] has been long used up in the contingencies of the bloody contest upon which we have entered; at any rate, the demand for lint from the operative lint-makers is at the present moment double what it was before the war broke out, and not a little difficulty is experienced by manufacturers and contractors, if their own complaints on the subject are to be relied on, in meeting the exigencies of the occasion.

The trade in lint is subject to one rather awkward condition, peculiar to no other linen manufacture that we are aware of. We advert to the fact, that it will not remunerate the producer of this article to forestall the demand for any length of time, or to any great extent, whatever his foresight, or however great may be his facilities for production – the reason being, that lint, long hoarded, is liable to become to a certain degree matted and lumpy, and therefore is less fit for use, of less value, to say nothing of the partial discoloration that will ensue upon long keeping, and which operates as a prejudice against its sale. As a general rule, therefore, lint may be said to be manufactured from hand to mouth to supply the wants of the hour.

Lint, as most persons know, and as the etymology of the word would imply, is made from linen. A popular definition of lint would be 'scraped rag,' and such is the definition actually given in some of our encyclopaedias. In domestic experience, we often see the housewife manufacturing her own lint, by scraping the rag

DOI: 10.4324/9780429274190-44

with a knife, to meet a sudden emergency. It may not be so generally known, however, that linen, in order to be appropriated to the manufacture of lint, must first become a rag – must at least have been worn and used, and tumbled and washed, again and again, into such a state as to be entitled to that appellation. New linen, even if it could be procured at the price of the old rags – a difficulty which might perhaps be overcome – would make but an inferior sort of lint, because it would be stiffer in the fibre than that which has been repeatedly worn and washed, and it would contain some definite amount of extraneous material existing in the form of grit, which, though it might be imperceptible to the eye, would yet be found irritating to the wound. Some years ago, an enterprising manufacturer produced a species of patent lint,[5] of a material entirely new, the surface of the linen cloth being scraped or linted in the process of making: when the necessity for lint, as at present, is great, it is probable that this product commands a remunerating price; but the apothecaries and surgeons raise a sad outcry against it, and the best that can be said in its favour is, that it is not preferred to the lint made by hand from rags – and that for the reasons above specified.

Linen rags, then, are the first and the indispensable essential for the production of lint; and the procuring of them at the present moment, especially when the paper-makers are raising such a hue-and-cry for the same material, is no easy matter: so difficult, in fact, has it become, that the price of rags applicable to the purposes of the lint-manufacturer has advanced full sixpence per pound – the advance alone being double the price which it will suit the paper-maker to pay. This is the lint-maker's great difficulty; and the profits to be realised will depend very largely upon his or her mode of dealing with it. If in a small way of business, he will have to collect his rags, as many of them do, by periodical pilgrimages to the rag-shops, which, under the patronage of the black doll that swings aloft over the door,[6] invite his inspection. The rag-dealer, who buys mixed rags in the mass, at a few half-pence per pound, knows the necessity the lint-maker is under, and is pretty sure to be prepared for his reception with rags selected from the mass, and suitable for his purpose, and for which at the present moment he will ask an exorbitant price. Others, who do a larger trade, employ collectors to procure the rags, who contract to supply them at a given rate, and pick them up where they can. But in this department of the lint trade, as in a hundred other trades to which we might refer, the Jew steps in to the relief of the manufacturer. There are in London, as everybody knows, a prodigious number of public institutions – benevolent, charitable, political, and educational – where multitudes of men, or women, or children, are congregated, at their own or other people's charges, from year's end to year's end – hospitals, infirmaries, lunatic asylums, prisons, police-stations, maisons-de-santé, charity-schools, penitentiaries, refuges for the destitute, and clubs for the aristocratic. Regarded from a peculiar and commercial point of view, each and all of these institutions may be looked upon as so many nurseries for the rearing of rags. It is in this light, at any rate, that certain tribes of the clever and far-seeing sons of Israel regard them; and of the entire rag product of the whole of the public institutions of the metropolis, the Jews, or their agents, may be considered to have almost the exclusive monopoly. They contract with the governors, managers, or trustees, of the several establishments, for the whole of the rags which each year produces; and not a shred is suffered to leave the premises but through their hands. It is to the Jew, therefore, that the wholesale lint-manufacturer looks for the supply of his raw material; and from him at all times he can procure it in abundance, for a very sufficient reason – namely, that the price he is ever willing to pay exceeds by a liberal margin that which any other purchaser of rags is known to disburse.

In default of a ready supply of linen rags, a considerable quantity of lint is made in London from cotton. Cotton-lint – the term is an etymological contradiction – is, however, no favourite with the surgical profession, because it is not so soft in fibre, nor so cooling to the wound, as that made from linen. It is no favourite either with the working lint-makers, for two very good reasons: in the first place, cotton is more troublesome under the machine, and more difficult to work, than lint; and in the next place, it weighs less, and therefore pays less, because the work is always paid as lint is sold – by the pound. Lastly, it is no favourite with the manufacturer, because it costs as much to make as that made from linen, and fetches a price too much inferior to be compensated by the lesser cost of the material.

Lint, like the linen cloth to which it owes its existence, is of various value, according to its various degrees of fineness. For all practical purposes, that which is made from rags of average texture or coarseness, is in every respect equal to that made from the finest linen. But fashion reigns and rules at the side of the sick man's couch as decidedly as elsewhere; and the wounds and sores of the scion of the aristocracy must be salved and swathed in the finest material that money can purchase. So, while the government contractor sends to the field of Alma or Inkermann,[7] lint at three-and-sixpence a pound, lint at seven or eight shillings a pound is hardly good enough for the accidental contusions of the 'gentleman who sits at home at ease.'[8]

But to proceed with the process of manufacture. Having procured the indispensable rags, the next thing is to prepare them for the operative lint-maker, who is invariably a woman, if she be not a child or a young girl. The seams have to be cut out, and such parts as are worn and triturated, thoroughly threadbare and ragged, are cut away. The average loss in weight from this operation, we are informed by an experienced dealer, is hardly less than twelve per cent. upon the amount of rags purchased in fragments from the rag-shops, though it is not more than half that upon old sheeting and linen of an analogous description. A further loss of two ounces in the pound is incurred in the process of linting under the machine, that being the extra weight allowed to the operative in weighing out the rags; so that if she can make the loss anything less, it is so much gain to herself. The rags being freed from seams, darns, &c., and cut to the width of the machine – some fourteen or fifteen inches – have next to be washed thoroughly clean. This is a measure of the utmost importance, and one upon which the quality of the lint to be made materially depends. Once made, lint can never be cleansed of any impurities it may chance to contract; and as its value in the market would be depreciated were it not in a pure and stainless condition, the utmost care is taken to insure, as far as possible, its ultimate appearance in a state of snowy whiteness. This desirable condition of cleanliness is dependent, however, much more on the skill and carefulness of the working-hands, than on the labours of the laundress; and in nothing do the females who employ themselves at this calling, differ so much as in their manner of turning out their work in this important particular. Where a woman works in a smoky, dusty apartment, with children around her, the lint she makes – which is, of all imaginable things, the readiest to contract the flying impurities – is sure to suffer; and if the work be broken off and interrupted from time to time, it is sure to become foul, and, as it is technically termed, 'grubby.' On the other hand, a tidy lass, working alone, or in company with a fellow-worker, and who carefully deposits each piece out of harm's way as it is liberated from the machine, will rival the lily in the purity of her wares.

The rags being cleansed, and reduced to convenient sizes, are now ready to be linted. Let us see in what that process consists. If the reader will take a piece of coarse lint in his hand, he will find, on endeavouring to pull it to pieces, that he can do so with the utmost ease in one direction, but not in another – that is, he can pull it into strips, but cannot break it into squares, pull as hard as he may. On examining it in a strong light, he will see the reason of this: he will perceive that all the threads which run in one direction (say the warp of the cloth) are but very slightly frayed or scraped, and remain nearly as strong, because nearly as entire, as they were when they came from the loom, and therefore it is vain for him to pull against their united strength; but he will see, also, that all the threads running across or perpendicular to them are, though none are cut through, reduced to hairs of infinitesimal thinness – mere single fibres of the flax – the rest of their substance being raised into a soft, filmy, pulpy 'fluff,' which constitutes the lint. In order to see how this process is accomplished, we must follow the lint-making operative to her home. We say to her home, because it is only in exceptional cases that the rags are really turned into lint on the premises of the manufacturer. Personally, we know but one manufacturer, who, supplying the public with the article, has the work done on his own premises, and by his own machines.[9] In the generality of cases, the work is given out to women who provide their own machines, at a cost of something under 30s. each, and who work their own hours. As the employment is not considered healthy – and hardly can be so, looking to the quantity of separated flax fibre floating in the atmosphere of the workroom – it is not much to be wondered at if, taking advantage of the comparatively lucrative nature of their industry, they sometimes refuse to labour more than a limited number of hours daily. Still their gains, when working for the 'middleman,' are not much to boast of. Half-a-crown a day is stated to be the utmost that a skilful workwoman can earn; and she, in order to do this, with the present imperfect means at her command, must have spent many years in constant practice at the machine. The services of the middleman, however, are by no means indispensable to the lint-maker, and, as a general rule, the older she grows, the less she has to do with him. Observation, inquiry, and experience, lead her in the end to form a connection of her own among the apothecaries and the members of the medical profession, by which she may chance nearly to double her earnings.

On visiting the lint-maker at her work, we find her seated in a lofty attic of a dingy house in a back-street, not far from the bank of the Thames, where the river runs towards Limehouse. In order to get at her apartment, we have to pass through a series of hanging gardens of damp rags, for the most part less than a foot square in size, and which, having been washed clean, are hung out to dry upon the staircase and landing, the weather being 'mizzly' out of doors. From such a manifold demonstration, we conclude that the lint-maker we have come to visit, by introduction of a friend who employs her, if she works for the middle-man, works also on her own account, and cultivates a connection. On entering the room, we find her seated in front of the linting-machine, a rude and primitive instrument, about the size of the stool of a banker's clerk, and not a whit more ingenious in its construction. The affair is just the shabbiest of all shabby contrivances for bringing the edge of a sharp blade, about fifteen inches in width, to bear upon a little platform beneath. There is a kind of treadle worked by the foot, which assists the hands of the manipulator in using the knife. Upon the flat surface of the little platform is stretched the rag, or that portion of it undergoing the operation, which has to be linted. A simple contrivance keeps the rag partially strained. As the knife hangs in its frame over the cloth, its edge is parallel with one line of the threads, and, of course, perpendicular to the other line. Several of these machines are at work in the room, and the blades are rising and falling with a dull, thumping, scraping sound continually. As the blade descends, it cannot much injure the threads whose course is parallel with itself, for obvious reasons; but it would, being very sharp, cut through the others, were it allowed to descend with sufficient force. The force of the descent, however, is regulated by the dexterity of the worker, so that it shall only partly sever the cross-threads; and at every fall, while the knife is down, and its edge imbedded in the partly severed threads, the blade is forcibly shifted in the direction of those threads for a certain small space. It is this horizontal shifting of the sharp and heavy blade of the knife upon the strained rag while it is half cut through, which by disintegrating those threads that cross the blade at a right angle, and raising nine-tenths or more of their entire substance into a soft woolly pile, produces the lint. It is worthy of remark, that the threads which, lying horizontally with the knife, escape serious injury by the process, render an important service by preventing the disintegrated pile from being detached from the surface of the rag by the violent passage of the blade.

The lint-maker tells us, that she served an apprenticeship of two years to the business; and that, in learning it, she did as most beginners do – that is, destroyed a good many rags in her first attempts. She has now been ten years at the trade, and is in her turn teaching apprentices of her own, one of whom sits at her side making coarse lint with a skill and rapidity hardly to be surpassed. She herself prefers the fine work, because she is accustomed to it, and it pays better. As a journey-woman she could, and did, earn half-a-crown a day, and might have earned more but for the loss of time in fetching the material, and taking home work when it was done, and the waiting which mostly takes place upon those occasions. The earnings of her oldest apprentice do not amount to that by more than a third. The work is not so easy as it appears, and requires long practice to be well learned. She adds, that she does not think it a healthy business by any means, as the severed fibres of the flax are apt to get into the lungs – two young girls, who commenced learning the business, were obliged to give it up on that account. But she objects more to the wearisomeness and monotonous character of the employment than to its unhealthiness, from which she is not sure that she has herself suffered to any extent. Lint-making, she is of opinion, requires more continuous attention than most other merely mechanical employments, because you never know what you are going to have under the knife till you come to try it, and are obliged constantly to act according to circumstances.

All this may be perfectly true, but there is a further truth of which the good woman is not conscious. A single glance at the machine with which the work is done, would be sufficient to convince any practical mechanic that the difficulty complained of is due to that, and to nothing else, and that it might be obviated as easily as the difficulty of eating with a pair of Chinese chopsticks would be obviated by recurrence to the knife and fork. There is no reason why machines should not be made, at a very trifling expense, to lint a surface of any convenient width at the rate of a yard a minute, or more if need be; and did a sufficient motive exist for the invention of such a machine, it would soon be in operation. The enormous margin of profit is surely a sufficient incentive for the inventor. It remains to be seen whether the fearful necessities of a general war – against which, as lovers of peace, we devoutly pray – will stimulate him to action. It is but fair to state, however, that from circumstances which have turned up in the course of our inquiries on this subject, we are not without a suspicion that lint is secretly making in the metropolis, and that in large quantities, by some already improved process. What these circumstances are, we do not feel at liberty to state; they warrant us, however, in indulging no more than a suspicion, which may be well or ill founded.

## Notes

1 The Crimean War began in October 1853.
2 The Euxine is an alternative name for the Black Sea.
3 Despite persistent searches, this article has not been found.
4 The firm of Savory and Moore, pharmaceutical chemists, New Bond Street, London, was established in 1811 out of a prior partnership. The principals were Thomas Field Savory (c1776–1847) and Thomas Moore.
5 In 1834, announcements were made of 'Messrs Toswell and Co.'s patent lint' (*Liverpool Mercury*, 7 Nov 1834, p. 6), and advertisements extolled its superior cleanliness because made of new material (*Globe*, 7 Nov 1834, p. 1). The patentees were Tosswill, Bailey

and Co., wholesale chemists, Garlick Hill, Cheapside; the principal was Robert Tosswill (1799–1860).

6 The black doll was the shop sign of the so-called 'marine store', giving rise to the name 'dolly shop'. Trench H. Johnson, in *Phrases and Names: Their Origins and Meanings* (Philadelphia: J. B. Lippincott, 1906) suggested this harked back to a practice of shipping old garments for 'negro' clothing in the southern states of America (pp. 78–79). However, Brewer's *Dictionary of Phrase and Fable* (London: Cassell, Petter and Galpin, 1870) traces the origin to the signs of shops selling India muslins.

7 These were Russian sites of Crimean War battles. The Battle of the Alma River was fought 20 September 1854, and the Battle of Inkerman was fought 5 November 1854.

8 This line is adapted from the broadside ballad 'Neptune's Raging Fury: or, the Gallant Seaman's Sufferings': 'You gentleman of England/who live at home at ease, Full little do you think upon/the dangers of the Seas'. In the form shown here, 'who sits at home at ease', the line was prolifically adopted to suit multifarious contexts contrasting upper and working classes in the last half of the nineteenth century.

9 The *Illustrated London News* ran a short article, 'Manufacturing Lint for the Army in the Crimea' with an illustration of a manufactory in Islington employing 'upwards of thirty hands, chiefly young girls from sixteen to twenty years of age; few of them, however, are at present engaged on the premises' (17 Mar 1855, p. 4). In the accompanying engraving, seven young women are shown at work on the premises.

## Editorial Headnote

### Smith, Charles Manby. 'Revelations About Sacks', *Chambers's Journal of Popular Literature, Science and Arts*, 1:1 (7 Jan 1854), pp. 14–16.

This article was chosen to complete the first issue of Chambers's new weekly journal. The article defied to some extent the journal's stated categories of literature, science and arts, but its London interest signalled the intended geographical reach of the new journal beyond its predecessor, *Chambers's Edinburgh Journal*. On 12 January, the *Nottinghamshire Guardian* revealed the 'interesting sketches from London life in this periodical are from the pen of Mr. Charles Manby Smith'. Indeed, Chambers's 'authors ledger' of 1846–1855 confirms Smith (1804–1880) as the contributor of this unusual piece of investigative journalism. Smith adopts here the successful approach of his contemporary Henry Mayhew (1812–1887) in combining urban vignettes with statistical information. Unlike Mayhew, rather than striving to capture the voice of the worker, Smith punctuates his writing with just a telling word or phrase from his informants. Here, 'evaporation' describes the unexplained disappearance of the hempen and jute sacks that are his subject, and a 'sack not worth the stealing' is the desire of their owners so as to prevent further depredations. Smith's article highlights a perennial problem of the free provision of recyclable containers, and proposes resumption of the prior deposit-and-return system as the most likely solution.

Unlike Mayhew, Smith was able to make a steady, comfortable living by his writing. Between 1861 and 1871, he and his wife moved from 23 Liverpool Terrace in Islington to a more substantial address at 45 Loraine Road. There, in his mid-sixties, Smith was enumerated in the census as a 'retired litterator', and on his death had a personal estate valued at nearly £4000.

*Chambers's Journal of Popular Literature, Science, and Arts* held sixteen pages, and was priced at 1½d., also available in monthly volumes for 7d. This article was reprinted, with credit to Chambers, in the American journal *Littell's Living Age*, published in Boston (40:512, 11 March 1854, pp. 507–509).

# 37

# SMITH, CHARLES MANBY. 'REVELATIONS ABOUT SACKS'

*Chambers's Journal* (7 Jan 1854), pp. 14–16.

Ever since the drinking-cup of Joseph was found in the sack of Benjamin,[1] and we don't know how long before, sacks have maintained a distinguished position among the commercial nations of the earth, as the receptacles of the food of man, and of a multitude of other things besides, which we are fortunately not under the necessity of enumerating. There can be but little doubt that a sack was the first portable depository for property constructed by human ingenuity, and that it was formed from the skin of an animal. Such were the bottles of ancient peoples, before the potter's or the glass-maker's art was known, or was extensively practised, or popularly adapted to meet the common want; and such, at the present day, are the vessels of many nomadic and pastoral tribes partially, if at all, acquainted with the ceramic or textile processes. But the cattle on a thousand hills, if every one of them surrendered his skin for the purpose, would not supply a thousandth part of the sacks which modern commerce demands for the reception of its merchandise. The millions stowed away in granaries and warehouses – the millions more constantly traversing the ocean in every direction – and, more than all, the millions in daily use wherever men are congregated – all these defy calculation to number, or the imagination to conceive. A sack is truly a comprehensive subject, and although it can be examined only on two sides – the outside and the inside – it may be considered from many and various points of view; but in order to keep ourselves within bounds, we shall confine our remarks, upon the present occasion, to the sacks which undergo a London experience.

The bulk of the sacks used in this country are woven by power-loom in Dundee, and by hand-loom in Norwich and various other places throughout the kingdom. The material is either hemp, which forms the best and most durable, or jute, a fibrous plant imported from the East Indies. The woven sacking, though partly made up in the provinces, is brought in great quantities to London, and being cut up into lengths, is sewn into sacks by women, who, working for very moderate wages upon a rough and cumbersome material, do not cut a very imposing figure among the fair professors of needlecraft. There is a large sack-manufactory in Tooley Street,[2] and the sack-making women may be seen at early morn and at eventide laden with piles of sacks, made or unmade, upon their heads, proceeding over London Bridge to and from the factory. These hard-working females

DOI: 10.4324/9780429274190-45

have latterly found a formidable rival in the new sewing-machine, which makes a sack in a fraction more than no-time, and threatens ultimately to throw them out of employment. Fortunately for them, however, there is an incessant demand for sacks – a demand which is always increasing in something like an arithmetical ratio. A question here naturally arises: What becomes of all the sacks? the answer to which, if it could be definitely given, would involve, we are afraid, an amount of moral delinquency which, if it could be measured by the sackful, would astound the questioner. Perhaps we shall arrive at some idea of the response by the time we have got to the end of our paper.

It might be reasonably supposed, that the immense demand for sacks would have the effect increased consumption has on other species of manufacture – the effect, namely, of improving their quality. But the fact happens to be just the reverse; the truth being, that the actual desideratum at the present time is, not a strong sack – not a tough, serviceable sack – not by any means a good sack, or any such kind of thing – but – hear it, ye men of inventive genius! – *a sack not worth the stealing!* Here is a field for enterprise! If any cunning contriver or persevering experimentalist can produce a sack which will barely carry its load once, and defy replenishing when empty, and sell it at a corresponding price – a price, that is, proportionate to the value of its temporary service – we will guarantee him a fortune. A good sack will cost 2s., or thereabouts, and will last for eight or ten years, and might be filled, perhaps, forty or fifty times or more; but the same 2s. spent in sacks at 4d. apiece, if such could be got, to be filled but once, would be beyond comparison a better investment on the part of the miller. We calculate by moral arithmetic.

Mention the word 'sack' to a metropolitan miller or corn-dealer, and down go the corners of his mouth instinctively. It is an ominous word, suggestive of a drawback upon his profits to an alarming but an indefinite amount, the sum-total of which he has no accurate notion of, and cannot have until the ceremony of stock-taking reveals the awful deficit. For we know not how long, but at least for some generations past, a property in sacks in use has been the most equivocal kind of property a man can possess. From the custom of the trade in corn, flour, grain, pulse, and agricultural productions of all kinds, the sacks in which they are contained are not chargeable to the purchaser, but are returnable to the owner when empty. Unhappily, they are liable to the other contingency, and a prodigious percentage of them never find their way back to the proprietors at all. It is marvellous to what a variety of uses such an apparently unmanageable material as a stray sack may, by a stretch of ingenuity, be applied. It becomes not merely a bed-sacking, a door-mat, fuel for the oven, roofing for the loft, but a pathway for the garden, wainscotting for the summer-house, raw material for the paper-mill, or daubed with pitch or tar, it finds its way from the warehouse of the corn-factor to the wagon of the coal-merchant, or from the shop of the baker to the hold of some outward-bound vessel, to be expatriated for ever. So outrageous is the tendency of sacks to a mysterious and unaccountable disappearance, which some owners term "evaporation," that we have known a single miller, doing no extraordinary trade, to lose, in the space of three years and a half, 16,500 sacks – a loss of nearly 5000 in a year, amounting to little less than a third of his entire issue. Between twenty and thirty years ago, the depredations upon this unprotected property had risen to such a pitch, that a few of the millers and factors who had suffered most severely resolved to submit to it no longer. They met together, and organised an association for the purpose of inflicting the penalty of the law upon transgressors. Writs were issued and warrants enforced against some of the petty plunderers, and not a few of them were brought to the slow and unwilling conviction, that to steal a sack was a theft, at least in the eye of the law; but they suffered the penalty with the air of martyrs enduring persecution, and were far from acknowledging its justice. But when a prosecution was threatened, and indeed commenced, against a wholesale purloiner, who was caught in the act of shipping a whole cargo of wheat in sacks belonging to his neighbours, proceedings were stopped by one of the most influential men in the association, who, doing a large business with the delinquent, preferred compromising the crime to disobliging a customer. As a consequence, that association fell to pieces.

Let us glance for a moment at the experience of a sack in London. When a baker or corn-chandler buys flour or grain from a factor in Mark Lane,[3] he receives an order upon the wharfinger for a specified number of sacks of flour or grain, as it may be. These, in the course of a few hours, are delivered at his place of business operations. He does not pay for the sacks, but they are returnable when empty – a consummation which may occur to-morrow, or six or twelve months hence. He is not, however, called upon to return them himself. There are in London at the present time – and have been for these fifty years past – sack-collectors, men, or firms, whose sole occupation is the collection of sacks and the delivering of them to their owners, or the agents of their owners. Some of these collectors keep a number of light carts continually driving about the town and suburbs on this errand. The collector charges 2s. 6d. a dozen, or 2½d. each, for every sack he rescues from the hands of the customer. In order to stimulate the baker or chandler to produce them as soon as empty, he is obliged to divide this premium with him, awarding him 1d., and sometimes 1½d. per sack for all he is able and disposed to surrender. It is the collector's business to sort them, to pack them in bundles, and forward them to the proprietors, before he presents his account for payment. At the period above alluded to, it is supposed that the collectors, or their agents, were principally concerned in the plunder carried on; although it was sufficiently shewn by the prosecutions of the day, that they did not want for countenance among dishonest tradesmen and dealers, rogues in grain, who profited by their complicity. Some years after the demise of the first association, the necessities of the commerce in grain called into existence another, which, under the designation of 'The Sack-protection Society,'[4] yet exists, and holds its periodical meetings at Jack's Coffee-house, Mark Lane.[5] It is a sort of guardian guild, enforcing the rigour of the law against sack-thieves. The members pay an annual subscription, we believe of two guineas each, to defray the cost of its proceedings, and have thereby reduced by a considerable percentage the loss by sack-plunder. They maintain a policeman in plain clothes, who, all-observant but unobserved, surveys the operations of suspected persons: he has, from long practice, a keen eye for a sack, can single out a corn or flour sack pressed into the service of the coal-merchant, or doing duty in a potato-shop; and it is his function to report all such malversations, in order to speed punishment and redress. By such and similar energetic measures, the Sack-protection Society secures some show of respect for sacks, and thereby, to a limited extent, benefits others as well as its own members. Still, however, the loss of sacks is enormous, and altogether unaccountable: we have heard it estimated variously at from seven to five-and-twenty per cent.; and it is characteristic, that the loss varies with the value of the article – the old and worthless returning to the proprietors, while the new and strong continue their travels. On this account, no miller, whose sacks go into the London market, dreams of paying a first-rate price for the article. At home, he will use sacks costing 2s. each, and will keep them for long years in use under his own eye; while those he sends out into the world may cost him less than half that sum, as he has but an uncertain prospect of seeing them again. Hence the desideratum we have hinted at above, of a species of sack which should cost a sum of money not more in amount than the present charge for collecting, plus the average loss by plunder, and which being thrown in gratis to the purchaser of its contents, would release both miller and factor from all anxiety respecting its ultimate fate.

The sack has other enemies in London besides the contraband dealers. Wharf-labourers and wagoners declare war against them, and invariably attack them with sharp iron hooks, with which they can lay hold of them more readily than with the fingers. The result is the rending of thousands of them, and the partial waste of their contents – a waste which, if it prevailed to a hundred times its present mischievous extent, would never prevent the use of the hook by the London wagoner, who would stand up for the privilege of his calling.

There is a prevailing and universal prejudice in favour of sacks among bakers and corn-chandlers. Barrels are to them an abomination – the reason being, that these cannot, like sacks, be folded up, and thrown aside when empty. Barrels take up as much room empty as full; and London tradesmen being proverbially short of room, would soon find themselves built out of their own premises by an accumulation of empty barrels. Large quantities of American flour are constantly imported in barrels, but the bakers, for the most part, will have nothing to do with it until it has been shot into sacks. This ceremony is continually going on at the wharfs on the banks of the Thames, and furnishes daily employment to a particular class of men. There is another objection to barrels: from lack of the occasional movement and shaking which it undergoes in sacks, the flour settles down in them, and, if untouched for a long period, has to be dug out in lumps, and pulverised again by rotating in a close wire cylinder set in rapid motion. Again, a third objection to their use is found in the negligence of the Americans, who, in their eagerness to do a fast trade, will, upon emergency, make them of green wood, in consequence of which the flour becomes impregnated with a disagreeable flavour. They are, in general, however, made remarkably well, with interiors astonishingly clean and neatly finished; but they are a drug to the English factor, who is often too glad to get rid of them at six or eight shillings a dozen.

The above revelations on the subject of sacks do not afford a very agreeable view of the practical morality of trade. But this is only one example, though an example on a large scale, of the imprudence of reposing confidence in a class, among whom it is impossible to distinguish the rogues from the honest men. There was a time when purchasers bought the sacks when they bought the flour or grain, and were credited with their value when they returned them empty. A return to that straightforward practice appears to be the only remedy for an evil which has resulted from its abandonment. It will deprive the rogues of the opportunity which has made so many of them what they are; it will put an end to the perplexities of the owners of the sacks; and, in abolishing the troublesome machinery contrived with a view to protect them, will remove from the honest members of the trade the odium of living under surveillance as the suspected custodians of other men's goods.

## Notes

1 Genesis 44:5.

2 In 1805, Thomas Edgington (1786–1857) established a warehouse at 244 Tooley Street, dealing largely in canvas products. By 1812, he had been joined by his brother Benjamin Edgington (1794–1869). Their partnership split in 1823, but Benjamin continued in the sack cloth trade at 5 Tooley Street. In 1835, he removed to 2 Duke Street, Tooley Street. Tallis's *Street Views* includes a vignette of Edgington's premises (no. 45). The firm was then more prominently known for its large marquees and tents, while maintaining its utilitarian range of tarpaulins and sacks. In 1898, the firm was merged within a limited company as S. W. Silver and Co. and Benjamin Edgington Ltd.

3 The Corn Exchange was situated in Mark Lane, north of the Tower of London, making this a centre for the milling trades. Flour merchants, corn factors, millstone manufacturers and milling engineers held business addresses there.

4 This London society was formed in 1844. The *Morning Post* reported a prosecution 'instituted by the "Sack Protecting Society," an association which has been formed for the protection of millers, whose losses in this respect are said to amount to the almost incredible sum of 20,000*l*. per annum'. The millers 'informed the magistrate that it was the intention of the society to prosecute to the utmost extent all persons found purloining their sacks, or not being able to give a satisfactory account of any found in their possession' (13 Nov 1844, p. 4). In the wake of the success of the London society, regional societies formed, with activities peaking in the mid-1860s.

5 Jack's Coffee House, Mark Lane, was a meeting place for millers as early as 1805 (*Morning Advertiser*, 12 Nov 1805, p. 3), and remained a place for business association into the 1870s.

## Editorial Headnote

### Wynter, Andrew. 'Old Clothes and What Becomes of Them', *The Times*, 3 Nov 1864, p. 6.

Andrew Wynter (1819–1876) was a physician who edited the *British Medical Journal* from 1855 to 1860, but he is better known as an author. He was a prolific contributor to periodicals, specialising in popular subjects that often were connected with topics of health or industry. The destination of discarded objects was one consistent theme. His 'Old Clothes' article covers some of the same ground as Henry Mayhew's 'Of the Street-sellers of Crockery and Glass-wares' in *London Labour and the London Poor* (vol. 1, pp. 405–409). However, Wynter's style is distinctive, abounding in evocative phrases, perhaps owing more to George Augustus Sala's topical treatments of modern urban life collected in his *Twice Round the Clock* (London: Houlston and Wright, 1859). Interest in urban 'low life' continued to proliferate in the 1860s, largely published anonymously in journals, such as 'Rough Sketches of London Life' in the *Temperance Magazine*, or 'Hole and Corner London' in *The Sportsman.*

Wynter's article, although lacking in reviews, certainly won approval as witnessed by its frequent quotation and reproduction. The *Sun* (London) printed the article the same day as *The Times*. On the following day, the *Manchester Guardian* noted the 'curious article' in the *Times*, and gave an abridged version, while the *Sheffield Independent* reprinted the whole article. Within ten days, a score of regional papers offered the article, from Edinburgh to Croydon, East Kent to West Somerset, Dublin and Cork. Continuing in following months, William Stevens's *Family Herald* carried the article in its 3 December issue (pp. 494–495), and James Macauley's family journal, *The Leisure Hour*, reprinted it on 18 March 1865 (pp. 172–174). Lengthy extracts were quoted in the entry for 'shoddy and mungo' in Charles Tomlinson's *Cyclopaedia of useful arts, and manufactures* (London: Virtue & Co., 1868, 3, p. 636). Peter Lund Simmonds was also to cite extensively from the article in his lecture on 'Waste Products and Undeveloped Substances'. Wynter included a new version of the article in the second volume of his compilation *Peeps into the Human Hive* (1874). From there, it was picked up for the article 'Waste Materials' printed in *Chambers's Journal* the same year (51:546, 13 Jun 1874, pp. 369–371).

# 38

# WYNTER, ANDREW. 'OLD CLOTHES AND WHAT BECOMES OF THEM'

## *The Times*, 3 Nov 1864, p. 6.

When the hawker working the suburban districts comes by with his barrow blooming with flowers and petitioning for old clothes, old hats, and old boots, &c., in exchange for them, the bargain seems so one-sided that most people are only too glad to begin the barter. We all get so sick of frowsy old clothes that it seems almost a mercy to get rid of them at any price, but to be able to translate them into geraniums and fuchsias, &c., to exchange musty, fusty gabardines for fresh odours and rainbow hues, is more than anybody ever expected to do. The coster who initiated this subtle method of weeding our wardrobes must have had a special insight into female character, ever ready to exchange the solid and useful for the brightly decorative – at all events, this almost poetical method of filling old clothes' bags deserves to be mentioned as one of the most abundant means of building up a trade which has now assumed enormous proportions. The great dealers into whose hands our cast-off skins ultimately fall have arrived at the dignified position of merchants. The value of their exports to foreign countries makes no inconsiderable item in our annual trade returns. The streams of old clothes that hour by hour are seductively drained, either by floral exchange, attractive advertisement, or by the downright pestering of "Old Ikeys,"[1] culminate in the great old-clothes mart in Houndsditch where Hebrews most do congregate. This inodorous spot has been so often described in popular works that people are now pretty familiar with it, by name at least. But having described the fierce contest which ensues over the mounds of old clothes therein daily deposited, our social statisticians seem to have had enough of them, and have proceeded no further. But the true interest in the story of old clothes begins just at the point where they leave off. To the question of what now becomes of them, we might answer that the greater part of them are now about to set out upon their travels, to enter new circles of society, and to see life both savage and civilized under a thousand new phases.

Those that are intended to remain in this country have to be tutored and transformed. The "clobberer," the "reviver," and the "translator" lay hands upon them. The duty of the "clobberer" is to patch, to sew up, and to restore as far as possible the garments to their pristine appearance; black cloth garments pass into the hands of the "revivers," who rejuvenate seedy black coats, and, for the moment, make them look as good as new. The "translator's" duty is of a higher order; his office is to transform one garment into another – the skirts of a cast-off coat being the least worn part of the garment make capital waistcoats and tunics for children, &c. Hats are revived in a still more wonderful manner; they are cut down to take out the grease marks, re-lined, and appear in the shops like new ones. The streets surrounding the old clothes' market are full of shops where these "clobbered" and "revived" goods are exposed for sale, and really a stranger to the trade would not know but that they were new goods. There is a department of the market also dedicated to old clothes, male and female, "clobbered" and revived. It is a touching sight to see the class of persons who frequent the men's market and turn over the seedy black garments that are doing their best to put on a good appearance – the toil-worn clerks, who for some social reason are expected to apparel themselves in black, and the equally careworn members of the clerical profession, chiefly curates whose meagre stipends do not permit of the extravagance of new suits of clothes. The ladies' market is a vast wardrobe of silk dresses, but if we are to believe the saleswoman the matrons of England are more thrifty than we gave them credit for. "Servants come here to purchase, Sir! No, indeed, Sir, ladies worth hundreds of pounds," was the reply we got to our inquiries as to the class of purchasers. Black cloth clothes that are too far gone to be "clobbered" and "revived" are always sent abroad to be cut up to make caps. France takes the best of these old clothes for this purpose. The linings are stripped out, and in this condition they are admitted duty free as old rags. Russia and Poland, where caps seem to be universally worn by the working population, are content with still more threadbare garments to be cut up for this purpose. The great bulk of our cast-off clothes of all kinds, however, find their way to two markets, – Ireland and Holland. The old clothes' bags of the collectors may, in fact, be said to be emptied out in the land of Erin,[2] as far as the ordinary order of clothes go, while to Holland only special articles of apparel are exported. Singularly enough, the destination of the red tunics of the whole British infantry is the chests of the sturdy Dutchman. There seems to be some popular belief or superstition in that waterlogged country that red cloth affords the best protection against rheumatism, consequently these jackets all find their way to the land of dykes. The sleeves are cut off, and they are made to button in a double-breasted fashion; thus remodelled they are worn next to the skin like a flannel waistcoat by all careful Dutchmen among the labouring classes. The Irish chiefly favour corduroys, and we suspect the worn-out legs of British pantaloons of this material are cut off and converted into breeches for Pat. Where he gets those wonderful swallow-tailed coats with brass buttons is a puzzle to all the dealers; it is very certain they do not come from this side of the Channel, and it is equally clear they are remnants of costume two generations back. Our readers will perhaps have noticed the special avidity the dealers in old clothes evince for all kinds of regimentals, full dress liveries, Volunteers' uniforms, beadles' coats, &c. Anything specially splendid in this line is marked by the collectors as a sportsman marks any rare and brilliantly plumaged bird, and ultimately it is sure to be bagged by them. One of the largest dealers in London in these showy dresses once said to us seeing a Guardsman going along the street, – "A thousand to one that coat comes into my hands." Really the inevitability there appears to be about the destination of these regimentals, if known to their wearers, should make them very uncomfortable. The dealers would, if they could, strip them off their backs just as an eel-woman skins an eel. A Lord Mayor's footman's full dress livery is viewed by these gentry with wolfish eyes. These are the great prizes of the profession – and their barbaric splendours are destined for a special market – the South Coast of Africa, where nature puts on her most gorgeous apparel, and the great ones of the land are determined to have something to match. Travellers often tell us of the marvellous appearance of the chiefs of these parts when in full mufti, but we scarcely expected to find our old clothes dealers the regular *costumiers* of these sable dignitaries, transmitting regimentals, laced liveries, and cocked hats, as regularly to them as a London tailor sends his clothes to his country customers. And Mumbo Jumbo[3] will not be put off with inferior articles – the slightest blemish in colour or inferiority in cloth is instantly detected and rejected by these semi-savages, hence the greatest care is necessary in catering for their wants. It is just possible that the Lord Mayors for these last dozen years would be able to recognize their own splendid liveries on the backs of a Council of these potentates if they could ever be got together for any purpose whatever. We ourselves saw an assortment of well-preserved liveries of the heir to the proudest throne in the world, just being packed for exportation to the grand destination of all fine liveries we have just mentioned. It should be some solace to the parish beadle that his clothes, instead of descending in the social scale like those of ordinary civilians, is destined to flame upon the back of some autocrat who holds the lives of thousands of men at his disposal, instead of only being the emblems of terror to poor parish boys. The vast majority of the scarlet coats of our officers that are a little worn find their way to the great annual fair at Leipsic. There is a belief in the trade that the destination of this bright scarlet cloth is the cuffs and facings of the civil officials in the Russian Government. However this may be, the fact of second-hand regimentals finding their way to the great German fair is undoubted. The pepper-and-salt great-coats of our infantry go to our agricultural districts and to the Cape, but the heavier and more valuable artillery cloaks find their way to Holland, and that country and Ireland absorb between them the cast-off clothes of the police. There is one odd item of old clothes that has a singular history. There are still a certain class in the community addicted to the use of silk-velvet waistcoats. This class is generally to be found among the well-to-do tradesmen of country towns. The longevity of a black silk velvet waistcoat is proverbial; it will not wear out. After adorning the respectable corporation of some provincial grocer until he is thoroughly tired of it, what does our reader think is its ultimate destination – the pate of some street German or Polish Jew! In obedience to a Rabbinical law it is not considered right by some of the more conscientious Hebrews to go uncovered, and these secondhand waistcoats are bought up to make skullcaps for their use.

But old clothes, after they have served the purpose of two or three classes of society, are yet far from closing their career; when they have seen their worst they take altogether a new lease of existence. As old Jason was renewed, in ancient story, by being ground in a mill,[4] so are our garments in the present day. When old clothes are too bad for anything else they are still good enough for Shoddy and Mungo. It is not many years since Mr. Ferrand denounced the "devil's dust" of the Yorkshire woollen manufacturers;[5] this devil's dust arises from the grand translation of old cloth into new. Batley, Dewsbury, and Leeds have been described as the grand centres of woollen rags – the tatterdemallion capitals, into which are drawn all the greasy, frowsy, cast-off clothes of Europe, and whence, issue the pilot cloths, the Petershams,[6] the beavers, the Talmas,[7] the Chesterfields,[8] and the Mohairs in which our modern dandies disport themselves. The old rags, after being reduced to the condition of wool by enormous toothed wheels, are mixed with a varying amount of fresh wool, and the whole is then worked up into the fabrics we have mentioned, which now have the run of fashion. It is estimated that shoddy and mungo supply the materials for a third of the woollen manufactures of this country. Here is a grand transformation. No man can say that the materials of the coat he is wearing has not been already on the back of some greasy beggar. In one corner of the "animal products department" in the South Kensington Museum[9] the visitor can see hundreds of specimens of this shoddy and mungo – a perfect resurrection of the old clothes from every country in Europe. The cast-off wardrobes of civilized man by a law of commerce are sucked into this country, and mainly into this metropolis, and in return we distribute it in perfect fabrics, destined to go once more the round of civilization; woollen fabrics are hard to die, and, for all we know, clothes are thus ground up over and over again.

The final destination, however, of all old clothes is the soil; when art can do no more for much-vexed woollen fibre it becomes a land rag.

We have pursued old clothes through so many shifting scenes that, having run them to earth at last, here, perhaps, it would be as well to leave them; but, no, they once more reappear in our beer. Hops, we are told, of a certain quality cannot be grown without the manure of land rags. Thus, the final destination of old clothes after all is the human frame, and we only finally lose sight of them when, instead of clothing this vile *corpus*, they are transmuted into the body itself, as we quaff the foaming tankard, or the more genteel bottled bitter of Bass or Allsopp.[10]

## Notes

1 Ike is a short form of the Jewish name Isaac. In the phrase here, the usage is derogatory.

2 In 'An Irish Stew', George Augustus Sala poses the question:

> What, then, becomes of the old clothes? . . . Step into the many old clothes depôts about Rag Fair, or the Clothes Exchange in London, and ask the dealer where the majority of his stock is to be exported to. He will tell you to Ireland – for the Irish market.

See *Looking at Life; or, Thoughts and Things* (London: Routledge, Warne, and Routledge, 1860), pp. 166–167.

3 A Mandingo judicial personality that Mungo Park described in his *Travels in the Interior of Africa* (London: J. W. Myers, 1799), pp. 36–37. Here, by association, the name designates an African dignitary, but derogatory in this context.

4 This renewal by grinding in a mill is not found in the story of Jason, but may refer to the Mesopotamian myth of Tammuz.

5 William Busfeild Ferrand (1809–1889), in a widely reported Parliamentary statement of 24 February 1842, denounced cheapened manufactures as a cause of decline in trade, citing 'devil's dust' of the Yorkshire shoddy trade.

6 A heavy, rough-napped overcoating cloth named after Charles Stanhope (1780–1851) when styled Viscount Petersham.

7 An overcoat style made fashionable by François-Joseph Talma (1763–1826), French actor.

8 The Chesterfield coat, traditionally made in heavy wool cloth, was named after George Stanhope, 6th Earl of Chesterfield (1805–1866).

9 Peter Lund Simmonds (1814–1897) catalogued the animal specimens from the Great Exhibition selected for a collection of trade products displayed at the South Kensington Museum, and later at Bethnal Green.

10 The Bass brewery founded by William Bass (1717–1787) in 1777, and the Allsopp brewery where Samuel Allsopp (1780–1838) began business in 1807, were the two largest breweries in England at the time.

## Editorial Headnote

### Matéaux, Clara L. 'Things that are done with', *The Wonderland of Work* (London: Cassell, Petter, Galpin and Co., 1881), 303–312.

The unusual surname of the author allows her identification as Clarisse Laverne Matéaux (c1836–1911), born in Chelsea, London. On the same basis, we can posit her relation to the dyer Louis Charles Matéaux (d. 1853), and Eliza Laverne Matéaux (d. 1864). If these were her parents, their deaths may have occasioned her entry upon an undisguised literary career. She began authoring books in her own name by 1870, enjoying an immediate popularity measured in the numerous editions of her works, all published by Cassell and Co. Matéaux's style was easy and directed at young people – didactic but entertaining. The content was often based upon other writings, but making these accessible and engaging for a juvenile audience. Her output ended in 1894, by which time Matéaux had probably gained sufficient income to retire; the 1911 census records her residence at 10 Bickerton Road, Holloway, living on 'Private means – Literary'. The census enumerator also confirmed that her father was of French nationality. Matéaux remained unmarried, and her probate records reveal a modest estate of £338, which she left to 'Margaret Andrews (wife of Edward Andrews)'.

Cassell announced *Wonderland of Work* as early as September 1880 as one of a number of books for young people projected for 'the coming season' (*Leeds Mercury*, 8 Sep 1880, p. 3). However, it was not until November 1881 that it was ready, a quarto-size work of 320 pages bound in 'cloth gilt' and priced at 7s. 6d. The *Scotsman* judged it

> a successful attempt at giving popular descriptions of modern industries. . . . It must be borne in mind that the descriptions of these industries are not given in any formal fashion, but are presented to the reader in a pleasant rapid form as if a story was being told.
>
> (3 Dec 1881, p. 10)

It was proposed as a serious and sensible gift book in contrast to flash Christmas titles. By 1883, a second edition was available at five shillings. The 1884 revised edition, published by Cassell in New York, was updated by the mechanical engineer Joshua Rose (c1845–1910), who added a totally incongruous account of the phonograph at the end of the 'Things that are done with' chapter. Finally, an abbreviated American edition from the New York publisher, possibly brought out for Christmas 1893, completely deselected the chapter.

Matéaux's chapter 'Things that are done with' harvests material from Lyon Playfair's 1852 lecture 'On the chemical principles involved in the manufactures of the Exhibition', and Peter Lund Simmonds's 1859 paper 'On the Utilization of Waste Substances'. In so doing, it embraces the *economy of nature* model whereby re-use of cast-off goods imitates nature's chemical breakdown and reincorporation of materials. The selection here is confined to the textile aspects of the far-reaching treatment in the original chapter.

# 39

# MATÉAUX, CLARA L: 'THINGS THAT ARE DONE WITH'

## *The Wonderland of Work* (London: Cassell, Petter, Galpin and Co., 1881), 303–312.

A curious subject with which to wind up, you may think, but what about those many varieties of greased rags, the shapeless, colourless remnants of many a smart suit, the almost legless knitted stocking without a foot, for instance, the thousand and one scraps of dingy wool and worsted?

. . .

Yet what *does* become of the masses of odds and ends that are daily thrust into the world's vast rag-bag, to be eagerly seized upon for some purpose or another by the numerous dealers in rags and bones, who offer so much a pound for all such dingy treasures? I do not, of course, mean cotton or linen rags – the merest child knows that they are transformed into paper – but the mixed remainder when these are all routed out, the shapeless, colourless, unfragrant bits, wrecked shadows of old coats, torn jackets, worn-out dresses, scraps and cuttings, and tangled woollen rubbish of all sorts, which every household helps to accumulate yet never finds a use for, however thrifty it may be.

Until quite recent years, the busy rag-sorters in search of materials for the paper-mills carefully avoided dirty woollen scraps, considering them as completely worthless, though in time a use was found for them by certain London mattress and cheap furniture makers, who had them torn up into fine pieces, and unravelled and reduced to loose "flocks," with which to stuff or cover the springs of very common furniture; they were afterwards used as padding for cheap harness and saddles. It was through this that they by chance attracted the attention of Mr. Lane,[1] a Yorkshire cloth manufacturer, who happened to notice a saddler busy stuffing handfuls of a soft, yielding, brown, woolly texture into some of his harness work, and wondered whatever this, to him, new sort of fluffy substance could be. Inquiring into the matter, he was informed that it was only a rubbishy kind of common flock, made up of the cast-aside remains of all sorts of old woollen refuse, such as worn-out stockings and bits of blankets and petticoats, washed, torn up, and unravelled into a soft mass that, being cheap, did very well to stuff ordinary saddles or things of that kind, but was of no use whatever for any other purpose.

As he stood listening, and stroking the soft, colourless, woolly fibres over his fingers, our shrewd observer felt of another opinion. It *was* wool, and being wool, why should it not be capable of being woven again into some sort of fresh tissue?

DOI: 10.4324/9780429274190-47

He inquired where this despised "flock" could be bought, sent an order that a quantity should be forwarded to his mill at Batley, near Leeds, where he lived, and on his return set to work with his purchase, mixing and weaving the old wool – at first by itself, then with new, until he at last produced a piece of cloth which surpassed all his expectation, and filled him with hopes of making a fair fortune out of the strange new invention he had so suddenly stumbled upon and introduced into our Wonderland.

But though he well deserved it, such success was not to be his, even though he invested all his time and money in the cause, and started a trade that has since made this village in Yorkshire the great cheap cloth market of the world; and you will understand what this means when I tell you that scarcely any cloth or fancy woollen material is now made without an admixture, more or less, of this preparation of "shoddy."

Before I begin to describe the process all woollen rags go through as they are being transformed into "shoddy" or "mungo" (not quite the same thing, though often confounded by outsiders), it may interest you to know that the old rags of all nations travel to us English folk, and that in this as in other things each country has its speciality. France, Holland, Germany, Belgium, Denmark, Italy, America, Australia, all favour us with their woollen refuse rubbish, for which they get large sums, the price of such rags varying, I am told, from a few shillings to £8 or £9 per hundredweight.

All these home and foreign rags, when collected, arrive at the various mills in and about Batley, tight hidden in great bales, the different styles of packing alone telling to accustomed eyes the places and countries from whence they come. These bales have each to be opened, and the contents to be scattered and spread out on the floor before a crowd of "sorters," women, boys, and girls, stick in hand, whose business it is to "sort" and class their miscellaneous contents – not an easy task, as you may fancy, for all these varied stores have to be arranged according to colour and quality of texture. From London come mostly "mixed softs" of a respectable kind, fragments of white flannels, stockings, carpets, army and tailors' clips and cuttings – these last much valued because they are new and clean. Scotland sends the remains of many tidy old rags and woollen stockings; Ireland fewer rags, but of the raggedest, dirty and darned. From Germany come motley ruins of numberless grey and white knitted socks and stockings; Italy, Russia, and other lands each helping the great rag-harvest with their own particular fragments "done with."

And all these shapeless oddments have to be selected and arranged judiciously by the busy sorters, who sit crouching on their low stools, half hidden by the mounds of woollens rising round them in hillocks of every shade of grime and shabbiness. The next performance is to "seam" all these ragged old clothes[2] – that is, to tear or cut off and set apart all the greasy lumps and thicknesses, which, though of no use for shoddy, have still to do some service to the world: for the better kind will be made into a very coarse flock, and used as of old for the stuffing of common couches; the rest, after being allowed to rot completely, will serve as a good manure for hop-growing and other purposes.

When they are all "sorted" and "seamed," the rags are gathered and put into huge canvas sacks suspended from the rafters; then they are pressed tight and even, trodden down by the boys' bare feet. When each sack is crammed quite full it is carried off to another large attic, known as the grinding-room, where its contents will be delivered over to the tender mercies of the "swift," or "devil," as the old workers here call it, and no wonder, for it is a great devouring monster, with an interior of huge iron cylinders, armed with some twelve thousand sharp teeth, which will tear and rend all that undainty woollen provender with which an attendant boy ceaselessly feeds it, until it is an undistinguishable mass of thick, soft, bewildered-looking fluff, ready to be carried off to the big "mixing-room," where the "flock," having been first sprinkled with oil,[3] is mixed with good new wool in different proportions according to the purposes for which it is intended; and here is a great saving of several sorts of wool, as some of the coarsest of Russian, Egyptian, and Turkish kinds – parts of "fleeces," the "shorts," and "noils," refuse of ordinary combings, almost useless in the ordinary worsted factories – can be worked with advantage into one or the other of the many materials which will be manufactured elsewhere.

You will imagine how various they are when I name tweeds, reversible cloth, many of those imitations of seal and fur used for ladies' jackets, army cloth, of which our soldiers' greatcoats are made, summer coatings, the well-known pilot cloths, common blankets and wraps, friezes, and others of which I do not know the names, down to the commonest house-flannel, or mop cloth, horse-cloth, linings for all kinds of things, but especially union cloths, that is, a mixture of cotton and shoddy, sold for boys' garments.

We left our once-despised but now valuable mixture at its first step as "new" wool. Its next was to be taken to the scribbling-machine, where, by being passed through rollers, it became twisted into long thick bands; then to the carding-machines and spindles, from whence we at last see it emerge, the fluffy, colourless, shapeless flock now changed into long and strong yarn, looking like any other wool, and ready and fit to be woven into any kind of cloth.

There is also another kind of well-known material that can be made out of the most worthless of these ground-up rags which is quite distinct from those I have yet mentioned, and that is the smooth felted cloth now so much used for table and crumb cloths, skirts, hats, and bonnet-boxes. The process of preparing the wool is just the same up to a certain point; but then, instead of being spun so as to form a fine yarn or thread, the wool is turned out, in one extremely thin and broad band, which is wound on to a roller. These rollers are placed on to a warping-machine and unwound, so that one band unrolls evenly on another, till the whole forms a thick, soft band of the required thickness, which as it leaves the warping-machine passes between a set of rollers into a trough of hot soapy water. The upper rollers, which are of solid wood, move and shake in a sort of uncomfortable, side-long fashion, while the lower rollers, which are filled with steam, revolve evenly; the fibre in the long band of wet wool passing in layers between these wheels is fretted and acted upon by their different motions and the heat, until it has become combined into one compact substance, and passes out a strip of thin, fine cloth, or rather "felt," which when dried, pressed, and printed upon will form a strong and pretty material.

. . .

Now, having explained matters a little, let us follow the leather-capped, noisy "dust-o-e-ys," who, having filled their cart, are rumbling off in the distance. A little beyond the city they will find a large enclosure into which they drive, and tilting up their vehicle, drop on a vacant space the whole of its contents in a big heap, which, as soon as the cloud of powdery dust has somewhat subsided, will be taken entire possession of by a number of grimy men and boys, known as "hill-people," who, settling down like a swarm of energetic ants, will instantly proceed to pick out, first of all the larger items, such as battered kettles, coal-scuttles, bricks, dead cats and dogs, old hats, bits of wood, straw, stones, odd boots and shoes; then shovel the pile in search of other treasures in the form of broken bottles, bones, rags, and the larger relics of numberless things flung aside as useless. This first clearance effected in an incredibly short space of time, the dark crowd of men and boys take sudden flight, most likely to settle like crows on a fresh heap ready for their inspection. As the carts follow each other in rapid succession, and as these workers are generally paid by the quantity they get sorted, they lose little time. One man only remains, spade in hand, to assist the next "sorters," a band of hard-working women, who now rush up, carrying sieves and baskets, and set to work as though they had no thought or time for anything but just earning a few pence as quickly as possible.

The man who has remained to aid in this sorting rapidly shovels the dust into the big wire sieves held out for the purpose, and the women shake the contents sharply, until only the larger bits are seen in them. This is then dropped into one of the ready baskets, being first cleared of extra good bits of coal, charred chips of wood, and other such valuables.[4]

Poor, toiling, industrious, dingy band! They are not very pleasant to look at, being almost hidden in those large, coarse, sacking leggings and aprons, their towzled hair poked out of sight under nightcaps, bent straw hats, and handkerchiefs of an undistinguishable hue. Little more is seen of their features than eyes and nose. Yet some of them sing at their disagreeable though useful work. Let us hope as the "heap" vanishes that "use is everything."

## Notes

1 This is a retelling of the story of Batley's Benjamin Law (1772–1837) and his experience of 1813. James Lane (1831–1906), the Batley waste dealer and rag merchant whose business began in the 1860s, is too late for the originator of Batley's shoddy trade.

2 Seaming was the process of cutting out seams sewn with silk or cotton thread, not quite understood in this account.

3 Oiling takes place before grinding in order to lessen the damage to the wool when pulling it apart.

4 This paragraph has been shifted up to give better continuity in this shortened extract.

# INDEX

Note: page numbers in *italics* indicate an image on the corresponding page. Page numbers followed by 'n' indicate notes.

www.ingramcontent.com/pod-product-compliance
Lightning Source LLC
LaVergne TN
LVHW010630300926
849162LV00001B/112